Lecture Notes in Computer Science 4963

Commenced Publication in 1973
Founding and Former Series Editors:
Gerhard Goos, Juris Hartmanis, and Jan

C.R. Ramakrishnan   Jakob Rehof (Eds.)

Tools and Algorithms for the Construction and Analysis of Systems

14th International Conference, TACAS 2008
Held as Part of the Joint European Conferences
on Theory and Practice of Software, ETAPS 2008
Budapest, Hungary, March 29-April 6, 2008
Proceedings

 Springer

Volume Editors

C.R. Ramakrishnan
Stony Brook University
Department of Computer Science
Stony Brook, NY 11794-4400, USA
E-mail: cram@cs.sunysb.edu

Jakob Rehof
Universität Dortmund
Fachbereich Informatik
Otto-Hahn-Str. 14, 44227 Dortmund, Germany
E-mail: rehof@cs.uni-dortmund.de

Library of Congress Control Number: 2008923178

CR Subject Classification (1998): F.3, D.2.4, D.2.2, C.2.4, F.2.2

LNCS Sublibrary: SL 1 – Theoretical Computer Science and General Issues

ISSN   0302-9743
ISBN-10   3-540-78799-2 Springer Berlin Heidelberg New York
ISBN-13   978-3-540-78799-0 Springer Berlin Heidelberg New York

Springer is a part of Springer Science+Business Media

springer.com

© Springer-Verlag Berlin Heidelberg 2008
Printed in Germany

Typesetting: Camera-ready by author, data conversion by Scientific Publishing Services, Chennai, India
Printed on acid-free paper   SPIN: 12245987   06/3180   5 4 3 2 1 0

Foreword

ETAPS 2008 was the 11th instance of the European Joint Conferences on Theory and Practice of Software. ETAPS is an annual federated conference that was established in 1998 by combining a number of existing and new conferences. This year it comprised five conferences (CC, ESOP, FASE, FOSSACS, TACAS), 22 satellite workshops (ACCAT, AVIS, Bytecode, CMCS, COCV, DCC, FESCA, FIT, FORMED, GaLoP, GT-VMT, LDTA, MBT, MOMPES, PDMC, QAPL, RV, SafeCert, SC, SLA++P, WGT, and WRLA), nine tutorials, and seven invited lectures (excluding those that were specific to the satellite events). The five main conferences received 571 submissions, 147 of which were accepted, giving an overall acceptance rate of less than 26%, with each conference below 27%. Congratulations therefore to all the authors who made it to the final programme! I hope that most of the other authors will still have found a way of participating in this exciting event, and that you will all continue submitting to ETAPS and contributing to make of it the best conference in the area.

The events that comprise ETAPS address various aspects of the system development process, including specification, design, implementation, analysis and improvement. The languages, methodologies and tools which support these activities are all well within its scope. Different blends of theory and practice are represented, with an inclination towards theory with a practical motivation on the one hand and soundly based practice on the other. Many of the issues involved in software design apply to systems in general, including hardware systems, and the emphasis on software is not intended to be exclusive.

ETAPS is a confederation in which each event retains its own identity, with a separate Programme Committee and proceedings. Its format is open-ended, allowing it to grow and evolve as time goes by. Contributed talks and system demonstrations are in synchronized parallel sessions, with invited lectures in plenary sessions. Two of the invited lectures are reserved for 'unifying' talks on topics of interest to the whole range of ETAPS attendees. The aim of cramming all this activity into a single one-week meeting is to create a strong magnet for academic and industrial researchers working on topics within its scope, giving them the opportunity to learn about research in related areas, and thereby to foster new and existing links between work in areas that were formerly addressed in separate meetings.

ETAPS 2008 was organized by the John von Neumann Computer Society jointly with the Budapest University of Technology and the Eötvös University, in cooperation with:

▷ European Association for Theoretical Computer Science (EATCS)
▷ European Association for Programming Languages and Systems (EAPLS)
▷ European Association of Software Science and Technology (EASST)

and with support from Microsoft Research and Danubius Hotels.

The organizing team comprised:

Chair	Dániel Varró
Director of Organization	István Alföldi
Main Organizers	Andrea Tósoky, Gabriella Aranyos
Publicity	Joost-Pieter Katoen
Advisors	András Pataricza, Joaõ Saraiva
Satellite Events	Zoltán Horváth, Tihamér Levendovszky, Viktória Zsók
Tutorials	László Lengyel
Web Site	Ákos Horváth
Registration System	Victor Francisco Fonte, Zsolt Berényi, Róbert Kereskényi, Zoltán Fodor
Computer Support	Áron Sisak
Local Arrangements	László Gönczy, Gábor Huszerl, Melinda Magyar, several student volunteers.

Overall planning for ETAPS conferences is the responsibility of its Steering Committee, whose current membership is:

Vladimiro Sassone (Southampton, Chair), Luca de Alfaro (Santa Cruz), Roberto Amadio (Paris), Giuseppe Castagna (Paris), Marsha Chechik (Toronto), Sophia Drossopoulou (London), Matt Dwyer (Nebraska), Hartmut Ehrig (Berlin), Chris Hankin (London), Laurie Hendren (McGill), Mike Hinchey (NASA Goddard), Paola Inverardi (L'Aquila), Joost-Pieter Katoen (Aachen), Paul Klint (Amsterdam), Kim Larsen (Aalborg), Gerald Luettgen (York) Tiziana Margaria (Göttingen), Ugo Montanari (Pisa), Martin Odersky (Lausanne), Catuscia Palamidessi (Paris), Anna Philippou (Cyprus), CR Ramakrishnan (Stony Brook), Don Sannella (Edinburgh), João Saraiva (Minho), Michael Schwartzbach (Aarhus), Helmut Seidl (Munich), Perdita Stevens (Edinburgh), and Dániel Varró (Budapest).

I would like to express my sincere gratitude to all of these people and organizations, the Programme Committee Chairs and members of the ETAPS conferences, the organizers of the satellite events, the speakers themselves, the many reviewers, and Springer for agreeing to publish the ETAPS proceedings. Finally, I would like to thank the Organizing Chair of ETAPS 2008, Dániel Varró, for arranging for us to have ETAPS in the most beautiful city of Budapest

January 2008   Vladimiro Sassone

Preface

This volume contains the proceedings of the 14th International Conference on Tools and Algorithms for the Construction and Analysis of Systems (TACAS 2008) which took place in Budapest, Hungary, March 31–April 3, 2008. TACAS is a forum for researchers, developers and users interested in rigorously based tools and algorithms for the construction and analysis of systems. The conference serves to bridge the gaps between different communities that share common interests in, and techniques for, tool development and its algorithmic foundations. The research areas covered by such communities include but are not limited to formal methods, software and hardware verification, static analysis, programming languages, software engineering, real-time systems, communications protocols, and biological systems. The TACAS forum provides a venue for such communities at which common problems, heuristics, algorithms, data structures and methodologies can be discussed and explored. In doing so, TACAS aims to support researchers in their quest to improve the utility, reliability, flexibility, and efficiency of tools and algorithms for building systems.

Topics covered by the conference included, but were not limited to, the following: specification and verification techniques for finite and infinite- state systems; software and hardware verification; theorem-proving and model-checking; system construction and transformation techniques; static and run-time analysis; abstraction techniques for modeling and validation; compositional and refinement-based methodologies; testing and test-case generation; analytical techniques for secure, real-time, hybrid, safety-critical, biological or dependable systems; integration of formal methods and static analysis in high-level hardware design or software environments; tool environments and tool architectures; SAT solvers; and applications and case studies.

TACAS traditionally considers two types of papers: research papers that describe in detail novel research within the scope of the TACAS conference; and short tool demonstration papers that give an overview of a particular tool and its applications or evaluation. A total of 121 research papers and 19 tool demonstration papers were submitted to TACAS 2008 (140 submissions in total). Of these, 31 research papers and 7 tool demonstration papers were accepted. Each submission was evaluated by at least three reviewers. After a seven-week reviewing process, the program selection was carried out in a two-week electronic Program Committee meeting. We believe that the committee deliberations resulted in a strong technical program. The TACAS 2008 Program Committee selected Sharad Malik (Princeton University, USA) as invited speaker, who kindly agreed and gave a talk entitled "Hardware Verification: Techniques, Methodology and Solutions," describing specification and validation techniques for verifying emerging computing systems.

We thank the authors of submitted papers, the Program Committee members, the additional reviewers, our Tools Chair Byron Cook, and the TACAS Steering Committee. Martin Karusseit gave us prompt support for the online conference management service used to prepare this program. TACAS 2008 was part of the 11th European Joint Conference on Theory and Practice of Software (ETAPS), whose aims, organization and history are detailed in the separate foreword by the ETAPS Steering Committee Chair. We would like to express our gratitude to the ETAPS Steering Committee chaired by Vladimiro Sassone, and the Organizing Committee led by Dániel Varró for their efforts in making ETAPS 2008 a successful event.

January 2008   C. R. Ramakrishnan
                                                              Jakob Rehof

Organization

Steering Committee

Ed Brinksma	ESI and Eindhoven University of Technology, The Netherlands
Rance Cleaveland	University of Maryland, College Park & Fraunhofer USA Inc, USA
Kim Larsen	Aalborg University, Aalborg, Denmark
Bernhard Steffen	University of Dortmund, Germany
Lenore Zuck	University of Illinois, Chicago, USA

Program Committee

Patricia Bouyer	CNRS, Ecole Normale Superieure de Cachan, France
Ed Brinksma	ESI & Eindhoven University of Technology, The Netherlands
Tevfik Bultan	University of California, Santa Barbara, USA
Rance Cleaveland	University of Maryland, College Park & Fraunhofer USA Inc, USA
Byron Cook	Microsoft Research, Cambridge, UK
Bruno Dutertre	SRI, Menlo Park, USA
Patrice Godefroid	Microsoft Research, Redmond, USA
Orna Grumberg	Technion, Haifa, Israel
Aarti Gupta	NEC Laboratories America Inc, USA
Fritz Henglein	University of Copenhagen, Denmark
Michael Huth	Imperial College, London, UK
Joxan Jaffar	National University of Singapore
Kurt Jensen	University of Aarhus, Denmark
Jens Knoop	Technical University, Vienna, Austria
Barbara König	University of Duisburg-Essen, Germany
Marta Kwiatkowska	Oxford University, UK
Kim Larsen	Aalborg University, Aalborg, Denmark
Nancy Lynch	MIT, Cambridge, USA
Kedar Namjoshi	Bell Labs, Murray Hill, USA
Paul Pettersson	Mälardalen University, Sweden
Sriram Rajamani	Microsoft Research, Bangalore, India
C.R. Ramakrishnan	Stony Brook University, USA
Jakob Rehof	University of Dortmund, Germany
Bill Roscoe	Oxford University, UK
Mooly Sagiv	Tel Aviv University, Israel
Stefan Schwoon	University of Stuttgart, Germany
Bernhard Steffen	University of Dortmund, Germany
Lenore Zuck	University of Illinois, Chicago, USA

Referees

Sara Adams
Daphna Amit
Philip Armstrong
Marco Bakera
Paolo Baldan
Calin Belta
Amir Ben-Amram
Nathalie Bertrand
Per Bjesse
Bruno Blanchet
Ahmed Bouajjani
Glenn Bruns
Sven Bünte
Sebastian Burckhardt
Doron Bustan
Jan Carlson
Chunqing Chen
Ling Cheung
Wei-Ngan Chin
Alexandre David
Cristina David
Leonardo de Moura
Jyotirmoy Deshmukh
Stefan Edelkamp
AnnMarie Ericsson
Javier Esparza
Sami Evangelista
Ansgar Faenker
Harald Fecher
Elena Fersman
Andrzej Filinski
Paul Fleischer
Martin Fraenzle
Laurent Fribourg
Zhaohui Fu
Silvio Ghilardi
Robert Glück
Michael Goldsmith
Dieter Gollmann
Georges Gonthier
Alexey Gotsman
Olga Grinchtein
Marcus Groesser
Radu Grosu

Sigrid Guergens
John Håkansson
Patrik Haslum
Keijo Heljanko
Espen Højsgaard
Gerard Holzmann
Graham Hughes
Hans Hüttel
Tom Hvitved
Franjo Ivancic
Himanshu Jain
Barbara Jobstmann
Sven Joerges
Colin Johnson
Marcin Jurdzinski
Albrecht Kadlec
Vineet Kahlon
Mark Kattenbelt
Sarfraz Khurshid
Stefan Kiefer
Raimund Kirner
Felix Klaedtke
Nils Klarlund
Gerwin Klein
Pavel Krcal
Lars M. Kristensen
Daniel Kroening
Orna Kupferman
Ken Friis Larsen
Ranko Lazic
Martin Leucker
Tal Lev-Ami
Vlad Levin
Shuhao Li
Birgitta Lindström
Yang Liu
Gerald Luettgen
Kristina Lundqvist
Michael Luttenberger
Sharad Malik
Roman Manevich
Nicolas Markey
Keneth McMillan
Yael Meller

Maik Merten
Marius Mikucionis
Peter Bro Miltersen
Sayan Mitra
Torben Mogensen
Ziv Nevo
Calvin Newport
Long Nguyen
Brian Nielsen
Lasse Nielsen
Mogens Nielsen
Morten Ib Nielsen
Michael Nissen
Thomas Nolte
Tina Nolte
Aditya Nori
Gethin Norman
Ulrik Nyman
Luke Ong
Ghassan Oreiby
Rotem Oshman
Joel Ouaknine
Sam Owre
David Parker
Corina Pasareanu
Nir Piterman
Franz Puntigam
Shaz Qadeer
Harald Raffelt
Venkatesh-Prasad
   Ranganath
Jacob Illum Rasmussen
Clemens Renner
Pierre-Alain Reynier
Noam Rinetzky
Abhik Roychoudhury
Oliver Rüthing
Michal Rutkowski
Andrey Rybalchenko
Hassen Saidi
Arnaud Sangnier
Sriram
   Sankaranarayanan
Andrew Santosa

Ursula Scheben
Markus Schordan
Carsten Schürmann
Cristina Seceleanu
Sanjit Seshia
Ohad Shacham
Natarajan Shankar
A. Prasad Sistla
Harald Sondergaard
Jeremy Sproston
Jiri Srba
Jan Strejcek
Jun Sun
Daniel Sundmark
Gregoire Sutre

Dejvuth
   Suwimonteerabuth
Ashish Tiwari
Simon Tjell
Rachel Tzoref
Shinya Umeno
Viktor Vafeiadis
Wim van Dam
Moshe Vardi
Kapil Vaswani
Martin Vechev
Miroslav Velev
Razvan Voicu
Chao Wang
Michael Weber

Lisa M. Wells
Ingomar Wenzel
Rafael Wisniewski
Uwe Wolter
James Worrell
Michael Westergaard
Ke Xu
Avi Yadgar
Eran Yahav
Roland Yap
Greta Yorsh
Fang Yu
Michael Zolda

Table of Contents

Invited Talk

Parameterized Systems

Model Checking – I

Applications

Model Checking – II

Static Analysis

Concurrent/Distributed Systems

Tools – I

Symbolic Execution

Abstraction, Interpolation

Tools – II

Trust, Reputation

Hardware Verification: Techniques, Methodology and Solutions

Sharad Malik

Dept. of Electrical Engineering
Princeton University
Princeton, NJ 08544, USA
`sharad@princeton.edu`

Abstract. Hardware verification has been one of the biggest drivers of formal verification research, and has seen the greatest practical impact of its results. The use of formal techniques has not been uniformly successful here — with equivalence checking widely used, assertion-based verification seeing increased adoption, and general property checking and theorem proving seeing only limited use. I will first examine the reasons for this varied success and show that for efficient techniques to translate to solutions they must be part of an efficient methodology and be scalable. Next I will describe specific efforts addressing each of these critical requirements for the verification of emerging computing systems.

A significant barrier in enabling efficient techniques to flow into efficient methodology is the need for human intervention in this process. I argue that in large part this is due to the gap between functional design specification, which is still largely in natural language, and structural design description at the register-transfer level (RTL). This gap is largely filled by humans, leading to a methodology which is error-prone, incomplete and inefficient. To overcome this, we need formal functional specification and a way to bridge the gap from this specification to structural RTL. In this direction I will present a modeling framework with design models at two levels — architectural and microarchitectural. The architectural model provides for a functional specification, and the microarchitectural model connects this to a physical implementation. I will illustrate how this enables greater automation in verification.

A major challenge in verification techniques providing scalable solutions is the inherent intractability of the problem. This is only getting worse with increasing complexity and is reflected in the increasing number of bug escapes into silicon. I argue that existing verification solutions need to be augmented with runtime validation techniques, through online error-checking and recovery in hardware. I will illustrate this with examples from emerging multi-core architectures. I will also discuss the complementary roles of formal techniques and runtime validation in a cooperative methodology.

C.R. Ramakrishnan and J. Rehof (Eds.): TACAS 2008, LNCS 4963, p. 1, 2008.

Extending Automated Compositional Verification to the Full Class of Omega-Regular Languages[*]

Azadeh Farzan[1], Yu-Fang Chen[2], Edmund M. Clarke[1], Yih-Kuen Tsay[2], and Bow-Yaw Wang[3]

[1] Carnegie Mellon University
[2] National Taiwan University
[3] Academia Sinica

Abstract. Recent studies have suggested the applicability of learning to automated compositional verification. However, current learning algorithms fall short when it comes to learning *liveness* properties. We extend the automaton synthesis paradigm for the infinitary languages by presenting an algorithm to learn an *arbitrary* regular set of infinite sequences (an ω-regular language) over an alphabet Σ. Our main result is an algorithm to learn a nondeterministic Büchi automaton that recognizes an unknown ω-regular language. This is done by learning a unique projection of it on Σ^* using the framework suggested by Angluin for learning regular subsets of Σ^*.

1 Introduction

Compositional verification is an essential technique for addressing the state explosion problem in Model Checking [1,7,8,11]. Most compositional techniques advocate proving properties of a system by checking properties of its components in an assume-guarantee style. The essential idea is to model check each component independently by making an assumption about its environment, and then discharge the assumption on the collection of the rest of the components. In the paradigm of automated compositional reasoning through learning [8], system behaviors and their requirements are formalized as regular languages. Assumptions in premises of compositional proof rules are often regular languages; their corresponding finite-state automata can therefore be generated by learning techniques for regular languages.

In automated compositional reasoning, a compositional proof rule is chosen *a priori*. The rule indicates how a system can be decomposed. Below is an example of a simple rule:

$$\frac{M_2 \models A \quad M_1 \| A \models P}{M_1 \| M_2 \models P}$$

[*] This research was sponsored by the iCAST project of the National Science Council, Taiwan, under the grant no. NSC96-3114-P-001-002-Y and the Semiconductor Research Corporation (SRC) under the grant no. 2006-TJ-1366.

C.R. Ramakrishnan and J. Rehof (Eds.): TACAS 2008, LNCS 4963, pp. 2–17, 2008.

for two components M_1 and M_2, and assumption A, and a property P. Intuitively, this rule says that if M_2 guarantees A, and M_1 guarantees P in an environment that respects A, then the system composed of M_1 and M_2 guarantees P. The goal is to automatically generate the assumption A by learning. One naturally wishes to verify all sorts of properties using this framework. However, all existing algorithms fall short when it comes to learning assumptions which involve *liveness* properties. In this paper, we present an algorithm that fills this gap and extends the learning paradigm to the full class of ω-regular languages. Soundness and completeness of the above proof rule with respect to *liveness properties* remains intact since ω-regular languages share the required closure properties of regular languages. Automation can be achieved following the framework of [8]. See [9] for a more detailed discussion.

The active learning model used in automated compositional reasoning involves a teacher who is aware of an unknown language, and a learner whose goal is to learn that language. The learner can put two types of queries to the teacher. A *membership query* asks if a string belongs to the unknown language. An *equivalence query* checks whether a conjecture automaton recognizes the unknown language. The teacher provides a counterexample if the conjecture is incorrect [2]. More specifically, in the process of learning an *assumption*, an initial assumption is generated by the learner through a series of membership queries. An equivalence query is then made to check if the assumption satisfies premises of the compositional proof rule. If it does, the verification process terminates with success. Otherwise, the learner refines the assumption by the returned counterexample and more membership queries. Since the weakest assumption either establishes or falsifies system requirements, the verification process eventually terminates when the weakest assumption is attained. A novel idea in [8] uses model checkers to resolve both membership and equivalence queries automatically. By using Angluin's L* [2] algorithm, the verification process can be performed without human intervention.

The product of the learning algorithm L* is a deterministic finite-state automaton recognizing the unknown regular language [2]. By the Myhill-Nerode Theorem, the minimal deterministic finite-state automaton can be generated from the equivalence classes defined by the coarsest right congruence relation of any regular language [13]. The L^* algorithm computes the equivalence classes by membership queries, and refines them with counterexamples returned by equivalence queries. It can, in fact, infer the minimal deterministic finite-state automaton for any unknown regular language with a polynomial number of queries in the size of the target automaton. The upper bound was later improved in [18].

Unfortunately, the L* algorithm cannot be directly generalized to learn ω-regular languages. Firstly, deterministic Büchi automata are less expressive than general Büchi automata. Inferred deterministic finite-state automata require more than the Büchi acceptance condition to recognize arbitrary ω-regular languages. Secondly, equivalence classes defined by the coarsest right congruence relation over an ω-regular language do not necessarily correspond to the states of its automaton. The ω-regular language $(a + b)^* a^\omega$ has only one equivalence class. Yet, there is no one-state ω-automaton with Büchi, Rabin, Streett, or even Muller acceptance conditions that can recognize this language.

Maler and Pnueli [14] made an attempt to generalize L* for the ω-regular languages. Their algorithm, L^ω, learns a proper subclass of ω-regular languages which is not expressive enough to cover liveness properties. This restricted class has the useful property of being uniquely identifiable by the syntactic right congruence. Thus, L^ω has the advantage of generating the minimal deterministic Muller automaton (isomorphic to the syntactic right congruence) recognizing a language in the restricted class. The syntactic right congruence, however, cannot be used to identify an arbitrary ω-regular language. Attempts to use more expressive congruences [3,21] have been unsuccessful.

Our main ideas are inspired by the work of Calbrix, Nivat, and Podelski [5]. Consider ultimately periodic ω-strings of the form uv^ω. Büchi [4] observed that the set of ultimately periodic ω-strings characterizes ω-regular languages; two ω-regular languages are in fact identical if and only if they have the same set of ultimately periodic ω-strings. Calbrix *et al.* [5] show that the finitary language $\{u\$v \mid uv^\omega \in L\}$ (where $ is a fresh symbol) is regular for any ω-regular language L. These properties help uniquely identify a Büchi automaton for the regular language corresponding to ultimately periodic ω-strings of an arbitrary ω-regular language. We develop a learning algorithm for the regular language $\{u\$v \mid uv^\omega \in L\}$ through membership and equivalence queries on the unknown ω-regular language L. A Büchi automaton accepting L can hence be constructed from the finite-state automaton generated by our learning algorithm.

2   Preliminaries

Let Σ be a finite set called the *alphabet*. A finite word over Σ is a finite sequence of elements of Σ. An empty word is represented by ϵ. For two words $u = u_1 \ldots u_n$ and $v = v_1 \ldots v_n$, define $uv = u_1 \ldots u_n v_1 \ldots v_m$. For a word u, u^n is recursively defined as uu^{n-1} with $u^0 = \epsilon$. Define $u^+ = \bigcup_{i=1}^\infty \{u^i\}$, and $u^* = \{\epsilon\} \cup u^+$. An infinite word over Σ is an infinite sequence of elements of Σ. For a finite word u, define the infinite word $u^\omega = uu \ldots u \ldots$. Operators $+$, $*$, and ω are naturally extended to sets of finite words.

A word u is a *prefix* (resp. *suffix*) of another word v if and only if there exists a word $w \in \Sigma^*$ such that $v = uw$ (resp. $v = wu$). A set of words S is called *prefix-closed* (resp. *suffix-closed*) if and only if for all $v \in S$, if u is a prefix (resp. suffix) of v then $u \in S$.

The set of all *finite* words on Σ is denoted by Σ^*. Σ^+ is the set of all nonempty words on Σ; therefore, $\Sigma^+ = \Sigma^* \backslash \{\epsilon\}$. Let u be a finite word. $|u|$ is the length of word u with $|\epsilon| = 0$. The set of all infinite words on Σ is denoted by Σ^ω. A language is a subset of Σ^*, and an ω-language is a subset of Σ^ω.

A finite automaton $\mathcal{A}$ is a tuple $(\Sigma, Q, I, F, \delta)$ where Σ is an alphabet, Q is a finite set of states, $I \subseteq Q$ is a set of *initial* states, $F \subseteq Q$ is a set of *final* states, and $\delta \subseteq Q \times \Sigma \times Q$ is the transition relation. A finite word $u = u_1 \ldots u_n$ is *accepted* by $\mathcal{A}$ if and only if there exists a sequence $q_{i_0} u_1 q_{i_1} u_2 \ldots u_n q_{i_n}$ such that

$q_{i_0} \in I$, $q_{i_n} \in F$, and for all j, we have $q_{i_j} \in Q$ and $(q_{i_{j-1}}, u_j, q_{i_j}) \in \delta$. Define $L(\mathcal{A}) = \{u \mid u \text{ is accepted by } \mathcal{A}\}$. A language $L \subseteq \Sigma^*$ is *regular* if and only if there exists an automaton $\mathcal{A}$ such that $L = L(\mathcal{A})$.

A Büchi automaton has the same structure as a finite automaton, except that it is intended for recognizing infinite words. An infinite word $u = u_1 \ldots u_n \ldots$ is *accepted* by a Büchi automaton $\mathcal{A}$ if and only if there exists a sequence $q_{i_0} u_1 q_{i_1} u_2 \ldots u_n q_{i_n} \ldots$ such that $q_{i_0} \in I$, $q_{i_j} \in Q$ and $(q_{i_{j-1}}, u_j, q_{i_j}) \in \delta$ (for all j), and there exists a state $q \in F$ such that $q = q_{i_j}$ for infinitely many j's. Again, define $L(\mathcal{A}) = \{u \mid u \text{ is accepted by } \mathcal{A}\}$. An ω-language $L \subseteq \Sigma^\omega$ is ω-*regular* if and only if there exists a Büchi automaton $\mathcal{A}$ such that $L = L(\mathcal{A})$. For an ω-language L, let $UP(L) = \{uv^\omega \mid u \in \Sigma^*, v \in \Sigma^+, uv^\omega \in L\}$. Words of the form uv^ω are called the *ultimately periodic*. Let α be an ultimately periodic word. A word $v \in \Sigma^+$ is a *period* of α if there exists a word $u \in \Sigma^*$ such that $\alpha = uv^\omega$.

Theorem 1. *(Büchi)[4] Let L and L' be two ω-regular languages. $L = L'$ if and only if $UP(L) = UP(L')$.*

The above theorem implies that the set of ultimately periodic words of an ω-regular language L uniquely characterizes L. Define $L_\$$ (read *regular image* of L) on $\Sigma \cup \{\$\}$ as

$$L_\$ = \{u\$v \mid uv^\omega \in L\}.$$

Intuitively, the symbol $\$$ marks the beginning of the period and separates it from the prefix of the ω-word uv^ω. Note that $L_\$ \subseteq \Sigma^*\$\Sigma^+$. We can then say that $L_\$$ uniquely characterizes L.

Theorem 2. *(Büchi)[4] If L is an ω-regular language, then there exist regular languages $L_1, \ldots, L_n$ and $L_1', \ldots, L_n'$ such that $L = \bigcup_{i=1}^{n} L_i(L_i')^\omega$.*

Theorem 3. *(Calbrix, Nivat, and Podelski)[5] $L_\$$ is regular.*

Moreover, one can show that the *syntactic congruence* of the regular language $L_\$$ and Arnold's congruence [3] for L coincide on the set Σ^+ [6].

3 Ultimately Periodic Words

Define an *equivalence* relation on the words in $\Sigma^*\$\Sigma^+$:

Definition 1. *The* equivalence *relation* $\stackrel{\circ}{=}$ *on* $\Sigma^*\$\Sigma^+$ *is defined by:*

$$u\$v \stackrel{\circ}{=} u'\$v' \iff uv^\omega = u'v'^\omega$$

$u, u' \in \Sigma^*$ *and* $v, v' \in \Sigma^+$.

Based on the ω-word ab^ω, we have $a\$b \stackrel{\circ}{=} ab\$b \stackrel{\circ}{=} ab\$bb \stackrel{\circ}{=} \ldots \stackrel{\circ}{=} ab^k\$b^{k'}$, for all k, k'. Therefore, the equivalence class $[a\$b]_{\stackrel{\circ}{=}}$ is equal to the set of words $ab^*\$b^+$.

Definition 2. *An equivalence relation $\equiv$ saturates a language L if and only if for two words u and v, where $u \equiv v$, we have $u \in L$ implies $v \in L$.*

Let L be an ω-regular language, and $L_\$$ its corresponding regular language as defined above. Let $u\$v$ be a word in $L_\$$ and $u'\$v' \in \Sigma^*\$\Sigma^+$ such that $u\$v \overset{\circ}{=} u'\$v'$. Since $uv^\omega = u'v'^\omega$, we have $u'v'^\omega \in L$, and therefore (by definition) $u'\$v' \in L_\$$. This implies the following Proposition:

Proposition 1. *The equivalence relation $\overset{\circ}{=}$ saturates $L_\$$.*

Let $R \subseteq \Sigma^*\$\Sigma^+$ be a regular language. Proposition 1 suggests that saturating $\overset{\circ}{=}$ is a necessary condition for R to be $L_\$$ for some ω-regular language L. The interesting point is that one can show that it is sufficient as well. This can be done by constructing a Büchi automaton $\mathcal{B}$ that recognizes L directly from the automaton $\mathcal{A}$ recognizing R [5]. Since this construction is used in our algorithm, we describe it here. We first need the following lemma:

Lemma 1. *(Calbrix, Nivat, and Podelski) [5] Let $L, L' \subseteq \Sigma^*$ be two regular languages such that $LL'^* = L$ and $L'^+ = L'$. Then, $\alpha \in UP(LL'^\omega)$ if and only if there exist $u \in L$ and $v \in L'$ such that $\alpha = uv^\omega$.*

Let $R \subseteq \Sigma^*\$\Sigma^+$ be a regular language. Let $\mathcal{A} = (\Sigma \cup \{\$\}, Q, I, F, \delta)$ be a deterministic automaton recognizing R. Define $Q_\$$ to be the set of states that can be reached by starting in an initial state and reading the part of a word $u\$v \in M$ that precedes the $\$$. Formally,

$$Q_\$ = \{q \in Q \mid \exists u\$v \in R, \exists q_i \in I, q = \delta(q_i, u)\}$$

For each state $q \in Q_\$$, let

$$M_q = \{u \mid \exists q_i \in I, \delta(q_i, u) = q\} \tag{1}$$
$$N_q = \{v \mid \exists q_f \in F, \delta(q, \$v) = q_f\}. \tag{2}$$

For each q, M_q and N_q are regular languages; one can easily construct an automaton accepting each by modifying $\mathcal{A}$. Moreover, the definitions of M_q and N_q along side the fact $R \subseteq \Sigma^*\$\Sigma^+$, implies that $R = \bigcup_{q \in Q_\$} M_q\$N_q$.

Next, we partition N_q based on the final states of the automaton. For each final state $q_f \in F$ and $q \in Q_\$$, let the regular language N_{q,q_f} be

$$N_{q,q_f} = \{v \mid \delta(q, v) = q \ \wedge \ \delta(q, \$v) = q_f \ \wedge \ \delta(q_f, v) = q_f\} \tag{3}$$

Finally, for the regular language $R \subseteq \Sigma^*\$\Sigma^+$, we define the ω-regular language $\omega(R)$ as

$$\omega(R) = \bigcup_{(q,q_f) \in Q_\$ \times F} M_q N_{q,q_f}^\omega. \tag{4}$$

We call this language $\omega(R)$ to indicate the fact that it is the corresponding ω-regular language of R. Next we show that $\omega(R)$ is the ω-regular language whose *regular imgage* is indeed R. The following theorem states this result:

Theorem 4. *Let $R \subseteq \Sigma^*\$\Sigma^+$ be a regular language that is saturated by $\stackrel{\circ}{=}$. Then, there exists an ω-regular language L such that $R = L_\$$.*

Proof. See [9] for the proof. □

In fact, $L = \omega(R)$ in the above theorem. One can directly build a Büchi automaton recognizing L from $\mathcal{A}$. The set $Q_\$$ can be effectively computed. For each state $q \in Q_\$$, the language M_q is recognized by the automaton $(\Sigma, Q, I, \{q\}, \delta)$. For each final state q_f, the language N_{q,q_f} is the intersection of the languages $L(\Sigma, Q, \{q\}, \{q\}, \delta)$, $L(\Sigma, Q, \{\delta(q, \$)\}, \{q_f\}, \delta)$, and $L(\Sigma, Q, \{q_f\}, \{q_f\}, \delta)$. For each pair (q, q_f), once we have DFAs recognizing M_q and N_{q,q_f}, we can easily construct[1] a Büchi automaton recognizing $M_q N_{q,q_f}^\omega$. The Büchi automaton recognizing L is the union of these automata. Each $M_q N_{q,q_f}^\omega$ is recognized by an automaton of size at most $|\mathcal{A}| + |\mathcal{A}|^3$, which means that L is recognized by an automata of size at most $|\mathcal{A}|^3 + |\mathcal{A}|^5$.

A question that naturally arises is what can one say about the result of the above construction if R is not saturated by $\stackrel{\circ}{=}$? As we will see in Section 4, we need to construct Büchi automata from DFAs guessed in the process of learning which may not be necessarily saturated by $\stackrel{\circ}{=}$. For a regular language $R \subseteq \Sigma^*\$\Sigma^+$ which is not saturated by $\stackrel{\circ}{=}$ and $L = \bigcup_{(q,q_f) \in Q_\$ \times F} M_q N_{q,q_f}^\omega$, it is not necessarily the case that $R = L_\$$ (compare with the statement of Theorem 4). For example, $R = \{a\$b\}$ is not saturated by $\stackrel{\circ}{=}$ since it contains an element of the class $[a\$b]_{\stackrel{\circ}{=}}$ (namely, $a\$b$), but does not contain the whole class (which is the set $ab^*\$b^+$). But, L has a number of essential properties:

Proposition 2. *Let $R = U_\$$ for some arbitrary ω-regular language U. Then, we have $\omega(R) = U$ (defined by (4)).*

Proof. Direct consequence of Theorem 4. □

Proposition 3. *Assume $R \subseteq \Sigma^*\$\Sigma^+$ is a regular language. Let $[u\$v]_{\stackrel{\circ}{=}}$ denote the equivalence class of the word $u\$v$ by the relation $\stackrel{\circ}{=}$. For each pair of words $(u, v) \in \Sigma^* \times \Sigma^+$, if $[u\$v]_{\stackrel{\circ}{=}} \cap R = \emptyset$ then $uv^\omega \notin \omega(R)$.*

Proof. If $uv^\omega \in \omega(R)$, there exist a string u' in some M_q and a string v' in some N_{q,q_f} such that $u'v'^\omega = uv^\omega$ (Lemma 1). Since u' is in M_q and v' is in N_{q,q_f}, we have $u'\$v'$ in R. Because $u'v'^\omega = uv^\omega$, we have $u'\$v' \in [u\$v]_{\stackrel{\circ}{=}}$, which contradicts $[u\$v]_{\stackrel{\circ}{=}} \cap R = \emptyset$. □

Proposition 4. *Assume $R \subseteq \Sigma^*\$\Sigma^+$ is a regular language. For each pair of words $(u, v) \in \Sigma^* \times \Sigma^+$, if $[u\$v]_{\stackrel{\circ}{=}} \subseteq R$ then $uv^\omega \in \omega(R)$.*

Proof. If $[u\$v]_{\stackrel{\circ}{=}} \subseteq R$, we can find k and k' satisfying $uv^k(v^{k'})^\omega \in \omega(R)$ (follows from proof of Theorem 4). Since $uv^\omega = uv^k(v^{k'})^\omega$, we have $uv^\omega \in \omega(R)$. □

---

[1] One can connect the final states of $\mathcal{A}(M_q)$ to the initial states of $\mathcal{A}^\omega(N_{q,q_F})$ by ϵ transitions, and let the final states of N_{q,q_f} be the final states of the resulting Büchi automaton. $\mathcal{A}^\omega(N_{q,q_F})$ can be obtained from $\mathcal{A}(N_{q,q_F})$ by normalizing it and connecting the final state to the initial state by an epsilon transition [17].

4   Learning ω-Regular Languages

In this section, we present an algorithm that *learns* an unknown ω-regular language and generates a nondeterministic Büchi automaton which recognizes L as the result. There are well-known and well-studied algorithms for learning a deterministic finite automaton (DFA) [2,18]. We propose an approach which uses the L* algorithm [2] as the basis for learning an unknown ω-regular language L.

The idea behind L* is learning by experimentation. The learner has the ability to make *membership queries*. An *oracle* (a *teacher* who knows the target language), on any input word v, returns a yes-or-no answer depending on whether v belongs to the target language. The learning algorithm thus chooses particular inputs to classify, and consequently makes progress. The learner also has the ability to make *equivalence* queries. A conjecture language is guessed by the learner, which will then be verified by the *teacher* through an equivalence check against the target language. The teacher returns *yes* when the conjecture is correct, or *no* accompanied by a counterexample to the equivalence of the conjecture and the target language. This counterexample can be a *positive* counterexample (a word that belongs to the target language but does not belong to the conjecture language) or a *negative* counterexample (a word that does not belong to the the target language but belongs to the conjecture language). We refer the reader unfamiliar with L* to [2] for more information on the algorithm.

The goal of our learning algorithm is to come up with a nondeterministic Büchi automaton that recognizes an unknown ω-regular language L. We assume that there is a teacher who can correctly answer the *membership* and *equivalence* queries on L as discussed above. The idea is to learn the language $L_\$$ instead of learning L directly. One can reuse the core of the L* algorithm here, but many changes have to be made. The reason is that the membership and equivalence queries allowed in the setting of our algorithm are for the ω-regular language L and not for the regular language $L_\$$. One has to translate the queries and their responses back and forth from the $L_\$$ level to the L level.

Membership Queries: The L* algorithm frequently needs to ask questions of the form: "does the string w belong to the target language $L_\$$?". We need to translate this query into one that can be posed to our teacher. The following simple steps perform this task:

1. Does w belong to $\Sigma^*\$\Sigma^+$? If no, then the answer is "NO". If yes, then go to the next step.
2. Let $w = u\$v$. Does uv^ω belong to L? if no, then the answer is "NO". If yes, then the answer is "YES".

We know that $L_\$ \subseteq \Sigma^*\$\Sigma^+$ which helps us filter out some strings without asking the teacher. If we have $w \in \Sigma^*\$\Sigma^+$, then w is of the form $u\$v$ which corresponds to the ultimately periodic word uv^ω. The teacher can respond to the membership query by checking whether uv^ω belongs to L. The answer to this query indicates whether $u\$v$ should belong to our current conjecture. Note that by the definition of $L_\$$, we have $u\$v \in L_\$ \Leftrightarrow uv^\omega \in L$.

Equivalence Queries: L* generates conjecture DFAs that need to be verified, and therefore a question of the form "Is the conjecture language M_i equivalent to the target language $L_\$$?" needs to be asked. We need to translate this query into an equivalent one that can be posed to the teacher:

1. Is M_i a subset of $\Sigma^*\$\Sigma^+$? If no, get the counterexample and continue with L*. If yes, then go the next step.
2. Is $\omega(M_i)$ (the corresponding ω-regular language of M_i) equivalent to L? If yes, we are done. If no, we get an ultimately periodic word c that is a (negative or positive) counterexample to the equivalence check. Return "NO" and a finitary interpretation of c (described below) to L*.

Again, the $M_i \subseteq \Sigma^*\$\Sigma^+$ check works as a preliminary test to filter out conjectures that are *obviously* not correct. If a conjecture language (DFA) M_i passes the first test, we construct its corresponding Büchi automaton $\omega(M_i)$. The teacher can then respond by checking the equivalence between L and $\omega(M_i)$. If they are not equivalent, the teacher will return a counterexample to the equivalence of the two languages. In order to proceed with L*, we have to translate these ω-words to finite words that are counterexamples to the equivalence of M_i and $L_\$$. To do this, for the counterexample uv^ω, we construct a DFA that accepts $[u\$v]_{\triangleq}$. There are two cases for each counterexample uv^ω:

- *The word uv^ω is a positive counterexample:* the word uv^ω should be in $\omega(M_i)$ but is not. Since $uv^\omega \notin \omega(M_i)$, by Proposition 4, $[u\$v]_{\triangleq} \not\subseteq M_i$ and there exists a word $u'\$v' \in [u\$v]_{\triangleq}$ such that $u'\$v'$ is not in M_i. Then $u'\$v'$ can serve as an effective positive counterexample for the L* algorithm. To find $u'\$v'$, it suffices to check the emptiness of the language $[u\$v]_{\triangleq} - M_i$. There are various ways in which one can compute $[u\$v]_{\triangleq}$. One way is by direct construction of a DFA accepting $[u\$v]_{\triangleq}$ from the Büchi automaton that accepts the language containing a single word uv^ω. There is a detailed description of this construction in [5] (note that although this construction has an exponential blow up in general, in this special case it is linear). We use a different construction in our implementation which is presented in [9].
- *The word uv^ω is a negative counterexample:* the word uv^ω should not be in $\omega(M_i)$, but it is. Since $uv^\omega \in L$, by Proposition 3, $[u\$v]_{\triangleq} \cap M_i \neq \emptyset$ and there exists a word $u'\$v' \in [u\$v]_{\triangleq}$ such that $u'\$v' \in M_i$. One can find this word by checking emptiness of $M_i \cap [u\$v]_{\triangleq}$. Then $u'\$v'$ works as a proper negative counterexample for the L* algorithm.

Here is why the above procedure works: A conjecture M may not be saturated by $\triangleq$. Consider the case presented in Figure 1(a). There are four equivalence classes: $[u_1\$v_1]_{\triangleq}$ is contained in M, $[u_2\$v_2]_{\triangleq}$ and $[u_3\$v_3]_{\triangleq}$ have intersections with M but are not contained in it, and $[u_4\$v_4]_{\triangleq}$ is completely outside M. Now assume $L' = \omega(M)$ (as defined by (4)) is the ω-regular language corresponding to M. Proposition 4 implies that $u_1v_1^\omega \in L'$. Proposition 3 implies that $u_4v_4^\omega \notin L'$. However, one cannot state anything about $u_2v_2^\omega$ and $u_3v_3^\omega$ with certainty; they may or may not be in L'. Let us assume (for the sake of the argument) that

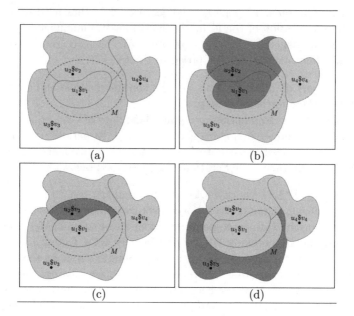

Fig. 1. The Case of Non-saturation

$u_2 v_2^\omega \in L'$ and $u_3 v_3^\omega \notin L'$. This means that $L'_\$$ (which is not equivalent to M) is actually the *shaded* area in Figure 1(b). Now, if L' is not the correct conjecture ($L' \neq L$), one will end up with an ω-word uv^ω as a counterexample. As mentioned above, we have one of the following two cases:

(1) The word uv^ω is a negative counterexample ($uv^\omega \in \omega(M)$ and $uv^\omega \notin L$). There are two possibilities for the class $[u\$v]_{\underline{\circ}}$:
   - $[u\$v]_{\underline{\circ}} \subseteq M$: This case is rather trivial. Any word in $[u\$v]_{\underline{\circ}}$, including $u\$v$, belongs to M while it should not. Therefore, $u\$v$ can serve as a *proper* negative counterexample for the next iteration of L*.
   - $[u\$v]_{\underline{\circ}} \not\subseteq M$: This case is more tricky. This means that $u_2 v_2^\omega$ was wrongly included in $\omega(M)$. But since some of the strings in $[u\$v]_{\underline{\circ}}$ do not belong to M, an arbitrary string from $[u\$v]_{\underline{\circ}}$ does not necessarily work as a negative counterexample for the next iteration of L*. One has to find a string which is in both $[u\$v]_{\underline{\circ}}$ and M, which means it belongs to $[u\$v]_{\underline{\circ}} \cap M$. The *shaded* area in Figure 1(c) demonstrates this set for the example. Note that $[u\$v]_{\underline{\circ}} \cap M$ cannot be empty; by Proposition 3, $[u\$v]_{\underline{\circ}} \cap M = \emptyset$ implies that $uv^\omega \notin L$ which is a contradiction.

(2) The word uv^ω is a positive counterexample ($uv^\omega \notin \omega(M)$ and $uv^\omega \in L$). There are two possibilities for the class $[u\$v]_{\underline{\circ}}$:
   - $[u\$v]_{\underline{\circ}} \cap M = \emptyset$: This case is rather trivial. All words in $[u\$v]_{\underline{\circ}}$, including $u\$v$, do not belong to M while they should. Therefore, $u\$v$ can serve as a *proper* positive counterexample for the next iteration of L*.

- $[u\$v]_{\doteq} \cap M \neq \emptyset$: This case is more tricky. This means that $u_3 v_3^\omega$ was wrongly left out of $\omega(M)$. But since some of the strings in $[u\$v]_{\doteq}$ do belong to M, an arbitrary string from that class is not necessarily going to work as a *proper* positive counterexample for the next iteration of L*. We have to make sure to find one that is in $[u\$v]_{\doteq}$ but not in M. The set $[u\$v]_{\doteq} - M$ contains such a string which is guaranteed to make L* *progress*. The *shaded* area in Figure 1(d) demonstrates this set for the example. Note that $[u\$v]_{\doteq} - M$ cannot be empty; $[u\$v]_{\doteq} - M = \emptyset$ implies that $[u\$v]_{\doteq} \subseteq M$ in which case by Proposition 4, we have $uv^\omega \in L$, which is a contradiction.

Below, we give a more technical description of our algorithm followed by an example for greater clarity.

Definition 3. *An observation table is a tuple $\langle S, E, T \rangle$ where S is a set of prefix-closed words in Σ^* such that each word in S represents a syntactic right congruence class of $L_\$$, E is a set of suffix-closed strings in Σ^* such that each word in E is a distinguishing word, and $T : (S \cup S\Sigma) \times E \longrightarrow \{-, +\}$ is defined as*

$$T(\alpha, \sigma) = \begin{cases} + & \text{if } \alpha\sigma \in L_\$ \\ - & \text{if } \alpha\sigma \notin L_\$. \end{cases}$$

An observation table is *closed* if for every word $s' \in S\Sigma$, there exists a word $s \in S$ such that $T(s, \bullet) = T(s', \bullet)$ (where $T(s, \bullet)$ indicates the row of the table which starts with s).

The goal of L* here is to learn $L_\$$ for an unknown ω-language L on alphabet $\Sigma \cup \{\$\}$. Our initial setting is the same as L*; the distinguishing experiment set $E = \{\lambda\}$ and the congruence class set $S = \{\lambda\}$. We fill the table by asking membership queries for each pair of strings $(\alpha, \sigma) \in (S \cup S\Sigma) \times E$; a "NO" response sets $T(\alpha, \sigma) = -$, and a "YES" response sets $T(\alpha, \sigma) = +$. Note that the membership queries are translated as discussed above to a format appropriate for the teacher.

When the observation table is closed, a conjecture DFA $A = (S, \Sigma, q_0, F, \delta)$, where $Q = \{u | u \in S\}$, $q_0 = \lambda$, $\delta = \{(u, a, u') | u' \in S \wedge T(u', \bullet) = T(ua, \bullet)\}$, and $F = \{u | T(u, \lambda) = +\}$ is constructed from the table.

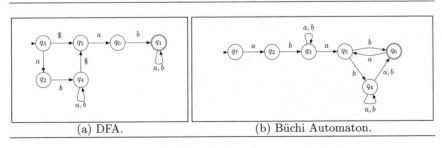

| | (a) DFA. | (b) Büchi Automaton. |

Fig. 2. First Iteration

We then check if $M_0 = L(A)$ is a subset of $\Sigma^*\$\Sigma^+$. If not, there is a counterexample in $L(A_\$) \cap \overline{\Sigma^*\$\Sigma^+}$ from the language containment check, all of whose suffixes are added to the set of distinguishing words E. If $M_0 \subseteq \Sigma^*\$\Sigma^+$, we construct a Büchi automaton B based on A (see Section 3), and perform the equivalence check. The counterexamples are interpreted (as discussed above) and the appropriate counterexamples are added to set E. We then proceed to another iteration of this algorithm, until the target language is found.

Example 1. We demonstrate our algorithm by showing the steps performed on a simple example. Assume that the target language is $ab((a + b)^*a)^\omega$. This ω-expression corresponds to the liveness property: "a happens infinitely often in a computation with the prefix ab" which cannot be learned using any of the existing algorithms.

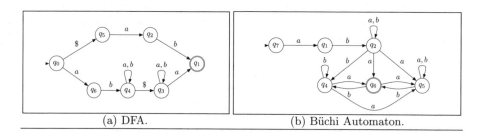

(a) DFA.   (b) Büchi Automaton.

Fig. 3. Second Iteration

Table 1(a) shows the closed observation from the first iteration of our algorithm. Figure 2(a) demonstrates the DFA that corresponds to this observation table, and Figure 2(b) demonstrates the Büchi automaton constructed form this DFA. The first conjecture is not correct; the word $ab(a)^\omega$ belongs to the target language, but is not accepted by the automaton in Figure 2(b). Therefore, the algorithm goes into a second iteration. The counterexample is translated into one appropriate for the L* ($ab\$a$), and all its suffixes are added to the top row of the table. Table 1(b) is the closed table which we acquire after adding the counterexample. Figure 3(a) shows the DFA corresponding to this table, and Figure 3(b) shows the Büchi automaton constructed based on this DFA. This Büchi automaton passes the equivalence check and the algorithm is finished learning the target language.

Complexity: Note that for the target ω-regular language L, our learning algorithm terminates by learning $L_\$$ (and hence L). We can show that our learning algorithm is polynomial (in terms of number of queries performed) on the size of $L_\$$ (and the size of the counter examples). However, one can show that $L_\$$, in the worst case, can be exponentially bigger that the minimal Büchi automaton accepting L. We refer the interested reader to [9] for a more detailed discussion.

5   Optimizations

In this section, we briefly discuss some practical optimizations that we have added to our implementation of the algorithm presented in Section 4 to gain a more efficient learning tool.

Equivalence query as the last resort: The equivalence query for an ω-regular language is expensive, even more than equivalence checking for regular languages. The main reason is that it requires complementing the Büchi automaton, which has a proven lower bound of $2^{O(n \log n)}$ [16]. Therefore, having fewer equivalence queries speeds up the process of learning. For each conjecture DFA A that is built during an iteration of the algorithm (more specifically, the incorrect conjectures), $L(A)$ may not be saturated by $\doteq$. If one could check for saturation and make $\doteq$ saturate $L(A)$ by adding/removing words, one could avoid going through with an (expensive) equivalence check that will most probably have a "NO" response. Unfortunately, there is no known way of effectively checking for saturation. But all is not lost. One can construct another DFA A' where $L(A') = (\Sigma^* \$ \Sigma^+) \cap \overline{L(A)}$. Since A is deterministic, A' can easily be constructed. Let B and B' be respectively the corresponding Büchi automata for A and A'. If $L(B) \cap L(B') \neq \emptyset$ then there is $uv^{\omega} \in L(B) \cap L(B')$, and we know that only a part of the equivalence class $[u\$v]_{\doteq}$ is in $L(A)$ and the rest of it is in $L(A')$. To decide whether the class should go into $L(A)$ (the conjecture) completely, or be altogether removed from

Table 1. Observation Tables

(a) First Iteration.

	λ	ab	b	$ab	a$ab	aba$ab	ba$ab
λ	−	−	−	+	−	−	+
a	−	−	−	−	−	+	−
b	−	−	−	−	−	−	−
$	−	−	+	−	−	−	−
ab	−	−	−	+	+	+	+
$a	−	+	−	−	−	−	−
$ab	+	+	+	−	−	−	−
aa	−	−	−	−	−	−	−
a$	−	−	−	−	−	−	−
ba	−	−	−	−	−	−	−
bb	−	−	−	−	−	−	−
b$	−	−	−	−	−	−	−
$b	−	−	−	−	−	−	−
$$	−	−	−	−	−	−	−
aba	−	−	−	+	+	+	+
abb	−	−	−	+	+	+	+
ab$	−	−	+	−	−	−	−
$aa	−	−	−	−	−	−	−
a	−	−	−	−	−	−	−
$aba	+	+	+	−	−	−	−
$abb	+	+	+	−	−	−	−
ab	−	−	−	−	−	−	−

(b) Second Iteration.

	λ	ab	b	$ab	a$ab	aba$ab	ba$ab	a	$a	b$a	ab$a
λ	−	−	−	+	−	−	+	−	−	−	+
a	−	−	−	−	−	+	−	−	−	+	−
b	−	−	−	−	−	−	−	−	−	−	−
$	−	−	+	−	−	−	−	−	−	−	−
ab	−	−	−	+	+	+	+	−	+	+	+
$a	−	+	−	−	−	−	−	−	−	−	−
$ab	+	+	+	−	−	−	−	+	−	−	−
ab$	−	−	+	−	−	−	−	+	−	−	−
aa	−	−	−	−	−	−	−	−	−	−	−
a$	−	−	−	−	−	−	−	−	−	−	−
ba	−	−	−	−	−	−	−	−	−	−	−
bb	−	−	−	−	−	−	−	−	−	−	−
b$	−	−	−	−	−	−	−	−	−	−	−
$b	−	−	−	−	−	−	−	−	−	−	−
$$	−	−	−	−	−	−	−	−	−	−	−
aba	−	−	−	+	+	+	+	−	+	+	+
abb	−	−	−	+	+	+	+	−	+	+	+
$aa	−	−	−	−	−	−	−	−	−	−	−
a	−	−	−	−	−	−	−	−	−	−	−
$aba	+	+	+	−	−	−	−	+	−	−	−
$abb	+	+	+	−	−	−	−	+	−	−	−
ab	−	−	−	−	−	−	−	−	−	−	−
ab$a	+	+	+	−	−	−	−	+	−	−	−
ab$b	−	−	+	−	−	−	−	+	−	−	−
ab$$	−	−	−	−	−	−	−	−	−	−	−

it, we can pose a membership query for uv^ω to the teacher. If $uv^\omega \in L$, then the class should belong to the conjecture, and therefore any word in $[u\$v]_{\doteq} \cap L(A')$ works as a positive counterexample for the next iteration of L*. If $uv^\omega \notin L$ then any word in $[u\$v]_{\doteq} \cap L(A)$ can serve as a negative counterexample for the next iteration of the L*. This check is polynomial in the size of A, and saves us an unnecessary equivalence query.

Minimization and Simplification: Our algorithm constructs and handles many DFAs during the construction of the Büchi automaton from the conjecture DFA (from M_q's and N_{q,q_f}'s). Hence, the algorithm can benefit from minimizing all those DFAs in order to reduce the overhead of working with them later on. DFA minimization can be done very efficiently; the complexity is $n \log n$ [12], where n is the size of the source DFA.

When the conjecture Büchi automaton is built, another useful technique is to simplify the Büchi automaton by detecting a simulation relation between states [19]. Intuitively, a state p simulates another state q in the Büchi automaton if all accepting traces starting from q are also accepting traces starting from p. If p simulates q and both transitions $r \xrightarrow{a} p$ and $r \xrightarrow{a} q$ are in the automaton, then $r \xrightarrow{a} q$ can be safely removed without changing the language of the Büchi automaton. Furthermore, if p and q simulate each other, then after redirecting all of q's incoming transitions to p, q can be safely removed. This technique is useful for reducing the size of the result automaton, because the structures of M_q and N_{q,q_f}^ω are usually very similar, which provides good opportunities for finding simulation relations.

6   Preliminary Experimental Results

We have implemented our algorithm using JAVA. DFA operations are delegated to the *dk.brics.automaton* package, and the Büchi automaton equivalence checking function is provided by the GOAL tool [20].

We check the performance of our tool by learning *randomly generated ω-regular languages*. More specifically, we combine the following 5 steps to get a target Büchi automaton:

1. Randomly generate LTL formulas with a length of 6 and with 1 or 2 propositions (which produces respectively Büchi automata with $|\Sigma| = 2$ and 4).
2. If the formula appeared before, discard it and go back to step 1.

Table 2. Results for Randomly Generated Temporal Formulas

	$|\Sigma| = 2$			$|\Sigma| = 4$		
	Avg	Min	Max	Avg	Min	Max
Target BA recognizing L	5.3	5	7	5.34	5	10
Learned DFA	7.98	3	21	8.7	5	16
Learned BA	6.78	3	11	12.92	5	35
Learned BA (after simplification)	5.36	2	8	9.38	3	24

(Unit: number of states)

3. Use the LTL2BA [10] algorithm to make them Büchi automata.
4. Apply the simplification [19] to make the Büchi automata as small as possible.
5. If the size of the automaton is smaller than 5, discard it and go to step 1.

Note that the combination of these steps does not guarantee the minimality of the resulting Büchi automaton.

Table 2 presents the performance of our algorithm on these randomly generated ω-regular languages. The sizes of the learned automata are compared with the sizes of the target automata. The result shows that the size the learned automaton is comparable with the size of the target automaton. Table 2 presents a summary of the results of 100 learning tasks. We have 50 are with $|\Sigma| = 2$ and another half of them with $|\Sigma| = 4$.

Table 3. Effectiveness for learning automata from selected temporal formulas

Property Classes	Canonical Formulas	Target St	Trans	Learned St	Trans	Responsive Formulas	Target St	Trans	Learned St	Trans	⊆ DB∩ coDB?
Reactive	$\mathbf{FG}p \vee \mathbf{GF}q$	5	26	7	37	$\mathbf{GF}p \to \mathbf{GF}q$	5	26	7	37	No
Persistence	$\mathbf{FG}p$	2	4	3	7	$\mathbf{G}(p \to \mathbf{FG}q)$	4	18	11	43	No
Recurrence	$\mathbf{GF}p$	2	12	3	9	$\mathbf{G}(p \to \mathbf{F}q)$	3	12	13	65	No
Obligation	$\mathbf{G}p \vee \mathbf{F}q$	4	15	6	25	$\mathbf{F}p \to \mathbf{F}q$	4	15	6	25	Yes
Safety	$\mathbf{G}p$	2	2	2	3	$p \to \mathbf{G}q$	3	9	9	32	Yes
Guarantee	$\mathbf{F}p$	2	4	3	8	$p \to \mathbf{F}q$	3	12	4	20	Yes

On a different note, we present the performance of our algorithm on learning properties that are often used in verification. Table 3 presents the result of these experiments. The target languages are described by temporal formulas selected from Manna and Pnueli [15] and classified according to the hierarchy of temporal properties which they proposed in the same paper. We translate those temporal formulas to Büchi automata by the LTL2BA algorithm. The first column of the table lists the six classes of the hierarchy. We select two temporal formulas for each class[2]. One of them is a formula in "canonical form"[3] and the other is a formula in "responsive form"[4]. Maler and Pnueli's algorithm [14] can only handle the bottom three levels of that hierarchy. Their algorithm cannot handle some important properties such as *progress* $\mathbf{G}(p \to \mathbf{F}q)$ and *strong fairness* $\mathbf{GF}p \to \mathbf{GF}q$, which can be handled by our algorithm.

7 Conclusions and Future Work

We have extended the learning paradigm of the infinitary languages by presenting an algorithm to learn an *arbitrary* ω-regular language L over an alphabet Σ.

---

[2] In this table, p and q are propositions. If one replaces p and q in a formula f with temporal formulas containing only past operators, f still belongs to the same class.

[3] The canonical formula is a simple representative formula for each class.

[4] A responsive formula usually contains two propositions p and q. The proposition p represents a stimulus and q is a response to p.

Our main result is an algorithm to learn a nondeterministic Büchi automaton that recognizes an unknown ω-regular language by learning a unique projection of it $(L_\$)$ on Σ^* using the L*[2] algorithm. We also presented preliminary experimental results that suggest that algorithms performs well on small examples.

In the future, we would like to extend our experiments by learning bigger Büchi automata. We would also like to use this learning algorithm as a core of a compositional verification tool to equip the tool with the capability to check liveness properties that have been missing from such tools so far. One way of improving our algorithm is to find an effective way of checking for saturation, which appears to be difficult and remains unsolved.

References

1. Alur, R., Madhusudan, P., Nam, W.: Symbolic compositional verification by learning assumptions. In: Etessami, K., Rajamani, S.K. (eds.) CAV 2005. LNCS, vol. 3576, pp. 548–562. Springer, Heidelberg (2005)
2. Angluin, D.: Learning regular sets from queries and counterexamples. Information and Computation 75(2), 87–106 (1987)
3. Arnold, A.: A syntactic congruence for rational omega-language. Theoretical Computer Science 39, 333–335 (1985)
4. Büchi, J.R.: On a decision method in restricted second-order arithmetic. In: Proceedings of the 1960 International Congress on Logic, Methodology and Philosophy of Science, pp. 1–11 (1962)
5. Calbrix, H., Nivat, M., Podelski, A.: Ultimately periodic words of rational ω-languages. In: Main, M.G., Melton, A.C., Mislove, M.W., Schmidt, D., Brookes, S.D. (eds.) MFPS 1993. LNCS, vol. 802, pp. 554–566. Springer, Heidelberg (1994)
6. Calbrix, H., Nivat, M., Podelski, A.: Sur les mots ultimement périodiques des langages rationnels de mots infinis. Comptes Rendus de l'Académie des Sciences 318, 493–497 (1994)
7. Chaki, S., Clarke, E., Sinha, N., Thati, P.: Automated assume-guarantee reasoning for simulation conformance. In: Etessami, K., Rajamani, S.K. (eds.) CAV 2005. LNCS, vol. 3576, pp. 534–547. Springer, Heidelberg (2005)
8. Cobleigh, J.M., Giannakopoulou, D., Păsăreanu, C.S.: Learning assumptions for compositional verification. In: Garavel, H., Hatcliff, J. (eds.) TACAS 2003. LNCS, vol. 2619, pp. 331–346. Springer, Heidelberg (2003)
9. Farzan, A., Chen, Y., Clarke, E., Tsay, Y., Wang, B.: Extending automated compositional verification to the full class of omega-regular languages. Technical Report CMU-CS-2008-100, Carnegie Mellon University, Department of Computer Science (2008)
10. Gastin, P., Oddoux, D.: Fast LTL to Büchi automata translations. In: Berry, G., Comon, H., Finkel, A. (eds.) CAV 2001. LNCS, vol. 2102, pp. 53–65. Springer, Heidelberg (2001)
11. Gupta, A., McMillan, K.L., Fu, Z.: Automated assumption generation for compositional verification. In: Damm, W., Hermanns, H. (eds.) CAV 2007. LNCS, vol. 4590, pp. 420–432. Springer, Heidelberg (2007)
12. Hopcroft, J.E.: A n logn algorithm for minimizing states in a finite automaton. Technical report, Stanford University (1971)
13. Hopcroft, J.E., Ullman, J.D.: Introduction to Automata Theory, Languages and Computation. Addison-Wesley, Reading (1979)

14. Maler, O., Pnueli, A.: On the learnability of infinitary regular sets. Information and Computation 118(2), 316–326 (1995)
15. Manna, Z., Pnueli, A.: A hierarchy of temporal properties. Technical Report STAN-CS-87-1186, Stanford University, Department of Computer Science (1987)
16. Michel, M.: Complementation is more difficult with automata on infinite words. In: CNET, Paris (1988)
17. Perrin, D., Pin, J.E.: Infinite Words: Automata, Semigroups, Logic and Games. Academic Press, London (2003)
18. Rivest, R.L., Schapire, R.E.: Inference of finite automata using homing sequences. Information and Computation 103(2), 299–347 (1993)
19. Somenzi, F., Bloem, R.: Efficient Büchi automata from LTL formulae. In: Emerson, E.A., Sistla, A.P. (eds.) CAV 2000. LNCS, vol. 1855, pp. 248–263. Springer, Heidelberg (2000)
20. Tsay, Y., Chen, Y., Tsai, M., Wu, K., Chan, W.: GOAL: A Graphical Tool for Manipulating Büchi Automata and Temporal Formulae. In: Grumberg, O., Huth, M. (eds.) TACAS 2007. LNCS, vol. 4424, pp. 466–471. Springer, Heidelberg (2007)
21. Van, D.L., Le Saëc, B., Litovsky, I.: Characterizations of rational omega-languages by means of right congruences. Theor. Comput. Sci. 143(1), 1–21 (1995)

Graph Grammar Modeling and Verification
of Ad Hoc Routing Protocols

Mayank Saksena, Oskar Wibling, and Bengt Jonsson

Dept. of Information Technology, P.O. Box 337, S-751 05 Uppsala, Sweden
{mayanks,oskarw,bengt}@it.uu.se

Abstract. We present a technique for modeling and automatic verification of network protocols, based on graph transformation. It is suitable
for protocols with a potentially unbounded number of nodes, in which
the structure and topology of the network is a central aspect, such as
routing protocols for ad hoc networks. Safety properties are specified as
a set of undesirable global configurations. We verify that there is no undesirable configuration which is reachable from an initial configuration,
by means of symbolic backward reachability analysis.

In general, the reachability problem is undecidable. We implement the
technique in a graph grammar analysis tool, and automatically verify
several interesting nontrivial examples. Notably, we prove loop freedom
for the DYMO ad hoc routing protocol. DYMO is currently on the IETF
standards track, to potentially become an Internet standard.

1 Introduction

The verification of network protocols has been one of the most important driving forces for the development of model checking technology. Most approaches
(e.g., [15]) analyze finite-state models of protocols, but an increasing number
of techniques are developed for analyzing parameterized or infinite-state models
(e.g., [2]). In this paper, we consider verification of protocols for networks with a
potentially unbounded number of nodes, possibly with a dynamically changing
topology. This is a large class of protocols, including protocols for wireless ad
hoc networks, many distributed algorithms, security protocols, telephone system
services, etc. Global configurations of such protocols are naturally modeled using
graphs, that are transformed by the protocol's dynamic behavior, and therefore
various forms of graph transformation systems have been used to model and
analyze them [19,7].

In this paper, we present a technique for modeling and verification of protocols using a variant of *graph transformation systems* (GTSs) [19,7]. We use
a general mechanism for expressing conditions on the applicability of a rule, in
the form of *negative application conditions (NACs)*. Sets of global configurations
are symbolically represented by *graph patterns* [7], which are graphs extended
with NACs. Intuitively, a graph pattern represents the set of configurations that
contain it as a subgraph, but none of the NACs. A safety property of a protocol is represented by a set of graph patterns that represent undesirable global
configurations.

C.R. Ramakrishnan and J. Rehof (Eds.): TACAS 2008, LNCS 4963, pp. 18–32, 2008.

We consider the problem of verifying safety properties. This can be reduced to the problem whether an undesirable configuration can be reached, by a sequence of graph transformation steps, from some initial global configuration. We present a method for automatically checking such a reachability problem by backward reachability analysis. Backward reachability analysis is a powerful verification technique, which has generated decidability results for many classes of parameterized and infinite-state systems (e.g., [3,2,13]) and proven to be highly useful also for undecidable verification problems (e.g., [1]). By fixed point computation, we compute an over-approximation of the set of configurations from which a bad configuration can be reached, and check that this set contains no initial configuration. The central part of the backward reachability procedure is to compute the predecessors of a set of configurations in this symbolic representation. Since the reachability problem is undecidable in general, the fixed point computation is not guaranteed to terminate. However, we show that the techniques are powerful enough for verifying several interesting nontrivial examples, indicating that the approach is useful for network protocols where the dynamically changing topology of the network is a central aspect.

A main motivation for our work is to analyze protocols for wireless ad hoc networks, including the important class of *routing protocols*. We have implemented our technique, and successfully verified that the DYMO protocol [10] will never generate routing loops. Verifying loop freedom for ad hoc routing protocols has been the subject of much work [8,12]; several previous protocol proposals have been incorrect in this respect [9,4]. Our verification method handles a detailed ad hoc routing protocol model, with relatively little effort. In our work, we have also found GTSs to be an intuitive and visually clear form of modeling.

For space limitations, proofs are not included in this paper; instead see the extended version [22].

Related work. There have been several efforts to verify loop freedom of routing protocols for ad hoc networks. Bhargavan et al. [8] verified AODV [21] to be loop free, using a combination of SPIN for model checking a finite network model, and HOL theorem proving for generalizing the proof. In contrast, we prove the same property automatically for an arbitrary number of nodes. Our experience is that modeling using GTSs is more intuitive than to separately construct SPIN models and HOL proofs. Das and Dill [12] developed automatic predicate discovery for use in predicate abstraction, and proved loop freedom for a simplified version of AODV, excluding timeouts. The construction of an abstract system and discovery of relevant abstraction predicates require many calls to a theorem prover; our method does not need to interact with a theorem prover. We check the graphs directly for inconsistencies.

There have been several other approaches to modeling and analysis using variants of GTSs. König and Kozioura [19] over-approximate graph transformation systems using Petri nets, successively constructed using forward counterexample guided abstraction refinement. Their technique does not support the use of NACs. We have found NACs to be an advantage during modeling and verification. For example, our first approach at verifying the DYMO protocol was without NACs, resulting in a more complex model with features not directly related to the central protocol function.

Kastenberg and Rensink [18] translate GTSs to finite-state models in the GROOVE tool by putting an upper bound on the number of nodes in a network. Becker et al. [7] verified safety properties of mechatronic systems, modeled by GTSs that are similar to ours. However, they only check that the set of non-bad configurations is an inductive invariant. That worked for their application, but for verifying safety properties in general it requires the user to supply an inductive invariant. Bauer and Wilhelm [6,5] use *partner abstraction* to verify dynamic communication systems; two nodes are not distinguished if they have the same labels and the sets of labels of their adjacent nodes are equal, respecting edge directions. That abstraction is not suited for ad hoc protocols, because nodes do not have dedicated roles.

Backward reachability analysis has also been used to verify safety properties in many parameterized and infinite-state system models, with less general connection patterns than those possible in GTSs. Examples include totally homogeneous topologies in which nodes can not identify different partners, resulting in Petri nets with variants (e.g., [13]), systems with linear structure and some extensions (e.g., [1]), and systems with binary connections between nodes, tailored for modeling telephone services [17].

Organization of paper. We give a brief outline of the DYMO protocol in Section 2. The graph transformation system formalism and the backward reachability procedure are presented in Sections 3 and 4. In Section 5 we describe how we modeled DYMO, and present our verification results in Section 6. Finally, Section 7 concludes the paper.

2 DYMO

We are interested in modeling and verification of ad hoc routing protocols. These protocols are used in networks that vary dynamically in size and topology. Every network node that participates in an ad hoc routing protocol acts as a router, using forwarding information stored in a routing table. The purpose of the ad hoc routing protocol is to dynamically update the routing tables so that they reflect the current network topology. DYMO [10] is one of two ad hoc routing protocols currently considered for standardization by the IETF MANET group [23]. The latest DYMO version at the time of writing is specified in version 10 of the DYMO Internet draft [11]. This is the version we have used as basis for our modeling. The following is a simplified description of the main properties of DYMO. The reader is referred to the Internet draft for the details.

In our protocol model, each DYMO network node A has an address, a routing table and a sequence number. The routing table of A contains the following fields for each destination node D.

- RouteNextHopAddress$_A(D)$ is the node to which A currently forwards packets, destined for node D.

- $\mathtt{RouteSeqNo}_A(D)$ is the sequence number that node A has recorded for the route to destination D. It is a measure of the freshness of a route; a higher number means more recent routing information. Note that this sequence number concerns the route to D from A, and is not related to the sequence number of A.
- $\mathtt{RouteHopCnt}_A(D)$ is the recorded distance between nodes A and D, in terms of number of hops.
- $\mathtt{Broken}_A(D)$ is an indicator of whether or not the route from A to D can be used. The protocol has a mechanism to detect when a link on a route is broken [11]. Information regarding broken links is propagated through route error messages ($\mathtt{RERR}$).

When a network node A wants to send a packet to another network node D, it first checks its routing table to see if it has an entry with $\mathtt{Broken}_A(D) = \mathit{false}$. If that is the case, it forwards the packet to node $\mathtt{RouteNextHopAddress}_A(D)$. Otherwise, node A needs to find a route to D, which it does by issuing a route request ($\mathtt{RREQ}$) message. The route request is flooded through the network. It contains the addresses of nodes A and D, the sequence number of A, and a hop counter. The hop counter contains the value 1 when the $\mathtt{RREQ}$ is issued; each re-transmitting node then increases it by one. Node A increases its own sequence number after each issued route request.

When the destination of a route request, D, receives it, it generates a route reply message ($\mathtt{RREP}$). The route reply contains the same fields as the request. Route replies are not flooded, but instead routed through the network using available routing table entries. $\mathtt{RREP}$s and $\mathtt{RREQ}$s are collectively referred to as routing messages (RMs).

Whenever a network node A receives an RM, the routing table of A is compared to the RM. If A does not have an entry pertaining to the originator of the RM, then the information in the RM is inserted into the routing table of A. Otherwise, the information in the RM replaces that of the routing table if the information is more recent, or equally recent but better, in terms of distance to the originator. The routing table update rules are detailed in Section 5.

3   Modeling Using Graph Transformation Systems

We model systems as transition systems of a particular form, in which configurations are hypergraphs, and transitions between configurations are specified by graph rewriting rules. Constraints on configurations are represented by so-called *patterns*, which are hypergraphs extended with a mechanism to describe the absence of certain hyperedges: *negative application conditions (NACs)*. Our definitions are similar to the ones used by, e.g., Becker et al. [7], but with a more general facility for expressing NACs.

Assume a finite set Λ of *labels*. A *hypergraph* is a pair $\langle N, E \rangle$, where N is a finite set of *nodes*, and $E \subseteq \Lambda \times N^*$ is a finite set of *hyperedges*. A hyperedge is a pair $(\lambda, \overrightarrow{n})$, where $\lambda \in \Lambda$ is its *label* and $\overrightarrow{n} \in N^*$. The length of $\overrightarrow{n}$ is called the *arity* of the hyperedge. A hyperedge is essentially a relation on nodes, and can be visualized as a box labeled λ, with connections to each node $n \in \overrightarrow{n}$.

A *pattern* is a tuple $\varphi = \langle N_\varphi, E_\varphi, \mathcal{G}_\varphi^- \rangle$, where $\langle N_\varphi, E_\varphi \rangle$ is a hypergraph, and $\mathcal{G}_\varphi^-$ is a set of NACs. Each *NAC* is a hypergraph $G^- = \langle N^-, E^- \rangle$, where N^- is a finite set of *negative nodes* disjoint from N_φ, and $E^- \subseteq \Lambda \times (N_\varphi \cup N^-)^*$ is a finite set of *negative hyperedges*. We refer to N_φ and E_φ as *positive* nodes and edges of φ. We define $\text{NODES}(E) = \{ n \in \overrightarrow{n} \mid (\lambda, \overrightarrow{n}) \in E \}$.

Example. Figure 1 shows a pattern — the left-hand side of one of the DYMO model routing table update rules. The pattern models a network node receiving routing information for a node to which it currently has no route. In the pattern, positive nodes are drawn as circles and negative nodes as double circles. Nodes have numeric names for identification. Positive and negative edges are drawn as boxes and double boxes. Edge connections are numbered, to indicate their order. The pattern contains a single NAC, consisting of the negative edges labeled `RouteEntry` and `RouteAddress` along with their connected nodes. Without the possibility to express non-existence, we would need to model traversal through the entries to conclude the absence of an entry. In more detail, the pattern consists of a network node A (node 3) and a routing message (node 1). A has a routing table (node 4) that contains no routing table entry pointing to network node D (node 6). The message has originator D, a hop count (node 7), a sequence number (node 5) and an IP source (node 2).

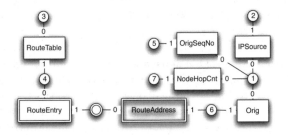

Fig. 1. A pattern containing a NAC

A hypergraph $g = \langle N_g, E_g \rangle$ is *subsumed by* a pattern $\varphi = \langle N_\varphi, E_\varphi, \mathcal{G}_\varphi^- \rangle$, written $g \preceq \varphi$, if there exists an injection $h : N_\varphi \to N_g$ satisfying:

1. for each $(\lambda, \overrightarrow{n}) \in E_\varphi$ we have $(\lambda, h(\overrightarrow{n})) \in E_g$ and
2. there exists no $\langle N^-, E^- \rangle \in \mathcal{G}_\varphi^-$ and no injection $k : N^- \to N_g$ such that $(\lambda, (h \cup k)(\overrightarrow{n})) \in E_g$ for each $(\lambda, \overrightarrow{n}) \in E^-$, where $(h \cup k)$ is defined as h on N_φ and as k on N^-.

Intuitively, a pattern $\varphi = \langle N_\varphi, E_\varphi, \mathcal{G}_\varphi^- \rangle$ is a constraint, saying that a hypergraph must contain $\langle N_\varphi, E_\varphi \rangle$ as a subgraph, which does not have a "match" for any NAC in $\mathcal{G}_\varphi^-$.

Above we let $f((n_1, \ldots, n_k)) = (f(n_1), \ldots, f(n_k))$ for a function on nodes applied to a vector of nodes. If an injection h satisfying the above conditions exists, we say that $g \preceq \varphi$ is *witnessed by* h, written $g \preceq_h \varphi$.

For a pattern φ we use $[\![\varphi]\!]$ to denote the set of hypergraphs g such that $g \preceq \varphi$. For a set of patterns Φ, we let $[\![\Phi]\!] = \cup\{[\![\varphi]\!] \mid \varphi \in \Phi\}$. We call φ *consistent* if there is no $\langle N^-, E^- \rangle \in \mathcal{G}_\varphi^-$ and no injection $k : N^- \to N_\varphi$ such that $(\lambda, k'(\overrightarrow{n})) \in E_\varphi$ for each $(\lambda, \overrightarrow{n}) \in E^-$, where k' extends k by the identity on N_φ. Informally, φ is consistent if none of its NACs contradicts its positive nodes and edges. An inconsistent pattern ψ represents an empty set, as $g \preceq \psi$ is not satisfied by any g.

A pattern φ is subsumed by the pattern ψ, denoted $\varphi \preceq \psi$, if $[\![\varphi]\!] \subseteq [\![\psi]\!]$. The relation $\preceq$ on patterns can be checked according to the following Proposition.

Proposition 1. *Given patterns* $\varphi = \langle N_\varphi, E_\varphi, \mathcal{G}_\varphi^- \rangle$ *and* $\psi = \langle N_\psi, E_\psi, \mathcal{G}_\psi^- \rangle$ *which are consistent, we have that* $\varphi \preceq \psi$ *iff there exists an injection* $h : N_\psi \to N_\varphi$, *such that* $\langle N_\varphi, E_\varphi \rangle \preceq_h \langle N_\psi, E_\psi, \emptyset \rangle$ *and for each NAC* $\langle M^-, F^- \rangle \in \mathcal{G}_\psi^-$ *there is a NAC* $\langle N^-, E^- \rangle \in \mathcal{G}_\varphi^-$ *and an injection* $k : N^- \to M^-$ *such that*

- $(\text{NODES}(E^-) \setminus N^-) \subseteq h(N_\psi)$, *and*
- *for each* $(\lambda, \overrightarrow{n}) \in E^-$, *we have* $(\lambda, (h^{-1} \cup k)(\overrightarrow{n})) \in F^-$. □

Intuitively, $\varphi \preceq \psi$ if and only if the positive part of ψ is a subgraph of the positive part of φ, and for each NAC in $\mathcal{G}_\psi^-$, there is a corresponding NAC in $\mathcal{G}_\varphi^-$ which is a subgraph of the former NAC.

In our system model, configurations are represented by hypergraphs. Transitions are specified by *actions*, which are (hypergraph) rewrite rules.

Definition 1. *An* action *is a pair* $\langle L, R \rangle$, *where* $L = \langle N_L, E_L, \mathcal{G}_L^- \rangle$ *is a pattern and* $R = \langle N_R, E_R \rangle$ *is a hypergraph with* $N_L \subseteq N_R$ *(i.e., actions can create nodes, but not delete them). The action* $\alpha = \langle L, R \rangle$ *denotes the set* $[\![\alpha]\!]$ *of pairs of configurations* (g, g'), *with* $g = \langle N_g, E_g \rangle$, $g' = \langle N_{g'}, E_{g'} \rangle$ *and* $N_g \subseteq N_{g'}$ *such that there is an injection* $h : N_R \to N_{g'}$ *satisfying:*

- $g \preceq L$ *is witnessed by the restriction of* h *to* N_L
- $N_{g'} = N_g \cup h(N_R)$
- $E_{g'} = (E_g \setminus h(E_L)) \cup h(E_R)$. □

Example. Figure 2(a) shows an action $\alpha = \langle L, R \rangle$. The pattern L is to the left of the arrow ($\Longrightarrow$) and R to the right. The action does not create any nodes, i.e., $N_L = N_R$. Figure 2(b) shows a pair $(g, g') \in [\![\alpha]\!]$, i.e., g can be rewritten via α to g'. The subsumption $g \preceq L$ is witnessed by the injection $h = \{1 \mapsto a, 2 \mapsto b\}$. The injection h satisfies $N_{g'} = N_g \cup h(N_R) = \{a, b\}$ and $E_{g'} = (E_g \setminus h(E_L)) \cup h(E_R) = h(E_R)$. Figure 2(c) shows a configuration g such that there is no g' with $(g, g') \in [\![\alpha]\!]$, since $g \not\preceq L$. In other words, g cannot be rewritten via α.

Definition 2. *A* system model *is a pair* $\langle \gamma_0, \mathcal{A} \rangle$ *consisting of an initial configuration* γ_0 *together with a finite set of actions* $\mathcal{A}$. □

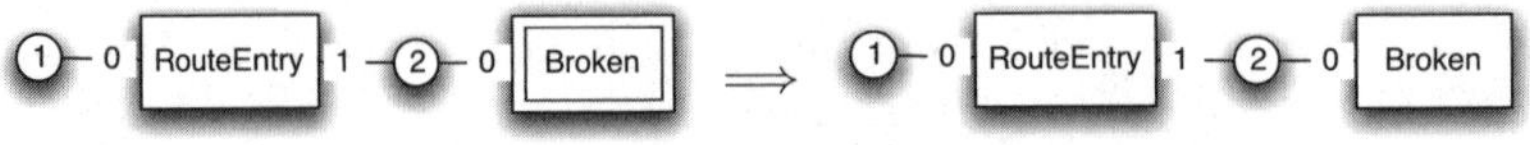

(a) Action α

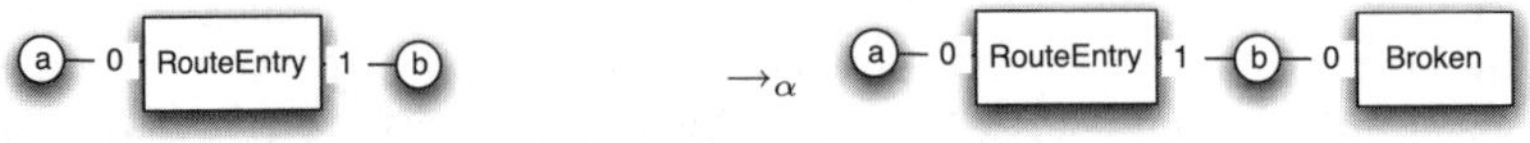

(b) Pair of configurations $(g, g') \in \llbracket \alpha \rrbracket$

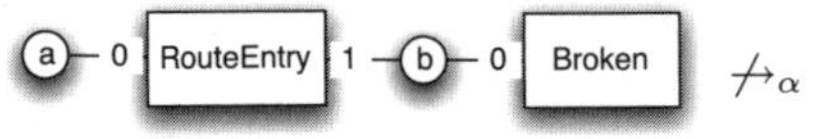

(c) Configuration g such that $\neg \exists g'.(g, g') \in \llbracket \alpha \rrbracket$

Fig. 2. Example of an action and its semantics

For a set Γ of configurations and an action α, let $pre(\alpha, \Gamma) = \{g \mid \exists g' \in \Gamma. \ (g, g') \in \llbracket \alpha \rrbracket\}$, i.e., the configurations which in one step can be rewritten to Γ using α. Similarly, for a set of actions $\mathcal{A}$, let $pre^*(\mathcal{A}, \Gamma)$ denote the set of configurations which can reach a configuration in Γ by a sequence of rewritings using actions in $\mathcal{A}$.

4   Symbolic Verification

We formulate a verification scenario as the problem whether a set of configurations, represented by a set of patterns, is reachable. More precisely, given a system model $\langle \gamma_0, \mathcal{A} \rangle$, and a set of patterns Φ, the *reachability problem* asks whether there is a sequence of transitions from γ_0 to some configuration in $\llbracket \Phi \rrbracket$.

In our approach, we analyze a reachability problem using *backward reachability analysis*, in which we compute an over-approximation of the set $pre^*(\mathcal{A}, \llbracket \Phi \rrbracket)$ of configurations, and check whether it includes γ_0. We clarify why and when the computation is not exact in the *Approximation* paragraph below. In general, the reachability problem is undecidable, and our analysis is not guaranteed to terminate. However, the technique is sufficiently powerful to verify several nontrivial network protocols (see Section 6).

We attempt to compute $pre^*(\mathcal{A}, \llbracket \Phi \rrbracket)$ by standard fixed point iteration, using predecessor computation, as shown in Procedure 1. In the procedure, V and W are sets of patterns whose predecessors already have (V) and have not (W) been computed. In each iteration of the while loop, we choose a pattern φ from W. If $\gamma_0 \in \llbracket \varphi \rrbracket$ then we have found a path from γ_0 to $\llbracket \Phi \rrbracket$. Otherwise, we check whether φ is redundant, meaning that it is subsumed by some other pattern which will be or has been explored. If not, we add to W a set of patterns over-approximating $pre(\mathcal{A}, \llbracket \varphi \rrbracket)$. As a further optimization, not shown in Procedure 1, at line 7 we also remove patterns from V and W that are subsumed by φ; keeping V and W small speeds up the procedure.

Procedure 1. Backward Reachability Analysis

Require: System model $\langle \gamma_0, \mathcal{A} \rangle$ and a set Φ of (bad) patterns
Ensure: If terminates; answers whether a configuration in $[\![\Phi]\!]$ is reachable from γ_0
1 $V := \emptyset,\ W := \Phi$
2 **while** $W \neq \emptyset$ **do**
3   **choose** $\varphi \in W$
4      $W := W \setminus \{\varphi\}$
5   **if** $\gamma_0 \in [\![\varphi]\!]$ **then**
6   **return** "Reachable"
7   **if** $\forall \psi \in (V \cup W).\ \neg(\varphi \preceq \psi)$ **then**
8          $V := V \cup \{\varphi\}$
9   **for each** $\alpha \in \mathcal{A}$ **do**
10             $W := W \cup \text{PRE}(\alpha, \varphi)$
11 **return** "Unreachable"

The central part of Procedure 1 is the (nontrivial) computation of predecessors of a pattern; it is done as in Procedure 2, whose description follows. Procedure 2 terminates on any input, as all loops are finite.

Procedure 2. $\text{PRE}(\alpha, \varphi)$

Require: Action $\alpha = \langle L, R \rangle$, pattern $\varphi = \langle N_\varphi, E_\varphi, \mathcal{G}_\varphi^- \rangle$
Ensure: Φ is a set of patterns satisfying $pre\,(\alpha, [\![\varphi]\!]) \subseteq [\![\Phi]\!]$
1 $\Phi := \emptyset$
2 Rename nodes in N_φ so that N_φ is disjoint from N_R
3 **for each** partial injection $h : N_R \to N_\varphi$ **do**
4   Rename each node $h(n)$ in the range of h to n
5   **if** $\exists n \in \text{DOMAIN}(h) - N_L\ .\ \text{EDGES}_+(n, \varphi) \not\subseteq \text{EDGES}_+(n, R)\ \vee$
       $\text{INCONSISTENT}(\varphi + R)$ **then**
6   **skip**
7   **else**
8          $\varphi' := (\varphi \ominus_\alpha R) + L$
9   **for each** $G^- \in \mathcal{G}_\varphi^-$ **do**
10   **if** $\text{INCONSISTENT}((L \ominus_E R) + G^-)$ **then**
11                 $\varphi' = \varphi' - G^-$
12   **if** $\neg\, \text{INCONSISTENT}(\varphi')$ **then**
13             $\Phi := \Phi \cup \varphi'$
14 **return** Φ

Let a *partial injection*, or *matching*, from a set N to a set N' be an injection from a nonempty subset of N to N'. For two patterns $\varphi = \langle N_\varphi, E_\varphi, \mathcal{G}_\varphi^- \rangle$ and $\psi = \langle N_\psi, E_\psi, \mathcal{G}_\psi^- \rangle$, we use $\varphi + \psi$ to denote $\langle N_\varphi \cup N_\psi, E_\varphi \cup E_\psi,\ \mathcal{G}_\varphi^- \cup \mathcal{G}_\psi^- \rangle$. When adding patterns, if the node and edge sets are not disjoint, the result is a "merge". No automatic renaming is assumed.

We use the following two subtraction operations in Procedure 2. First, for a pattern $\varphi = \langle N_\varphi, E_\varphi, \mathcal{G}_\varphi^- \rangle$, and an action $\alpha = \langle L, R \rangle$, let $\varphi \ominus_\alpha R$ be the pattern

$\psi = \langle N_\psi, E_\psi, \mathcal{G}_\varphi^- \rangle$, with $E_\psi = E_\varphi \setminus E_R$ and $N_\psi = N_\varphi \setminus (N_R \setminus N_L)$. Second, for a pattern $\varphi = \langle N_\varphi, E_\varphi, \mathcal{G}_\varphi^- \rangle$, and a hypergraph $g = \langle N_g, E_g \rangle$, let $\varphi \ominus_E g$ be the pattern $\psi = \langle N_\psi, E_\psi, \mathcal{G}_\varphi^- \rangle$, with $E_\psi = E_\varphi \setminus E_g$ and $N_\psi = \text{NODES}(E_\psi)$.

For a NAC G^-, we use $\varphi + G^-$ to denote $\langle N_\varphi, E_\varphi, \mathcal{G}_\varphi^- \cup G^- \rangle$ and $\varphi - G^-$ to denote $\langle N_\varphi, E_\varphi, \mathcal{G}_\varphi^- \setminus G^- \rangle$. If $n \in N_\varphi$, let $\text{EDGES}_+(n, \langle N_\varphi, E_\varphi, \mathcal{G}_\varphi^- \rangle)$ denote the set of edges in E_φ connected to n.

Procedure 2 first renames the nodes (line 2) to avoid unintended node collisions between φ and α. Thereafter, the loop starting at line 3 performs a sequence of operations for each possible matching between some nodes of N_R and N_φ.

On line 4 each node $h(n)$ in the range of h is renamed to n, in order to "merge" R and φ according to h. Since nodes that are created by α must also have all their edges created by α, we should discard matchings which violate this (line 5). On line 5 we also discard inconsistent matchings. The procedure $\text{INCONSISTENT}(\varphi)$ returns true iff pattern φ is not consistent.

On line 8 the action α is "executed" backwards to obtain a pattern φ' that is a potential predecessor of φ. Using the special subtraction $\ominus_\alpha$ nodes and edges created by α are removed from φ. On lines 9–11, we remove all NACs from φ' which contradict subgraphs removed by α. This may introduce approximation (see the paragraph below). Since by definition α cannot remove nodes, we use the special subtraction $\ominus_E$ which ignores nodes not connected to edges. On line 12, we discard the resulting predecessor pattern if it is inconsistent – this can happen if a NAC in L contradicts a positive subgraph of φ'. Finally, if we reach line 13, we have found a predecessor pattern, which is added to Φ.

Approximation. The predecessor computation in Procedure 2 sometimes introduces an approximation at line 11. If α removes a subgraph which is forbidden by φ, then $pre(\alpha, \llbracket \varphi \rrbracket)$ should say that there is exactly one subgraph of this form. However, patterns cannot express "exactly one" occurrence of a subgraph. In this situation, Procedure 2 therefore lets the resulting pattern say that "there is at least one occurrence" of this subgraph. As an example, consider the simple situation in Figure 3, where α, shown in Figure 3(a), removes an RM-edge between two nodes, and φ, the rightmost pattern in Figure 3(b), says that there is no RM-edge. The exact predecessor of φ is: "there is exactly one RM-edge between two nodes". However, the resulting predecessor (the leftmost pattern in Figure 3(b)) represents that there is *at least* one RM-edge connected to graph node 1. To illustrate the effect of lines 9–11 of Procedure 2, an intermediate pattern, where the contradiction has not yet been resolved, is shown in Figure 3(b).

Optimizations. To make the analysis more efficient, we have (implemented) two mechanisms for the user to specify simple type constraints. One is to annotate nodes with types that are respected in the analysis, with the semantics that nodes may only "match" nodes of same type. Another is to add patterns that describe multiplicity constraints on edges. For example, our DYMO models use "a network node can have at most one routing table", by specifying a pattern where a node has two routing tables as "impossible".

We need to model integer-valued variables, as DYMO uses sequence numbers and hop counts. This is done by representing integers as nodes, and greater

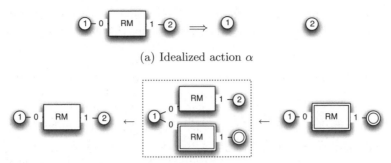

(a) Idealized action α

(b) Predecessor computation showing intermediate pattern

Fig. 3. Approximation due to upwards-closure

than ($>$) and equality ($=$) relations as edges between these nodes. We do not represent concrete integer values. Hence, we cannot compare integers which are not connected by a relational edge. We have extended our tool to handle the transitive closure of $>$ and $=$, as part of the predecessor computation. For each predecessor pattern generated, the closure of all transitive numerical relations present in the pattern is computed. New relational edges are then added to the pattern accordingly. The reason is that our syntactic subsumption check cannot deduce such semantic information about relations. The check for created nodes on line 5 of Procedure 2 was also extended to take into account the transitivity of numerical relations.

5   Modeling and Verification of DYMO

In this section we describe how we modeled the DYMO protocol (more precisely, the latest version at the time of writing, version 10 [11], and version 5). See our project home page [14] for the complete models. In total, our DYMO v10 model consists of one initial graph ("an empty network") and 77 actions. Of these, 38 actions model routing table update rules, similar to the one in Figure 4 below. We have only used unary and binary hyperedges in our models, although our implementation supports hyperedges of any arity.

Modeling network topology and message transmission. We represent arbitrary network topologies by letting the initial system configuration be an empty network (i.e., an empty graph), and including an action for creating an arbitrary network node; thus any initial topology can be formed. We do not explicitly model connectivity in the network. Instead all nodes can potentially react on all messages in the network; this reaction on a message can be postponed indefinitely, corresponding to a node being out of range or otherwise incapable of receiving the message. Messages can also be non-deterministically removed, corresponding to message loss. In our modeling of message transmission, messages are left in the network after a node has handled them (until they are potentially dropped): this accounts for messages being duplicated.

Handling of timeouts and hop limits. DYMO uses timeouts to determine if a RREQ should be retransmitted, if a link is broken, or if a routing table entry should be removed. We over-approximate timeouts as "event x can happen at any time", which covers all possibilities for a timeout. It is known from previous work on the AODV protocol [8], that if entries are removed from the routing table, loops may form. The reason is that obsolete information can then be accepted. In DYMO, routing table entries are invalidated (set to broken) after some time, and later removed; temporary loops are thus tolerated. We exclude removal of routing table entries from our analysis; they can only be invalidated. In practice, we thus verify loop-freedom under the assumption that routing table entries are kept "long enough".

We do not model DYMO hop limits [11], used to limit packet traversal. However, since we include actions for arbitrary dropping of RMs and RERRs, we implicitly cover all possible hop limit settings.

Routing table update rules. The DYMO specification [11] prescribes when a node should update its own routing table upon receiving routing data, i.e., when received routing data should replace existing data. Existing data is represented by a routing table entry, with fields `RouteSeqNo`, `RouteHopCnt`, and `Broken`. Received data is represented by a routing message with fields `OrigSeqNo`, `NodeHopCnt` and message type `RM` – either a route request (`RREQ`) or a route reply (`RREP`). The table entry should be updated in the following cases:

1. `OrigSeqNo` > `RouteSeqNo`
2. `OrigSeqNo` = `RouteSeqNo` ∧ `NodeHopCnt` < `RouteHopCnt`
3. `OrigSeqNo` = `RouteSeqNo` ∧ `NodeHopCnt` = `RouteHopCnt` ∧ `RM` = `RREP`
4. `OrigSeqNo` = `RouteSeqNo` ∧ `NodeHopCnt` = `RouteHopCnt` ∧ `Broken`

The rules say that an update is allowed if (1) the message has a higher sequence number for the destination, or (2) the message has the same sequence number, but a shorter route, or (3) the message has the same routing metric value, and the message is a route reply, or (4) the table entry is broken. See Figure 4 for an illustration of how we model the update rules. The figure corresponds to rule (2). In our framework, we have to model each combination of network nodes used in the rules, such as when `IPSource` equals `Orig`, or `RouteNextHopAddress` equals `RouteAddress`, etc., as separate actions; however, we have tool support for doing this.

Formalizing the non-looping property. A central property of ad hoc routing protocols is that they never cause routing loops, as a routing loop prevents a packet from reaching its intended destination. A routing loop is a nonempty finite sequence of nodes $n_1, \ldots, n_k$ such that for some destination D it holds that for all $i : 1 \leq i \leq k$ node $n_{(i+1)(mod\ k)}$ is the next hop towards D from node n_i, and $n_i \neq D$.

We define the ordering $<_D$ on nodes in a configuration as: $n <_D n'$ iff $\text{RouteSeqNo}_n(D) > \text{RouteSeqNo}_{n'}(D) \vee (\text{RouteSeqNo}_n(D) = \text{RouteSeqNo}_{n'}(D) \wedge \text{RouteHopCnt}_n(D) < \text{RouteHopCnt}_{n'}(D))$. There can be no routing loops towards a destination D, if each hop from a node n towards D goes to a node n' with

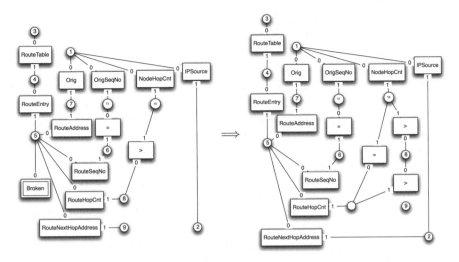

Fig. 4. Action modeling a routing table update

$n' <_D n$. Since $<_D$ is a partial order, any routing path towards D can contain a node at most once. The same ordering was used in the proof of loop freedom for AODV in [8]. The following property, LP, implies the pairwise ordering along routing paths; if LP is invariant for DYMO, there are no routing loops.

$$
\begin{array}{c|c}
\forall\, A, B, D & \\
A \neq B, B \neq D, & \texttt{RouteNextHopAddress}_A(D) = B \implies B <_D A \qquad (LP)\\
A \neq D &
\end{array}
$$

By negating the loop property (LP), we obtain a characterization of the bad system configurations. Loops may thus form if the sequence number strictly decreases, or the sequence number stays the same but the hop count does not decrease, between a node A and its next hop B on a route towards a destination node D. In our verification of DYMO, we verify unreachability for a set of six bad patterns. Three represent a disjunct of $(\neg LP)$ under quantification; two represent a network node with a routing table entry pointing to the node itself; and one pattern represents that a node has a next hop (which is not D) towards some destination D, but the next hop has no entry for D. As an example, a pattern representing one of the disjuncts of $(\neg LP)$ is shown in Figure 5.

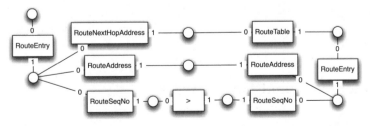

Fig. 5. Graph pattern representing a set of bad system configurations in DYMO

6   Experimental Results

We have modeled and verified the DYMO protocol as described in Sections 5 and 4. Recall that the analysis is under an assumption of routing table entries not being removed. The analysis has been performed using our tool GBT (Graph Backwards Tool). GBT and the models are available at our project home page [14]. The tool uses the `.dot` format for describing hypergraphs and patterns (input and output). If the initial configuration can be reached, an error trace, showing a sequence of actions leading to one of the bad patterns, is provided. Note that this trace may be spurious, due to over-approximation.

We have verified the latest DYMO version at the time of writing, namely version 10 of the Internet draft [11], as well as an older draft (version 5). Our results are presented in Table 1. In the "dest. reply" models, only the destination node replies to an RREQ, whereas in "interm. reply", intermediate nodes may also reply (in case they have a fresh enough route, see [11]). Column *Actions* contains the number of actions in the model. *Checked* contains the total number of unique non-impossible patterns generated by the predecessor computation, plus the ones given as input. *Covered* contains the patterns which were subsumed (see Section 4). *Left* contains the patterns left after the analysis has finished; none of them contain the initial graph. *Time* contains the total verification time (GBT start to end) on a machine with an AMD Opteron 2220 2.8 GHz processor.

Table 1. Measurement results from using GBT

Protocol	Actions	Checked	Covered	Left	Verified	Time
DYMO draft 10						
- dest. reply	56	185751	185695	56	Yes	2h 24 min
- interm. reply	77	295164	295108	56	Yes	4h 31 min
DYMO draft 05	50	118685	118637	48	Yes	1h 20 min
Pub/priv srv I	12	498	484	14	Yes	0.73 s
Pub/priv srv II	13	629	609	20	Yes	0.94 s
Firewall I	6	129	126	3	Yes	0.11 s
Firewall II	6	129	126	3	Yes	0.11 s

In Table 1 we have also included GBT verification results for the "Public/private servers" and "Firewall" examples, used by König and Kozioura [19]. These examples required modifications to work with our tool: a NAC was added to the left hand side of an action in "Public/private servers II" and the transitivity handling in our tool was extended to include communication channels.

7   Conclusions and Future Work

We have described and implemented a general framework for modeling and verification of protocols using a variant of graph transformation systems, and applied it to automatically prove loop freedom of the DYMO v10 ad hoc routing protocol. We expect that several of the actions used in our DYMO model need only small modifications to work for other ad hoc routing protocols categorized as reactive (i.e., on-demand). The reason is that reactive ad hoc routing protocols generally use the same kind of flooding route discovery mechanism; examples include AODV[21], DSR[16], and LUNAR[24] (see [20] for an extensive list).

As GTSs with NACs make up quite a generic modeling framework, there should be possibilities for interesting case studies, and further development. Directions for future work include further optimizations of the predecessor computation, e.g., by early detection of unfruitful matchings. We are currently working on a new DYMO model, to investigate the effect on run-time performance when using hyperedges of arity greater than two. Termination of the reachability analysis can be obtained by bounding and truncating the generated patterns, at the cost of over-approximation, e.g., by enforcing a maximum size. The possibility of spurious counter-examples, due to approximations in the predecessor computation, motivates looking at counter-example guided abstraction refinement.

Acknowledgments. We would like to thank Barbara König for valuable help on the Augur tool and related issues. We also thank Parosh Abdulla, Joachim Parrow, and the anonymous referees for their many helpful comments.

References

1. Abdulla, P.A., Delzanno, G., Rezine, A., Ben Henda, N.: Regular model checking without transducers (On Efficient Verification of Parameterized Systems). In: Grumberg, O., Huth, M. (eds.) TACAS 2007. LNCS, vol. 4424, pp. 721–736. Springer, Heidelberg (2007)
2. Abdulla, P.A., Čerāns, K., Jonsson, B., Yih-Kuen, T.: Algorithmic analysis of programs with well quasi-ordered domains. Information and Computation 160, 109–127 (2000)
3. Abdulla, P.A., Jonsson, B.: Verifying programs with unreliable channels. Information and Computation 127(2), 91–101 (1996)
4. Abolhasan, M., Wysocki, T., Dutkiewicz, E.: A review of routing protocols for mobile ad hoc networks. Ad Hoc Networks 2(1), 1–22 (2004)
5. Bauer, J.: Analysis of Communication Topologies by Partner Abstraction. PhD thesis, Universität des Saarlandes (2006)
6. Bauer, J., Wilhelm, R.: Static Analysis of Dynamic Communication Systems. In: 14th International Static Analysis Symposium, Springer, Heidelberg (2007)
7. Becker, B., Beyer, D., Giese, H., Klein, F., Schilling, D.: Symbolic invariant verification for systems with dynamic structural adaptation. In: Proc. ICSE 2006, 28th Int. Conf. on Software Engineering, pp. 72–81. ACM Press, New York (2006)
8. Bhargavan, K., Obradovic, D., Gunter, C.A.: Formal verification of standards for distance vector routing protocols. Journal of the ACM 49(4), 538–576 (2002)
9. Broch, J., Maltz, D.A., Johnson, D.B., Hu, Y.-C., Jetcheva, J.: A performance comparison of multi-hop wireless ad hoc network routing protocols. In: Proceedings of MobiCom 1998 (October 1998)
10. Chakeres, I.D., Perkins, C.E.: DYMO - Dynamic MANET On-demand Routing Protocol home page (2007), http://www.ianchak.com/dymo/

11. Chakeres, I.D., Perkins, C.E.: Dynamic MANET On-demand (DYMO) Routing. In: Internet draft (July 2007), `draft-ietf-manet-dymo-10.txt`

12. Das, S., Dill, D.L.: Counter-example based predicate discovery in predicate abstraction. In: Aagaard, M.D., O'Leary, J.W. (eds.) FMCAD 2002. LNCS, vol. 2517, pp. 19–32. Springer, Heidelberg (2002)

13. Esparza, J., Finkel, A., Mayr, R.: On the verification of broadcast protocols. In: Proc. LICS 1999 14th IEEE Int. Symp. on Logic in Computer Science (1999)

14. GBT - Graph Backwards Tool project home page. `http://www.it.uu.se/research/group/mobility/adhoc/gbt`

15. Holzmann, G.: The model checker SPIN. IEEE Trans. on Software Engineering SE-23(5), 279–295 (1997)

16. Johnson, D.B., Maltz, D.A., Broch, J.: DSR: The dynamic source routing protocol for multi-hop wireless ad hoc networks. In: Ad Hoc Networking, ch. 5, pp. 139–172. Addison-Wesley, Reading (2001)

17. Jonsson, B., Kempe, L.: Verifying safety properties of a class of infinite-state distributed algorithms. In: Wolper, P. (ed.) CAV 1995. LNCS, vol. 939, pp. 42–53. Springer, Heidelberg (1995)

18. Kastenberg, H., Rensink, A.: Model checking dynamic states in GROOVE. In: SPIN Workshop, pp. 299–305. Springer, Heidelberg (2006)

19. König, B., Kozioura, V.: Counterexample-guided abstraction refinement for the analysis of graph transformation systems. In: Hermanns, H., Palsberg, J. (eds.) TACAS 2006. LNCS, vol. 3920, pp. 197–211. Springer, Heidelberg (2006)

20. List of ad-hoc routing protocols - Wikipedia, the free encyclopedia, `http://en.wikipedia.org/wiki/Ad_hoc_routing_protocol_list`

21. Perkins, C.E., Belding-Royer, E.M.: Ad-hoc on-demand distance vector routing. In: Proc. 2nd Workshop on Mobile Computing Systems and Applications (WMCSA 1999), pp. 90–100. IEEE Computer Society Press, Los Alamitos (1999)

22. Saksena, M., Wibling, O., Jonsson, B.: Graph grammar modeling and verification of ad hoc routing protocols. Technical Report 2007-035, Dept. of Information Technology, Uppsala University, Sweden (2007)

23. The official IETF MANET working group web page, `http://www.ietf.org/html.charters/manet-charter.html`

24. Tschudin, C., Gold, R., Rensfelt, O., Wibling, O.: LUNAR: a lightweight underlay network ad-hoc routing protocol and implementation. In: Proc. Next Generation Teletraffic and Wired/Wireless Advanced Networking (NEW2AN) (February 2004)

Proving Ptolemy Right: The Environment Abstraction Framework for Model Checking Concurrent Systems*

Edmund Clarke[1], Murali Talupur[2], and Helmut Veith[3,4]

[1] School of Computer Science, Carnegie Mellon University, USA
[2] Intel Strategic CAD Labs, Portland, USA
[3] Fachbereich Informatik, Technische Universität Darmstadt, Germany
[4] Institut für Informatik, Technische Universität München, Germany

Abstract. The parameterized verification of concurrent algorithms and protocols has been addressed by a variety of recent methods. Experience shows that there is a trade-off between techniques which are widely applicable but depend on non-trivial human guidance, and fully automated approaches which are tailored for narrow classes of applications. In this spectrum, we propose a new framework based on environment abstraction which exhibits a large degree of automation and can be easily adjusted to different fields of application. Our approach is based on two insights: First, we argue that natural abstractions for concurrent software are derived from the "Ptolemaic" perspective of a human engineer who focuses on a single reference process. For this class of abstractions, we demonstrate soundness of abstraction under very general assumptions. Second, most protocols in given a class of protocols – for instance, cache coherence protocols and mutual exclusion protocols – can be modeled by small sets of compound statements. These two insights allow to us efficiently build precise abstract models for given protocols which can then be model checked. We demonstrate the power of our method by applying it to various well known classes of protocols.

1 Introduction

In many areas of system engineering, distributed concurrent computation has become an essential design principle. For instance, the controllers on an automobile have to be necessarily distributed. Further, in fundamental areas like chip design, distributed computation often offers the best way to increased performance. Protocols like cache coherence protocols, mutual exclusion protocols, synchronization protocols form the bedrock on which these distributed systems are built. Experience has shown however that designing such protocols correctly is a non-trivial task for human engineers and should be supported by computer-aided verification methods. Although non-rigorous verification techniques such as testing are very effective in finding many obvious errors, they cannot explore all interleaving behaviors, and may miss subtle errors. Consequently,

---

* This research was sponsored by the Gigascale Systems Research Center (GSRC), Semiconductor Research Corporation (SRC), the National Science Foundation (NSF), the Office of Naval Research (ONR), the Naval Research Laboratory (NRL), the Defense Advanced Research P rojects Agency, the Army Research Office (ARO), and the General Motors Collaborative Research Lab at CMU, and the Deutsche Forschungsgemeinschaft (DFG) under grant FORTAS.

C.R. Ramakrishnan and J. Rehof (Eds.): TACAS 2008, LNCS 4963, pp. 33–47, 2008.

rigorous formal verification techniques are indispensable in ensuring the correctness of such protocols.

Important classes of distributed protocols are designed *parametrically*, i.e., for an unlimited number of concurrent processes. For example, cache coherence protocols are designed to be correct independently of the exact number of caches. Verifying a protocol parametrically is however difficult, and is known to be undecidable [24]. Nonetheless, parameterized verification has received considerable attention in the recent years. Parameterized verification of cache coherence protocols is a pressing problem for the hardware industry and has been considered by [11,17,6,4,12]. Another important class of protocols that has been widely studied is mutual exclusion protocols [18,14,2,20].

The approaches by McMillan [17], Chou et al. [6], which have been successfully applied to industrial-strength cache coherence protocols require significant human guidance during verification. On the other hand, researchers have not been able to apply largely automatic methods like the ones by Lahiri et al [14] and Pnueli et al [20,2] to large protocols. Thus, while the ideal is to have a single automatic method to handle the whole class of real life protocols, it has come to be accepted that any practically useful tool will involve some human intervention. The goal then is to minimize the amount of effort and ingenuity required to guide a verification tool successfully. In this paper, we are proposing a framework that addresses this issue.

Our method is built around two insights which we describe in the following subsections: (1) humans tend to reason about distributed systems from the "Ptolemaic" viewpoint of an individual process, and (2) natural classes of protocols can be captured by a small number of compound statements. Combined, these two insights lead to an abstraction framework which accounts for the specifics of distributed systems and can be easily adjusted to different classes of protocols.

Ptolemaic System Analysis. The success of the Ptolemaic system (where earth is the center of the cosmos) over many centuries reveals an innate reasoning principle which the human mind applies to complex systems: we tend to imagine complex systems with the human observer in the center. Although this Ptolemaic intuition is wrong for many systems we encounter in nature, it is naturally built into the systems we *construct*.

Let us look more closely at the case of concurrent systems. During the construction of such a system, the programmer arguably imagines him/herself in the position of one *reference process*, around which the other processes – which constitute *the environment* – evolve. In fact, we usually consider a program to be well written when its correctness can be intuitively understood from the Ptolemaic viewpoint of a single process. Thus, an abstract model that reflects the viewpoint of a reference process is likely to contain sufficient information for asserting system correctness. The goal of environment abstraction is to put this intuition into a formal and practically useful framework.

Our concrete models are concurrent parameterized systems, where the number of processes is the parameter, and all processes execute the same program. We write $P(K)$ to denote a system with $K > 1$ processes. Thus, the formal verification question is

$$\forall K > 1. P(K) \models \forall x. \varphi(x)$$

where $\forall x \varphi(x)$ is an indexed temporal logic specification [5].

Each abstract state in our framework can be described by a formula $\Delta(x)$ where x stands for the process chosen to act as the reference process. The abstract state $\Delta(x)$ will contain (i) a detailed description of the internal state of process x and (ii) a concise abstract description of x's *environment* consisting of other processes. The *abstract transition relation* is defined by a new form of existential abstraction which quantifies over the parameter K and the variable x: If some concrete system $P(K)$ has a process p and a transition from state s_1 to s_2 such that $\Delta_1(p)$ holds in state s_1, and $\Delta_2(p)$ hols in state s_2, then we include a transition from $\Delta_1(x)$ to $\Delta_2(x)$ in the abstract model. Thus, every abstract transition is induced by a concrete transition in some concrete model $P(K)$. Note that $\Delta_1(x)$ and $\Delta_2(x)$ have to satisfy the <u>same</u> process p before and after the transition, i.e., the Ptolemaic reference point does not change during a transition.

The main mathematical contribution of this paper is a soundness result which shows that for a suitably chosen language of descriptions $\Delta(x)$, environment abstraction preserves universally quantified indexed temporal logic specifications, see Section 4. The requirements for choosing the $\Delta(x)$ are quite general: first, each concrete situation has to be covered by at least one $\Delta(x)$ (*coverage*), and second, the $\Delta(x)$ have to be sufficiently expressive to imply truth or falsity of atomic specifications (*completeness*). Our soundness result naturally carries over to the case of multiple reference processes.

While this definition of the abstract model reflects our intuition about distributed system design and ensures soundness of our approach, it is clearly not operational. Since the parameter K is unbounded, it is often not possible to compute the abstract transition relation exactly. It is here that our second insight comes into play.

Abstraction Templates for Compound Statements. The communication and coordination mechanisms between the processes in a distributed system are usually confined to a few basic patterns characteristic for each system type. Thus, when we focus on a particular class of protocols like cache coherence protocols or mutual exclusion protocols, the protocols in that class can be described in terms of a small number of *compound* transactions or statements. For example, to describe cache coherence protocols we need at most six compound statements [25], to describe mutex protocols we need only two statements [8,25], and to describe semaphore based algorithms, we just need a single statement, cf. Sections 4 and 5.

This insight allows us to approximate the abstract transition relation for a given parameterized system in an efficient manner. We know that all transitions of the system fall under a few compound statements. From the general construction principle for Ptolemaic environment abstraction we also know the structure of the abstract domain. Thus, *for each of these compound statements, we can provide an abstraction template.* Technically, we describe this abstraction template in terms of an abstract transition invariant, i.e., a formula expressing the relationship between the variables for the current abstract state and the next abstract state. Note that this invariant is given in a generic fashion, independently of the protocol in which it is used. For each concrete statement, we just have to plug in the specific parameters of that transition into the template invariant. Thus, the template invariants have to be written only once for each statement type. Since there are only a small number of compound statements for each class of protocols, writing the abstract template invariants is usually easy.

Tool Flow of the Environment Abstraction Framework . Once the compound statements for a protocol class are integrated in the framework, the tool flow is as follows:

1. The *user* describes $P(K)$ as a program in terms of the compound statements.
2. The *user* writes an indexed specification $\forall x.\Phi(x)$.
3. The *abstraction tool* computes the abstract model $P^{\mathcal{A}}$ from the protocol description. In our prototype implementation, this abstract model is an *SMV* model.
4. A *model checker* verifies $P^{\mathcal{A}} \models \varphi(x)$. Note that in $P^{\mathcal{A}}$, x is interpreted as the reference process. If $P^{\mathcal{A}} \models \varphi(x)$, then $\forall x.\varphi(x)$ holds for all $P(K), K > 1$. Otherwise, the model checker outputs an abstract counterexample for further analysis.

Structure of the Paper. In Section 3, we describe the environment abstraction framework in a rigorous and general way. In Section 4, we apply environment abstraction to the semaphore based mutual exclusion algorithms by Courtois et al. [10]; these protocols were posed to us as a challenge problem by Peter O'Hearn. In Section 5 we survey our experiences with other classes of protocols.

2   Related Work

In previous work, we used a specific instance of environment abstraction for the verification of the Bakery procotol and Szymanski's algorithm [8]. Although our paper [8] contains several seminal ideas about environment abstraction, it is very different in scope and generality. In particular, the methods in [8] are tailored towards a specific application and a hardwired set of specifications, without a general soundness result.

The method of counter abstraction [20] inspired our approach, and can be seen as a specific, but limited form of environment abstraction. Invisible invariants [19,2] provide another novel method for verifying parameterized systems. Both these methods are restricted to systems without unbounded integer variables.

The Indexed Predicates method [14,15] is similar to predicate abstraction with the crucial difference that predicates can contain free index variables (variables that range over process indices). These indexed predicates are used to construct complex (universally) quantified invariants for parameterized systems. The abstract descriptions used in our abstraction are Indexed Predicates in that they contain free index variables. But the similarity ends there. While we build an abstract transition relation over these descriptions, in the Indexed Predicates method they don't have an abstract transition relation. They only have an abstract reachability relation, which specifies what set of abstract states can one reach starting from another set of abstract states.

The series of papers [16,17,18,6] by McMillan and Chou et al. introduced an important and successful approach for parameterized verification. In this approach, which is based on circular compositional reasoning, a model checker is used as a proof assistant to carry out parameterized verification. The user however has the burden of coming up with *non-interference* lemmas [17] which can be non-trivial and require a deep understanding of the protocol under verification.

The TVLA method by Reps et al. [21] is a widely applicable abstract interpretation based approach for shape analysis, and also for verification of safety properties of multi-threaded systems, cf. Yahav's method [26]. TVLA's canonical abstraction is a generalization of predicate abstraction similar in spirit to the description formulas in environment abstraction. To make verification of unbounded systems possible, TLVA uses summarization, which is related to the idea of counting abstraction. Special predicates called *instrumentation* predicates are used to focus on particular processes in detail.

In recent work, [13] proposes a method to find network invariants using finite automata learning algorithms due to Angluin and Beirmann. The paper [9] uses a new completion procedure to strengthen split invariants. While parameterized verification is not their primary aim, the method is able to produce parameterized proofs for protocols like the Bakery protocol. Other classical approaches to parameterized verification include regular model checking [1] and the WS1S based method [3]. Early work on parameterized verification was done by Clarke et al [5].

3   A Generic Framework for Environment Abstraction

3.1   System Model

We consider parameterized concurrent systems $P(K)$, where the parameter $K \geq 2$ denotes the number of replicated processes. The processes are distinguished by unique indices in $\{1, \ldots, K\}$ which serve as process id's. Each process executes the same program which has access to its process *id*. We do not make any specific assumptions about the processes, in particular we do not require them to be finite state processes.

Consider a system $P(K)$ with a set S_K of states. Each state $s \in S_K$ contains the entire state information for each of the K concurrent processes, i.e., s is a vector $\langle s_1, \ldots, s_K \rangle$. Technically, $P(K)$ is a Kripke structure (S_K, I_K, R_K, L_K) where I_K is the set of initial states and R_K is the transition relation. We will discuss the labeling L_K for the states in S_K below.

It is easy to extend our framework to parameterized systems which contain one or several *non-replicated processes* in addition. In this case, the states s will be vectors $\langle s_1, \ldots, s_K, t_1, \ldots, t_{\text{const}} \rangle$ where the t_i are the states of the non-replicated processes. In the following exposition, we will for simplicity omit this easy extension.

3.2   Ptolemaic Specifications

The change of focus brought upon by environment abstraction most visibly affects the specification language: We use a variation of indexed ACTL* where the atomic formulas are able to express not only properties of individual processes, but also properties of processes in the environment. In our practical examples, the following two atomic formulas (where c is a constant value) have been most relevant:

Formula	Meaning
$\text{pc}[x] = c$	**the program counter of process** x **has value** c
$c \in \text{env}(\mathsf{x})$	**there is a process** $y \neq x$ **with program counter value** c
	"The <u>environment</u> of x contains a process with program counter value c."

In this language, we can specify mutual exclusion

$$\forall x.\ \mathbf{AG}\ (pc[x] = 5 \rightarrow \neg(5 \in env(x)))$$

and many other important properties with a single quantifier $\forall x$ that ranges over the processes in the system. Intuitively, this is the reason why a single reference process in the abstract model is able to assert correctness of the specification. Below we will discuss what properties are expressible with a single quantifier.

3.3 Environment Abstraction

Our examples of atomic formulas motivate the construction of the abstract model: At each state, we must be able to assert the truth or falsity of the atomic propositions $pc[x] = c$ and $c \in env(x)$. Consequently, the expressions $pc[x] = c$ and $c \in env(x)$ are used as *labels* in the abstract model. We will write L to denote the finite set of atomic formulas, and will call them *labels* further on. Note that L can contain formulas different from the two examples mentioned above.

The *states of the abstract model are formulas* $\Delta(x)$ (called "descriptions") which describe properties of process x and its environment. Similar to the atomic labels, the $\Delta(x)$ also have a free variable referring to the reference process. In contrast to the atomic labels, however, the descriptions will usually be relatively large and intricate formulas which give a quite detailed picture of the global system state from the point of view of reference process x. Intuitively, an abstract state $\Delta(x)$ represents all concrete system states where some process p satisfies $\Delta(p)$. In our running example, the simplest natural choice for the abstract states are descriptions of the form

$$pc[x] = c \land (\bigwedge_{i \in A} \underbrace{\exists y \neq x.pc[y] = i}_{i \in env(x)}) \land (\bigwedge_{i \in B} \underbrace{\neg \exists y \neq x.pc[y] = i}_{\neg(i \in env(x))})$$

where c is a program counter position, and $A \dot\cup B$ is a partition of all program counter positions. (Note that this simple base case is a form of counter abstraction; the descriptions we use in applications are often much richer – depending on the complexity of the problem.) Intuitively, this description says that *"the reference process x is in program counter location c, and the set of program counter locations of the other processes in the system is A"*. Since these formulas all belong to a simple syntactic class, it is easy to identify $\Delta(x)$ with a tuple, as usually in predicate abstraction, for instance $\langle c, A, B \rangle$. In the logical framework of this section, it is more natural to view descriptions as formulas. In the applications, however, we will usually prefer an appropriate tuple notation.

In the rest of this section, we will assume that we have a fixed *finite* set of descriptions D which constitute the abstract state space.

Soundness Requirements for Labels and Descriptions. Given a label or description $\varphi(x)$, we write $s \models \varphi(c)$ to express that in state s, process c has property φ. We next describe two requirements on the set D of descriptions and the set L of labels to make them useful as building blocks for the abstract model.

1. **Coverage.** For each system $P(K)$, each state s in S_K and each process c there is some description $\Delta(x) \in D$ which describes the properties of c, i.e.,

$$s \models \Delta(c).$$

In other words, every concrete situation is reflected by some abstract state.

2. **Completeness.** For each description $\Delta(x) \in D$ and each label $l(x) \in L$ it holds that either

$$\Delta(x) \to l(x) \qquad \text{or} \qquad \Delta(x) \to \neg l(x).$$

In other words, the descriptions in D contain enough information about a process to conclude whether a label holds true for this process or not. The completeness property enables us to give natural labels to each state of the abstract system: An abstract state $\Delta(x)$ has label $l(x)$ if $\Delta(x) \to l(x)$.

Description of the Abstract System P^A. Given two sets D and L of descriptions and labels which satisfy the two criteria *coverage* and *completeness*, the abstract system P^A is a Kripke structure

$$\langle D, I^A, R^A, L^A \rangle$$

where each $\Delta(x) \in D$ has a label $l(x) \in L$ if $\Delta(x) \to l(x)$, i.e., $L^A(\Delta(x)) = \{l(x) : \Delta(x) \to l(c)\}$. Before we describe I^A and R^A, we state the following lemma about preservation of labels which motivates our definition of the abstraction function below:

Lemma 1. *Suppose that $s \models \Delta(c)$. Then the concrete state s has label $l(c)$ iff the abstract state $\Delta(x)$ has label $l(x)$.*

Definition 1. *Given a concrete state s and a process c, the abstraction of s with reference process c is given by the set $\alpha_c(s) = \{\Delta(x) \in D : s \models \Delta(c)\}$.*

Remark 1. (i) The coverage requirement guarantees that $\alpha_c(s)$ is always non-empty. (ii) If the $\Delta(x)$ are mutually exclusive, then $\alpha_c(s)$ always contains exactly one description $\Delta(x)$. (iii) Two processes c, d of the same state s will in general give rise to different abstractions, i.e., $\alpha_c(s) = \alpha_d(s)$ is, in general, not true.

Now we define the *transition relation* of the abstract system by a variation of existential abstraction: R^A contains a transition between $\Delta_1(x)$ and $\Delta_2(x)$ if there exist a concrete system $P(K)$, two states s_1, s_2 and a process r such that

1. $\Delta_1(x) \in \alpha_r(s_1)$ [or, equivalently, $s_1 \models \Delta_1(r)$]
2. $\Delta_2(x) \in \alpha_r(s_2)$ [or, equivalently, $s_2 \models \Delta_2(r)$]
3. there is a transition from s_1 to s_2 in $P(K)$, i.e., $(s_1, s_2) \in R_K$.

We note three important properties of this definition:

(a) We existentially quantify over K, s_1, s_2, and r. This is different from standard existential abstraction where we only quantify over s_1, s_2. For fixed K and r, our definition is essentially equivalent to existential abstraction. The only difference is the obvious change in the labels: the concrete structure has labels of the form $l(c)$, while the abstract structure has labels of the form $l(x)$.

(b) Since $\Delta_1(x) \in \alpha_r(s_1)$ and $\Delta_2(x) \in \alpha_r(s_2)$, both abstractions Δ_1 and Δ_2 use the same process r. Thus, the Ptolemaic viewpoint of the reference process is not changed in the transition.

(c) The process which is active in the transition from s_1 to s_2 can be any process in $P(K)$, it does not have to be r.

Finally, the set I^A of abstract initial states is the union of the abstractions of concrete states, i.e., $\Delta(x) \in I^A$ if there exists a system $P(K)$ with state $s \in I_K$ and process r such that $\Delta(x) \in \alpha_r(s)$.

For environment abstractions that satisfy coverage and completeness we have the following general soundness theorem.

Theorem 1 (Soundness of Environment Abstraction). *Let $P(K)$ be a parameterized system and P^A be its abstraction as described above. Then for single indexed $ACTL^\star$ specifications $\forall x.\varphi(x)$, the following holds:*

$$P^A \models \varphi(x) \quad \text{implies} \quad \forall K.P(K) \models \forall x.\varphi(x).$$

The reader is referred to the full version of this paper [7] for a proof; the full version also contains the formal generalization of environment abstraction to multiple reference processes.

3.4   Trade-Off between Expressivity of Labels and Number of Index Variables

In this section, we discuss how a well-chosen set of labels L often makes it possible to use a *single* index variable. The Ptolemaic system view explains why we seldom find more than *two* indices in practical specifications: When we specify a system, we tend to track properties *our* process has in relation to other processes in the system, one at a time. Thus, double-indexed specifications of the form $\forall x \neq y.\varphi(x,y)$ often suffice to express the specifications of interest. Properties involving *three* or more processes at a time are rare, as they consider triangles of processes and their relationships. (Note however that our method can, in principle, handle an arbitrary number of index variables, cf. [7].) Let us return to our example specification. Mathematically, we can write this formula in three ways:

(1) $\forall x, y.x \neq y \rightarrow \mathbf{AG}\ (pc[x] = 5) \rightarrow (pc[y] \neq 5)$
(2) $\forall x.\mathbf{AG}\ (pc[x] = 5) \rightarrow \neg(\exists y \neq x.pc[y] = 5)$
(3) $\forall x.\mathbf{AG}\ (pc[x] = 5) \rightarrow \neg(5 \in env(x))$

Going from (1) to (3) we see that the universal quantifier is *distributed* over $\mathbf{AG}$ and *hidden* inside the label $5 \in env(x)$. The Ptolemaic viewpoint again explains why such situations are likely to happen: In many specifications, we consider *our* process along the time axis, but only at each individual time point, we evaluate its relationship to other processes; thus, a *quantification scope inside the temporal operator* suffices.

Formally, it is easy to see that the translation from (1) to (3) depends on the distributivity of conjunction over $\mathbf{AG}(\alpha \rightarrow \beta)$ with respect to β, i.e., $\mathbf{AG}(\alpha \rightarrow (\varphi \wedge \psi))$ is equivalent to $\mathbf{AG}(\alpha \rightarrow \varphi) \wedge \mathbf{AG}(\alpha \rightarrow \psi)$. We give a syntactic characterization of formulas with this property in [7]. Our characterization relies on previous work [22,23] in the context of temporal logic query languages.

4   Verification of the Reader and Writer Algorithms

In this section we apply our framework to two classical semaphore based distributed algorithms by Courtois et al. [10]. The algorithms ensure mutual exclusion of multiple concurrent *readers* and *writers*. To our knowledge, these algorithms – which were posed as challenge problems to us by Peter O'Hearn – have not been verified parametrically. Figure 1 shows the code for a reader process in the simpler of the two algorithms.

L1: P(mutex)
L2: readcount := readcount + 1
L3: if readcount = 1 then P(w)
L4: V(mutex)
L5: * reading is performed ****

L6: P(mutex)
L7: readcount := readcount - 1
L8: if readcount = 0 then V(w)
L9: V(mutex)

Fig. 1. The Reader Algorithm

We first give a single compound statement that suffices to describe the semaphore based algorithms. Then we introduce an appropriate abstract template invariant, and show how to verify the two algorithms in practice.This example should illustrate all the ingredients that go into our method and demonstrate the ease of application.

Compound Statement for Semaphore Based Algorithms. A semaphore is a low-level hardware or OS construct for ensuring mutual exclusion. By design, a semaphore variable can be accessed by only one process at any given time. The basic operations on a semaphore variable w are $P(w)$, which *acquires* the semaphore, and $R(w)$, which *releases* the semaphore.

We model a semaphore w as a boolean variable b_w that can be accessed by all processes. The acquire and release actions $P(w)$ and $R(w)$ are modeled by setting b_w to 1 and 0 respectively. A semaphore based algorithm has N identical local processes corresponding to the readers and writers. Readers and writers do not have the same code but we can create a union of the two syntactically to obtain a single larger process with two possible start states; depending on which state is chosen as the start state the compound process either acts as a reader or as a writer. The state space of each local process is finite. Instead of having multiple local variables, we will assume for simplicity there is only one local variable pc per process.

In addition to the local processes there is one central process C. The central process essentially consists of the shared variables, including the boolean variables used to model the semaphores. As with the local processes, we roll up all the variables of the central process into a single variable st_{cen} for the sake of simplicity. Note that st_{cen} can be an unbounded variable. We will denote the parameterized system by $P(N)$.

The reader and writer algorithms of [10] have three different types of transitions:

1. A simple transition by a local process. For example, the transition at $L5$ in Figure 1.
2. A local transition conditioned on acquiring or releasing a semaphore, e.g. $L1$, $L4$.
3. A transition in which a process modifies a shared variable, e.g., $L2$, $L7$.

All three types of transitions can be guarded by a condition on the central variables. The three types of transitions can be modeled using the compound statement

$$pc = L_1 : \textbf{if } st_{cen} = C_1 \textbf{ then goto } st_{cen} = f(st_{cen}) \wedge pc = L_2$$
$$\textbf{else goto } st_{cen} = g(st_{cen}) \wedge pc = L_3.$$

The semantics of this statement is intuitive: if the local process is in control location L_1, it checks if the *central process* is in state C_1. In this case, it modifies the central process to a new state $f(st_{cen})$ (where f is a function, see below) and goes to L_2. Otherwise, the central process is modified to $g(st_{cen})$ and the local process goes to L_3.

In the semaphore algorithms we consider, the functions f, g are simple linear functions. For instance, in the transition $L2 : readcount := readcount + 1$ of Figure 1 the new value for the central variable $readcount$ is a linear function of the previous value.

In the longer version of this paper [7] we present the two algorithms from [10] in our input language. For example, the semaphore acquire action at $L1$ in Figure 1 can be modelled as

$$pc = L_1 : \text{ if } b_{mutex} = 0 \text{ then goto } b_{mutex} = 1 \wedge pcl = L_2 \text{ else goto } pc = L_1$$

Abstract Domain. Our description formulas $\Delta(x)$ are very similar to the example of Section 3, except for an additional conjunct Δ_{cen}:

$$pc[x] = \textbf{pc} \wedge (\bigwedge_{i \in A} \exists y \neq x.pc[y] = i) \wedge (\bigwedge_{i \in B} \neg \exists y \neq x.pc[y] = i) \wedge \Delta_{\text{cen}}$$

Here, Δ_{cen} is a predicate which describes properties of the central process, analogous to classical predicate abstraction. Since the central process does not depend on the reference process x, the formula Δ_{cen} does not contain the free variable x.

The structure of Δ_{cen} is automatically extracted from the program code. For instance, for the program of Figure 1, Δ_{cen} describes the semaphore variables $w, mutex$ and the two predicates $readcount = 0$ and $readcount = 1$. Thus, Δ_{cen} has the form

$$[\neg]w \wedge [\neg]mutex \wedge [\neg](readcount = 0) \wedge [\neg](readcount = 1).$$

Here, $[\neg]$ stands for a possibly negated subformula. We write D_{cen} to denote the set of all these Δ_{cen} formulas; in our example, D_{cen} has $2^4 = 16$ elements.

As argued above, it is more convenient in the applications to describe an abstract state $\Delta(x)$ as a tuple. Specifically, we will use the tuple

$$\langle \textbf{pc}, e_1, \ldots, e_n, \Delta_{\text{cen}} \rangle$$

to describe an abstract state $\Delta(x)$. Intuitively, $\textbf{pc}$ refers to the control location of the reference process, and Δ_{cen} is the predicate abstraction for the central process. The bits e_i describe the presence of an environment process in control location i, i.e., e_i is 1 if $i \in A$. (Equivalently, e_i is 1 if $\Delta(x) \rightarrow i \in env(x)$.)

We note that the abstract descriptions $\Delta(x)$ and the corresponding tuples can be constructed automatically and syntactically from the protocol code. Since our labels of interest are of the form $pc[x] = c$ and $c \in env(x)$, it is easy to see that the *coverage* and *completeness* properties are satisfied by construction.

Abstraction Template Invariants. To describe the abstract template invariant, we will consider two cases: (i) the executing process is the reference process and (ii) the executing process is an environment process. For both cases, we will describe a suitable abstract invariant, and take their disjunction. Recall the general form

$$pc = L_1 : \text{ if } st_{\text{cen}} = C_1 \text{ then goto } st_{\text{cen}} = f(st_{\text{cen}}) \wedge pc = L_2$$
$$\text{else goto } st_{\text{cen}} = g(st_{\text{cen}}) \wedge pc = L_3.$$

of the compound statement. We will give an invariant for the abstract transition

$$\langle \textbf{pc}, e_1, \ldots, e_n, \Delta_{\text{cen}} \rangle \qquad \text{to} \qquad \langle \textbf{pc}', e_1', \ldots, e_n', \Delta_{\text{cen}}' \rangle$$

Case 1: Reference Process Executing. The invariant I_{ref} in this case is

$$\textbf{pc} = L_1 \wedge \tag{1}$$

$$\left[(C_1 \models \Delta_{\text{cen}} \wedge \Delta'_{\text{cen}} \in \textbf{f}(\Delta_{\text{cen}}) \wedge \textbf{pc}' = L_2) \bigvee \right. \tag{2}$$

$$\left. (C_1 \not\models \Delta_{\text{cen}}) \wedge \Delta'_{\text{cen}} \in \textbf{g}(\Delta_{\text{cen}}) \wedge \textbf{pc}' = L_3) \right] \tag{3}$$

Condition (1) says that the reference process is at control location L_1. Condition (2) corresponds to the **then** branch: it says that the central process is approximated to be in state C_1; in the next state, the reference process is in control location L_2 and the new approximation of the central process is non-deterministically picked from the set $\textbf{f}(\Delta_{\text{cen}})$. As usually in predicate abstraction, $\textbf{f}$ is an over-approximation of function f:

$$\textbf{f}(\Delta_{\text{cen}}) = \{\Delta'_{\text{cen}} \in D_{\text{cen}} \mid \exists st_{\text{cen}}.\ st_{\text{cen}} \models \Delta_{\text{cen}} \text{ and } f(st_{\text{cen}}) \models \Delta'_{\text{cen}}\}$$

Usually the operations on variables in a protocol are not more complicated than simple linear operations; consequently, the predicates involved in our environment abstraction are simple, too. Therefore, computing $\textbf{f}$ is trivial with standard decision procedures.

Condition (3), which corresponds to the **else** branch, is similar to condition (2).

Case 2: Environment Process Executing. The invariant I_{env} in this case is

$$e_{L_1} = 1 \wedge \tag{4}$$

$$\left[(C_1 \models \Delta_{\text{cen}} \wedge \Delta'_{\text{cen}} \in \textbf{f}(\Delta_{\text{cen}}) \wedge e'_{L_2} = 1) \bigvee \right. \tag{5}$$

$$\left. (C_1 \not\models \Delta_{\text{cen}}) \wedge \Delta'_{\text{cen}} \in \textbf{g}(\Delta_{\text{cen}}) \wedge e'_{L_3} = 1) \right] \tag{6}$$

Condition (4) says that some environment process is in control location L_1). Condition (5) is similar to Condition (2) of *Case 1* above, with the exception that $e'_{L_2} = 1$ forces a process in the environment to go to location L_2. Condition (6) is analogous to (5).

The invariant I for the compound statement is the disjunction $I = I_{\text{ref}} \vee I_{\text{env}}$ of the invariants in the two cases. Given a protocol with compound statements $cs_1, \ldots, cs_m$ we first find invariants $I(cs_1), \ldots, I(cs_m)$ by plugging in the concrete parameters of each statement into the template invariant I. The disjunction of these individual invariants gives us the abstract transition relation.

We denote the abstract system obtained from the template invariant as $P^{\mathscr{A}}$ and the abstract system obtained from the definition of environment abstraction by $P^{\mathcal{A}}$. Our construction is a natural over-approximation of $P^{\mathcal{A}}$:

Fact 1. *Every state transition from $\Delta(x)$ to $\Delta'(x)$ in $P^{\mathcal{A}}$ also occurs in $P^{\mathscr{A}}$.*

Practical Application. For our experiments, we already had a prototype implementation of environment abstraction to deal with cache coherence and mutual exclusion protocols. We added new procedures to allow our tool to read in protocols using the new compound statement and to perform automatic abstraction of the protocol, as described in the previous section.

The procedure to compute next values for Δ_{cen}, i.e., $\textbf{f}(\Delta_{\text{cen}})$, was handled by an internal decision procedure. (This is a carry over from our previous work with environment abstraction. In hindsight, calling an external decision procedure is a better option).

Our tool, written in Java, takes less than a second to find the abstract models given the concrete protocol descriptions. We use Cadence SMV to verify the abstract model.

For both algorithms in [10], we verified the safety property

$$\forall x \neq y.\mathbf{AG}\big(pc[x] \in \{LR, LW\} \;\rightarrow\; \neg LW \in env(x)\big)$$

where LR and LW are the program locations for reading and writing respectively.

Our first attempt to verify the protocol produced a spurious counterexample. To understand the reason for this counterexample, consider the protocol shown in Figure 1. Each time a reader enters the section between lines $L3$ and $L7$, $readcount$ is incremented. When a reader exits the section, $readcount$ is decremented. The semaphore w, which controls a writer's access to the critical section, is released only when $readcount = 0$ and this happens only when no reader is between lines $L3$ and $L7$. Our abstract model tracks only the predicate $readcount = 0$. The decrement operation on readcount in line $L7$ is abstracted to a non-deterministic choice over $\{0, 1\}$ for the value of the predicate $(readcount = 0)$. Thus, the predicate can become true (i.e., take value 1) even when there are readers between lines $L3$ and $L7$ and this leads to the spurious counter example. To eliminate this spurious counterexample we make use of the invariant

$$pc[x] \in [L3..L7] \rightarrow readcount \neq 0$$

This invariants essentially says that for a process between lines $L3$ and $L7$, $readcount$ has to be non-zero. We abstract this invariant into two invariants

$$\mathbf{pc} \in [L3..L7] \rightarrow \neg(readcount = 0) \quad \text{and} \quad \Big(\bigvee_{L \in [L3..L7]} .e_L\Big) \rightarrow \neg(readcount = 0).$$

for the reference process and the environment respectively. Constraining the abstract model with these two invariants, we are able to prove the safety property. The model checking time is less than a minute for both semaphore algorithms.

There still remains an important question: *How do we know that the invariant added to the abstract model is true?* First, we note that the invariant is a local invariant in that it refers only to one process and it is quite easy to convince ourselves that it holds. To prove formally that the invariant holds, we proceed as follows: Running the model checker on the *original abstract model* establishes $\mathbf{pc} \in [L3..L7]\neg(\rightarrow readcount = 0)$. From Theorem 1 we can conclude that $\forall x.pc[x] \in [L3..L7] \rightarrow readcount \neq 0$, and thus we are justified in using this invariant as assumption in proving the safety property. Note that this approach is close in spirit to adding *non-interference* lemmas, as described by McMillan and Chou et al. [17,6].

5 Survey of Other Environment Abstraction Applications

In this section, we survey other, more involved applications of the environment abstraction principle. For a more detailed discussion of these applications, we refer the reader to Talupur's thesis [25], and our predecessor paper [8].

Mutual Exclusion Protocols. In [8], we have shown how to verify mutual exclusion protocols such as the Bakery protocol and Szymanski's algorithm. We need two compound statements which are more complex than in Section 4:

Guarded Transition
$pc = L_1 :$ **if** $\forall otr \neq x.\mathcal{G}(x, otr)$ **then goto** $pc = L_2$ **else goto** $pc = L_3$
Semantics: In control location L_1, the process evaluates the guard and changes to control loca-tion L_2 or L_3 accordingly.

Update Transition
$pc = L_1 :$ **for all** $otr \neq x$ **if** $\mathcal{T}(x, otr)$ **then** $u_k := \varphi(otr)$ **goto** $pc = L_2$
Semantics: At location L_1, the process scans over all other processes otr to check if formula $\mathcal{T}(x, otr)$ is true. In this case, the process changes the value of its data variable u_k according to $u_k := \varphi(otr)$. Finally, the process changes to location L_2.

The abstract domain is also more complex, because each process can have unbounded data variables. To account for these variables, the $\Delta(x)$ include *inter-predicates* $IP_j(x, y)$, i.e., predicates that span multiple processes. Thus, the $\Delta(x)$ have the form

$$pc[x] = c \quad \wedge \bigwedge_{(i,j)\in A} \exists y \neq x.pc[y] = i \wedge IP_j(x, y) \wedge \bigwedge_{(i,j)\in B} \neg \exists y \neq x.pc[y] = i \wedge IP_j(x, y)$$

for suitable A and B. The inter-predicates are automatically picked from the program code. For example, a typical inter-predicate for Bakery is $t[x] > t[y]$, which says that the ticket variable of process x is greater than the ticket variable of process y.

The abstraction templates for this language are quite involved, providing a quite precise abstract semantics which is necessary for this protocol class. While [8] assumed that the compound statements are atomic, we later improved the abstraction to verify the mutex property of Bakery without this assumption. We defer a full discussion of these results to a future publication, and refer the reader to [25].

Cache Coherence Protocols. For cache coherence protocols we require six compound statements. Like semaphore based protocols, cache coherence systems also have a central process. The replicated processes, i.e., the caches, have very simple behaviors, and essentially move from one control location to another. This is modeled by the trivial *local transition* $pc = L_1 :$ **goto** $pc = L_2$. Unlike semaphore based protocols, the directory (central process) can exhibit complex behaviors, as it has pointer variables and set variables referring to caches. The *compound statement for the directory* has the form

$$guard : \textbf{do actions } A_1, A_2, .., A_k$$

where $A_1, \ldots, A_k$ are *basic actions* and *guard* is a condition on the directory's control location and its pointer and set variables. The basic actions comprise *goto, assign, add, remove, pick* and *remote* actions, cf. [7].

The descriptions $\Delta(x)$ used for cache coherence are similar to those of Section 4, but owing to the complexity of the directory process, Δ_{cen} is more elaborate than in the semaphore case. We have used this framework to verify the coherence property of several versions of German's protocol and a simplified version of the Flash protocol [25].

Our experiments with the original Flash protocol showed that the abstract model can become very large. The reason is the high precision of the abstract domain based on *all* control conditions from the protocol code. There is a promising approach to alleviate this problem: instead of building the best possible abstract model we build a coarser model which we refine using the circular reasoning scheme of [16,17,6]. Such a hybrid approach combines the strengths of our approach and the circular reasoning approach.

6   Conclusion

Environment abstraction provides a uniform platform for different types of parame-terized systems. To adjust our tool to a new class of protocols, we have to identify the compound statements for that class, and specify the actions of compound statements in terms of abstraction templates. This task requires ingenuity, but is a one time task. Once a 'library' for a class of protocols is built, it can be used to verify any protocol in the class automatically or with minimum user guidance.

Let us address some common questions we have encountered.

Human involvement present in too many places ? The end user who applies our tool to a specific protocol can be different from the verification engineer who builds the library. To verify a protocol, the user has to know only the compound statements; providing the abstract template invariants is the task of the tool builder.

Compound statements too complex ? The compound statements try to pack as many basic patterns as possible in a single statement and thus can be complex. But it is easy to create familiar looking syntactic sugar for often used instances of the compound statements.

Correctness of the abstraction templates ? This question is not much different from asking if a source code model checker is correct. It is easier to convince ourselves about the correctness of a small number of declarative transition invariants than to reason about a huge piece of software. In future work, we plan to investigate formal methods to ensure correctness of the abstraction.

Abstraction refinement ? There are many ways of refining our abstract model. In partic-ular, we can (i) enrich the environment predicates to count the number of processes in a certain environment, (ii) increase the number of reference processes, and (iii) enrich the $\Delta(x)$ descriptions by additional predicates. This is a natural part of our future work.

In conclusion, the environment abstraction framework works well for a variety of protocols by striking what we believe is the right balance between automation and class specific reasoning. As part of future work, we plan to apply this framework to real time and time triggered systems to further illustrate this point.

References

1. Abdullah, P., Buojjani, A., Jonsson, B., Nilsson, M.: Handling Global Conditions in Pa-rameterized System Verification. In: Halbwachs, N., Peled, D.A. (eds.) CAV 1999. LNCS, vol. 1633, pp. 134–145. Springer, Heidelberg (1999)
2. Arons, T., Pnueli, A., Ruah, S., Zuck, L.: Parameterized Verification with Automatically Computed Inductive Assertions. In: Berry, G., Comon, H., Finkel, A. (eds.) CAV 2001. LNCS, vol. 2102, Springer, Heidelberg (2001)
3. Baukus, K., Bensalem, S., Lakhnech, Y., Stahl, K.: Abstracting WS1S Systems to Ver-ify Parameterized Networks. In: Schwartzbach, M.I., Graf, S. (eds.) TACAS 2000. LNCS, vol. 1785, Springer, Heidelberg (2000)
4. Stahl, K., Baukus, K., Lakhnech, Y.: Parameterized Verification of a Cache Coherence Pro-tocol: Safety and Liveness. In: Cortesi, A. (ed.) VMCAI 2002. LNCS, vol. 2294, Springer, Heidelberg (2002)
5. Browne, M.C., Clarke, E.M., Grumberg, O.: Reasoning about Networks with Many Identical Finite State Processes. Information and Computation 81, 13–31 (1989)

6. Chou, C.-T., Mannava, P.K., Park, S.: A Simple Method for Parameterized Verification of Cache Coherence Protocols. In: Hu, A.J., Martin, A.K. (eds.) FMCAD 2004. LNCS, vol. 3312, Springer, Heidelberg (2004)
7. Clarke, E., Talupur, M., Veith, H.: Proving Ptolemy Right: The Environment Abstraction Framework for Model Checking Concurrent Systems, www.cs.cmu.edu/~tmurali/tacas08.pdf
8. Clarke, E., Talupur, M., Veith, H.: Environment Abstraction for Parameterized Verification. In: Emerson, E.A., Namjoshi, K.S. (eds.) VMCAI 2006. LNCS, vol. 3855, pp. 126–141. Springer, Heidelberg (2005)
9. Cohen, A., Namjoshi, K.: Local Proofs for Global Safety Properties. In: Damm, W., Hermanns, H. (eds.) CAV 2007. LNCS, vol. 4590, pp. 55–67. Springer, Heidelberg (2007)
10. Courtois, P.J., Heymans, F., Parnas, D.L.: Concurrent Control with "Readers" and "Writers". Communication of the ACM 14 (1971)
11. Delzanno, G.: Automated Verification of Cache Coherence Protocols. In: Emerson, E.A., Sistla, A.P. (eds.) CAV 2000. LNCS, vol. 1855, Springer, Heidelberg (2000)
12. German, S.M., Sistla, A.P.: Reasoning about Systems with Many Processes. Journal of the ACM 39 (1992)
13. Grinchtein, O., Leucker, M., Piterman, N.: Inferring Network Invariants Automatically. In: Furbach, U., Shankar, N. (eds.) IJCAR 2006. LNCS (LNAI), vol. 4130, pp. 483–497. Springer, Heidelberg (2006)
14. Lahiri, S.K., Bryant, R.: Constructing Quantified Invariants. In: Jensen, K., Podelski, A. (eds.) TACAS 2004. LNCS, vol. 2988, Springer, Heidelberg (2004)
15. Lahiri, S.K., Bryant, R.: Indexed Predicate Discovery for Unbounded System Verification. In: Alur, R., Peled, D.A. (eds.) CAV 2004. LNCS, vol. 3114, pp. 135–147. Springer, Heidelberg (2004)
16. McMillan, K.L.: Verification of an implementation of tomasulo's algorithm by compositional model checking. In: Y. Vardi, M. (ed.) CAV 1998. LNCS, vol. 1427, pp. 110–121. Springer, Heidelberg (1998)
17. McMillan, K.L.: Parameterized Verification of the FLASH Cache Coherence Protocol by Compositional Model Checking. In: Margaria, T., Melham, T.F. (eds.) CHARME 2001. LNCS, vol. 2144, Springer, Heidelberg (2001)
18. McMillan, K.L., Qadeer, S., Saxe, J.B.: Induction in Compositional Model Checking. In: Emerson, E.A., Sistla, A.P. (eds.) CAV 2000. LNCS, vol. 1855, pp. 312–327. Springer, Heidelberg (2000)
19. Pnueli, A., Ruah, S., Zuck, L.: Automatic Deductive Verification with Invisible Invariants. In: Margaria, T., Yi, W. (eds.) TACAS 2001. LNCS, vol. 2031, Springer, Heidelberg (2001)
20. Pnueli, A., Xu, J., Zuck, L.: Liveness with $(0, 1, \infty)$-Counter Abstraction. In: Brinksma, E., Larsen, K.G. (eds.) CAV 2002. LNCS, vol. 2404, Springer, Heidelberg (2002)
21. Sagiv, S., Reps, T.W., Wilhelm, R.: Parametric Shape Analysis via 3-valued Logic. In: TOPLAS (2002)
22. Samer, M., Veith, H.: A Syntactic Characterization of Distributive LTL Queries. In: Díaz, J., Karhumäki, J., Lepistö, A., Sannella, D. (eds.) ICALP 2004. LNCS, vol. 3142, pp. 1099–1110. Springer, Heidelberg (2004)
23. Samer, M., Veith, H.: Deterministic CTL Query Solving. In: Proc. of the 12th International Symposium on Temporal Representation and Reasoning (TIME) (2005)
24. Suzuki, I.: Proving Properties of a Ring of Finite State Machines. Information Processing Letters 28, 213–214 (1988)
25. Talupur, M.: Abstraction Techniques for Infinite State Verification. PhD thesis, Carnegie Mellon University, Computer Science Department (2006)
26. Yahav, E.: Verifying safety properties of concurrent Java programs using 3-valued logic. In: The Proceedings of 18th Symposium on Principles of Programming Languages (2001)

Revisiting Resistance Speeds Up I/O-Efficient
LTL Model Checking[*]

J. Barnat[1], L. Brim[1], P. Šimeček[1], and M. Weber[2]

[1] Masaryk University Brno, Czech Republic
[2] University of Twente, The Netherlands

Abstract. Revisiting resistant graph algorithms are those, whose correctness is not vulnerable to repeated edge exploration. Revisiting resistant I/O efficient graph algorithms exhibit considerable speed-up in practice in comparison to non-revisiting resistant algorithms. In the paper we present a new revisiting resistant I/O efficient LTL model checking algorithm. We analyze its theoretical I/O complexity and we experimentally compare its performance to already existing I/O efficient LTL model checking algorithms.

1 Introduction

Model checking real-life industrial systems is a memory demanding and computation intensive task. Utilizing the increase of computational resources available for the verification process is indispensable to handle these complex systems. The three major approaches to gain more computational power include the usage of parallel computers, clusters of workstations and the usage of external memory devices (hard disks), as well as their combination.

In this paper, we focus on external memory devices, where the goal is to develop algorithms that reduce the number of I/O operations an algorithm has to perform to complete its task. This is because the access to information stored on an external device is orders of magnitude slower than the access to information stored in main memory. Thus, the complexity of I/O efficient algorithms is measured in the number of I/O operations [1].

The automata-theoretic approach [2] to model checking finite-state systems against linear-time temporal logic (LTL) reduces to the detection of reachable accepting cycles in a directed graph. Recently, two I/O efficient LTL model-checking algorithms that allow verification of both safety and liveness properties have been proposed in [3] and in [4]. Both algorithms build on breadth-first traversal through the graph and employ the *delayed duplicate detection* technique [5,6,7,8]. The traversal procedure has to maintain a set of visited vertices (*closed set*) to prevent their re-exploration. Since the graphs are large, the closed set cannot be kept completely in main memory. Most of it is stored on an external memory device. When a new vertex is generated (into the *open set*) it is checked against the closed set to avoid its re-exploration. The idea of the delayed duplicate detection technique is to postpone the individual checks and perform them

[*] This work has been partially supported by the Grant Agency of Czech Republic grant No. 201/06/1338 and the Academy of Sciences grant No. 1ET408050503.

C.R. Ramakrishnan and J. Rehof (Eds.): TACAS 2008, LNCS 4963, pp. 48–62, 2008.

together in a group, for the price of a single scan operation. We assume that the de-layed vertices are stored in the main memory as *candidate set*. In order to minimize the number of scan operations which merge the closed set on disk with the candidate set, it is important that the candidate set is as large as possible. In the case of BFS traversal, candidate sets are formed typically from a single BFS level. However, if the level is small, the utility of delaying the duplicate check drops down. A possible solution is to maximize the size of the candidate set by exploring more BFS levels at once. This, in general, leads to revisiting of vertices due to cycles and might violate the correctness of the algorithm. Whether correctness is preserved depends on the algorithm itself. E.g., if an algorithm uses BFS to traverse the reachable part of a graph, revisiting of vertices does not disturb its correctness, while the algorithm for computing a topological sort is not resistant to such revisits.

It is important to note that even though vertex revisits result in performing more (cheap) RAM operations, it might significantly reduce the number of expensive I/O operations. Thus, *revisiting resistant* algorithms are expected to be more I/O efficient than non-resistant ones in practice. In the first part of the paper we explore the notion of a revisiting resistant graph algorithm in more detail.

We are interested in LTL model-checking algorithms for very large *implicit graphs*, i.e., graphs defined by an initial vertex and a successor function. In previous work, we provided an I/O efficient LTL model checking algorithm that builds on topological sort [4]. The algorithm does not work on-the-fly, however, which limits its applicability. In addition, the algorithm is not revisiting resistant. The main contribution of this paper is to overcome these obstacles by providing a new algorithm. The algorithm adapts the idea of the on-the-fly MAP algorithm [9], which is revisiting resistant. In particular, we exploit the algorithm's property of decomposing a graph into several independently processable, smaller sub-graphs. This, in combination with revisiting resistance, sig-nificantly improves its practical behavior. We consider several heuristics that guide the decomposition.

Related work. Regarding I/O efficient LTL model-checking, we explicitly compare our work to all existing approaches in Sections 5 and 6. Works on improving the effi-ciency of delayed duplicate detection (DDD) include hash-based DDD [10], structured DDD [11], graph compression, lossy hash tables and bit-state hashing [12]. All these techniques are orthogonal to our approach and can be combined with the revisiting resistance principle. We have not implemented these other techniques to provide an empirical evaluation.

Main Results. The contribution of this paper can be summarized as follows:

– We explore the notion of a revisiting resistant algorithm and show that the I/O efficient algorithm from [4] is not revisiting resistant (Section 2).
– We present a revisiting resistant I/O efficient reachability algorithm (Section 3).
– We describe the I/O efficient MAP algorithm for LTL model-checking that works *on-the-fly* (Section 4), analyze its theoretical complexity (Section 5), and compare it to other algorithms, both in terms of asymptotic complexity (Section 5) and ex-perimental behavior (Section 6).

2   Revisiting Resistance

In this section, we explain that some algorithms exhibit a quite distinct property that can be of use when adapting the algorithm to an I/O efficient setting. We will refer to this property as *revisiting resistance* and will brand algorithms satisfying the property as *revisiting resistant algorithms*.

We start with a brief description of a general graph search algorithm. Basically, a search algorithm maintains two data structures: a set of vertices that await processing (*open set*) and a set of vertices that have been processed already (*closed set*). The way in which vertices are manipulated by a general algorithm is depicted in Fig. 1(a). A vertex from the open set is selected and its immediate successors are generated (by traversing edges originating from the vertex). The newly generated vertices are checked against the closed set, to ensure that information stored in the closed set is properly updated. Also, if there is need for further processing of some vertices, they are inserted into the open set along with all necessary information for the processing.

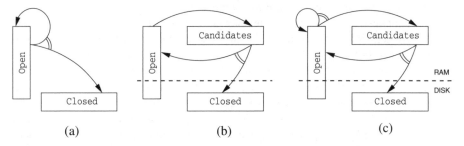

(a)   (b)   (c)

Fig. 1. Vertex work flow: (a) Standard search algorithm, (b) I/O search algorithm with delayed duplicate detection, (c) I/O search algorithm with delayed duplicate detection and revisiting

An I/O efficient search algorithm utilizing the delayed duplicate detection technique has a different vertex work flow. A vertex is picked from the open set and its successors are generated. Then they are inserted into the set of *candidates*, i. e., vertices for which the corresponding check against the closed set has been postponed. In our approach, the set of candidates is kept completely in memory. Candidates are flushed to disk using a *merge* operation under two different circumstances: Either the open set runs empty and the algorithm has to perform a merge to get new vertices into it, or the candidate set is too large and cannot be kept in memory anymore. The merge operation performs the duplicate check of candidate vertices against closed vertices, and inserts those vertices that require further processing into the open set. A schema of the vertex work flow is depicted in Fig. 1(b).

As explained, the merge operation is performed every time the algorithm empties the set of open vertices. Under the standard I/O efficient approach to BFS graph exploration this happens at least after every BFS level. We have observed that for many particular runs of the I/O efficient BFS algorithm, the fact that the merge operation appears after every BFS level is actually a weak point in the practical performance of the algorithm. This is because often a single BFS level contains a relatively small number of vertices,

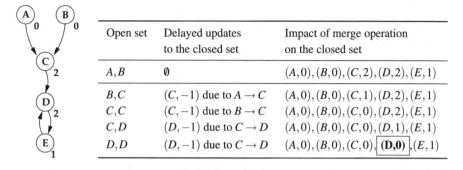

Open set	Delayed updates to the closed set	Impact of merge operation on the closed set
A,B	$\emptyset$	$(A,0),(B,0),(C,2),(D,2),(E,1)$
B,C	$(C,-1)$ due to $A \to C$	$(A,0),(B,0),(C,1),(D,2),(E,1)$
C,C	$(C,-1)$ due to $B \to C$	$(A,0),(B,0),(C,0),(D,2),(E,1)$
C,D	$(D,-1)$ due to $C \to D$	$(A,0),(B,0),(C,0),(D,1),(E,1)$
D,D	$(D,-1)$ due to $C \to D$	$(A,0),(B,0),(C,0),\boxed{(D,0)},(E,1)$

Fig. 2. Example computation of the topological-sort based cycle detection algorithm. Values associated with a vertex correspond to the number of immediate predecessors that have not been processed yet. After the computation, vertices that are associated with a zero value lie outside cycles. The algorithm is not revisiting resistant, as vertex D is labeled with a zero value after the merge operation, although it does lie on a cycle.

in comparison to the full graph. Processing them means that the merge operation has to traverse a large disk file, which is costly.

To fight this inefficiency, we suggest a modification in the vertex work flow of an I/O efficient algorithm, as depicted in Fig. 1(c). A vertex, when generated, is inserted not only into the set of candidates, but also into the open set. This causes some of the vertices stored in the candidate set to be revisited. I.e., the "visit" procedure is performed repeatedly for a vertex *without* properly updating its associated information in the closed set residing in external memory. Consequently, some graph algorithms may exhibit incorrect behavior. Revisiting resistant external memory graph algorithms are those, whose correctness is not vulnerable to repeated edge exploration from vertices in the open set. Below, we demonstrate that some algorithms are vulnerable to the revisiting of candidates and become incorrect, while others cope with the revisiting without problems.

We exemplify the concept of revisiting resistance on the *single source shortest path* (SSSP) and the *topological-search based cycle detection* (OWCTY) [13,14,15] algorithms. As for the SSSP algorithm, the procedure that is bound to edge exploration computes a new value for the target vertex, or updates it if the newly computed value is better (lower in this case) than the value stored before. For example: suppose, an edge (u,v) is labeled with the value t, and vertex u is stored in the open set with an associated value $d(u)$, representing the length of the currently shortest known path to vertex u from the source vertex. The procedure computes a new value for vertex v using the formula $d(v) = d(u) + t$. The new pair $(v, d(v))$ is stored in the candidate set and awaits merging with the value stored in the closed set. After the merge, the value stored in the closed set corresponds to the minimum of the originally stored value and the newly computed value. Note, that the resulting value in the closed set is independent from the number of re-explorations of edge (u,v), and, in other words, the number of merges. Even if performed several times, the computation of the minimum among several possible values remains correct. Therefore, we consider the SSSP algorithm as revisiting resistant.

The situation is quite different in the case of the I/O-efficient OWCTY algorithm. The algorithm performs a cycle detection that is based on the recursive elimination of vertices with zero predecessors. At first, the algorithm computes the number of immediate predecessors for every reachable vertex, and then eliminates vertices whose predecessor count drops to zero. During vertex elimination, the predecessor count is decreased for all immediate successors of the eliminated vertex. Thus, when visiting a vertex v from vertex u, the predecessor count stored at vertex v has to be decreased by one. Unfortunately, the value stored for vertex v can be maintained correctly only by costly access to external memory. One way around this dilemma is to only store a delta alongside v in the candidate set. E. g., a pair $(v, -1)$ indicates that there is a new eliminated predecessor of v, and so the value associated with v should be decreased by one. If we now allow the algorithm to further explore vertices below v, it may happen that the edge (u, v) is re-explored again and another pair $(v, -1)$ is inserted into the set of candidates. However, when the set of candidates is merged with the closed set on disk, the predecessor count of vertex v gets decreased *twice*. This violates the correctness of the algorithm. The problem is exemplified in Fig. 2. Therefore, the algorithm is not revisiting resistant.

3   Revisiting Resistant Reachability

This section explains a simple revisiting resistant algorithm, an I/O efficient breadth-first search (Alg. REACHABILITY). The algorithm's sole task is to traverse all vertices, thus we only have to remember for each vertex whether it has been visited or not. Clearly, once a vertex is marked as visited, additional visits do not change this property.

We introduce revisiting resistance to the standard I/O efficient breadth-first search (BFS) procedure as follows. After a single BFS level is fully generated, a decision is made whether the set of candidates will be merged with the closed set, or whether another BFS level will be processed without prior merging. The pseudo-code of function OPENISNOTEMPTY makes this more precise.

According to our observations, omitting the merge operation as long as there is still some unused memory left is not the optimal strategy. Merging with a small closed set might be cheaper than repeatedly re-exploring vertices of the candidate set. We avoid postponing merge operations on small closed sets by introducing a decision formula that builds upon the estimated time needed to fully generate the next BFS level $(n + 1)$, and the estimated time needed to perform the merge operation. These estimations are denoted as $estim(t_{n+1}^{gen})$ and $estim(t_{n+1}^{merge})$, respectively, and they are computed from the sizes of open and closed sets as follows:

$$estim(t_{n+1}^{gen}) = t_n^{gen} \cdot \frac{|Open_{n+1}|}{|Open_n|} \quad \text{and} \quad estim(t_{n+1}^{merge}) = t_n^{merge} \cdot \frac{|Closed_n| + |Open_n|}{|Closed_n|},$$

where $|Open_{n+1}|$ refers to the number of newly discovered vertices w.r.t. *Candidates*. The decision formula is then a simple comparison of the estimated values:

$$estim(t_{n+1}^{gen}) < estim(t_{n+1}^{merge})$$

Finally, note that in our approach the entire set of candidates is kept in memory. However, there is a different approach to I/O efficient reachability, in which both, the

---

Algorithm 1. REACHABILITY

 1: *OmittedMergeCount* ← 0
 2: *Candidates* ← ∅
 3: *s* ← GETINITIALVERTEX()
 4: *Closed* ← {*s*}
 5: *Open*.push(*s*)
 6: **while** OPENISNOTEMPTY() **do**
 7:     *s* ← *Open*.pop()
 8:     **for all** *t* ∈ GETSUCCESSORS(*s*) **do**
 9:         **if** *t* ∉ *Candidates* **then**
10:             *Candidates* ← *Candidates* ∪ {*t*}
11:             *LastLevel* ← *LastLevel* ∪ *t*
12:             **if** MEMORYISFULL() **then**
13:                 MERGE()

Algorithm 2. OPENISNOTEMPTY

1: **if** *Open*.isEmpty() **then**
2:     **if** ESTIMGEN() < ESTIMMERGE() **then**
3:         *Open*.swap(*LastLevel*)
4:         *OmittedMergeCount* ← *OmittedMergeCount* + 1
5:     **else**
6:         MERGE()
7: **return** ¬*Open*.isEmpty()

Algorithm 3. MERGE

 1: **for all** *s* ∈ *Closed* **do**
 2:     **if** *s* ∈ *Candidates* **then**
 3:         *Candidates* ← *Candidates* \ {*s*}
 4: **if** *OmittedMergeCount* > 0 **then**
 5:     *Open* ← (*Open* ∪ *LastLevel*) \ *Closed*
 6:     *OmittedMergeCount* ← 0
 7: **for all** *s* ∈ *Candidates* **do**
 8:     **if** *OmittedMergeCount* = 0 **then**
 9:         *Open*.push(*s*)
10:     *Closed* ← *Closed* ∪ {*s*}
11: *LastLevel*.clear()
12: *Candidates* ← ∅

---

candidate and the closed set are stored in external memory [3]. It is possible to combine revisiting resistant algorithms with that approach by employing a similar decision formula to trigger the merge operation.

4 I/O Efficient MAP Algorithm

In this section we design a new revisiting resistant, I/O efficient algorithm for detecting reachable accepting cycles in an implicitly given, directed graph. The algorithm is derived from the *Maximal Accepting Predecessors* (MAP) algorithm [9,16]. We discuss advantages and disadvantages of the algorithm in comparison to other I/O efficient LTL model checking algorithms.

The main idea behind the MAP algorithm is based on the fact that each accepting vertex lying on an accepting cycle is its own accepting predecessor. Instead of expensive computing and storing of all accepting predecessors for each (accepting) vertex, the algorithm computes and stores a single representative accepting predecessor for each vertex, namely the maximal one in a suitable ordering of vertices.

Let $G = (V, E, s_0, F)$ be a directed graph, where V is a set of vertices, E is a set of edges, s_0 is an initial vertex, and F a set of accepting vertices. For technical reasons we assume s_0 is not accepting. Let $\prec$ be a linear order on vertices with minimal element $\bot$. Let $u \leadsto^+ v$ denote that there is a directed path from u to v. Then the *maximal accepting predecessor* function map_G is defined as:

$$map_G(v) = \max\left(\{u \in F \mid u \leadsto^+ v\} \cup \{\bot\}\right)$$

Accepting cycle detection is based on the fact that if $v = map_G(v)$, then v lies on an accepting cycle. While the condition is sufficient, it is not necessary—it is possible that $v \neq map_G(v)$ but v lies on an accepting cycle. Moreover, if v is accepting and $map_G(v) \prec v$ then v does not lie on an accepting cycle. Therefore, the MAP algorithm repeatedly removes vertices for which $map_G(v) \prec v$ and recomputes map_G for all vertices.

There is another feature of the MAP algorithm that can be exploited in designing its I/O efficient version. If $map_G(u) \neq map_G(v)$, then u and v cannot lie on the same accepting cycle. This property allows to decompose the graph G into disjoint subgraphs each time map_G values are computed. Let $P(u) = \{v \mid map_G(v) = u\}$. The vertex u is called a *seed* of a *partition* $P(u)$. For any two vertices u, v we have that either $P(u) = P(v)$ or $P(u) \cap P(v) = \emptyset$. The subgraphs are given by disjoint partitions and it is enough to search for accepting cycles in each partition separately. The algorithm thus maintains a queue of pairs $(seed, partition)$, which is initialized with the partition containing all vertices of G and the initial vertex s_0 as its seed. On each partition P the algorithm computes map_G values. If there is a vertex u such that $map_G(u) \in P$, an accepting cycle is detected, otherwise P is split into smaller partitions which are stored for further processing. Note that sub-partitions with $map_G = \bot$ are dropped immediately.

The algorithm obtains the necessary linear ordering on vertices by assigning a unique number to every vertex. This also allows us to store for each vertex the *order value* of its maximal accepting predecessor rather than the maximal accepting predecessor itself.

The basic structure of our new algorithm follows the original MAP algorithm. We maintain a queue *Partitions* of unprocessed partitions as produced by computing map_G. For each partition the algorithm also records its size. If a partition fits into the main memory, we call a standard in-memory algorithm searching accepting cycles, for example, *nested depth-first search* [17].

Procedure MAP propagates the highest order values across the graph in order to compute map_G values for all vertices in a given partition. In essence, the procedure is very similar to external BFS, but it allows to enqueue already explored vertices if it increases their map_G value. We return to this point in the explanation of procedure UPDATEMAP.

Algorithm 4. DETECTACCEPTINGCYCLE(G)

Require: $G = (V, E, s_0, F)$
1: *Partitions.push*(s_0, V)
2: **while** *Partitions* $\neq \emptyset$ **do**
3:         $(s, Partition) \leftarrow Partitions.pop()$
4:         **if** $\|Partition\| > MEMORY\_CAPACITY$ **then**
5:                 MAP($s, Partition$)
6:         **else**
7:                 NESTED-DFS($s, Partition$)
8:         FINDPARTITIONS($Partition$)
9: **return** No accepting cycle!

Algorithm 5. MAP($seed, Partition$)

1: *Open.push*($\langle seed, \bot \rangle$)
2: *Closed* $\leftarrow \{seed\}$
3: *Closed.setMap*($seed, \bot$)
4: **while** OPENISNOTEMPTY() **do**
5:         $(s, propagate) \leftarrow Open.pop()$
6:         **for all** $t \in$ GETSUCCESSORS(s) **do**
7:                 STOREORCOMBINE($t, propagate$)

Algorithm 6. STOREORCOMBINE(s, map)

1: **if** $s \in Candidates$ **then**
2:         $map' \leftarrow Candidates.getMap(s)$
3:         *Candidates.setMap*(s, MAX(map, map'))
4: **else**
5:         **if** MEMORYISFULL() **then**
6:                 MERGE()
7:         *Candidates* $\leftarrow Candidates \cup \{s\}$
8:         *Candidates.setMap*(s, map)

In procedure STOREORCOMBINE, we ensure that the currently highest known accepting predecessor for vertex s is stored: if some accepting predecessor for s has been encountered already, we compare it to *map* and store the higher one. Otherwise, we store s and *map*, possibly first making enough memory available through the MERGE operation.

The MERGE procedure joins data stored in internal memory with an external repository. To identify which vertices are new or having their maximal accepting predecessor updated, the procedure traverses all vertices stored on disk and checks whether they are present in the candidate set. For each vertex found in internal memory, MERGE also compares whether the newly found accepting predecessor is higher than the one stored on disk.

Finally, new vertices and vertices with updated accepting predecessor are appended to the open set. New vertices are added to the *Closed* repository, too.

Algorithm 7. MERGE

1: *Candidates ← Candidates ∩ Partition* {Intersection is made trivially by a single traversal across *Partition*}
2: *Updated = ∅*
3: **for all** *s ∈ Closed* **do**
4:         **if** *s ∈ Candidates* **then**
5:                 UPDATEMAP(*s*)
6: **for all** *s ∈ Candidates* **do**
7:         *Open.push(⟨s, Candidates.getMap(s)⟩)*
8: *New ← Candidates \ Updated*
9: *Closed ← Closed ∪ New*
10: *Candidates ← ∅*

Procedure UPDATEMAP is called from MERGE to compare accepting predecessors of a given vertex *s*, this time taking *all* known information into account. We compare the (so far) highest accepting predecessor for *s* stored with the candidate set (in memory), the closed set (on disk), and *s* itself if it is an accepting vertex. Out of those, the maximal vertex (w.r.1t. ≺) is stored as new accepting predecessor for *s*.

We discard *s* from memory if its accepting predecessor stored with the candidate set is not higher than the one stored with the closed set, as it does not yield any useful information.

After the loop between lines 3–5 in MERGE finishes, the candidate set contains only new vertices and vertices whose accepting predecessor in memory has been greater than the one stored on disk. In addition, we return the set of vertices whose accepting predecessor has been changed.

Algorithm 8. UPDATEMAP(*s*)

1: *map ← Candidates.getMap(s)*
2: *map' ← Closed.getMap(s)*
3: **if** ISACCEPTING(*s*) **then**
4:         *map' ← MAX(map', s)*
5: *Closed.setMap(s, MAX(map, map'))*
6: *Candidates.setMap(s, MAX(map, map'))*
7: **if** *map ≻ map'* **then**
8:         **if** *s = map* **then**
9:                 **exit** Accepting cycle found!
10:         *Updated ← Updated ∪ {s}*
11: **else**
12:         *Candidates ← Candidates \ {s}*
13: **return** *Updated*

Procedure FINDPARTITIONS is called from DETECTACCEPTINGCYCLE to identify new sub-partitions in a given partition. Therefore, the procedure sorts vertices in the partition by their *map_G* values. After that, it only traverses the sorted list of vertices sequentially (loop 4–13) to find the beginning and end of partitions, and also to find the maximal accepting predecessor in the given partition, which is from this moment on regarded to be non-accepting (see line 3 of MAP). Note that the condition on line 6 leaves out a partition with map_G value set to $\bot$, since it does not contain any accepting vertex and thus cannot contain an accepting cycle.

Algorithm 9. FINDPARTITIONS$(Partition)$

1: *Partition.sortByMap()*
2: *newPartition* $\leftarrow \emptyset$
3: *lastMap* $\leftarrow \bot$ $\{\bot$ is the lowest possible value $\}$
4: **for all** $(s, map, order) \in Partition$ **do**
5:      **if** *lastMap* $\neq$ *map* **then**
6:          **if** *lastMap* $\neq \bot$ **then**
7:              *Partitions.push(seed, newPartition)*
8:          *newPartition* $\leftarrow \emptyset$
9:      **else**
10:          *newPartition* $\leftarrow$ *newPartition* $\cup \{s\}$
11:      **if** *map* $=$ *order* **then**
12:          *seed* $\leftarrow s$
13:      *lastMap* $\leftarrow$ *map*
14: *Partitions.push(seed, newPartition)* $\{$Adding last partition$\}$

MAP is a revisiting resistant algorithm because it simply traverses the state space and updates map_G values, which are computed as maximum of the values propagated to it. The order and repetition of vertices does not matter, as the maximum stays the same. Henceforward we will refer to the revisiting resistant version of the I/O efficient MAP algorithm as MAP-rr.

Changes in the algorithm are analogous to the modification of the reachability algorithm presented in Sec. 3, but we have to take care of accepting vertices in a special way: between lines 11 and 12 of function UPDATEMAP we put another line:

if $map' = $ ORDERNUMBER(s) **then** *Updated* $\leftarrow$ *Updated* $\cup \{s\}$

5 Complexity Analysis and Comparison

A widely accepted model for the complexity analysis of I/O algorithms is the model of Aggarwal and Vitter [1], in which the complexity of an I/O algorithm is measured solely in terms of the numbers of external I/O operations. This is motivated by the fact that a single I/O operation is approximately six orders of magnitude slower than a computation step performed in main memory [18]. Therefore, an algorithm that does not perform the optimal amount of work but has lower I/O complexity may be faster in practice, when compared to an algorithm that performs the optimal amount of work, but has higher I/O complexity. The complexity of an I/O algorithm in the model of Aggarwal and Vitter is further parametrized by M, B, and D, where M denotes the number of items that fits into the internal memory, B denotes the number of items that can be transferred in a single I/O operation, and D denotes the number of blocks that can

Table 1. I/O complexity of algorithms for both modes of candidate set storage. Parameter p_{max} denotes the longest path in the graph going through trivial strongly connected components (without self-loops), l_{SCC} denotes the length of the longest path in the SCC graph, h_{BFS} denotes the height of its BFS tree, and d denotes the diameter of the graph.

Algorithm	Worst-case I/O Complexity
Candidate set in main memory	
EJ'	$O((l + |F| \cdot |E|/M) \cdot scan(|F| \cdot |V|))$
OWCTY	$O(l_{SCC} \cdot (h_{BFS} + |p_{max}| + |E|/M) \cdot scan(|V|))$
MAP	$O(|F| \cdot ((d + |E|/M + |F|) \cdot scan(|V|) + sort(|V|)))$
Candidate set in external memory	
EJ	$O(l \cdot scan(|F| \cdot |V|) + sort(|F| \cdot |E|))$
OWCTY'	$O(l_{SCC} \cdot ((h_{BFS} + |p_{max}|) \cdot scan(|V|) + sort(|E|)))$
MAP'	$O(|F| \cdot ((d + |F|) \cdot scan(|V|) + sort(|F| \cdot |E|)))$

be transferred in parallel, i.e., the number of independent parallel disks available. The abbreviations $sort(n)$ and $scan(n)$ stand for $\Theta(N/(DB) \log_{M/B}(N/B))$ and $\Theta(N/(DB))$, respectively. In this section we give the I/O complexity of our algorithm and compare it with the complexity of the algorithm by Edelkamp and Jabbar [3].

Theorem 1. *The I/O complexity of algorithm* DETECTACCEPTINGCYCLE *is*

$$O(|F| \cdot ((d + |E|/M + |F|) \cdot scan(|V|) + sort(|V|)))$$

where d is the diameter of a given graph.

Proof. Since each partition is identified by its maximal accepting vertex, at most $|F|$ partitions can be found during traversal. Thus, lines 2–8 in DETECTACCEPTINGCYCLE are repeated at most $|F|$ times, and consequently, procedures MAP and FINDPARTITIONS are called at most $|F|$ times as well. Each call of FINDPARTITIONS costs at most $O(scan(|V|) + sort(|V|))$, because of the dominating sort operation on line 1 and the linear scan in loop 4–13. The I/O complexity of MERGE is $O(scan(|V|))$, because it is dominated by the scan operation across the closed set (loop 3–5) and writing of new and updated vertices to the open set.

There are two main sources of I/O operations in procedure MAP: merge operations and open set manipulation. MERGE is indirectly called on lines 4 and 7. It is called whenever the memory becomes full (at most $|E|/M$ times) or the open set becomes empty (at most d times). Reading of *Open* on line 5 costs at most $O(scan(|F| \cdot |V|)) = O(|F|scan(|V|))$, because each vertex can appear in the open set as many times as its associated accepting predecessor changes. □

For the purpose of comparison, we denote our new algorithm as MAP, the algorithm proposed in [4] as OWCTY and the algorithm of Edelkamp and Jabbar [3] as EJ. MAP and OWCTY store the candidate set internally, while EJ stores it externally by default. In the case the candidate set is sorted externally, it is possible to perform the merge operation on a BFS level independently of the size of the main memory. This approach

Table 2. Partitions after the first iteration of MAP algorithm. Maximums are taken over partitions with some accepting vertex in them.

Experiment	Graph Size	Number of Partitions	Max. Partition Size		Vertices with $map_G = \perp$	
Lamport(5),P4	74,413,141	838,452	454,073	< 1%	38,717,846	52%
MCS(5),P4	119,663,657	3,373,145	108,092	< 1%	60,556,519	51%
Peterson(5),P4	284,942,015	11,451	12,029,114	4%	142,471,098	50%
Phils(16,1),P3	61,230,206	336,339	129,023	< 1%	43,046,721	70%
Rether(16,8,4),P2	31,087,573	33,353	5	< 1%	30,920,813	99%
Szymanski(5),P4	419,183,762	20,064	131,441,308	31%	209,596,444	50%

is suitable for those cases where memory is small, or the graph is orders of magnitude larger. A disadvantage of the approach is the need to sort during each merge operation. Furthermore, it cannot be combined with heuristics, such as Bloom filters and a lossy hash table [12]. Fortunately, all three algorithms are modular enough to be able to work in both modes. Tab. 1 shows the I/O complexities for all three algorithms in both variants.

It can be seen that the upper bound for the complexity of MAP is worse than the one of EJ and OWCTY (in both modes of the candidate set). Nevertheless, we claim that the complexity is reasonable in most cases, for a number of reasons. First, the algorithm usually performs at most two iterations of the loop between lines 2–8 in procedure DETECTACCEPTINGCYCLE: if an accepting cycle was not found during the first iteration, the state space is partitioned into many partitions (as shown in Tab. 2). Furthermore, if the state space was partitioned evenly, then 1000 partitions would be enough to divide a 1 Terabyte state space into blocks sufficiently small to fit into very modestly sized internal memory, by today's standards. Even if some partitions would not fit into main memory yet, another partitioning round usually decreases the maximal partition size enough such that all remaining partitions fit into internal memory. Therefore, it is reasonable to expect that the algorithm becomes fully internal after a very small number of iterations.

Second, d is commonly not proportional to the size of the state space and is usually not much higher than h_{BFS}.

Third, the upper bound $|F| \cdot |V|$ on the number of vertices revisited due to updates of a map_G value is quite coarse. We have measured the amount of map_G updates for the MAP algorithm with a reverse-BFS ordering of vertices. We found that map updates take commonly not more than 20% of the graph exploration (see Tab. 4).

Taking this into account, the complexity of MAP could be very close to

$$O((h_{BFS} + |E|/M) \cdot scan(|V|) + sort(|V|))$$

in most practical cases. We note that this equals the complexity of I/O efficient reachability plus sorting the set of vertices. Our measurements confirm this claim, as shown in Tab. 4.

Table 3. Comparison of revisiting techniques and simple I/O efficient reachability

Experiment	Normal (hours)	Revisiting Resistant (hours)	
Lamport(5),P4	02:51:09	01:19:32	46%
MCS(5),P4	03:56:26	02:41:45	68%
Peterson(5),P4	19:38:32	09:02:37	46%
Phils(16,1),P3	02:09:45	01:41:24	77%
Rether(16,8,4),P2	13:54:29	00:29:19	3%
Szymanski(5),P4	51:20:32	17:54:14	34%
On average	100%		46%

Table 4. Run times of reachability and MAP algorithm

Model	Reachability (hours)	MAP (hours)	
Lamport	2:51:09	3:12:09	112%
MCS	3:56:26	4:28:06	113%
Phils	2:09:45	2:29:26	115%

6   Experiments

In order to obtain experimental evidence about the behavior of our algorithm in practice, we implemented an I/O efficient reachability procedure and three I/O efficient LTL model checking algorithms.

All algorithms have been implemented on top of the DIVINE library [19], providing the state space generator, and the STXXL library [20], providing the needed I/O primitives. Experiments were run on 2 GHz Intel Xeon PC, the main memory was limited to 2 GB, the disk space to 60 GB and wall clock time limit was set to 120 hours. Algorithm MAP-rr is a variant of MAP exploiting its revisiting resistance. Algorithm EJ was implemented as a procedure that performs the graph transformation as suggested in [3] and then employs I/O efficient breadth-first search to check for a counter example. Note, that our implementation of [3] does not include the A^* heuristics and hence can be less efficient when searching for an existing counter example. The procedure is referred to as *Liveness as Safety with BFS* (LaS-BFS) [21].

First of all, we have measured the impact of revisiting resistance on procedure REACHABILITY. We have obtained results that demonstrate significant speed-up, as shown in Tab. 3. We have also measured run times and memory consumption of LaS-BFS, OWCTY, MAP and MAP-rr. The experimental results are listed in Tab. 5. We note that just before the unsuccessful termination of LaS-BFS due to exhausting the disk space, the BFS level size still tended to grow. This suggests that the computation would last substantially longer if sufficient disk space would have been available. For the same input graphs, algorithms OWCTY, MAP and MAP-rr manage to perform the verification using a few Gigabytes of disk space only. All the models and their LTL properties are taken from the BEEM project [22].

Measurements on models with valid properties demonstrate that MAP is able to successfully prove their correctness, while LaS-BFS fails. Additionally, MAP's

Table 5. Run times in `hh:mm:ss` format and memory consumption on a single workstation. "OOS" means "out of space".

Experiment	LaS-BFS		OWCTY		MAP		MAP-rr	
	Time	Disk	Time	Disk	Time	Disk	Time	Disk
Valid Properties								
Lamport(5),P4	(OOS)		02:37:17	5.5 GB	03:16:36	5.7 GB	02:37:56	8.5 GB
MCS(5),P4	(OOS)		03:27:05	9.8 GB	04:59:17	10 GB	04:13:21	11 GB
Peterson(5),P4	(OOS)		18:20:03	26 GB	25:09:35	26 GB	15:24:29	27 GB
Phils(16,1),P3	(OOS)		01:49:41	6.2 GB	02:31:33	7.8 GB	02:19:20	8.1 GB
Rether(16,8,4),P2	53:06:44	12 GB	07:22:05	3.2 GB	12:31:18	6.3 GB	00:39:07	6.3 GB
Szymanski(5),P4	(OOS)		45:52:25	38 GB	59:35:25	38 GB	29:09:12	39 GB
Invalid Properties								
Anderson(5),P2	00:00:17	50 MB	07:14:23	3.3 GB	00:00:07	2 MB	00:00:01	4 MB
Bakery(5,5),P3	00:25:59	5.4 GB	68:23:34	38 GB	00:00:09	16 MB	00:00:23	54 MB
Szymanski(4),P2	00:00:50	203 MB	00:20:07	253 MB	00:00:04	2 MB	00:00:02	4 MB
Elevator2(7),P5	00:01:02	130 MB	00:00:25	6 MB	00:00:05	2 MB	00:00:01	3 MB

performance does not differ much from the performance of OWCTY. Moreover, with the use of revisiting resistant techniques, MAP-rr is able to outperform OWCTY in many cases. We observe that specifically in cases with high h_{BFS}—e.g., Rether(16,8,4),P2—time savings are substantial.

A notable weakness of OWCTY is its slowness on models with invalid properties. It does not work on-the-fly, and is consequently outperformed by LaS-BFS in the aforementioned class of inputs. Algorithms MAP and MAP-rr do not share OWCTY's drawbacks, and in fact they outperform both, OWCTY and LaS-BFS on those inputs. This can be attributed to their on-the-fly nature: On all our inputs, a counter example, if existing, is found during the first iteration.

7   Conclusions

We described *revisiting resistance*, a distinct property of graph algorithms, and showed how it can be of practical use to the I/O efficient approach of processing very large graphs. In particular, we described how a simple I/O efficient reachability procedure with delayed duplicate detection can be extended to exploit its revisiting resistance and showed that the extension is valuable in practice. Furthermore, we analyzed existing I/O efficient algorithms for LTL model checking and showed that the OWCTY algorithm is not revisiting resistant. We introduced a new I/O efficient revisiting resistant algorithm for LTL model checking that employs the *Maximal Accepting Predecessor* function to detect accepting cycles. We analyzed the I/O complexity of the new algorithm, and showed that due to the revisiting resistance, the algorithm exhibits competitive runtimes for verification of valid LTL properties while preserving its on-the-fly nature. According to our experimental results, the algorithm outperforms other I/O efficient algorithms on invalid LTL properties even if it is being slowed down with the vertex revisiting.

References

1. Aggarwal, A., Vitter, J.S.: The input/output complexity of sorting and related problems. Commun. ACM 31(9), 1116–1127 (1988)
2. Vardi, M.Y., Wolper, P.: An Automata-Theoretic Approach to Automatic Program Verification. In: Proc. of LICS 1986, pp. 332–344. Computer Society Press (1986)
3. Edelkamp, S., Jabbar, S.: Large-Scale Directed Model Checking LTL. In: Valmari, A. (ed.) SPIN 2006. LNCS, vol. 3925, pp. 1–18. Springer, Heidelberg (2006)
4. Barnat, J., Brim, L., Šimeček, P.: I/O Efficient Accepting Cycle Detection. In: Damm, W., Hermanns, H. (eds.) CAV 2007. LNCS, vol. 4590, pp. 281–293. Springer, Heidelberg (2007)
5. Korf, R.E., Schultze, P.: Large-Scale Parallel Breadth-First Search. In: Proc. of AAAI, pp. 1380–1385. AAAI Press / The MIT Press (2005)
6. Korf, R.E.: Best-First Frontier Search with Delayed Duplicate Detection. In: Proc. of AAAI, pp. 650–657 (2004)
7. Stern, U., Dill, D.L.: Using Magnetic Disk Instead of Main Memory in the Murphi Verifier. In: Y. Vardi, M. (ed.) CAV 1998. LNCS, vol. 1427, pp. 172–183. Springer, Heidelberg (1998)
8. Munagala, K., Ranade, A.: I/O-complexity of graph algorithms. In: Proc. of SODA, Society for Industrial and Applied Mathematics, pp. 687–694 (1999)
9. Brim, L., Černá, I., Moravec, P., Šimša, J.: Accepting Predecessors Are Better than Back Edges in Distributed LTL Model-Checking. In: Hu, A.J., Martin, A.K. (eds.) FMCAD 2004. LNCS, vol. 3312, pp. 352–366. Springer, Heidelberg (2004)
10. Korf, R.E.: Best-First Frontier Search with Delayed Duplicate Detection. In: Proc. of AAAI, pp. 650–657. AAAI Press / The MIT Press (2004)
11. Zhou, R., Hansen, E.A.: Structured Duplicate Detection in External-Memory Graph Search. In: Proc. of AAAI, pp. 683–689 (2004)
12. Hammer, M., Weber, M.: To Store or Not To Store. In: Brim, L., Haverkort, B.R., Leucker, M., van de Pol, J. (eds.) FMICS 2006 and PDMC 2006. LNCS, vol. 4346, pp. 51–66. Springer, Heidelberg (2007)
13. Černá, I., Pelánek, R.: Distributed Explicit Fair Cycle Detection. In: Ball, T., Rajamani, S.K. (eds.) SPIN 2003. LNCS, vol. 2648, pp. 49–73. Springer, Heidelberg (2003)
14. Fisler, K., Fraer, R., Kamhi, G., Vardi, M.Y., Yang, Z.: Is There a Best Symbolic Cycle-Detection Algorithm? In: Margaria, T., Yi, W. (eds.) ETAPS 2001 and TACAS 2001. LNCS, vol. 2031, pp. 420–434. Springer, Heidelberg (2001)
15. Ravi, K., Bloem, R., Somenzi, F.: A Comparative Study of Symbolic Algorithms for the Computation of Fair Cycles. In: Johnson, S.D., Hunt Jr., W.A. (eds.) FMCAD 2000. LNCS, vol. 1954, pp. 143–160. Springer, Heidelberg (2000)
16. Brim, L., Černá, I., Moravec, P., Šimša, J.: How to Order Vertices for Distributed LTL Model-Checking Based on Accepting Predecessors. In: Proc. of PDMC (2005)
17. Holzmann, G., Peled, D., Yannakakis, M.: On Nested Depth First Search. In: The SPIN Verification System, American Mathematical Society, pp. 23–32 (1996)
18. Vitter, J.S.: External memory algorithms and data structures: dealing with massive data. ACM Comput. Surv. 33(2), 209–271 (2001)
19. Barnat, J., Brim, L., Černá, I., Šimeček, P.: DiVinE – The Distributed Verification Environment. In: Proc. of PDMC, pp. 89–94 (2005)
20. Dementiev, R., Kettner, L., Sanders, P.: STXXL: Standard Template Library for XXL Data Sets. In: Brodal, G.S., Leonardi, S. (eds.) ESA 2005. LNCS, vol. 3669, pp. 640–651. Springer, Heidelberg (2005)
21. Schuppan, V., Biere, A.: Efficient Reduction of Finite State Model Checking to Reachability Analysis. International Journal on Software Tools for Technology Transfer (STTT) 5(2–3), 185–204 (2004)
22. Pelánek, R.: BEEM: Benchmarks for Explicit Model Checkers. In: Bošnački, D., Edelkamp, S. (eds.) SPIN 2007. LNCS, vol. 4595, pp. 263–267. Springer, Heidelberg (2007)

Antichains: Alternative Algorithms for LTL Satisfiability and Model-Checking*

M. De Wulf[1], L. Doyen[2], N. Maquet[1,**], and J.-F. Raskin[1]

[1] CS, Université Libre de Bruxelles (ULB), Belgium
[2] I&C, Ecole Polytechnique Fédérale de Lausanne (EPFL), Switzerland

Abstract. The linear temporal logic (LTL) was introduced by Pnueli as a logic to express properties over the computations of reactive systems. Since this seminal work, there have been a large number of papers that have studied deductive systems and algorithmic methods to reason about the correctness of reactive programs with regard to LTL properties. In this paper, we propose new efficient algorithms for LTL satisfiability and model-checking. Our algorithms do not construct nondeterministic automata from LTL formulas but work directly with alternating automata using efficient exploration techniques based on antichains.

1 Introduction

A model for an LTL formula over a set P of propositions is an infinite word w over the alphabet $\Sigma = 2^P$. An LTL formula ϕ defines a set of words $\llbracket \phi \rrbracket = \{w \in \Sigma^\omega \mid w \models \phi\}$. The *satisfiability problem* for LTL asks, given an LTL formula ϕ, if $\llbracket \phi \rrbracket$ is empty. The *model-checking problem* for LTL asks, given an omega-regular language $\mathcal{L}$ (e.g., the set of all computations of a reactive system) and a LTL formula ϕ, if $\mathcal{L} \subseteq \llbracket \phi \rrbracket$.

The link between LTL and omega-regular languages is at the heart of the *automata-theoretic approach* to LTL [24]. Given a LTL formula ϕ, we can construct a nondeterministic Büchi automaton (NBW) $\mathcal{A}_\phi$ whose language, noted $\mathsf{L_b}(\mathcal{A}_\phi)$, corresponds exactly to the models of ϕ, i.e., $\mathsf{L_b}(\mathcal{A}_\phi) = \llbracket \phi \rrbracket$. This reduces the satisfiability and model-checking problems to automata-theoretic questions.

This elegant framework has triggered a large body of works that have been implemented in explicit state model-checking tools such as SPIN [19] and in symbolic state model-checking tools such as SMV [15] and NuSMV [2].

The translation from LTL to NBW is central to the automata-theoretic approach to model-checking. When done explicitly, this translation is *worst-case exponential*. Explicit translation is required for explicit state model-checking, while in the symbolic approach to LTL model-checking [3] the NBW is symbolically encoded using boolean constraints. In [18], Rozier and Vardi have extensively compared symbolic and explicit approaches to satisfiability checking using a large number of tools. From their experiments, the symbolic approach scales better.

---

* This research was supported by the Belgian FNRS grant 2.4530.02 of the FRFC project "Centre Fédéré en Vérification" and by the project "MoVES", an Interuniversity Attraction Poles Project of the Belgian Federal Government.
** This authorw is supported by a FNRS-FRIA grant.

C.R. Ramakrishnan and J. Rehof (Eds.): TACAS 2008, LNCS 4963, pp. 63–77, 2008.

Efficient algorithms to reason on large LTL formulas are highly desirable. First, as writing formal requirements is a difficult task, verifying consistency is an issue for which efficient satisfiability checking would be highly valuable. Second, when model-checking a system and especially in the "debugging" phase, we may want to check properties that are true only under a set of assumptions, in which case specifications are of the form $\rho_1 \wedge \rho_2 \wedge \cdots \wedge \rho_n \rightarrow \phi$, and are usually very large. The reader will find such large formulas for example in [1] and in the experiments reported here.

In this paper, we present a new approach to LTL satisfiability and model-checking. Our approach avoids the explicit translation to NBW and does not resort to pure boolean reasoning as in the symbolic approach. Instead, we associate to every LTL formula an alternating Büchi automaton over a symbolic alphabet (sABW) that recognizes the models of the formula. The use of alternation instead of nondeterminism, and of symbolic alphabets allows for the construction of compact automata (the number of states and symbolic transitions are linear in the size of the LTL formula). While this construction is well-known and is an intermediate step in several translators from LTL to explicit NBW [23], we provide a new efficient way to analyze sABW. This new algorithm is an extension of [7], where we have shown how to efficiently decide the emptiness problem for (non-symbolic) ABW. The efficiency of our new algorithm relies on avoiding the explicit construction of a NBW and on the existence of pre-orders that can be exploited to efficiently compute fixpoint expressions directly over the transition relation of ABW.

Contributions. The three main contributions of the paper are as follows. First, we adapt the algorithm of [7] for checking emptiness of symbolic ABW. The algorithm in [7] enumerates the alphabet Σ, which is impractical for LTL where the alphabet $\Sigma = 2^P$ is of exponential size. To cope with this, we introduce a way to combine BDD-based techniques with antichain algorithms, taking advantage of the strengths of BDDs for boolean reasoning. Second, we extend the combination of BDDs and antichains to model-checking of LTL specifications over symbolic Kripke structures. In [7], only explicit-state models and specifications given as NBWs were handled. Third, we have implemented and extensively tested our new algorithms. While the previous evaluations of antichain algorithms [6,7] were performed on randomly generated models, we experiment here our new algorithms on concrete (i.e., with a meaningful semantics as opposed to randomly generated instances) satisfiability and model-checking examples. Most of our examples are taken in [18] and [20] where they are presented as benchmarks to compare model-checking algorithms. Our new algorithms outperform standard classical symbolic algorithms of the highly optimized industrial-level tools like NUSMV for both satisfiability and model-checking.

Related works. We review the recent related works about LTL satisfiability and model-checking. For many years, great efforts have been devoted to reduce the cost of the explicit translation from LTL to NBW (see e.g., [8,9,22,4]). The existing translators are now very sophisticated and it is questionable that they can still be drastically improved. According to [18], the current explicit tools are suitable for relatively small formulas but do not scale well. Rozier and Vardi advocate the use of symbolic methods as defined in [3] and tools like NUSMV for LTL satisfiability checking. They can handle much larger formulas than explicit tools. Therefore, we compare our new algorithms with NUSMV on benchmarks proposed by Rozier and Vardi, with very good results.

In [20], Vardi *et al.* propose a *hybrid approach* to model-checking: the system is represented symbolically using BDDs and the LTL formula is translated explicitly as a NBW. Their method has the nice property to partition the usually huge symbolic state space into pieces associated to each state of the NBW (this heuristic is called *property-driven partitioning* in [18]). Our approach also gains from this interesting feature, but in contrast to Vardi *et al.*, we do not need the expensive construction of the explicit NBW from the LTL formula.

Structure of the paper. The paper is structured as follows. In Section 2, we recall the definitions of LTL and ABW. In Section 3, we present a forward semi-symbolic algorithm for satisfiability checking of LTL and we evaluate its performance in Section 4. In Section 5, we present a similar algorithm for model-checking and we show in Section 6 that it has performances that are better than the best existing tools. We draw some conclusion in Section 7.

2   LTL and Alternating Automata

Linear Temporal Logic. Given a finite set P of propositions, a *Kripke structure* over P is a tuple $\mathcal{K} = \langle Q, q_\iota, \rightarrow_\mathcal{K}, \mathcal{L} \rangle$ where Q is a finite set of states, $q_\iota \in Q$ is the initial state, $\rightarrow_\mathcal{K} \subseteq Q \times Q$ is a transition relation, and $\mathcal{L} : Q \rightarrow 2^P$ is a labeling function. A *run* of $\mathcal{K}$ is an infinite sequence $\rho = q_0 q_1 \ldots$ such that $q_0 = q_\iota$ and for all $i \geq 0$, $(q_i, q_{i+1}) \in \rightarrow_\mathcal{K}$. Let $\mathcal{L}(\rho) = \mathcal{L}(q_0)\mathcal{L}(q_1) \ldots$ and define the *language* of $\mathcal{K}$ as $\mathsf{L}(\mathcal{K}) = \{\mathcal{L}(\rho) \mid \rho \text{ is a run of } \mathcal{K}\}$.

The *LTL formulas* over P are defined by $\phi ::= p \mid \neg\phi \mid \phi \vee \phi \mid \mathcal{X}\phi \mid \phi\mathcal{U}\phi$ where $p \in P$. Given an infinite word $w = \sigma_0\sigma_1 \cdots \in \Sigma^\omega$ where $\Sigma = 2^P$, and an LTL formula ϕ over P, we say that w *satisfies* ϕ (written $w \models \phi$) if and only if (recursively):

- $\phi \equiv p$ and $p \in \sigma_0$,
- or $\phi \equiv \neg\phi_1$ and $w \not\models \phi_1$,
- or $\phi \equiv \phi_1 \vee \phi_2$ and $w \models \phi_1$ or $w \models \phi_2$,
- or $\phi \equiv \mathcal{X}\phi_1$ and $\sigma_1\sigma_2 \ldots \models \phi_1$,
- or $\phi \equiv \phi_1\mathcal{U}\phi_2$ and for some $k \in \mathbb{N}$, $\sigma_k\sigma_{k+1} \ldots \models \phi_2$ and for all $i, 0 \leq i < k$, $\sigma_i\sigma_{i+1} \ldots \models \phi_1$.

Additional formulas such as true, false and $\phi_1 \wedge \phi_2$ can be derived from the definition in the usual way, as well as the following temporal operators: let $\Diamond\phi = \mathsf{true}\mathcal{U}\phi$, $\Box\phi = \neg\Diamond\neg\phi$ and $\phi_1\mathcal{R}\phi_2 = \neg(\neg\phi_1\mathcal{U}\neg\phi_2)$.

Let $\llbracket\phi\rrbracket = \{w \in \Sigma^\omega \mid w \models \phi\}$ be the *language* defined by the LTL formula ϕ. The *satisfiability-checking problem* asks, given an LTL formula ϕ whether $\llbracket\phi\rrbracket \neq \varnothing$ (if so, we say that ϕ is *satisfiable*). Given an LTL formula ϕ and a Kripke structure $\mathcal{K}$ over P, we say that $\mathcal{K}$ satisfies ϕ (written $\mathcal{K} \models \phi$) if and only if $\mathsf{L}(\mathcal{K}) \subseteq \llbracket\phi\rrbracket$, that is for all runs ρ of $\mathcal{K}$, we have $\mathcal{L}(\rho) \models \phi$. The *model-checking problem* asks, given a Kripke structure $\mathcal{K}$ and an LTL formula ϕ, whether $\mathcal{K} \models \phi$. Satisfiability and model-checking of LTL are both PSPACE-COMPLETE. The time complexity of LTL model-checking is linear in the number of states of the Kripke structure and exponential in the size of the LTL formula.

Symbolic Alternating Büchi Automata. The automata-based approach to satisfiability is to transform the formula ϕ to an automaton $\mathcal{A}_\phi$ that defines the same language, and then to check the emptiness of $\mathsf{L_b}(\mathcal{A}_\phi)$. Similarly for model-checking, we check the emptiness of $\mathsf{L}(\mathcal{K}) \cap \mathsf{L_b}(\mathcal{A}_{\neg\phi})$. These automata are defined over a symbolic alphabet of propositional formulas. Intuitively, a transition labeled by a formula φ encodes all the transitions that are labeled by a set of propositions that satisfies φ.

Given a finite set Q, let $\mathsf{Lit}(Q) = Q \cup \{\neg q \mid q \in Q\}$ be the set of *literals* over Q, and $\mathcal{B}^+(Q)$ be the set of *positive boolean formulas* over Q, that is formulas built from elements in $Q \cup \{\mathsf{true}, \mathsf{false}\}$ using the boolean connectives $\wedge$ and $\vee$. Given $R \subseteq Q$ and $\varphi \in \mathcal{B}^+(Q)$, we write $R \models \varphi$ if and only if the truth assignment that assigns true to the elements of R and false to the elements of $Q \setminus R$ satisfies φ.

A *symbolic alternating Büchi automaton* (sABW) over the set of propositions P is a tuple $\mathcal{A} = \langle \mathsf{Loc}, I, \Sigma, \delta, \alpha \rangle$ where:

- Loc is a finite set of states (or locations);
- $I \in \mathcal{B}^+(\mathsf{Loc})$ defines the set of possible initial sets of locations. Intuitively, a set $s \subseteq \mathsf{Loc}$ is initial if $s \models I$;
- $\Sigma = 2^P$ is the alphabet;
- $\delta : \mathsf{Loc} \rightarrow \mathcal{B}^+(\mathsf{Lit}(P) \cup \mathsf{Loc})$ is the transition function. The use of formulas to label transitions in δ allows a compact representation of δ', e.g., using BDD. We write $\ell \xrightarrow{\sigma}_\delta s$ whenever $\sigma \cup s \models \delta(\ell)$;
- $\alpha \subseteq \mathsf{Loc}$ is the set of accepting states.

A *run* of $\mathcal{A}$ on an infinite word $w = \sigma_0 \sigma_1 \cdots \in \Sigma^\omega$ is a DAG $T_w = \langle V, V_\iota, \rightarrow \rangle$ where:

- $V \subseteq \mathsf{Loc} \times \mathbb{N}$ is the set of nodes. A node (ℓ, i) represents the location ℓ after the first i letters of w have been read by A. Nodes of the form (ℓ, i) with $\ell \in \alpha$ are called α-*nodes*;
- $V_\iota \subseteq \mathsf{Loc} \times \{0\}$ is such that $V_\iota \subseteq V$ and $\{\ell \mid (\ell, 0) \in V_\iota\} \models I$;
- and $\rightarrow \subseteq V \times V$ is such that (*i*) if $(\ell, i) \rightarrow (\ell', i')$ then $i' = i + 1$ and (*ii*) $\sigma_i \cup \{\ell' \mid (\ell, i) \rightarrow (\ell', i + 1)\} \models \delta(\ell)$ for all $(\ell, i) \in V$.

A run $T_w = \langle V, v_\iota, \rightarrow \rangle$ of $\mathcal{A}$ on an infinite word w is *accepting* if all its infinite paths visit α-nodes infinitely often. An infinite word $w \in \Sigma^\omega$ is *accepted* by $\mathcal{A}$ if there exists an accepting run on it. We denote by $\mathsf{L_b}(\mathcal{A})$ the set of infinite words accepted by $\mathcal{A}$.

A *nondeterministic Büchi automaton* (sNBW) is an sABW $\mathcal{A} = \langle \mathsf{Loc}, I, \Sigma, \delta, \alpha \rangle$ such that I is a disjunction of locations, and for each $\ell \in \mathsf{Loc}$, $\delta(\ell)$ is a disjunction of formulas of the form $\varphi \wedge \ell'$ where $\varphi \in \mathcal{B}^+(\mathsf{Lit}(P))$ and $\ell' \in \mathsf{Loc}$. In the sequel, we often identify I with the set of locations that appear in I and δ as a the set of all transitions (ℓ, σ, ℓ') such that $\sigma \cup \{\ell'\} \models \delta(\ell)$. Runs of sNBW reduce to (linear) sequences of locations as a single initial state can be chosen in I, and each node has at most one successor. We define the *reverse* automaton of $\mathcal{A}$ as the sNBW $\mathcal{A}^{-1} = \langle \mathsf{Loc}, \alpha, \Sigma, \delta^{-1}, I \rangle$ where $\delta^{-1} = \{(\ell, \sigma, \ell') \mid (\ell', \sigma, \ell) \in \delta\}$.

There exists a simple translation from LTL to sABW [9,23]. We do not recall the translation but we give an example hereafter. The construction is defined recursively over the structure of the formula and it gives a compact automata representation of LTL formulas (the number of states of the automaton is linear in the size of the formula). The succinctness results from the presence of alternation in the transition function, and from the use of propositional formulas (the symbolic alphabet) to label the transitions.

Example. Fig. 1 shows the sABW for the negation of the formula $\Box\Diamond p \rightarrow \Box(\neg p \rightarrow \Diamond r)$, which is equivalent to the conjunction of $\phi_1 \equiv \Box\Diamond p$ and $\phi_2 \equiv \Diamond(\neg p \wedge \Box\neg r)$. The accepting states are $\alpha = \{\ell_1, \ell_4\}$. Intuitively, the states ℓ_4, ℓ_3 check that ϕ_1 holds, and states ℓ_2, ℓ_1 check that ϕ_2 holds. The conjunction is enforced by the initial condition $\ell_4 \wedge \ell_2$. We write transitions in disjunctive normal form and we consider two parts in each conjunction, one for the propositions and one for the locations. E.g., the transition from ℓ_4 is $\delta(\ell_4) = (p \wedge \ell_4) \vee (\text{true} \wedge \ell_3 \wedge \ell_4)$, and from ℓ_3 it is $\delta(\ell_3) = (\text{true} \wedge \ell_3) \vee (p \wedge \text{true})$. We use true to emphasize when there is no constraint on either propositions or locations. In the figure, a conjunction of locations is depicted by a

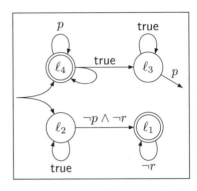

Fig. 1. Alternating automaton for $\varphi \equiv \neg(\Box\Diamond p \rightarrow \Box(\neg p \rightarrow \Diamond r))$

forked arrow, the conjunction of literals is labelling the arrow. One arrow from ℓ_3 has an empty target as $\varnothing \models$ true. If the control of the automaton is in ℓ_4 and the automaton reads some $\sigma \in 2^P$ such that $p \notin \sigma$, then the control moves simultaneously to location ℓ_4 and location ℓ_3. As ℓ_3 is not accepting, the control has to leave ℓ_3 eventually by reading some σ' such that $p \in \sigma'$. So every run accepted from ℓ_4 satisfies $\Box\Diamond p$.

3 Satisfiability-Checking of LTL

By the above translation from LTL to sABW, the satisfiability-checking problem reduces to emptiness of sABW (that is to decide, given an sABW $\mathcal{A}$, whether $L_b(\mathcal{A}) = \varnothing$) which can be solved using a translation from sABW to sNBW that preserves the language of the automaton [16]. This construction involves an exponential blow-up that makes straight implementations infeasible in practice. We do not construct this automaton, but the correctness of our approach relies on its existence.

Miyano-Hayashi construction. The construction transforms an sABW into a sNBW that accepts the same language. It has the flavor of the subset construction for automata over finite words. Intuitively, the sNBW maintains a set s of states of the sABW that corresponds to a whole level of a guessed run DAG of the sABW. In addition, the sNBW maintains a set o of states that "owe" a visit to an accepting state. Whenever the set o gets empty, meaning that every path of the guessed run has visited at least one accepting state, the set o is initiated with the current level of the guessed run. The Büchi condition asks that o gets empty infinitely often in order to ensure that every path of the run DAG visits accepting states infinitely often. The construction is as follows (we adapt it for symbolic sABW).

Given an sABW $\mathcal{A}=\langle \mathsf{Loc}, I, \Sigma, \delta, \alpha \rangle$ over P, let $\mathsf{MH}(\mathcal{A})=\langle Q, I^{\mathsf{MH}}, \Sigma, \delta^{\mathsf{MH}}, \alpha^{\mathsf{MH}} \rangle$ be a sNBW where:

- $Q = 2^{\mathsf{Loc}} \times 2^{\mathsf{Loc}}$;
- I^{MH} is the disjunction of all the pairs $\langle s, \varnothing \rangle$ such that $s \models I$;
- δ^{MH} is defined for all $\langle s, o \rangle \in Q$ as follows:
  - If $o \neq \varnothing$, then $\delta^{\mathsf{MH}}(\langle s, o \rangle)$ is the disjunction of all the formulas $\varphi \wedge \langle s', o' \setminus \alpha \rangle$ with $\varphi \in \mathcal{B}^+(\mathsf{Lit}(P))$ such that:
    - (i) $o' \subseteq s'$;
    - (ii) $\forall \ell \in s \cdot \forall \sigma \subseteq P :$ if $\sigma \models \varphi$ then $\sigma \cup s' \models \delta(\ell)$;
    - (iii) $\forall \ell \in o \cdot \forall \sigma \subseteq P :$ if $\sigma \models \varphi$ then $\sigma \cup o' \models \delta(\ell)$.
  - If $o = \varnothing$, then $\delta^{\mathsf{MH}}(\langle s, o \rangle)$ is the disjunction of all the formulas $\varphi \wedge \langle s', s' \setminus \alpha \rangle)$ with $\varphi \in \mathcal{B}^+(\mathsf{Lit}(P))$ such that:
    $\forall \ell \in s \cdot \forall \sigma \subseteq P :$ if $\sigma \models \varphi$ then $\sigma \cup s' \models \delta(\ell)$;
- $\alpha^{\mathsf{MH}} = 2^{\mathsf{Loc}} \times \{\varnothing\}$.

The number of states of the Miyano-Hayashi construction is exponential in the number of states of the original automaton.

Theorem 1 ([16]). *For all sABW $\mathcal{A}$, we have $\mathsf{L_b}(\mathsf{MH}(\mathcal{A})) = \mathsf{L_b}(\mathcal{A})$.*

Fixpoint formulas. To check the satisfiability of an LTL formula ϕ we check the emptiness of $\mathsf{MH}(\mathcal{A}_\phi) = \langle Q, I^{\mathsf{MH}}, \Sigma, \delta^{\mathsf{MH}}, \alpha^{\mathsf{MH}} \rangle$.

It is well-known that $[\![\phi]\!] = \mathsf{L_b}(\mathcal{A}_\phi) = \varnothing$ iff $I^{\mathsf{MH}} \cap \mathcal{F}_\phi = \varnothing$ where $\mathcal{F}_\phi$ is the following fixpoint formula [5]:

$$\mathcal{F}_\phi \equiv \nu y \cdot \mu x \cdot (\mathsf{Pre}(x) \cup (\mathsf{Pre}(y) \cap \alpha^{\mathsf{MH}}))$$

where $\mathsf{Pre}(L) = \{q \in Q \mid \exists \sigma \in \Sigma \cdot \exists q' \in L : \sigma \cup \{q'\} \models \delta^{\mathsf{MH}}(q)\}$.

We call $\mathcal{F}_\phi$ a *backward* algorithm as it uses the predecessor operator $\mathsf{Pre}(\cdot)$. The set of states that are computed in the iterations of the fixpoints may be unreachable from the initial states [12]. Therefore, a *forward* algorithm based on the successor operator $\mathsf{Post}(\cdot)$ would have the advantage of exploring only the reachable states of the automaton. Moreover, the number of successors is often smaller than the number of predecessors, especially when the LTL formula "specifies" initial conditions that reduce the forward non-determinism.

The following fixpoint formulas compute the accepting reachable states R_α and then the set $\mathcal{F}'_\phi$ in a forward fashion.

$$R_\alpha \equiv \alpha^{\mathsf{MH}} \cap \mu x \cdot (\mathsf{Post}(x) \cup I^{\mathsf{MH}})$$
$$\mathcal{F}'_\phi \equiv \nu y \cdot \mu x \cdot (\mathsf{Post}(x) \cup (\mathsf{Post}(y) \cap R_\alpha))$$

where $\mathsf{Post}(L) = \{q \in Q \mid \exists \sigma \in \Sigma \cdot \exists q' \in L : \sigma \cup \{q\} \models \delta^{\mathsf{MH}}(q')\}$.

Theorem 2. $\mathsf{L_b}(\mathcal{A}_\phi) = \varnothing$ iff $\mathcal{F}'_\phi = \varnothing$.

Proof. Define $\Delta^{\mathsf{MH}} : Q \times \Sigma^+$ the extension of the transition relation δ^{MH} to nonempty words as follows (recursively): $\Delta^{\mathsf{MH}}(q, \sigma) = \delta^{\mathsf{MH}}(q, \sigma)$ and $\Delta^{\mathsf{MH}}(q, w\sigma) = \{q' \in Q \mid \exists q'' \in \Delta^{\mathsf{MH}}(q, w) : \sigma \cup \{q'\} \models \delta^{\mathsf{MH}}(q'')\}$ for each $q \in Q$, $w \in \Sigma^+$ and $\sigma \in \Sigma$.

Let $\mathcal{C}^{\mathsf{MH}} = \{q \in Q \mid \exists w \in \Sigma^+ : q \in \Delta^{\mathsf{MH}}(q, w)\}$ be the set of *looping* states in $\mathsf{MH}(\mathcal{A}_\phi)$. From the definition of Büchi acceptance condition for NBW, we have $\mathsf{L_b}(\mathcal{A}_\phi) = \varnothing$ iff $\mathcal{C}^{\mathsf{MH}} \cap R_\alpha = \varnothing$. Let $\mathsf{HM}(\mathcal{A}_\phi)$ be the reverse automaton[1]. The following equivalences (the first one being well-known) establish the theorem:

$$\nu y \cdot \mu x \cdot (\mathsf{Pre}(x) \cup (\mathsf{Pre}(y) \cap R_\alpha)) = \varnothing$$
iff $\mathcal{C}^{\mathsf{MH}} \cap R_\alpha = \varnothing$
iff $\mathcal{C}^{\mathsf{HM}} \cap R_\alpha = \varnothing$
iff $\nu y \cdot \mu x \cdot (\mathsf{Post}(x) \cup (\mathsf{Post}(y) \cap R_\alpha)) = \varnothing$
iff $\mathcal{F}'_\phi = \varnothing$

∎

Closed Sets and Antichains. Remember that Q is exponential in the size of ϕ. Following the lines of [7], we show that $\mathcal{F}'_\phi$ can be computed more efficiently. Let $\preceq \subseteq Q \times Q$ be a preorder and let $q_1 \prec q_2$ iff $q_1 \preceq q_2$ and $q_2 \not\preceq q_1$. A set $R \subseteq Q$ is $\preceq$-*closed* iff for all $q_1, q_2 \in Q$, if $q_1 \preceq q_2$ and $q_2 \in R$ then $q_1 \in R$. The $\preceq$-*closure* of R, is the set $[\![R]\!]_{\preceq} = \{q \in Q \mid \exists q' \in R : q \preceq q'\}$. Let $\lceil R \rceil_{\preceq} = \{q \in R \mid \nexists q' \in R : q \prec q'\}$ be the set of $\preceq$-*maximal elements* of R, and dually let $\lfloor R \rfloor_{\succeq} = \{q \in R \mid \nexists q' \in R : q \succ q'\}$ be the set of $\succeq$-*minimal elements* of R.

For all $\preceq$-closed sets $R \subseteq Q$, we have $R = [\![\lceil R \rceil_{\preceq}]\!]_{\preceq}$ and for all $\succeq$-closed sets $R \subseteq Q$, we have $R = [\![\lfloor R \rfloor_{\preceq}]\!]_{\succeq}$. Furthermore, if $\preceq$ is a partial order, then $\lceil R \rceil_{\preceq}$ is an *antichain* and it is a canonical representation of R.

Let $\mathcal{A} = \langle \mathsf{Loc}, I, \Sigma, \delta, \alpha \rangle$ be a NBW. A preorder $\preceq \subseteq \mathsf{Loc} \times \mathsf{Loc}$ is a *forward-simulation* for $\mathcal{A}$ (q_1 forward-simulates q_2 if $q_1 \preceq q_2$) if for all $q_1, q_2, q_3 \in \mathsf{Loc}$, for all $\sigma \in \Sigma$, (i) if $q_1 \preceq q_2$ and $q_2 \xrightarrow{\sigma}_\delta q_3$ then there exists $q_4 \in \mathsf{Loc}$ such that $q_1 \xrightarrow{\sigma}_\delta q_4$ and $q_4 \preceq q_3$, and (ii) if $q_1 \preceq q_2$ and $q_2 \in \alpha$ then $q_1 \in \alpha$. A *backward-simulation* for $\mathcal{A}$ is a forward-simulation for $\mathcal{A}^{-1}$. It is not true in general that $\succeq$ is a backward-simulation for $\mathcal{A}$ if $\preceq$ is a forward-simulation for $\mathcal{A}$ (consider a state q_c that has no predecessor and such that $q_b \preceq q_c$). However, the following lemma shows that the language of a sNBW is unchanged if we add a transition from a state q_a to a state q_c which is forward-simulated by one of the successors of q_a. By adding in this way all the possible transitions, we obtain a sNBW for which $\succeq$ is a backward-simulation.

Lemma 3. *Let $\mathcal{A}$ be a sNBW with transition relation δ_A and $\preceq$ be a forward-simulation relation for $\mathcal{A}$. If $(q_a, \sigma, q_b) \in \delta_A$ and $q_b \preceq q_c$, then the sNBW $\mathcal{A}'$ that differs from $\mathcal{A}$ only by its transition relation $\delta_{A'} = \delta_A \cup \{(q_a, \sigma, q_c)\}$ defines the same language as $\mathcal{A}$, that is $\mathsf{L_b}(\mathcal{A}') = \mathsf{L_b}(\mathcal{A})$.*

As a dual of the results of [7], it is easy to show that given a backward-simulation $\succeq$ for $\mathsf{MH}(\mathcal{A}_\phi)$, all the sets that are computed to evaluate R_α and $\mathcal{F}'_\phi$ are $\succeq$-closed, that is I^{MH} and α^{MH} are $\succeq$-closed, and $x \cap y$, $x \cup y$ and $\mathsf{Pre}(x)$ are $\succeq$-closed whenever x and y are $\succeq$-closed [7]. The relation $\preceq_{\mathsf{alt}}$ defined by $\langle s, o \rangle \preceq_{\mathsf{alt}} \langle s', o' \rangle$ iff (i) $s \subseteq s'$, (ii)

---

[1] In the sequel, $\mathsf{Pre}(\cdot)$ and $\mathsf{Post}(\cdot)$ are always computed on $\mathsf{MH}(\mathcal{A}_\phi)$ and never on $\mathsf{HM}(\mathcal{A}_\phi)$.

$o \subseteq o'$, and (iii) $o = \varnothing$ iff $o' = \varnothing$ is a forward-simulation for $\mathsf{MH}(\mathcal{A}_\phi)$. Therefore, the relation $\succeq_{\mathsf{alt}}$ (which is $\preceq_{\mathsf{alt}}^{-1}$) is a backward-simulation if we modify the transition relation of $\mathsf{MH}(\mathcal{A}_\phi)$ as follows: if $\delta^{\mathsf{MH}}(\langle s, o \rangle)$ is a disjunction of formulas of the form $\varphi \wedge \langle s', o' \rangle$ with $\varphi \in \mathcal{B}^+(\mathsf{Lit}(P))$, then we disjunctively add all the formulas $\varphi \wedge \langle s'', o'' \rangle$ to $\delta^{\mathsf{MH}}(\langle s, o \rangle)$ such that $\langle s', o' \rangle \preceq_{\mathsf{alt}} \langle s'', o'' \rangle$. According to Lemma 3, this preserves the language of $\mathsf{MH}(\mathcal{A}_\phi)$. We keep only the $\succeq_{\mathsf{alt}}$-minimal elements of $\succeq_{\mathsf{alt}}$-closed sets to evaluate $\mathcal{F}'_\phi$ and so we dramatically reduce the size of the sets that are handled by the algorithms.

Remark 1. The intuition for keeping only minimal elements is as follows. Let A be a sABW, along a run of $\mathsf{MH}(A)$ that reads a word w, a pair $\langle s, o \rangle$ keeps track of the set of locations from which the sABW has to accept the suffix and to pass by accepting states. Clearly, if there is no accepting run from $\langle s, o \rangle$ then there is no accepting run from any pair $\langle s', o' \rangle$ where $\langle s', o' \rangle \succeq_{\mathsf{alt}} \langle s, o \rangle$. In short, the antichain algorithm concentrates on the most promising pairs that can be part of an accepting run by only keeping track of minimal elements.

Elements of efficient implementation. The efficient computation of the $\succeq_{\mathsf{alt}}$-minimal elements of $\mathsf{Post}(\llbracket \cdot \rrbracket_{\succeq_{\mathsf{alt}}})$ is not trivial. For instance, the algorithm of [7] would have to enumerate all the truth assignments of propositional formulas over P appearing on transitions. To mitigate this problem, we propose to combine BDDs and antichains as follows. Antichains of pairs $\langle s, o \rangle$ are represented *explicitly* (as a list of pairs of sets of locations) while computation of the successors of a pair $\langle s, o \rangle$ is done *symbolically*. This is why, in the following, we call our algorithm *semi-symbolic*.

Given a BDD B over a set of variables V (seen as a boolean formula over V), let $\llbracket B \rrbracket$ be the set of truth assignments over V that satisfy B. Given a pair $\langle s, o \rangle$, Algorithm 1 computes the set $L_{\mathsf{Post}} = \lfloor \mathsf{Post}(\llbracket \{\langle s, o \rangle\} \rrbracket_{\succeq_{\mathsf{alt}}}) \rfloor_{\succeq_{\mathsf{alt}}}$. When computing the successors of a pair $\langle s, o \rangle$, the algorithm uses the intermediate boolean variables $x_1, \ldots, x_n, y_1, \ldots, y_n$ and $y'_1, \ldots, y'_n$ to encode respectively the sets s', $o' \setminus \alpha$ and o' where $\langle s', o' \setminus \alpha \rangle \in \mathsf{Post}(\llbracket \{\langle s, o \rangle\} \rrbracket_{\succeq_{\mathsf{alt}}})$. We write $\delta(\ell)[x_1 \ldots x_n]$ to denote the formula $\delta(\ell)$ in which each occurrence of a location ℓ_i is replaced by variable x_i for all $1 \leq i \leq n$. The computations at lines 1–6 match exactly the definition of the Miyano-Hayashi construction. The BDD $\theta(y, y')$ is used to remove the accepting states from the sets o' in B_L, and the existential quantification over the set P of propositions matches the definition of the $\mathsf{Post}(\cdot)$ operator. Then, using a BDD $\omega(x, y, x', y')$ that encodes the relation $\preceq_{\mathsf{alt}}$ (we have $\langle s', o' \rangle \preceq_{\mathsf{alt}} \langle s, o \rangle$ in ω where s, o, s', o' are encoded respectively with variables x, y, x', y'), we eliminate the non-minimal elements in B_L and we reconstruct the explicit set of pairs $\langle s', o' \rangle$ from $B_L^{\mathsf{min}}(x, y)$.

The encoding that we have chosen uses a number of variables linear in the size of the set of locations of the sABW and number of propositions. Preliminary experiments have shown that this approach is faster than an enumerative algorithm implemented in a clever way. The combinatorial blow-up that is hidden in the quantification $\exists P$ over propositions is likely to be the reason for this, as it is well known that for this purpose symbolic algorithms are faster in practice.

Algorithm 1. Semi-symbolic Algorithm for Post$(\cdot)$

Data	: An sABW $\mathcal{A} = \langle \text{Loc}, I, \Sigma, \delta, \alpha \rangle$, and a pair $\langle s, o \rangle$ such that $o \subseteq s$.
Result	: The set $L_{\text{Post}} = \lfloor \text{Post}([\![\{ \langle s, o \rangle \}]\!]_{\succeq_{\text{alt}}}) \rfloor_{\succeq_{\text{alt}}}$.

begin

1   if $o \neq \varnothing$ then

2   $\quad B_L(x, y') \leftarrow \exists P : \begin{cases} \bigwedge_{i=1}^{n} y'_i \rightarrow x_i & // \ o' \subseteq s' \\ \wedge \bigwedge_{\ell \in s} \delta(\ell)[x_1 \ldots x_n] & // \ \sigma \cup s' \models \delta(\ell) \text{ for all } \ell \in s \\ \wedge \bigwedge_{\ell \in o} \delta(\ell)[y'_1 \ldots y'_n] & // \ \sigma \cup o' \models \delta(\ell) \text{ for all } \ell \in o \end{cases}$

3   $\quad \theta(y, y') \leftarrow \bigwedge_{\ell_i \in \alpha} \neg y_i \wedge \bigwedge_{\ell_i \notin \alpha} y_i \leftrightarrow y'_i \qquad // \ o' \setminus \alpha$

4   $\quad B_L(x, y) \leftarrow \exists y' : B_L(x, y') \wedge \theta(y, y')$

5   else

6   $\quad B_L(x, y) \leftarrow \exists P : \begin{cases} \bigwedge_{\ell_i \in \alpha} \neg y_i \wedge \bigwedge_{\ell_i \notin \alpha} y_i \leftrightarrow x_i & // \ o' \text{ is } s' \setminus \alpha \\ \wedge \bigwedge_{\ell \in s} \delta(\ell)[x_1 \ldots x_n] & // \ s' \models \delta(\ell) \text{ for all } \ell \in s \end{cases}$

7   $\omega(x, y, x', y') \leftarrow \begin{cases} \bigwedge_{i=1}^{n} (x'_i \rightarrow x_i \wedge y'_i \rightarrow y_i) \\ \wedge \bigvee_{i=1}^{n} (x_i \neq x'_i \vee y_i \neq y'_i) \\ \wedge (\bigvee_{i=1}^{n} y_i) \leftrightarrow (\bigvee_{i=1}^{n} y'_i) \end{cases} \qquad // \ \omega \text{ encodes } \prec_{\text{alt}}$

8   $B_L^{\min}(x, y) \leftarrow B_L(x, y) \wedge \neg(\exists x', y' : \omega(x, y, x', y') \wedge B_L(x', y'))$

9   $L_{\text{Post}} \leftarrow \{ \langle s', o' \rangle \mid \exists v \in [\![B_L^{\min}]\!] : s' = \{ \ell_i \mid v(x_i) = \text{true} \}, o' = \{ \ell_i \mid v(y_i) = \text{true} \} \}$

end

---

4 Satisfiability: Performance Evaluation

We have implemented our new forward semi-symbolic satisfiability algorithm in a prototype written in Python[2]. Before evaluating the fixpoint expression, the prototype performs the following steps: the LTL formula is parsed, standard fast heuristical rewriting rules are applied [22], and the formula is then translated to a sABW [9]. This sABW contains n locations, where n is linear in the size of the LTL formula. To compactly represent the symbolic transitions associated to each location, we use BDDs over $n + k$ boolean variables where k is the number of propositions that appear in the formula. Usually, the BDDs that are associated to the locations of the sABW are small because they are typically expressing constraints over few locations. This is usually in sharp contrast with the size of the BDDs that represent the underlying NBW of a LTL formula in fully-symbolic model-checking. The BDD package used by our prototype is CuDD [21] which is available through a python binding called PyCuDD[3].

Comparison with the state-of-the-art algorithms. According to the extensive survey of Vardi and Rozier [18] NuSMV is the most efficient available tool for LTL satisfiability. We therefore compare our prototype with NuSMV. Satisfiability checking with NuSMV is done simply by model checking the negation of the formula against a

---

[2] Python is an interpreted object-oriented language. See http://www.python.org
[3] http://www.ece.ucsb.edu/bears/pycudd.html

universal Kripke structure. In all our experiments, we used NuSMV 2.4 with the default options. [4] No variable reordering techniques were activated in either tool.

Benchmarks. We have compared both tools on four families of LTL formulas. Our satisfiability-checking prototype is reported as "sat.py" in the figures. All the experiments were performed on a single Intel Xeon CPU at 3.0 GHz, with 4 GB of RAM, using a timeout of 10 min and a maximum memory usage limit of 2.5 GB (all experiments timed out before exceeding the memory limit). All the LTL formulas tested here can be found in the long version of this paper[14].[5]

The first family is a parametric specification of a lift system with n floors that we have taken from Harding's thesis [11]. Two encodings are used: one ("lift") that uses a linear number of variables per floor, and another ("lift-b") which uses a number of variables that is logarithmic in the number of floors (resulting in larger formulas). As seen in figure 2(a), our algorithm scales much better than NuSMV for both encodings. For more than 7-floor (a formula with 91 temporal operators and 17 distinct boolean propositions), NuSMV is more than 60 times slower than our tool.

The second family of formulas was referenced in [20] as examples of difficult LTL to NBW translation and describes liveness properties for the Szymanski mutual exclusion protocol and for a variant of this protocol due to Pnueli. We have run both our prototype and NuSMV on these four formulas (pos) and their negation (neg), all of which can be found in [14]. Again, our tool shows better performances (by factors of 50 and higher), as reported in figure 2(b).

The third family we used is a random model described in [4] and also used in [18]. Random LTL formulas are generated according to the following parameters: the length of the formula (L), the number of propositions (N) each with equal probability of occurrence, and the probability (P) of choosing a temporal operator ($\mathcal{U}$ or $\mathcal{R}$). As in [18], we fix $P = 0.5$ and compare execution times for $L \in \{10, 20, \ldots, 100\}$ and for both $N = 2$ and $N = 4$. As indicated by figure 2(c), our algorithm copes much better with the joint increase in formula length and number of propositions[6]. For $L = 100$, going from $N = 2$ to $N = 4$ multiplies the time needed by NuSMV by 7, while our prototype only exhibits an 8% increase in execution time.

Finally, the last set of formulas (also taken in [18]) describes how a binary counter, parameterized by its length, is incremented. Two ways of formalizing the increment are considered ("count", "count-l"). Those formulas are quite particular as they all define a unique model: for $n = 2$, the model is $(00 \cdot 01 \cdot 10 \cdot 11)^{\omega}$. In this benchmark, the classical fully-symbolic algorithm behaves much better than our antichain algorithm. This is not surprising for two reasons. First, the efficiency of our antichain-based algorithms comes from the ability to identify prefixes of runs in the ABW which can be ignored because they impose more constraints than others on the future (see Remark 1). As there is only one future allowed by the formula, the locations of the NBW defined by the Miyano-Hayashi construction are incomparable for the simulation relation defined in Section 3, causing very long antichains and poor performances. This can be considered as a pathological and maybe not very interesting case.

---

[4] The options are numerous, check the NuSMV user manual for full details.

[5] They can also be downloaded at http://www.ulb.ac.be/di/ssd/nmaquet/tacas.

[6] We report only the mean execution times, but the standard deviation is similar for both tools.

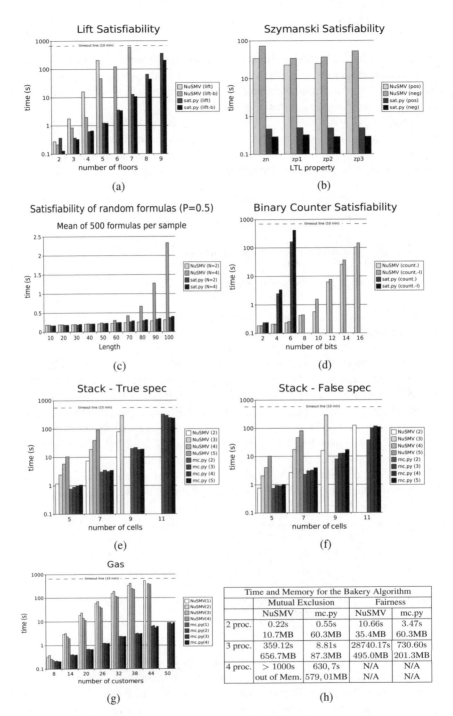

Fig. 2. Experimental results comparing NuSMV with our algorithms

5   LTL Model-Checking

Our algorithm for LTL model-checking is based on forward exploration and semi-symbolic representations. It is also related to the hybrid approach proposed by Vardi *et al.* in [20] with the essential difference that we work directly on the sABW for the LTL formula, avoiding the construction of a NBW.

Given a Kripke structure $\mathcal{K} = \langle Q, q_\iota, \to_\mathcal{K}, \mathcal{L} \rangle$ and an LTL formula ϕ, the model-checking problem for $\mathcal{K}$ and ϕ reduces to the emptiness of $L(\mathcal{K}) \cap L_b(\mathcal{A}_{\neg\phi})$ (where $\mathcal{A}_{\neg\phi} = \langle \mathsf{Loc}, I, \Sigma, \delta, \alpha \rangle$ is the sABW for $\neg\phi$) which can be checked by computing the following fixpoint formulas over the lattice of subsets of $Q \times 2^{\mathsf{Loc}} \times 2^{\mathsf{Loc}}$:

$$R_\alpha^\mathcal{K} \equiv \alpha' \cap \mu x \cdot (\mathsf{Post}_{\mathsf{MC}}(x) \cup I')$$
$$\mathcal{F}_\phi^\mathcal{K} \equiv \nu y \cdot \mu x \cdot (\mathsf{Post}_{\mathsf{MC}}(x) \cup (\mathsf{Post}_{\mathsf{MC}}(y) \cap R_\alpha^\mathcal{K}))$$

where $\mathsf{Post}_{\mathsf{MC}}(L) = \{(q', \langle s', o' \rangle) \mid \exists (q, \langle s, o \rangle) \in L : q \to_\mathcal{K} q' \wedge \mathcal{L}(q) \cup \{\langle s', o' \rangle\} \models \delta^{\mathsf{MH}}(\langle s, o \rangle)\}$, $I' = \{q_\iota\} \times I^{\mathsf{MH}}$ and $\alpha' = Q \times \alpha^{\mathsf{MH}}$ (where the MH superscript refers to the sABW $\mathsf{MH}(\mathcal{A}_{\neg\phi})$). As before, we have $\mathcal{F}_\phi^\mathcal{K} = \varnothing$ iff $L(\mathcal{K}) \cap L_b(\mathcal{A}_{\neg\phi}) = \varnothing$ iff $\mathcal{K} \not\models \phi$.

Moreover, there exists a partial order $\succeq_{\mathsf{MC}}$ for which all the sets that are computed to evaluate $\mathcal{F}_\phi^\mathcal{K}$ are $\succeq_{\mathsf{MC}}$-closed. The relation $\succeq_{\mathsf{MC}}$ is defined by $(q, \langle s, o \rangle) \succeq_{\mathsf{MC}} (q', \langle s', o' \rangle)$ iff $q = q'$ and $\langle s, o \rangle \succeq_{\mathsf{alt}} \langle s', o' \rangle$.

We use a semi-symbolic forward algorithm for model-checking as this is the most promising combination, in the light of our experiences with satisfiability. We assume a symbolic representation of $\mathcal{K}$ where each state $q \in Q$ is a valuation for a finite set of boolean variables $V = \{z_1, \ldots, z_m\}$ such that $P \subseteq V$. The labeling function $\mathcal{L}$ is defined as the projection of 2^V to 2^P in the natural way. The transition relation is given by a BDD $T(V, V')$ over $V \cup V'$ where the set $V' = \{z' \mid z \in V\}$ of primed variables is used to define the value of the variables after the transition.

To efficiently compute $\mathcal{F}_\phi^\mathcal{K}$, we need a compact representation of $\succeq_{\mathsf{MC}}$-antichains. Under the hypothesis that the huge size of Q is the main obstacle, we consider a semi-symbolic representation of antichains, as a set of pairs $(B, \langle s, o \rangle)$ where B is a BDD over V. A pair $(B, \langle s, o \rangle)$ represents the set $[[(B, \langle s, o \rangle)]] = \{(q, \langle s, o \rangle) \mid q \in [[B]]\}$.

Let $L = \{(q_1, \langle s_1, o_1 \rangle), (q_2, \langle s_2, o_2 \rangle), \ldots\}$ be an $\succeq_{\mathsf{MC}}$-antichain. Let $S_L = \{\langle s, o \rangle \mid \exists (q, \langle s, o \rangle) \in L\}$. We define $R(L) = \{(B, \langle s, o \rangle) \mid \langle s, o \rangle \in S_L \wedge [[B]] = \{q \mid (q, \langle s, o \rangle) \in L\}$. It is easy to establish the following property of this encoding.

Lemma 4. *If L is an $\succeq_{\mathsf{MC}}$-antichain for all $(B_1, \langle s_1, o_1 \rangle), (B_2, \langle s_2, o_2 \rangle) \in R(L)$, if $\langle s_1, o_1 \rangle \succ_{\mathsf{alt}} \langle s_2, o_2 \rangle$, then $[[B_1]] \cap [[B_2]] = \varnothing$.*

We say that $R(L)$ is a *semi-symbolic* and *canonical* representation of $[[L]]_{\succeq_{\mathsf{MC}}}$. The algorithm to compute $\mathsf{Post}_{\mathsf{MC}}(\cdot)$ follows the lines of Algorithm 1, using $2n$ boolean variables to encode a pair $\langle s, o \rangle$. The existential quantification over V is performed after synchronization over propositions P with the Kripke structure. Let $B_L(x, y, V)$ be the BDD that encodes with variables x, y the successors of $\langle s, o \rangle$ over a symbolic label encoded by variables V. We compute the BDD $C_L(x, y, V') = \exists V : B(V) \wedge T(V, V') \wedge B_L(x, y, V)$ and then we construct the encoding $R(\cdot)$ of its minimal elements.

6   Model-Checking: Performance Evaluation

Implementation. We have implemented the forward semi-symbolic model-checking algorithm using the same technology as for satisfiability (i.e., Python and PYCUDD). The sABW of the negation of the LTL formula is obtained as described in Section 3. We have interfaced our prototype with NUSMV in order to get the BDDs[7] obtained from models written in the SMV input language. This has two advantages. First, we can effectively run our algorithm on any available SMV model, making direct comparisons with NUSMV easy. Second, we are guaranteed to use *exactly* the same BDDs for the Kripke structure (with the same ordering on variables) than NUSMV, making comparisons with this tool very meaningful.

On the use of NUSMV. As for satisfiability, all our experiments were performed using NuSMV 2.4 without any option except "-dcx" which disables the creation of counterexamples. By default, NUSMV implements the following version of the LTL symbolic algorithm: it precomputes the reachable states of the Kripke structure and then evaluates a backward fixpoint expression (the Emerson-Lei algorithm) for checking emptiness of the product of the structure and the NBW of the formula (encoded with BDDs). Guiding the backward iterations with reachable states usually improves execution times dramatically. It also makes the comparison with our algorithm fair as it also only visits reachable states.

Benchmarks. We have compared our prototype with NUSMV on three families of scalable SMV models. The experiments were performed using the same environment as for satisfiability (see Section 4). Again, additional information about models and formulas can be found in[14].

The first family describes a gas station with an operator, one pump, and n customers (n is a parameter) waiting in line to use the pump. The operator manages the customer queue and activates or deactivates the pump. This resource-access protocol was used in [20] as an LTL model-checking benchmark. We have used the same LTL formulas as in [20]. The running times for n between 2 and 50 are given in Fig. 2(g). The difference in scalability is striking. While our tool is slower than NUSMV for $n=2$ (probably due to the overhead of using an interpreted language instead of C), it scales much better. For instance, for $n = 38$ NUSMV needs several minutes (between 233 and 418 seconds depending on the property), while our algorithm completes in just over 3 seconds for all properties. NUSMV is not able to verify models with 50 customers within 10 minutes while our algorithm handles them in less than 10 seconds.

The second family of models also comes from [20] and represents a stack, on which push, pop, empty and freeze operations can be performed. Each cell of the stack can hold a value from the set $\{1,2\}$ and a freeze operation allows to permanently freeze the stack, after which the model runs a pointer along the stack from top to bottom repeatedly. At each step of this infinite loop, a "call" predicate indicates the value currently pointed.[8] As we needed a scalable set of formulas for at least one model to compare the

---

[7] These are essentially: the predicates appearing in the LTL formula, the initial constraints, the transition relation and the invariant constraints.

[8] For example, if the stack contains, from bottom to top, $\{1,2\}$ then after the freeze operation, the model will behave like this : call2, call1, call2, call1, ...

scalability of our algorithm with NuSMV, we have provided and used our own specifications for this model. These specifications simply enforce that if the sequence of
push operations "$12 \ldots n$" is performed and not followed by any pop until the freeze
operation, then the subsequence of call operations "$n \ldots 21$" appears infinitely often.

Finally, the last family of models that we consider is a finite state version of the
Lamport's bakery mutex protocol [13]. This protocol is interesting because it imposes
fairness among all processes and again it is parametric in the number n of participating
processes. Our model is large and grows very rapidly with the number of processes.
For 2 processes, it uses 42 boolean variables and requires BDDs with a total of 7750
nodes to encode the model, for 4 processes, it uses 91 variables and BDDs with more
than 20 million nodes. Again, our algorithm scales much better than the classical fully
symbolic algorithm. For 3 processes, we are able to verify the fairness requirement in
730.6 seconds while NuSMV needs 28740.17s. Also, our algorithm requires much less
memory than NuSMV, see Table 2(h) for the details.

7   Conclusion

In this paper, we have defined new algorithms for LTL satisfiability and model-checking.
The new algorithms use a clever combination of the antichain method defined in [7] and
BDDs. Our method differs fundamentally from the explicit and hybrid approach to LTL
as it does not require the explicit construction of a NBW, and from the symbolic approach as it does not encode the NBW with BDDs.

With a prototype implementation written in Python, we outperform in time and memory usage the state-of-the-art implementation in NuSMV of the classical fully symbolic
approach on all but one benchmark. More importantly, our implementation is able to
handle LTL formulas and models that are too large for NuSMV.

There are several lines of future works to consider both on the theoretical side and on
the practical side. First, we should investigate how we can take advantage of the structure of sABW that are produced from the LTL formula. Indeed, those sABW are weak
in the sense of [17], a property that we do not exploit currently. Second, we use a notion
of simulation which is called the direct simulation in the terminology of [10]. Weaker
notions of simulation exist for NBW like the *fair simulation* or the *delayed simulation*.
We should investigate their possible use instead of the direct simulation. This would allow for more pruning as antichains for those orders would be smaller. Third, high level
heuristics should be investigated. Let us take an example. A pair of locations $\{l_1, l_2\}$ is an
incompatible pair of locations in a sABW A if there is no word w such that w is accepted
in A simultaneously from l_1 and l_2. In the forward satisfiability algorithm, it is easy to
see that we can stop the exploration of any pairs $\langle s, o \rangle$ such that s contains an incompatible pair. We should look for easily (polynomial-time) checkable sufficient conditions
for incompatibility. Finally, a first release of our prototype (codenamed ALASKA) is
available for download at http://www.ulb.ac.be/di/ssd/nmaquet/alaska/.

References

1. Baukus, K., Bensalem, S., Lakhnech, Y., Stahl, K.: Abstracting wsls systems to verify parameterized networks. In: Schwartzbach, M.I., Graf, S. (eds.) TACAS 2000. LNCS,
   vol. 1785, pp. 188–203. Springer, Heidelberg (2000)

2. Cimatti, A., Clarke, E., Giunchiglia, F., Roveri, M.: Nusmv: A new symbolic model checker. STTT 2(4), 410–425 (2000)
3. Clarke, E., Grumberg, O., Hamaguchi, K.: Another look at LTL model checking. In: Dill, D.L. (ed.) CAV 1994. LNCS, vol. 818, pp. 415–427. Springer, Heidelberg (1994)
4. Daniele, M., Giunchiglia, F., Vardi, M.: Improved automata generation for linear temporal logic. In: Halbwachs, N., Peled, D.A. (eds.) CAV 1999. LNCS, vol. 1633, pp. 249–260. Springer, Heidelberg (1999)
5. de Alfaro, L., Henzinger, T.A., Majumdar, R.: From verification to control: Dynamic programs for omega-regular objectives. In: LICS, pp. 279–290. IEEE, Los Alamitos (2001)
6. De Wulf, M., Doyen, L., Henzinger, T.A., Raskin, J.-F.: Antichains: A new algorithm for checking universality of finite automata. In: Ball, T., Jones, R.B. (eds.) CAV 2006. LNCS, vol. 4144, pp. 17–30. Springer, Heidelberg (2006)
7. Doyen, L., Raskin, J.-F.: Improved algorithms for the automata-based approach to model-checking. In: Grumberg, O., Huth, M. (eds.) TACAS 2007. LNCS, vol. 4424, pp. 451–465. Springer, Heidelberg (2007)
8. Fritz, C.: Constructing Büchi automata from LTL using simulation relations for alternating Büchi automata. In: H. Ibarra, O., Dang, Z. (eds.) CIAA 2003. LNCS, vol. 2759, pp. 35–48. Springer, Heidelberg (2003)
9. Gastin, P., Oddoux, D.: Fast LTL to Büchi automata translation. In: Berry, G., Comon, H., Finkel, A. (eds.) CAV 2001. LNCS, vol. 2102, pp. 53–65. Springer, Heidelberg (2001)
10. Gurumurthy, S., Kupferman, O., Somenzi, F., Vardi, M.: On complementing nondeterministic Büchi automata. In: Geist, D., Tronci, E. (eds.) CHARME 2003. LNCS, vol. 2860, pp. 96–110. Springer, Heidelberg (2003)
11. Harding, A.: Symbolic Strategy Synthesis For Games With LTL Winning Conditions. PhD thesis, University of Birmingham (2005)
12. Henzinger, T.A., Kupferman, O., Qadeer, S.: From prehistoric to postmodern symbolic model checking. In: Y. Vardi, M. (ed.) CAV 1998. LNCS, vol. 1427, pp. 195–206. Springer, Heidelberg (1998)
13. Lamport, L.: A new solution of dijkstra's concurrent programming problem. ACM 17(8), 453–455 (1974)
14. Maquet, N., De Wulf, M., Doyen, L., Raskin, J.-F.: Antichains: Alternative algorithms for LTL satisfiability and model-checking. Technical Report, 84, CFV, Belgium (2008)
15. McMillan, K.L.: Symbolic Model Checking. Kluwer Academic Publishers, Dordrecht (1993)
16. Miyano, S., Hayashi, T.: Alternating finite automata on omega-words. In: CAAP, pp. 195–210 (1984)
17. Rohde, S.: Alternating Automata and the Temporal Logic of Ordinals. PhD thesis, University of Illinois at Urbana-Champaign (1997)
18. Rozier, K., Vardi, M.: Ltl satisfiability checking. In: Bošnački, D., Edelkamp, S. (eds.) SPIN 2007. LNCS, vol. 4595, pp. 149–167. Springer, Heidelberg (2007)
19. Ruys, T., Holzmann, G.: Advanced Spin tutorial. In: Graf, S., Mounier, L. (eds.) SPIN 2004. LNCS, vol. 2989, pp. 304–305. Springer, Heidelberg (2004)
20. Sebastiani, R., Tonetta, S., Vardi, M.: Symbolic systems, explicit properties: On hybrid approaches for LTL symbolic model checking. In: Etessami, K., Rajamani, S.K. (eds.) CAV 2005. LNCS, vol. 3576, pp. 350–363. Springer, Heidelberg (2005)
21. Somenzi, F.: CUDD: CU Decision Diagram Package, University of Colorado (1998)
22. Somenzi, F., Bloem, R.: Efficient Büchi automata from LTL formulae. In: Emerson, E.A., Sistla, A.P. (eds.) CAV 2000. LNCS, vol. 1855, pp. 248–263. Springer, Heidelberg (2000)
23. Vardi, M.: An automata-theoretic approach to linear temporal logic. In: Moller, F., Birtwistle, G. (eds.) Logics for Concurrency. LNCS, vol. 1043, pp. 238–266. Springer, Heidelberg (1996)
24. Vardi, M., Wolper, P.: Reasoning about infinite computations. Information and Computation 115(1), 1–37 (1994)

On-the-Fly Techniques for Game-Based Software Model Checking*

Adam Bakewell and Dan R. Ghica

University of Birmingham, UK
{a.bakewell,d.r.ghica}@cs.bham.ac.uk

Abstract. We introduce on-the-fly composition, symbolic modelling and lazy iterated approximation refinement for game-semantic models. We present MAGE, an experimental model checker implementing this new technology. We discuss several typical examples and compare MAGE with BLAST and GAMECHECKER, which are the state-of-the-art tools in on-the-fly software model checking, and game-based model checking.

1 Introduction and Background

Automated software verification evolved rapidly in the last few years, culminating in the development of industry-strength verification toolkits such as SLAM [6] and BLAST [19]. These toolkits represent impressive feats of engineering, combining techniques from model checking [10] and theorem proving, especially satisfiability. They employ various methods intended to alleviate the so-called *state-explosion problem*, i.e. the fact that the space complexity of the software verification problem is very high. Some the most effective such methods are:

On-the-fly model checking. Also known as *lazy* model checking [10, Sec. 9.5], it is used whenever a larger (finite-state) model needs to be constructed from the intersection of two (or more) models; after that, a reachability test is performed. In lazy model checking, the test is conducted while the intersection is performed, rather than after. If the test succeeds then the rest of the intersection is not computed, hence the gain in efficiency.

Symbolic model checking. This terminology is overloaded. We mean representing a model by equations, rather than explicitly by concrete states and transitions [8].

Abstract interpretation. The key idea [11] is to construct, in a precisely defined sense, *best safe approximations* of systems. That is, an "abstracted" system that is smaller than the system to be verified but has richer behaviour than it. Very large economies of space can be achieved by this method; indeed, finite-state approximations can be found for infinite-state systems. The tradeoff is that additional behaviour in the "abstracted" system may lead to "false positives," i.e. it may report errors that do not exist in the original.

---

* Work supported by EPSRC grants EP/D070880/1 and EP/D034906/1.

C.R. Ramakrishnan and J. Rehof (Eds.): TACAS 2008, LNCS 4963, pp. 78–92, 2008.

Iterated refinement. This technique is used in conjunction with the previous one: if an approximation is too coarse and results in false positives, the false positives are used to *refine* the approximation, i.e. to make it more precise [9].

The success of the combination of methods enumerated above has been extraordinary, allowing tools to perform such feats as fully-automated verification of device drivers and other important programs. However, to scale up automated verification to large and complex software projects, modelling and verification cannot remain monolithic operations. Instead, they must be done compositionally, but in such a way that the above methods can be utilised.

A promising new approach to software verification uses game semantics [3,20]. This technique of modelling programming languages is inherently compositional, and known to give models both sound and complete (*fully abstract*) for many languages. Subsequent research showed that game models can be given effective algorithmic representations [15] and used as a basis for model checking.

Even a naïve implementation of game-based model checking was surprisingly effective in verifying challenging programs such as sorting, or certain abstract data types [2]. In a step towards fully automated verification a counterexample-guided refinement technique was adapted to the game model [13], and a prototype tool was developed [14]. However, all these efforts focus on model extraction, and use off-the-shelf back-ends for the heavy-duty model checking.

Older, more established model checking techniques benefit from elaborate implementations. In order for games-based model checking to close the gap it needs to adapt the state-of-the-art methods for mitigating the state-explosion problem to the particular context of game models. We make significant steps in this paper by introducing *on-the-fly composition, symbolic modelling and lazy iterated refinement for game models.*

Game-based models are defined inductively on syntax and use *composition* of models of sub-terms to generate the model of a given term. This indicates that the scope for gains through lazy modelling is considerable. We push this method to the extreme: we do not explicitly construct any of the component models, only a *tree of automata*, then we combine a search through the tree with searches in the models which are at the leaves of the tree using an algorithm that is compatible with composition of game models.

We take a similar lazy approach to approximation and refinement. Rather than refining whole models, we only refine along those paths that yield counterexamples, refining further when the counterexample is potentially spurious and backtracking whenever refinement leads into a dead end.

Last, but not least, our model-checker, MAGE, has a simple (but not simplistic!) and elegant implementation. It uses no external tools or libraries, so it may serve as a concise, self-contained, example of the most effective state-of-the-art model checking techniques in action. Programming MAGE in Haskell allowed us to take advantage of lazy evaluation, and naturally resulted in a compact implementation.[1] A compact presentation of our early results with MAGE is given in [4]. More detail on the material here is given in [5].

---

[1] Get MAGE and a test suite at http://www.cs.bham.ac.uk/~axb/games/mage/

2   Idealized Algol: Syntax and Semantics

We analyse IA^2, the procedural programming language presented in [13]. IA has boolean and integer constants, the usual arithmetic and logical operators, sequencing, branching and iteration commands, first (base-type) and second order (function-type) variables, λ-abstraction of first-order variables, term application and block variable declaration.

The operational semantics is standard, see [13]. The game-semantic model is fully abstract and can be expressed as an algebra of languages. We briefly present this model using notation taken from [2].

Game models of terms are languages R over alphabets of moves $\mathcal{A}$. They include the standard languages consisting of: the empty language $\emptyset$; the empty sequence ϵ; concatenation $R \cdot S$; union $R + S$; Kleene star R^* and the elements of the alphabet taken as sequences of unit length. In addition we use: intersection $R \cap S$; direct image under homomorphism ϕR and inverse image $\phi^{-1} R$. The languages defined by these extensions are the obvious ones. It is a standard result that languages constructed from regular languages using these operations are regular and can be recognised by a finite automaton effectively constructable from the language [21].

The disjoint union of two alphabets creates a larger alphabet $\mathcal{A}_1 + \mathcal{A}_2$. Disjoint union gives rise to canonical inclusion maps $in_i : \mathcal{A}_i \to \mathcal{A}_1 + \mathcal{A}_2$. Concretely, these maps are *tagging* operations. We use the same notation for the homomorphism $in_i : \mathcal{A}_i \to (\mathcal{A}_1 + \mathcal{A}_2)^*$ and take $out_i : \mathcal{A}_1 + \mathcal{A}_2 \to \mathcal{A}_i^*$ to be the homomorphism defined by $out_i a = a_i$ if a is in the image of in_i and ϵ otherwise. If $\phi_1 : \mathcal{A}_1 \to \mathcal{B}_1^*$ and $\phi_2 : \mathcal{A}_2 \to \mathcal{B}_2^*$ are homomorphisms then their sum $\phi_1 + \phi_2 : \mathcal{A}_1 + \mathcal{A}_2 \to (\mathcal{B}_1 + \mathcal{B}_2)^*$ as $(\phi_1 + \phi_2)a = in_i(\phi_i a)$ if a_i is in the image of in_i.

Definition 1 (Composition). *If R is a language over alphabet $\mathcal{A} + \mathcal{B}$ and S a language over alphabet $\mathcal{B} + \mathcal{C}$ we define the* composition *$S \circ R$ as the language $S \circ R = out_3\big(out_1^{-1}(R) \cap out_2^{-1}(S)\big)$, over alphabet $\mathcal{A} + \mathcal{C}$, with maps*

$$\mathcal{A} + \mathcal{B} \xrightleftharpoons[out_1]{in_1} \mathcal{A} + \mathcal{B} + \mathcal{C} \ , \ \mathcal{B} + \mathcal{C} \xrightleftharpoons[out_2]{in_2} \mathcal{A} + \mathcal{B} + \mathcal{C} \ and \ \mathcal{A} + \mathcal{C} \xrightleftharpoons[out_3]{in_3} \mathcal{A} + \mathcal{B} + \mathcal{C} \ .$$

Type θ is interpreted by a language over alphabet $\mathcal{A}[\![\theta]\!]$, containing the *moves* from the game model. Terms are functionalized, so $C; D$ is treated as $\mathsf{seq}\, C\, D$ and $\mathsf{int}\, x; C$ is treated as $\mathsf{newvar}(\lambda x.C)$ and so on. Term $\Gamma \vdash M : \theta$, with typed free identifiers $\Gamma = \{x_i : \theta_i\}$, is interpreted by a language $R = \mathcal{R}[\![\Gamma \vdash M : \theta]\!]$ over alphabet $\sum_{x_i : \theta_i \in \Gamma} \mathcal{A}[\![\theta_i]\!] + \mathcal{A}[\![\theta]\!]$. This interpretation is defined compositionally, by induction on the syntax of the functionalized language.

See [2,13] for full details of the semantic model. Here we only emphasise the aspect that is most relevant to the model-checking algorithm: function application. The semantics of application is defined by

$$\mathcal{R}[\![\Gamma, \Delta \vdash MN : \theta]\!] = \mathcal{R}[\![\Delta \vdash N : \tau]\!]^* \circ \mathcal{R}[\![\Gamma \vdash M : \tau \to \theta]\!],$$

---

[2] See the webpage for example programs.

with the composition $- \circ -$ of Def. 1. This application model uses three operations: (1) homomorphisms (tagging and de-tagging); (2) Kleene-star; (3) intersection. At the automata level: (1) is linear time; (2) the second is constant time; (3) is $\mathcal{O}(m \cdot n)$ where m, n are the sizes of the automata to be composed. Clearly intersection dominates. For a term with k syntactic elements, therefore, calculating the game model needs $k-1$ automata intersections. Computing them explicitly incurs a huge penalty if, in the end, we only want a safety check (e.g. that some bad action never occurs). Hence on-the-fly techniques are particularly useful in this context.

3   Automata Formulation: On-the-Fly Composition

We reformulate composition (Def. 1) to be explicitly automata-oriented, in a way that emphasises on-the-fly composition.

Let a *lazy automaton* $\mathbf{A} : A \to B$ be a tuple $\mathbf{A} = \langle S, A, B, X, \delta, s_0 \rangle$ where: S is a set of states; A, B are sets of symbols called *active* symbols; X is a set of symbols called *passive* symbols; $\delta : (A + B + X) \to S \to \mathbb{N} \to S_\perp$, where $S_\perp = S + \{\perp\}$, such that $\delta msn = \perp$ implies $\delta ms(n+1) = \perp$ is a next-state function that gives the ith next-state (rather than giving a set of all next states); $s_0 \in S$ is a distinguished *initial state*.

If $|S| \in \mathbb{N}$ then the lazy automaton is *finite-state*. Lazy automaton $\mathbf{A}$ *accepts a string* $t \in (A + B + X)^*$ *from a set of states* S_0 iff $t = \epsilon$ and $S_0 \neq \emptyset$ or $t = m \cdot t'$ with $m \in A + B + X$ and $t' \in (A + B + X)^*$ such that $\mathbf{A}$ accepts t' from a state in $\delta m S_0$. If $S_0 = \{s_0\}$ we say just that $\mathbf{A}$ *accepts* t. We denote by $\mathcal{L}(\mathbf{A})$ the set of strings accepted by $\mathbf{A}$.

The monotonicity of next-state function δ ensures that if requesting the jth next state returns "none" then requesting any $j + k$th next state returns "none".

Definition 2 (Lazy composition of automata). *Given two lazy automata* $\mathbf{A}_1 : A \to B = \langle S, A, B, X, \delta, s_0 \rangle$ *and* $\mathbf{A}_2 : B \to C = \langle T, B, C, Y, \lambda, t_0 \rangle$ *their* lazy composition *is* $\mathbf{A}_2 \circ \mathbf{A}_1 = \langle S \times T, A, C, B + X + Y, \lambda \cdot \delta, \langle s_0, t_0 \rangle \rangle$ *where*

$$(\lambda \star \delta)m\langle s, t\rangle\langle n_1, n_2\rangle = \langle (\textit{if } m \in \text{in}_1(A + B + X) \textit{ then } \delta msn_1 \textit{ else } s),$$
$$(\textit{if } m \in \text{in}_2(B + C + Y) \textit{ then } \lambda mtn_2 \textit{ else } t)\rangle$$
and $\lambda \cdot \delta = (\lambda \star \delta) \circ \langle \text{id}, \simeq \rangle$
and $\perp = \langle s, \perp \rangle = \langle \perp, t \rangle$
and $A + B + X \xrightarrow{\text{in}_1} A + B + C + X + Y$
and $B + C + Y \xrightarrow{\text{in}_2} A + B + C + X + Y.$

Above, id is the identity function and $\simeq : \mathbb{N} \to \mathbb{N} \times \mathbb{N}$ any monotonic bijection. The language of composed lazy automata is that required:[3]

Proposition 1. *Given two lazy automata* $\mathbf{A}_1 : A \to B$ *and* $\mathbf{A}_2 : B \to C$, $\text{out}_2(\mathcal{L}(\mathbf{A}_2)) \circ \text{out}_1(\mathcal{L}(\mathbf{A}_1)) = \text{out}(\mathcal{L}(\mathbf{A}_2 \circ \mathbf{A}_1))$, *where* $A + B + X \xrightarrow{\text{out}_2} A + B$, $B + C + Y \xrightarrow{\text{out}_1} B + C$, $A + B + C + X + Y \xrightarrow{\text{out}} A + C$.

---

[3] The propositions have elementary proofs, which are omitted.

Above, we need to "project" the languages of the composite automata on their active symbols, because automata compose "without hiding." This move from the "black-box" models of game semantics to "grey-box" models allows some exposure of internal actions and is needed to identify spurious counterexamples.

In game models it is more natural to reduce safety to event reachability rather than to state reachability. Given lazy automaton $\mathbf{A}$ we say that event m is *reachable* if there exists string t such that $tm \in \mathcal{L}(\mathbf{A})$. Now we give an algorithm for (lazy) reachability of move m_0 in lazy automaton $\mathbf{A}$, using the composition defined above.

Definition 3 (Lazy reachability for lazy automata)

> visited := $\emptyset$
> frontier := $[s_0]$
> *iterate* state *over* frontier
>   visited := visited $\cup$ {state}
>   *iterate* move *over* $(A + B + X)$
>   *iterate* state$'$ *over* δ move state
>   *if* move = m_0 *then return REACHABLE*
>   *if* state$'$ $\notin$ visited *then* frontier := [state$'$] : frontier
> *return UNREACHABLE.*

This algorithm is a depth-first-search (DFS) through the automata tree, generating only necessary transitions. The lazy implementation of δ ensures that iteration over δ move state returns one state at a time, rather than sets of states, until $\bot$ is produced and it stops.

3.1 Symbolic Automata

In the tree of automata that models a term, the leaves are automata representing the constants of the language and the free identifiers. These can all be defined *symbolically*, further reducing memory requirements: instead of constructing the transition system corresponding to the leaf automata explicitly, as in the older games-based model checkers [2,14] we only represent the transition function of the automaton. This may sound silly, because the transition function *is* the automaton, and they have the same size (theoretically). However, many of the automata involved have particular structures (copy-cat, arithmetic, logic) and their transition functions have efficient implementations in the programming language in which the model checker is implemented (and, of course, on the underlying hardware). Addition of finite integers, for example, is implemented far more efficiently than a table of all possible pairs of operands and their results!

For example, the symbolic automaton of any arithmetic operator $\oplus$ has state set $S = \mathbb{N} \times \mathbb{Z} \times \mathbb{Z}$, initial state $s_0 = (0, 0, 0)$ and, for $m, n \in \mathbb{Z}$, transitions:

$$\delta \mathsf{q}\,(0,0,0) = \{(1,0,0)\}, \qquad \delta \mathsf{q}\,(3,m,0) = \{(4,m,0)\},$$
$$\delta \mathsf{q}\,(1,0,0) = \{(2,0,0)\}, \qquad \delta n\,(4,m,0) = \{(5,m,n)\},$$
$$\delta m\,(2,0,0) = \{(3,m,0)\}, \qquad \delta(m \oplus n)\,(5,m,n) = \{(6,0,0)\},$$

3.2 Implementing Efficient Lazy Composition

The automata-theoretic formulation of lazy composition in Definition 2 omits a key aspect of the original game model which leads to serious inefficiency if implemented literally.

The problem occurs for active symbols common to the automata being composed: the definition suggests that both sub-automata should be queried about their transition for each such symbol. By analogy with abstract machines, this is like implementing application by taking each value v in the argument type, asking the argument term if it can produce v, and asking the function what it will do with v, and proceeding whenever both respond positively!

The key aspect that must be restored is the "proponent/opponent" (i.e. input/output) polarity of the game-semantic moves. At every composite state, one component must be asked about its next move and the other component asked only about particular moves. MAGE records the necessary polarity information and acts accordingly.

Another key inefficiency in Definition 2 is the iteration over *all* moves in $A + B + X$. In practice, knowing which leaf in the automata tree will be asked about its next move dramatically reduces the set of possible next moves: there is only really a choice when a free variable reads from the environment.

4 CEGAR: On-the-Fly Approximation and Refinement

Because they involve large subsets of the integers, automata representing game-semantic models are defined over enormous alphabets and, consequently, have huge state sets. [13] shows how to apply approximation-refinement in the context of games. We develop the ideas there in several directions by generalising the definition of data abstraction from games to automata in general and by giving a general and efficient criterion for recognising genuine counterexamples in approximated automata. This fast detection criterion plays in important role in the efficient implementation of approximation-refinement in MAGE.

Two apparently insurmountable problems prevent us using the popular abstract interpretation framework of [12]. Firstly, the automata-theoretic and game-theoretic formulations of the model seem to be at odds with the lattice-theoretic semantics of abstract interpretation. Secondly, abstract interpretation is compositional but not *functorial* — applying the abstract interpretation of a function to the abstract interpretation of an argument does not necessarily yield the same as the abstract interpretation of the result of the application in the concrete domain [1]. [12] argues convincingly that the practical consequences of the requirement to preserve functoriality are too restrictive.

Therefore we use a simplified framework based only on *approximation*. An approximation of language $\mathcal{L}$ is a function $\alpha : \mathcal{L} \to \hat{\mathcal{L}}$. Interesting approximations are, obviously, non-injective. An *automaton approximation* for automaton $\mathbf{A} = \langle S, A, B, X, \delta, s_0 \rangle$ is a tuple $\alpha = \langle \alpha_S : S \to \hat{S}, \alpha_{A+B+X} : A+B+X \to \hat{A}+\hat{B}+\hat{X} \rangle$ which defines an automaton $\hat{\mathbf{A}} = \alpha(\mathbf{A}) = \langle \hat{S}, \hat{A}, \hat{B}, \hat{X}, \hat{\delta}, \hat{s}_0 \rangle$ where $\hat{s}_0 = \alpha_S(s_0)$

and $\hat{\delta}$ is any function such that $\hat{\delta}\hat{m}\hat{s} \supseteq \alpha_S(\delta m s)$ for any $m \in A + B$, $s \in S$, $\hat{m} = \alpha_{A+B+X}m$, $\hat{s} = \alpha_S s$. Approximation is sound in the following sense:

Proposition 2. *If $m \in A + B + X$ is reachable in automaton **A** then for any automata approximation α, $\alpha_{A+B+X}(m)$ is reachable in $\alpha(\mathbf{A})$.*

Given two automata $\mathbf{A} : A \to B = \langle S, A, B, X, \delta, s_0 \rangle$ and $\mathbf{B} : B \to C = \langle T, B, C, Y, \lambda, t_0 \rangle$ and two approximations α and β the resulting automata $\alpha\mathbf{A} : \alpha_A A \to \alpha_B B$ and $\beta\mathbf{B} : \beta_B B \to \beta_C C$ are not immediately composable. However, we can use a "glue" automaton $\mathbf{I} : \alpha_B B \to \beta_B B$ to perform the composition as indicated by the diagram below

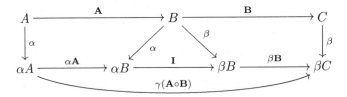

A *glue automaton* $\mathbf{I} : \alpha B \to \beta B$ is an approximation of the "copy-cat" automaton on $B \to B$, i.e. an automaton that accepts strings of shape $(\Sigma_{m \in B} mm)^*$ which uses α_B to approximate the domain alphabet and β_B the co-domain alphabet. Using glue automata we can show that approximation is compositional.

Proposition 3. *For any automata $\mathbf{A} : A \to B = \langle S, A, B, X, \delta, s_0 \rangle$ and $\mathbf{B} : B \to C = \langle T, B, C, Y, \lambda, t_0 \rangle$ and approximations α, β there exists an approximation γ such that $\beta\mathbf{B} \circ \alpha\mathbf{A} = \gamma(\mathbf{B} \circ \mathbf{A})$.*

This flexible approximation framework allows each automaton in an automata tree to be approximated individually, in a compositional and sound way.

Definition 4. *Given a language $\mathcal{L}$ and approximation $\alpha : \mathcal{L} \to \hat{\mathcal{L}}$, we call $\alpha' : \mathcal{L} \to \hat{\mathcal{L}}'$ a refinement of the approximation α if there exists a map $\alpha'' : \hat{\mathcal{L}}' \to \hat{\mathcal{L}}$ such that $\alpha = \alpha'' \circ \alpha'$.*

4.1 Approximating Game Automata

Approximation of our game automata is most naturally done by finitely approximating the alphabets and using an approximation of the set of states induced by the alphabet approximation.

Definition 5 (Data approximation). *An approximation α, is termed a data approximation of automaton **A** if*

- $\hat{S} = S/\cong$, *and α_S is its representation function, where $\cong \subseteq S \times S$ is the least reflexive relation such that $s_1 \cong s_2$ if $s_1' \cong s_2'$, $s_1 \in \delta m_1 s_1'$, $s_2 \in \delta m_2 s_2'$ and $\alpha_{A+B}(m_1) = \alpha_{A+B}(m_2)$.*
- $\hat{\delta}\hat{m}\hat{s} = \alpha_S(\delta m s)$.

This means that the states of $\hat{S}$ are the equivalence classes of S under $\cong$. So states are identified by a data abstraction only when they are targets of transitions with identified moves from already identified states.

The definition of data approximation is not algorithmic, because it depends in a non-trivial way on the automaton itself. However, the following property along with the fact that we can rather easily find data approximations for the particular automata that represent game-semantic models ensures that we can use data approximation in our models:

Proposition 4. *If automata* $\mathbf{A} : A \to B$ *and* $\mathbf{B} : B \to C$ *are data-approximated as* $\alpha(\mathbf{A})$ *and* $\beta(\mathbf{B})$ *then there exists a data approximation* γ *for* $\mathbf{B} \circ \mathbf{A}$ *such that* $\alpha(\mathbf{B}) \circ \mathbf{I} \circ \beta(\mathbf{A}) = \gamma(\mathbf{B} \circ \mathbf{A})$, *with* $\mathbf{I} : \alpha B \to \beta B$ *a data-approximated glue automaton.*

In other words, a composition of data-approximate automata is itself a data-approximated automaton. Data-approximation can lead to finite-state automata.

Proposition 5. *For any automaton* $\mathbf{A}$ *representing a game-semantic model of IA and for any data approximation such that* $|\text{range}\,\alpha_{A+B+X}| \in \mathbb{N}$, *the automaton* $\hat{\mathbf{A}}$ *is finite-state.*

We approximate game automata using data approximation. More precisely, we use partitions of the set of integers into a finite set of intervals, wherever necessary. The refinement of such an approximation using intervals is the obvious one: using smaller intervals.

This approximation is compatible with the symbolic representation discussed in Sec. 3.1. Moreover, approximate symbolic automata can be parameterized lazily by the approximation scheme. This is only interesting for arithmetic and logical operators. To implement their lazy and symbolic approximations we extend the operators from acting on integers to intervals, in the obvious way. Every arithmetic operation $\oplus : \mathbb{Z} \to \mathbb{Z} \to \mathbb{Z}$ becomes a *finite relation* $\hat{\oplus} \subseteq \alpha\mathbb{Z} \times \alpha'\mathbb{Z} \times \alpha''\mathbb{Z}$, defined as follows: $([m_1, m_1'], [m_2, m_2'], [m, m']) \in \hat{\oplus}$ if and only if $[m, m'] \in \alpha''([\min\{x_1 \oplus x_2 \mid x_i \in [m_i, m_i']\}, \max\{x_1 \oplus x_2 \mid x_i \in [m_i, m_i']\}])$.

4.2   Fast Early Detection of Counterexamples

As is well known, the converse of Prop. 2 is not true, since approximation can introduce new behaviour. A reachability test in an approximate automaton will return a string that needs to be "certified" for authenticity, i.e. that it indeed is the image, under approximation, of a string in the original automaton.

The usual approach in model checking is to analyse a counterexample trace using a SAT solver. We could follow that approach. However, by using domain-specific knowledge about the automata and the approximations we obtain a simpler and more efficient solution. A trivial test for identifying valid counterexamples can be implemented starting from the following fact:

Proposition 6. *For any interface automaton* $\mathbf{A}$ *and data approximation* α, *if* $\hat{m}_0 \cdots \hat{m}_k \in \mathcal{L}(\hat{\mathbf{A}})$ *and* $\alpha^{-1}(\hat{m}_i) = \{m_i\}$ *then* $m_0 \cdots m_k \in \mathcal{L}(\mathbf{A})$.

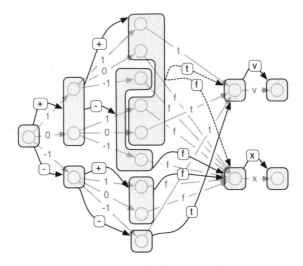

Fig. 1. Data-approximated automaton

In words, a trace is valid if it contains no approximated symbols. This is only true of data-approximated automata. This test is linear time, but it requires a very "deep" refinement of a model. MAGE uses a test that accepts traces with approximate symbols when the approximation does not cause non-determinism in the approximated automaton for transitions that are deterministic in the precise version. Fig. 1 shows a simple data approximation of an automaton[4] that checks for equality on the set $\{-1, 0, 1\}$ by accepting two symbols then t if they are equal and f otherwise; if f, we mark "success" by symbol v and otherwise we mark "failure" by x. The data approximation is induced by $\alpha = \{-1 \mapsto -, 0 \mapsto +, 1 \mapsto +, t \mapsto t, f \mapsto f, x \mapsto x, v \mapsto v\}$. The precise automaton is greyed out and the approximated version superimposed. Approximated transitions that introduce nondeterminism are dashed (e.g. $+.+.f.x$); approximated transitions not introducing non-determinism (and which pass the test) are solid (e.g. $+.-.f.x$).

To apply this new criterion the counterexample must contain the visited states (as well as the symbols in the trace), but that only adds a constant-factor time and space algorithmic overhead.

Definition 6. *Given an automaton* $\mathbf{A}$, *a state* $s \in S$ *is said to be* forced *if for all* $(s, m', s'), (s, m'', s'') \in \delta$, $m' = m''$ *and* $s' = s''$.

Proposition 7. *For any automaton* $\mathbf{A}$, *data approximation* α *and sequence* $(\hat{s}_0, \hat{m}_0) \cdots (\hat{s}_k, \hat{m}_k)$ *such that* $(\hat{s}_j, \hat{m}_j, \hat{s}_{j+1}) \in \hat{\delta}$, *if* $\hat{s}_i$ *is forced whenever some state* $s \in \alpha_S^{-1}(\hat{s}_i)$ *is forced then* $m_0 \cdots m_k \in \mathcal{L}(\mathbf{A})$.

As before, this criterion is only valid for data approximation, and it spares the need for an expensive SAT test. Instead, we can use a simple, linear-time test. When automata compose, forced states in the components correspond to forced

---

[4] For brevity, it is more concise than the corresponding IA game model.

states in the composite automaton. It thus suffices to recognise when forced
states become non-forced through approximation in leaf automata, and record
this information whenever such states are visited, in order to indicate a trace
that fails the test of Prop. 7 and requires further refinement.

5   Mage: Empirical Results and Comparisons

We present a small selection of simple case studies to illustrate our main techniques; and to compare MAGE with both non-lazy game-based model checking
and lazy non-game-based model checking. The example programs are given in
the appendix. They and many more are also available on the webpage.

5.1   Lazy Precise Models

```
uflo : com,            // exception called when empty stack popped
oflo : com,            // exception called when full stack pushed
input : nat1,          // free var in {0,1} supplying pushed values
output : nat1,         // free var in {0,1} receiving popped values
check : com -> com -> com                    // arbitrary context
|-
new nat32[size] buffer in          // fixed-size stack of numbers
new nat(log size) top := 0 in         // first free buffer element
let push be
  if top=size then oflo                    // raise oflo if full
  else buffer[top] := input; top := top+1 fi   // push and inc top
in let pop be
  if top=0 then uflo                      // raise uflo if empty
  else top := top-1; output := buffer[top] fi   // pop and dec top
in check(pop,push)     // context can do any seq of pushes and pops
```

The first example searches the model of the fixed-size integer stack ADT above
for sequences of calls of its push and pop methods that will result in uflo (i.e.
'pop empty') or oflo (i.e. 'push full'), for different stack sizes. This example is
a classic model checking problem with a history in the games-literature making
it suitable for comparison in later sections, as well as being a good example
of how we can verify open terms. It is also a good example for testing our lazy
techniques because it presents a huge model in which a few specific paths exhibit
the properties of interest.

While checking the unapproximated model we make the stack elements be
naturals in $\{0, 1\}$ — bigger integer types makes the precise models far too big.
Table 1 presents the time for MAGE to search the lazy model for various stack
sizes.[5] The rapid generation of counterexamples clearly demonstrates the benefit
of lazy model building. The times depend on stack size and model search order:
with the pop method given priority, the obvious uflo counterexample ("pop")
is generated immediately. With push prioritised, a longer counterexample that

---

[5] MAGE is compiled with GHC6.4.2 and run with a 250MB heap on a 1.86GHz PC.

Table 1. Lazy precise stack model verification with MAGE

stack size	fixed-order search times (sec)				randomized search averaged times (sec)	
	push prioritised		pop prioritised			
	oflo	uflo	oflo	uflo	oflo	uflo
2	0.04	0.04	0.04	0.03	0.04	0.03
4	0.05	0.05	0.06	0.03	0.06	0.03
8	0.08	0.09	0.10	0.03	0.09	0.04
16	0.17	0.21	0.21	0.04	0.20	0.06
32	0.49	0.61	0.77	0.04	0.64	0.22
64	1.57	2.05	1.96	0.05	1.78	0.82
128	5.96	7.62	7.13	0.06	6.38	1.43
256	23.20	30.44	28.09	0.08	25.57	7.35
512	96.42	127.14	115.73	0.14	106.37	22.91
1024	433.43	575.56	525.27	0.30	501.02	189.26

fills then empties then underflows the stack is found. Similarly, search order affects the harder `oflo` search problem. MAGE can mitigate this effect by choosing transitions (when iterating over frontier in the terminology of Def. 3) in a randomised order instead; the last two columns in Table 1 show how this tends to average out differences in search time caused by order.

5.2 Approximated Models and On-Demand Refinement

Switching from precise to approximate model building cuts model size, introduces non-determinism and introduces possible false counterexamples. The MAGE approximation/refinement scheme begins by setting the approximated domain of each program variable to contain one value (the full range, determined by declared size).

In the very best cases, searching the starting approximated model quickly reveals safety. The starting approximated model of the term

```
new nat32 x := i in assert (x<1000000000 | x>1000)
```

exhibits a typical false counterexample. After three refinement iterations the domain of x is precise enough for MAGE to prove the assertion.

In addition to the early stopping, refinement is lazy in that only paths in the automata that indicate potential counterexamples get refined. Spurious counterexample makes the search backtrack to the next most-precise potential counterexample and forget recent refinements. Consider this constraint problem:

> Bill is twice as old as Ben was when Bill was as old as Ben is now.
> Their combined ages are 84.

```
bill:nat7, ben:nat7 |-                    // 7-bit natural inputs
new nat7 y := bill in new nat7 ny := ben in    // read the inputs
(y + ny = 84) & (y = 2 * (ny - (y - ny)))      // age constraint
```

The above program returns true when its inputs are a solution. Searching its precise model with MAGE finds the correct ages in 256.5 seconds. Using approximation/refinement, the ages are found in only 6.5 seconds after four backtracks and six refinement iterations.

5.3   Comparison of Precise vs. Approximate Modelling in Mage

Returning to the stack example, we make the elements realistic 32-bit integers and show in Table 2 the iterated-refinement times. This exposes some pros and cons of approximation-refinement, compared to the precise model verification in Table 1. uflo search is even quicker, despite the increase in element domain size. The oflo searches get somewhat slower than the precise search. While the increased element size would make the precise search task impossible, this is not a major factor in the time increase seen here because, as with uflo, repeatedly pushing *any* value causes an oflo — indeed, the times are not much changed by reducing the element type right down to nat1. What is going on instead, is that each iteration identifies that a chain of pushes (of any value) could lead to oflo so the refinement "learns" to keep the approximation domain of the array elements vague, and each iteration makes the array index domain more precise; each array index must be written for an oflo, so over log(size) iterations the array index types are refined to be fully precise; this roughly doubles the number of distinct indices each time, so the refinement amounts to the same thing as searching for oflo in arrays with a tiny element domain and an index domain of size 2^i for each i from 0 to log(size).

It happens that the oflo counterexample is easy to find in that no backtracking from false counterexamples is needed. However, the search algorithm retains a backtrack queue, so search with approximation/refinement tends to incur further slowing as the memory gradually fills with the backtrack queue. There is clearly potential to optimise the search process, perhaps with significant performance gains.

5.4   Comparison with GameChecker

GAMECHECKER [13,14] is a recent game-based model checker that incorporates approximation and refinement. The main theoretical difference is that it does not use our on-the-fly or symbolic techniques; the main practical difference is that it is a Java front-end coupled to an industrial model checker whereas MAGE is implemented directly in Haskell. For a fair comparison we modify the stack ADT program so the stack elements are 32-bit integers and search for oflo's and uflo's using MAGE with approximation/refinement on, and with GAMECHECKER using counterexample-guided refinement (on infinite integers). The results in Table 2 support the expectation that the lazy techniques should reap massive rewards: the GAMECHECKER times show that building even approximate full models before analysing them incurs a severe penalty. As stack size increases, building a full model of stack behaviour before searching is almost all wasted work.

A secondary reason for GAMECHECKER's poorer performance is that it always uses infinite integers, and to avoid infinite refinement of spurious counterexamples it uses clever refinement schedules. This involves finding the smallest counterexample relative to a rather complex order. This is not an issue with the finite types in MAGE, and the resultant performance gain seems to vindicate the decision to use realistically large (i.e. 32-bit or more) integers.

Table 2. CEGAR stack verification with MAGE, GAMECHECKER and BLAST

stack size	MAGE				GAMECHECKER				BLAST	
	oflo	(iters)	uflo	(iters)	oflo	(iters)	uflo	(iters)	oflo	(iters)
2	0.1	(2)	0.03	(2)	10.1	(4)	5.31	(2)	1.6	(2)
4	0.1	(3)	0.03	(2)	27.6	(6)	8.21	(2)	3.3	(4)
8	0.2	(4)	0.03	(2)	112.6	(10)	20.29	(2)	4.6	(8)
16	0.4	(5)	0.03	(2)	780.7	(18)	78.26	(2)	7.8	(16)
32	1.2	(6)	0.03	(2)	12,268.1	(36)	494.20	(2)	17.3	(32)
64	3.9	(7)	0.03	(2)	>7 hrs	-	8,982.13	(2)	43.7	(64)
128	13.9	(8)	0.03	(2)	-	-	>7 hrs	-	145.3	(128)
224	19.1	(9)	0.03	(2)	-	-		-	506.4	(224)
225	19.3	(9)	0.03	(2)	-	-		-	-	-
256	54.8	(9)	0.03	(2)	-	-		-	-	-
512	215.3	(10)	0.03	(2)	-	-		-	-	-
1024	864.7	(11)	0.03	(2)	-	-		-	-	-

5.5   Comparison with Other Model Checkers

From the multitude of non-game-based approaches to model checking, in this section we focus on what we regard as the leading tool based on *predicate abstraction*, BLAST. This is a useful comparison because BLAST has achieved significant performance improvements over SLAM, by incorporating laziness into the cycle of abstraction, verification and refinement. Thus we can think of MAGE vs. GAMECHECKER as a game-based analogue of BLAST vs. SLAM.

Of course, the game-based tools are experiments in pure model checking for a simple language whereas SLAM and BLAST are quite mature tools that handle the C language. As a simple example of a defect of pure model checking compared to the predicate abstraction tools, verifying the following with MAGE requires a search of all 2^{32} possible inputs whereas BLAST can declare the corresponding C code safe in a fraction of a second.

```
input : nat32 |- new nat32 x := input in assert (x != 1+x)
```

Approaches to laziness. Laziness in BLAST consists in rearranging the perfectly eager CEGAR cycle of SLAM which: (1) constructs a predicate-abstraction of the program [7]; (2) model-checks; (3) refines the abstraction using the counterexample. Instead, BLAST updates the predicate-abstraction while constructing the model, informed by a continuous examination of the counterexamples yielded.This makes tremendous savings by zooming in on program parts that need close examination and leaving the rest suitably abstract.

The incremental model building in MAGE is very different but like BLAST it builds and refines only the parts needed. The other big separation is that MAGE does not pick up "interesting" predicates from the program as a starting point; it just partitions the integers. Then refinement requires no syntactic manipulation of source code; instead we just change the model semantics. This allows spurious counterexamples to be identified without using an external theorem prover. In BLAST the theorem prover ends up dominating the verification process [18, p. 3].

The potential disadvantage is that the initial approximation in MAGE is blind to any useful features in the program being analysed.

Stacks. Like MAGE, BLAST can detect uflo's in less than a second for stack sizes into billions of elements. BLAST detects oflo in a stack of size n after n iterations. Table 2 shows that we were able to do this without exhausting our resources for stacks up to 224 elements. Much of the poor performance of BLAST with larger stacks is because it only generates a precise analysis of the first n iterations of a loop, and only extends n by one at each refinement iteration, so failures occurring only after very large numbers of iterations can be hard for it to find. By comparison, the MAGE data refinement tends to home loop counters in on the number needed to generate the failure.

6   Conclusion

Games-based software model checking offers the advantage of compositionality, which we believe essential for scaling to larger programs. Early work in this area showed how the technique can be used in principle [2], and how the essential method of iterated refinement can be adapted to the model [13]. The present paper takes the next step in making this technique practical by incorporating lazy/on-the-fly modelling techniques, with apparent massive efficiency gains. We implemented, and made available, the first model checker specifically targeted to take advantage of the multi-layered compositional nature of game models.

Our choice of target language was dictated by a desire to compare MAGE to previous work; a switch to call-by-value can be easily accomplished. Concurrency can be also added using the work in [16]. Genuinely new developments that seem compatible with our approach are the introduction of recursion and higher-order functions, the game models of which admit finite-state over-approximations.

Comparison with the state-of-the art model checker BLAST suggests that for unsafe programs MAGE is able to zoom in on the error faster. On safe programs MAGE's total ignorance of specific predicates used in the program gives BLAST a substantial edge. It should be noted that MAGE consists of 2,250 lines of Haskell code, whereas BLAST's source distribution is 64MB, excluding the required external theorem prover. Finding common ground between the semantic-direct approach of MAGE and the syntax-oriented techniques of predicate abstraction might be the best way forward in automated software verification.

References

1. Abramsky, S.: Abstract interpretation, logical relations and kan extensions. J. Log. Comput. 1(1), 5–40 (1990)
2. Abramsky, S., Ghica, D.R., Murawski, A.S., Ong, C.-H.L.: Applying game semantics to compositional software modeling and verification. In: Jensen, K., Podelski, A. (eds.) TACAS 2004. LNCS, vol. 2988, pp. 421–435. Springer, Heidelberg (2004)
3. Abramsky, S., Jagadeesan, R., Malacaria, P.: Full abstraction for PCF. Inf. Comput. 163(2), 409–470 (2000)

4. Bakewell, A., Ghica, D.R.: Game-Based Safety Checking with Mage. In: SAVCBS, pp. 85–87 (2007)
5. Bakewell, A., and Ghica, D. R. On-the-Fly Techniques for Game-Based Software Model Checking (extended report). Technical Report TR-07-8, School of Computer Science, University of Birmingham (2007)
6. Ball, T., Cook, B., Levin, V., Rajamani, S.K.: SLAM and static driver verifier: Technology transfer of formal methods inside microsoft. In: Boiten, E.A., Derrick, J., Smith, G.P. (eds.) IFM 2004. LNCS, vol. 2999, pp. 1–20. Springer, Heidelberg (2004)
7. Ball, T., Majumdar, R., Millstein, T.D., Rajamani, S.K.: Automatic predicate abstraction of c programs. In: SIGPLAN Conference on Programming Language Design and Implementation, pp. 203–213 (2001)
8. Ball, T., Rajamani, S.K.: Bebop: A symbolic model checker for boolean programs. In: Havelund, K., Penix, J., Visser, W. (eds.) SPIN 2000. LNCS, vol. 1885, pp. 113–130. Springer, Heidelberg (2000)
9. Clarke, E.M., Grumberg, O., Jha, S., Lu, Y., Veith, H.: Counterexample-guided abstraction refinement. In: Emerson, E.A., Sistla, A.P. (eds.) CAV 2000. LNCS, vol. 1855, pp. 154–169. Springer, Heidelberg (2000)
10. Clarke, E.M., Grumberg, O., Peled, D.: Model Checking. The MIT Press, Cambridge (1999)
11. Cousot, P., Cousot, R.: Abstract interpretation: A unified lattice model for static analysis of programs by construction or approximation of fixpoints. In: POPL, pp. 238–252 (1977)
12. Cousot, P., Cousot, R.: Higher-order abstract interpretation, invited paper. In: Proc. 1994 International Conference on Computer Languages, pp. 95–112. IEEE Computer Society Press, Los Alamitos (1994)
13. Dimovski, A., Ghica, D.R., Lazic, R.: Data-abstraction refinement: A game semantic approach. In: Hankin, C., Siveroni, I. (eds.) SAS 2005. LNCS, vol. 3672, pp. 102–117. Springer, Heidelberg (2005)
14. Ghica, D.R., Lazić, R.S., Dimovski, A.: A counterexample-guided refinement tool for open procedural programs. In: Valmari, A. (ed.) SPIN 2006. LNCS, vol. 3925, pp. 288–292. Springer, Heidelberg (2006)
15. Ghica, D.R., McCusker, G.: The regular-language semantics of second-order idealized Algol. Theor. Comput. Sci. 309(1-3), 1–3 (2003)
16. Ghica, D.R., Murawski, A.S.: Compositional model extraction for higher-order concurrent programs. In: Hermanns, H., Palsberg, J. (eds.) TACAS 2006. LNCS, vol. 3920, pp. 303–317. Springer, Heidelberg (2006)
17. Henzinger, T., Jhala, R., Majumdar, R., Sanvido, M.: Extreme model checking (2003)
18. Henzinger, T., Jhala, R., Majumdar, R., Sutre, G.: Software verification with Blast (2003)
19. Henzinger, T.A., Jhala, R., Majumdar, R.: The BLAST software verification system. In: Godefroid, P. (ed.) SPIN 2005. LNCS, vol. 3639, pp. 25–26. Springer, Heidelberg (2005)
20. Hyland, J.M.E., Ong, C.-H.L.: On full abstraction for PCF: I, II, and III. Inf. Comput. 163(2), 285–408 (2000)
21. Hopcroft, J.E., Ullman, J.D.: Introduction to Automata Theory, Languages and Computation. Addison-Wesley, Reading (1979)
22. Laird, J.: A fully abstract game semantics of local exceptions. In: LICS, pp. 105–114 (2001)

Computing Simulations over Tree Automata
(Efficient Techniques for Reducing Tree Automata)

Parosh A. Abdulla[1], Ahmed Bouajjani[2], Lukáš Holík[3], Lisa Kaati[1], and Tomáš Vojnar[3]

[1] University of Uppsala, Sweden
{parosh,lisa.kaati}@it.uu.se
[2] LIAFA, University Paris 7, France
abou@liafa.jussieu.fr
[3] FIT, Brno University of Technology, Czech Republic
{holik,vojnar}@fit.vutbr.cz

Abstract. We address the problem of computing simulation relations over tree automata. In particular, we consider downward and upward simulations on tree automata, which are, loosely speaking, analogous to forward and backward relations over word automata. We provide simple and efficient algorithms for computing these relations based on a reduction to the problem of computing simulations on labelled transition systems. Furthermore, we show that downward and upward relations can be combined to get relations compatible with the tree language equivalence, which can subsequently be used for an efficient size reduction of nondeterministic tree automata. This is of a very high interest, for instance, for symbolic verification methods such as regular model checking, which use tree automata to represent infinite sets of reachable configurations. We provide experimental results showing the efficiency of our algorithms on examples of tree automata taken from regular model checking computations.

1 Introduction

Tree automata are widely used for modelling and reasoning about various kinds of structured objects such as syntactical trees, structured documents, configurations of complex systems, algebraic term representations of data or computations, etc. (see [9]). For instance, in the framework of regular model checking, tree automata are used to represent and manipulate sets of configurations of infinite-state systems such as parameterized networks of processes with a tree-like topology, or programs with dynamic linked data-structures [7,3,5,6].

In the above context, checking language equivalence and reducing automata wrt. the language equivalence is a fundamental issue, and performing these operations efficiently is crucial for all practical applications of tree automata. Computing a minimal canonical tree automaton is, of course, possible, but it requires determinisation, which may lead to an exponential blow-up in the size of the automaton. Therefore, even if the resulting automaton can be small, we may not be able to compute it in practice due to the very expensive determinisation step, which is, indeed, a major bottleneck when using canonical tree automata.

A reasonable and pragmatic approach is to consider a notion of equivalence that is stronger than language equivalence, but which can be checked efficiently, using a polynomial algorithm. Here, a natural trade-off between the strength of the considered

C.R. Ramakrishnan and J. Rehof (Eds.): TACAS 2008, LNCS 4963, pp. 93–108, 2008.

equivalence and the cost of its computation arises. In the case of word automata, an equivalence which is widely considered as a good trade-off in this sense is simulation equivalence. It can be checked in polynomial time, and efficient algorithms have been designed for this purpose (see, e.g., [10,14]). These algorithms make the computation of simulation equivalence quite affordable even in comparison with the one of bisimulation, which is cheaper [13], but which is also stronger, and therefore leads in general to less significant reductions in the sizes of the automata.

In this paper, we study notions of entailment and equivalence between tree automata, which are suitable in the sense discussed above, and we also provide efficient algorithms for their computation.

We start by considering a basic notion of tree simulation, called *downward simulation*, corresponding to a natural extension of the usual notion of simulation defined on *or*-structures to *and-or* structures. This relation can be shown to be compatible with the tree language equivalence.

The second notion of simulation that we consider, called *upward simulation*, corresponds intuitively to a generalisation of the notion of backward simulation to and-or structures. The definition of an upward simulation is parametrised by a downward simulation: Roughly speaking, two states q and q' are upward similar if whenever one of them, say q, considered within some vector $(q_1, \ldots, q_n)$ at position i, has an upward transition to some state s, then q' appears at position i of some vector $(q'_1, \ldots, q'_n)$ that has also an upward transition to a state s', which is upward similar to s, and moreover, for each position $j \neq i$, q_j is downward similar to q'_j.

Upward simulation is not compatible with the tree language equivalence. It is rather compatible with the so-called context language equivalence, where a context of a state q is a tree with a hole on the leaf level such that if we plug a tree in the tree language of q into this hole, we obtain a tree recognised by the automaton. However, we show an interesting fact that when we restrict ourselves to upward relations compatible with the set of final states of automata, the downward and upward simulation equivalences can be *combined* in such a way that they give rise to a new equivalence relation which is compatible with the tree language equivalence. This combination is not trivial. It is based on the idea that two states q_1 and q_2 may have different tree languages and different context languages, but for every t in the tree language of one of them, say q_1, and every C in the context language of the other, here q_2, the tree $C[t]$ (where t is plugged into C) is recognised by the automaton. The combined relation is coarser than (or, in the worst case, as coarse as) the downward simulation and according to our practical experiments, it usually leads to significantly better reductions of the automata.

In this way, we obtain two candidates for simulation-based equivalences for use in automata reduction. Then, we consider the issue of designing efficient algorithms for computing these relations. A deep examination of downward and upward simulation equivalences shows that they can be computed using essentially the same algorithmic pattern. Actually, we prove that, surprisingly, computing downward and upward tree simulations can be reduced in each case to computing simulations on standard labelled transition systems. These reductions provide a simple and elegant way of solving in a uniform way the problem of computing tree simulations by reduction to computing simulations in the word case. The best known algorithm for solving the latter problem, published recently in [14], considers simulation relations defined on Kripke structures. The use of this algorithm requires its adaptation to labelled transition systems. We provide such an adaptation and we provide also a proof for this algorithm which can be seen as an alternative, more direct, proof of the algorithm of [14]. The combination of our reductions with the labelled transition systems-based simulation algorithm leads to efficient algorithms for our equivalence relations on tree automata, whose precise complexities are also analysed in the paper.

We have implemented our algorithms and performed experiments on automata computed in the context of regular tree model checking (corresponding to representations of the set of reachable configurations of parametrised systems). The experiments show that, indeed, the relations proposed in this paper provide significant reductions of these automata and that they perform better than (existing) bisimulation-based reductions [11].

Related work. As far as we know, this is the first work which addresses the issue of computing simulation relations for tree automata. The downward and upward simulation relations considered in this work have been introduced first in [4] where they have been used for proving soundness of some acceleration techniques used in the context of regular tree model checking. However, the problem of computing these relations has not been addressed in that paper. A form of combining downward and upward relations has also been defined in [4]. However, the combinations considered in that paper require some restrictions which are computationally difficult to check and that are not considered in this work. Bisimulations on tree automata have been considered in [2,11]. The notion of a backward bisimulation used in [11] corresponds to what can be called a downward bisimulation in our terminology.

Outline. The rest of the paper is organised as follows. In the next section, we give some preliminaries on tree automata, labelled transition systems, and simulation relations. Section 3 describes an algorithm for checking simulation on labelled transition systems. In Section 4 resp. Section 5, we translate downward resp. upward simulation on tree automata into corresponding simulations on labelled transition systems. Section 6 gives methods for reducing tree automata based on equivalences derived form downward and upward simulation. In Section 7, we report some experimental results. Finally, we give conclusions and directions for future research in Section 8.

Remark. For space reasons, all proofs are deferred to [1].

2 Preliminaries

In this section, we introduce some preliminaries on trees, tree automata, and labelled transition systems (LTS). In particular, we recall two simulation relations defined on tree automata in [4], and the classical (word) simulation relation defined on LTS. Finally, we will describe an encoding which we use in our algorithms to describe pre-order relations, e.g., simulation relations.

For an equivalence relation $\equiv$ defined on a set Q, we call each equivalence class of $\equiv$ a *block*, and use $Q/\equiv$ to denote the set of blocks in $\equiv$.

Trees. A *ranked alphabet* Σ is a set of symbols together with a function $Rank : \Sigma \to \mathbb{N}$. For $f \in \Sigma$, the value $Rank(f)$ is said to be the *rank* of f. For any $n \geq 0$, we denote by Σ_n the set of all symbols of rank n from Σ. Let ε denote the empty sequence. A *tree t* over an alphabet Σ is a partial mapping $t : \mathbb{N}^* \to \Sigma$ that satisfies the following conditions:

- $dom(t)$ is a finite, prefix-closed subset of $\mathbb{N}^*$, and
- for each $p \in dom(t)$, if $Rank(t(p)) = n > 0$, then $\{i \mid pi \in dom(t)\} = \{1, \ldots, n\}$.

Each sequence $p \in dom(t)$ is called a *node* of t. For a node p, we define the ith *child* of p to be the node pi, and we define the ith *subtree* of p to be the tree t' such that $t'(p') = t(pip')$ for all $p' \in \mathbb{N}^*$. A *leaf* of t is a node p which does not have any children, i.e., there is no $i \in \mathbb{N}$ with $pi \in dom(t)$. We denote by $T(\Sigma)$ the set of all trees over the alphabet Σ.

Tree Automata. A (finite, non-deterministic, bottom-up) *tree automaton* (TA) is a 4-tuple $A = (Q, \Sigma, \Delta, F)$ where Q is a finite set of states, $F \subseteq Q$ is a set of final states, Σ is a ranked alphabet, and Δ is a set of transition rules. Each transition rule is a triple of the form $((q_1, \ldots, q_n), f, q)$ where $q_1, \ldots, q_n, q \in Q$, $f \in \Sigma$, and $Rank(f) = n$. We use $(q_1, \ldots, q_n) \xrightarrow{f} q$ to denote that $((q_1, \ldots, q_n), f, q) \in \Delta$. In the special case where $n = 0$, we speak about the so-called *leaf rules*, which we sometimes abbreviate as $\xrightarrow{f} q$. We use $Lhs(A)$ to denote the set of *left-hand sides* of rules, i.e., the set of tuples of the form $(q_1, \ldots, q_n)$ where $(q_1, \ldots, q_n) \xrightarrow{f} q$ for some f and q. Finally, we denote by $Rank(A)$ the smallest $n \in \mathbb{N}$ such that $n \geq m$ for each $m \in \mathbb{N}$ where $(q_1, \ldots, q_m) \in Lhs(A)$ for some $q_i \in Q$, $1 \leq i \leq m$.

A *run* of A over a tree $t \in T(\Sigma)$ is a mapping $\pi : dom(t) \to Q$ such that for each node $p \in dom(t)$ where $q = \pi(p)$, we have that if $q_i = \pi(pi)$ for $1 \leq i \leq n$, then Δ has a rule $(q_1, \ldots, q_n) \xrightarrow{t(p)} q$. We write $t \xRightarrow{\pi} q$ to denote that π is a run of A over t such that $\pi(\varepsilon) = q$. We use $t \Longrightarrow q$ to denote that $t \xRightarrow{\pi} q$ for some run π. The *language* of a state $q \in Q$ is defined by $L(q) = \{t \mid t \Longrightarrow q\}$, while the *language* of A is defined by $L(A) = \bigcup_{q \in F} L(q)$.

Labelled Transition Systems. A (finite) *labelled transition system (LTS)* is a tuple $T = (S, \mathcal{L}, \to)$ where S is a finite set of states, $\mathcal{L}$ is a finite set of labels, and $\to \subseteq S \times \mathcal{L} \times S$ is a transition relation.

Given an LTS $T = (S, \mathcal{L}, \to)$, a label $a \in \mathcal{L}$, and two states $q, r \in S$, we denote by $q \xrightarrow{a} r$ the fact that $(q, a, r) \in \to$. We define the set of *a-predecessors* of a state r as $pre_a(r) = \{q \in S \mid q \xrightarrow{a} r\}$. Given $X, Y \subseteq S$, we denote $pre_a(X)$ the set $\bigcup_{s \in X} pre_a(s)$, we write $q \xrightarrow{a} X$ iff $q \in pre_a(X)$, and $Y \xrightarrow{a} X$ iff $Y \cap pre_a(X) \neq \emptyset$.

Simulations. For a tree automaton $A = (Q, \Sigma, \Delta, F)$, a *downward simulation D* is a binary relation on Q such that if $(q, r) \in D$ and $(q_1, \ldots, q_n) \xrightarrow{f} q$, then there are $r_1, \ldots, r_n$ such that $(r_1, \ldots, r_n) \xrightarrow{f} r$ and $(q_i, r_i) \in D$ for each i such that $1 \leq i \leq n$. It is easy to show [4] that any downward simulation can be closed under reflexivity and transitivity. Moreover, there is a unique maximal downward simulation over a given tree automaton, which we denote as $\preceq_{down}$ in the sequel.

Given a TA $A = (Q, \Sigma, \Delta, F)$ and a downward simulation D, an *upward simulation* U induced by D is a binary relation on Q such that if $(q, r) \in U$ and $(q_1, \ldots, q_n) \xrightarrow{f} q'$ with $q_i = q$, $1 \leq i \leq n$, then there are $r_1, \ldots, r_n, r'$ such that $(r_1, \ldots, r_n) \xrightarrow{f} r'$ where $r_i = r$, $(q', r') \in U$, and $(q_j, r_j) \in D$ for each j such that $1 \leq j \neq i \leq n$. In [4], it is shown that any upward simulation can be closed under reflexivity and transitivity. Moreover, there is a unique maximal upward simulation with respect to a fixed downward simulation over a given tree automaton, which we denote as $\preccurlyeq_{up}$ in the sequel.

Given an *initial* pre-order $I \subseteq Q \times Q$, it can be shown that there are unique maximal downward as well as upward simulations included in I on the given TA, which we denote $\preccurlyeq_x^I$ in the sequel, for $x \in \{down, up\}$. Further, we use $\cong_x$ to denote the equivalence relation $\preccurlyeq_x \cap \preccurlyeq_x^{-1}$ on Q for $x \in \{down, up\}$. Likewise, we define the equivalence relations $\cong_x^I$ for an initial pre-order I on Q and $x \in \{down, up\}$.

For an LTS $T = (S, \mathcal{L}, \rightarrow)$, a *(word) simulation* is a binary relation R on S such that if $(q, r) \in R$ and $q \xrightarrow{a} q'$, then there is an r' with $r \xrightarrow{a} r'$ and $(q', r') \in R$. In a very similar way as for simulations on trees, it can be shown that any given simulation on an LTS can be closed under reflexivity and transitivity and that there is a unique maximal simulation on the given LTS, which will we denote by $\preccurlyeq$. Moreover, given an *initial* pre-order $I \subseteq S \times S$, it can be shown that there is a unique maximal simulation included in I on the given LTS, which we denote $\preccurlyeq^I$ in the sequel. We use $\cong$ to denote the equivalence relation $\preccurlyeq \cap \preccurlyeq^{-1}$ on S and consequently $\cong^I$ to denote $\preccurlyeq^I \cap (\preccurlyeq^I)^{-1}$.

Encoding. Let S be a set. A *partition-relation pair* over S is a pair (P, Rel) where (1) $P \subseteq 2^S$ is a partition of S (i.e., $S = \cup_{B \in P} B$, and for all $B, C \in P$, if $B \neq C$, then $B \cap C = \emptyset$), and (2) $Rel \subseteq P \times P$. We say that a partition-relation pair (P, Rel) over S *induces* (or defines) the relation $\delta = \cup_{(B,C) \in Rel} B \times C$.

Let $\preceq$ be a pre-order defined on a set S, and let $\equiv$ be the equivalence $\preceq \cap \preceq^{-1}$ defined by $\preceq$. The pre-order $\preceq$ can be represented—which we will use in our algorithms below—by a partition-relation pair (P, Rel) over S such that $(B, C) \in Rel$ iff $s_1 \preceq s_2$ for all $s_1 \in B$ and $s_2 \in C$. In this representation, if the partition P is as coarse as possible (i.e., such that $s_1, s_2 \in B$ iff $s_1 \equiv s_2$), then, intuitively, the elements of P are blocks of $\equiv$, while Rel reflects the partial order on P corresponding to $\preceq$.

3 Computing Simulations on Labelled Transition Systems

We now introduce an algorithm to compute the (unique) maximal simulation relation $\preccurlyeq^I$ on an *LTS* for a given initial pre-order I on states. Our algorithm is a re-formulation of the algorithm proposed in [14] for computing simulations over *Kripke structures*.

3.1 An Algorithm for Computing Simulations on LTS

For the rest of this section, we assume that we are given an LTS $T = (S, \mathcal{L}, \rightarrow)$ and an initial pre-order $I \subseteq S \times S$. We will use Algorithm 1 to compute the maximum simulation $\preccurlyeq^I \subseteq S \times S$ included in I. In the algorithm, we use the following notation. Given $\rho \subseteq S \times S$ and an element $q \in S$, we denote $\rho(q)$ the set $\{r \in S \mid (q, r) \in \rho\}$.

The algorithm performs a number of iterations computing a sequence of relations, each induced by a partition-relation pair (P, Rel). During each iteration, the states belonging to a block $B' \in P$ are those which are currently assumed as capable of simulating those from any B with $(B, B') \in Rel$. The algorithm starts with an initial partition-relation pair (P_{init}, Rel_{init}) that induces the initial pre-order I on S. The partition-relation pair is then gradually refined by splitting blocks of the partition P and by restricting the relation Rel on P. When the algorithm terminates, the final partition-relation pair (P_{sim}, Rel_{sim}) induces the required pre-order $\preccurlyeq^I$.

The refinement performed during the iterations consists of splitting the blocks in P and then updating the relation Rel accordingly. For this purpose, the algorithm maintains a set $Remove_a(B)$ for each $a \in L$ and $B \in P$. Such a set contains states that do not have an a-transition going into states that are in B nor to states of any block B' with $(B, B') \in Rel$. Clearly, the states in $Remove_a(B)$ cannot simulate states that have an a-transition going into $\bigcup_{(B,B') \in Rel} B'$. Therefore, for any $Remove_a(B) \neq \emptyset$, we can split each block $C \in P$ to $C \cap Remove_a(B)$ and $C \setminus Remove_a(B)$. This is done using the function $Split$ on line 6.

After performing the $Split$ operation, we update the relation Rel and the $Remove$ sets. This is carried out in two steps. First, we compute an approximation of the next values of Rel and $Remove$. More precisely, after a split, all Rel relations between the original "parent" blocks of states are inherited to their "children" resulting from the split (line 8)—the notation $\mathtt{parent}_{P_{prev}}(C)$ refers to the parent block from which C arose within the split. On line 10, the remove sets are then inherited from parent blocks to their children. To perform the second step, we observe that the inheritance of the original relation Rel on parent blocks to the children blocks is not consistent with the split we have just performed. Therefore, on line 14, we subsequently prune Rel such that blocks C that have an a-transition going into B states cannot be considered as simulated by blocks D which do not have an a-transition going into $\bigcup_{(B,B') \in Rel} B'$—notice that due to the split that we have performed, the D blocks are now included in $Remove$. This pruning can then cause a necessity of further refinements as the states that have some b-transition into a D block (that was freshly found not to simulate C), but not to C nor any block that is still viewed as capable of simulating C, have to stop simulating states that can go into $\bigcup_{(C,C') \in Rel} C'$. Therefore, such states are added into $Remove_b(C)$ on line 17.

3.2   Correctness and Complexity of the Algorithm

In the rest of the section, we assume that Algorithm 1 is applied on an LTS $T = (S, L, \rightarrow)$ with an initial partition-relation pair (P_{init}, Rel_{init}). The correctness of the algorithm is formalised in Theorem 1.

Theorem 1. *Suppose that I is the pre-order induced by (P_{init}, Rel_{init}). Then, Algorithm 1 terminates and the final partition-relation pair (P_{sim}, Rel_{sim}) computed by it induces the simulation relation $\preccurlyeq^I$, and, moreover, $P_{sim} = S/\cong^I$.*

A similar correctness result is proved in [14] for the algorithm on Kripke structures, using notions from the theory of abstract interpretation. In [1], we provide an alternative, more direct proof, which is, however, beyond the space limitations of this paper. Therefore, we will only mention the key idea behind the termination argument. In particular, the key point is that if we take any block B from P_{init} and any $a \in L$, if B or any

---

Algorithm 1. Computing simulations on states of an LTS

Input: An LTS $T = (S, L, \rightarrow)$, an initial partition-relation pair (P_{init}, Rel_{init}) on S inducing a pre-order $I \subseteq S \times S$.

Data: A partition-relation pair (P, Rel) on S, and for each $B \in P$ and $a \in L$, a set $Remove_a(B) \subseteq S$.

Output: The partition-relation pair (P_{sim}, Rel_{sim}) inducing the maximal simulation on T contained in I.

```
   /* initialisation */
1  (P,Rel) ← (Pinit,Relinit);
2  forall a ∈ L,B ∈ P do Removea(B) ← S\prea(⋃Rel(B));

   /* computation */
3  while ∃a ∈ L. ∃B ∈ P. Removea(B) ≠ ∅ do
4      Remove ← Removea(B);Removea(B) ← ∅;
5      Pprev ← P;Bprev ← B;Relprev ← Rel;
6      P ← Split(P,Remove);
7      forall C ∈ P do
8          Rel(C) ← {D ∈ P | D ⊆ ⋃Relprev(parentPprev(C))};
9          forall b ∈ L do
10             Removeb(C) ← Removeb(parentPprev(C))
11     forall C ∈ P. C ─a→ Bprev do
12         forall D ∈ P. D ⊆ Remove do
13             if (C,D) ∈ Rel then
14                 Rel ← Rel\{(C,D)};
15                 forall b ∈ L do
16                     forall r ∈ preb(D)\preb(⋃Rel(C)) do
17                         Removeb(C) ← Removeb(C)∪{r}
18 (Psim,Relsim) ← (P,Rel);
```

---

of its children B', which arises by splitting, is repeatedly selected to be processed by the while loop on line 3, then the $Remove_a(B)$ (or $Remove_a(B')$) sets can never contain a single state $s \in S$ at an iteration i of the while loop as well as on a later iteration j, $j > i$. Therefore, as the number of possible partitions as well as the number of states is finite, the algorithm must terminate.

The complexity of the algorithm is equal to that of the original algorithm from [14], up to the new factor L that is not present in [14] (or, equivalently, $|L| = 1$ in [14]). The complexity is stated in Theorem 2.

Theorem 2. *Algorithm 1 has time complexity $O(|L|.|P_{sim}|.|S| + |P_{sim}|.| \rightarrow |)$ and space complexity $O(|L|.|P_{sim}|.|S|)$.*

A proof of Theorem 2, based on a similar reasoning as in [14], can be found in [1]. Here, let us just mention that the result expects the input LTS and the initial partition-relation pair be encoded in suitable data structures. This fact is important for the complexity analyses presented later on as they build on using Algorithm 1.

In particular, the input LTS is represented as a list of records about its states—we call this representation as the *state-list* representation of the LTS. The record about each state $s \in S$ contains a list of nonempty $pre_a(s)$ sets[1], each of them encoded as a list of its members. The partition P_{init} (and later any of its refinements) is encoded as a doubly-linked list (DLL) of blocks. Each block is represented as a DLL of (pointers to) states of the block. The relation Rel_{init} (and later any of its refinements) is encoded as a Boolean matrix $P_{init} \times P_{init}$.

4   Computing Downward Simulation

In this section, we describe algorithms for computing downward simulation on tree automata. Our approach consists of two parts: (1) we translate the maximal downward simulation problem over tree automata into a corresponding maximal simulation problem over LTSs (i.e., basically word automata), and (2) we compute the maximal word simulation on the obtained LTS using Algorithm 1. Below, we describe how the translation is carried out.

We translate the downward simulation problem on a TA $A = (Q, \Sigma, \Delta, F)$ to the simulation problem on a derived LTS $A^\bullet$. Each state and each left hand side of a rule in A is represented by one state in $A^\bullet$, while each rule in A is simulated by a set of rules in $A^\bullet$. Formally, we define $A^\bullet = (Q^\bullet, \Sigma^\bullet, \Delta^\bullet)$ as follows:

- The set $Q^\bullet$ contains a state $q^\bullet$ for each state $q \in Q$, and it also contains a state $(q_1, \ldots, q_n)^\bullet$ for each $(q_1, \ldots, q_n) \in Lhs(A)$.
- The set $\Sigma^\bullet$ contains each symbol $a \in \Sigma$ and each index $i \in \{1, 2, \ldots, n\}$ where n is the maximal rank of any symbol in Σ.
- For each transition rule $(q_1, \ldots, q_n) \xrightarrow{f} q$ of A, the set $\Delta^\bullet$ contains both the transition $q^\bullet \xrightarrow{f} (q_1, \ldots, q_n)^\bullet$ and transitions $(q_1, \ldots, q_n)^\bullet \xrightarrow{i} q_i^\bullet$ for each $i : 1 \leq i \leq n$.
- The sets $Q^\bullet$, $\Sigma^\bullet$, and $\Delta^\bullet$ do not contain any other elements.

The following theorem shows correctness of the translation.

Theorem 3. *For all $q, r \in Q$, we have $q^\bullet \preccurlyeq r^\bullet$ iff $q \preccurlyeq_{down} r$.*

Due to Theorem 3, we can compute the simulation relation $\preccurlyeq_{down}$ on Q by constructing the LTS $A^\bullet$ and running Algorithm 1 on it with the initial partition-relation pair being simply $(P^\bullet, Rel^\bullet) = (\{Q^\bullet\}, \{(Q^\bullet, Q^\bullet)\})^2$.

4.1   Complexity of Computing the Downward Simulation

The complexity naturally consists of the price of compiling a given TA $A = (Q, \Sigma, \Delta, F)$ into its corresponding LTS $A^\bullet$, the price of building the initial partition-relation pair $(P^\bullet, Rel^\bullet)$, and the price of running Algorithm 1 on $A^\bullet$ and $(P^\bullet, Rel^\bullet)$.

We assume the automata not to have unreachable states and to have at most one (final) state that is not used in the left-hand side of any transition rule—general automata

---

[1] We use a list rather than an array having an entry for each $a \in L$ in order to avoid a need to iterate over alphabet symbols for which there is no transition.

[2] We initially consider all states of the LTS $A^\bullet$ equal, and hence they form a single class of $P^\bullet$, which is related to itself in $Rel^\bullet$.

can be easily pre-processed to satisfy this requirement. Further, we assume the input automaton A to be encoded as a list of states $q \in Q$ and a list of the left-hand sides $l = (q_1, ..., q_n) \in Lhs(A)$. Each left-hand side l is encoded by an array of (pointers to) the states $q_1, ..., q_n$, plus a list containing a pointer to the so-called f-list for each $f \in \Sigma$ such that there is an f transition from l in Δ. Each f-list is then a list of (pointers to) all the states $q \in Q$ such that $l \xrightarrow{f} q$. We call this representation the *lhs-list* automata encoding. Then, the complexity of preparing the input for computing the downward simulation on A via Algorithm 1 is given by the following lemma.

Lemma 1. *For a TA $A = (Q, \Sigma, \Delta, F)$, the LTS $A^\bullet$ and the partition-relation pair $(P^\bullet, Rel^\bullet)$ can be derived in time and space $O(Rank(A) \cdot |Q| + |\Delta| + (Rank(A) + |\Sigma|) \cdot |Lhs(A)|)$.*

In order to instantiate the complexity of running Algorithm 1 for $A^\bullet$ and $(P^\bullet, Rel^\bullet)$, we first introduce some auxiliary notions. First, we extend $\preccurlyeq_{down}$ to the set $Lhs(A)$ such that $(q_1, ..., q_n) \preccurlyeq_{down} (r_1, ..., r_n)$ iff $q_i \preccurlyeq_{down} r_i$ for each $i : 1 \le i \le n$. We notice that $P_{sim} = Q^\bullet / \cong$. From an easy generalisation of Theorem 3 to apply not only for states from Q, but also the left-hand sides of transition rules from $Lhs(A)$, i.e., from the fact that $\forall l_1, l_2 \in Lhs(A).l_1 \preccurlyeq_{down} l_2 \Leftrightarrow l_1^\bullet \preccurlyeq l_2^\bullet$, we have that $|Q^\bullet / \cong| = |Q / \cong_{down}| + |Lhs(A) / \cong_{down}|$.

Lemma 2. *Given a tree automaton $A = (Q, \Sigma, \Delta, F)$, Algorithm 1 computes the simulation $\preccurlyeq$ on the LTS $A^\bullet$ for the initial partition-relation pair $(P^\bullet, Rel^\bullet)$ with the time complexity $O((|\Sigma| + Rank(A)) \cdot |Lhs(A)| \cdot |Lhs(A) / \cong_{down}| + |\Delta| \cdot |Lhs(A) / \cong_{down}|)$ and the space complexity $O((|\Sigma| + Rank(A)) \cdot |Lhs(A)| \cdot |Lhs(A) / \cong_{down}|)$.*

The complexity of computing the downward simulation for a tree automaton A via the LTS $A^\bullet$ can now be obtained by simply adding the complexities of computing $A^\bullet$ and $(P^\bullet, Rel^\bullet)$ and of running Algorithm 1 on them.

Theorem 4. *Given a tree automaton A, the downward simulation on A can be computed in time $O((|\Sigma| + Rank(A)) \cdot |Lhs(A)| \cdot |Lhs(A) / \cong_{down}| + |\Delta| \cdot |Lhs(A) / \cong_{down}|)$ and space $O((|\Sigma| + Rank(A)) \cdot |Lhs(A)| \cdot |Lhs(A) / \cong_{down}| + |\Delta|)$.* [3]

Moreover, under the standard assumption that the maximal rank and size of the alphabet are constants, we get the time complexity $O(|\Delta| \cdot |Lhs(A) / \cong_{down}|)$ and the space complexity $O(|Lhs(A)| \cdot |Lhs(A) / \cong_{down}| + |\Delta|)$.

5   Computing Upward Simulation

In a similar manner to the downward simulation, we translate the upward simulation problem on a tree automaton $A = (Q, \Sigma, \Delta, F)$ to the simulation problem on an LTS $A^\odot$. To define the translation from the upward simulation, we first make the following definition. An *environment* is a tuple of the form $((q_1, ..., q_{i-1}, \Box, q_{i+1}, ..., q_n), f, q)$ obtained

---

[3] Note that in the special case of $Rank(A) = 1$ (corresponding to a word automaton viewed as a tree automaton), we have $|Lhs(A)| = |Q|$, which leads to the same complexity as Algorithm 1 has when applied directly on word automata.

by removing a state q_i, $1 \leq i \leq n$, from the ith position of the left hand side of a rule $((q_1, \ldots, q_{i-1}, q_i, q_{i+1}, \ldots, q_n), f, q)$, and by replacing it by a special symbol $\square \notin Q$ (called a *hole* below). Like for transition rules, we write $(q_1, \ldots, \square, \ldots, q_n) \xrightarrow{f} q$ provided $((q_1, \ldots, q_{i-1}, q_i, q_{i+1}, \ldots, q_n), f, q) \in \Delta$ for some $q_i \in Q$. Sometimes, we also write the environment as $(q_1, \ldots, \square_i, \ldots, q_n) \xrightarrow{f} q$ to emphasise that the hole is at position i. We denote the set of all environments of A by $Env(A)$.

The derivation of $A^{\odot}$ differs from $A^{\bullet}$ in two aspects: (1) we encode environments (rather than left-hand sides of rules) as states in $A^{\odot}$, and (2) we use a non-trivial initial partition on the states of $A^{\odot}$, taking into account the downward simulation on Q. Formally, we define $A^{\odot} = (Q^{\odot}, \Sigma^{\odot}, \Delta^{\odot})$ as follows:

- The set $Q^{\odot}$ contains a state $q^{\odot}$ for each state $q \in Q$, and it also contains a state $((q_1, \ldots, \square_i, \ldots, q_n) \xrightarrow{f} q)^{\odot}$ for each environment $(q_1, \ldots, \square_i, \ldots, q_n) \xrightarrow{f} q$.
- The set $\Sigma^{\odot}$ contains each symbol $a \in \Sigma$ and also a special symbol $\lambda \notin \Sigma$.
- For each transition rule $(q_1, \ldots, q_n) \xrightarrow{f} q$ of A, the set $\Delta^{\odot}$ contains both the transitions $q_i^{\odot} \xrightarrow{\lambda} ((q_1, \ldots, \square_i, \ldots, q_n) \xrightarrow{f} q)^{\odot}$ for each $i \in \{1, \ldots, n\}$ and the transition $((q_1, \ldots, \square_i, \ldots, q_n) \xrightarrow{f} q)^{\odot} \xrightarrow{f} q^{\odot}$.
- The sets $Q^{\odot}$, $\Sigma^{\odot}$, and $\Delta^{\odot}$ do not contain any other elements.

We define I to be the smallest binary relation on $Q^{\odot}$ containing all pairs of states of the automaton A, i.e., all pairs $(q_1^{\odot}, q_2^{\odot})$ for each $q_1, q_2 \in Q$, as well as all pairs of environments $(((q_1, \ldots, \square_i, \ldots, q_n) \xrightarrow{f} q)^{\odot}, ((r_1, \ldots, \square_i, \ldots, r_n) \xrightarrow{f} r)^{\odot})$ such that $(q_j, r_j) \in D$ for each $j : 1 \leq j \neq i \leq n$.

The following theorem shows correctness of the translation.

Theorem 5. *For all $q, r \in Q$, we have $q \preccurlyeq_{up} r$ iff $q^{\odot} \preccurlyeq^I r^{\odot}$.*

The relation I is clearly a pre-order and so the relation $\imath = I \cap I^{-1}$ is an equivalence. Due to Theorem 5, we can compute the simulation relation $\preccurlyeq_{up}$ on Q by constructing the LTS $A^{\odot}$ and running Algorithm 1 on it with the initial partition-relation pair $(P^{\odot}, Rel^{\odot})$ inducing I, i.e., $P^{\odot} = Q^{\odot}/\imath$ and $Rel^{\odot} = \{(B, C) \in P^{\odot} \times P^{\odot} \mid B \times C \subseteq I\}$.

5.1 Complexity of Computing the Upward Simulation

Once the downward simulation $\preccurlyeq_{down}$ on a given TA $A = (Q, \Sigma, \Delta, F)$ is computed, the complexity of computing the simulation $\preccurlyeq_{up}$ naturally consists of the price of compiling A into its corresponding LTS $A^{\odot}$, the price of building the initial partition-relation pair $(P^{\odot}, Rel^{\odot})$, and the price of running Algorithm 1 on $A^{\odot}$ and $(P^{\odot}, Rel^{\odot})$.

We assume the automaton A to be encoded in the same way as in the case of computing the downward simulation. Compared to preparing the input for computing the downward simulation, the main obstacle in the case of the upward simulation is the need to compute the partition $P_e^{\odot}$ of the set of environments $Env(A)$ wrt. I, which is a subset of the partition $P^{\odot}$ (formally, $P_e^{\odot} = P^{\odot} \cap 2^{Env(A)}$). If the computation of $P_e^{\odot}$ is done naively (i.e., based on comparing each environment with every other environment), it can introduce a factor of $|Env(A)|^2$ into the overall complexity of the procedure. This would dominate the complexity of computing the simulation on $A^\odot$ where, as we will see, $|Env(A)|$ is only multiplied by $|Env(A)/\cong_{up}|$.

Fortunately, this complexity blowup can be to a large degree avoided by exploiting the partition $Lhs(A)/\cong_{down}$ computed within deriving the downward simulation as shown in detail in [1]. Here, we give just the basic ideas.

For each $1 \leq i \leq Rank(A)$, we define an i-weakened version D_i of the downward simulation on left-hand sides of A such that $((q_1,\ldots,q_n),(r_1,\ldots,r_m)) \in D_i \iff n = m \geq i \wedge (\forall 1 \leq j \leq n. \ j \neq i \implies q_j \preccurlyeq_{down} r_j)$. Clearly, each D_i is a pre-order, and we can define the equivalence relations $\approx_i = D_i \cap D_i^{-1}$. Now, a crucial observation is that there exists a simple correspondence between $P_e^\odot$ and $Lhs(A)/\approx_i$. Namely, we have that $L \in Lhs(A)/\approx_i$ iff for each $f \in \Sigma$, there is a block $E_{L,f} \in P_e^\odot$ such that $E_{L,f} = $

$$\{(q_1,\ldots,\Box_i,\ldots,q_n) \xrightarrow{f} q \mid \exists q_i, q \in Q. \ (q_1,\ldots,q_i,\ldots,q_n) \in L \wedge (q_1,\ldots,q_i,\ldots,q_n) \xrightarrow{f} q\}.$$

The idea of computing $P_e^\odot$ is now to first compute blocks of $Lhs(A)/\approx_i$ and then to derive from them the $P_e^\odot$ blocks. The key advantage here is that the computation of the $\approx_i$-blocks can be done on blocks of $Lhs(A)/\cong_{down}$ instead of directly on elements of $Lhs(A)$. This is because, for each i, blocks of $Lhs(A)/\cong_{down}$ are sub-blocks of blocks of $Lhs(A)/\approx_i$. Moreover, for any blocks K, L of $Lhs(A)/\cong_{down}$, the test of $K \times L \subseteq D_i$ can simply be done by testing whether $(k,l) \in D_i$ for any two representatives $k \in K, l \in L$. Therefore, all $\approx_i$-blocks can be computed in time proportional to $|Lhs(A)/\cong_{down}|^2$.

From each block $L \in Lhs(A)/\approx_i$, one block $E_{L,f}$ of $P_e^\odot$ is generated for each symbol $f \in \Sigma$. The $E_{L,f}$ blocks are obtained in such a way that for each left-hand side $l \in L$, we generate all the environments which arise by replacing the ith state of l by $\Box$, adding f, and adding a right-hand side state $q \in Q$ which together with l form a transition $l \xrightarrow{f} q$ of A. This can be done efficiently using the lhs-list encoding of A. An additional factor $|\Delta| \cdot \log|Env(A)|$ is, however, introduced due to a need of not having duplicates among the computed environments, which could result from transitions that differ just in the states that are replaced by $\Box$ when constructing an environment. The factor $\log|Env(A)|$ comes from testing a set membership over the computed environments to check whether we have already computed them before or not.

Moreover, it can be shown that $Rel^\odot$ can be computed in time $|P^\odot|^2$. The complexity of constructing $A^\odot$ and $(P^\odot, Rel^\odot)$ is then summarised in the below lemma.

Lemma 3. *Given a tree automaton* $A = (Q, \Sigma, \Delta, F)$, *the downward simulation* $\preccurlyeq_{down}$ *on* A, *and the partition* $Lhs(A)/\cong_{down}$, *the LTS* $A^\odot$ *and the partition-relation pair* $(P^\odot, Rel^\odot)$ *can be derived in time* $O(|\Sigma| \cdot |Q| + Rank(A) \cdot (|Lhs(A)| + |Lhs(A)/\cong_{down}|^2) + Rank(A)^2 \cdot |\Delta| \cdot \log|Env(A)| + |P^\odot|^2)$ *and in space* $O(|\Sigma| \cdot |Q| + |Env(A)| + Rank(A) \cdot |Lhs(A)| + |Lhs(A)/\cong_{down}|^2 + |P^\odot|^2)$.

In order to instantiate the complexity of running Algorithm 1 for $A^\odot$ and $(P^\odot, Rel^\odot)$, we again first introduce some auxiliary notions. Namely, we extend $\preccurlyeq_{up}$ to the set $Env(A)$ such that $(q_1,\ldots,\Box_i,\ldots,q_n) \xrightarrow{f} q \preccurlyeq_{up} (r_1,\ldots,\Box_j,\ldots,r_m) \xrightarrow{f} r \iff m = n \wedge i = j \wedge q \preccurlyeq_{up} r \wedge (\forall k \in \{1,\ldots,n\}. \ k \neq i \implies q_k \preccurlyeq_{down} r_k)$. We notice that $P_{sim} = Q^\odot/\cong^I$. From an easy generalisation of Theorem 5 to apply not only for states from Q, but also environments from $Env(A)$, i.e., from the fact that $\forall e_1, e_2 \in Env(A). \ e_1 \preccurlyeq_{up} e_2 \iff e_1^\odot \preccurlyeq^I e_2^\odot$, we have that $|Q^\odot/\cong^I| = |Q/\cong_{up}| + |Lhs(A)/\cong_{up}|$.

Lemma 4. *Given a tree automaton $A = (Q, \Sigma, \Delta, F)$, the upward simulation $\preccurlyeq_{up}$ on A can be computed by running Algorithm 1 on the LTS $A^{\odot}$ and the partition-relation pair $(P^{\odot}, Rel^{\odot})$ in time $O(Rank(A) \cdot |\Delta| \cdot |Env(A)/\cong_{up}| + |\Sigma| \cdot |Env(A)| \cdot |Env(A)/\cong_{up}|)$ and space $O(|\Sigma| \cdot |Env(A)| \cdot |Env(A)/\cong_{up}|)$.*

The complexity of computing upward simulation on a TA A can now be obtained by simply adding the price of computing downward simulation, the price of computing $A^{\odot}$ and $(P^{\odot}, Rel^{\odot})$, and the price of running Algorithm 1 on $A^{\odot}$ and $(P^{\odot}, Rel^{\odot})$.

Theorem 6. *Given a tree automaton $A = (Q, \Sigma, \Delta, F)$, let $T_{down}(A)$ and $S_{down}(A)$ denote the time and space complexity of computing the downward simulation $\preccurlyeq_{down}$ on A. Then, the upward simulation $\preccurlyeq_{up}$ on A can be computed in time*

$$O(((|\Sigma| \cdot |Env(A)| + Rank(A) \cdot |\Delta|) \cdot \|Env(A)/\cong_{up}| + Rank(A)^2 \cdot |\Delta| \cdot \log |Env(A)| + T_{down}(A))$$

and in space $O(|\Sigma| \cdot |Env(A)| \cdot |Env(A)/\cong_{up}| + S_{down}(A))$.[4]

Finally, from the standard assumption that the maximal rank and the alphabet size are constants and from observing that $|Env(A)| \leq Rank(A) \cdot |\Delta| \leq Rank(A) \cdot |\Sigma| \cdot |Q|^{Rank(A)+1}$, we get the time complexity $O(|\Delta| \cdot (|Env(A)/\cong_{up}| + \log |Q|) + T_{down}(A))$ and the space complexity $O(|Env(A)| \cdot |Env(A)/\cong_{up}| + S_{down}(A))$.

6 Reducing Tree Automata

In this section, we describe how to reduce tree automata while preserving the language of the automaton. The idea is to identify suitable equivalence relations on states of tree automata, and then collapse the sets of states which form equivalence classes. We will consider two reduction methods: one which uses downward simulation, and one which is defined in terms of both downward and upward simulation. The choice of the equivalence relation is a trade-off between the amount of reduction achieved and the cost of computing the relation. The second mentioned equivalence is heavier to compute as it requires that both downward and upward simulation are computed and then suitably composed. However, it is at least as coarse as—and often significantly coarser than—the downward simulation equivalence, and hence can give much better reductions as witnessed even in our experiments.

Consider a tree automaton $A = (Q, \Sigma, \Delta, F)$ and an equivalence relation $\equiv$ on Q. The *abstract tree automaton* derived from A and $\equiv$ is $A\langle\equiv\rangle = (Q\langle\equiv\rangle, \Sigma, \Delta\langle\equiv\rangle, F\langle\equiv\rangle)$ where:

- $Q\langle\equiv\rangle$ is the set of blocks in $\equiv$. In other words, we collapse all states which belong to the same block into one abstract state.
- $(B_1, \ldots, B_n) \xrightarrow{f} B$ iff $(q_1, \ldots, q_n) \xrightarrow{f} q$ for some $q_1 \in B_1, \ldots, q_n \in B_n, q \in B$. This is, there is a transition in the abstract automaton iff there is a transition between states in the corresponding blocks.
- $F\langle\equiv\rangle$ contains a block B iff $B \cap F \neq \emptyset$. Intuitively, a block is accepting if it contains at least one state which is accepting.

---

[4] Note that in the special case of $Rank(A) = 1$ (corresponding to a word automaton viewed as a tree automaton), we have $|Env(A)| \leq |\Sigma| \cdot |Q|$, which leads to almost the same complexity (up to the logarithmic component) as Algorithm 1 has when applied directly on word automata.

6.1 Downward Simulation Equivalence

Given a tree automaton $A = (Q, \Sigma, \Delta, F)$, we consider the abstract automaton $A\langle \cong_{down} \rangle$ constructed by collapsing states of A which are equivalent with respect to $\cong_{down}$. We show that the two automata accept the same language, i.e., $L(A) = L(A\langle \cong_{down} \rangle)$. Observe that the inclusion $L(A) \subseteq L(A\langle \cong_{down} \rangle)$ is straightforward. We can prove the inclusion in the other direction as follows. Using a simple induction on trees, one can show that downward simulation implies language inclusion. In other words, for states $q, r \in Q$, if $q \preccurlyeq_{down} r$, then $L(q) \subseteq L(r)$. This implies that for any $B \in Q\langle \cong_{down} \rangle$, it is the case that $L(B) \subseteq L(r)$ for any $r \in B$. Now suppose that $t \in L(A\langle \cong_{down} \rangle)$. It follows that $t \in L(B)$ for some $B \in F\langle \cong_{down} \rangle$. Since $B \in F\langle \cong_{down} \rangle$, there is some $r \in B$ with $r \in F$. It follows that $t \in L(r)$, and hence $t \in L(A)$. This gives the following Theorem.

Theorem 7. $L(A) = L(A\langle \cong_{down} \rangle)$ *for each tree automaton A.*

In fact, $A\langle \cong_{down} \rangle$ is the minimal automaton which is equivalent to A with respect to downward simulation and which accepts the same language as A.

6.2 Composed Equivalence

Consider a tree automaton $A = (Q, \Sigma, \Delta, F)$. Let I_F be a partitioning of Q such that $(q, r) \in I_F$ iff $q \in F \implies r \in F$. Consider a reflexive and transitive downward simulation D, and a reflexive and transitive upward simulation U induced by D. Assume that $U \subseteq I_F$. We will reduce A with respect to relations of the form $\equiv_R$ which preserve language equivalence, but which may be much coarser than downward simulations. Here, each $\equiv_R$ is an equivalence relation $R \cap R^{-1}$ defined by a pre-order R satisfying certain properties. More precisely, we use $D \oplus U$ to denote the set of relations on Q such that for each $R \in (D \oplus U)$, the relation R satisfies the following two properties: (i) R is transitive and (ii) $D \subseteq R \subseteq (D \circ U^{-1})$. For a state $r \in Q$ and a set $B \subseteq Q$ of states, we write $(B, r) \in D$ to denote that there is a $q \in B$ with $(q, r) \in D$. We define $(B, r) \in U$ analogously. We will now consider the abstract automaton $A\langle \equiv_R \rangle$ where the states of A are collapsed according to $\equiv_R$. We will relate the languages of A and $A\langle \equiv_R \rangle$.

To do that, we first define the notion of a *context*. Intuitively, a context is a tree with "holes" instead of leaves. Formally, we consider a special symbol $\bigcirc \notin \Sigma$ with rank 0. A *context* over Σ is a tree c over $\Sigma \cup \{\bigcirc\}$ such that for all leaves $p \in c$, we have $c(p) = \bigcirc$. For a context c with leaves $p_1, \ldots, p_n$, and trees $t_1, \ldots, t_n$, we define $c[t_1, \ldots, t_n]$ to be the tree t, where

- $dom(t) = dom(c) \bigcup \{p_1 \cdot p' \mid p' \in dom(t_i)\} \bigcup \cdots \bigcup \{p_n \cdot p' \mid p' \in dom(t_n)\}$,
- for each $p = p_i \cdot p'$, we have $t(p) = t_i(p')$, and
- for each $p \in dom(c) \setminus \{p_1, \ldots, p_n\}$, we have $t(p) = c(p)$.

In other words, $c[t_1, \ldots, t_n]$ is the result of appending the trees $t_1, \ldots, t_k$ to the holes of c. We extend the notion of runs to contexts. Let c be a context with leaves $p_1, \ldots, p_n$. A *run* π of A on c from $(q_1, \ldots, q_n)$ is defined in a similar manner to a run on a tree except that for a leaf p_i, we have $\pi(p_i) = q_i$, $1 \le i \le n$. In other words, each leaf labelled with $\bigcirc$ is annotated by one q_i. We use $c[q_1, \ldots, q_n] \xRightarrow{\pi} q$ to denote that π is a run of A on c from $(q_1, \ldots, q_n)$ such that $\pi(\varepsilon) = q$. The notation $c[q_1, \ldots, q_n] \implies q$ is explained in a similar manner to runs on trees.

Using the notion of a context, we can relate runs of A with those of the abstract automaton $A\langle\equiv_R\rangle$. More precisely, we can show that for blocks $B_1,\ldots,B_n,B \in Q\langle\equiv_R\rangle$ and a context c, if $c[B_1,\ldots,B_n] \Longrightarrow B$, then there exist states $r_1,\ldots,r_n,r \in Q$ such that $(B_1,r_1) \in D,\ldots,(B_n,r_n) \in D, (B,r) \in U$, and $c[r_1,\ldots,r_n] \Longrightarrow r$. In other words, each run in $A\langle\equiv_R\rangle$ can be simulated by a run in A which starts from larger states (with respect to downward simulation) and which ends up at a larger state (with respect to upward simulation). This leads to the following lemma.

Lemma 5. *If $t \Longrightarrow B$, then $t \Longrightarrow w$ for some w with $(B,w) \in U$. Moreover, if $B \in F\langle\equiv_R\rangle$, then also $w \in F$.*

In other words, each tree t which leads to a block B in $A\langle\equiv_R\rangle$ will also lead to a state in A which is larger than (some state in) the block B with respect to upward simulation. Moreover, if t can be accepted at B in $A\langle\equiv_R\rangle$ (meaning that B contains a final state of A, i.e., $B \cap F \neq \emptyset$), then it can be accepted at w in A (i.e., $w \in F$) too.

Notice that Lemma 5 holds for any downward and upward simulations satisfying the properties mentioned in the definition of $\oplus$. We now instantiate the lemma for the maximal downward and upward simulation to obtain the main result. We take D and U to be $\preccurlyeq_{down}$ and $\preccurlyeq_{up}^{I_F}$, respectively, and we let $\preccurlyeq_{comp}$ be any relation from the set of relations $(\preccurlyeq_{down} \oplus \preccurlyeq_{up}^{I_F})$. We let $\cong_{comp}$ be the corresponding equivalence.

Theorem 8. $L(A\langle\cong_{comp}\rangle) = L(A)$ *for each tree automaton A.*

Proof. The inclusion $L(A\langle\cong_{comp}\rangle) \supseteq L(A)$ is trivial. Let $t \in L(A\langle\cong_{comp}\rangle)$, i.e., $t \Longrightarrow B$ for some block B where $B \cap F \neq \emptyset$. Lemma 5 implies that $t \Longrightarrow w$ such that $w \in F$. $\square$

Note that it is clearly the case that $\cong_{down} \subseteq \cong_{comp}$. Moreover, note that a relation $\preccurlyeq_{comp} \in (\preccurlyeq_{down} \oplus \preccurlyeq_{up}^{I_F})$ can be obtained, e.g., by a simple (random) pruning of the relation $\preccurlyeq_{down} \circ (\preccurlyeq_{up}^{I_F})^{-1}$ based on iteratively removing links not being in $\preccurlyeq_{down}$ and at the same time breaking transitivity of the so-far computed composed relation. Such a way of computing $\preccurlyeq_{comp}$ does not guarantee that one obtains a relation of the greatest cardinality possible among relations from $\preccurlyeq_{down} \oplus \preccurlyeq_{up}^{I_F}$, but, on the other hand, it is cheap (in the worst case, cubic in the number of states). Moreover, our experiments show that even this simple way of computing the composed relation can give us a relation $\cong_{comp}$ that is much coarser (and yields significantly better reductions) than $\cong_{down}$.

Remark. Our definition of a context coincides with the one of [8] where all leaves are holes. On the other hand, a context in [9] and [3] is a tree with a *single* hole. Considering single-hole contexts, one can define the *language of contexts* $L_c(q)$ of a state q to be the set of contexts on which there is an accepting run if the hole is replaced by q. Then, for all states q and r, it is the case that $q \preccurlyeq_{up} r$ implies $L_c(q) \subseteq L_c(r)$.

7 Experiments with Reducing Tree Automata

We have implemented our algorithms in a prototype tool written in Java. We have run the prototype on a number of tree automata that arise in the framework of *tree regular model checking*. Tree regular model checking is the name of a family of techniques for analysing infinite-state systems in which states are represented by trees, (infinite) sets of states by

Table 1. Reduction of the number of states and rules using different reduction algorithms

Protocol	original		$\cong_{down}$		$\cong_{comp}$		backward bisimulation	
	states	rules	states	rules	states	rules	states	rules
percolate	10	72	7	45	7	45	10	72
	20	578	17	392	14	346	20	578
	28	862	13	272	13	272	15	341
arbiter	15	324	10	248	7	188	11	252
	41	313	28	273	19	220	33	285
	109	1248	67	1048	55	950	83	1116
leader	17	153	11	115	6	47	16	152
	25	384	16	235	6	59	23	382
	33	876	10	100	7	67	27	754

finite tree automata, and transitions by tree transducers. Most of the algorithms in the framework rely crucially on efficient automata reduction methods since the size of the generated automata often explodes, making computations infeasible without reduction. The (nondeterministic) tree automata that we have considered arose during verification of the *Percolate* protocol, the *Arbiter* protocol, and the *Leader* election protocol [4].

Our experimental evaluation was carried out on an AMD Athlon 64 X2 2.19GHz PC with 2.0 GB RAM. The time for minimising the tree automata varied from a few seconds up to few minutes. Table 1 shows the number of states and rules of the various considered tree automata before and after computing $\cong_{down}$, $\cong_{comp}$, and the backward bisimulation from [11]. Backward bisimulation is the bisimulation counterpart of downward simulation. The composed simulation equivalence $\cong_{comp}$ was computed in the simple way based on the random pruning of the relation $\preccurlyeq_{down} \circ (\preccurlyeq_{up}^{I_F})^{-1}$ as mentioned at the end of Section 6.2. As Table 1 shows, $\cong_{comp}$ achieves the best reduction (often reducing to less than one-third of the size of the original automaton). As expected, both $\cong_{down}$ and $\cong_{comp}$ give better reductions than backward bisimulation in all test cases.

8   Conclusions and Future Work

We have presented methods for reducing tree automata under language equivalence. For this purpose, we have considered two kinds of simulation relations on the states of tree automata, namely downward and upward simulation. We give procedures for efficient translation of both kinds of relations into simulations defined on labelled transition systems. Furthermore, we define a new, language-preserving equivalence on tree automata, derived from compositions of downward and upward simulation, which (according to our experiments) usually gives a much better reduction on the size of automata than downward simulation.

There are several interesting directions for future work. First, we would like to implement the proposed algorithms in a more efficient way, perhaps over automata encoded in a symbolic way using BDDs like in MONA [12], in order to be able to experiment with bigger automata. Further, for instance, we can define *upward* and *downward bisimulation* for tree automata in an analogous way to the case of simulation. It is straightforward to show that the encoding we use in this paper can also be used to translate bisimulation problems on tree automata into corresponding ones for LTSs. Although reducing according to a bisimulation does not give the same reduction as for a simulation, it is relevant since it generates more efficient algorithms. Also, we plan to investigate coarser relations for better reductions of tree automata by refining the ideas behind the definition of the composed relation introduced in Section 6. We believe that it is possible to define a refinement scheme allowing one to define an increasing family of such relations between downward simulation equivalence and tree language equivalence. Finally, we plan to consider extending our reduction techniques to the class of unranked trees which are used in applications such as reasoning about structured documents or about configurations of dynamic concurrent processes.

Acknowledgement. The work was supported by the ANR-06-SETI-001 French project AVERISS, the Czech Grant Agency (projects 102/07/0322 and 102/05/H050), the Czech-French Barrande project 2-06-27, and the Czech Ministry of Education by the project MSM 0021630528 *Security-Oriented Research in Information Technology.*

References

1. Abdulla, P., Bouajjani, A., Holík, L., Kaati, L., Vojnar, T.: Computing Simulations over Tree Automata. Technical report, FIT-TR-2007-001, FIT, Brno University of Technology, Czech Republic (2007)
2. Abdulla, P., Högberg, J., Kaati, L.: Bisimulation Minimization of Tree Automata. In: H. Ibarra, O., Yen, H.-C. (eds.) CIAA 2006. LNCS, vol. 4094, Springer, Heidelberg (2006)
3. Abdulla, P., Jonsson, B., Mahata, P., d'Orso, J.: Regular Tree Model Checking. In: Brinksma, E., Larsen, K.G. (eds.) CAV 2002. LNCS, vol. 2404, Springer, Heidelberg (2002)
4. Abdulla, P., Legay, A., d'Orso, J., Rezine, A.: Tree Regular Model Checking: A Simulation-based Approach. The Journal of Logic and Algebraic Programming 69(1-2), 93–121 (2006)
5. Bouajjani, A., Habermehl, P., Rogalewicz, A., Vojnar, T.: Abstract Regular Tree Model Checking. In: ENTCS, vol. 149(1), pp. 37–48. Elsevier, Amsterdam (2006)
6. Bouajjani, A., Habermehl, P., Rogalewicz, A., Vojnar, T.: Abstract Regular Tree Model Checking of Complex Dynamic Data Structures. In: Yi, K. (ed.) SAS 2006. LNCS, vol. 4134, Springer, Heidelberg (2006)
7. Bouajjani, A., Touili, T.: Extrapolating Tree Transformations. In: Brinksma, E., Larsen, K.G. (eds.) CAV 2002. LNCS, vol. 2404, Springer, Heidelberg (2002)
8. Bouajjani, A., Touili, T.: Reachability Analysis of Process Rewrite Systems. In: Pandya, P.K., Radhakrishnan, J. (eds.) FSTTCS 2003. LNCS, vol. 2914, Springer, Heidelberg (2003)
9. Comon, H., Dauchet, M., Gilleron, R., Jacquemard, F., Lugiez, D., Tison, S., Tommasi, M.: Tree Automata Techniques and Applications (1997), Available on: http://www.grappa.univ-lille3.fr/tata
10. Henzinger, M., Henzinger, T., Kopke, P.: Computing simulations on finite and infinite graphs. In: Proc. of FOCS 1995, IEEE, Los Alamitos (1995)
11. Maletti, A., Högberg, J., May, J.: Backward and forward bisimulation minimisation of tree automata. In: Holub, J., Žd'árek, J. (eds.) CIAA 2007. LNCS, vol. 4783, pp. 109–121. Springer, Heidelberg (2007)
12. Klarlund, N., Møller, A.: MONA Version 1.4 User Manual, BRICS, Department of Computer Science, University of Aarhus, Denmark (2001)
13. Paige, R., Tarjan, R.: Three Partition Refinement Algorithms. SIAM Journal on Computing 16, 973–989 (1987)
14. Ranzato, F., Tapparo, F.: A New Efficient Simulation Equivalence Algorithm. In: Proc. of LICS 2007, IEEE CS, Los Alamitos (2007)

Formal Pervasive Verification of a Paging Mechanism

Eyad Alkassar*, Norbert Schirmer **, and Artem Starostin ***

Computer Science Department - Saarland University
{eyad,nschirmer,starostin}@wjpserver.cs.uni-sb.de

Abstract. Memory virtualization by means of demand paging is a crucial component of every modern operating system. The formal verification is challenging since reasoning about the page fault handler has to cover two concurrent computational sources: the processor and the hard disk. We accurately model the interleaved executions of devices and the page fault handler, which is written in a high-level programming language with inline assembler portions. We describe how to combine results from sequential Hoare logic style reasoning about the page fault handler on the low-level concurrent machine model. To the best of our knowledge this is the first example of pervasive formal verification of software communicating with devices.

1 Introduction

With a comparably small code base of only some thousand lines of code, and implementing important safety and security abstractions as process isolation, microkernels seem to offer themselves as perfect candidates for a feasible approach to formal verification. The most challenging part in microkernel verification is memory virtualization, i.e., to ensure that each user process has the notion of an own, large and isolated memory. User processes access memory by virtual addresses, which are then translated to physical ones. Modern computer systems implement virtual memory by means of paging: small consecutive chunks of data, called pages, are either stored in a fast but small physical memory or in a large but slower auxiliary memory (usually a hard disk), called swap memory. The page table, a data structure both accessed by the processor and by software, maintains whether a page is in the swap or the physical memory. Whenever the process accesses a page located in the swap memory, either by a store/load instruction or by an instruction fetch, the processor signals a page fault interrupt. On the hardware side, the memory management unit (MMU) triggers the interrupt and translates from virtual to physical page addresses. On the software side, the *page fault handler* reacts to a page fault interrupt by moving the requested page to the physical memory. In case the physical memory is full, some other page is swapped out (cf. Fig. 1).

The aim of the Verisoft project[1] is a pervasive formal correctness result. The grand challenge is to integrate various levels of abstraction and computational models. The

---

* Work was supported by the German Research Foundation (DFG) within the program 'Performance Guarantees for Computer Systems'.
** Work was supported by the German Federal Ministry of Education and Research (BMBF) in the framework of the Verisoft project.
*** Work was supported by the International Max Planck Research School for Computer Science.
[1] http://www.verisoft.de

C.R. Ramakrishnan and J. Rehof (Eds.): TACAS 2008, LNCS 4963, pp. 109–123, 2008.
© Springer-Verlag Berlin Heidelberg 2008

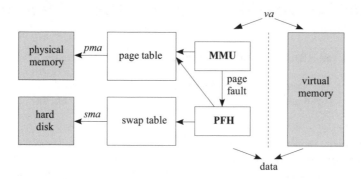

Fig. 1. Concept of paging

physical machine on the lower end, which comprises the concurrent computation of at least the processor and the devices, in the middle, portions of assembler code to implement the device drivers, and on the upper end a high-level sequential programming language, in our case C0, a subset of C. The decisive contribution of this paper is the integration of devices into a pervasive system verification methodology. This comprises dealing with interleaved I/O devices and integration of inline assembler code even in the high-level Hoare logics. All computational models and abstraction layers and almost all proofs are mechanized in the theorem prover Isabelle/HOL, which gives us the highest possible assurance that all parts fit together. At submission of the paper not finished proofs include the read case of the driver.

Related Work. Hillebrand [7] presents paper and pencil formalisations and proofs for memory virtualisation. First attempts to use theorem provers to specify and even prove correct operating systems were made as early as the seventies in PSOS [11] and UCLA Secure Unix [16]. However a missing or to a large extend underdeveloped tool environment made mechanized verification futile. With the CLI stack [2], a new pioneering approach for pervasive system verification was undertaken.

Most notably the simple kernel KIT was developed and its machine code implementation was proven. Compared to modern kernels KIT was very limited, in particular it lacked the interaction with devices. The project L4.verified [6] focuses on the verification of an efficient microkernel, rather than on formal pervasiveness, as no compiler correctness or an accurate device interaction is considered. The microkernel is implemented in a larger subset of C, including pointer arithmetic and an explicit low-level memory model [15]. However with inline assembler code we gain an even more expressive semantics as machine registers become visible if necessary. So far only exemplary portions of kernel code were reported to be verified, the virtual memory subsystem uses no demand paging [14]. For code verification L4.verified relies on Verisoft's Hoare environment [13]. In the FLINT project, an assembly code verification framework is developed and code for context switching on a x86 architecture is formally proven [12]. Although a verification logic for assembler code is presented, no integration of results into high-level programming languages is undertaken. The VFiasco project [9] aims at the verification of the microkernel Fiasco implemented in a subset of C++. Code verification is performed in a embedding of C++ in PVS and there is no attempt to map the results down to the machine level.

Overview. Sect. 2 elaborates on the virtualization problem, gives an overview of our general approach and states the required page fault handler correctness property. In Sect. 3 a page fault handler implementation, specification and its code verification is presented. In Sect. 4 we integrate the code verification into the Verisoft system stack to obtain the desired correctness result. Finally we conclude in Sect. 5.

2   Virtual Memory Simulation Problem

One of the most challenging verification objectives of Verisoft is to prove that the physical machine correctly implements memory virtualization towards user processes: the physical memory and the swap space of the hard disk are organized by the page fault handler to provide separate uniform linear memories towards user processes. This is expressed as a simulation theorem between a physical machine and a virtual machine model and is described in this section. The other sections are concerned with its proof.

Most crucially the correctness of the simulation theorem depends on the correctness of the page fault handler. This proof ties together various key results of the Verisoft system stack. Besides the physical machine this also includes semantics for C0 and a Hoare logic. The physical machine model is quite fine grained and executes instructions and devices concurrently, whereas the page fault handler is basically a high-level sequential C0 program. We avoid conducting the whole proof on the low-level of the physical machine, by proving the page fault handler correct in a Hoare logic for C0. The soundness theorem of the Hoare logic [13] composed with the correctness theorem of the C0 compiler [10] allows to transfer the page fault handler correctness down to the physical machine. However, we have to consider one peculiarity of the page fault handler (and low-level systems code in general): there are small portions of inline assembler code that break the high-level C0 semantics. In case of the page fault handler this is the device driver code for communication with the hard disk. We encapsulate these pieces of inline assembler code into so called 'XCall's. On the level of the Hoare logic these are represented as atomic state updates (cf. Sect. 3.1) on an extended state that comprises both the C0 memory and the current configuration of the hard drive. We prove that the assembler implementation of the XCall adheres to this abstraction (cf. Sect. 4.2).

Another major step is to bridge the gap from the sequential C0 model to the concurrent execution of the processor and the devices on the physical machine. This is achieved by means of a reordering theorem (cf. Sect. 4.2). The memory virtualization theorem is a property that has to hold for all possible interleavings. The reordering theorem allows us to focus only on those execution traces where the relevant actions of the device driver and the device happen consecutively.

2.1   Basic Definitions

We denote the set of boolean values by $\mathbb{B}$ and set of natural numbers including zero by $\mathbb{N}$. For any natural x we denote the set of natural numbers less then x by $\mathbb{N}_x$. We denote the unbounded abstract list with elements of type T by T^* and the list of length n by T^n. The length of a list x is denoted by $|x|$, its element access by $x[i]$, and the tail, e.g., the part of the list without the first element, by $tl(x)$. The operator $\langle x \rangle$ yields for a bit string $x \in \mathbb{B}^*$ the natural number represented by x. The fragment of a bit list from a position a to b is denoted by $x[b : a]$. For a record x the set of all its possible configurations is defined by C_x. A memory m is modeled as a mapping from addresses a to byte values $m[a]$. An access to d consecutive memory cells starting at address a is abbreviated as $m_d[a] = m[a+d-1], \ldots, m[a]$.

We deal with an abstract model of computation, where N user processes are virtual machines that run on a single physical machine. The memories of machines are logically organized in pages of size $P = 4K$ bytes. For a virtual address $va \in \mathbb{B}^{32}$ we define by $px(va) = va[31 : 12]$ and $bx(va) = va[11 : 0]$ its page and byte indexes, respectively. Represented as natural number we get $px(va) = va/P$ and $bx(va) = va \mod P$.

2.2 Physical Machine Specification

The physical machine is the sequential programming model of the VAMP hardware [3] as seen by a system software programmer. It is parameterized by (i) the set $SAP \subseteq \mathbb{B}^5$ of special purpose register addresses visible to physical machines, and (ii) the number TPP of total physical memory pages which defines the set $PMA = \{a \mid 0 \leq \langle a \rangle < TPP \cdot P\} \subseteq \mathbb{B}^{32}$ of accessible physical memory addresses. The machines are records $pm = (pc, dpc, gpr, spr, m)$ with the following components: (i) the normal $pm.pc \in \mathbb{B}^{32}$ and the delayed $pm.dpc \in \mathbb{B}^{32}$ program counters used to implement the delayed branch mechanism, (ii) the general purpose register file $pm.gpr \in \mathbb{B}^5 \mapsto \mathbb{B}^{32}$, and the special purpose register file $pm.spr \in SAP \mapsto \mathbb{B}^{32}$, and (iii) the byte addressable physical memory $pm.m \in PMA \mapsto \mathbb{B}^8$. We demand SAP to contain the following addresses: (i) *mode*, for the mode register, and (ii) *pto* and *ptl*, for the page table origin resp. length registers whose values are measured in pages. For any address $a \in SAP$ we will abbreviate $pm.spr[a] = pm.a$. A physical machine is running in *system mode* if $pm.mode = 0^{32}$ and in *user mode* if $pm.mode = 0^{31}1$.

Address Translation and Page Faults. In user mode a memory access to a virtual address va is subject to address translation. It either redirects to the translated physical memory address $pma(pm, va)$ or generates a page fault.

The physical memory address is computed as follows. We interpret the memory region $pm.m_{pm.ptl \cdot P}[pm.pto \cdot P]$ as the current page table. Let $ptea(pm, va) = pm.pto \cdot P + 4 \cdot px(va)$ be the page table entry address for virtual address va and $pte(pm, va) = pm.m_4[ptea(pm, va)]$ be its page table entry. The page table entry is composed of three components, the physical page index $ppx(pm, va) = pte(pm, va)[31 : 12]$, the valid bit $v(pm, va) = pte(pm, va)[11]$, and the protected bit $p(pm, va) = pte(pm, va)[10]$. Concatenation of the physical page index and the byte index yields the physical memory address $pma(pm, va) = ppx(pm, va) \circ bx(va)$.

In order to define page faults, let $w \in \mathbb{B}$ be active on write operations. The page fault $pf(pm, va, w)$ is raised if (i) the valid bit $v(pm, va)$ is not set, or (ii) the write flag w and the protected bit $p(pm, va)$ are active.

Semantics. The semantics of a physical machine is formally given by the transition function $\delta_{pm}(pm) = pm'$ yielding the next state configuration. If no page fault occurs the effects of a transition are defined by the underlying instruction set architecture (ISA). In case $pf(pm, va, w)$ the program counters are set to the start address of the page fault handler. We switch to system mode and the execution of the handler is triggered. After its termination the mode is changed back and the user computation resumes.

2.3 Devices

From the viewpoint of the operating system the hard disk is a device . Before describing the hard disk model, we sketch our general framework for memory-mapped devices (we do not consider DMA here). A device x is a finite transition system which communicates with (i) an unspecified external environment, and (ii) the processor. Examples for input and output from and to the environment are incoming key press events and outgoing network packages. We denote inputs from the environment with $eifi_x$ and outputs with $eifo_x$. The processor reads and writes from and to a device by load- and store-word operations to specific address regions. Both operations are signaled by an output function ω of the processor: $\omega(pm) = mifi$. In case of a read operation, the device returns requested data in form of an output called $mifo$. The transition of a device of type C_x is then given by: $\delta_{devs}(x, eifi_x, mifi) = (x', mifo, eifo_x)$.

For all modeled device types DT and a set of device identifiers DI, the configuration $pmd = (pm, devs : DI \rightarrow DT)$ describes the state of the processor and of all devices. The processor and devices are executed in an interleaved way. An oracle, called *execution sequence* (seq) determines for a given step number i whether the processor, i.e., $seq(i) = Proc$ or some device d makes a step, in which case the sequence also provides the input from the environment: $seq(i) = (d, eifi_{xd})$. The function δ_{pmd} describes the execution of the overall system. It takes as input the combined state of the processor and of all devices, a step number and an execution sequence. A detailed description of the device framework can be found in [1]. Next we instantiate one device with the hard disk.

Hard Disk Description. We model a hard disk based on the ATA/ATAPI protocol. Hard disks are parameterized over the number of sectors S. Each sector has a size of 128 words. We assume that the hard disk is large enough to store the total virtual page space of all user processes. The processor can issue read or write commands to a range of sectors, by writing the start address and the count of sectors to a special port. Each sector is then read/written word by word from/to a sector buffer. After a complete sector is written or read to the sector buffer, the hard disk needs some time to transfer data to the sector memory. This amount of time is modeled as non-determinism by an oracle input from the external environment, indicating the end of the transfer. In this case the input $eifi_{hd}$ is set to one. The hard disk can be run either in interrupt or polling mode. We chose the second type.

In the following we only need the sector memory of the hard disk. Its domain ranges over $S \cdot 128$ words: $hd = (sm : \mathbb{N}_{S \cdot 128} \mapsto \mathbb{N}_{256}, \dots)$. A hard disk is necessarily an item of the device system $pmd.devs$. We abbreviate an access to the hard disk of a physical machine with devices as $pmd.hd$. A detailed description of the hard disk, its transitions and a simple driver can be found in [8].

2.4   Virtual Machine Specification

Virtual machines are the hardware model visible for user processes. They give an user the illusion of an address space exceeding the physical memory. No address translation is required, hence page faults are invisible. The virtual machine's parameters are: (i) the number TVP of total virtual memory pages which defines the set of virtual memory addresses $VMA = \{a \mid 0 \le \langle a \rangle < TVP \cdot P\} \subseteq \mathbb{B}^{32}$, and (ii) the set $SAV \subseteq SAP \setminus \{mode, pto, ptl\}$ of special purpose register addresses visible to virtual machines. Their configuration, formally, is a record $vm = (pc, dpc, gpr, spr, m)$ where only the $vm.spr \in SAV \mapsto \mathbb{B}^{32}$ and $vm.m \in VMA \mapsto \mathbb{B}^8$ differ from the physical machines. The semantics is completely specified by the ISA.

2.5   Simulation Relation

A physical machine maintaining a page fault handler with a hard disk can simulate virtual machines. The simulation relation, called the $\mathscr{B}$-relation, specifies a (pseudo-) parallel computation of N user processes $up \in C_{vm}^N$ modeled as virtual machines on one system pmd composed out of a physical machine, a hard disk, and other devices. The computation proceeds as follows.

The physical machine maintains a variable cp designating which of the user processes is meant to make a step. Unless a page fault occurs, the process $up[cp]$ is updated according to the semantics of virtual machines. Otherwise, the physical machine invokes the page fault handler. After its execution, the user process continues the computation. An appropriate page fault handler obeys the following rules: (i) it maintains the list of N *process control blocks (PCB)* (described below), which permanently reside in the memory of the physical machine, (ii) it is able to access page tables of processes which lie consecutively in the physical memory, (iii) it has a data structure, called the *swap table* which maps virtual addresses to swap page indexes. A swap memory address $sma(pm, a)$ is computed via an access to such a table.

Process control blocks implement the user processes. They contain fields for storing the content of gpr and spr register files of all processes. When a user process currently being run on the physical machine is interrupted by a page fault, the content of the registers is copied into the PCBs *before* the execution of the page fault handler. Accordingly, after the handler terminates the interrupted user process is restored by copying the content of appropriate PCB fields back to the registers of the physical machine.

Now we define the $\mathscr{B}$-relation. First, we must reconstruct virtual machines from the contexts stored in PCBs. The function $virt(pid, pmd) = vm$ yields the virtual machine for process pid by taking the register values from the corresponding PCB fields. The memory component of the built virtual machine is constructed out of physical memory and the data on the hard disk depending where a certain memory page lies:

$$vm.m[a] = \begin{cases} pmd.pm.m[pma(pm, a)] & \text{if } v(pm, a) \\ pmd.hd.sm[sma(pm, a)] & \text{otherwise} \end{cases}.$$

Then, the $\mathscr{B}$-relation is: $\mathscr{B}(pmd, up) = \forall pid \in \mathbb{N}_N : virt(pid, pmd) = up[pid]$.

There is a small number of additional correctness relations omitted due to the lack of space. The reader should refer to [5] for them.

Proving the correctness of memory virtualization is a one-to-n-step simulation between the virtual and the physical machine. One has to show that each step of a virtual machine, can be simulated by n steps of the physical machine, while the $\mathscr{B}$-relation is preserved. The only interesting case in the proof is the occurrence of a page fault during the execution of a load or store instruction. In all other cases, the semantics of the virtual and the physical machines almost coincide. In the following we describe the crucial part of the proof: the page fault handler execution leads to a non-page faulting configuration maintaining the $\mathscr{B}$-relation.

3   Page Fault Handler Implementation and Code Verification

3.1   Extended Hoare Logic

Our page fault handler is implemented in a high-level programming language with small portions of inline assembler code for communication with the hard disk and to access portions of memory that are not mapped to program variables (e.g., memory of user processes). As programming language we use C0, which has been developed for and is extensively used within the Verisoft project. In short C0 is Pascal with C syntax, i.e., its type-system is sound and it supports references but no pointer-arithmetic. Syntax and semantics of C0 are fully formalized in Isabelle/HOL. Moreover, a compiler is implemented and formally verified [10].

We use Hoare logic as an effective means of C0 program verification. Unfortunately the inline assembler portions, that make hardware details visible towards the programming language, break the abstractions C0 provides. We deal with the low-level inline assembler parts, without breaking the Hoare logic abstraction for C0, by encapsulated them into an atomic step on an extended state, a so called *XCall*. The extended state can only be modified via a XCall.

We apply an instance of Schirmer's Hoare logic environment [13] implemented in Isabelle/HOL. He defines a set of Hoare rules, for a generic programming language *Simpl*, and formally proves the soundness of this logic. Hoare rules describe a triple $\{P\}S\{Q\}$, where precondition P defines the set of valid initial states of the C0 variables, S is the statement to execute and postcondition Q is guaranteed to hold for the states after execution of S. We prove total correctness and hence termination is guaranteed.

Additionally to the embedding of C0 into Simpl, we introduce some special treatment for XCalls and refer to the resulting system as *extended Hoare logic*. First we have to deal with the extended state space, i.e., the physical memory and the swap. In Simpl we treat them analogous to C0 variables, with the only difference that they are not restricted to C0 types. It is not necessary to introduce a new Hoare rule into Simpl to handle XCalls. Instead we can use the '*Basic*' construct of Simpl, a general assignment which can deal with an arbitrary state update function f: $\{f(s) \in Q\}$ *Basic f* $\{Q\}$. On the level of Simpl every XCall is modelled as such a state update, representing the abstract semantics of the XCall.

The specification of the page fault handler and its operations, and data types in general, are not directly formulated on the level of the extended C0 state. Instead the C0 state is lifted to a more abstract model. For example a linked pointer structure may be mapped to a HOL list. An abstraction relation *abs* relates the model *a* and the extended C0 state *xc*. The pre- and postconditions of Hoare triples then typically express that the abstraction relation is preserved by the abstract operation and the corresponding C0 implementation. When the operation on the abstract model transfers *a* to *a'* then the extended C0 state has to make the analogous transition. Hence we prove simulation of the abstraction and the C0 program by the following specification scheme: $\{abs(a,xc)\}S\{abs(a',xc')\}$.

In Sect. 3.2 we describe the C0 implementation of the page fault handler using XCalls. Then we continue in Sect. 3.3 with the specification of the page fault handler by an abstract model. The aforementioned Hoare logic verification ensures the simulation of the implementation and the abstract model.

3.2   Implementation

Our page fault handler implementation [4] maintains several global data structures to manage the physical and the swap memories. These data structures permanently reside in the memory of a physical machine. They are used to support mechanisms of virtual memory de- and allocation, and the page replacement strategy. The necessary data structures comprise: (i) the process control blocks, (ii) the page and swap tables, and (iii) *active* and *free* lists managing allocated and free user memory pages, respectively.

On the software level we distinguish the following page faults: (i) an *invalid access* occurring when a desired page is not present in the physical memory, and (ii) the *zero protection* page fault which signals a write access to a newly allocated page.

On the reset signal a page fault handler initialization code is executed. It brings the data structures to a state where all the user physical pages are free, and page resp. swap tables are filled with zeros. The page table lengths of all user processes are nulled, and their origins are uniformly distributed inside the page table space.

When a memory page is allocated for a virtual machine it must be filled with zeros. In order to avoid heavy swapping and zero-copying at a particular page index, we optimize the allocation process by making all of the newly allocated pages point to the *zero filled page* residing at page address ad_{zfp}. This page is always protected. Whenever one reads from such a page a zero content is provided. At a write attempt to such a page a zero protection page fault is raised. Thus, an allocation leaves the *active* and *free* lists unchanged, possibly modifying the PCBs and the page table space in case a movement of origins is needed. On the memory free, the descriptors of the released pages are moved back to the *free* list, and the corresponding entries in the page tables are invalidated.

On a page fault the handling routine is called. The free list is examined in order to find out whether any unused page resides in the physical memory and could be given to a page faulting process. If not, a page from an active list is evicted. An obtained vacant page is then either filled with the desired data loaded from the disk, or with zeros depending on the kind of page fault. The page table entry of an evicted page is invalidated while the valid bit of a loaded page is set. We use the FIFO-eviction strategy, which guarantees that the page swapped in during the previous call to the handler will not be swapped out during the current call. This property is crucial for liveness of the page fault handler since a single instruction can cause up to two page faults on the physical machine — one during the fetch phase, the other during a load/store operation.

Programming Model and Extended State. The semantics of C0 is defined as a small step transition system on configurations c. In small step semantics, C0 configurations are records $c = (pr, s)$ where $c.pr$ is the program rest and $c.s$ is the 'state'. The page fault handler manipulates and hence must have access to the following components:

- Program variables as the *free*, and *active* lists, maintained only by the page fault handler. These are ordinary C0 variables.
- The page tables which are used by the hardware for address translation. We simply map them to an ordinary array variable in C0, where we solely have to ensure that the allocation address of this array coincides with the page table origin used by the physical machine during address translation. All the C0 data structures together with the handler code consume *TSP* total system pages of physical memory.
- Physical memory of the machine running the handler. The page fault handler transfers memory pages from the hard disk to the non-system region of physical memory which consists of $TUP = TPP - TSP$ total user pages of physical memory, and hence it must be able to manipulate the region $pm.m_{TUP \cdot P}[TSP \cdot P]$. As in C0 the memory is not explicitly visible (e.g., through pointer arithmetic) we employ the extended state to manipulate physical memory.
- The swap memory of the hard disk. An elementary device driver which swaps pages from memory to the hard disk is an integral part of the page fault handler. Similar to the virtual memory, the hard disk is out of the scope of the pure C0 machine, and is handled by the extended state.

Access to the physical memory and the elementary device driver of the hard disk are both implemented as *inline assembler code* in C0. As detailed in Sect. 3.1 we encapsulate inline code by atomic primitives, the XCalls. We augment the C0 small step semantics to handle XCalls which results in a new transition system on extended configurations $xc = (c, mem \in \mathbb{N}_{TUP} \mapsto \mathbb{N}^P_{256}, swap \in \mathbb{N}_{TVP \cdot N} \mapsto \mathbb{N}^P_{256})$.

The semantics δ_{xc} of the new machine executes the small step transition function of the C0 machine in case the head of the program rest is an ordinary C0 statement. Otherwise the effects of the primitives are applied, i.e., in case the next statement is a read command: $xc.c.pr = readPage(xc, ad_{mem}, ad_{swap})$ we copy a page from the swap to the virtual memory: $xc'.mem(ad_{mem}) = xc.swap(ad_{swap})$. Whereas in case of a write primitive $xc.c.pr = writePage(xc, ad_{swap}, ad_{mem})$ we copy a page from physical memory to the swap: $xc'.swap(ad_{swap}) = xc.mem(ad_{mem})$.

The implementations of these primitives, mainly the elementary drivers, are verified separately against their specification. Note, that at this point we even abstracted interleaved device execution to one atomic step. In Sect. 4.2 we justify this abstraction by stating the correctness of our driver implementation.

3.3 Specification

Abstract Page Fault Handler. An abstract page fault handler is a high-level concept of: (i) data structures from the implementation, (ii) physical memory of the machine running a page fault handler, and (iii) hard disk of this machine. Before the formal specification of the page fault handler two auxiliary concepts are formalized. They are page descriptors and translation tables.

Page Descriptors. A page descriptor is a record $pd = (pid, vpx, ppx)$ holding the information about one user page. Its fields are: (i) $pd.pid \in \mathbb{N}_N$, a process identifier which denotes to which virtual machine an associated physical page belongs, (ii) $pd.vpx \in \mathbb{N}_{TVP}$, a virtual page index showing to which virtual page the corresponding physical page belongs, and (iii) $pd.ppx \in \mathbb{N}_{TPP}$, a physical page index which points to the user page in the physical memory.

Translation Table. We abstract the page and the swap tables to the concept of a translation table. It allows us to easily determine the address of a virtual page in physical or swap memories. A *translation table entry* is a record $tte = (ppx, spx, v)$ with $tte.ppx \in \mathbb{N}_{TPP}$, $tte.spx \in \mathbb{N}_{TVP}$ and $tte.v \in \mathbb{B}$. The components are the physical page index, the swap page index, and the valid bit, respectively.

Configuration. The abstracted configuration of a page fault handler is a record $pfh = (active, free, tt, pto, ptl, mem, swap)$. The meaning of the components is: (i) the active list $pfh.active \in C^*_{pd}$ of page descriptors associated with user memory pages that store a virtual page, (ii) the free list $pfh.free \in \mathbb{N}^*_{TPP}$ of unused physical page indexes. We demand $|pfh.active| + |pfh.free| = TUP$ since both lists describe physical memory pages potentially accessible by a user, (iii) the translation table $pfh.tt \in C^{TVP}_{tte}$ is an abstraction of the physical memory region that stores page tables and swap tables. Each entry corresponds exactly to one virtual page, (iv) the vectors of the processes' page table origins $pfh.pto \in \mathbb{N}^N_{TVP}$ and page table lengths $pfh.ptl \in \mathbb{N}^N_{TVP}$, (v) page addressable representations of the non-system part of the physical memory $pfh.mem \in \mathbb{N}_{TUP} \mapsto \mathbb{N}^P_{256}$, and the hard disk content $pfh.swap \in \mathbb{N}_{TVP \cdot N} \mapsto \mathbb{N}^P_{256}$.

   The components $pfh.(mem, swap)$ are supposed to be mapped one-to-one to the corresponding components of the implementation configuration xc.

Page Faults Visible to the Software. A page fault handler guarantees that after its call a page associated with a virtual address va and a process pid will be in the physical memory. The translation table entry address for a virtual page index $px(va)$ and a process pid is defined as $ttea(pfh, pid, px(va)) = pfh.pto[pid] \cdot P + px(va)$, and the corresponding translation table entry is $tte(pfh, pid, px(va)) = pfh.tt[ttea(pfh, pid, px(va))]$. We shorten an access to an entry's component $x \in \{ppx, spx, v\}$ as $x(pfh, pid, px(va)) = tte(pfh, pid, px(va)).x$. By $pf(pfh, pid, va) = v(pfh, pid, px(va)) \vee ppx(pfh, pid, px(va)) = ad_{zfp}$ we define the page fault signal. The disjuncts denote the invalid access and the zero protection page faults, respectively.

Obtaining a Non-Page Faulting Configuration. A page fault handling routine invoked in a configuration pfh with $pf(pfh, pid, va)$ steps to a configuration pfh' with $pf(pfh', pid, va)$ according to the following algorithm. First, a *victim* page descriptor vic is selected depending on the length of the free list. Let $E(pfh)$ hold in case the free list in the configuration pfh is empty, i.e., $|pfh.free| = 0$. We set $vic = pfh.active[0]$ if $E(pfh)$, and $vic = (*, *, pfh.free[0])$ otherwise. If the free list is empty the descriptor of the page to be swapped in is removed from the head of the active list, otherwise from the head of the free list, and is appended to the active list. The vpx field of the descriptor is set to the $px(va)$ value. Formally,

$pfh'.active = tl(pfh.active) \circ (pid, px(va), vic.ppx)$ and $pfh'.free = pfh.free$ if $E(pfh)$, and $pfh'.active = pfh.active \circ (pid, px(va), vic.ppx)$ and $pfh'.free = tl(pfh.free)$ otherwise. Further, in case of the empty free list the victim page is written to the swap memory. Formally, $pfh'.swap = swap\_out(pfh, vic.pid, vic.ppx, vic.vpx)$ if $E(pfh)$, where $swap\_out(pfh, pid, ppx, vpx)$ yields the modified swap component replacing the swap page at address $spx(pfh, pid, vpx)$ by $pfh.mem[ppx]$. The (obtained) free space in the physical memory is either filled with zeros in case of the zero protection page fault or with the page loaded from the swap memory. We set $pfh'.mem = zfp(pfh, vic.ppx)$ if $ppx(pfh, pid, px(va)) = ad_{zfp}$, and $pfh'.mem = swap\_in(pfh, pid, vic.ppx, px(va))$ otherwise. The $swap\_in(pfh, pid, ppx, vpx)$ returns a memory component where a page at address ppx is updated with $pfh.swap[spx(pfh, pid, vpx)]$, and $zfp(pfh, ppx)$ yields a memory where the page ppx is filled with zeros. Finally, the translation table entry of the evicted page is invalidated while the valid bit and the page index of the swapped in page are appropriately set:

$$pfh'.tt[i].(ppx, v) = \begin{cases} (ppx(pfh, vic.pid, vic.vpx), 0) & \text{if } i = ttea(pfh, vic.pid, vic.vpx) \\ (vic.ppx, 1) & \text{if } i = ttea(pfh, pid, px(va)) \\ pfh.tt[i].(ppx, v) & \text{otherwise} \end{cases}.$$

4   Correctness of the Page Fault Handler: Integrating Results

Conceptually, there are two correctness criteria for a page fault handler. Invoked in the configuration pfh with the parameters (pid, va) it must guarantee, first of all, a page fault no longer occurs at the address va. Secondly, it must preserve the $\mathscr{B}$-relation which is established for the first time after the page fault handler initialization code. Both properties follow from the functional correctness of the page fault handler implementation.

Mapping Implementation to Abstraction. In order to state that the handler implementation respects abstraction we define the predicate $map(c, pmd, pfh)$ which is, basically, a conjunction of the three following statements: (i) the variables of the implementation C0 machine c encode the data structures $pfh.(active, free, tt, pto, ptl)$ of the abstraction, (ii) the memory $pmd.pm.m$ of the physical machine starting from the page TSP encodes the abstract memory component $pfh.mem$, and (iii) the hard disk content $pmd.hd.sm$ stores the swap pages $pfh.swap$ of the abstraction. This mapping is established for the first time with the initial configuration of the abstract page fault handler and has to be preserved under each call to the handler.

Mapping C0 to the Physical Machine. Since the overall paging mechanism correctness is stated on the level of the physical machine with devices, we relate C0 configurations to the physical machine states. Given an allocation function $alloc$ mapping variable names to memory locations, we relate a C0 configuration to its physical machine implementation. We use the compiler simulation relation $consis(alloc)(c, pm)$, which relates values of variables and pointers to memory regions and the program to some code region of the physical machine. A further condition is control-consistency, which states that the delayed PC of the physical machine (used to fetch instructions) points to the start of the translated code of the program rest $c.pr$ of the C0 machine.

Validity of the Abstract Page Fault Handler. We demand a variety of properties to hold over the page fault handler abstraction. These properties reflect the functional correctness and are necessary for the $\mathscr{B}$-relation proof. The predicate $valid(pfh)$ claims, among others, the following: (i) all virtual addresses are translated into physical addresses outside the page fault handler code range, (ii) translation tables do not overlap, (iii) page table origins of user processes are monotonic, and $ttea(pfh, pid, px(va))$ always addresses a value inside the translation table, (iv) the active list describes only valid pages, and all the valid pages are described by the active list, (v) none of the virtual pages of a given process might be stored by two or more active pages, and (vi) all physical page indexes in active and free lists are distinct. Now we state the overall correctness theorem of a paging mechanism.

Theorem 1 (Paging Mechanism Correctness). Let c be the C0 machine calling the handler function: $c.pr = handler(pid, va); r$, and let pfh be the abstract page fault handler configuration. Let up be the user processes, and $pmd = (pm, devs)$ be the physical machine with devices. Assuming that (i) c is simulated by pm: $consis(alloc)(c, pm)$, (ii) the relation $\mathscr{B}(pmd, up)$ holds, (iii) c and pmd encode a valid configuration pfh: $map(c, pmd, pfh) \wedge valid(pfh)$, and (iv) a page fault takes place: $pf(pfh, pid, va)$, then there exists a number of steps T, s.t. $pmd' = (pm', devs') = \delta_{pmd}^{T}(pmd)$ after which (i) the handler function is executed and the C0 machine remains consistent with the physical one: $\exists c', alloc'.\ consis(alloc')(c', pm') \wedge c'.pr = r$, (ii) the relation $\mathscr{B}(pmd', up)$ is preserved, and (iii) c' and pmd' encode a valid non-page faulting configuration pfh': $map(c', pmd', pfh') \wedge valid(pfh') \wedge pf(pfh', pid, va)$.

4.1 Compiler Correctness: From C0 to the Physical Machine

The compiler correctness theorem states that the execution of a given C0 program simulates the execution of the compiled program running on the hardware. It is formally proven correct in Isabelle/HOL by Leinenbach [10].

Theorem 2. $\forall t.\ consis(alloc)(c, pm) \implies \exists s, alloc'.\ consis(alloc')(c^t, pm^s)$

4.2 Driver Correctness

Implementation Model. The driver calls are implemented as C0 functions with inline assembler code, where the inline code portion accesses the hard disk and manipulates the physical memory. An assembler instruction list il can be integrated by a special statement $Asm(il)$ into the C0 code. The control-consistency is extended in a straightforward way to the new statement: an instruction list at the head of the program rest maps to a memory region pointed at by the delayed PC of the physical machine: $c.pr = Asm(il); r \wedge consis(alloc)(c, pm) \implies pm.m_{4 \cdot length(il)}(pm.dpc) = il$

The semantics of inline assembler is defined over the combined configuration of a C0 and a physical machine with device state (c, pmd). We execute C0 transitions as long as no assembler is met. In case of assembler instructions we switch, via the compiler consistency relation, to the physical machine, execute the assembler code and switch back to the C0 machine. For the last step, we only have to state how the C0 variables are

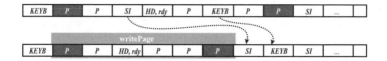

Fig. 2. Reordering of device steps, with hard disk, serial interface and keyboard

manipulated by the assembler code. This combination of assembler and C0 semantics is the driver's implementation model. Out of the two driver calls *readPage* and *writePage* the latter and more complex one was formally verified.

Simulation Relation. This paragraph outlines the correctness of the elementary hard disk driver. First we have to define a simulation relation between our abstract state xc and the implementation state (c, pmd). This relation is called $xConsis(xc, c, pmd)$ and it maps: (i) the abstract swap component to the sector memory defined in the hard disk: $xc.swap_{TUP}[0] = pmd.hd.sm_{TUP.K}[0]$, (ii) the abstract memory component to total user pages of physical memory: $xc.mem_{TUP}[0] = pm.m_{TUP.P}[TSP \cdot P]$, (iii) the program rest of xc to the C0 program rest by substituting XCalls by their C0 with inline assembler implementation, and (iv) machine c to the physical machine pm: $consis(alloc)(c, pm)$. Next we can state the simulation theorem, where $pmd^{t,seq}$ denotes the execution of t steps under the oracle seq of the physical machine with devices:

Theorem 3. $\forall seq.\ xConsis(xc, c, pmd) \implies \exists c',\ t.\ xConsis(\delta_{xc}(xc), c', pmd^{t,seq})$

The most challenging part of the correctness prove, is dealing with the interleaved device execution. We need a programmer's model without unnecessary interleaving, and we have to prove some atomicity of driver execution.

Non-Interference of Devices. All devices take interleaved steps triggered by the environment. However we want to verify Theorem 3, ignoring all devices except the hard disk. In the best case the proof would split in sequential assembler execution and device steps analyzed separately. In principle we want to ensure that: (i) the execution of the driver does not interfere with other devices than the hard disk, and (ii) the execution of the driver can be considered as one atomic step.

These two properties follow from a simple observation of device execution. If the processor is not accessing a device x and if device x is not triggering an interrupt we can simply swap the execution of the processor and the device without changing the final configuration. A similar lemma holds for swapping steps of two different devices.

We generalized this basic observations to a reordering theorem (see Fig. 2): if all interrupts are disabled and if the processor only accesses some device x during executing a given instruction list, we can move all other device steps after the time when the instruction list is executed.

4.3   Proof Sketch of the Paging Mechanism Correctness

With the described methodology we are able to show Theorem 1. In brief, the proof idea is as follows: we show the functional correctness of the page fault handler by reasoning

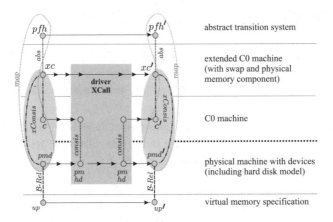

Fig. 3. Page fault handler correctness: putting it all together

in Hoare logic, lift the results down to the level of the physical machine via the soundness theorem of the Hoare logic [13] and Theorems 3 and 2, and infer the $\mathcal{B}$-relation by reasoning about the physical machine memory content. An overview is depicted in Fig. 3. The order of proof steps of the paging mechanism are as follows. 1. Show the validity of the Hoare triple $\{abs(pfh, xc)\}$ $handler(pid, va)$ $\{abs(pfh', xc')\}$. 2. Justify the implication $valid(pfh) \implies valid(pfh')$. 3. From Theorem 3 obtain the number of steps T and the implementation machine c' in order to instantiate the existential quantifiers in the conclusion: (a) via $xConsis$ and (1) obtain the user part memories' contents $pmd'.pm'.m$ and $pmd'.hd'.sm$ that respect pfh', and (b) via $xConsis$ get that c' is mapped to pfh'. 4. Apply Theorem 2 in order to lift (3.c) down to the system part of the physical memory $pmd'.pm'.m_{TSP}[0]$. 5. We have mapped the user and system parts of physical memory and hard disk content to the valid non-pagefaulting configuration pfh'. From $valid(pfh')$ we are able to claim the properties about physical memory content sufficient to show $\mathcal{B}(pmd', up)$, which follows by case splitting on the page fault types.

5   Conclusion

The verification of 500 lines of C0 and 30 lines of assembler code and the reordering theorems took us about 2 person years[2]. Not classical verification problems, as finding invariants, appeared to be the major problem. Rather unexpected and tedious work as 'simple' bitvector operations turned out to be very time consuming. A lot of further effort, not elaborated in this paper, amounts to the integration of models, in particular lifting properties to the overall kernel correctness result, as well as a language stack covering different big- and small step semantics of C0.

This paper not only presents the methodology to deal with pervasive system verification, including inline assembler and driver code accessing interleaved devices, we also verify an important piece of a kernel, running on a real and verified processor.

---

[2] Isabelle/HOL theories are available from http://www.verisoft.de/

By that we give a strong argument for the feasibility of formal verification beyond its application to abstract models and toy implementations.

References

1. Alkassar, E., Hillebrand, M., Knapp, S., Rusev, R., Tverdyshev, S.: Formal device and programming model for a serial interface. In: Proc. 4th International Verification Workshop (VERIFY). CEUR-WS Workshop Proc. (2007)
2. Bevier, W., Hunt Jr., W., Moore, J.S., Young, W.: An approach to systems verification. Journal of Automated Reasoning 5(4), 411–428 (1989)
3. Beyer, S., Jacobi, C., Kroening, D., Leinenbach, D., Paul, W.: Putting it all together: Formal verification of the VAMP. International Journal on Software Tools for Technology Transfer 8(4–5), 411–430 (2006)
4. Condea, C.: Design and implementation of a page fault handler in C0. Master's thesis, Saarland University (July 2006)
5. Gargano, M., Hillebrand, M., Leinenbach, D., Paul, W.: On the correctness of operating system kernels. In: Hurd, J., Melham, T. (eds.) TPHOLs 2005. LNCS, vol. 3603, pp. 1–16. Springer, Heidelberg (2005)
6. Heiser, G., Elphinstone, K., Kuz, I., Klein, G., Petters, S.: Towards trustworthy computing systems: Taking microkernels to the next level. In: Operating Systems Review (July 2007)
7. Hillebrand, M.: Address Spaces and Virtual Memory: Specification, Implementation, and Correctness. PhD thesis, Saarland University, Computer Science Department (June 2005)
8. Hillebrand, M., In der Rieden, T., Paul, W.: Dealing with I/O devices in the context of pervasive system verification. In: ICCD 2005, pp. 309–316. IEEE Computer Society Press, Los Alamitos (2005)
9. Hohmuth, M., Tews, H., Stephens, S.: Applying source-code verification to a microkernel: the vfiasco project. In: Proc. 10th ACM SIGOPS, pp. 165–169. ACM Press, New York (2002)
10. Leinenbach, D., Petrova, E.: Pervasive compiler verification – from verified programs to verified systems. In: 3rd SSV 2008, Elsevier Science B. V (to appear, 2008)
11. Neumann, P., Feiertag, R.: PSOS revisited. In: Omondi, A.R., Sedukhin, S. (eds.) ACSAC 2003. LNCS, vol. 2823, Springer, Heidelberg (2003)
12. Shao, Z., Yu, D., Ni, Z.: Using xcap to certify realistic systems code: Machine context management. In: Schneider, K., Brandt, J. (eds.) TPHOLs 2007. LNCS, vol. 4732, pp. 189–206. Springer, Heidelberg (2007)
13. Schirmer, N.: Verification of Sequential Imperative Programs in Isabelle/HOL. PhD thesis, Technische Universität München (April 2006)
14. Tuch, H., Klein, G.: Verifying the L4 virtual memory subsystem. In: Proc. NICTA Formal Methods Workshop on Operating Systems Verification, NICTA, pp. 73–97 (2004)
15. Tuch, H., Klein, G., Norrish, M.: Types, bytes, and separation logic. In: Proc. 34th POPL, pp. 97–108. ACM Press, New York (2007)
16. Walker, B., Kemmerer, R., Popek, G.: Specification and verification of the UCLA Unix security kernel. Commun. ACM 23(2), 118–131 (1980)

Analyzing Stripped Device-Driver Executables*

Gogul Balakrishnan[1],[**] and Thomas Reps[2],[3]

[1] NEC Laboratories America, Inc.
[2] University of Wisconsin
[3] GrammaTech, Inc.
bgogul@nec-labs.com, reps@cs.wisc.edu

Abstract. This paper sketches the design and implementation of Device-Driver Analyzer for x86 (DDA/x86), a prototype analysis tool for finding bugs in stripped Windows device-driver executables (i.e., when neither source code nor symbol-table/debugging information is available), and presents a case study. DDA/x86 was able to find known bugs (previously discovered by source-code-based analysis tools) along with useful error traces, while having a reasonably low false-positive rate.

This work represents the first known application of automatic program verification/analysis to stripped industrial executables, and allows one to check that an executable does not violate known API usage rules (rather than simply trusting that the implementation is correct).

1 Introduction

A device driver is a program in the operating system that is responsible for managing a hardware device attached to the system. In Windows, a (kernel-level) device driver resides in the address space of the kernel, and runs at a high privilege level; therefore, a bug in a device driver can cause the entire system to crash. The Windows kernel API [27] requires a programmer to follow a complex set of rules: (1) a call to the functions *IoCallDriver* or *PoCallDriver* must occur only at a certain interrupt request level, (2) the function *IoCompleteRequest* should not be called twice with the same parameter, etc.

The device drivers running in a given Windows installation are one of the sources of instability in the Windows platforms: according to Swift et al. [31], bugs in kernel-level device drivers cause 85% of the system crashes in Windows XP. Because of the complex nature of the Windows kernel API, the probability of introducing a bug when writing a device driver is high. Moreover, drivers are typically written by less-experienced or less-skilled programmers than those who wrote the Windows kernel itself.

Several approaches to improve the reliability of device drivers have been previously proposed [10,12,15,31]. Swift et al. [30,31] propose a runtime approach that works on executables; they isolate the device driver in a light-weight protection domain to reduce the possibility of whole-system crashes. Because their method

---

* Supported by NSF under grants CCF-0540955 and CCF-0524051.
** Work performed while at the University of Wisconsin.

C.R. Ramakrishnan and J. Rehof (Eds.): TACAS 2008, LNCS 4963, pp. 124–140, 2008.

is applied at runtime, it may not prevent all bugs from causing whole-system crashes. Other approaches [10,11,12,22] are based on static program analysis of a device driver's source code. Ball et al. [10,12] developed the Static Driver Verifier (SDV), a tool based on model checking to find bugs in device-driver source code. A kernel API usage rule is described as a finite-state machine (FSM), and SDV analyzes the source code for the driver to determine whether there is a path in the driver that violates the rule.

Our work, which is incorporated in a prototype tool called Device-Driver Analyzer for x86 (DDA/x86), is also based on static analysis, but in contrast to the work cited above, DDA/x86 checks properties of stripped Windows device-driver executables; i.e., neither source code nor symbol-table/debugging information need be available (although DDA/x86 can use debugging information, such as Windows .pdb files, if it is available). Thus, DDA/x86 can provide information that is useful in the common situation where one needs to install a device driver for which source code has not been furnished.

Microsoft has a program for signing Windows device drivers, called Windows Hardware Quality Lab (WHQL) testing. Device vendors submit driver executables to WHQL, which runs tests on different hardware platforms with different versions of Windows, reviews the results, and, if the driver passes the tests, creates a digitally signed certificate for use during installation that attests that Microsoft has performed some degree of testing. However, there is anecdotal evidence that device vendors have tried to cheat [2]. A tool like DDA/x86 could allow static analysis to play a role in such a certification process.

Even if you have a driver's source code (and can build an executable) and also have tools for examining executables equipped with symbol-table/debugging information, this would not address the effects of the optimizer. If you want to look for bugs in an optimized version, you would have a kind of "partially stripped" executable, due to the loss of debugging information caused by optimization. This is a situation where our techniques for analyzing stripped executables should be of assistance.

A skeptic might question how well an analysis technique can perform on a stripped executable. §4 presents some quantitative results about how well the answers obtained by DDA/x86 compare to those obtained by SDV; here we will just give one example that illustrates the ability of DDA/x86 to provide information that is qualitatively comparable to the information obtained by SDV. Fig. 1 shows fragments of the witness traces reported by SDV (Fig. 1(a)) and DDA/x86 (Fig. 1(b)) for one of the examples in our test suite. Fig. 1 shows that in this case the tools report comparable information: the three shaded areas in Fig. 1(b) correspond to those in Fig. 1(a).

Although not illustrated by Fig. 1, there are ways in which DDA/x86 can provide higher-fidelity answers than tools based on analyzing source code. This may seem counterintuitive, but the reason is that DDA/x86 works at a level in which many platform-specific features are revealed, such as memory-layout details (e.g., the offsets of variables in activation records and padding between fields of a struct). Because the compiler is in charge of such choices, and may

(a)

(b)

Fig. 1. (a) SDV trace; (b) DDA/x86 trace. The three shaded areas in (b) correspond to those in (a).

also restructure the computation in certain ways, the machine-code level at which DDA/x86 works is closer than the source-code level to what is actually executed.

Elsewhere [4,8], we have called this the WYSINWYX phenomenon (**W**hat **Y**ou **S**ee **I**s **N**ot **W**hat **Y**ou e**X**ecute): computers execute the instructions of programs that have been complied, and not the source code itself; compilation effects can be important if one is interested in better diagnosis of the causes of bugs, or in detecting security vulnerabilities. A Microsoft report on writing kernel-mode drivers in C++ recommends examining "... the object code to be sure it matches your expectations, or at least will work correctly in the kernel environment" [3]. As discussed in §4, we encountered a few cases of the WYSINWYX phenomenon in our experiments, although these concerned the hand-written environment harnesses that we picked up from SDV [10,12].

This paper describes the design and implementation of DDA/x86, and presents a case study in which we used it to find problems in Windows device drivers by analyzing the drivers' stripped executables. The key idea that allows DDA/x86 to achieve a substantial measure of success was to combine the algorithm for memory-access analysis [4,5,6] from CodeSurfer/x86 [7] with the path-sensitive method of interpreting property automata from ESP [17]. The resulting algorithm explores an over-approximation of the set of reachable states, and hence can verify correctness by determining that all error configurations are unreachable. The contributions of the work include

- DDA/x86 can analyze *stripped device-driver executables*, and thus provides a capability not found in previous tools for analyzing device drivers [11,22].
- Our case study shows that this approach is viable. DDA/x86 was able to identify some known bugs (previously discovered by source-code-based analysis tools) along with useful error traces, while having a reasonably low false-positive rate: On a corpus of 17 device-driver executables, 10 were found to pass the *PendedCompletedRequest* rule (definitely no bug), 5 false positives were reported, and 2 were found to have real bugs—for which DDA/x86 supplied feasible error traces.
- We developed a novel, low-cost mechanism for instrumenting a dataflow-analysis algorithm to provide witness traces.

One of the challenges that we faced was to find ways of coping with the differences that arise when property checking is performed at the machine-instruction level, rather than on an IR created from source code. In particular, the domains of discourse—the alphabets of actions to which the automata respond—are different in the two situations. This issue is discussed in §4.

The remainder of the paper is organized as follows: §2 provides background on recovering intermediate representations (IRs) from executables. §3 describes the extensions that we made to our algorithm for IR-recovery from low-level code to perform path-sensitive property checking. §4 presents experimental results. Related work is discussed in §5.

2   Background on Intermediate-Representation Recovery

DDA/x86 makes use of the IR-recovery algorithms of CodeSurfer/x86 [4,5,6,7]. This section explains some of the ideas used in those algorithms that are important to understanding how they were extended to support path-sensitivity.

The IR-recovery algorithms of CodeSurfer/x86 recover from a device-driver executable IRs that are similar to those that would be available had one started from source code. CodeSurfer/x86 recovers IRs that represent control-flow graphs (CFGs), with indirect jumps resolved; a call graph, with indirect calls resolved; information about the program's variables; possible values of pointer variables; sets of used, killed, and possibly-killed variables for each CFG node; and data dependences. The techniques employed by CodeSurfer/x86 do not rely on debugging information being present, but can use available debugging information (e.g., Windows .pdb files) if directed to do so.

The analyses used in CodeSurfer/x86 (see [4,5,6]) are a great deal more ambitious than even relatively sophisticated disassemblers, such as IDAPro [24]. At the technical level, they address the following problem: *Given a (possibly stripped) executable E, identify the procedures, data objects, types, and libraries*

*that it uses, and, for each instruction I in E and its libraries, for each inter-
procedural calling context of I, and for each machine register and variable V in
scope at I, statically compute an accurate over-approximation to the set of values
that V may contain when I executes.*

Variable and Type Discovery. One of the major stumbling blocks in analyzing executables is the difficulty of recovering information about variables
and types, especially for aggregates (i.e., structures and arrays). When performing source-code analysis, the programmer-defined variables provide us with the
compartments for tracking data manipulations. When debugging information is
absent, an executable's data objects are not easily identifiable. Consider, for instance, an access on a source-code variable x in some source-code statement. At
the machine-instruction level, an access on x is performed either directly—by
specifying an absolute address—or indirectly—through an address expression of
the form "[*base + index × scale + offset*]", where *base* and *index* are registers
and *scale* and *offset* are integer constants. The variable and type-discovery phase
of CodeSurfer/x86 [4,6] recovers information about variables that are allocated
globally, locally (i.e., on the run-time stack), and dynamically (i.e., from the
heap). The recovered variables, called *a-locs* (for "abstract locations") are the
basic variables used in the extension of the VSA algorithm described in §3.

To accomplish this task, CodeSurfer/x86 makes use of a number of analyses,
and the sequence of analyses performed is itself iterated [4,6]. On each round,
CodeSurfer/x86 uses VSA to identify an over-approximation of the memory
accesses performed at each instruction. Subsequently, the results of VSA are
used to perform aggregate structure identification (ASI) [28], which identifies
commonalities among accesses to different parts of an aggregate data value, to
refine the current set of a-locs. The new set of a-locs are used to perform another
round of VSA. If the over-approximation of memory accesses computed by VSA
improves from the previous round, the a-locs computed by the subsequent round
of ASI may also improve. This process is repeated as long as desired, or until
the process converges. By this means, CodeSurfer/x86 bootstraps its way to a
set of a-locs that serve as proxies for the program's original variables.

3   Property Checking in Executables Using VSA

This section describes the extensions that we made to our IR-recovery algorithm
to perform path-sensitive property checking. Consider the following memory-
safety property: p should not be dereferenced if its value is NULL. Fig. 2 shows
an FSM that checks for property violations. One approach to determining if there
is a null-pointer dereference in the executable is to start from the initial state
(UNSAFE) at the entry point of the executable, and find an over-approximation
of the set of reachable states at each statement in the executable. This can be
done by determining the states for the successors at each statement based on
the transitions in the FSM that encodes the memory-safety property.

Another approach is to use abstract interpretation to determine the abstract
memory configurations at each statement in the routine, and use the results to

check the memory-safety property. For executables, we could use the information computed by the IR-recovery algorithms of CodeSurfer/x86 [7]. For instance, for each instruction I in an executable, the value-set analysis (VSA) algorithm [4,5,6] used in CodeSurfer/x86 determines an over-approximation of the set of memory addresses and numeric values held in each register and variable when I executes.

Suppose that we have the results of VSA and want to use them to check the memory-safety property; the property can be checked as follows:

*If the abstract set of addresses and numeric values computed for **p** possibly contains **NULL** just before a statement, and the statement dereferences **p**, then the memory-safety property is potentially violated.*

Unfortunately, the approaches described above would result in a lot of false positives because they are not path-sensitive. To overcome the limitations of the two approaches described above, DDA/x86 follows Das et al. [17] and Fischer et al. [20], who showed how to obtain a degree of path-sensitivity by combining the propagation of automaton states with the propagation of abstract-state values during abstract interpretation. The remainder of this section describes how the propagation of property-automaton states can be incorporated into the VSA algorithm to obtain a degree of path-sensitivity.

To simplify the discussion, the ideas are initially described for a simplified version of VSA, called *context-insensitive* VSA [5]; the combination of automaton-state propagation with the context-sensitive version of VSA [4, Ch. 3] is discussed at the end of the section. The context-insensitive VSA algorithm associates each program point with an AbsEnv value [4,6], which represents a set of concrete (i.e., run-time) states of a program. An element in the AbsEnv domain associates each a-loc and register in the executable with an abstract value that represents a set of memory addresses and numeric values. Let State

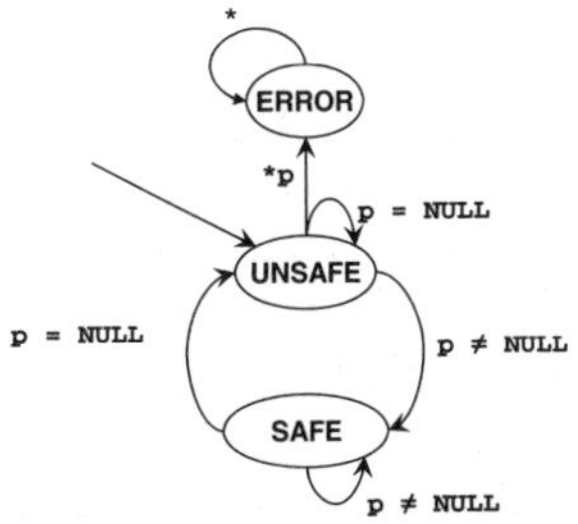

Fig. 2. An FSM that encodes the rule that pointer p should not be dereferenced if it is NULL

denote the set of property-automaton states. The path-sensitive VSA algorithm associates each program point with an AbsMemConfig^{ps} value, where AbsMemConfig^{ps} = ((State × State) → AbsEnv$_\perp$).

In the pair of property-automaton states at a node n, the first component refers to the state of the property automaton at the enter node of the procedure to which node n belongs, and the second component refers to the current state of the property automaton at node n. If an AbsEnv entry for the pair $\langle s_0, s_{cur} \rangle$ exists at node n, then n is possibly reachable with the property automaton in state s_{cur} from a memory configuration at the enter node of the procedure in which the property automaton was in state s_0.

The path-sensitive VSA algorithm is shown in Fig. 3. The worklist consists of triples of the form $\langle$State, State, Node$\rangle$. A triple $\langle enter\_state, cur\_state, n \rangle$ is selected from the worklist, and for each successor edge of node n, a new AbsEnv value is computed by applying the corresponding abstract transformer (line[11]).

After computing a new AbsEnv value, the set of pairs of states for the successor is identified (see the *GetSuccStates* procedure in Fig. 3). For an intraprocedural edge *pred→succ*, the set of pairs of states for the target of the edge is obtained by applying the *NextStates* function to ⟨*enter_state, cur_state*⟩ (line[34]). The *NextStates* function pairs *enter_state* with all possible second-component states according to the property automaton's transition relation for edge *pred→succ*. For a call→enter edge, the only new state pair is the pair ⟨*cur_state, cur_state*⟩ (line[30]). For an exit→end-call edge, the set of pairs of states for the end-call node is determined by examining the set of pairs of states at the corresponding call (line[24]-[28]); for each ⟨*call_enter_state, call_cur_state*⟩ at the call node such that (*call_cur_state = enter_state*), the pair ⟨*call_enter_state, cur_state*⟩ is added to the result.

Note that the condition (*call_cur_state = enter_state*) at line[25] checks if ⟨*enter_state, cur_state*⟩ at the exit node is reachable, according to the property automaton, from ⟨*call_enter_state, call_cur_state*⟩ at the call node. The need to check the condition (*call_cur_state = enter_state*) at an exit node is the reason for maintaining a pair of states at each node. If we do not maintain a pair of states, it would not be possible to determine the property-automaton states at the call that reach the given property-automaton state at the exit node. (In essence, we are doing a natural join a tuple at a time: the subset of State × State at the call node represents a reachability relation R_1 for the property automaton's possible net change in state as control moves from the caller's enter node to the call site; the subset of State × State at the exit node represents a reachability relation R_2 for the automaton's net change in state as control moves from the callee's enter node to the exit node. The subset of State × State at the end-call node, representing a reachability relation R_3, is their natural join, given by $R_3(x, y) = \exists z.\ R_1(x, z) \wedge R_2(z, y)$. Thus, technically our extension amounts to the use of the reduced cardinal power [16,17,20] of the edges in the transitive closure of the automation's transition relation and the original VSA domain.)

Finally, in the AbsMemConfig^{ps} value for the successor node, the AbsEnv values for all the pairs of states that were identified by *GetSuccStates* are updated with the newly computed AbsEnv value (see the *Propagate* function in Fig. 3).

It is trivial to combine the path-sensitive VSA algorithm in Fig. 3 and the context-sensitive VSA algorithm to get a VSA algorithm that can distinguish paths as well as calling contexts to a limited degree. In the combined algorithm, each node is associated with a value from the following domain (where CallString$_k$ represents the set of call-string suffixes of length up to k [29]):

AbsMemConfig^{ps-cs} = ((CallString$_k$ × State × State) → AbsEnv$_\perp$).

4   Experiments

This section presents a case study in which we used DDA/x86 to analyze the executables of Windows device drivers. The study was designed to test how well different extensions of the VSA algorithm could detect problems in Windows device drivers by analyzing device-driver executables—without accessing source

```
 1: decl worklist: set of ⟨State, State, Node⟩
 2:
 3: proc PathSensitiveVSA()
 4:     worklist := {⟨StartState, StartState, enter⟩}
 5:     absMemConfig^ps_enter[⟨StartState, StartState⟩] := Initial values of global a-locs and esp
 6:     while (worklist ≠ ∅) do
 7:         Select and remove a triple ⟨enter_state, cur_state, n⟩ from worklist
 8:         m := Number of successors of node n
 9:         for i = 1 to m do
10:             succ := GetSuccessor(n, i)
11:             edge_amc := AbstractTransformer(n → succ, absMemConfig^ps_n[⟨enter_state, cur_state⟩])

12:             succ_states := GetSuccStates(enter_state, cur_state, n, succ)
13:             for (each ⟨succ_enter_state, succ_cur_state⟩ ∈ succ_states) do
14:                 Propagate(enter_state, succ_enter_state, succ_cur_state, succ, edge_amc)
15:             end for
16:         end for
17:     end while
18: end proc
19:
20: proc GetSuccStates(enter_state: State, cur_state: State, pred: Node, succ: Node): set of
    ⟨State, State⟩
21:     result := ∅
22:     if (pred is an exit node and succ is an end-call node) then
23:         Let c be the call node associated with succ
24:         for each ⟨call_enter_state, call_cur_state⟩ in absMemConfig^ps_c do
25:             if (call_cur_state = enter_state) then
26:                 result := result ∪ {⟨call_enter_state, cur_state⟩}
27:             end if
28:         end for
29:     else if (pred is a call node and succ is an enter node) then
30:         result := {⟨cur_state, cur_state⟩}
31:     else
32:         // Pair enter_state with all possible second-component states according to
33:         // the property automaton's transition relation for input edge pred → succ
34:         result := NextStates(pred→succ, ⟨enter_state, cur_state⟩)
35:     end if
36:     return result
37: end proc
38:
39: proc Propagate(pred_enter_state: State, enter_state: State, cur_state: State, n: Node, edge_amc:
    AbsEnv)
40:     old := absMemConfig^ps_n[⟨enter_state, cur_state⟩]
41:     if n is an end-call node then
42:         Let c be the call node associated with n
43:         edge_amc := MergeAtEndCall(edge_amc, absMemConfig^ps_c[⟨enter_state, pred_enter_state⟩])
44:     end if
45:     new := old ⊔^ae edge_amc
46:     if (old ≠ new) then
47:         absMemConfig^ps_n[⟨enter_state, cur_state⟩] := new
48:         worklist := worklist ∪ {⟨enter_state, cur_state, n⟩}
49:     end if
50: end proc
```

Fig. 3. Path-sensitive VSA algorithm. (The function *MergeAtEndCall* merges information from the abstract state at an exit node with information from the abstract state at the call node (cf. [25]). Underlining indicates an action that manages or propagates property-state information.)

code, symbol-tables, or debugging information. In particular, if DDA/x86 were successful at finding the bugs that the Static Driver Verifier (SDV) [10,12] tool finds in Windows device drivers, that would be powerful evidence that our approach is viable—i.e., that it will be possible to find previously undiscovered bugs in device drivers for which source code is not available, or for which compiler/optimizer effects make source-code analysis unsafe. We selected a subset of drivers from the Windows Driver Development Kit (DDK) [1] release 3790.1830 for the case study. For each driver, we obtained an executable by compiling the driver source code along with the harness and the OS environment model [10] of the SDV toolkit. (Thus, as in SDV and other source-code-analysis tools, the harness and OS environment models are analyzed; however, DDA/x86 analyzes the executable code that the compiler produces for the harness and the models. This creates certain difficulties, which are discussed below.)

A device driver is analogous to a library that exports a collection of subroutines. Each subroutine exported by a driver implements an action that needs to be performed when the OS makes an I/O request (on behalf of a user application or when a hardware-related event occurs). For instance, when a new device is attached to the system, the OS invokes the `AddDevice` routine provided by the device driver; when new data arrives on a network interface, the OS calls the `DeviceRead` routine provided by the driver; etc. For every I/O request, the OS creates a structure called the "I/O Request Packet (IRP)", which contains such information as the type of the I/O request, the parameters associated with the request, etc.; the OS then invokes the appropriate driver's dispatch routine. The dispatch routine performs the necessary actions, and returns a value that indicates the status of the request. For instance, if a driver successfully completes the I/O request, the driver's dispatch routine calls the *IoCompleteRequest* API function to notify the OS that the request has been completed, and returns the value `STATUS_SUCCESS`. Similarly, if the I/O request is not completed within the dispatch routine, the driver calls the *IoMarkPending* API function and returns `STATUS_PENDING`.

A harness in the SDV toolkit is C code that simulates the possible calls to the driver that could be made by the OS. An application generates requests, which the OS passes on to the device driver. Both levels are modeled by the harness. The harness defined in the SDV toolkit acts as a client that exercises all possible combinations of the dispatch routines that can occur in two successive calls to the driver. The harness that was used in our experiments calls the following driver routines (in the order given below):

1. `DriverEntry`: initializes the driver's data structures and the global state.
2. `AddDevice`: simulates the addition of a device to the system.
3. The plug-and-play dispatch routine (called with an `IRP_MN_START_DEVICE` I/O request packet): simulates the starting of the device by the OS.
4. Some dispatch routine, deferred procedure call, interrupt service routine, etc.: simulates various actions on the device.
5. The plug-and-play dispatch routine (called with an `IRP_MN_REMOVE_DEVICE` I/O request packet): simulates the removal of the device by the OS.
6. `Unload`: simulates the unloading of the driver by the OS.

The OS environment model in the SDV toolkit consists of a collection of functions (written in C) that conservatively model the API functions in the Windows DDK. The models are conservative in the sense that they simulate all possible behaviors of an API function. For instance, if an API function Foo returns the value 0 or 1 depending upon the input arguments, the model for Foo consists of a non-deterministic if statement that returns 0 in the true branch and 1 in the false branch. Modeling the API functions conservatively enables a static-analysis tool to explore all possible behaviors of the API.

WYSINWYX. We had to make some changes to the OS models used in the SDV toolkit because SDV's models were never meant to be compiled and used, in compiled form, as models of the OS environment by an analyzer that works on machine instructions, such as DDA/x86. These problems showed up as instances of the WYSINWYX phenomenon. For instance, each driver has a device-extension structure that is used to maintain extended information about the state of each device managed by the driver. The number of fields and the type of each field in the device-extension structure is specific to a driver. However, in SDV's OS model, a single integer variable is used to represent the device-extension object. Therefore, in a driver executable built using SDV's models, when the driver writes to a field at offset o of the device-extension structure, it would appear as a write to the memory address that is offset o bytes from the memory address of the integer that represents the device-extension object.

We also encountered the WYSINWYX phenomenon while using SDV's OS models. For instance, the OS model uses a function named SdvMakeChoice to represent non-deterministic choice. However, the body of SdvMakeChoice only contains a single "return 0" statement.[1] Consequently, instead of exploring all possible behaviors of an API function, DDA/x86 would explore only a subset of the behaviors of the API function. We had to modify SDV's OS environment model to avoid such problems.

Case Study. We chose the following "*PendedCompletedRequest*" rule for our case study:
  A driver's dispatch routine should not return STATUS_PENDING *on an I/O Request Packet (IRP) if it has called IoCompleteRequest on the IRP, unless it has also called IoMarkIrpPending.*
Fig. 4 shows the FSM for this rule.[2]
We used the three different variants of the VSA algorithm listed in Tab. 1 for our experiments on a 64-bit Xeon 3GHz processor with 16GB (only 4GB/process) of memory, and Tab. 2 presents the results. The column labeled "Result" indicates whether the VSA algorithm reported that there is some node n at which the ERROR state in the *PendedCompletedRequest* FSM is reachable, when one starts from the initial memory configuration at the entry node of the executable.

Configuration '⊖' uses an algorithm that is similar to the one used in IDAPro to recover variable-like entities. That algorithm does not provide variables of the

---

[1] According to T. Ball [9], the C front end used by SDV treats SdvMakeChoice specially.
[2] According to the Windows DDK documentation, *IoMarkPending* has to be called before *IoCompleteRequest*; however, the FSM defined for the rule in SDV is the one shown in Fig. 4. We used the same FSM for our experiments.

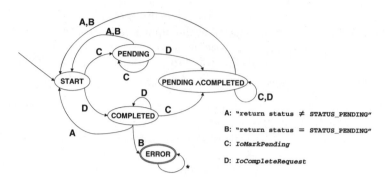

Fig. 4. Finite-state machine for the rule *PendedCompletedRequest*

Table 1. Variants of the VSA algorithm used in the experiments

Config.	A-locs	Property Automaton
⊖	IDAPro-based algorithm	Fig. 4
⊙	ASI-based algorithm	Fig. 4
★	ASI-based algorithm	Cross-product of the automata in Figs. 4 and 6

Table 2. Results of checking the *PendedCompletedRequest* rule in Windows device drivers. ($\surd$: passes rule; ×: a real bug found; FP: false positive.) See Tab. 1 for an explanation of ⊖, ⊙, and ★. (For the examples that pass the rule, "Rounds" represents the number of VSA-ASI rounds required to prove the absence of the bug; for the other examples, the maximum number of rounds was set to 5.)

			⊖		⊙		★			
Driver	Procedures	Instructions	Result	Feasible Trace?	Result	Feasible Trace?	Result	Feasible Trace?	Time	Rounds
src/vdd/dosioctl/krnldrvr	70	2824	FP	-	$\surd$	-	$\surd$	-	14s	2
src/general/ioctl/sys	76	3504	FP	-	$\surd$	-	$\surd$	-	13s	2
src/general/tracedrv/tracedrv	84	3719	FP	-	$\surd$	-	$\surd$	-	16s	2
src/general/cancel/startio	96	3861	FP	-	$\surd$	-	$\surd$	-	12s	2
src/general/cancel/sys	102	4045	FP	-	$\surd$	-	$\surd$	-	10s	2
src/input/moufiltr	93	4175	×	No	×	No	×	Yes	3m 3s	5
src/general/event/sys	99	4215	FP	-	$\surd$	-	$\surd$	-	20s	2
src/input/kbfiltr	94	4228	×	No	×	No	×	Yes	2m 53s	5
src/general/toaster/toastmon	123	6261	FP	-	FP	-	$\surd$	-	4m 1s	3
src/storage/filters/diskperf	121	6584	FP	-	FP	-	$\surd$	-	3m 17s	3
src/network/modem/fakemodem	142	8747	FP	-	FP	-	$\surd$	-	11m 6s	3
src/storage/fdc/flpydisk	171	12752	FP	-	FP	-	FP	-	1h 6m	5
src/input/mouclass	192	13380	FP	-	FP	-	FP	-	40m 26s	5
src/input/mouser	188	13989	FP	-	FP	-	FP	-	1h 4m	5
src/kernel/serenum	184	14123	FP	-	FP	-	$\surd$	-	19m 41s	2
src/wdm/1394/driver/1394diag	171	23430	FP	-	FP	-	FP	-	1h33m	5
src/wdm/1394/driver/1394vdev	173	23456	FP	-	FP	-	FP	-	1h38m	5

right granularity and expressiveness, and therefore, not surprisingly, configuration '⊖' reports many false positives for all of the drivers.[3]

---

[3] In this case, a false positive reports that the ERROR state is (possibly) reachable at some node n, when, in fact, it is never reachable. This is sound (for the reachability question), but imprecise.

```
int dispatch_routine(...) {
    int status, c = 0;
    .
    .
    status = STATUS_PENDING;
    P1:if(...) {
        status = STATUS_SUCCESS;
        c = 1;
    }
    P2:
    .
    .
    if(c == 1) {
        IoCompleteRequest(...)
    }
    P3: return status;
}
```

Information at P3 with the FSM shown in Fig. 4
START:
$c \mapsto \{0,1\}$
status $\mapsto \{$STATUS_SUCCESS, STATUS_PENDING$\}$
COMPLETED:
$c \mapsto \{0,1\}$
status $\mapsto \{$STATUS_SUCCESS, STATUS_PENDING$\}$

Information at P3 with the FSM shown in Fig. 6
ST_PENDING:
$c \mapsto \{0\}$
status $\mapsto \{$STATUS_PENDING$\}$
ST_NOT_PENDING:
$c \mapsto \{1\}$
status $\mapsto \{$STATUS_SUCCESS$\}$

Fig. 5. An example illustrating false positives in device-driver analysis

Configuration '⊙', which uses only the *PendedCompletedRequest* FSM, also reports a lot of false positives. Fig. 5 shows an example that illustrates one of the reasons for the false positives in configuration '⊙'. As shown in the right column of Fig. 5, the set of values for status at the return statement (P3) for the property-automaton state COMPLETED contains both STATUS_PENDING and STATUS_SUCCESS. Therefore, VSA reports that the dispatch routine possibly violates the *PendedCompletedRequest* rule. The problem is as follows: because the state of the *PendedCompletedRequest* automaton is the same after both branches of the if statement at P1 are analyzed, VSA merges the information from both of the branches, and therefore the correlation between c and status is lost after the statement at P2.

Fig. 6 shows an FSM that enables VSA to maintain the correlation between c and status. Basically, the FSM changes the abstraction in use, and enables VSA to distinguish paths in the executable based on the contents of the variable status. We refer to a variable (such as status in Fig. 6) that is used to keep track of the current status of the I/O request in a dispatch routine as the *status-variable*. To be able to use the FSM in Fig. 6 for analyzing an executable, it is necessary to determine the status-variable for each procedure. However, because debugging information is usually not available, we use the following heuristic to identify the status-variable for each procedure in the executable:

By convention, eax holds the return value in the x86 architecture. Therefore, the local variable (if any) that is used to initialize the value of eax just before returning from the dispatch routine is considered to be the status-variable.

Configuration '★' uses the automaton obtained by combining the *PendedCompletedRequest* FSM and the FSM shown in Fig. 6 (instantiated using the above heuristic) using a cross-product construction. As shown in Tab. 2, for configuration '★', the number of false positives is substantially reduced.

It required substantial manual effort to find an abstraction that had sufficient fidelity to reduce the number of false positives reported by DDA/x86. To create a practical tool, it would be important to automate the process of refining the abstraction based on the property be checked. The model-checking community has developed many techniques that could be applicable, although the discussion above shows that the definition of a suitable refinement can be quite subtle.

As a point of comparison, SDV also found the bugs in both "moufiltr" and "kbfiltr", but had no false positives in any of the examples. However, one should not leap to the conclusion that machine-code-analysis tools are necessarily inferior to source-code-analysis tools.

- The basic capabilities are different: DDA/x86 can analyze stripped device-driver executables, which goes beyond the capabilities of SDV.
- The analysis techniques used in SDV and in DDA/x86 are incomparable: SDV uses predicate-abstraction-based abstractions [21], plus abstraction refinement; DDA/x86 uses a combined numeric-plus-pointer analysis [5], together with a different kind of abstraction refinement [6]. Thus, there may be examples for which DDA/x86 outperforms SDV.

Moreover, SDV is a multiple man-year effort, with a professional team at Microsoft devoted to its development. In contrast, the prototype DDA/x86 was created in only a few man-months (although multiple man-years went into building the underlying CodeSurfer/x86 infrastructure).

Property Automata for the Analysis of Machine Code. Property automata for the analysis of machine code differ from the automata used for source-level analysis. In particular, the domain of discourse—the alphabet of actions to which an automaton responds—is different when property checking is performed at the machine-code level, rather than on an IR created from source code.

In some cases, it is possible to recognize a source-level action based on information available in the recovered IR. For instance, a source-code procedure call with actual parameters is usually implemented as a sequence of instructions that evaluate the actuals, followed by a `call` instruction to transfer control to the starting address of the procedure. The IR-recovery algorithms used in CodeSurfer/x86 will identify the call along with its arguments.

In other cases, a source-level action is not identifiable. One contributing factor is that a source-level action can correspond to a sequence of instructions. Moreover, the instruction sequences for two source-level actions could be interleaved. We did not have a systematic way to cope with such problems except to rewrite the automaton of interest based on instruction-level actions.

Fortunately, most of the instruction-level actions that need to be tracked boil down to memory accesses/updates. Because VSA is precise enough to interpret many memory accesses [4, §7.5], it is possible for DDA/x86 to perform property checking using the extended version of VSA described in §3. In our somewhat limited experience, we found that for many property automata it is possible to rewrite them based on memory accesses/updates so that they can be used for the analysis of executables.

Finding a Witness Trace. If the VSA algorithm reports that the ERROR state in the property automaton is reachable, it is useful to find a sequence of

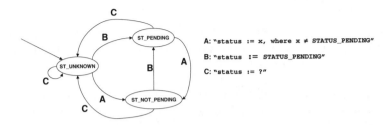

Fig. 6. Finite-state machine that tracks the contents of the variable `status`

instructions that shows how the property automaton can be driven to ERROR. Rather than extending the VSA implementation to generate and manage explicitly the information required for reporting witness traces, we exploited the fact that the standard algorithms for solving reachability problems in pushdown systems (PDSs) [14,19] provide a witness-trace capability to show how a given (reachable) configuration is reachable.

The algorithm described in §3 was augmented to emit the rules of a PDS on-the-fly. The PDS constructed is equivalent to a PDS that would be obtained by a cross-product of the property automaton and a PDS that models the interprocedural control-flow graph, except that, by emitting the PDS on-the-fly as VSA variant '★' is run, the cross-product PDS is pruned according to what the VSA algorithm and the property automaton both agree on as being reachable. The PDS is constructed as follows:

PDS rules	Control flow modeled
$\langle q, [n_0, s]\rangle \hookrightarrow \langle q, [n_1, s']\rangle$	Intraprocedural CFG edge from node n_0 in state s to node n_1 in state s'
$\langle q, [c, s]\rangle \hookrightarrow \langle q, [enter_{\mathsf{P}}, s][r, s']\rangle$ $\langle q_{[x_{\mathsf{P}}, s']}, [r, s']\rangle \hookrightarrow \langle q, [r, s']\rangle$	Call to procedure P from c in state s that returns to r in state s'.
$\langle q, [x_{\mathsf{P}}, s']\rangle \hookrightarrow \langle q_{[x_{\mathsf{P}}, s']}, \epsilon\rangle$	Return from P at exit node x_{P} in state s'

In our case, to obtain a witness trace, we merely use the witness trace returned by the PDS reachability algorithm to determine if a PDS configuration $\langle q, [n, \text{ERROR}]\rangle$—where n is a node in the interprocedural CFG—is reachable from the configuration $\langle q, enter_{\text{main}}\rangle$.

Because the PDS used for reachability queries is based on the results of VSA, which computes an *over-approximation* of the set of reachable concrete memory states, the witness traces provided by the reachability algorithm may be infeasible. In our experiments, only for configuration '★' were the witness traces for `kbfiltr` and `moufiltr` feasible. (Feasibility was checked by hand.)

This approach is not specific to VSA; it can be applied to essentially any worklist-based dataflow-analysis algorithm when it is extended with a property automaton, and provides a conceptually low-cost mechanism for augmenting such algorithms to provide witness traces.

5   Related Work

DDA/x86 is the first known application of program analysis/verification techniques to stripped industrial executables. Among other techniques, it combines the IR-recovery algorithms from CodeSurfer/x86 [4,5,6] with the path-sensitive method of interpreting property automata from ESP [17].

A number of algorithms have been proposed in the past for verifying properties of programs when source code is available [10,12,13,17,20,22]. Among these techniques, SDV [10,12] and ESP [17] are closely related to DDA/x86. SDV builds a Boolean representation of the program using predicate abstraction; it reports a possible property violation if an error state is reachable in the Boolean model. In contrast, DDA/x86 uses value-set analysis [5,4] (along with property simulation) to over-approximate the set of reachable states; it reports a possible property violation if the error state is reachable at any instruction in the executable. To eliminate spurious error traces, SDV uses counter-example-guided abstraction refinement, whereas DDA/x86 leverages path sensitivity obtained by combining property simulation and abstract interpretation. In this respect, DDA/x86 is more closely related to ESP—in fact, the algorithm in §3 was inspired by ESP. However, unlike ESP, DDA/x86 provides a witness trace for a possible bug, as described in §4. Moreover, DDA/x86 uses a different kind of abstraction refinement [6].

Although combining the propagation of property-automaton states and abstract interpretation provides a degree of path sensitivity, it was not always sufficient to eliminate all of the false positives for the examples in our test suite. Therefore, we also distinguished paths based on the abstract state (using the automaton shown in Fig. 6) in addition to distinguishing paths based on property-automaton states. While the results of our experiments are encouraging, it required a lot of manual effort to reduce the number of false positives: spurious error traces were examined by hand, and the automaton in Fig. 6 was introduced to refine the abstraction in use. For DDA/x86 to be usable on a day-to-day basis, it would be important to automate the process of reducing the number of false positives. Several techniques have been proposed to reduce the number of false positives in abstract interpretation, including trace partitioning [26], qualified dataflow analysis [23], and the refinement techniques of Fisher et al. [20] and Dhurjati et al. [18]. All of these techniques are potentially applicable in DDA/x86.

References

1. http://www.microsoft.com/whdc/devtools/ddk/default.mspx
2. Defrauding the WHQL driver certification process, March (2004),
   http://blogs.msdn.com/oldnewthing/archive/2004/03/05/84469.aspx
3. C++ for kernel mode drivers: Pros and cons, WHDC web site (February 2007),
   http://www.microsoft.com/whdc/driver/kernel/KMcode.mspx
4. Balakrishnan, G.: WYSINWYX: What You See Is Not What You eXecute. PhD thesis, C.S. Dept. Univ. of Wisconsin, Madison, WI, August, TR-1603 (2007)

5. Balakrishnan, G., Reps, T.: Analyzing memory accesses in x86 executables. In: Duesterwald, E. (ed.) CC 2004. LNCS, vol. 2985, pp. 5–23. Springer, Heidelberg (2004)

6. Reps, T., Balakrishnan, G.: DIVINE: DIscovering Variables IN Executables. In: Cook, B., Podelski, A. (eds.) VMCAI 2007. LNCS, vol. 4349, pp. 1–28. Springer, Heidelberg (2007)

7. Reps, T., Melski, D., Lal, A.K., Teitelbaum, T., Balakrishnan, G., Gruian, R., Kidd, N., Lim, J., Yong, S., Chen, C.-H.: Model checking x86 executables with CodeSurfer/x86 and WPDS++. In: Etessami, K., Rajamani, S.K. (eds.) CAV 2005. LNCS, vol. 3576, pp. 158–163. Springer, Heidelberg (2005)

8. Balakrishnan, G., Reps, T., Melski, D., Teitelbaum, T.: WYSINWYX: What You See Is Not What You eXecute. In: IFIP Working Conf. on VSTTE (2005)

9. Ball, T.: Personal communication (February 2006)

10. Ball, T., Bounimova, E., Cook, B., Levin, V., Lichtenberg, J., McGarvey, C., Ondrusek, B., Rajamani, S.K., Ustuner, A.: Thorough static analysis of device drivers. In: EuroSys. (2006)

11. Ball, T., Rajamani, S.K.: Bebop: A symbolic model checker for Boolean programs. In: Spin Workshop (2000)

12. Rajamani, S.K., Ball, T.: The SLAM Toolkit. In: Berry, G., Comon, H., Finkel, A. (eds.) CAV 2001. LNCS, vol. 2102, Springer, Heidelberg (2001)

13. Blanchet, B., Cousot, P., Cousot, R., Feret, J., Mauborgne, L., Miné, A., Monniaux, D., Rival, X.: A static analyzer for large safety-critical software. In: PLDI (2003)

14. Bouajjani, A., Esparza, J., Maler, O.: Reachability analysis of pushdown automata: Application to model checking. In: Mazurkiewicz, A., Winkowski, J. (eds.) CONCUR 1997. LNCS, vol. 1243, Springer, Heidelberg (1997)

15. Chou, A., Yang, J., Chelf, B., Hallem, S., Engler, D.: An empirical study of operating systems errors. In: SOSP (2001)

16. Cousot, P., Cousot, R.: Systematic design of program analysis frameworks. In: POPL (1979)

17. Das, M., Lerner, S., Seigle, M.: ESP: Path-sensitive program verification in polynomial time. In: PLDI (2002)

18. Das, M., Yang, Y., Dhurjati, D.: Path-Sensitive Dataflow Analysis with Iterative Refinement. In: Yi, K. (ed.) SAS 2006. LNCS, vol. 4134, pp. 425–442. Springer, Heidelberg (2006)

19. Finkel, A., Willems, B., Wolper, P.: A direct symbolic approach to model checking pushdown systems. Elec. Notes in Theor. Comp. Sci. 9 (1997)

20. Fischer, J., Jhala, R., Majumdar, R.: Joining dataflow with predicates. In: Gilbert, H., Handschuh, H. (eds.) FSE 2005. LNCS, vol. 3557, Springer, Heidelberg (2005)

21. Graf, S., Saïdi, H.: Construction of abstract state graphs with PVS. In: Grumberg, O. (ed.) CAV 1997. LNCS, vol. 1254, Springer, Heidelberg (1997)

22. Henzinger, T.A., Jhala, R., Majumdar, R., Sutre, G.: Lazy abstraction. In: POPL (2002)

23. Holley, L.H., Rosen, B.K.: Qualified data flow problems. TSE 7(1), 60–78 (1981)

24. IDAPro disassembler, http://www.datarescue.com/idabase/

25. Knoop, J., Steffen, B.: The interprocedural coincidence theorem. In: Pfahler, P., Kastens, U. (eds.) CC 1992. LNCS, vol. 641, Springer, Heidelberg (1992)

26. Mauborgne, L., Rival, X.: Trace Partitioning in Abstract Interpretation Based Static Analyzers. In: Sagiv, M. (ed.) ESOP 2005. LNCS, vol. 3444, pp. 5–20. Springer, Heidelberg (2005)

27. Oney, W.: Programming the Microsoft Windows Driver Model. In: Microsoft (2003)
28. Ramalingam, G., Field, J., Tip, F.: Aggregate structure identification and its application to program analysis. In: POPL (1999)
29. Sharir, M., Pnueli, A.: Two approaches to interprocedural data flow analysis. In: Program Flow Analysis: Theory and Applications, Prentice-Hall, Englewood Cliffs (1981)
30. Swift, M.M., Annamalai, M., Bershad, B.N., Levy, H.M.: Recovering device drivers. In: OSDI (2004)
31. Swift, M.M., Bershad, B.N., Levy, H.M.: Improving the reliability of commodity operating systems. ACM Trans. Comput. Syst. 23(1) (2005)

Model Checking-Based Genetic Programming with an Application to Mutual Exclusion

Gal Katz and Doron Peled

Department of Computer Science
Bar Ilan University
Ramat Gan 52900, Israel

Abstract. Two approaches for achieving correctness of code are verification and synthesis from specification. Evidently, it is easier to check a given program for correctness (although not a trivial task by itself) than to generate algorithmically correct-by-construction code. However, formal verification may give quite limited information about how to correct the code. Genetic programming repeatedly generates mutations of code, and then selects the mutations that remain for the next stage based on a fitness function, which assists in converging into a correct program. We use a model checking procedure to provide the fitness value in every stage. As an example, we generate algorithms for mutual exclusion, using this combination of genetic programming and model checking. The main challenge is to select a fitness function that will allow constructing correct solutions with minimal effort. We present our considerations behind the selection of a fitness function based not only on the classical outcome of model checking, i.e., the existence of an error trace, but on the complete graph constructed during the model checking process.

1 Introduction

The challenge in automatic programming is synthesizing programs automatically from their set of requirements. Genetic programming (GP) is an automatic program generation methodology; a population of programs is randomly created, and evolves by a biologically inspired process; the fitness of each program is usually calculated by running the program on some test cases, and evaluating its performance. Orthogonally, model checking [1] can be used to analyze a given program, verifying that it satisfies its specification, or providing a counterexample of that fact.

One of the possibilities of program synthesis is based on a brute force generation and analysis of the possible solutions. For example, Perrig and Song [2] successfully synthesized security protocols, while Bar-David and Taubenfeld [3] used a similar approach for the generation of mutual exclusion algorithms. Checking all the possibilities one by one guarantees that given enough time, a correct solution will be found. However, synthesis is an intractable problem in nature, which becomes quite quickly prohibitively expensive. This is also the case for synthesis algorithms that are not based on enumeration.

C.R. Ramakrishnan and J. Rehof (Eds.): TACAS 2008, LNCS 4963, pp. 141–156, 2008.

Genetic programming is often appropriate for solving sequential optimization related problems, where providing better solutions for some inputs than for others is acceptable. GP is less used traditionally for designing communication protocols, concurrent or reactive systems, where there is a specification on the behavior of the system over time, which must not be violated. Recently, Johnson [4] experimented with using the results of model checking for providing the fitness function for synthesizing a reactive system with GP. Using model checking for providing the fitness function has the advantage over testing that *all* the executions of the generated code are checked, rather than sampled. However, finding a fitness function with enough values to allow the gradual improvements typical to GP is not an easy task.

We provide a framework for genetic programming that is based on intensive analysis of a model checking procedure. The main challenge is to provide a fitness function that will improve the chances and speed of convergence towards a correct solution. For that, model checking is not only used to decide whether some properties of the specification hold or not (as in [4]), but the graph generated during model checking is analyzed, in order to extract more information. Finally, we provide experimental results of applying our framework to the mutual exclusion algorithm generation problem.

We experimented with several alternative analysis methods based on the result of state based model checking, such as probabilistic [5] and quantitative [6] model checking. In our experiments, these methods have not led to convergence toward solutions. Our method for calculating a fitness function is based on an analysis of the strongly connected components in the model checking graph. We show experimental results where this analysis leads to the generation of mutual exclusion algorithms. While the stochastic nature of GP eliminates the ability of finding all solutions, or proving that no such exists, it drastically reduces the average time and search steps required for finding a solution, compared to the enumeration methods. This is especially true when the solution programs are long, resulting in an extremely large search space.

In particular, our analysis gives a lower fitness weight to the case where an error can occur after a finite number of steps and a higher fitness weight to the case where infinite number of choices is needed in order for it to occur. The intuition behind this distinction is that the first kind of errors is more basic, whereas the second kind of errors is due to subtle scheduling.

The rest of the paper is organized as follows: Section 2 gives background on Genetic Programming and Model Checking. A description of the combined approach is given in Sect. 3. The mutual exclusion example is described in Sect. 4, followed by conclusions and future work in Sect. 5.

2   Background

2.1   Genetic Programming

Genetic Programming [7] is a method for automatic synthesis of computer programs by an evolutionary process. GP is derived from the field of Genetic

Algorithms (GA) [8], and uses a similar methodology. An initial population of candidate solutions is randomly generated and gradually improved by various biologically inspired operations. The main advantages of GP over GA are the explicit use of computer programs in the solution space, and the flexible structure of the solutions, usually represented as trees (although other representation are possible as well). The GP algorithm we use in this work goes through the following steps (described in details below):

1. Create initial population of candidate solutions.
2. Randomly choose μ candidate solutions.
3. Create λ new candidates by applying mutation (and optionally crossover) operations (as explained below) to the above μ candidates.
4. Calculate the fitness function for each of the new candidates.
5. Based on the calculated fitness, choose μ individuals from the obtained set of size $\mu + \lambda$ candidates, and use them to replace the old μ individuals selected at step 2.
6. Repeat steps 2-5 until a perfect candidate is found, or until the maximal permitted number of iterations is reached.

Programs are represented as trees, where an instruction or an expression is represented by a single node, having its parameters as its offspring, and terminal nodes represent constants. Examples of the instructions we use are *assignment*, *while* (with or without a body), *if* and *block*. The latter is a special node that takes two instructions as its parameters, and runs them sequentially.

A strongly-typed GP [9] is used, which means that every node has a type, and also enforces the type of its offspring. It also affects the genetic operations which must preserve the program typing rules.

At the first step, an initial population of candidate programs is generated. Each program is generated recursively, starting from the root, and adding nodes until the tree is completed. The root node is chosen randomly from the set of instruction nodes, and each child node is chosen randomly from the set of nodes allowed by its parent type, and its place in the parameter list. A "grow" method [7] is used, meaning that either terminal or non-terminal nodes can be chosen, unless the maximum tree depths is reached, which enforces the choice of terminals. This method can create trees with various forms. Figure 1(i) shows an example of a randomly created program tree. The tree represents the following program:

```
while (A[2] != 0)
    A[me] = 1
```

Nodes in bold belong to instructions, while the other nodes are the parameters of those instructions.

Mutation is the main operation we use. It allows making small changes on existing program trees. The mutation includes the following steps:

1. Randomly choose a node (internal or leaf) from the program tree.
2. Apply one of the following operations to the tree with respect to the chosen node:

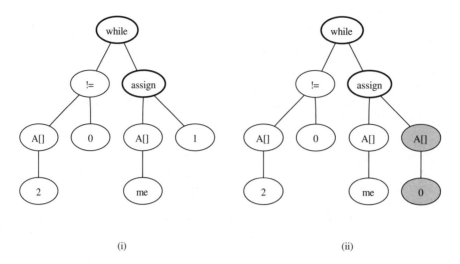

(i)   (ii)

Fig. 1. (i) Randomly created program tree, (ii) the result of a replacement mutation

(a) Replace the subtree rooted by the node with a new randomly generated subtree.
(b) Add an immediate parent to the node. Randomly create other offspring to the new parent, if needed.
(c) Replace the node by one of its offspring. Delete the remaining offspring of that node.
(d) Delete the subtree rooted by the node. The node ancestors should be updated recursively (possible only for instruction nodes).

Mutation of type (a) can replace either a single terminal or an entire subtree. For example, the terminal "1" in the tree of Fig. 1(i), is replaced by the grayed subtree in (ii), changing the assignment instruction into A[me] = A[0]. Mutations of type (b) can extend programs in several ways, depending on the new parent node type. In case a "block" type is chosen, a new instruction(s) will be inserted before or after the mutation node. For instance, the grayed part of Fig. 2 represents a second assignment instruction inserted into the original program. Similarly, choosing a parent node of type "while" will have the effect of wrapping the mutation node with a while loop. Another situation occurs when the mutation node is a simple condition which can be extended into a complex one, extending, for example, the simple condition in Fig. 1 into the complex condition: A[2] != 0 and A[other] == me. Mutation type (c) has the opposite effect, and can convert the tree in Fig. 2 back into the original tree of Fig. 1(i). Mutation of type (d) allows the deletion of one or more instructions. It can recursively change the type, or even cause the deletion of ancestor nodes.

Mutation type is randomly selected, but all mutations must obey strongly typing rules of nodes. This affects the possible mutation type for the chosen node, and the type of new generated nodes.

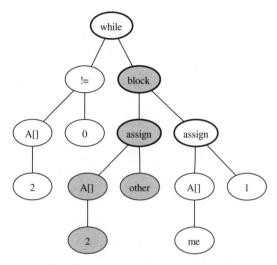

Fig. 2. Tree after insertion mutation

The crossover operation creates new individuals by merging building blocks of two existing programs. The crossover steps are:

1. Randomly choose a node from the first program.
2. Randomly choose a node from the second program that has the same type as the first node.
3. Exchange between the subtrees rooted by the two nodes, and use the two new programs created by this method.

While traditional GP is heavily based on crossover, it is quite a controversial operation (see [10], for example), and may cause more damage than benefit in the evolutionary process, especially in the case of small and sensitive programs that we investigate. Thus, crossover is barely used in our work.

Fitness is used by GP in order to choose which programs have a higher probability to survive and participate in the genetic operations. In addition, the success termination criterion of the GP algorithm is based on the fitness value of the most fitted individual. Traditionally, the fitness function is calculated by running the program on some set of inputs (a training set) which suppose to represent all of the possible inputs. This can lead to programs which work only for the selected inputs (overfitting), or to programs that may fail for some inputs, which might be unacceptable in some domains. In contrast, our fitness function is not based on running the programs on sample data, but on an enhanced model checking procedure, as described later.

We use a fitness-proportional selection [8] that gives each program a probability of being chosen that is proportional to its fitness value. In traditional GP, after the μ programs are randomly chosen, the selection method is applied in order to decide which of them will participate in the genetic operations. The selected programs are then used in order to create a new set of μ programs that will replace the original ones.

We use another method, which is more similar to the Evolutionary Strategies [11] $\mu + \lambda$ style. In this method, genetic operations are applied to all of the μ programs, in order to produce a much larger set of λ offspring. The fitness proportional selection is then used in order to chooses μ programs from the set of parents and offspring that will replace the original μ parents.

2.2   Model Checking

A *finite ω-automaton* is a tuple $A = (\Sigma, S, S_0, \Delta, L, \Omega)$ where:

- Σ is a finite alphabet.
- S is a finite set of states.
- $S_0 \subseteq S$ is a set of initial states.
- $\Delta \subseteq S \times S$ is a transition relation.
- $L : S \rightarrow \Sigma$ is a labeling function of the states.
- Ω is the acceptance condition (defined later).

Note that in the automaton type defined here, the labels are on the states instead of on the arcs. Nevertheless, it is easy to transform one type of the automaton into another. An automaton can be treated as a directed graph $G_A = (V, E)$ by setting $V = S$ and $E = \Delta$.

A *run p of A* over an infinite word $w = w_0 w_1 w_2... \in \Sigma^\omega$ is the sequence $s = s_0 s_1 s_2... \in S^\omega$ such that: $s_0 \in S_0$, for all $i \geq 0$, $(s_i, s_{i+1}) \in \Delta$, and $w_i = L(s_i)$. We denote by *Inf(p)* the set of states appearing infinitely on the run p.

A *maximal strongly connected component (SCC)* is a maximal set of nodes $C \subseteq S$ such that for each $s, t \in C$ there is a path from s to t. An SCC is *non-trivial* if it has at least one edge. A graph can be decomposed into SCCs by a linear time algorithm, such as Tarjan's. The SCCs in a graph can be converted into a directed acyclic graph (DAG) where each SCC is represented by a simple node, and edges between these latter nodes represent paths from one corresponding SCC to another. A *bottom SCC (BSCC)* is an SCC that has no paths to other SCCs, i.e. it is associated with a leaf in the SCCs DAG defined in the previous paragraph. A *Büchi automaton* is an ω-automaton with the acceptance condition defined as a set of states $F \subseteq S$ where a run p over a word w is accepted if $\text{Inf}(p) \cap F \neq \emptyset$.

A *Streett automaton* is an ω-automaton with the acceptance condition defined as a set of k ordered pairs (E_i, F_i), where $E_i, F_i \subseteq S, 1 \leq i \leq k$. A run p over a word w is accepted if $\text{Inf}(p) \cap E_i \neq \emptyset \rightarrow \text{Inf}(p) \cap F_i \neq \emptyset$ for all pairs. Every Streett automaton can be converted into a Büchi automaton accepting the same language, and vice versa [12]. Streett automata are closed under determinization [13], but this is not the case for Büchi automata where their nondeterministic version is more expressive than their deterministic one. The *language* of A, denoted by *L(A)* is defined as the set of all words accepted by A. A is *nonempty* if $L(A) \neq \emptyset$, i.e. A accepts at least one word. An *accepting SCC* is defined as an SCC C, for which there exists an accepting run p such that $\text{Inf}(p) \subseteq C$. We say that this SCC is *not empty*.

Algorithm 1. Checking non-emptiness of a Streett automaton or SCC

IsNonempty(A, IsEntireAutomaton)
(1)   if IsEntireAutomaton
(2)   Decompose A into SCCs reachable from S_0
(3)   repeat
(4)   changed = FALSE
(5)   for each pair $(E_i, F_i) \in \Omega$
(6)   for each nontrivial SCC C
(7)   if $C \cap E_i \neq \emptyset$ and $C \cap F_i = \emptyset$
(8)   remove from C all states $\{e \mid e \in E_i\}$
(9)   rebuild the decomposition of C into SCCs
(10)   changed = TRUE
(11)   until changed = FALSE
(12)   if A contains nontrivial components return TRUE
(13)   else return FALSE

Algorithm 1 can check in polynomial time the non-emptiness of an entire Streett automaton or a single SCC [14]. The second parameter should be set to TRUE of FALSE respectively.

Street automata are closed under intersection, i.e. if

$$A = (\Sigma, S_A, S_A^0, \Delta_A, L_A, \Omega_A) \quad , \quad B = (\Sigma, S_B, S_B^0, \Delta_B, L_B, \Omega_B)$$

are two Street automata using the same alphabet, then there exists a Street automaton C such that $L(C) = L(A) \cap L(B)$. C is constructed as follows:

$$C = (\Sigma, S_A \times S_B, S_A^0 \times S_B^0, \Delta_C, L_C, \Omega_C) \text{ where}$$

- $\Delta_C = \{(s, s'), (t, t') \mid (s, t) \in \Delta_A \text{ and } (s', t') \in \Delta_B \text{ and } L(s) = L(s') \text{ and } L(t) = L(t')\}$.
- For each state (s, s') of C, $L(s, s') = L(s)$.
- $\Omega_C = \{(E \times S_B, F \times S_B) \mid (E, F) \in \Omega_A\} \cup \{(S_A \times E, S_A \times F) \mid (E, F) \in \Omega_B\}$.

Büchi automata are closed under intersection as well.

A *finite-state system* M can be represented as an ω-automaton A_M by using the following settings:

- $\Sigma = 2^{AP}$ where AP denote a set of atomic propositions that may hold on the system states.
- S is a set of the system states, where a system state consists of the values of its variables, program counter, buffers, etc. at a specific time.
- S_0 is the initial state of the system.
- $\Delta \subseteq S \times S$ is a set of state pairs (s, r) such that r can be obtained from s by an atomic transition of M.
- $L : S \to 2^{AP}$ assigns to each state a set of propositions that hold in that state.
- Ω is set to accept all runs. This can be done on Büchi automata by setting $\Omega = S$, and on Street automata by setting $\Omega = \emptyset$. Another option is to set Ω to some fairness conditions that will allow only fair runs of the system.

In order to define the specification properties we use *Linear Temporal Logic (LTL)*. LTL is a modal logic having the following syntax:

$$\varphi ::= p \mid (\varphi) \mid \neg\varphi \mid \varphi \vee \varphi \mid \varphi \wedge \varphi \mid \varphi \to \varphi \mid \Box\varphi \mid \Diamond\varphi \mid \bigcirc\varphi \mid \varphi\mathcal{U}\varphi$$

where $p \in AP$, a set of atomic propositions. LTL formulas are interpreted over an infinite sequence of states $\xi = s_0 s_1 s_2 \ldots$, where we denote by ξ_i the suffix $s_i s_{i+1} s_{i+2} \ldots$ of ξ. For a suffix ξ_k of ξ, the LTL semantics is defined as follows:

- $\xi_i \models p$ iff $s_i \in p$.
- $\xi_i \models \neg\varphi$ iff not $\xi_i \models \varphi$.
- $\xi_i \models \varphi \vee \psi$ iff $\xi_i \models \varphi$ or $\xi_i \models \phi$.
- $\xi_i \models \bigcirc\varphi$ iff $\xi_{i+1} \models \varphi$.
- $\xi_i \models \varphi\mathcal{U}\psi$ iff for some $j \geq i$, $\xi_j \models \psi$. and for all $i \leq k < j$, $\xi_k \models \varphi$.

The rest of connectives can be defined by using the following identities:

$$true = p \vee \neg p, \quad \varphi \wedge \psi = \neg(\neg\varphi \vee \neg\psi), \quad \varphi \to \psi = \neg\varphi \vee \psi, \quad \Diamond\varphi = true\,\mathcal{U}\varphi, \quad \Box\varphi = \neg\Diamond\neg\varphi$$

We say that $\xi \models \varphi$ if $\xi_0 \models \varphi$, i.e. the complete sequence ξ satisfies the LTL formula φ. For a finite-state system M, $M \models \varphi$ if for every fair run ξ on M, $\xi \models \varphi$.

Specification properties defined as LTL formulas can be converted into ω-automata. For nondeterministic Büchi automata, this can be done by a direct construction algorithm in time exponential to the formula size [15]. For deterministic Streett automata, the process may involve a construction of a Büchi automaton, and a determinization process that ends with a deterministic Streett automaton [13]. The translation may result in a doubly exponential blowup [16].

A standard Model Checking procedure checks whether a system M satisfies a specification φ [17]. This is done by building the automata A_M and A_φ of M and φ respectively, and checking whether $L(M) \subseteq L(\varphi)$. Since

$$L(M) \subseteq L(\varphi) \leftrightarrow L(M) \cap \overline{L(\varphi)} = \emptyset \leftrightarrow L(M) \cap L(\neg\varphi) = \emptyset$$

it is possible to use the negation of φ, build $A_{\neg\varphi}$, and check whether the language $L(M) \cap L(\neg\varphi)$ is empty. The Model Checking process is usually performed using Büchi automata, since the conversion from LTL, and the language emptiness checking are easier with these automata. However, for our purposes we will use Streett automata, as explained in the next section.

3   Combining GP and Model Checking

The standard model checking procedure gives a yes/no answer to the satisfaction of a system M by a specification formula φ (in addition to a counterexample, when φ is not satisfied). As we wish to base the fitness function on the model checking results, using a function with just two values may give a limited ability to gradually improve the programs ([4], for instance). Therefore, we try to quantify the level of satisfaction, by comparing the system computations on which the specification is satisfied, with those on which it is not. This can be done by checking the intersection graph of the system and the specification, for accepting and non-accepting paths.

However, when using a nondeterministic (such as Büchi) automaton, finding a non-accepting path of a computation does not necessarily mean that the computation itself is not accepted, since there might be another accepting path for the same computation. For this reason, we use deterministic Streett automata, on which each computation is represented by a single path. While this choice has an additional cost on the size of the specification automata, and on the model checking procedure performance, the symmetry between accepting and non-accepting paths is crucial for our analysis.

Having a system M and a specification formula φ, we perform the enhanced model checking procedure showed below.

Algorithm 2. Enhanced model checking

ENHANCEDMC(M, φ)
- (1)   univ := FALSE
- (2)   Construct Streett automata A_M and A_φ for M and φ respectively.
- (3)   Create the intersection automaton $A_{pos} = A_M \cap A_\varphi$.
- (4)   Decompose A_{pos} into SCCs reachable from its initial states
- (5)   For each SCC $C \in A_{pos}$:
- (6)   acc(C) := IsNonempty(C, FALSE)
- (7)   if for each SCC C, acc(C) = TRUE
- (8)   Construct Streett automaton $A_{\neg\varphi}$ for the negation of φ
- (9)   Create the intersection automaton $A_{neg} = A_M \cap A_{\neg\varphi}$
- (10)   univ := $\neg$ IsNonempty(A_{neg}, TRUE)

The algorithm first checks the non-emptiness of every SCC of the graph and stores the result in the SCC's *acc* variable (lines (1) - (6)). In the case that all of the SCCs are accepting, an additional step is performed in order to check the automaton for universality (stored in the *univ* variable) (lines (7) - (10)).

The results of the algorithm are used for setting the value of the fitness function, as detailed in Table 1. In order to assign a fitness level, we assume that the choice of program transitions is made by a hostile scheduler (or environment) that tries to cause the violation of the checked property. The amount of choices the scheduler has to make during an execution determines the fitness level (for a related approach for analyzing counterexamples, see [18]). The lowest fitness level of 0 is given when the checked property is never satisfied (thus, no hostile scheduling choices are needed to violate the property). Level 1 is assigned when the graph contains a non-accepting bottom SCC. In this case, a finite number of choices can lead to that BSCC, from which the failure is unavoidable. A higher level of 2 is assigned where all BSCCs are accepting, hence, a violation can be caused only by an infinite scheduler choices that will consistently skip the accepting paths. The highest level of 3 indicates that the property is always satisfied (thus, even a hostile scheduler cannot cause a violation of the property).

Table 1. Fitness Levels

Fitness level	Condition	Description	Hostile scheduler choices	Score
0	For all SCCs, acc(C)=FALSE	The property is not satisfied on any execution	None	0
1	At least one SCC with acc(C)=TRUE. At least one BSCC with acc(C)=FALSE	The program can reach a state from which the violation of the property is unavoidable	Finite	70
2	For all BSCCs, acc(C)=TRUE, univ=FALSE	Property violation is always avoidable. It can be violated only by an infinite scheduler choices	Infinite	80
3	univ=TRUE	The property is always satisfied	Impossible	100

The scores assigned to each fitness level are intended to encourage the gradual evolution of programs among the various levels. The specific score values were chosen so that two or more partially satisfied properties will have a higher score than a single fully satisfied property. This gives a better chance to a more parallel and smooth evolution.

A class of properties that need a special treatment are properties of the form $\square(P \rightarrow \diamond Q)$. These properties can be vacuously satisfied by a run on which P never happens (see [19]). When comparing the accepting and non-accepting paths of the program, we wish to ignore those vacuous runs, and concentrate only on runs where P eventually happens.

Consider for instance the property $\square\ (p\ in\ \texttt{Pre} \rightarrow \diamond\ (p\ in\ \texttt{CS}))$ (defined at Sect. 4), requiring that a process trying to enter the critical section will eventually enter it. We do not wish to give extra score for program runs that stay infinitely on the $\texttt{Non Critical Section}$. Neither can we just add "$\wedge \diamond\ (p\ in\ \texttt{Pre})$" to the property, since this will treat the above runs as violating the property. Instead, we wish to evaluate only runs where the process enters the $\texttt{Pre Protocol}$ section, and ignore other runs and their related SCCs.

In order to achieve that, a prior step is added before line (3) of algorithm 2 . In this step A_M is intersected with the automaton of the property $\diamond P$, and the intersection is used instead of A_M. In the special case when the intersection is empty, all runs are vacuously satisfied, and a predefined fitness level (usually 0) is assigned to the program, without running the rest of the algorithm.

Another reason for restricting program runs is related to fairness. In this work we use weak process fairness by adding Streett conditions to the program automaton (strong fairness can be applied as well with Streett conditions).

On cases when not all of the program runs are accepted by the program automaton A_M (such as the two cases above), algorithm 2 needs a refinement. Prior to the non-emptiness check at lines (5) - (6), we run a similar check, but only with the Streett conditions derived from A_M. Empty SCCs found at this stage are considered *not-relevant*, and are not used by further steps of the algorithm and the scoring analysis. After this stage, the standard check of lines

(5) - (6) is performed on the *relevant* SCCs, including all of the Streett conditions (derived from both the program and the specification).

Deadlocks in programs are considered a fundamental failure, and are usually tested at early stages along with other safety properties. In our case, however, programs can evolve to a certain fitness score, even if they contain deadlocks. This is a result of the fact that as shown on the previous section regarding vacuity, some liveness properties can be relevant only in some parts of the state space, and may not be affected by other parts with deadlocks.

For this reason, we do not check for deadlocks explicitly. Instead, when the graph of a specific liveness property contains a deadlock, it will be detected by the above algorithm as a non-accepting BSCC, and will be assigned fitness level 1. In order to distinguish this case from the usual cases of level 1, we slightly decrease the score given to the property if the BSCC contains only a single node (which is the case when a deadlock occurs). While programs may simply raise their score by adding lines that turn the deadlock into a livelock, adding these lines increases the probability of a mutation in the program lines related to the deadlock, which may help in eliminating it. This was the case on the run described later.

The procedure above is performed for each of the properties included in the specification, resulting in multiple fitness functions. These values have to be merged into a single fitness score. This can be done by summing up the values of all functions (as done in [4]). However, our experience shows that some properties may depend on other more basic properties, and may become trivially satisfied where those basic properties are not satisfied. In order to prevent this biased fitness calculation, we assign a level to each property, starting from 1 for the most basic properties, and checking properties by the order of levels. If at level i, not all of the properties are fully satisfied, the checking process is stopped, and all properties at levels greater than i receive a score of 0. This also saves time by not checking unneeded properties. The total fitness value is then divided by the total number of properties (including those that were not checked) in order to get an average fitness value.

GP programs tend to grow in size over time until they reach the maximum allowed tree depth. This phenomena [20,21], known as "bloating" is caused by non-relevant portions of code which are called "introns" after the analogous biological term for non-relevant DNA. While there is evidence that introns may help the evolutionary process [10], they may hurt performance and even prevent the convergence, especially in areas such as protocols and concurrent programs, where programs has to be small and accurate. One of the ways of preventing introns from appearing is giving a penalty to large programs by decreasing their fitness.

We use parsimony as a secondary fitness measure by subtracting from the total score the number of program nodes multiplied by a small constant (0.1). The constant is chosen to be small enough, so that programs with various length can evolve, and the distinction between fitness levels is preserved, but still large enough to affect programs at the same level to have a reduced size. Note that this means programs cannot get a perfect score of 100, but only get closer to it. Instead, we mark programs as perfect when all properties are fully satisfied. Shorter programs can be created as a result of the genetic operations, as well as by removing dead-code detected by the model checking process.

4   Example - The Mutual Exclusion Problem

As an example, we use our method in order to automatically generate solutions to several variants of the Mutual Exclusion Problem. In this problem, first described and solved by Dijkstra [22], two or more processes are repeatedly running critical and non-critical sections of a program. The goal is to avoid the simultaneous execution of the critical section by more than one process. We limit our search for solutions to the case of only two processes. The problem is modeled using the following program parts that are executed in an infinite loop:

```
Non Critical Section
Pre Protocol
Critical Section
Post Protocol
```

The Non Critical Section part represents the process part on which it does not require an access to the shared resource. A process can make a nondeterministic choice whether to stay in that part, or to move into the Pre Protocol part. From the Critical Section part, a process always has to move into the Post Protocol part. The Non Critical Section and Critical Section parts are fixed, while our goal is to automatically generate code for the Pre Protocol and Post Protocol parts, such that the entire program will fully satisfy the problem's specification.

We use a restricted high level language based on the C language. Each process has access to its id (0 or 1) by the me literal, and to the other process' id by the other literal. The processes can use an array of shared bits with a size depended on the exact variant of the problem we wish to solve. The two processes run the same code. The available node types are: *assignment, if, while, empty-while, block, and ,or* and *array*. Terminals include the constants: *0, 1, 2, me* and *other*.

Table 2 describes the properties which define the problem specification. The four program parts are denoted by NonCS, Pre, CS and Post respectively. Property 1 is the basic safety property requiring the mutual exclusion. Properties displayed

Table 2. Mutual Exclusion Specification

No.	Type	Definition	Description	Level
1	Safety	$\Box\neg(p_0$ in CS $\land p_1$ in CS$)$	Mutual Exclusion	1
2,3	Liveness	$\Box(p_{me}$ in Post $\to \Diamond(p_{me}$ in NonCS$))$	Progress	2
4,5		$\Box(p_{me}$ in Pre $\land \Box(p_{other}$ in NonCS$)) \to \Diamond(p_{me}$ in CS$))$	No Contest	3
6		$\Box((p_0$ in Pre $\land p_1$ in Pre$) \to \Diamond(p_0$ in CS $\lor p_1$ in CS$))$	Deadlock Freedom	4
7,8		$\Box(p_{me}$ in Pre $\to \Diamond(p_{me}$ in CS$))$	Starvation	4

in pairs are symmetrically defined for the two processes. Properties 2 and 3 guarantee that the processes are not hung in the Post Protocol part. Similar properties for the Critical Section are not needed, since it is a fixed part without an evolved code. Properties 4 and 5 require that a process can enter the critical section, if it is the only process trying to enter it. Property 4 requires that if both processes are trying to enter the critical section, at least one of them will eventually succeed. This property can be replaced by the stronger requirements 7 and 8 that guarantee that no process will starve.

There are several known solutions to the Mutual Exclusion problem, depending on the number of shared bits in use, the type of conditions allowed (simple / complex) and whether starvation-freedom is required. The variants of the problem we wish to solve are showed in Table 3.

Table 3. Mutual Exclusion Variants

Variant No.	Number of bits	Conditions	Requirement	Relevant properties	Known algorithm
1	2	Simple	Deadlock Freedom	1,2,3,4,5,6	One bit protocol [23]
2	3	Simple	Starvation Freedom	1,2,3,4,5,7,8	Dekker [22]
3	3	Complex	Starvation Freedom	1,2,3,4,5,7,8	Peterson [24]

4.1 Experimental Results

We used a specially designed model check and GP engine which implements the methods described earlier. Three different configurations where used, in order to search for solutions to the variants described in Table 3. Each run included the creation of 150 initial programs by the GP engine, and the iterative creation of new programs until a perfect solution was found, or until a maximum of 2000 iterations. At each iteration, 5 programs were randomly selected, bred, and replaced using mutation and crossover operations, as described on Sect. 2.1. The values $\mu = 5, \lambda = 150$ where chosen. The tests were performed on a 2.6 GHz Pentium Xeon Processor. For each configuration, multiple runs were performed. Some of the runs converged into perfect solutions, while others found only partial solutions. The results are summarized on Table 4.

Table 4. Test results

Variant No.	Successful runs (%)	Avg. run durtaion (sec)	Avg. no. of tested programs per run
1	40	128	156600
2	6	397	282300
3	7	363	271950

Test 1. At the first test, we tried to find a deadlock-free algorithm solving the mutual exclusion problem. The programming language in this case was set to allow the use of two shared bits, and only simple conditions. Followed is an

analysis of one of the successful runs. The numbers in the square brackets under each program below represent the program fitness scores.

The initial population contained 150 randomly generated programs with various fitness scores. Many programs did not satisfy even the basic mutual exclusion safety property 1, and thus achieved a fitness score of zero.

The programs were gradually improved by the genetic operations, until program (a) was created. This program fully satisfies all of the properties, which makes it a correct solution. At this stage, we could end the run; however, we kept it for some more iterations. Due to the parsimony pressure caused by the secondary fitness measure, the program is finally evolved by a series of deletion and replacement mutations into program (b). This program is a perfect solution to the requirements, which is actually the known one bit protocol [23].

```
Non Critical Section           Non Critical Section
A[me] = 1                      A[me] = 1
While (A[other] != 0)          While (A[other] != 0)
    A[me] = me                     A[me] = me
    While (A[other] != A[0])        While (A[other] == 1)
        While (A[1] != 0)          A[me] = 1
    A[me] = 1                  Critical Section
Critical Section               A[me] = 0
A[me] = 0
```

(a) [96.50]   (b) [97.10]

Test 2. At the second test we changed the configuration to support three shared bits. This allowed the creation of algorithms like Dekker's [22] which uses the third bit to set turns between the two processes. Since the requirements were similar to those of the previous test (accept the change of property 6 by 7 and 8), many runs initially converged into deadlock-free algorithms using only two bits. Those algorithms have execution paths at which one of the processes starve, hence only partially satisfying properties 7 or 8. Program (c) shows one of those algorithms, which later evolved into program (d). The evolution first included the addition of the a second line to the *post protocol* section (which only slightly decreased its fitness level due to the parsimony measure). A replacement mutation then changed the inner while loop condition, leading to a perfect solution similar to Dekker's algorithm.

Another interesting algorithm generated by one of the runs is program (e). This algorithm (also reported at [3]) is a perfect solution too, but it is shorter than Dekker's algorithm.

```
Non Critical Section    Non Critical Section    Non Critical Section
A[me] = 1               A[me] = 1               A[other] = other
While (A[other] == 1)   While (A[other] == 1)   if (A[2] == other)
    While (A[0] != other)    While (A[2] == me)      A[2] = me
        A[me] = 0                A[me] = 0           While (A[me] == A[2])
    A[me] = 1               A[me] = 1           Critical Section
Critical Section        Critical Section        A[other] = me
```

```
A[me] = 0                       A[2] = me
                                A[me] = 0
```

    (c) [94.34]   (d) [96.70]   (e) [97.50]

Test 3. At this test, we added the *and* and *or* operators to the function set, allowing the creation of complex conditions. Some of the runs evolved into program (f) which is the known Peterson's algorithm [24].

```
Non Critical Section
A[me] = 1
A[2] = me
While (A[other] == 1 and A[2] != other)
Critical Section
A[me] = 0
```

    (f) [97.60]

5   Conclusions and Future Work

One of the main features of our scoring system is that a failure of a property to hold in a program is considered to be more severe where there is a finite prefix from which the property would not be fixable. On the other hand, when failure involves infinitely many choices that would steer away the execution from a correct one, the failure is considered to be "weaker". This provides an interesting dichotomy in analysis of correctness, and can be further refined (e.g., by recognizing the case when *all* of the executions are of the same severe failure, rather than that there exists at least one such).

Experimentally, this distinction turned out to provide good scoring results with a high probability of convergence. On the other hand, the disadvantage of using GP for generating solutions for problems like mutual exclusion is that because GP involves probabilistic decisions, one does not know when and whether the search space is exhausted.

Further work includes refining the scoring system, and making experiments with other concurrent or distributed algorithms.

References

1. Clarke, E.M., Grumberg, O., Peled, D.A.: Model Checking. MIT Press, Cambridge (2000)
2. Perrig, A., Song, D.: Looking for diamonds in the desert - extending automatic protocol generation to three-party authentication and key agreement protocols. In: CSFW, pp. 64–76 (2000)
3. Bar-David, Y., Taubenfeld, G.: Automatic discovery of mutual exclusion algorithms. In: Fich, F.E. (ed.) DISC 2003. LNCS, vol. 2848, pp. 136–150. Springer, Heidelberg (2003)

4. Johnson, C.G.: Genetic programming with fitness based on model checking. In: Ebner, M., O'Neill, M., Ekárt, A., Vanneschi, L., Esparcia-Alcázar, A.I. (eds.) EuroGP 2007. LNCS, vol. 4445, pp. 114–124. Springer, Heidelberg (2007)
5. Kwiatkowska, M.Z., Norman, G., Parker, D.: PRISM: Probabilistic symbolic model checker. In: Field, T., Harrison, P.G., Bradley, J., Harder, U. (eds.) TOOLS 2002. LNCS, vol. 2324, pp. 200–204. Springer, Heidelberg (2002)
6. Grosu, R., Smolka, S.A.: Monte carlo model checking. In: Halbwachs, N., Zuck, L.D. (eds.) TACAS 2005. LNCS, vol. 3440, pp. 271–286. Springer, Heidelberg (2005)
7. Koza, J.R.: Genetic Programming: On the Programming of Computers by Means of Natural Selection. MIT Press, Cambridge (1992)
8. Holland, J.H.: Adaptation in Natural and Artificial Systems: An Introductory Analysis with Applications to Biology, Control and Artificial Intelligence. MIT Press, Cambridge (1992)
9. Montana, D.J.: Strongly typed genetic programming. Evolutionary Computation 3(2), 199–230 (1995)
10. Banzhaf, W., Nordin, P., Keller, R.E., Francone, F.D.: Genetic Programming – An Introduction; On the Automatic Evolution of Computer Programs and its Applications, 3rd edn. Morgan Kaufmann, San Francisco (2001)
11. Schwefel, H.P.P.: Evolution and Optimum Seeking: The Sixth Generation. John Wiley & Sons, Inc. New York (1993)
12. Safra, S., Vardi, M.Y.: On ω automata and temporal logic. In: 21th Annual Symp. on Theory of Computing, pp. 127–137 (1989)
13. Safra, S.: Complexity of automata on infinite objects. PhD thesis, Rehovot, Israel (1989)
14. Emerson, E.A.: Automata, tableaux and temporal logics. In: Parikh, R. (ed.) Logic of Programs 1985. LNCS, vol. 193, pp. 79–88. Springer, Heidelberg (1985)
15. Vardi, M.Y., Wolper, P.: Reasoning about infinite computations. Information and Computation 115(1), 1–37 (1994)
16. Kupferman, O., Vardi, M.Y.: Model checking of safety properties. Formal Methods in System Design 19(3), 291–314 (2001)
17. Vardi, M.Y., Wolper, P.: An automata-theoretic approach to automatic program verification. In: Proc. IEEE Symp. on Logic in Computer Science, Boston, July 1986, pp. 332–344 (1986)
18. Jin, H., Ravi, K., Somenzi, F.: Fate and free will in error traces. In: Katoen, J.-P., Stevens, P. (eds.) TACAS 2002. LNCS, vol. 2280, pp. 445–459. Springer, Heidelberg (2002)
19. Beatty, D.L., Bryant, R.E.: Formally verifying a microprocessor using a simulation methodology. In: DAC, pp. 596–602 (1994)
20. Angeline, P.J.: Genetic programming and emergent intelligence. In: Advances in Genetic Programming, pp. 75–98. MIT Press, Cambridge (1994)
21. Tackett, W.A.: Recombination, selection, and the genetic construction of computer programs. PhD thesis, Los Angeles, CA, USA (1994)
22. Dijkstra, E.W.: Solution of a problem in concurrent programming control. Commun. ACM 8(9), 569 (1965)
23. Burns, J.E., Lynch, N.A.: Bounds on shared memory for mutual exclusion. Information and Computation 107(2), 171–184 (1993)
24. Peterson, G.L., Fischer, M.J.: Economical solutions to the critical section problem in a distributed system. In: ACM Symposium on Theory of Computing (STOC), pp. 91–97 (1977)

Conditional Probabilities over Probabilistic and Nondeterministic Systems

Miguel E. Andrés and Peter van Rossum

Institute for Computing and Information Sciences,
Radboud University Nijmegen, The Netherlands
{mandres,petervr}@cs.ru.nl

Abstract. This paper introduces the logic cpCTL, which extends the probabilistic temporal logic pCTL with conditional probability, allowing one to express that the probability that φ is true given that ψ is true is at least a. We interpret cpCTL over Markov Chain and Markov Decision Processes. While model checking cpCTL over Markov Chains can be done with existing techniques, those techniques do not carry over to Markov Decision Processes. We present a model checking algorithm for Markov Decision Processes. We also study the class of schedulers that suffice to find the maximum and minimum probability that φ is true given that ψ is true. Finally, we present the notion of counterexamples for cpCTL model checking and provide a method for counterexample generation.

1 Introduction

Conditional probabilities are a fundamental concept in probability theory. In system validation these appear for instance in anonymity, risk assessment, and diagnosability. Typical probabilities here are the probability that a certain message was sent by Alice, given that an intruder observes a certain traffic pattern; the probability that the dykes break, given that it rains heavily; the probability that component A has failed, given error message E.

This paper introduces the logic cpCTL extending the probabilistic temporal logic pCTL [HJ89] with new probabilistic operators of the form $\mathbf{P}_{\leq a}[\varphi|\psi]$, which expresses that the probability that φ is true given that ψ is true is at most a. We interpret cpCTL formulas over Markov Chains (MCs) and Markov Decision Processes (MDPs). Model checking cpCTL over MCs can be done with model checking techniques for pCTL*, using the equality $\mathbf{P}[\varphi|\psi] = \mathbf{P}[\varphi \wedge \psi]/\mathbf{P}[\psi]$.

For MDPs, cpCTL model checking is significantly more complex. Writing $\mathbf{P}_\eta[\varphi|\psi]$ for the probability $\mathbf{P}[\varphi|\psi]$ under scheduler η, model checking $\mathbf{P}_{\leq a}[\varphi|\psi]$ boils down to computing $\mathbf{P}^+[\varphi|\psi] = \max_\eta \mathbf{P}_\eta[\varphi|\psi] = \max_\eta \mathbf{P}_\eta[\varphi \wedge \psi]/\mathbf{P}_\eta[\psi]$. Thus, we have to maximize a non-linear function. (Note that in general it is not true that $\mathbf{P}^+[\varphi|\psi] = \mathbf{P}^+[\varphi \wedge \psi]/\mathbf{P}^+[\psi]$). Therefore, we cannot reuse the efficient machinery for pCTL model checking, which heavily relies on linear optimization techniques [BA95].

In particular we show that, unlike for pCTL [BA95], memoryless schedulers are not sufficient for optimizing reachability properties. We introduce the class

C.R. Ramakrishnan and J. Rehof (Eds.): TACAS 2008, LNCS 4963, pp. 157–172, 2008.
© Springer-Verlag Berlin Heidelberg 2008

of semi history-independent schedulers and show that these suffice to attain the optimal conditional probability. We also show that in cpCTL optimizing schedulers are not determined by the local structure of the system. That is, the choices made by the scheduler in one branch may influence the optimal choices in other branches. Surprisingly, deterministic schedulers still suffice to find the optimal conditional probability. This is remarkable indeed, since many non-linear optimization problems attain their optimal value in the interior of a convex polytope (which correspond to randomized schedulers in our setting).

Based on these properties, we present an exponential algorithm for checking if a given system satisfies a formula in the logic. We also present two heuristic optimizations of this algorithm: one trades time for space by exploiting the semi-history-independentness of optimizing schedulers; the other uses the fact that in certain cases optimal decisions can be decided locally. Finally, we present the notion of counterexamples for cpCTL model checking as pairs of sets of paths and provide a method for counterexample generation.

1.1 Applications

Complex Systems. One application of the techniques in this paper can be found in the area of complex system behavior. Modeling naturally occurring events as probabilistic choices and operator actions as non-deterministic choices, computing maximum and minimum conditional probabilities can help optimize run-time behavior. For instance, suppose that the desired behavior of the system is expressed as a pCTL formula φ and that during run-time we are making an observation about the system, expressed as a pCTL formula ψ. The techniques in this paper allow us to compute the maximum probability of obtaining φ given that ψ is true and compute the corresponding actions (non-deterministic choices) that have to be taken to achieve this probability.

Anonymizing Protocols. Another application can be found in anonymizing protocols. These protocols such as Onion Routing [CL05], Dining Cryptographers [Cha88], voting protocols [FOO92] try to hide the originator of a message rather than the content. Strong anonymity is commonly formulated [Cha88, BP05] in terms of conditional probability: A protocol is considered strongly anonymous if no information about the sender of a message can be derived from observations of the network traffic. Formally, this is expressed by saying that the (random variable representing) sender of a specific message is independent of the (random variable representing) the observations the adversary makes. That is, for all users u and all observations of the adversary o:

$$\mathbf{P}[\text{sender} = u \mid \text{observations} = o] = \mathbf{P}[\text{sender} = u].$$

It is customary to give the adversary full control over the network [DY83] and model the capabilities of the adversary as nondeterministic choices in the system; probabilistic choices model user behavior and random choices in the protocol. Since anonymity should be guaranteed for all possible attacks of the adversary, equality should hold for all schedulers. That is: for all schedulers η, all users u and all adversarial observations o:

$$\mathbf{P}_\eta[\text{sender} = u \mid \text{observations} = o] = \mathbf{P}_\eta[\text{sender} = u]$$

In practic e, $\mathbf{P}_\eta[\text{sender} = u]$ does not depend on the adversary. Since the techniques in this paper allow us to compute the maximal and minimal conditional probabilities, we can use them to prove strong anonymity.

Similarly, probable innocence is often formulated as saying that a user is (at worst) as likely to have not sent a message as to have sent it. In cpCTL this can immediately be expressed as $\mathbf{P}_{\leq 1/2}[\text{sender} = u \mid \text{observations} = o]$.

1.2   Organization of the Paper

In Section 2 we present the necessary background on MDPs. In Section 3 we introduce conditional probabilities over MDPs and cpCTL is introduced in Section 4. Section 5 introduces the class of semi history-independent schedulers and Section 6 explains how to compute maximum and minimum conditional probabilities. In Section 7, we investigate the notion of counterexamples. Finally, in Section 8 we give directions for future research.

2   Markov Decision Processes

Markov Decision Processes constitute a formalism that combines nondeterministic and probabilistic choices. They are a dominant model in corporate finance, supply chain optimization and system verification and optimization. While there are many slightly different variants of this formalism (e.g., action-labeled MDPs [Bel57, FV97], probabilistic automata [SL95, SV04]), we work with the state-labeled MDPs from [BA95].

The set of all discrete probability distributions on a set S is denoted by $\mathrm{Distr}(S)$. The Dirac distribution on an element $s \in S$ is written as 1_s. We also fix a set $\mathcal{P}$ of propositions.

Definition 2.1. *A Markov Decision Process (MDP) is a four-tuple $\Pi = (S, s_0, \tau, L)$, where S is the finite state space of the system; $s_0 \in S$ is the initial state; $L: S \to \wp(\mathcal{P})$ is a labeling function that associates to each state $s \in S$ a subset of $\mathcal{P}$; $\tau: S \to \wp(\mathrm{Distr}(S))$ is a function that associates to each $s \in S$ a non-empty and finite subset of $\mathrm{Distr}(S)$ of successor distributions.*

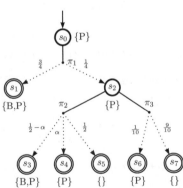

Fig. 1. Markov Decision Process

We define a *successor* relation $\rho \subseteq S \times S$ by $\rho \triangleq \{(s,t) | \exists \pi \in \tau(s) \ . \ \pi(t) > 0\}$ and for each state $s \in S$ we define the sets $\Omega_s \triangleq \{s_0 s_1 s_2 \ldots \in S^\omega | s_0 = s \wedge \forall n \in \mathbb{N} \ . \ \rho(s_n, s_{n+1})\}$, and $\Omega_s^* \triangleq \{s_0 s_1 \ldots s_n \in S^* | s_0 = s \wedge \forall 0 \leq i < n \ . \ \rho(s_n, s_{n+1}) .$ of paths and finite paths resp. beginning at s. For $\omega \in \Omega_s$, we write the n-th state of ω as ω_n. As usual, we let $\mathcal{B}_s \subseteq \wp(\Omega_s)$ be the Borel σ-algebra on the basic cylinders $\langle s_0 \ldots s_n \rangle \triangleq \{\omega \in \Omega_s | \omega_0 = s_0 \wedge \ldots \wedge \omega_n = s_n\}$.

Example 2.2. Figure 1 shows a MDP. Absorbing states (i.e., states s with $\tau(s) = \{1_s\}$) are represented by double lines. This MDP features a single non-deterministic decision, to be made in state s_2.

Schedulers (also called strategies, adversaries, or policies) resolve the nondeterministic choices in a MDP [PZ93, Var85, BA95].

Definition 2.3. Let $\Pi = (S, s_0, \tau, L)$ be a MDP and $s \in S$. An s-scheduler η on Π is a function from Ω_s^* to $\mathrm{Distr}(\wp(\mathrm{Distr}(S)))$ such that for all $\sigma \in \Omega_s^*$ we have $\eta(\sigma) \in \mathrm{Distr}(\tau(\mathrm{last}(\sigma)))$. We denote the set of all s-schedulers on Π by $\mathrm{Sch}_s(\Pi)$. When $s = s_0$ we omit it.

Note that our schedulers are randomized, i.e., in a finite path σ a scheduler chooses an element of $\tau(\mathrm{last}(\sigma))$ probabilistically. Under a scheduler η, the probability that the next state reached after the path σ is t, equals $\sum_{\pi \in \tau(\mathrm{last}(\sigma))} \eta(\sigma)$ $(\pi) \cdot \pi(t)$. In this way, a scheduler induces a probability measure on $\mathcal{B}_s$ as usual.

Definition 2.4. Let Π be a MDP, $s \in S$, and η an s-scheduler on Π. We define the probability measure $\mu_{s,\eta}$ as the unique measure on $\mathcal{B}_s$ such that for all $s_0 s_1 \dots s_n \in \Omega_s^*$

$$\mu_{s,\eta}(\langle s_0 s_1 \dots s_n \rangle) = \prod_{i=0}^{n-1} \sum_{\pi \in \tau(s_i)} \eta(s_0 s_1 \dots s_i)(\pi) \cdot \pi(s_{i+1}).$$

We recall the notions of deterministic and history independent schedulers.

Definition 2.5. Let Π be a MDP, $s \in S$, and η an s-scheduler of Π. We say that η is deterministic if $\eta(\sigma)(\pi_i)$ is either 0 or 1 for all $\pi_i \in \tau(\mathrm{last}(\sigma))$ and all $\sigma \in \Omega_s^*$. We say that a scheduler is history independent (HI) if for all finite paths σ_1, σ_2 of Π with $\mathrm{last}(\sigma_1) = \mathrm{last}(\sigma_2)$ we have $\eta(\sigma_1) = \eta(\sigma_2)$ The set of all deterministic and HI s-schedulers will be denoted by $\mathrm{Sch}_s^{\mathrm{HI}}(\Pi)$.

Definition 2.6. Let Π be a MDP, $s \in S$, and $\Delta \in \mathcal{B}_s$. Then the maximal and minimal probabilities of Δ, $\mu_s^+(\Delta), \mu_s^-(\Delta)$, are defined by

$$\mu_s^+(\Delta) \triangleq \sup_{\eta \in \mathrm{Sch}_s(\Pi)} \mu_{s,\eta}(\Delta) \quad and \quad \mu_s^-(\Delta) \triangleq \inf_{\eta \in \mathrm{Sch}_s(\Pi)} \mu_{s,\eta}(\Delta).$$

A scheduler that attains $\mu_s^+(\Delta)$ or $\mu_s^-(\Delta)$ is called a maximizing or minimizing scheduler respectively.

We define the notion of (finite) convex combination of schedulers.

Definition 2.7. Let Π be a MDP, $s \in S$. An s-scheduler η is a convex combination of the s-schedulers $\eta_1, \dots, \eta_n$ if there are $\alpha_1, \dots, \alpha_n \in [0, 1]$ with $\alpha_1 + \dots + \alpha_n = 1$ such that for all $\Delta \in \mathcal{B}_s$, $\mu_{s,\eta}(\Delta) = \alpha_1 \mu_{s,\eta_1}(\Delta) + \dots + \alpha_n \mu_{s,\eta_n}(\Delta)$.

Note that taking the convex combination η of η_1 and η_2 as functions, i.e., $\eta(\sigma)(\pi) = \alpha \eta_1(\sigma)(\pi) + (1 - \alpha)\eta_2(\sigma)(\pi)$, does not imply that η is a convex combination of η_1 and η_2 in the sense above.

3   Conditional Probabilities over MDPs

The conditional probability $P(A \mid B)$ is the probability of an event A, given the occurrence of another event B. Recall that given a probability space (Ω, F, P) and two events $A, B \in F$ with $P(B) > 0$, $P(A \mid B)$ is defined as $P(A \cap B)/P(B)$. If $P(B) = 0$, then $P(A \mid B)$ is undefined. In particular, given a MDP Π, a scheduler η and a state s, $(\Omega_s, \mathcal{B}_s, \mu_{s,\eta})$ is a probability space. So, for two sets of paths $\Delta_1, \Delta_2 \in \mathcal{B}_s$ with $\mu_{s,\eta}(\Delta_2) > 0$, the conditional probability of Δ_1 given Δ_2 is $\mu_{s,\eta}(\Delta_1 \mid \Delta_2) = \mu_{s,\eta}(\Delta_1 \cap \Delta_2)/\mu_{s,\eta}(\Delta_2)$. If $\mu_{s,\eta}(\Delta_2) = 0$, then $\mu_{\eta,s}(\Delta_1 \mid \Delta_2)$ is undefined. For technical reasons, we define the maximum and minimum conditional probabilities for all $\Delta_2 \in \mathcal{B}_s$.

Definition 3.1. *Let Π be a MDP. The* maximal *and* minimal *conditional probabilities* $\mu_s^+(\Delta_1|\Delta_2)$, $\mu_s^-(\Delta_1|\Delta_2)$ *of sets of paths* $\Delta_1, \Delta_2 \in \mathcal{B}_s$ *are defined by*

$$\mu_s^+(\Delta_1|\Delta_2) \triangleq \begin{cases} \sup_{\eta \in \mathrm{Sch}_{\Delta_2}^{>0}} \mu_{s,\eta}(\Delta_1|\Delta_2) & \text{if } \mathrm{Sch}_{\Delta_2}^{>0} \neq \emptyset, \\ 0 & \text{otherwise}, \end{cases}$$

$$\mu_s^-(\Delta_1|\Delta_2) \triangleq \begin{cases} \inf_{\eta \in \mathrm{Sch}_{\Delta_2}^{>0}} \mu_{s,\eta}(\Delta_1|\Delta_2) & \text{if } \mathrm{Sch}_{\Delta_2}^{>0} \neq \emptyset, \\ 1 & \text{otherwise}, \end{cases}$$

where $\mathrm{Sch}_{\Delta_2}^{>0} = \{\eta \in \mathrm{Sch}_s(\Pi) \mid \mu_{s,\eta}(\Delta_2) > 0\}$.

The following lemma generalizes Lemma 6 of [BA95] to conditional probabilities.

Lemma 3.2. *Given* $\Delta_1, \Delta_2 \in \mathcal{B}_s$, *its maximal and minimal conditional probabilities are related by:* $\mu_s^+(\Delta_1|\Delta_2) = 1 - \mu_s^-(\Omega_s - \Delta_1|\Delta_2)$.

4   Conditional Probabilistic Temporal Logic

The logic cpCTL extends pCTL with formulas of the form $\mathbf{P}_{\bowtie a}[\varphi|\psi]$. Intuitively, $\mathbf{P}_{\leq a}[\varphi|\psi]$ holds if the probability that φ holds given that ψ holds is at most a.

Definition 4.1. *The cpCTL logic is defined as the set of state and path formulas, i.e.,* cpCTL $\triangleq$ Stat $\cup$ Path, *where* Stat *and* Path *are defined inductively:*

$$\mathcal{P} \subseteq \mathrm{Stat},$$
$$\varphi, \psi \in \mathrm{Stat} \Rightarrow \varphi \wedge \psi, \neg\varphi \in \mathrm{Stat},$$
$$\varphi, \psi \in \mathrm{Path} \Rightarrow A\varphi, E\varphi, \mathbf{P}_{\bowtie a}[\varphi], \mathbf{P}_{\bowtie a}[\varphi|\psi] \in \mathrm{Stat},$$
$$\varphi, \psi \in \mathrm{Stat} \Rightarrow \varphi\,\mathcal{U}\psi, \Diamond\varphi, \Box\,\varphi \in \mathrm{Path}.$$

Here $\bowtie \in \{<, \leq, >, \geq\}$ *and* $a \in [0, 1]$.

Semantics. Satisfiability of state-formulas ($s \models \varphi$ for a state s) and path-formulas ($\omega \models \psi$ for a path ω) is defined as an extension of satisfiability for pCTL. Satisfiability of the logical, temporal, and pCTL operators is defined in the usual way. For the conditional probabilistic operators we define

$$s \models \mathbf{P}_{\leq a}[\varphi|\psi] \Leftrightarrow \mu_s^+(\{\omega \in \Omega_s \mid \omega \models \varphi\}|\{\omega \in \Omega_s \mid \omega \models \psi\}) \leq a,$$
$$s \models \mathbf{P}_{\geq a}[\varphi|\psi] \Leftrightarrow \mu_s^-(\{\omega \in \Omega_s \mid \omega \models \varphi\}|\{\omega \in \Omega_s \mid \omega \models \psi\}) \geq a,$$

and similarly for $s \models \mathbf{P}_{<a}[\varphi|\psi]$ and $s \models \mathbf{P}_{>a}[\varphi|\psi]$. Following [BA95] we define

$$\mathbf{P}_s^+[\varphi] \triangleq \mu_s^+(\{\omega \in \Omega_s \mid \omega \models \varphi\}),$$
$$\mathbf{P}_s^+[\varphi|\psi] \triangleq \mu_s^+(\{\omega \in \Omega_s \mid \omega \models \varphi\}|\{\omega \in \Omega_s \mid \omega \models \psi\}),$$
$$\mathbf{P}_{s,\eta}[\varphi|\psi] \triangleq \mu_{s,\eta}(\{\omega \in \Omega_s \mid \omega \models \varphi\}|\{\omega \in \Omega_s \mid \omega \models \psi\})$$

and we define $\mathbf{P}_s^-[\varphi|\psi]$ and $\mathbf{P}_s^-[\varphi]$ analogously.

Observation 4.2. *As usual, for checking if* $s \models \mathbf{P}_{\bowtie a}[\varphi|\psi]$, *we only need to consider the cases where* $\varphi = \varphi_1 \mathcal{U} \varphi_2$ *and where* ψ *is either* $\psi_1 \mathcal{U} \psi_2$ *or* $\Box \psi_1$. *This follows using* $\Box\varphi \leftrightarrow \neg\Diamond\neg\varphi$, $\Diamond\varphi \leftrightarrow \mathbf{true}\,\mathcal{U}\varphi$, *and the relations*

$$\mathbf{P}_s^+[\neg\varphi|\psi] = 1 - \mathbf{P}_s^-[\varphi|\psi] \qquad \mathbf{P}_s^-[\neg\varphi|\psi] = 1 - \mathbf{P}_s^+[\varphi|\psi]$$

derived from Lemma 3.2. Because there is no way to relate $\mathbf{P}^+[\varphi|\psi]$ *and* $\mathbf{P}^+[\varphi|\neg\psi]$, *we have to provide two algorithms, one to compute* $\mathbf{P}^+[\varphi|\psi_1\mathcal{U}\psi_2]$ *and one to compute* $\mathbf{P}^+[\varphi|\Box\psi_1]$

5   Deterministic and Semi History-Independent Schedulers

Recall that there exist maximizing and minimizing schedulers on pCTL that are deterministic and HI [BA95]. We show that for cpCTL deterministic schedulers still suffice to reach optimal conditional probability. Because we now have to solve a non-linear optimization problem, the proof differs from the pCTL case in an essential way. We also show that HI schedulers do not suffice and we introduce semi history-independent schedulers that do attain optimal conditional probability.

To simplify notation, for a deterministic scheduler η, we use $\eta(\sigma)$ to denote the unique distribution $\pi \in \tau(\text{last}(\sigma))$ such that $\eta(\sigma)(\pi) = 1$.

5.1   Semi History-Independent Schedulers

The following example shows that maximizing schedulers are not necessarily HI.

Example 5.1. Let Π be the MDP of Figure 2 and the conditional probability $\mathbf{P}_{s_0,\eta}[\Diamond B|\Diamond P]$. There are only three deterministic history independent schedulers, choosing π_1, π_2, or π_3 in s_0. For the first one, the conditional probability is undefined and for the second and third it is 0. The scheduler η that maximizes $\mathbf{P}_{s_0,\eta}[\Diamond B|\Diamond P]$ satisfies $\eta(s_0) = \pi_3$, $\eta(s_0 s_3) = \pi_5$, and $\eta(s_0 s_3 s_0) = \pi_1$. Since η chooses on s_0 first π_2 and later π_1, η is not history independent.

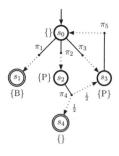

Fig. 2. MDP

However, there exists a maximizing scheduler that is "nearly HI" in the sense that it always takes the same decision *before* the system reaches a certain condition φ and also always takes the same decision *after* φ. This family of schedulers is called φ-semi history independent (φ-sHI for short).

Definition 5.2. *Let $\Pi = (S, s_0, \tau, L)$ be a MDP, $s \in S$, η a scheduler of Π, and $\varphi \in$ Stat. We say that η is a φ-sHI s-scheduler if it satisfies*

1. *for all $\sigma_1, \sigma_2 \in \Omega_s^*$, if $\mathrm{last}(\sigma_1) = \mathrm{last}(\sigma_2)$ and $\sigma_1, \sigma_2 \not\models \Diamond\varphi$, then $\eta(\sigma_1) = \eta(\sigma_2)$;*
2. *for all $\sigma \in \Omega_s^*$, if $\sigma \models \Diamond\varphi$, then for all $\sigma', \sigma'' \in \Omega_{\mathrm{last}(\sigma)}^*$ such that $\sigma \sqsubseteq \sigma'$, $\sigma \sqsubseteq \sigma''$, and $\mathrm{last}(\sigma') = \mathrm{last}(\sigma'')$ we have $\eta(\sigma') = \eta(\sigma'')$.*

Here $\mathrm{last}(s_0 s_1 \ldots s_n) = s_n$, $\mathrm{tail}(s_0 s_1 \ldots s_n) = s_1 \ldots s_n$, and $\sqsubseteq$ denotes the prefix order over finite paths, i.e. $\sigma' \sqsubseteq \sigma \Leftrightarrow \sigma = \sigma'\sigma''$ for some σ''.

Theorem 5.3. *Let Π be a MDP, $s \in S$, and $\varphi_1\mathcal{U}\varphi_2$, $\psi_1\mathcal{U}\psi_2$, $\Box\psi_1 \in$ cpCTL. There exists a $(\neg\varphi_1 \vee \varphi_2 \vee \neg\psi_1 \vee \psi_2)$-sHI s-scheduler η' such that*

$$\mathbf{P}_{s,\eta'}[\varphi_1\mathcal{U}\varphi_2|\psi_1\mathcal{U}\psi_2] = \mathbf{P}_s^+[\varphi_1\mathcal{U}\varphi_2|\psi_1\mathcal{U}\psi_2]$$

and a $(\neg\varphi_1 \vee \varphi_2 \vee \neg\psi_1)$-sHI s-scheduler η'' such that

$$\mathbf{P}_{s,\eta''}[\varphi_1\mathcal{U}\varphi_2|\Box\psi_1] = \mathbf{P}_s^+[\varphi_1\mathcal{U}\varphi_2|\Box\psi_1].$$

We define $\varphi_U \triangleq \neg\varphi_1 \vee \varphi_2 \vee \neg\psi_1 \vee \psi_2$ and $\varphi_\Box \triangleq \neg\varphi_1 \vee \varphi_2 \vee \neg\psi_1$. We refer to φ_U (resp. $\varphi_\Box$) as the until (resp. globally) stopping condition.

5.2 Deterministic Schedulers

Lemma 5.4. *Let $v_1, v_2 \in [0, \infty)$ and $w_1, w_2 \in (0, \infty)$. Then the function $f: \mathbb{R} \to \mathbb{R}$ defined by $f(x) \triangleq \frac{xv_1 + (1-x)v_2}{xw_1 + (1-x)w_2}$ is monotonous.*

Proof. $f'(x) = \frac{v_1 w_2 - v_2 w_1}{(xw_1 - (1-x)w_2)^2}$ which is always ≥ 0 or always ≤ 0.

The following result states that taking the convex combination of schedulers does not increase the conditional probability $\mathbf{P}[\varphi|\psi]$.

Lemma 5.5. *Let Π be a MDP, s a state, and φ, ψ path formulas. Suppose that the s-scheduler η is a convex combination of η_1 and η_2. Then $\mathbf{P}_{s,\eta}[\varphi|\psi] \leq \max(\mathbf{P}_{s,\eta_1}[\varphi|\psi], \mathbf{P}_{s,\eta_2}[\varphi|\psi])$.*

Proof. Applying the above lemma to

$$[0, 1] \ni \alpha \mapsto \frac{\alpha\mathbf{P}_{s,\eta_1}[\varphi \wedge \psi] + (1-\alpha)\mathbf{P}_{s,\eta_2}[\varphi \wedge \psi]}{\alpha\mathbf{P}_{s,\eta_1}[\psi] + (1-\alpha)\mathbf{P}_{s,\eta_2}[\psi]}$$

we get that the maximum is reached at $\alpha = 0$ or $\alpha = 1$. Because η is a convex combination of η_1 and η_2, $\mathbf{P}_{s,\eta}[\varphi|\psi] \leq \mathbf{P}_{s,\eta_2}[\varphi|\psi]$ (in the first case) or $\mathbf{P}_{s,\eta}[\varphi|\psi] \leq \mathbf{P}_{s,\eta_1}[\varphi|\psi]$ (in the second case).

Theorem 5.6. *Let Π be a MDP, s a state, and φ a path formula. Then every s-scheduler on Π is a convex combination of deterministic φ-sHI s-schedulers.*

Theorem 5.7. *Let Π be a MDP, $s \in S$, and $\varphi_1\mathcal{U}\varphi_2$, $\psi_1\mathcal{U}\psi_2$, $\Box\psi_1 \in$ cpCTL. There exists a deterministic φ_U-sHI s-scheduler η' such that*

$$\mathbf{P}_{s,\eta'}[\varphi_1 \mathcal{U} \varphi_2 | \psi_1 \mathcal{U} \psi_2] = \mathbf{P}_s^+[\varphi_1 \mathcal{U} \varphi_2 | \psi_1 \mathcal{U} \psi_2]$$

and a deterministic $\varphi_\square$-sHI s-scheduler η'' such that

$$\mathbf{P}_{s,\eta''}[\varphi_1 \mathcal{U} \varphi_2 | \square \psi_1] = \mathbf{P}_s^+[\varphi_1 \mathcal{U} \varphi_2 | \square \psi_1],$$

where $\varphi_\mathcal{U}$ and $\varphi_\square$ are the stopping conditions.

Example 5.8 *Consider the MDP and* cpCTL *formula of Example 5.1. According to Theorem 5.7 there exists a deterministic and $(B \vee P)$-sHI scheduler that maximizes $\mathbf{P}_{s_0,\eta}[\lozenge B | \lozenge P]$. In this case, a maximizing scheduler will take always the same decision (π_3) before the system reaches s_3 (a state satisfying the until stopping condition $(B \vee P)$) and always the same decision (π_1) after the system reaches s_3.*

6   Model Checking cpCTL

Model checking cpCTL means checking if a state s satisfies a certain state formula φ. We focus on formulas of the form $\mathbf{P}_{\leq a}[\varphi | \psi]$ and show how to compute $\mathbf{P}_s^+[\varphi | \psi]$ given $\varphi, \psi \in \mathrm{Path}$. The case $\mathbf{P}_s^-[\varphi | \psi]$ is similar.

Recall that model checking pCTL is based on the Bellman-equations. For instance, $\mathbf{P}_s^+[\lozenge B] = \max_{\pi \in \tau(s)} \sum_{t \in \mathrm{succ}(s)} \pi(t) \mathbf{P}_t^+[\lozenge B]$ whenever $s \not\models B$. So a scheduler η that maximizes $\mathbf{P}_s[\lozenge B]$ chooses $\pi \in \tau(s)$ maximizing $\sum_{t \in \mathrm{succ}(s)} \pi(t) \cdot \mathbf{P}_t^+[\lozenge B]$. In a successor state t, η still behaves as a scheduler that maximizes $\mathbf{P}_t[\lozenge B]$. As shown below, such a local Bellman-equation is not true for conditional probabilities: a scheduler that maximizes a conditional probability such as $\mathbf{P}_s[\lozenge B | \square P]$ does not necessarily maximize $\mathbf{P}_t[\lozenge B | \square P]$ for successors t of s.

Example 6.1 *Again, consider the MDP and* cpCTL *formula $\mathbf{P}_{\leq a}[\lozenge B | \square P]$ of Figure 1. There are only two deterministic schedulers. The first one, η_1, chooses π_2 when the system reaches the state s_2 and the second one, η_2, chooses π_3 when the system reaches s_2. For the first one $\mathbf{P}_{s_0,\eta_1}[\lozenge B | \square P] = 1 - \frac{2\alpha}{7}$, and for the second one $\mathbf{P}_{s_0,\eta_2}[\lozenge B | \square P] = \frac{30}{31}$. So $\mathbf{P}_{s_0}^+[\lozenge B | \square P] = \max(1 - \frac{2\alpha}{7}, \frac{30}{31})$. Therefore, if $\alpha \geq \frac{7}{62}$ the scheduler that maximizes $\mathbf{P}_{s_0}[\lozenge B | \square P]$ is η_2 ($\mathbf{P}_{s_0,\eta_2}[\lozenge B | \square P] = \mathbf{P}_{s_0}^+[\lozenge B | \square P]$) and otherwise it is η_1 ($\mathbf{P}_{s_0,\eta_1}[\lozenge B | \square P] = \mathbf{P}_{s_0}^+[\lozenge B | \square P]$).*

Furthermore, $\mathbf{P}_{s_1}^+[\lozenge B | \square P] = 1$ and $\mathbf{P}_{s_2}^+[\lozenge B | \square P] = 1 - 2\alpha$; the scheduler that obtains this last maximum is the one that chooses π_2 in s_2.

So, if $\alpha \geq \frac{7}{62}$ the scheduler that maximizes the conditional probability from s_0 is taking a different decision than the one that maximize the conditional probability from s_2. Furthermore, for all α, $\max(1 - \frac{2\alpha}{7}, \frac{30}{31}) = \mathbf{P}_{s_0}^+[\lozenge B | \square P] \neq \frac{3}{4}\mathbf{P}_{s_1}^+[\lozenge B | \square P] + \frac{1}{4}\mathbf{P}_{s_2}^+[\lozenge B | \square P] = 1 - \frac{1}{2}\alpha$, showing that the Bellman-equation from above does not generalize to cpCTL.

An obvious way to compute $\mathbf{P}_s^+[\varphi | \psi]$ is by computing the pairs $(\mathbf{P}_{s,\eta}[\varphi \wedge \psi], \mathbf{P}_{s,\eta}[\psi])$ for all sHI schedulers η, and taking the maximum quotient $\mathbf{P}_{s,\eta}[\varphi \wedge \psi] / \mathbf{P}_{s,\eta}[\psi]$. We present two methods to avoid the computation of certain pairs of acyclic MDPs. We can use these for a MDP with cycles by first transforming it to an equivalent acyclic one using the strongly connected component structure.

6.1   Acyclic MDP

Note that every MDP has cycles associated to absorbing states. We call a MDP acyclic if it the only if the only cycles are selfloops taken with probability one.

Definition 6.2. *A MDP Π is called* acyclic *if for all states $s \in S$ and all $\pi \in \tau(s)$ we have $\pi(s) = 0$ or $\pi(s) = 1$ and for all paths ω and all $i < j$ such that $\omega_i = \omega_j$ we have $\omega_i = \omega_{i+1} = \cdots = \omega_j$.*

The idea behind the algorithm for acyclic MDPs is as follows. We label each state s by a sequence $(p_1, q_1), \ldots, (p_n, q_n)$ of pairs of probabilities, where $p_i = \mathbf{P}_{s, \eta_i}[\varphi \wedge \psi]$ and $q_i = \mathbf{P}_{s, \eta_i}[\psi]$ for a certain sHI s-scheduler η_i. The algorithm starts by labeling each leaf s with a single pair $(\mathbf{P}_{s, \eta}[\varphi \wedge \psi], \mathbf{P}_{s, \eta}[\psi])$ for the unique deterministic sHI s-scheduler η. The labeling is propagated towards the root node s_0. We obtain the maximum conditional probability $\mathbf{P}_{s_0}^+[\varphi | \psi]$ as the maximum quotient p/q for all (p, q) in the labeling of s_0. Section 6.3 shows that certain pairs can be discarded when propagating the labeling.

Definition 6.3. *Let L be the set of expressions of the form $(p_1, q_1) \vee \cdots \vee (p_n, q_n)$ where $p_i, q_i \in [0, \infty)$ and $q_i \geq p_i$, for all $n \in \mathbb{N}^\star$. On L we consider the smallest congruence relation $\equiv_1$ satisfying (Idempotence) $(p_1, q_1) \vee (p_1, q_1) \equiv_1 (p_1, q_1)$, (Associativity) $((p_1, q_1) \vee (p_2, q_2)) \vee (p_3, q_3) \equiv_1 (p_1, q_1) \vee ((p_2, q_2) \vee (p_3, q_3))$, (Commutatitivity) $(p_1, q_1) \vee (p_2, q_2) \equiv_1 (p_2, q_2) \vee (p_1, q_1)$. Note that $(p_1, q_1) \vee \cdots \vee (p_n, q_n) \equiv_1 (p'_1, q'_1) \ldots (p'_{n'}, q'_{n'})$ if and only if $\{(p_1, q_1), \ldots, (p_n, q_n)\} = \{(p'_1, q'_1), \ldots, (p'_{n'}, q'_{n'})\}$.*

Fig. 3. δ-values

We let L_1 be the set of equivalence classes and denote the projection map $L \to L_1$ that maps each expression to its equivalence class by f_1. On L we also define maximum quotient $\top : L \to [0, \infty)$, *and* minimum quotient $\bot : L \to [0, \infty)$ *by* $\top(\bigvee_{i=1}^n (p_i, q_i)) \triangleq \max(\{\frac{p_i}{q_i} | q_i \neq 0, i = 1, \ldots, n\} \cup \{0\})$ *and* $\bot(\bigvee_{i=1}^n (p_i, q_i)) \triangleq \min(\{\frac{p_i}{q_i} | q_i \neq 0, i = 1, \ldots, n\} \cup \{1\})$.

Note that $\top$ and $\bot$ induce maps $\top_1 : L_1 \to [0, \infty)$ and $\bot_1 : L_1 \to [0, \infty)$ such that $\top_1 \circ f_1 = \top$ and $\bot_1 \circ f_1 = \bot$.

Definition 6.4. *Let Π be a MDP. We define the function $\delta : S \times \text{Stat} \times \text{Path} \times \text{Path} \to L$ by $\delta(s, \varphi, \varphi, \psi) \triangleq \bigvee_{\eta \in \text{Sch}_s^\varphi(\Pi)} (\mathbf{P}_{s, \eta}[\varphi \wedge \psi], \mathbf{P}_{s, \eta}[\psi])$ and we define $\delta_1 : S \times \text{Stat} \times \text{Path} \times \text{Path} \to L_1$ by $\delta_1 \triangleq f_1 \circ \delta$.*

When no confusion arises, we omit the subscripts 1 and omit the projection map f_1, writing $(p_1, q_1) \vee \cdots \vee (p_n, q_n)$ for the equivalence class it generates.

Example 6.5. In Figure 3 we show the value $\delta(s, B \vee \neg P, \Diamond B, \Box P)$ associated to each state s of the MDP previously presented in Figure 1.

The following result says that we can compute maximum conditional probability from $\delta_s^{\mathcal{U}}$ or $\delta_s^{\Box}$.

Theorem 6.6. *Given* $\Pi = (S, s_0, L, \tau)$ *an acyclic MDP, and* $\varphi_1, \varphi_2, \psi_1, \psi_2 \in$ Stat. *Then*

$$\mathbf{P}_s^+[\varphi_1 \mathcal{U} \varphi_2 | \psi_1 \mathcal{U} \psi_2] = \top(\overbrace{\delta(s, \varphi_U, \varphi_1 \mathcal{U} \varphi_2, \psi_1 \mathcal{U} \psi_2)}^{\triangleq \delta_s^{\mathcal{U}}(\varphi_1, \varphi_2, \psi_1, \psi_2)})$$

and

$$\mathbf{P}_s^+[\varphi_1 \mathcal{U} \varphi_2 | \Box \psi_1] = \top(\overbrace{\delta(s, \varphi_\Box, \varphi_1 \mathcal{U} \varphi_2, \Box \psi_1)}^{\triangleq \delta_s^{\Box}(\varphi_1, \varphi_2, \psi_1)}).$$

6.2   Extension to General MDP

Now, we extend our results to general, not necessarily acyclic, MDPs. We first reduce all cycles in Π and create a new acyclic reduced MDP $[\Pi]$ such that the probabilities involved in the computation of $\mathbf{P}^+[-|-]$ are preserved. We do so by removing every strongly connected component (SCC) c of (the graph of) a MDP Π, keeping only input states and transitions to output states. We show that $\mathbf{P}^+[-|-]$ on $[\Pi]$ is equal to the corresponding value on Π. For this, we have to make sure that states satisfying the stopping condition are ignored when we are removing the SCCs.

Identifying SCCs. Our first step is to make stopping condition states absorbing.

Definition 6.7. *Let* $\Pi = (S, s_0, \tau, L)$ *be a MDP and* $\varphi \in$ Stat *a state formula. We define a new MDP* $\langle \Pi \rangle_\varphi = (S, s_0, \langle \tau \rangle_\varphi, L)$ *where* $\langle \tau \rangle_\varphi(s)$ *is equal to* $\tau(s)$ *if* $s \not\models \varphi$ *and to* 1_s *otherwise.*

Typically φ will be either the until stopping condition (φ_U) or the globally stopping condition $(\varphi_\Box)$.

To recognize cycles in the MDP we define a graph associated to it.

Definition 6.8. *Let* $\Pi = (S, s_0, \tau, L)$ *be MDP and* $\varphi \in$ Stat. *We define the digraph* $G = G_{\Pi,\varphi} = (S, \rightarrow)$ *associated to* $\langle \Pi \rangle_\varphi = (S, s_0, \langle \tau \rangle_\varphi, L)$ *where* $\rightarrow$ *satisfies* $u \rightarrow v \Leftrightarrow \exists \pi \in \langle \tau \rangle_\varphi(u).\pi(v) > 0$.

Now we let SCC = $\text{SCC}_{\Pi,\varphi} \subseteq \wp(S)$ be the set of SCC of G. For each SCC c we define the sets Inp_c of all states in c that have an incoming transition of Π from a state outside of c; we also define the set Out_c of all states outside of c that have an incoming transition from a state of c. Formally, for each $c \in$ SCC we define

$$Inp_c \triangleq \{u \in c \mid \exists s \in S - c.\exists \pi \in \tau(s).\pi(u) > 0\},$$

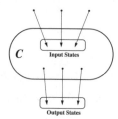

$$Out_c \triangleq \{s \in S - c \mid \exists u \in c.\exists \pi \in \tau(u).\pi(s) > 0\}.$$

We then associate a MDP Π_c to each SCC c of G. The space of states of Π_c is $c \cup Out_c$ and the transition relation is induced by the transition relation of Π.

Definition 6.9. *Let Π be a MDP and $c \in$ SCC be a scc in Π. We pick an arbitrary element s_c of Inp_c and define the MDP $\Pi_c = (S_c, s_c, \tau_c, L)$ where $S_c = c \cup Out_c$ and $\tau_c(s)$ is equal to $\{1_s\}$ if $s \in Out_c$ and to $\tau(s)$ otherwise.*

Defining the new acyclic MDP. To obtain a reduced acyclic MDP from the original one we first define the probability of reaching one state from another according to a given HI scheduler in the following way.

Definition 6.10. *Let $\Pi = (S, s_0, \tau, L)$ be a MDP, and η be a HI scheduler on Π. Then for each $s, t \in S$ we define the function R such that $R_\Pi(s \overset{\eta}{\rightsquigarrow} t) \triangleq \mu_{s,\eta}(\{\omega \in \Omega_s \mid \exists i.\omega_i = t\})$.*

Now we are able to define an acyclic MDP $[\Pi]$ related to Π such that $\mathbf{P}^+_{[\Pi]}[-|-] = \mathbf{P}^+_\Pi[-|-]$.

Definition 6.11. *Let $\Pi = (S, s_0, \tau, L)$ be a MDP. Then we define $[\Pi]$ as $([S], s_0, [\tau], L)$ where*

$$[S] = S - \overbrace{\bigcup_{c \in \text{SCC}} c}^{S_{com}} \cup \overbrace{\bigcup_{c \in \text{SCC}} Inp_c}^{S_{inp}}$$

and for all $s \in [S]$ the set $[\tau](s)$ of probabilistic distributions on $[S]$ is given by

$$[\tau](s) = \begin{cases} \tau(s) & \text{if } s \in S_{com}, \\ \{\lambda \in [S].R_{\Pi_{c_s}}(s \overset{\eta}{\rightsquigarrow} t)) \mid \eta \in \text{Sch}^{\text{HI}}_s(\Pi_{c_s})\} & \text{if } s \in S_{inp}. \end{cases}$$

Here c_s is the SCC associated to s.

Theorem 6.12. *Let $\Pi = (S, s_0, \tau, L)$ be a MDP, and $\mathbf{P}_{<a}[\varphi|\psi] \in$ cpCTL. Then $[\Pi]$ is an acyclic MDP and $\mathbf{P}^+_{s_0,\Pi}[\varphi|\psi] = \mathbf{P}^+_{s_0,[\Pi]}[\varphi|\psi]$, where $\mathbf{P}^+_{s,\Pi'}[-|-]$ represents $\mathbf{P}^+_s[-|-]$ on the MDP Π'.*

Finally we can use the technique for acyclic MDPs on the reduced MDP in order to obtain $\mathbf{P}^+_{s_0}[-|-]$. Note that to compute $\mathbf{P}^+_{s_0}[-|-]$ it is not necessary to compute reachability properties on SCC that are not reachable on G from its initial state, so in model checking we avoid that.

6.3   Optimizations

We have already shown that δ is computable. Now we show two optimizations in order to compute δ in a more efficient way.

Optimization 1: Reusing Information. We now show how to compute $\delta^{\mathcal{U}}_s(\varphi_1, \varphi_2, \psi_1, \psi_2)$ and $\delta^{\square}_s(\varphi_1, \varphi_2, \psi_1, \psi_2)$ recursively in s. The base cases of the recursion are the states where the stopping condition holds. Because there exists an optimizing scheduler that is sHI, we only need to consider HI (and determininstic) schedulers in such a state. In the recursive case we can express $\delta^{\mathcal{U}}_s$

(resp. $\delta_s^\square$) in terms of the $\delta_t^\mathcal{U}$ (resp. $\delta_t^\square$) of the successor states t of s. Therefore, if we encounter the same state t in more than one branch of the recursive computation, we can reuse the previously computed value of $\delta_t^\mathcal{U}$ (resp. $\delta_t^\square$).

To do this, we now define a *scalar multiplication operator* $\odot$ and an *addition operator* $\oplus$ on L.

Definition 6.13. *We define* $\odot : [0, \infty) \times L \to L$ *and* $\oplus : L \times L \to L$ *by* $c \odot \bigvee_{i=1}^n (p_i, q_i) \triangleq \bigvee_{i=1}^n (c \cdot p_i, c \cdot q_i)$ *and* $\bigvee_{i=1}^n (p_i, q_i) \oplus \bigvee_{j=1}^m (p_j', q_j') \triangleq \bigvee_{i=1}^n \bigvee_{j=1}^m (p_i + p_j', q_i + q_j')$.

Note that $\odot$ and $\oplus$ induce maps $\odot_1 : [0, \infty) \times L_1 \to L_1$ and $\oplus_1 : L_1 \times L_1 \to L_1$. As before, we omit the subscript 1 if that will not cause confusion.

The following result gives recursive equations for the values of $\delta_s^\mathcal{U}$ and $\delta_s^\square$. If the MDP is acyclic, it can be used to compute these values.

Theorem 6.14. *Let* Π *be a MDP,* $s \in S$, *and* $\varphi_1 \mathcal{U} \varphi_2, \psi_1 \mathcal{U} \psi_2, \square \psi_1 \in \text{Path}$. *Then* $\delta_s^\mathcal{U}(\varphi_1, \varphi_2, \psi_1, \psi_2) =$

$$\begin{cases} \bigvee_{\eta \in \text{Sch}_s^{\text{HI}}(\Pi)} (\mathbf{P}_{s,\eta}[\psi_1 \mathcal{U} \psi_2], \mathbf{P}_{s,\eta}[\psi_1 \mathcal{U} \psi_2]) & \text{if } s \models \varphi_2, \\ \bigvee_{\eta \in \text{Sch}_s^{\text{HI}}(\Pi)} (\mathbf{P}_{s,\eta}[\varphi_1 \mathcal{U} \varphi_2], 1) & \text{if } s \models \neg\varphi_2 \wedge \psi_2, \\ \bigvee_{\eta \in \text{Sch}_s^{\text{HI}}(\Pi)} (0, \mathbf{P}_{s,\eta}[\psi_1 \mathcal{U} \psi_2]) & \text{if } s \models \neg\varphi_1 \wedge \neg\varphi_2 \wedge \neg\psi_2, \\ (0, 0) & \text{if } s \models \varphi_1 \wedge \neg\varphi_2 \wedge \neg\psi_1 \wedge \neg\psi_2, \\ \bigvee_{\pi \in \tau(s)} \left(\bigoplus_{t \in \text{succ}(s)} \pi(t) \odot \delta_t^\mathcal{U}(\varphi_1, \varphi_2, \psi_1, \psi_2) \right) & \text{if } s \models \varphi_1 \wedge \neg\varphi_2 \wedge \psi_1 \wedge \neg\psi_2, \end{cases}$$

and $\delta_s^\square(\varphi_1, \varphi_2, \psi_1) =$

$$\begin{cases} \bigvee_{\eta \in \text{Sch}_s^{\text{HI}}(\Pi)} (\mathbf{P}_{s,\eta}[\square \psi_1], \mathbf{P}_{s,\eta}[\square \psi_1]) & \text{if } s \models \varphi_2, \\ (0, 0) & \text{if } s \models \neg\varphi_2 \wedge \neg\psi_1, \\ \bigvee_{\eta \in \text{Sch}_s^{\text{HI}}(\Pi)} (0, \mathbf{P}_{s,\eta}[\square \psi_1]) & \text{if } s \models \neg\varphi_1 \wedge \neg\varphi_2 \wedge \psi_1, \\ \bigvee_{\pi \in \tau(s)} \left(\bigoplus_{t \in \text{succ}(s)} \pi(t) \odot \delta_t^\square(\varphi_1, \varphi_2, \psi_1) \right)) & \text{if } s \models \varphi_1 \wedge \neg\varphi_2 \wedge \psi_1. \end{cases}$$

Optimization 2: Using pCTL algorithms after the stopping condition.
Up to now we have computed $(\mathbf{P}_{s_0,\eta}[\varphi \wedge \psi], \mathbf{P}_{s_0,\eta}[\psi])$ for all sHI schedulers. The reason for this is that the (local) Bellman-equations do not hold for cpCTL. Therefore, it is not enough to know the values $\mathbf{P}_t^+[\varphi|\psi]$ for all successors t of s. However, in some cases, we can locally decide that one sHI scheduler is guaranteed to be better than another one. We now give some intuition for this; a formal claim is in Lemma 6.16 below.

For instance, let s be a state that is reachable from s_0. Assume that η' and η'' are sHI s-schedulers such that $\mathbf{P}_{s,\eta'}[\varphi \wedge \psi] = \mathbf{P}_{s,\eta''}[\varphi \wedge \psi]$ and $\mathbf{P}_{s,\eta'}[\psi] \leq \mathbf{P}_{s,\eta''}[\psi]$. Furthermore, assume that η_1 and η_2 are sHI s_0-schedulers that are equal except that η_1 behaves like η' "below" s and η_2 behaves like η'' "below" s. One can easily see that $\mathbf{P}_{s_0,\eta_1}[\varphi|\psi] \geq \mathbf{P}_{s_0,\eta_2}[\varphi|\psi]$. Therefore, when computing $\mathbf{P}_{s_0}^+[\varphi|\psi]$ we do not have to consider all sHI s-schedulers, but, in this case, we can omit η'' from consideration.

Similarly, if $\mathbf{P}_{s,\eta'}[\varphi \wedge \psi] \leq \mathbf{P}_{s,\eta''}[\varphi \wedge \psi]$ and $\mathbf{P}_{s,\eta'}[\psi] = \mathbf{P}_{s,\eta''}[\psi]$, then we do not have to consider the scheduler η'.

Finally, it follows from Lemma 5.4 that we don't have to consider the scheduler η'' if $\mathbf{P}_{s,\eta'}[\varphi \wedge \psi] + a = \mathbf{P}_{s,\eta''}[\varphi \wedge \psi]$ and $\mathbf{P}_{s,\eta'}[\psi] + a = \mathbf{P}_{s,\eta''}[\psi]$. This is used to show that when we reach a state s satisfying the stopping condition, we only have to compute $\mathbf{P}_s^+[\psi]$ and we do not have to consider conditional probabilities anymore.

As a consequence of these facts we do not have to compute $(\mathbf{P}_{s_0,\eta}[\varphi \wedge \psi]$, $\mathbf{P}_{s_0,\eta}[\psi])$ for all sHI schedulers. In particular, if we reach a state satisfying the stopping condition we can always choose a scheduler that maximizes or minimizes one pCTL formula.

Definition 6.15. *Consider the set of expressions L defined in Definition 6.3. On L we now consider the smallest congruence relation $\equiv_2$ containing $\equiv_1$ and satisfying (1) $(p_1, q_1) \vee (p_1, q_2) \equiv_2 (p_1, \min(q_1, q_2))$, (2) $(p_1, q_1) \vee (p_2, q_1) \equiv_2 (\max(p_1, p_2), q_1)$, (3) $(p_1 + a, q_1 + a) \vee (p_1, q_1) \equiv_2 (p_1 + a, q_1 + a)$, where $a \in [0, \infty)$. We write L_2 for the set of equivalence classes and denote the projection map $L_2 \to L$ by f_2.*

Since $\equiv_1 \subseteq \equiv_2$, this projection maps factors through f_1, say $g \colon L_1 \to L_2$ is the unique map such that $g \circ f_1 = f_2$. The following seemingly innocent lemma is readily proven, but it contains the heart of this optimization. The fact that $\top$ and $\bot$ induce operations on L_2 means that it is correct to "simplify" expressions using $\equiv_2$ when we are interested in the maximum or minimum quotient. After that, we show that this implies that we do not have to consider *all* sHI schedulers when computing maximum or minimum conditional probabilities, but can on-the-fly omit some from consideration.

Lemma 6.16. *The operators $\odot$, $\oplus$, $\top$, and $\bot$ on L induce operators $\odot_2$, $\oplus_2$, $\top_2$, and $\bot_2$ on L_2.*

Definition 6.17. *We define $\delta_2 \colon S \times \text{Stat} \times \text{Path} \times \text{Path} \to L_2$ by $\delta_2 \triangleq f_2 \circ \delta$.*

As usual, we omit subscripts 2 when confusion is unlikely. Note that with this convention Theorem 6.6 still holds. Finally, the following theorem allow us to recursively compute $\delta_s^{\mathcal{U}}$ and $\delta_s^{\square}$ considering these last optimizations.

Theorem 6.18. *Let Π be a MDP, $s \in S$, and $\varphi_1 \mathcal{U} \varphi_2, \psi_1 \mathcal{U} \psi_2, \square \psi_1 \in \text{Path}$. Then $\delta_s^{\mathcal{U}}(\varphi_1, \varphi_2, \psi_1, \psi_2) =$*

$$\begin{cases} (\mathbf{P}_s^+[\psi_1 \mathcal{U} \psi_2], \mathbf{P}_s^+[\psi_1 \mathcal{U} \psi_2]) & \text{if } s \models \varphi_2, \\ (\mathbf{P}_s^+[\varphi_1 \mathcal{U} \varphi_2], 1) & \text{if } s \models \neg\varphi_2 \wedge \psi_2, \\ (0, \mathbf{P}_s^-[\psi_1 \mathcal{U} \psi_2]) & \text{if } s \models \neg\varphi_1 \wedge \neg\varphi_2 \wedge \neg\psi_2, \\ (0,0) & \text{if } s \models \varphi_1 \wedge \neg\varphi_2 \wedge \neg\psi_1 \wedge \neg\psi_2, \\ \bigvee_{\pi \in \tau(s)} \left(\bigoplus_{t \in \text{succ}(s)} \pi(t) \odot \delta_t^{\mathcal{U}}(\varphi_1, \varphi_2, \psi_1, \psi_2) \right) & \text{if } s \models \varphi_1 \wedge \neg\varphi_2 \wedge \psi_1 \wedge \neg\psi_2, \end{cases}$$

and $\delta_s^{\square}(\varphi_1, \varphi_2, \psi_1) =$

$$\begin{cases} (\mathbf{P}_s^+[\square\psi_1], \mathbf{P}_s^+[\square\psi_1]) & \text{if } s \models \varphi_2, \\ (0,0) & \text{if } s \models \neg\varphi_2 \wedge \neg\psi_1, \\ (0, \mathbf{P}_s^-[\square\psi_1]) & \text{if } s \models \neg\varphi_1 \wedge \neg\varphi_2 \wedge \psi_1, \\ \bigvee_{\pi \in \tau(s)} \left(\bigoplus_{t \in \text{succ}(s)} \pi(t) \odot \delta_t^{\square}(\varphi_1, \varphi_2, \psi_1) \right) & \text{if } s \models \varphi_1 \wedge \neg\varphi_2 \wedge \psi_1. \end{cases}$$

7 Counterexamples

Counterexamples in model checking provide important diagnostic information used, among others, for debugging, abstraction-refinement [CGJ+00], and scheduler synthesis [LBB+01]. For systems without probability, a counterexample typically consists of a path violating the property under consideration. Counterexamples in MCs are sets of paths. E.g, a counterexample for the formula $\mathbf{P}_{\leq a}[\varphi]$ is a set Δ of paths, none satisfying φ, and such that the probability mass of Δ is greater than a [HK07, And06, AL06].

In MDPs, we first have to find the scheduler achieving the optimal probability. Both for pCTL and cpCTL, this scheduler can be derived from the algorithms computing the optimal probabilities [And06]. Once the optimal scheduler is fixed, the MDP can be turned into a Markov Chain and the approaches mentioned before can be used to construct counterexamples for pCTL. For cpCTL however, the situation is slightly more complex. It follows directly from the semantics that:

$$s \not\models \mathbf{P}_{\leq a}[\varphi|\psi] \quad \text{iff} \quad \exists \eta \in \mathrm{Sch}_s(\Pi). \frac{\mu_{s,\eta}(\{\omega \in \Omega_s | \omega \models \varphi \wedge \psi\})}{\mu_{s,\eta}(\{\omega \in \Omega_s | \omega \models \psi\})} > a.$$

Lemma 7.1. *Let* $a \in [0,1]$ *and consider the formula* $\mathbf{P}_{\leq a}[\varphi|\psi]$. *Let* $\Delta_\varphi \triangleq \{\omega \in \Omega \mid \omega \models \varphi\}$, $\Delta_1 \subseteq \Delta_{\varphi \wedge \psi}$, *and* $\Delta_2 \subseteq \Delta_{\neg\psi}$. *Then* $a < \mu_\eta(\Delta_1)/(1 - \mu_\eta(\Delta_2))$ *implies* $a < \mathbf{P}_\eta[\varphi|\psi]$.

Proof. The proof follows from $\mu_\eta(\Delta_1) \leq \mu_\eta(\Delta_{\varphi\wedge\psi})$ and $\mu_\eta(\Delta_2) \leq \mu_\eta(\Delta_{\neg\psi})$. Then $a < \frac{\mu_\eta(\Delta_1)}{1-\mu_\eta(\Delta_2)} \leq \frac{\mu_\eta(\Delta_{\varphi\wedge\psi})}{1-\mu_\eta(\Delta_{\neg\psi})} = \frac{\mu_\eta(\Delta_{\varphi\wedge\psi})}{\mu_\eta(\Delta_\psi)} = \mathbf{P}_\eta[\varphi|\psi]$. $\square$

This leads to the following notion of counterexample.

Definition 7.2. *A counterexample for* $\mathbf{P}_{\leq a}[\varphi|\psi]$ *is a pair* (Δ_1, Δ_2) *of measurable sets of paths satisfying* $\Delta_1 \subseteq \Delta_{\varphi\wedge\psi}$, $\Delta_2 \subseteq \Delta_{\neg\psi}$, *and* $a < \mu_\eta(\Delta_1)/(1 - \mu_\eta(\Delta_2))$, *for some scheduler* η.

Note that such sets Δ_1 and Δ_2 can be computed using the techniques on Markov Chains mentioned above.

Example 7.3. Consider the evaluation of $s_0 \models \mathbf{P}_{\leq 3/4}[\Diamond B|\Box P]$ on the MDP obtained by taking $\alpha = \frac{1}{10}$ in Example 2.2 (see Figure 4(a)). In this case the maximizing scheduler, say η, chooses π_2 in s_2. In Figure 4(b) we show the Markov Chain derived from MDP using η. In this setting we have $\mathbf{P}_{s_0,\eta}[\Diamond B|\Box P] = \frac{68}{70}$ and consequently s_0 does not satisfy this formula.

We show this fact with the notion of counterexample of Definition 7.2. Note that $\Delta_{\Diamond B \wedge \Box P} = \langle s_0 s_1 \rangle \cup \langle s_0 s_2 s_3 \rangle$ and $\Delta_{\neg \Box P} = \langle s_0 s_2 s_5 \rangle$. Using Lemma 7.1 with $\Delta_1 = \langle s_0 s_1 \rangle$ and $\Delta_2 = \langle s_0 s_2 s_5 \rangle$ we have $\frac{3}{4} < \frac{\mu_\eta(\Delta_1)}{1-\mu_\eta(\Delta_2)} = \frac{3/4}{1-1/8} = \frac{6}{7}$. Consequently $\frac{3}{4} < \mathbf{P}_{s_0,\eta}[\Diamond B|\Box P]$, which proves that $s_0 \not\models \mathbf{P}_{\leq 3/4}[\Diamond B|\Box P]$.

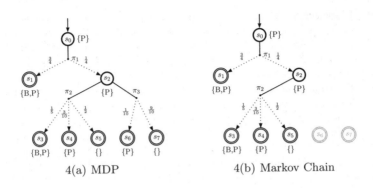

4(a) MDP   4(b) Markov Chain

8   Conclusion and Future Work

In this paper we extended the probabilistic temporal logic pCTL to cpCTL, in which it is possible to express conditional probabilities. We showed that optimal scheduling decisions can always be reached by a deterministic and semi history-independent scheduler. Using this we presented an algorithm to check if a MDP satisfies a cpCTL-formula. Our algorithm first reduces the MDP to an acyclic MDP and then computes optimal conditional probabilities in over this reduction. Counterexamples for conditional formulas consist of two sets of paths in the MDP or MC. We have sketched an algorithm for counterexample generation.

A natural direction for future research is to extend pCTL* to cpCTL* and find algorithms for model checking cpCTL*. Furthermore, we plan to investigate ways to find better counterexamples in cpCTL model checking. Finally, we intend to implement our algorithms in a probabilistic model checker and apply cpCTL model checking to verify the correctness of anonymity protocols.

Acknowledgement. The authors thank Mariëlle Stoelinga for helpful comments on an earlier version of this paper.

References

[AL06]   Aljazzar, H., Leue, S.: Extended directed search for probabilistic timed reachability. In: Asarin, E., Bouyer, P. (eds.) FORMATS 2006. LNCS, vol. 4202, pp. 33–51. Springer, Heidelberg (2006)

[And06]   Andrés, M.E.: Derivation of counterexamples for quantitative model checking. Master's thesis, National University of Córdoba (2006)

[BA95]   Bianco, A., de Alfaro, L.: Model checking of probabilistic and nondeterministic systems. In: Thiagarajan, P.S. (ed.) FSTTCS 1995. LNCS, vol. 1026, pp. 499–513. Springer, Heidelberg (1995)

[Bel57]   Bellman, R.E.: A Markovian decision process. J. Math. Mech. 6, 679–684 (1957)

[BP05]   Bhargava, M., Palamidessi, C.: Probabilistic anonymity. In: Abadi, M., de Alfaro, L. (eds.) CONCUR 2005. LNCS, vol. 3653, pp. 171–185. Springer, Heidelberg (2005)

[CGJ+00] Clarke, E.M., Grumberg, O., Jha, S., Lu, Y., Veith, H.: Counterexample-guided abstraction refinement. In: Emerson, E.A., Sistla, A.P. (eds.) CAV 2000. LNCS, vol. 1855, pp. 154–169. Springer, Heidelberg (2000)

[Cha88] Chaum, D.: The dining cryptographers problem: Unconditional sender and recipient untraceability. Journal of Cryptology 1(1), 65–75 (1988)

[CL05] Camenisch, J., Lysyanskaya, A.: A formal treatment of onion routing. In: Shoup, V. (ed.) CRYPTO 2005. LNCS, vol. 3621, pp. 169–187. Springer, Heidelberg (2005)

[DY83] Dolev, D., Yao, A.C.: On the security of public key protocols. IEEE Transactions on Information Theory 29(2), 198–208 (1983)

[FOO92] Fujioka, A., Okamoto, T., Ohta, K.: A practical secret voting scheme for large scale elections. In: Zheng, Y., Seberry, J. (eds.) AUSCRYPT 1992. LNCS, vol. 718, pp. 244–251. Springer, Heidelberg (1993)

[FV97] Filar, J., Vrieze, K.: Competitive Markov Decision Processes. Springer, Heidelberg (1997)

[HJ89] Hansson, H., Jonsson, B.: A framework for reasoning about time and reliability. In: Proceedings of Real Time Systems Symposium, pp. 102–111. IEEE, Los Alamitos (1989)

[HK07] Han, T., Katoen, J.-P.: Counterexamples in probabilistic model checking. In: Grumberg, O., Huth, M. (eds.) TACAS 2007. LNCS, vol. 4424, pp. 60–75. Springer, Heidelberg (2007)

[LBB+01] Larsen, K.G., Behrmann, G., Brinksma, E., Fehnker, A., Hune, T.S., Petterson, P., Romijn, J.: As cheap as possible: Efficient cost-optimal reachability for priced timed automata. In: Berry, G., Comon, H., Finkel, A. (eds.) CAV 2001. LNCS, vol. 2102, Springer, Heidelberg (2001)

[PZ93] Pnueli, A., Zuck, L.D.: Probabilistic verification. Information and Computation 103(1), 1–29 (1993)

[SV04] Sokolova, A., de Vink, E.P.: Probabilistic automata: System types, parallel composition and comparison. In: Baier, C., Haverkort, B.R., Hermanns, H., Katoen, J.-P., Siegle, M. (eds.) Validation of Stochastic Systems. LNCS, vol. 2925, pp. 1–43. Springer, Heidelberg (2004)

[SL95] Segala, R., Lynch, N.: Probabilistic simulations for probabilistic processes. Nordic Journal of Computing 2(2), 250–273 (1995)

[Var85] Vardi, M.Y.: Automatic verification of probabilistic concurrent finite-state systems. In: Proc. 26th IEEE Symp. Found. Comp. Sci, pp. 327–338 (1985)

On Automated Verification of Probabilistic Programs

Axel Legay[1], Andrzej S. Murawski[2], Joël Ouaknine[2], and James Worrell[2]

[1] Institut Montefiore, Université de Liège, Belgium
[2] Oxford University Computing Laboratory, UK

Abstract. We introduce a simple procedural probabilistic programming language which is suitable for coding a wide variety of randomised algorithms and protocols. This language is interpreted over finite datatypes and has a decidable equivalence problem. We have implemented an automated equivalence checker, which we call APEX, for this language, based on game semantics. We illustrate our approach with three non-trivial case studies: (i) Herman's self-stabilisation algorithm; (ii) an analysis of the average shape of binary search trees obtained by certain sequences of random insertions and deletions; and (iii) the problem of anonymity in the Dining Cryptographers protocol. In particular, we record an exponential speed-up in the latter over state-of-the-art competing approaches.

1   Introduction

Ever since Michael Rabin's seminal paper on probabilistic algorithms [23], it has been widely recognised that introducing randomisation in the design of algorithms can yield substantial benefits. Unfortunately, randomised algorithms and protocols are notoriously difficult to get right, let alone to analyse and prove correct. In this paper, we propose a simple prototype programming language which we believe is suitable for coding a wide variety of algorithms, systems, and protocols that make use of probability.

Our language incorporates several high-level programming constructs, such as procedures (with local scoping) and arrays, but is predicated on finite datatypes and enjoys some key decidability properties. From our perspective the most important of these is *probabilistic contextual equivalence*, which can be used to express a broad range of interesting specifications on various systems.

We have developed an automated equivalence checker, APEX, for our probabilistic programming language. Our approach is based on game semantics, and enables us to verify *open* programs (i.e., programs with undefined components), which is often essential for the modular analysis of complex systems. Game semantics itself has a strong compositional flavour, which we have exploited by incorporating a number of state-space reduction procedures that are invoked throughout a verification task.

We illustrate our framework with three non-trivial case studies. The first is Herman's algorithm, a randomised self-stabilising protocol. The second is a problem about the average shape of binary search trees obtained by certain

C.R. Ramakrishnan and J. Rehof (Eds.): TACAS 2008, LNCS 4963, pp. 173–187, 2008.

sequences of random insertions and deletions. Finally, our third case study is an analysis of anonymity in the Dining Cryptographers protocol. In the latter, we record an exponential speed-up over state-of-the-art competing approaches.

Main Contributions.[1] Our main contributions are twofold: First, we define a simple imperative, non-recursive call-by-name procedural probabilistic language, interpreted over finite datatypes, and show that it has a decidable contextual equivalence problem. Our language is related to second-order Probabilistic Idealized Algol, as studied in [19], and our decidability proof relies in important ways on results from [6, 19]. Among the new ingredients are direct automata constructions (rather than reliance on abstract theoretical results, as was done in [19]), in particular with respect to epsilon-elimination.

Our second—and arguably most significant—contribution lies in the novel application of our framework in the treatment of the case studies. In particular, we use contextual equivalence for *open* programs in a key way in two of the three instances. As discussed in greater details below and in Section 6, our use of contextual equivalence in the Dining Cryptographers protocol results in a dramatic improvement in both verification time and memory consumption over current alternative approaches.

Related Work. Proposals for imperative probabilistic programming languages, along with associated semantics, go back several decades (see, e.g., [16]). As noted in [8], most of the semantic models in the literature are variants of Markov chains, where the states of the Markov chain are determined by the program counter and the values of the variables.

While such treatments are perfectly adequate for model checking closed (monolithic) programs, they are usually ill-suited to handle open programs, in which certain variables or even procedures are left undefined. Moreover, such semantic approaches are also generally of no help in establishing (probabilistic) contextual equivalence: the indistinguishability of two open programs by any (program) context. Contextual equivalence, in turn, is arguably one of the most natural and efficient ways to specify various properties such as anonymity—see Section 6 for further details and background on this point.

As we explain in Section 3, our approach, in contrast, is based on game semantics, and differs radically from the various 'probabilistic state-transformer' semantics discussed above. The main benefit we derive is an algorithm for deciding contextual equivalence.

We note that many probabilistic model checkers, such as PRISM [11] and LiQuor [4], have been reported upon in the literature—see [18] for a partial survey. Most of these tools use probabilistic and continuous-time variants of Computation Tree Logic, although Linear Temporal Logic is also occasionally supported.

---

[1] A full version of this paper, which will include all the formal definitions, constructions, and proofs that have been omitted here, is currently in preparation [18].

2 A Probabilistic Programming Language

Code fragments accepted by APEX are written in a probabilistic procedural language with call-by-name evaluation, whose full syntax is given below.

```
const ::= [0-9]+
id ::= [a-z]+
gr_type ::= 'void' | 'int%' const | 'var%' const
gr_list ::= gr_type {',' gr_list }
type ::= { gr_type '->' | '(' gr_list ') ->' } gr_type
rand_dist ::= const ':' const '/' const {',' rand_dist }
gr_params ::= gr_type id {',' gr_params }
params ::= gr_type id { '(' gr_list ')' } {',' params }
program_list ::= program {',' program_list }
binop ::= '+' | '-' | '*' | '/' | 'and' | 'or' | '<=' | '<' | '='
unop ::= 'not'
typable_val ::= const | 'coin' | 'rand[' rand_dist ']'

program ::=
   'skip' | typable_val | '( int%'const typable_val ')' |
   id | id '(' { program_list } ')' | id '[' program ']' |
   'int%'const id | 'int%'const id '[' const ']' |
   'if' program 'then' program { 'else' program } |
   'case' '(' program ')' '[' program_list ']' |
   program ';' program | 'while' program 'do' program |
   program ':=' program | program binop program | unop program |
   gr_type id '(' {gr_params} ') {' program '}' program |
   '(' program ')' | '{' program '}'

input ::= type 'main(' { params } ') {' program '}'
```

This language has two simple mechanisms for specifying random values. First, the 'probabilistic' constant coin represents the fair coin: it returns value 0 or 1, each with probability $\frac{1}{2}$. More generally, one can specify arbitrary finite distributions using rand, e.g., rand[1:1/3, 2:1/3, 3:1/3] stands for the fair three-sided die. Other syntactic elements are intended to resemble C in order to make it easier to analyse pieces of code; for example, blocks are delimited by braces ({...}). The language is predicated on finite integer datatypes, which support modulo arithmetic (+,-,*,/). Local variables can be declared using statements of the form int%n i, where n indicates the modulus and i is a variable name. Similarly, arrays are defined using declarations such as int%n a[m], where m represents the size of the array. int%2 can double as the Boolean type with the associated logical operations (and, or, not). Procedures can be introduced with syntax such as

$$\text{void procname(int\%4 i, var\%7 j) } \{...\}$$

where i is a $\{0, 1, 2, 3\}$-valued parameter (modulo 4) and j is a reference parameter (analogous to 'int &j' in C++) modulo 7. Functions are defined in the same way except that int%n should be used instead of void for some $n \in \mathbb{N}^+$. Procedures/functions can be declared locally within other procedures/functions, but recursive calls are not allowed. Iteration is provided in the form of while loops.

Our framework also supports *open* code with undefined variables, procedures or functions (also known as undefined parameters). Their names together with types (e.g., var%6 x, or void f(int%3,var%7)) have to be declared as part of the input statement whose general shape is as follows:

$$type \; \text{main}(\textit{undefined\_parameters}) \; \{\textit{open\_code}\}.$$

3   Contextual Equivalence

As a result of randomisation, closed programs of type void terminate with some probability, whereas closed programs of type int%m generate a sub-distribution on $\{0, \ldots, m-1\}$. In addition to closed programs, we also consider open program fragments in which some parts are not specified and are represented by undefined parameters, as discussed earlier. Open programs cannot be executed on their own and become executable only when put in a program context that makes them closed, i.e., provides instantiations for the undefined parts. Note that open programs can alternatively be viewed as higher-order procedures.

We say that two (open or closed) programs P_1 and P_2 are *equivalent* iff they behave the same way inside all program contexts, i.e., for any context C such that $C[P_1]$, $C[P_2]$ are closed programs of type void, $C[P_1]$ and $C[P_2]$ terminate with the same probability[2]. Thus equivalent programs exhibit the same observable behaviour. The observable behaviour of closed programs is determined simply by the sub-distribution generated by termination. That of open programs can be said to correspond to the ways the program can use its undefined components. This intuition is made precise by game semantics [1, 12, 6, 19], which we briefly examine below.

Intuitively, probabilistic contextual equivalence is a linear-time (as opposed to branching-time) and statistical (as opposed to possibilistic) notion of program equivalence. We remark that it is an especially powerful instrument in the case of open programs, which we make full use of in the case studies presented in Sections 5 and 6.

The main theoretical result underpinning the work we present here is the following.

Theorem 1. *Probabilistic contextual equivalence is decidable for the programming language given in Section 2.*

The proof of Theorem 1 is based on game semantics and relies heavily on the results of [6, 19]. Full details will appear in [18].

---

[2] The probability of termination is formally computed using an operational semantics; we refer the reader to [18] for the precise details.

Game semantics is a modelling theory for a wide range of programming paradigms. It associates to any given (probabilistic) open program a (probabilistic) *strategy*, which in turn gives rise to a set of (probabilistic) *complete plays*. *Full abstraction* is then the assertion that two open programs are contextually equivalent iff they exhibit precisely the same set of complete plays. Theorem 1 is established via a full abstraction result, in which moreover the relevant sets of complete plays can be represented using probabilistic automata [22]. Probabilistic program equivalence therefore reduces to language equivalence for probabilistic automata, which can be decided in polynomial time [25].

We note that the probabilistic automata arising from game semantics are radically different from the Markov chains that arise in the various probabilistic state-transformer semantics discussed in Section 1. Whereas the latter essentially correspond to an operational unwinding of a program, the game-semantical probabilistic automata capture the ways in which a program can interact with its environment, i.e., the broader context in which the program lies. For a more detailed account of game semantics as used in this paper, we refer the reader to [18].

Our tool APEX generates the probabilistic automata representing open programs in a compositional manner, by executing bespoke automata operations for each of the syntactic constructs of our language. The state spaces of the resultant intermediate automata are reduced using a variety of algorithmic techniques, including reachability analysis, decomposition into strongly connected components, and quotienting by probabilistic bisimulation [17].

We remark that closed programs always give rise to single-state automata, whereas open programs yield non-trivial automata. Of course, in both cases the intermediate automata produced can be arbitrarily large[3] and complex, hence the need for efficient implementations of the constructions and the use of state-space reduction techniques.

As an example, consider the following open program P_1:

```
void main(var%2 x) { x:=rand[0:1/3, 1:2/3]; x:=coin }
```

P_1 has a single free identifier, x, which is a variable ranging over $\{0, 1\}$. In the program code, x is first assigned 0 or 1 with respective probabilities of $\frac{1}{3}$ and $\frac{2}{3}$, and is then again assigned 0 or 1, but with equal probability.

The open program P_2, below, is similar to P_1 except that the two assignments to x are both made by a fair coin:

```
void main(var%2 x) { x:=coin; x:=coin }
```

P_1 and P_2, it turns out, are not equivalent; indeed, it is possible to manufacture a context which (probabilistically) distinguishes them by observing the sequence of assignments to x.[4] By full abstraction, the complete plays of P_1

---

[3] More precisely, the automata can have size exponential in the size of the code fragment.

[4] An instance of such a context could, for example, instantiate the free occurrences of x with the sequential composition of a command followed by a variable; in effect, assignments to x then induce side-effects, which can be detected by the context.

and P_2, captured respectively by the two probabilistic automata depicted below, must therefore differ:

Each automaton consists of three states. Initial states are shaded, and accepting states are doubly circled. Transitions are labelled by the corresponding assignments to x together with the associated probabilities.

The probabilistic languages of the two automata are plainly different; for instance, the word $\langle write(0)\_x, write(0)\_x \rangle$ is accepted by the first automaton with probability $\frac{1}{6}$ and by the second automaton with probability $\frac{1}{4}$.

P_1 and P_2 both contain a free identifier x, and are therefore not closed programs. It is of course possible to declare x as a local variable instead, as in the following:

```
void main() { int%2 x; x:=coin[0:1/3, 1:2/3]; x:=coin }
```

The above program is closed, and terminates with probability 1; it is therefore equivalent to `void main() { skip }`, and its set of complete plays is captured by the following probabilistic automaton:

The second component of the label on the accepting state, the number '1', represents the probability of termination. This automaton therefore accepts the empty word with probability 1 (and all other words with probability 0).

It should be clear that, if P_1 and P_2 are modified by making x a local variable rather than a free identifier, then no context can possibly distinguish them and they therefore become equivalent (in accordance with one's intuition). Hence the way in which variables are declared, whether as free identifiers or locally, intuitively corresponds to whether they are visible or not to the outside world. We will make use of this idea when we consider the notion of anonymity in Section 6.

The current version of APEX relies on manipulating text files with a library of automata routines. APEX takes as input a text file containing a description of an open probabilistic program which comprises the program type, the list of its free identifiers, and the program code. The output is a probabilistic automaton. After the automata have been generated they can be inspected immediately, or fed to other automata-theoretic procedures such as Tzeng's equivalence-checking algorithm [25].

4   Herman's Self-stabilisation Algorithm

Self-stabilisation is an important area of research in distributed systems that originated with Dijkstra's seminal 1974 paper [7]. Roughly speaking, a self-stabilising system is one that always eventually recovers in finite time from transient faults and operates correctly.

Herman's algorithm is a classical example of a randomised self-stabilisation protocol [9]. Imagine a network of processes, arranged in a ring, with each process possibly holding a token. 'Legitimate' configurations are those in which a token is held by exactly one process. The aim of a self-stabilisation protocol is to guide the network towards legitimate configurations.

Let us assume that each process possesses a distinguished two-valued variable, and let us adopt the convention that a process is deemed to hold a token if its distinguished variable has the same value as that of its immediate right-hand neighbour. (Note that in order for this representation scheme to make sense, there must be an odd number of processes in the network.)

The algorithm works as follows. At every time step, each process determines whether or not it holds a token. If it does, it flips its distinguished variable with probability $\frac{1}{2}$, and otherwise sets its distinguished variable equal to that of its right-hand neighbour. We assume that processes execute synchronously.

What we would like to show is that such a protocol is *correct*, i.e., that it always eventually leads the system to a legitimate, single-token configuration.

To this end, we implemented Herman's algorithm in our probabilistic programming language for various numbers of processes in the network. The code for a 15-process network is given below.

```
void main() {
  int%2 x[15]; int%2 z; int%3 token; int%15 i;
  token:=2;
  while(not (token=1)) do {
    token:=0;
    i:=0;
    z:=x[0];
    while (i+1) do {
      if (x[i]=x[i+1]) then
        x[i]:=coin else x[i]:=x[i+1];
      if (i>0) and (x[i-1]=x[i]) then
        token:=case(token)[1,2,2];
      i:=i+1
    };
    if (x[i]=z) then x[i]:=coin else x[i]:=z;
    if (x[i-1]=x[i]) then token:=case(token)[1,2,2];
    if (x[i]=x[0]) then token:=case(token)[1,2,2]
  }
}
```

Most of the syntax is self-explanatory, perhaps with the exception of the statement `token:=case(token)[1,2,2];`. This is similar to the `switch` construct in C, and is equivalent to

```
if token=0 then token:=1 else
  if token=1 then token:=2 else
    if token=2 then token:=2;
```

In the program, the distinguished variables of processes are held in a 15-element array x of two-valued variables. The inner `while` loop simulates the synchronous execution of the network over a single time step. In this loop, the variable `token` is used to count the total number of tokens present in the network, with the value 2 representing 'two or more'. Recall the use of modulo arithmetic so that variables that overflow simply cycle through 0. The outer `while` loop ensures that the code is executed until the network contains just a single token.

Note that our implementation is a closed program of type `void`. It should be clear that the correctness of Herman's algorithm (a single-token configuration is always eventually reached) corresponds to the assertion that our program terminates with probability 1. And indeed, when running APEX, the output is the one-state automaton corresponding to `void main() { skip }` already depicted in Section 3.

We remark that it is trivial to modify the code to model networks with different numbers of processes: it suffices to replace the two occurrences of the number '15' in the first line by whatever other value is desired.

Although all instances of our program ultimately give rise to the same single-state automaton, the computation times of APEX increase with the sizes of the networks modelled. This is not surprising since an n-process network has 2^n distinct configurations (ignoring symmetries). The intermediate automata generated by APEX reflect this growth, although this is mitigated to some extent by the use of state-space reduction techniques throughout the computation.

5   Hibbard's Algorithm and Random Trees

APEX makes it possible to compare various finite-state distribution generators. For instance, one can easily verify that the standard iterative algorithm for simulating a six-sided die using a fair coin is correct.

In this section we analyse a more complicated example, having to do with the average shape of binary search trees generated by sequences of random insertions and deletions. This is a classical problem in the theory of algorithms, in which a central concern is to ensure that the random trees generated within a particular scheme have low average height.

Binary search trees have been used and studied by computer scientists since the 1950s. In 1962, Hibbard proposed a simple algorithm to dynamically delete an element from a binary tree [10]. Moreover, he also proved that a random deletion from a random tree, using his algorithm, leaves a random tree. Although the statement might seem self-evident, we will see shortly that this is not quite the case. More precisely, Hibbard's theorem can be stated as follows: "If $n+1$ items are inserted into an initially empty binary tree, in random order, and if one of those items (selected at random) is deleted, the probability that the resulting binary tree has a given shape is the same as the probability that this tree shape would be obtained by inserting n items into an initially empty tree, in random order."

Hibbard's paper was remarkable in that it contained one of the first formal theorems about algorithms. Furthermore, the proof was not simple. Interestingly, for more than a decade it was subsequently believed that Hibbard's theorem in fact proved that trees obtained through arbitrary sequences of random insertions and deletions are automatically random, i.e., have shapes whose distribution is the same as if the trees had been generated directly using random insertions only; see [10, 15].

Quite surprisingly, it turns out that this intuition was wrong. In 1975, Knott showed that, although Hibbard's theorem establishes that $n + 1$ random insertions followed by a deletion yield the same distribution on tree shapes as n insertions, we cannot conclude that a subsequent random insertion yields a tree whose shape has the same distribution as that obtained through $n + 1$ random insertions [14].

As Jonassen and Knuth point out, this result came as a shock. In [13], they gave a careful counterexample (based on Knott's work) using trees having size no greater than three. More precisely, they showed that three insertions, followed by a deletion and a subsequent insertion (all random) give rise to different tree shapes from those obtained by three random insertions. Despite the small sizes of the trees involved and the small number of random operations performed, their presentation showed that the analysis at this stage is already quite intricate. This suggests a possible reason as to why an erroneous belief was held for so long: carrying out even small-scale experiments on discrete distributions is inherently difficult and error-prone. For example, it would be virtually impossible to carry out by hand Jonassen and Knuth's analysis for trees of size no greater than five (i.e., five insertions differ from five insertions followed by a deletion and then another insertion), and even if one used a computer it would be quite tricky to correctly set up a bespoke exhaustive search.

Our goal here is to show that such analyses can be carried out almost effortlessly with APEX. It suffices to write programs that implement the relevant operations and subsequently print the shape of the resultant tree, and then ask whether the programs are equivalent or not.

As an example, we describe how to use APEX to reproduce Jonassen and Knuth's counterexample, i.e., three insertions differ from three insertions followed by a deletion and an insertion. Since APEX does not at present support pointers, we represent binary trees of size n using arrays of size $2^n - 1$, following a standard encoding (see, e.g., [5]): the left and right children of an i-indexed array entry are stored in the array at indices $2i + 1$ and $2i + 2$ respectively.

It is then possible to write a short program that inserts three elements at random into a tree, then sequentially prints out the tree shape in breadth-first manner into a free identifier ch. The actual code is omitted here for lack of space, and can be found in [18]. From this open program, APEX generates the following probabilistic automaton:

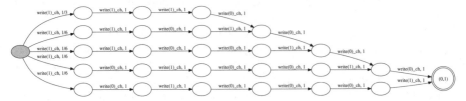

The upper path in this automaton, for example, represents the balanced three-element tree shape ⌢. The probability that this shape occurs can be determined by multiplying together the weights of the corresponding transitions, yielding a value of $\frac{1}{3}$.

It is likewise straightforward to produce a program implementing three insertions followed by a deletion and an insertion, all of them random—the code can be found in [18]. The corresponding probabilistic automaton is the following:

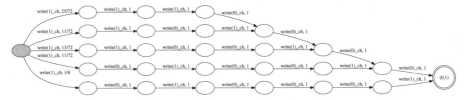

The reader will note that the balanced three-element tree shape occurs with slightly greater probability: $\frac{25}{72}$. Thus the two programs are indeed not equivalent.

Note that none of this, of course, contradicts Hibbard's theorem, to the effect that the distribution on tree shapes upon performing two random insertions is the same as that obtained from three random insertions followed by a random deletion. The reason is that, although the distribution on tree *shapes* is the same, that on *trees* is not. This is then witnessed by performing an additional random insertion, which in the second case very slightly biases the resulting tree shape towards balance, as compared to the first case.

6   The Dining Cryptographers

Anonymity is a key concept in computer security. It arises in a wide range of contexts, such as voting, blogging, making donations, passing on sensitive information, etc. A celebrated toy example illustrating anonymity is that of the 'Dining Cryptographers protocol' [3]. Imagine that a certain number of cryptographers are sharing a meal at a restaurant around a circular table. As the end of the meal, the waiter announces that the bill has already been paid. The cryptographers conclude that it is either one of them who has paid, or the organisation that employs them. They resolve to determine which of the two alternatives is the case, with the proviso that for the former the identity of the payer should remain secret.

A possible solution goes as follows. A coin is placed between each pair of adjacent cryptographers. The cryptographers flip the coins and record the outcomes for the two coins that they can see, i.e., the ones that are to their immediate left and right. Each cryptographer then announces whether the two outcomes *agree* or *disagree*, except that the payer (if there is one) says the opposite. When all cryptographers have spoken, they count the number of *disagrees*. If that number is odd, then one of them has paid, and otherwise, their organisation has paid. Moreover, if the payer is one of the cryptographers, then no other cryptographer is able to deduce who it is.

There are many formalisations of the concept of anonymity in the literature. The earliest approaches ignored probabilities and relied instead on nondeterminism; anonymity was then equated with 'confusion', or more precisely with notions of equivalence between certain processes [24]. For example, in the case of the dining cryptographers, every possible behaviour visible to one of the cryptographers (i.e., outcomes of the two adjacent coin flips and subsequent round of announcements) should be consistent with any of the other cryptographers having paid, provided the number of *disagrees* is odd.

A more sophisticated treatment takes probabilities into account. In our example, assuming the coins are fair, it can be shown that the *a posteriori* probability of having paid, given a particular protocol run, is the same for all cryptographers. Note that this does not hold if the coins are biased, which highlights one of the advantages of using probability over nondeterminism. A survey of the literature, as well as an in-depth treatment using process algebra, can be found in [2].

We show how to model the Dining Cryptographers protocol in our probabilistic programming language, and verify anonymity using APEX. Let us consider the case of three cryptographers, numbered 1, 2, and 3, from the point of view of the first cryptographer; the open program below enacts the protocol. This program has a local variable whopaid that can be set to 2 or 3, to model the appropriate situation. All events meant to be visible to the first cryptographer, i.e., the outcomes of his two adjacent coins, as well as the announcements of all cryptographers, are written to the free identifiers cn and ch respectively. (Probabilistic) anonymity with respect to the first cryptographer corresponds to the assertion that the program in which whopaid has been set to 2 is equivalent to the program in which whopaid has been set to 3.

```
void main(var%2 ch, var%2 cn) {
  int%4 whopaid; int%2 first; int%2 right; int%2 left; int%4 i;
  whopaid:=2; first:=coin; right:=first; i:=1;
  while (i) do {
    left := if (i=3) then first else coin;
    if (i=1) then { cn:=right; cn:=left };
    if ((left=right)+(i=whopaid)) then ch:=1 else ch:=0;
    right:=left;
    i:=i+1
  }
}
```

From this code, APEX produces the following probabilistic automaton:

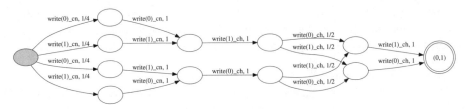

It turns out that setting `whopaid` to 3 in the above program yields precisely the same automaton. The two programs are therefore equivalent, which establishes anonymity of the protocol with three cryptographers.

One can easily investigate larger instances of the protocol, through very minor modifications of the code. For example, the probabilistic automaton below corresponds to an instance of the protocol comprising 10 cryptographers. It is interesting to note that the size of the state space of the automata grows only linearly with the number of cryptographers, despite the fact that the raw cryptographers state space is ostensibly exponential (due to the set of possible outcomes of the coin flips). Note however that this complexity is in our case reflected in the number of *paths* of the automata rather than in the number of their states. In fact, in our experiments (see Figure 1), the state spaces of the intermediate automata as well as the total running times grew linearly as well. This unexpected outcome arose partly from APEX's use of bisimulation reduction throughout the construction, in which most symmetries were factored out.

We can also show that probabilistic anonymity fails when the coins are biased, as described in [18]. Note that thanks to full abstraction, whenever two probabilistic programs are not equivalent, their corresponding probabilistic automata will disagree on the probability of accepting some particular word. This word, whose length need at most be linear in the sizes of the automata, can be thought of as a *counterexample* to the assertion of equivalence of the original programs, and can potentially be used to 'debug' them. In the case at hand, such a word would illustrate why anonymity fails when the coins are biased, albeit only in a probabilistic sense. A would-be spymaster could then return to the programs and attempt to fix the problem.

Although APEX does not at present generate counterexamples in instances of inequivalence, we remark that it would be straightforward and computationally inexpensive to instrument it to do so.

Related Work. Although the Dining Cryptographers protocol was proposed almost twenty years ago and has been extensively studied since[5], it had until

---

[5] Google Scholar lists over 500 papers dealing with the Dining Cryptographers!

recently never been verified[6] in a fully automated way. In the last few weeks, we have become aware of two automated verification instances (other than that proposed in the present paper): [21] and [20].

As explained earlier, assertions of anonymity are most commonly and naturally expressed as *equivalences*; in [24], for example, trace equivalence in (non-probabilistic) CSP is used, whereas [2] is based on bisimulation equivalence for a probabilistic extension of the π-calculus. Most probabilistic verification engines, however, focus on *model checking*, i.e., whether a particular probabilistic system satisfies a given specification, where the latter is usually given in some (probabilistic) temporal logic such as PCTL.

As regards anonymity, model checking is considerably less convenient than equivalence checking. In [21], for example, the authors establish anonymity of the Dining Cryptographers protocol by considering all possible visible behaviours, and proving for each that the likelihood of its occurrence is the same regardless of the payer. This leads to exponentially large specifications, and correspondingly intractable model-checking tasks.[7] In practice, a proper verification of the protocol can only be carried out for a handful of cryptographers—see the experimental results reported in Figure 1, running on a Fujitsu-Siemens Lifebook P7120 at 1.2 GHz, with 1 GB RAM, under Windows XP. In particular, PRISM takes over an hour to handle 10 cryptographers, and runs out of memory for larger instances. By contrast, we can handle 100 cryptographers in approximately 125 seconds.

The same difficulties beset the framework of [20], which gives an algorithm for PCTL model checking of the probabilistic π-calculus, along with a PRISM-based implementation. Again, the combinatorial explosion (of both the model and the specification) severely limits the sizes of the protocol instances that can be verified. We believe that the work presented in this section makes a forceful case for the development of probabilistic equivalence checkers alongside model-checking tools.

7   Future Work

There are many avenues for further research. We are currently implementing support for pointers, which would enable more flexible modelling of algorithms that use dynamic data structures. We would also like to extend APEX to handle programs that feature *parameterised* random constants, representing undetermined sub-distributions, which can be viewed as a form of nondeterminism. For instance, in a version of Herman's protocol with biased coins, one could verify termination for all possible biases at once.

---

[6] By *verification* of the protocol we refer here to the automated handling of instances in which the number of cryptographers is fixed; the *parameterised* verification problem, which deals at once with all possible numbers of cryptographers, is substantially more difficult to achieve in fully automated fashion.

[7] The state space of the underlying Markov chain generated by PRISM also grows exponentially, but this is mitigated by PRISM's use of symbolic representations in the form of MTBDDs.

# crypt.	PRISM	APEX
3	4	7
4	4	8
5	7	8
6	39	9
7	95	9
8	282	10
9	964	10
10	> 1h	11
15	OOM	13
50	OOM	56
100	OOM	125

Fig. 1. Dining Cryptographers protocol verification times. Timeout was set at one hour, all other times reported in seconds. OOM indicates 'out of memory'.

To support such an extension, we believe that Tzeng's algorithm for language equivalence of probabilistic automata [25] can be generalised to a randomised polynomial-time algorithm for determining *universal equivalence* of parameterised probabilistic automata: 'Are two automata equivalent for all possible instantiations of their parameters, subject to a set of linear constraints?'

We also aim to extend the capabilities of APEX beyond equivalence checking, by exploiting the probabilistic automata it generates in different ways. Model checking and counterexample generation are the most obvious examples, but refinement checking and performance analysis, among others, would also be very useful.

A more ambitious line of research would consist in extending the current approach to handle concurrency, which would facilitate the modelling of distributed systems and protocols.

Acknowledgements. We would like to thank Marta Kwiatkowska, Gethin Norman, and Dave Parker for useful discussions and their help with PRISM, and the London Mathematical Society for financial support.

References

[1] Abramsky, S., Jagadeesan, R., Malacaria, P.: Full abstraction for PCF. Inf. Comput. 163, 409–470 (2000)

[2] Bhargava, M., Palamidessi, C.: Probabilistic anonymity. In: Abadi, M., de Alfaro, L. (eds.) CONCUR 2005. LNCS, vol. 3653, pp. 171–185. Springer, Heidelberg (2005)

[3] Chaum, D.: The dining cryptographers problem: Unconditional sender and recipient untraceability. J. Cryptology 1(1), 65–75 (1988)

[4] Ciesinski, F., Baier, C.: LiQuor: A tool for qualitative and quantitative linear time analysis of reactive systems. In: Proceedings of QEST, IEEE Computer Society Press, Los Alamitos (2006)

[5] Cormen, T.H., Leiserson, C.E., Rivest, R.L., Stein, C.: Introduction to Algorithms, 2nd edn. MIT Press, Cambridge (2001)

[6] Danos, V., Harmer, R.: Probabilistic game semantics. ACM Trans. Comput. Log. 3(3), 359–382 (2002)

[7] Dijkstra, E.W.: Self-stabilizing systems in spite of distributed control. Commun. ACM 17(11), 643–644 (1974)

[8] Esparza, J., Etessami, K.: Verifying probabilistic procedural programs. In: Lodaya, K., Mahajan, M. (eds.) FSTTCS 2004. LNCS, vol. 3328, pp. 16–31. Springer, Heidelberg (2004)

[9] Herman, T.: Probabilistic self-stabilization. Inf. Process. Lett. 35(2), 63–67 (1990)

[10] Hibbard, T.N.: Some combinatorial properties of certain trees with applications to searching and sorting. J. ACM 9(1), 13–28 (1962)

[11] Hinton, A., Kwiatkowska, M.Z., Norman, G., Parker, D.: PRISM: A Tool for Automatic Verification of Probabilistic Systems. In: Hermanns, H., Palsberg, J. (eds.) TACAS 2006. LNCS, vol. 3920, pp. 441–444. Springer, Heidelberg (2006)

[12] Hyland, J.M.E., Ong, C.-H.L.: On Full Abstraction for PCF: I. Models, observables and the full abstraction problem, II. Dialogue games and innocent strategies, III. A fully abstract and universal game model. Inf. Comput. 163(2), 285–408 (2000)

[13] Jonassen, A.T., Knuth, D.E.: A trivial algorithm whose analysis isn't. J. Comput. Syst. Sci. 16(3), 301–322 (1978)

[14] Knott, G.D.: Deletion in Binary Storage Trees. PhD thesis, Stanford University, Computer Science Technical Report STAN-CS-75-491 (1975)

[15] Knuth, D.E.: Sorting and searching. In: The Art of Computer Programming (first printing), vol. 3, Addison-Wesley, Reading (1973)

[16] Kozen, D.: Semantics of probabilistic programs. J. Comput. Syst. Sci. 22(3), 328–350 (1981)

[17] Larsen, K., Skou, A.: Compositional verification of probabilistic processes. In: Cleaveland, W.R. (ed.) CONCUR 1992. LNCS, vol. 630, Springer, Heidelberg (1992)

[18] Legay, A., Murawski, A.S., Ouaknine, J., Worrell, J.: Verification of probabilistic programs via equivalence checking. (preparation)

[19] Murawski, A.S., Ouaknine, J.: On Probabilistic Program Equivalence and Refinement. In: Abadi, M., de Alfaro, L. (eds.) CONCUR 2005. LNCS, vol. 3653, pp. 156–170. Springer, Heidelberg (2005)

[20] Norman, G., Palamidessi, C., Parker, D., Wu, P.: Model checking the probabilistic π-calculus. In: Proceedings of QEST, IEEE Computer Society Press, Los Alamitos (2007)

[21] PRISM case study: Dining Cryptographers. www.prismmodelchecker.org/casestudies/dining_crypt.php

[22] Rabin, M.O.: Probabilistic automata. Information and Control 6(3), 230–245 (1963)

[23] Rabin, M.O.: Probabilistic algorithms. In: Proceedings of the Symposium on Algorithms and Complexity, Academic Press, London (1976)

[24] Schneider, S., Sidiropoulos, A.: CSP and anonymity. In: Martella, G., Kurth, H., Montolivo, E., Bertino, E. (eds.) ESORICS 1996. LNCS, vol. 1146, Springer, Heidelberg (1996)

[25] Tzeng, W.-G.: A polynomial-time algorithm for the equivalence of probabilistic automata. SIAM J. Comput. 21(2), 216–227 (1992)

Symbolic Model Checking of Hybrid Systems Using Template Polyhedra

Sriram Sankaranarayanan[1], Thao Dang[2], and Franjo Ivančić[1]

[1] NEC Laboratories America, Princeton, NJ, USA
[2] Verimag, Grenoble, France
{srirams,ivancic}@nec-labs.com,thao.dang@imag.fr

Abstract. We propose techniques for the verification of hybrid systems using template polyhedra, i.e., polyhedra whose inequalities have fixed expressions but with varying constant terms. Given a hybrid system description and a set of template linear expressions as inputs, our technique constructs over-approximations of the reachable states using template polyhedra. Therefore, operations used in symbolic model checking such as intersection, union and post-condition across discrete transitions over template polyhedra can be computed efficiently using template polyhedra without requiring expensive vertex enumeration.

Additionally, the verification of hybrid systems requires techniques to handle the continuous dynamics inside discrete modes. We propose a new flowpipe construction algorithm using template polyhedra. Our technique uses higher-order Taylor series expansion to approximate the time trajectories. The terms occurring in the Taylor series expansion are bounded using repeated optimization queries. The location invariant is used to enclose the remainder term of the Taylor series, and thus truncate the expansion. Finally, we have implemented our technique as a part of the tool TimePass for the analysis of affine hybrid automata.

1 Introduction

Symbolic model checking of infinite state systems requires a systematic representation for handling infinite sets of states. Commonly used representations include difference matrices, integer/rational polyhedra, Presburger arithmetic, polynomials, nonlinear arithmetic and so on. Expressive representations can better approximate the underlying sets. However, the basic operations required for symbolic execution such as intersection, image (post-condition) and so on are harder to compute on such representations.

Convex polyhedra over reals (rationals) are a natural representation of sets of states for the verification of hybrid systems [15,30,2,10,11,12]. However, basic algorithms required to manipulate polyhedra require worst-case exponential complexity. This fact has limited the practical usefulness of symbolic model checking tools based on polyhedra. Therefore, restricted forms of polyhedra such as *orthogonal polyhedra* [3] and *zonotopes* [11] are used to analyze larger systems at a level of precision that is useful for proving some properties of interest. Other

C.R. Ramakrishnan and J. Rehof (Eds.): TACAS 2008, LNCS 4963, pp. 188–202, 2008.

techniques, such as *predicate abstraction*, use Boolean combinations of a fixed set of predicates $p_1, \ldots, p_m$, to represent sets of states [1,16]. Such techniques enable the refinement of the representation based on counterexamples.

In this paper, we propose *template polyhedra* as a representation of sets of states. Given a set of *template expressions* $e_1, \ldots, e_m$, we obtain a family of *template polyhedra*, each of which is represented by the constraints $\bigwedge_i e_i \leq c_i$ [29]. As with predicate abstraction, our approach assumes that the template expressions are provided as an input to the reachability problem. We then use the family of polyhedra defined by the given template expressions as our representation for sets of states. The advantage of restricting our representation to a family of template polyhedra is that operations such as join, meet, discrete post-condition and time elapse can be performed efficiently, without requiring expensive vertex enumeration. Furthermore, our initial experience suggests that commonly used domains in software analysis such as *intervals* and *octagons* provide a good initial set of templates. This set can be further refined using simple heuristics for deriving additional expressions.

In order to analyze hybrid systems, we additionally require techniques to over-approximate the continuous dynamics at some location. This paper proposes a sound flowpipe construction technique based on a Taylor series approximation. Our approach works by solving numerous linear programs. The solutions to these linear programs correspond to bounds on the terms involved in the Taylor series expansion. The expansion itself is bounded by enclosing the remainder term using the location invariant. The flowpipe construction results in a series of template polyhedra whose disjunctions over-approximate the time trajectories.

Finally, we have implemented our methods in our prototype tool TIMEPASS for verifying safety properties of affine hybrid systems. We use our tool to analyze many widely studied benchmark systems and report vastly improved performance on them.

Related Work

Hybrid systems verification is a challenge even for small systems. Numerous approaches have been used in the past to solve reachability problems: the HyTech tool due to Henzinger et al. uses polyhedra to verify rectangular hybrid systems [15]. More complex dynamics are handled using approximations. Kurzhanski and Variaya construct ellipsoidal approximations [17]; Mitchell et al. use level-set methods [20]; the d/dt system uses orthogonal polyhedra and face lifting [2]; Piazza et al. [22] propose approximations using constraint solving based on quantifier elimination over the reals along with Taylor series expansions to handle the continuous dynamics. Lanotte & Tini [18] present approximations based on Taylor series that can be made as accurate as possible, approaching the actual trajectories in the limit.

Girard uses zonotopes to construct flowpipes [11]. The PHAVer tool due to Frehse extends the HyTech approach by repeatedly subdividing the invariant region and approximating the dynamics inside each subdivision by piece-wise constant dynamics [10]. Tiwari [31] presents interesting techniques for proving safety by symbolically integrating the dynamics of the system. Symbolic techniques for proving unreachability without the use of an explicit flowpipe approximation [28,32,26,23]. These techniques can handle interesting nonlinear systems beyond the reach of many related techniques.

The problem of flowpipe construction for template polyhedra has been studied previously by Chutinan & Krogh [5]. Their technique has been implemented as a part of the tool CheckMate [30]. Whereas the CheckMate approach solves global non convex optimization problems using gradient descent, our approach solves simple convex optimization problems to bound the coefficients of the Taylor series expansion. Furthermore, our technique can be extended to some nonlinear systems to construct ellipsoidal and polynomial flowpipes. The CheckMate technique simply yields a harder nonconvex optimization problem for these cases. On the other hand, our approach loses in precision due to its approximation of functions by Taylor polynomials; CheckMate, however, is more robust in this regard.

Template polyhedra are commonly used in static analysis of programs for computing invariants. Range analysis can be regarded as template polyhedra over expressions of the form $\pm x$ [7] . Similarly, the octagon domain due to Miné [19] uses template polyhedron of the form $\bigwedge x_i - x_j \leq c$. General template polyhedra were used as an abstract domain to represent sets of states by Sankaranarayanan et al. [29].

2   Preliminaries

Let $\mathcal{R}$ denote the set of reals, and $\mathcal{R}_+ = \mathcal{R} \cup \{\pm\infty\}$. A first order assertion $\varphi[x_1, \ldots, x_n]$, over the theory of reals, represents a set $[\![\varphi]\!] \subseteq \mathcal{R}^n$. A column vector, denoted $\langle x_1, \ldots, x_n \rangle$, is represented succinctly as $\boldsymbol{x}$. Capital letters A, B, C and X, Y, Z denote matrices; A_i denotes the ith row of a matrix A. A linear function $f(x)$ is the inner product of vectors $\boldsymbol{c}^T \boldsymbol{x}$. Similarly, an affine function is represented as $\boldsymbol{c}^T \boldsymbol{x} + d$.

Polyhedra. A polyhedron is a conjunction of finitely many linear inequalities $\bigwedge_i e_i \leq c$, represented succinctly as $A\boldsymbol{x} \leq \boldsymbol{b}$, where A is a $m \times n$ matrix, $\boldsymbol{b}$ is a $m \times 1$ column vector and $\leq$ is interpreted entry-wise.

A linear program(LP) $P :$ max. $\boldsymbol{c}^T \boldsymbol{x}$ subject to $A\boldsymbol{x} \leq \boldsymbol{b}$ seeks to optimize a linear objective $\boldsymbol{c}^T \boldsymbol{x}$ over the convex polyhedron $[\![A\boldsymbol{x} \leq \boldsymbol{b}]\!]$. If $[\![A\boldsymbol{x} \leq \boldsymbol{b}]\!]$ is nonempty and bounded then the optimal solution always exists. LPs are solved using techniques such as Simplex [8] and interior point techniques [4]. The former technique is polynomial time for most instances, whereas the latter can solve LPs in polynomial time.

Vector Fields and Lie Derivatives. A *vector field* $\mathbf{D}$ over $\mathcal{R}^n$ associates each point $\boldsymbol{x} \in \mathcal{R}^n$ with a derivative vector $\mathbf{D}(\boldsymbol{x}) \in \mathcal{R}^n$. Given a system of differential equations of the form $\dot{x}_i = f_i(x_1, \ldots, x_n)$, we associate a vector field $\mathbf{D}(\boldsymbol{x}) = \langle f_1(\boldsymbol{x}), \ldots, f_n(\boldsymbol{x}) \rangle$. A vector field is *affine* if the functions $f_1, \ldots, f_n$ are all affine in $\boldsymbol{x}$. For instance, the vector field $\mathbf{D}_0(x, y) : \langle x + y, x - 2y - 3 \rangle$ is affine.

Let $D(\boldsymbol{x}) = \langle f_1(\boldsymbol{x}), \ldots, f_n(\boldsymbol{x}) \rangle$ be a vector field over $\mathcal{R}^n$. The *Lie derivative* of a continuous and differentiable function $h : \mathcal{R}^n \mapsto \mathcal{R}$ is $\mathcal{L}_D(f) = (\nabla h) \cdot D(\boldsymbol{x}) = \sum_{i=1}^{n} \frac{\partial h}{\partial x_i} \cdot f_i(\boldsymbol{x})$. The Lie derivative of the function $x + 2y - 2$ over the vector field $\mathbf{D}_0(x, y)$ shown above is given by

$$\mathcal{L}_{D_0}(x + 2y - 2) = 1 \cdot (x + y) + 2 \cdot (x - 2y - 3) = 3x - 3y - 6 \,.$$

Hybrid Systems. To model hybrid systems we use hybrid automata [14].

Definition 1 (Hybrid Automaton). *A hybrid automaton Ψ : $\langle n, \mathbf{L}, \mathcal{T}, \Theta, \mathbf{D}, \mathbf{I}, \ell_0 \rangle$ consists of the following components:*

- *n is the number of continuous variables. These variables are denoted by the set $V = \{x_1, \ldots, x_n\}$.*
- *$\mathbf{L}$, a finite set of locations; $\ell_0 \in L$ is the initial location;*
- *$\mathcal{T}$, a set of (discrete) transitions. Each transition $\tau : \langle \ell_1 \to \ell_2, \rho_\tau \rangle \in \mathcal{T}$ consists of a move from $\ell_1 \in \mathbf{L}$ to $\ell_2 \in \mathbf{L}$, and an assertion ρ_τ over $V \cup V'$, representing the transition relation;*
- *Assertion Θ, specifying the* initial *values of the continuous variables;*
- *$\mathbf{D}$, mapping each $\ell \in \mathbf{L}$ to a vector field $\mathbf{D}(\ell)$, specifying the continuous evolution in location ℓ;*
- *$\mathbf{I}$, mapping each $\ell \in \mathbf{L}$ to a location invariant, $\mathbf{I}(\ell)$.*

A *computation* of a hybrid automaton is an infinite sequence of states $\langle l, \boldsymbol{x} \rangle \in \mathbf{L} \times \mathcal{R}^n$ of the form $\langle l_0, \boldsymbol{x}_0 \rangle$, $\langle l_1, \boldsymbol{x}_1 \rangle$, $\langle l_2, \boldsymbol{x}_2 \rangle$, ..., such that initially $l_0 = \ell_0$ and $\boldsymbol{x}_0 \in [\![\Theta]\!]$; and for each consecutive state pair $\langle l_i, \boldsymbol{x}_i \rangle$, $\langle l_{i+1}, \boldsymbol{x}_{i+1} \rangle$, satisfies one of the *consecution* conditions:

Discrete Consecution: There exists a transition $\tau : \langle \ell_1, \ell_2, \rho_\tau \rangle \in \mathcal{T}$ such that $l_i = \ell_1$, $l_{i+1} = \ell_2$, and $\langle \boldsymbol{x}_i, \boldsymbol{x}_{i+1} \rangle \models \rho_\tau$, or

Continuous Consecution: $l_i = l_{i+1} = \ell$, and there exists a time interval $[0, \delta)$, $\delta > 0$, and a *time trajectory* $\tau : [0, \delta] \mapsto \mathcal{R}^n$, such that τ evolves from $\boldsymbol{x}_i$ to $\boldsymbol{x}_{i+1}$ according to the vector field at location ℓ, while satisfying the location condition $\mathbf{I}(\ell)$. Formally,

1. $\tau(0) = \boldsymbol{x}_1$, $\tau(\delta) = \boldsymbol{x}_2$, and $(\forall\, t \in [0, \delta])$, $\tau(t) \in [\![\mathbf{I}(\ell)]\!]$,
2. $(\forall t \in [0, \delta))$, $\frac{d\tau}{dt} = \mathbf{D}(\ell)|_{\boldsymbol{x} = \tau(t)}$.

Definition 2 (Affine Hybrid Automaton). *A hybrid automaton Ψ is affine if the initial condition, location invariants and transition relations are all represented by a conjunction of linear inequalities; and furthermore, the dynamics at each location $\mathbf{D}(\ell)$ is an affine vector field.*

The rest of the paper focuses solely on affine systems. However, our results also extend to the non-affine case.

Example 1. Affine hybrid systems are used to represent a variety of useful systems. Consider the oscillator circuit shown in Figure 1(a). The circuit consists of

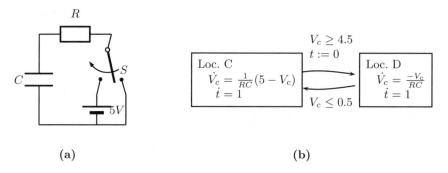

Fig. 1. An oscillator circuit (left) and its affine hybrid automaton model

a capacitor that may be charged or discharged using a voltage triggered switch S that is controlled by the voltage across the capacitor V_c. The corresponding affine hybrid automaton H has two modes C and D corresponding to the charging and discharging; and two variables V_c modeling the voltage of the capacitor and t modeling time. Switching between each mode takes place when the capacitor has charged (or discharged) to 90% (10%) of its final charge. We assume the mode invariants $\mathbf{I}(C) :\ 0 \leq V_c \leq 4.5$ and $\mathbf{I}(D) :\ 0.5 \leq V_c \leq 5$.

The *post-condition* and *time elapse* operations are the two fundamental primitives for over-approximating the reachable sets of a given hybrid automaton. Given an assertion φ over the continuous variables, its *post-condition* across a transition $\tau :\ \langle \ell, m, \rho \rangle$ is given by $\mathsf{post}(\varphi, \tau)[\boldsymbol{y}] :\ (\exists\ \boldsymbol{x})\ (\varphi(\boldsymbol{x}) \ \wedge\ \rho(\boldsymbol{x}, \boldsymbol{y}))$. The post-condition of a polyhedron is also polyhedral. It is computed using intersection and existential quantification.

Similarly, given an assertion φ, the set of possible time trajectories inside a location ℓ with invariant $\mathbf{I}(\ell)$ and dynamics $\mathbf{D}(\ell)$ is represented by its *time elapse* $\psi :\ \mathsf{timeElapse}(\varphi, \langle \mathbf{D}, \mathbf{I} \rangle)$. However, for affine hybrid systems, the time elapse of a polyhedron need not be a polyhedron. Therefore, the time elapse operator is hard to compute and represent exactly. It is over-approximated by the union of a set of polyhedra. Such an approximation is called a *flowpipe approximation*.

Using post-conditions and time elapse operators as primitives, we can prove unreachability of unsafe states using a standard forward propagation algorithm. Such an algorithm is at the core of almost all safety verification tools for hybrid systems [15,2,30,10].

Template Polyhedra. The goal of this paper is to implement symbolic model checking on hybrid systems using template polyhedra. We now present the basic facts behind template polyhedra, providing algorithms for checking inclusion, intersection, union and post-condition. Additional details and proofs are available from our previous work [29].

A *template* is a set $H = \{h_1(\boldsymbol{x}), \ldots, h_m(\boldsymbol{x})\}$ of linear expressions over $\boldsymbol{x}$. We represent a template as an $m \times n$ matrix H, s.t. each row H_i corresponds to the linear expression h_i. Given a template, a family of template polyhedra may be obtained by considering conjunctions of the form $\bigwedge_i h_i(\boldsymbol{x}) \leq c_i$. Each

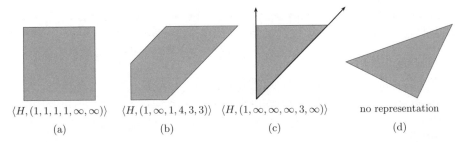

$\langle H, (1, 1, 1, 1, \infty, \infty) \rangle$ $\langle H, (1, \infty, 1, 4, 3, 3) \rangle$ $\langle H, (1, \infty, \infty, \infty, 3, \infty) \rangle$ no representation

(a)   (b)   (c)   (d)

Fig. 2. Polyhedra (a), (b) and (c) are template instances for the template H shown in Example 2, whereas (d) is not

polyhedron in the family may be obtained by choosing the constant coefficients $c_1, \ldots, c_m$.

Definition 3 (Template Polyhedron). *A template polyhedron over a template H is a polyhedron of the form $H\boldsymbol{x} \leq \boldsymbol{c}$, wherein $\boldsymbol{c} \in \mathcal{R}_+^m$. Such a polyhedron will be represented as $\langle H, \boldsymbol{c} \rangle$.*

Example 2. Consider the template $H = \{x, -x, y, -y, y - x, x - y\}$. The unit square $-1 \leq x \leq 1 \wedge -1 \leq y \leq 1$ may be represented by the template polyhedron $\langle H, (1, 1, 1, 1, \infty, \infty) \rangle$. Figure 2 shows three polyhedra that are instances, and one that is not.

Let $\boldsymbol{c}_1 \leq \boldsymbol{c}_2$ signify that for each row $i \in [1, |\boldsymbol{c}_1|]$, $\boldsymbol{c}_{1i} \leq \boldsymbol{c}_{2i}$.

Lemma 1. *If $\boldsymbol{c}_1 \leq \boldsymbol{c}_2$ then $\langle H, \boldsymbol{c}_1 \rangle \subseteq \langle H, \boldsymbol{c}_2 \rangle$. However, the converse need not hold.*

Example 3. The set $C : x = 0 \wedge y = 0$ may be represented using the template $H = \{x, -x, y, -y, x + y\}$ using the instances vectors $\boldsymbol{c} : \langle 0, 0, 0, 0, 0 \rangle$, $\boldsymbol{c}_1 : \langle 0, 0, 0, 0, 100 \rangle$, $\boldsymbol{c}_2 : \langle -10, 0, 0, 0, 0 \rangle$, and $\boldsymbol{c}_3 : \langle 0, -100, 0, 0, 0 \rangle$. In each case $\langle H, \boldsymbol{c}_i \rangle \subseteq \langle H, \boldsymbol{c} \rangle$. However $\boldsymbol{c}_i \not\leq \boldsymbol{c}$. Intuitively, "fixing" any four of the rows to 0 renders the remaining constraint row redundant.

Consider a region $C \subseteq \mathcal{R}^n$ and template H. There exists a smallest template polyhedron $\langle H, \boldsymbol{c} \rangle$, with the least instance vector $\boldsymbol{c}$, that over-approximates C, denoted $\boldsymbol{c} = \alpha_H(C)$. Furthermore, for any template polyhedra $\langle H, \boldsymbol{d} \rangle$ that over-approximates C, $\boldsymbol{c} \leq \boldsymbol{d}$. Each component c_i of $\alpha_H(C)$ may be computed using the optimization problem $c_i : \mathsf{max.}\ h_i(\boldsymbol{x})\ \mathsf{s.t.}\ \boldsymbol{x} \in C$. Note that if C is a polyhedron, then its best over-approximation according to a template H is obtained by solving $|H|$ linear programs.

Lemma 2. *For any closed set $C \subseteq \mathcal{R}^n$, the polyhedron $H\boldsymbol{x} \leq \alpha_H(\boldsymbol{c})$ is the smallest template polyhedron that includes C.*

Example 4. Let $H = \{x, -x, y, -y\}$ be a template. Consider the set $C : (x^2 + y^2 \leq 1)$ of all points inside the unit circle. The smallest template polyhedron containing C is the unit square that may be represented with the instance vector $\langle 1, 1, 1, 1 \rangle$. Additionally, if the expressions $x + y, x - y, -x - y, x + y$ are added to the set H, the smallest template polyhedron representing C is the octagon inscribed around the circle.

It is algorithmically desirable to have a unique representation of each set by a template polyhedron. Given a template polyhedron $\langle H, c \rangle$, its *canonical form* is given by $\mathsf{can}_H(c) = \alpha_H(Hx \leq c)$. An instance vector is *canonical* iff $c = \mathsf{can}_H(c)$.

Lemma 3. *(a)* $\langle H, c \rangle \equiv \langle H, d \rangle$ *iff* $\mathsf{can}_H(c) = \mathsf{can}_H(d)$*, and (b)* $\langle H, c \rangle \subset \langle H, d \rangle$ *iff* $\mathsf{can}_H(c) < \mathsf{can}_H(d)$*.*

Thus, canonicity provides an unique representation of template polyhedra. Any representation can be converted into a canonical representation in polynomial time using optimization problems.

The *union* of $\langle H, c_1 \rangle$ and $\langle H, c_2 \rangle$ (written $c_1 \sqcup c_2$) is defined as $c = \max(c_1, c_2)$, where max denotes the entry-wise minimum. Similarly, intersection of two polyhedra c_1, c_2 is represented by $c = \min(c_1, c_2)$.

Given a template polyhedron $P_0 : \langle J, c \rangle$, and a discrete transition relation τ, we wish to compute the smallest template polyhedron $P_1 : \langle H, d \rangle$ that over-approximates the post-condition $\mathsf{post}(P_0, \tau)$. Note that the templates J and H need not be identical. The *post-condition* $d : \mathsf{post}_H(\langle J, c \rangle, \tau)$ is computed by posing an optimization query for each d_i: max. $H_i y$ subj. to $Jx \leq c \wedge \rho_\tau(x, y)$. The resulting d is always guaranteed to be canonical.

Lemma 4. *The polyhedron* $\mathsf{post}_H(P_0, \tau)$ *is the smallest template polyhedron containing* $\mathsf{post}(P_0, \tau)$*.*

In program analysis, template polyhedra with a fixed set of template have been used previously. For instance, given variables $x_1, \ldots, x_n$, intervals are obtained as template polyhedra over the set $H_I = \{x_1, -x_1, x_2, \ldots, x_n, -x_n\}$ [7]. Similarly, the *octagon* domain is obtained by considering the template expressions $H_O = H_I \cup \{\pm x_i \pm x_j | 1 \leq i < j \leq n\}$ [19]. Other domains based on template polyhedra include the *octahedron* domain consisting of all linear expressions involving the variables $x_1, \ldots, x_n$ with unit coefficients [6].

3   Flowpipe Construction

We now consider flowpipe construction techniques to over-approximate the time trajectories of affine differential equations. An instance of flowpipe construction problem: $\langle H, c_0, \mathsf{inv}, \mathbf{D}, \delta \rangle$ consists of the template H, an initial region $\langle H, c_0 \rangle$, the location invariant $\langle H, \mathsf{inv} \rangle$ and an affine vector field $\mathbf{D}$ representing the dynamics and a *time step* $\delta \geq 0$. We assume that $\langle H, \mathsf{inv} \rangle$ and $\langle H, c_0 \rangle$ are nonempty and bounded polyhedra.

Example 5. Consider the oscillator circuit model from Example 1. An instance consists of a template $H = \{v, -v, t, -t, v - t, t - v\}$, initial condition $v \in [0, 0.1], t = 0$ and location invariant $v \in [0, 5], t \in [0, 100]$.

Let $\mathfrak{F}(t)$ denote the set of states reachable, starting from $\langle H, c_0 \rangle$, at some time instant $t \geq 0$. Similarly, $\mathfrak{F}[t, t+\delta)$ denotes the set of reachable states for the time interval $[t, t+\delta)$.

Formally, we wish to construct a series of flowpipe segments

$$\langle H, d_0 \rangle, \langle H, d_1 \rangle, \langle H, d_2 \rangle, \ldots, \langle H, d_N \rangle, \ldots$$

such that each segment d_j over-approximates $\mathfrak{F}[j\delta, (j+1)\delta)$. There are two parts to our technique:

Flowpipe Approximation: Approximate $\mathfrak{F}[0, \delta)$ given $\langle H, c_0 \rangle$.
Set Integration: Given an approximation $\mathfrak{F}[i\delta, (i+1)\delta)$, approximate the next segment $\mathfrak{F}[(i+1)\delta, (i+2)\delta)$.

Together, they may be used to incrementally construct the entire flowpipe.
Set Integration. By convention, the jth order Lie derivative of a function f is written $f^{(j)}$. Let $f : c^T x$ be a linear function. By convention, we denote its jth order derivative as $c^{(j)} x$.

Definition 4 (Taylor Series). *Let h be a continuous function and differentiable at least to order $m + 1$. It follows that*

$$h(t) = h(0) + h^{(1)}(0)t + h^{(2)}(0)\frac{t^2}{2!} + \cdots + h^{(m)}(0)\frac{t^m}{m!} + h^{(m+1)}(\theta)\frac{t^{m+1}}{(m+1)!},$$

where $\theta \in [0, t)$. The last term of the series is known as the remainder.

Let $S_k : \langle H, d_k \rangle$ be an over-approximation of $\mathfrak{F}[k\delta, (k+1)\delta)$. We wish to compute an approximation S_{k+1} for the time interval $[(k+1)\delta, (k+2)\delta)$. In other words, we require an upper bound for the value of each template row $H_i x$. Let $x(t)$ be the state at time instant t. Using a Taylor series expansion, we get:

$$H_i x(t+\delta) = H_i x(t) + \cdots + \frac{\delta^m}{m!} H_i^{(m)} x(t) + \frac{\delta^{m+1}}{(m+1)!} H_i^{(m+1)} x(t+\theta), \quad (1)$$

where $0 \leq \theta < \delta$. Note that the first m terms are functions of $x(t)$, whereas the remainder term, is a function of $x(t+\theta)$. The exact value of θ is not known and is conservatively treated as a nondeterministic input. In other words, we may write $H_i x(t+\delta)$ as a sum of two expressions $H_i x(t+\delta) = g_i^T x(t) + r_i^T x(t+\theta)$, wherein g_i represents the sum of the first m terms of the Taylor series and r_i represents the remainder term.

Assuming $t \in [j\delta, (j+1)\delta)$, we have $x(t) \in S_k$. Therefore, an upper bound on g_i is obtained by solving the following LP:

$$g_i^{max} = \mathsf{max.} \ g_i^T x \ \text{subj.to.} \ x \in S_k \quad (2)$$

Similarly, even though the remainder term cannot be evaluated with certainty, we know that $x(t+\theta) \in \langle H, \mathsf{inv} \rangle$. A bound on $r_i x(t+\delta)$ is, therefore, obtained by solving the optimization problem

$$r_i^{max} = \mathsf{max.} \ r_i^T y \ \text{subj.to} \ y \in \langle H, \mathsf{inv} \rangle \quad (3)$$

The overall bound on $H_i \boldsymbol{x}(t+\delta)$ is $g_i^{max} + r_i^{max}$. Finally, the over-approximation S_{k+1} is obtained by computing $g_i^{max} + r_i^{max}$ for each template row $i \in [1, |H|]$.

Note that in the optimization problem above, the time step δ is an user-input constant, each Lie-derivative $g_i^{(m)}$ is affine and S_k is a template polyhedron. As a result, the optimization problems for affine vector fields are linear programs.

Example 6. Following Example 5, consider a flowpipe segment $v \in [0, 0.2] \wedge t \in [0, 0.1]$ by $\delta = 0.1$, according to the differential equation $\dot{v} = \frac{5-v}{2}, \dot{t} = 1$. The first row of the template is $H_1 : v$. The first 6 Lie derivatives of H_1 are tabulated below:

0	1	2	3	4	5	6
v	$\frac{5-v}{2}$	$\frac{-5+v}{4}$	$\frac{5-v}{8}$	$\frac{-5+v}{16}$	$\frac{5-v}{32}$	$\frac{-5+v}{64}$

Following, Eq. 1, we use exact arithmetic to obtain

$$v(t+\delta) = v + \frac{5-v}{2}\delta + \frac{-5+v}{4}\frac{\delta^2}{2!} + \cdots + \frac{5-v}{32}\delta^5 5! + \frac{-5+v(\theta)}{64}\frac{\delta^6}{6!}$$
$$\sim \underbrace{0.951229424479167 v(0) + 0.24385288020833}_{g_0} + \underbrace{0.131 \times 10^{-7} v(\theta)}_{r_0}$$

Now observing that $v(0) \in [0, 0.2]$, we obtain $g_0^{max} = 0.4341$ (upto 4 decimal places). Similarly, using the location invariant $v(\theta) \in [0, 5]$, we obtain $r_0^{max} = 0.131 \times 10^{-8} \times 5$. As a result, we obtain a bound $v(t+0.1) \leq 0.4341$ (upto 4 decimal digits). Repeating this process for every template row gives us the required flowpipe approximation for the segment $[0.1, 0.2]$.

Flowpipe Approximation

We now seek an approximation $\langle H, \boldsymbol{d}_0 \rangle$ for $\mathfrak{F}[0, \delta)$. Therefore, for each template row H_i, we wish to bound the function $H_i \boldsymbol{x}$ as an univariate polynomial of degree $m+1$ over the time interval $[0, \delta)$. Let $a_{i,j}$, $0 \leq j \leq m$ be the result of the optimization $a_{i,j} = \max \frac{H_i^{(j)}(\boldsymbol{x})}{j!}$ subj.to. $\boldsymbol{x} \in \langle H, \boldsymbol{c}_0 \rangle$ and $a_{i,m+1} = \max \frac{H_i^{(m+1)}(\boldsymbol{y})}{m+1!}$ subj.to. $\boldsymbol{y} \in \langle H, \mathsf{inv} \rangle$.

Each optimization problem is an LP and can be solved efficiently. Consider the polynomial $p_i(t) = \sum_{j=0}^{m} a_{ij} t^j + a_{i,m+1} t^{m+1}$.

Lemma 5. *For $t \geq 0$ and $\boldsymbol{x} \in \langle H, \boldsymbol{c}_0 \rangle$, $H_i \boldsymbol{x}(t) \leq p_i(t)$.*

$$H_i \boldsymbol{x}(t) = H_i \boldsymbol{x}(0) + t H_i^{(1)} \boldsymbol{x}(0) + \cdots + t^m \frac{H_i^{(m)}(\boldsymbol{x}(0))}{m!} + t^{m+1}\frac{H_i^{(m+1)}(\boldsymbol{x}(\theta))}{(m+1)!}$$
$$\leq a_{i0} + a_{i1}t + \cdots + a_{im}t^m + a_{i,m+1}t^{m+1} \quad \because \frac{H_i^{(j)}\boldsymbol{x}(0)}{j!} \leq a_{ij} \text{ and } t \geq 0$$
$$\leq p_i(t)$$

The required bound for the function $H_i \boldsymbol{x}$ for the time interval $t \in [0, \delta)$ may now be approximated by maximizing the univariate polynomial $p_i(t)$ over the interval $[0, \delta)$. The maximum value of an univariate polynomial p in a time interval $[T_1, T_2]$ may be computed by evaluating the polynomial at the end points T_1, T_2 and the roots (if any) of its derivative p' lying in that interval. The maxima in the interval is guaranteed to be achieved at one of these points.

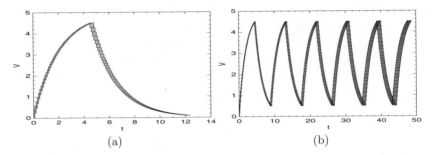

Fig. 3. Flowpipes for Example 1: (a) one complete charge/discharge cycle and (b) the time interval $[0, 49]$

Example 7. Consider the problem instance shown in Example 5. We wish to compute an over-approximation of $\mathfrak{F}[0, 0.1)$ given $v(0) \in [0, 0.1]$ and $t(0) = 0$. We consider a bound $H_1 : v$ over $t \in [0, 0.1)$. Example 6 shows the lie derivatives. The following table shows the bounds $a_1, \ldots, a_6$ corresponding to the initial condition and invariant regions (accurate to 4 decimal places).

0	1	2	3	4	5	6
0.1	2.5	−0.6125	0.1058	−0.01276	0.0013	−0.00106

As a result, we have that $v(t) \leq -0.00106t^6 + 0.0013t^5 - 0.01276t^4 + \cdots + 0.1$ for all $t \in [0, 0.1)$. This polynomial is increasing in this range and has its maximum value at $t = 0.1$. This yields a bound $v \leq 0.3439$ for the segment $\mathfrak{F}[0, 0.1)$. Similarly, we can compute bounds for all the rows in the template.

Thus, given an instance of the flowpipe problem, we compute an initial flow-pipe segment $\langle H, \boldsymbol{d}_0 \rangle \supseteq \mathfrak{F}[0, \delta)$ by computing univariate polynomials, one per template row, that upper bound the Taylor series and in turn finding the maxima of these polynomials. This initial flowpipe segment is then advanced by using set integration. Following this scheme, Fig. 3 shows the flowpipe constructed for the instance in Example 5. Let $\boldsymbol{d}_0, \ldots, \boldsymbol{d}_N$ be the results of the flowpipe construction on a given instance.

Theorem 1. *The disjunction $\bigvee_{i=0}^{N} \langle H, \boldsymbol{d}_i \rangle$ contains all the time trajectories starting from $\langle H, \boldsymbol{c}_0 \rangle$ and evolving according to $\mathbf{D}$ inside $\langle H, \mathsf{inv} \rangle$.*

Termination. In theory, the flowpipe construction produces infinitely many segments. However, we may stop this process if the flowpipe "exits" the invariant, i.e, $\langle H, \boldsymbol{d}_N \rangle \cap \langle H, \mathsf{inv} \rangle = \emptyset$ for some $N > 0$; or "cycles" back into itself, i.e., $\langle H, \boldsymbol{d}_N \rangle \subseteq \langle H, \boldsymbol{d}_j \rangle$ for $j < N$. The flowpipe construction can be stopped upon encountering a cycle since each subsequent segment will lie inside a previously encountered segment.

Extensions. Our technique is directly applicable to cases where the templates may consist of nonlinear functions and the dynamics may be nonlinear. In each

Table 1. Optimization problems for flowpipe construction

Dynamics (**D**)	Template (h_i)	Invariants (**I**)	Optimization Problem.
Affine	Linear	Polyhedral	Linear Programming
Affine	Ellipsoidal	Polyhedral	Quadratic Programming [4]
Polynomial	Polynomial	Semi-Algebraic	Sum-of-Squares Optimization (SOS) [21]
Continuous	Continuous	Rectangular	Interval Arithmetic [13]

case, we encounter different types of optimization problems with differing objectives and constraints. Table 1 summarizes the different optimization problems that are encountered.

Matrix Exponentiation. Set integration can also be computed using *matrix exponentiation* for affine systems [5]. In this approach, we compute a matrix exponential $T = e^{A\delta}$, corresponding to the dynamics $\mathbf{D}(x) = Ax$. Given the initial segment S_0, approximating $\mathfrak{F}[0, \delta)$, we may compute successive sets as $S_{i+1} = TS_i$. However, computing this transformation requires an expensive vertex representation of S_i. On the other hand, our approach works purely on the constraint representation of template polyhedra using LPs for set integration.

Location Invariant Strengthening. The location invariant bounds the remainder term in our construction. Therefore, tighter bounds on the remainder can result from stronger location invariants. Such a strengthening can be computed prior to each flowpipe construction using a *policy iteration* technique. Using invariant strengthening, each flowpipe construction instance can be performed more accurately using a better bound for the location invariant. Curiously, a stronger invariant region may result in fewer flowpipe segments and quicker termination, thus reducing the overall time taken by our technique. The details of the invariant strengthening technique appear elsewhere [27].

4   Experiments

Our prototype tool TimePass implements the techniques described in this paper using template polyhedra for safety verification.

Template Construction. A larger set of template expressions provides a richer representation of template polyhedra. However, the size of each LP instance encountered is linear in the number of templates. Therefore, too many templates impacts performances.

Our template construction strategy uses two basic sources of template expressions: (a) Fixed templates such as boxes and octagons; and (b) Expressions occurring in the hybrid system description. Fixed templates used include *box templates* which include the expressions $\pm x_i$, for each continuous variable x_i in the system, and *octagon templates* of the form $\pm x_i \pm x_j$ for all $x_i \neq x_j$.

Additionally, we enrich templates by computing their Lie derivatives. This process is important since the key flowpipe construction steps involve finding

Table 2. Performance of our tool on hybrid systems benchmarks. All timings are in seconds and memory in MBs. Legend: **Inv. Str.**: Invariant Strengthening, **H**: Template size, δ: step size, **T**:Time, **Mem:** memory, **Prf?**: Property proved.

Name	Description	Size/Params					w/o Inv. Str.		Inv. Str.	
		#Var	#Loc	#Trs	H	δ	T	Prf?	T	Prf?
focus	[24]	2	2	1	28	0.2	0	Y	0	Y
reigen	-	3	2	1	54	0.2	0.1	Y	0.2	Y
flow	-	3	2	1	54	0.2	0.1	Y	0.1	Y
convoi	-	5	1	1	90	0.2	10	Y	18	Y
therm	[1]	2	3	4	28	0.05	1.1	Y	1.2	Y
nav01	Benchmark [9]	4	8	18	64	0.2	260	Y	22	Y
nav02	-	4	8	18	64	0.2	362	Y	23	Y
nav03	-	4	8	18	64	0.2	390	Y	20	Y
nav04	-	4	8	18	64	0.2	1147	Y	18	Y
nav05	-	4	8	18	64	0.1	7	N	513	Y
nav06	-	4	8	18	64	0.2	45	N	1420	N
nav07	-	4	15	39	64	0.2	1300	N	572	Y
nav08	-	4	15	39	64	0.2	139	N	572	Y

bounds on the Lie derivatives of the template rows (and their convex combinations). Therefore, tracking bounds for such rows as part of the template can lead to tighter bounds. The *eigenvectors* corresponding to the real eigenvalues of the RHS matrix of the differential equations also form an interesting set of template expressions. The Lie derivatives of such expressions yield back the original expression upto a constant scale factor. As a result, the Taylor polynomials for such expressions can be computed precisely without truncation.

Numerical Issues. It is possible to implement most of the algorithms described in this paper using exact arithmetic. In our experience, however, exact arithmetic LP solvers exhibit large performance overheads. Hence, our tool primarily uses a floating point implementation of the simplex algorithm. The LP solution can then be verified using the Karush-Kuhn-Tucker (KKT) conditions to lie within an error tolerance bound ($\sim 10^{-7}$). Failing, the error tolerance bounds, the verification may be performed an exact arithmetic simplex implementation. All our experiments, however, were performed with a floating point solver.

Parameters. The time step δ for flowpipe construction has the largest impact on the performance. A large time step speeds up the convergence but results in a coarser approximation. In general, the ideal choice of time step is hard to realize. Therefore, we use a trial-and-error approach to successively reduce/increase δ to arrive at a large enough time step that proves the property of interest.

Experiments. Table 2 shows the performance of our tool on some hybrid systems benchmarks consisting of small but complex systems, designed to test the accuracy of the flowpipe construction and its propagation. A detailed description is available elsewhere [24,9]. We report on our performance with and without the use of invariant strengthening. Our tool successfully proves safety for a most of the benchmarks instances. Note that invariant strengthening plays a key role,

Table 3. Flowpipe results on systems with many variables. Note: Timeout is set to 1h.

n	#Sys	$\|H\|$	#Loc	#Trs	Time(sec)			Mem (Mb)			Proved?
					Avg.	Max	Min	Avg.	Max	Min	
10	10	80	7	6	21	52	1	5	7	3	10/10
20	10	160	14	13	30	91	8	11	13	5	10/10
40	10	320	21	20	192	975	44	105	88	126	10/10
80	6	640	29	28	1386	$> 1h$	420	700	743	608	5/6

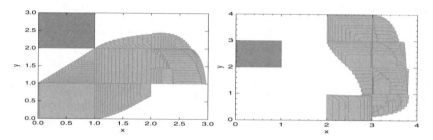

Fig. 4. Reach sets (projected over x, y) along with the unsafe cell for the NAV05 (left) and NAV08 (right) benchmarks

especially for the larger examples. As expected, the use of invariant strengthening vastly reduces the time taken to prove many properties. Our timings on the other examples are quite competitive with those of PHaVer [10] and HSolver [25]. Our approach also provides the first known verification for benchmarks nav05-nav08. Figure 4 depicts the reach sets computed by our tool for the NAV05 and the NAV08 benchmark examples.

We stress test our flowpipe construction on systems with a large number of variables. Since we do not have access to meaningful models in a suitable format, we use a scheme for generating a family of systems with known behaviors and verify these using our tool. Each system H_n has $n > 0$ variables. It has a *primary mode* ℓ_0, and secondary modes $\ell_1, \ldots, \ell_m$.

The dynamics at location ℓ_0 are $\boldsymbol{x}' = A(\boldsymbol{x} - \boldsymbol{t})$, where A is an invertible matrix with negative real eigenvalues and $\boldsymbol{t}$ is a target point. These dynamics ensure that $\boldsymbol{t}$ is a stable equilibrium point. The mode invariant $\mathbf{I}(\ell_0)$ is a hypercube $|\boldsymbol{x}| \leq \boldsymbol{t} + \boldsymbol{\epsilon}$ for a parameter $\epsilon > 0$. To generate A, we choose negative eigenvalues Λ at random, and compute $A = X^{-1}\Lambda X$ for invertible X.

The secondary modes consist of regions around the corners of the primary mode hypercube, which are unreachable from the interior of the primary mode. The initial location is ℓ_0 and $\Theta : \boldsymbol{x} \in [-\epsilon_0, \epsilon_0]$. We seek to verify that the secondary modes are unreachable. We first generate many instances with varying dynamics A, target vectors $\boldsymbol{t}$ and number of secondary modes. We also fix $\epsilon = 1$ and $\epsilon_0 = 0.1$. Table 3 shows the results of running our tool on systems of varying sizes. To minimize the run-time overhead especially for large systems, these experiments were carried out without using policy iteration to strengthen the invariant region. It clearly demonstrates the scalability of our approach. Also, it demonstrates that our flowpipe is accurate enough to prove a vast majority of instances.

5   Conclusion

Template polyhedra are shown to be an effective tool for the verification of hybrid systems by avoiding the need to perform costly vertex enumerations using template polyhedra. In the future, we hope to study heuristics for choosing template expressions that would enable application of our technique to the counterexample guided refinement (CEGAR) framework. We hope to extend our techniques to nonlinear systems and apply it to more meaningful examples.

References

1. Alur, R., Dang, T., Ivančić, F.: Counterexample-guided predicate abstraction of hybrid systems. Theor. Comput. Sci. 354(2), 250–271 (2006)
2. Asarin, E., Dang, T., Maler, O.: The d/dt tool for verification of hybrid systems. In: Brinksma, E., Larsen, K.G. (eds.) CAV 2002. LNCS, vol. 2404, pp. 365–370. Springer, Heidelberg (2002)
3. Bournez, O., Maler, O., Pnueli, A.: Orthogonal polyhedra: Representation and computation. In: Vaandrager, F.W., van Schuppen, J.H. (eds.) HSCC 1999. LNCS, vol. 1569, pp. 46–60. Springer, Heidelberg (1999)
4. Boyd, S., Vandenberghe, S.: Convex Optimization. Cambridge University Press, Cambridge (2004), http://www.stanford.edu/~boyd/cvxbook.html
5. Chutinan, A., Krogh, B.: Computing polyhedral approximations to flow pipes for dynamic systems. In: Proceedings of IEEE CDC, IEEE press, Los Alamitos (1998)
6. Clarisó, R., Cortadella, J.: The Octahedron Abstract Domain. In: Giacobazzi, R. (ed.) SAS 2004. LNCS, vol. 3148, pp. 312–327. Springer, Heidelberg (2004)
7. Cousot, P., Cousot, R.: Static determination of dynamic properties of programs. In: Proceedings of the Second International Symposium on Programming, Dunod, Paris, France, pp. 106–130 (1976)
8. Dantzig, G.B.: Programming in Linear Structures. In: USAF (1948)
9. Fehnker, A., Ivančić, F.: Benchmarks for Hybrid Systems Verification. In: Alur, R., Pappas, G.J. (eds.) HSCC 2004. LNCS, vol. 2993, pp. 326–341. Springer, Heidelberg (2004)
10. Frehse, G.: PHAVer: Algorithmic verification of hybrid systems past HyTech. In: Tomlin, C.J., Greenstreet, M.R. (eds.) HSCC 2002. LNCS, vol. 2289, pp. 258–273. Springer, Heidelberg (2002)
11. Girard, A.: Reachability of uncertain linear systems using zonotopes. In: Morari, M., Thiele, L. (eds.) HSCC 2005. LNCS, vol. 3414, pp. 291–305. Springer, Heidelberg (2005)
12. Halbwachs, N., Proy, Y., Roumanoff, P.: Verification of real-time systems using linear relation analysis. Formal Methods in System Design 11(2), 157–185 (1997)
13. Hentenryck, P.V., Michel, L., Benhamou, F.: Newton: Constraint programming over nonlinear real constraints. Science of Computer Programming 30(1-2), 83–118 (1998)
14. Henzinger, T.A.: The theory of hybrid automata. In: Logic In Computer Science (LICS 1996), IEEE Computer Society Press, Los Alamitos (1996)

15. Henzinger, T.A., Ho, P.: HYTECH: The Cornell hybrid technology tool. In: Antsaklis, P.J., Kohn, W., Nerode, A., Sastry, S.S. (eds.) HS 1994. LNCS, vol. 999, pp. 265–293. Springer, Heidelberg (1995)
16. Ivančić, F. Modeling and Analysis of Hybrid Systems. PhD thesis, University of Pennsylvania (December 2003)
17. Kurzhanski, A.B., Varaiya, P.: Ellipsoidal techniques for reachability analysis. In: Lynch, N.A., Krogh, B.H. (eds.) HSCC 2000. LNCS, vol. 1790, pp. 202–214. Springer, Heidelberg (2000)
18. Lanotte, R., Tini, S.: Taylor approximation for hybrid systems. In: Morari, M., Thiele, L. (eds.) HSCC 2005. LNCS, vol. 3414, pp. 402–416. Springer, Heidelberg (2005)
19. Miné, A.: A new numerical abstract domain based on difference-bound matrices. In: Danvy, O., Filinski, A. (eds.) PADO 2001. LNCS, vol. 2053, pp. 155–172. Springer, Heidelberg (2001)
20. Mitchell, I., Bayen, A., Tomlin, C.: Computing reachable sets for continuous dynamic games using level set methods. IEEE Transactions on Automatic Control 50(7), 947–957 (2005)
21. Parillo, P.A.: Semidefinite programming relaxation for semialgebraic problems. Mathematical Programming Ser. B 96(2), 293–320 (2003)
22. Piazza, C., Antoniotti, M., Mysore, V., Policriti, A., Winkler, F., Mishra, B.: Algorithmic algebraic model checking I: Challenges from systems biology. In: Etessami, K., Rajamani, S.K. (eds.) CAV 2005. LNCS, vol. 3576, pp. 5–19. Springer, Heidelberg (2005)
23. Prajna, S., Jadbabaie, A.: Safety verification using barrier certificates. In: Alur, R., Pappas, G.J. (eds.) HSCC 2004. LNCS, vol. 2993, pp. 477–492. Springer, Heidelberg (2004)
24. Ratschan, S., She, Z.: Benchmarks for safety verification of hybrid systems. cf. (viewed October, 2007), http://hsolver.sourceforge.net/benchmarks
25. Ratschan, S., She, Z.: Safety verification of hybrid systems by constraint propagation based abstraction refinement. In: Morari, M., Thiele, L. (eds.) HSCC 2005. LNCS, vol. 3414, pp. 573–589. Springer, Heidelberg (2005)
26. Rodriguez-Carbonell, E., Tiwari, A.: Generating polynomial invariants for hybrid systems. In: Morari, M., Thiele, L. (eds.) HSCC 2005. LNCS, vol. 3414, pp. 590–605. Springer, Heidelberg (2005)
27. Sankaranarayanan, S., Dang, T., Ivancic, F.: A policy iteration technique for time elapse over template polyhedra (Extended Abstract). In: HSCC 2008. LNCS, vol. 4981, Springer, Heidelberg (to appear, 2008)
28. Sankaranarayanan, S., Sipma, H.B., Manna, Z.: Constructing invariants for hybrid systems. In: Alur, R., Pappas, G.J. (eds.) HSCC 2004. LNCS, vol. 2993, pp. 539–555. Springer, Heidelberg (2004)
29. Sankaranarayanan, S., Sipma, H.B., Manna, Z.: Scalable analysis of linear systems using mathematical programming. In: Cousot, R. (ed.) VMCAI 2005. LNCS, vol. 3385, Springer, Heidelberg (2005)
30. Silva, B., Richeson, K., Krogh, B.H., Chutinan, A.: Modeling and verification of hybrid dynamical system using checkmate. In: ADPM (2000), http://www.ece.cmu.edu/~webk/checkmate
31. Tiwari, A.: Approximate reachability for linear systems. In: Maler, O., Pnueli, A. (eds.) HSCC 2003. LNCS, vol. 2623, pp. 514–525. Springer, Heidelberg (2003)
32. Tiwari, A., Khanna, G.: Non-linear systems: Approximating reach sets. In: Alur, R., Pappas, G.J. (eds.) HSCC 2004. LNCS, vol. 2993, pp. 477–492. Springer, Heidelberg (2004)

Fast Directed Model Checking Via Russian Doll Abstraction

Sebastian Kupferschmid[1], Jörg Hoffmann[2], and Kim G. Larsen[3]

[1] University of Freiburg, Germany
kupfersc@informatik.uni-freiburg.de
[2] University of Innsbruck, STI, Austria
joerg.hoffmann@sti2.at
[3] Aalborg University, Denmark
kgl@cs.aau.dk

Abstract. Directed model checking aims at speeding up the search for bugs in a system through the use of heuristic functions. Such a function maps states to integers, estimating the state's distance to the nearest error state. The search gives a preference to states with lower estimates. The key issue is how to generate good heuristic functions, i.e., functions that guide the search quickly to an error state. An arsenal of heuristic functions has been developed in recent years. Significant progress was made, but many problems still prove to be notoriously hard. In particular, a body of work describes heuristic functions for model checking timed automata in UPPAAL, and tested them on a certain set of benchmarks. Into this arsenal we add another heuristic function. With previous heuristics, for the largest of the benchmarks it was only just possible to find some (unnecessarily long) error path. *With the new heuristic, we can find provably shortest error paths for these benchmarks in a matter of seconds.* The heuristic function is based on a kind of Russian Doll principle, where the heuristic for a given problem arises through using UPPAAL itself for the complete exploration of a simplified instance of the same problem. The simplification consists in removing those parts from the problem that are distant from the error property. As our empirical results confirm, this simplification often preserves the characteristic structure leading to the error.

1 Introduction

When model checking safety properties, the ultimate goal is to prove the absence of error states. This can be done by exploring the entire reachable state space. UPPAAL is a tool doing this for networks of extended timed automata. It has a highly optimized implementation, but still the reachable state space often is too large in realistic applications. A potentially much easier task is to try to *falsify* the safety property, by identifying an error path: for this, we can use a *heuristic* that determines in what order the states are explored. In our work, we enhance error detection in UPPAAL following such a strategy.

A heuristic, or *heuristic function*, is a function h that maps states to integers, estimating the state's distance to the nearest error state. The heuristic is called *admissible* if it provides a lower bound on the real error state distance. The search gives a preference to states with lower h value. There are many different ways of doing the latter.

C.R. Ramakrishnan and J. Rehof (Eds.): TACAS 2008, LNCS 4963, pp. 203–217, 2008.

The A^* method, where the search queue is a priority queue over start state distance plus the value of h, guarantees to find an optimal (shortest possible) error path if the heuristic is admissible. An alternative is *greedy best-first search*. There, the search queue is a priority queue over the value of h. This does not give any guarantee on the solution length, but is often (yet not always) faster than A^* in practice. Note that short error paths are important in practice, since the error path will be used for debugging purposes. The application of heuristic search to model checking was introduced a few years ago by Edelkamp et al. [1,2], naming this research direction *directed model checking*, and inspiring various other approaches of this sort, e. g. [3,4,5,6,7]. The main difference between these approaches is how they define and compute the heuristic function: *How does one estimate the distance to an error state?*

The following gives an overview of the heuristic functions defined so far. Edelkamp et al. [1] base their heuristics on the "graph distance" within each automaton – the number of edge traversals needed, disregarding synchronization and all state variables. This yields a rather simplistic estimation, but can be computed very quickly. Groce and Visser [3] define heuristics inspired from the area of testing, with the idea to prefer covering yet unexplored branches in the program. Qian and Nymeyer [4,8] ignore some of the state variables to define heuristics which are then used in a pattern database approach (see below). Kupferschmid et al. [5] adapt a heuristic method from the area of AI Planning, based on a notion of "monotonicity" where it is assumed that a state variable accumulates, rather than changes, its values. Dräger et al. [6] iteratively "merge" a pair of automata, i. e., compute their product and then merge locations until there are at most N locations left, where N is an input parameter. The heuristic function is read off the overall merged automaton. Hoffmann et al. [7] compute the state space of a predicate abstraction of the system to be checked, and use a mapping from real states into abstract states to compute the heuristic values.

We add another kind of heuristic functions into the above arsenal. Like Qian and Nymeyer's [4] techniques, our heuristic functions belong into the family of *pattern databases* (PDB), which were first explored in AI [9], more precisely for hard search problems in single agent games such as Rubik's Cube. A PDB heuristic function abstracts a problem by ignoring some of the relevant symbols, e. g., some of the state variables [4]. The state space of the abstracted problem is built completely as a pre-process to search, and is used as a look-up table for the heuristic values during search.

The main question to answer is, of course, which symbols should be ignored? How should we abstract the problem to obtain our PDB? In AI, see e. g. [9,10], most strategies are aimed at exploiting parts of the problem that are largely independent – the idea being to generate a separate PDB for each part, and accumulate the heuristic values. Indeed, Edelkamp et al.'s [1,2] heuristic can be viewed as an instance of this, where each PDB ignores all symbols except the program counter of one single automaton.

In our work, we extend and improve upon a new kind of strategy to choose a PDB abstraction. The strategy is particularly well suited for model checking; a first version of it was explored by Qian and Nymeyer [8]. It is based on what we call a *Russian Doll* principle. Rather than trying to split the entire system up into (more or less) independent parts, one homes in on the part of the system that is most relevant to the safety property, and *leaves that part entirely intact.*[1] Intuitively, this is more suitable for model checking than traditional AI techniques because *a particular combined behavior of the automata nearest to the safety property is often essential in how the error arises.* The child Russian Doll preserves such combined behaviors, and should hence provide useful search guidance. The excellent results we obtained in our benchmarks indicate that this is indeed the case, even with rather small abstractions/"child dolls".

Given the key idea of the Russian Doll strategy – keep all and only symbols that are of "immediate relevance" to the safety property to be checked – the question remains what is "relevant". Answering this question precisely involves solving the problem in the first place. However, one can design computationally easy strategies that are intuitively very adequate for model checking. The basic idea is to do some form of abstract cone-of-influence [11] computation, and ignore those symbols that do not appear in the cone-of-influence. Qian and Nymeyer [8] use a simple syntactic backward chaining process that iteratively collects variable names and requires the user to specify a threshold on the maximal considered "distance" – number of iterations – of the kept variables from the safety property. In our work, we use a more sophisticated procedure based on the abstraction techniques of Kupferschmid et al. [5]. The procedure selects a subset of the relevant symbols (automata, synchronization actions, clock variables, integer variables) based on an abstract error path. No user input is required. Once it is decided which parts to keep, our implementation outputs those parts in UPPAAL input language. In Russian Doll style, UPPAAL itself is then used to compute the entire state space of the abstracted problem, and that state space is stored and used as a look-up table for heuristic values during search.

With half of the related work discussed above, namely [5,6,7], we share the fact that we are working with UPPAAL, and we also share the set of benchmarks with these works. The benchmarks are meaningful in that they stem from two industrial case studies [12,13]. Table 1 gives a preview of our results with our "Russian Doll" approach; we re-implemented the two heuristic functions defined in [1]; for each of [5,6,7], we could run the original implementation; finally, we implemented the abstraction strategy of [8], for comparison with our more sophisticated abstraction strategy (we created the pattern database with UPPAAL for our strategy). Every entry in Table 1 gives the total runtime (seconds), as well as the length of the found error path. The result shown is the best one that could be achieved, on that instance, with the respective technique: from the data points with shortest error path length, we selected the one with the smallest runtime (detailed empirical results are given in Section 5). A dash means the technique runs out of memory on a 4 GByte machine. Quite evidently, our approach drastically outperforms all the other approaches. This signifies a real boost in the performance of directed model checking, at least on these benchmarks.

The paper is organized as follows. Section 2 introduces notations. Section 3 explains some technicalities regarding possible sets of symbols to be ignored, and regarding the generation of a pattern database using UPPAAL. Section 4 introduces our Russian Doll strategy for choosing the symbols to be ignored. Section 5 contains our empirical evaluation, Section 6 discusses related work, and Section 7 concludes.

---

[1] We chose the name "Russian Doll" based on the intuition that the part left intact resembles the child Russian Doll, which is smaller but still characteristically similar to the parent.

Table 1. Results preview: total runtime / error path length

Exp.	[1]-best	[5]-best	[6]-best	[7]-best	[8]-best	Russian Doll
C_5	114.2 / 57	114.1 / 57	21.8 / 57	13.7 / 57	121.5 / 57	1.1 / 57
C_6	–	1211.7 / 57	291.5 / 57	85.2 / 57	–	1.3 / 57
C_7	–	–	309.1 / 855	204.5 / 1064	–	2.1 / 57
C_8	–	427.0 / 433	293.8 / 707	153.5 / 976	–	2.2 / 57
C_9	–	875.8 / 614	–	–	–	2.1 / 58

2   Notations

We assume the reader is roughly familiar with timed automata (TA) and their commonly used extensions; however, an in-depth familiarity is not necessary to understand the key contribution of this paper. Here, we give a brief description of the TA variant treated in our current implementation loosely following the terminology given by Behrmann et al. [14].

We treat networks of timed automata with binary synchronisation and integer variables. Our notations are as follows (all sets are finite). Each automaton i is a tuple $(L_i, X_i, V_i, A_i, E_i)$ where L_i is a set of locations, X_i is a set of clock variables, V_i is a set of integer variables, A_i is a set of actions, and E_i is a set of edges; these constructs will be explained below. The network consists of a set I of automata. By X, V, and A we denote $\bigcup_{i \in I} X_i$, $\bigcup_{i \in I} V_i$, and $\bigcup_{i \in I} A_i$, respectively. Importantly, each $x \in X$, $v \in V$, and $a \in A$ may appear in more than one automaton $i \in I$. In our Russian Doll abstractions, as stated, we ignore a set of "symbols". More precisely, such an *abstraction set* $\mathcal{A}$ will be a subset of $I \cup X \cup V \cup A$.

To denote the current locations of the automata, we assume a location variable loc_i for each $i \in I$, where the range of loc_i is L_i. A *state*, or *system state*, of the network is then given by a valuation of the variables loc_i, X, and V. Each $x \in X$ ranges over the non-negative reals. Each $v \in V$ has a finite domain dom_v. The action set A contains the internal action τ, and for each action $a? \in A$ there is a corresponding co-action $a! \in A$; for $a \in A$, we denote the co-action with $\bar{a}$. For each $i \in I$, the edges E_i are given as a subset of $L_i \times L_i$. Each edge $e \in E_i$ is annotated with an action $a_e \in A$, with a guard g_e, and with an effect f_e. The guard is a conjunction of conditions, each having the form of either $x \bowtie c$, or $x - y \bowtie c$, or $lfn(V') \bowtie c$, where $x, y \in X_i$, $\bowtie \in \{<, \leq, =, \geq, >\}$, c is a constant (a number), and $lfn(V')$ is a linear function in a variable set $V' \subseteq V_i$. The effect is a list of assignments, each of which either has the form $x := c$ or $v := lfn(V') + c$, where $v \in V_i$ and the other notations remain the same. Each variable $x \in X_i$ and $v \in V_i$ occurs on the left hand side of one such assignment at most. The semantics are defined as usual. Transitions are either asynchronous and triggered by an edge e where $a_e = \tau$, or synchronous and triggered by two edges $e \in E_i$ and $e' \in E_j$, $i \neq j$, so that $a_e = a?$ and $a_{e'} = a!$ for some $a?, a! \in A$. Each $i \in I$ has a start location $l_i^0 \in L_i$; each $v \in V$ has a start value $c_v^0 \in dom_v$; the start value of all clocks is 0.

As stated, we address the falsification of safety properties, also commonly referred to as invariants; in CTL, these properties take the form $AG\phi$. In our current implementation, ϕ takes the form $g \wedge (\bigvee_{i \in I'} \neg loc_i = l_i)$ where g has the same form as a guard, $I' \subseteq I$, and $l_i \in L_i$. A path of transitions is called an *error path* if it leads from the start state to a state that satisfies $\neg\phi$. An error path is *optimal* if there is no other error path that contains less transitions.

The above notations correspond to a subset of the UPPAAL input language; that language allows more powerful constructs such as non-binary synchronization, committed locations, and array manipulations. It is important to note that the restrictions imposed by the language subset are by no means inherent to our approach. Indeed, the only "language bottleneck" in our current implementation is the method choosing the abstraction set $\mathcal{A}$; as detailed in Section 4, this is based on methods from [5] which are as yet restricted to the above input language. Once $\mathcal{A}$ is chosen, UPPAAL itself is used to solve the abstracted problem, and so of course the whole of UPPAAL's input language can be handled. Hence, one can extend our technique simply by devising more generally applicable techniques for choosing $\mathcal{A}$.

3   Russian Doll Abstraction

This section presents the technicalities of generating the simplified problem in UPPAAL input language, and using UPPAAL itself to compute the heuristic function. We show how the simplified problem is generated based on an abstraction set $\mathcal{A}$, how the pattern database is built and used, and that the resulting heuristic estimates are admissible (i. e., lower bounds) provided $\mathcal{A}$ satisfies a certain property.

3.1   Abstraction Sets

Assume a network I of timed automata with the notations as specified, and a safety property $AG\phi$. As mentioned, an abstraction set is a set $\mathcal{A} \subseteq I \cup X \cup V \cup A$. The abstracted problem is generated as follows.

Definition 1. *Given a network I of timed automata and an abstraction set $\mathcal{A}$, the abstraction of I under $\mathcal{A}$, $\mathcal{A}(I)$, is defined as*

$$\{(L_i, X_i \setminus \mathcal{A}, V_i \setminus \mathcal{A}, A_i \setminus \mathcal{A}, \{\mathcal{A}(e) \mid e \in E_i\}) \mid i \in I \setminus \mathcal{A}\}$$

where $\mathcal{A}(e)$ is initialized to be equal to e and then modified as follows: if $a_e \in \mathcal{A}$ or $\overline{a_e} \in \mathcal{A}$, then $a_{\mathcal{A}(e)} := \tau$; if $x \in \mathcal{A}$ or $y \in \mathcal{A}$ for a guard or effect $x \bowtie c$, $x - y \bowtie c$, or $x := c$, then this guard/effect is removed; if $(\{v\} \cup V') \cap \mathcal{A} \neq \emptyset$ for a guard or effect lfn$(V') \bowtie c$ or $v := $ lfn$(V') + c$, then this guard/effect is removed.

Given a safety property $AG\phi$, $\phi = g \wedge (\bigvee_{i \in I'} \neg loc_i = l_i)$, the abstraction of ϕ under $\mathcal{A}$, $\mathcal{A}(\phi)$, is defined as $\mathcal{A}(g) \wedge (\bigvee_{i \in I' \setminus \mathcal{A}} \neg loc_i = l_i)$, where $\mathcal{A}(g)$ is defined as for guards above.

In words, given an abstraction set $\mathcal{A}$, we simply ignore any automaton that appears in $\mathcal{A}$, as well as any guards or effects that involve variables or actions from $\mathcal{A}$.

It is important to note that this simple strategy does not always have the desired effect. Consider the case where automaton i has an edge e where $a_e = a?$ and automaton j has an edge e' where $a_{e'} = a!$. Say $i \in \mathcal{A}$ but $a! \notin \mathcal{A}$. Then potentially j can never traverse the edge e' because there is no one to synchronize with. A similar situation arises if f_e sets $v := v'$ and $g_{e'}$ demands $v = 7$, but $v' \in \mathcal{A}$ and $v \notin \mathcal{A}$. The following is a sufficient condition on $\mathcal{A}$ ensuring that such things do not happen.

Definition 2. *Given a network I of timed automata and an abstraction set $\mathcal{A}$, $\mathcal{A}$ is closed iff all of the following hold:*

- *If $i \in I \cap \mathcal{A}$ and $a \in A_i$, then $\bar{a} \in \mathcal{A}$*
- *If $i \in I \cap \mathcal{A}$ and $e \in E_i$ so that f_e sets $x := c$, then $x \in \mathcal{A}$*
- *If $i \in I \cap \mathcal{A}$ and $e \in E_i$ so that f_e sets $v := \text{lfn}(V') + c$, then $v \in \mathcal{A}$*
- *If $i \in I \setminus \mathcal{A}$ and $e \in E_i$ so that f_e sets $v := \text{lfn}(V') + c$ where $V' \cap \mathcal{A} \neq \emptyset$, then $v \in \mathcal{A}$*

We will see below that closed $\mathcal{A}$ yield admissible heuristic functions. Obviously, any $\mathcal{A}$ can be closed by extending it according to Definition 2.

3.2 Pattern Databases

As explained, pattern databases in our approach are obtained as the result of a complete state space exploration using UPPAAL. One subtlety to consider here is that, due to the continuous nature of the set of possible system states in timed automata, UPPAAL's search space does *not* coincide with the set of possible system states. Rather, each state s that UPPAAL considers corresponds to a set of system states where all automata locations and integer variables are fixed but the clock valuation can be any of a particular clock *region*. A clock region is given in the form of a (normalized) set of unary or binary constraints on the clock values, called *difference bound matrix*, which we denote by DBM_s. By $[s]$, we denote the set of system states corresponding to s.[2]

Our basic notions regard state spaces and error distances.

Definition 3. *Given a network I of timed automata, the* UPPAAL *state space for I, $\mathcal{S}(I)$, is a tuple (S, T, s_0), where S is the set of search states explored by* UPPAAL *when verifying a safety property $AG\phi$ with $\phi \equiv \top$, $T \subseteq S \times S$ are the possible transitions between those search states, and $s_0 \in S$ is the start state.*

Given also a safety property $AG\phi$, an error state *is a state $s \in S$ so that $s \models \neg\phi$. Given an arbitrary state $s \in S$, the* error distance *of s in I with ϕ, $d^{I,\phi}(s)$, is the length of a shortest path in (S, T) that leads from s to an error state, or $d^{I,\phi}(s) = \infty$ if there is no such path.*

Given Definition 3, it is now easy to state precisely what our pre-process to search does, when given a network I and a safety property $AG\phi$. First, an abstraction set $\mathcal{A}$ is chosen (with the techniques detailed below in Section 4). Then, UPPAAL is called to generate $\mathcal{S}(\mathcal{A}(I))$. The resulting tuple (S', T', s_0') is redirected into a file, in a simple format. Once UPPAAL has stopped, an external program finds all error states in S', and computes $d^{\mathcal{A}(I),\mathcal{A}(\phi)}(s')$ for all $s' \in S'$, using a version of Dijkstra's algorithm with multiple sources. In other words, UPPAAL computes the state space of the abstracted problem, and an external program finds the distances to the abstracted error states.

It remains to specify how $\mathcal{S}(\mathcal{A}(I))$ and the $d^{\mathcal{A}(I),\mathcal{A}(\phi)}(s')$ are used to implement a heuristic function for solving I and $AG\phi$. The core operation is to map a state in $\mathcal{S}(I)$ onto a set of corresponding states in $\mathcal{S}(\mathcal{A}(I))$. For a UPPAAL state s, by $[s]|_{\mathcal{A}}$ we denote the projection of the system states in $[s]$ onto the variables not contained in $\mathcal{A}$.

---

[2] For the reader unfamiliar with timed automata, we want to add that our techniques apply also to discrete state spaces, in a manner that should become obvious in the following.

Definition 4. *Given a network I of timed automata with $\mathcal{S}(I) = (S, T, s_0)$, an abstraction set $\mathcal{A}$ with $\mathcal{S}(\mathcal{A}(I)) = (S', T', s_0')$, and a state $s \in S$, the abstraction of s under $\mathcal{A}$, $\mathcal{A}(s)$, is defined as $\{s' \in S' \mid [s'] \cap [s]|_{\mathcal{A}} \neq \emptyset\}$. Given a safety property $AG\phi$, the heuristic value of s under $\mathcal{A}$, $h^{\mathcal{A}}(s)$, is defined as $min\{d^{\mathcal{A}(I),\mathcal{A}(\phi)}(s') \mid s' \in \mathcal{A}(s)\}$.*

Note that $[s'] \cap [s]|_{\mathcal{A}} \neq \emptyset$ may be the case for more than one s' because, and only because, UPPAAL's search states do not commit to one particular clock valuation. We have $[s'] \cap [s]|_{\mathcal{A}} \neq \emptyset$ if and only if s' and s agree completely on the automata locations of $I \setminus \mathcal{A}$ and on the values of $V \setminus \mathcal{A}$, and $DBM_{s'}$ is consistent with DBM_s.[3] Testing consistency of two DBMs is a standard operation for which UPPAAL provides a highly efficient implementation. Consequently, in our implementation, we store $\mathcal{S}(\mathcal{A}(I))$ in a hash table indexed on $I \setminus \mathcal{A}$ and $V \setminus \mathcal{A}$, where each table entry contains a list of DBMs, one for each corresponding abstract state s'; of course, $d^{\mathcal{A}(I),\mathcal{A}(\phi)}(s')$ is also stored in each list entry. Lookup of heuristic values is then realized via hash table lookup plus DBM consistency checks in the list, selecting the smallest $d^{\mathcal{A}(I),\mathcal{A}(\phi)}(s')$ of those s' for which the check succeeded.

Lemma 1. *Let I be a network of timed automata with $\mathcal{S}(I) = (S, T, s_0)$, let $\mathcal{A}$ be a closed abstraction set $\mathcal{A}$, and let $s \in S$ be a state. Then $h^{\mathcal{A}}(s) \leq d^{I,\phi}(s)$.*

Proof Sketch: Let $\mathcal{S}(\mathcal{A}(I)) = (S', T', s_0')$. The key property is that, in the terms of [15], (S', T', s_0') approximates (S, T, s_0): for any transition $(s_1, s_2) \in T$, either s and s' agree on the symbols not in $\mathcal{A}$, or there is a corresponding transition $(s_1', s_2') \in T'$. So transitions are preserved, and error path length can only get shorter in the abstraction. ∎

Lemma 1 does *not* hold if $\mathcal{A}$ is not closed. This can be seen easily based on examples like those mentioned above Definition 2, where a symbol that is abstracted away can contribute to changing the status of a symbol that is not abstracted away. The importance of Lemma 1 is that, plugging our heuristic function into A^*, we can guarantee to find a shortest possible – an optimal – error path.

4   Choosing Abstraction Sets

Having specified how to proceed once an abstraction set $\mathcal{A}$ is chosen, it remains to clarify how that choice is made. In AI, the traditional design principle for pattern databases is to look for different parts of the problem that are largely independent, and to construct a separate pattern database for each of them, accumulating the heuristic values. This principle has been shown to be powerful (see e. g. [16,10]). Now, consider this design principle in model checking. An error typically arises due to some complex interaction between several automata. If one tears those automata apart, the information about this interaction is lost. A different approach, first mentioned by Qian and Nymeyer [8], is to keep only one pattern database that includes as much as possible of those parts of the network that are of immediate relevance to the safety property. The intuition is that the particular combined behavior responsible for the error should be preserved.

---

[3] In a discrete state space, s' and s agree completely on all non-abstracted variables, and so the mapping becomes simpler.

To realize this idea, one needs a definition of what is "close" to the safety property, and what is "distant". The notion of cone-of-influence [11] computation lends itself naturally to obtain such a definition. Qian and Nymeyer [8] use a simple method based on syntactic backward chaining over variable names. Herein, we introduce a more sophisticated method based on the abstraction techniques of Kupferschmid et al. [5]. As we shall see, this method leads to much better empirical behavior, at least in our tests with UPPAAL on networks of timed automata.

Qian and Nymeyer's [8] method starts with the symbols – automata, variables – mentioned in the safety property; this set of symbols forms layer 0. Then, iteratively, new layers are added, where layer $t + 1$ arises from layer t by including any symbol y that does not occur in a layer $t' \leq t$, and that may be involved in modifying the status of a symbol x in layer t, e. g., x and y may be variables and there may exist an assignment $x := exp(\bar{y})$ where $y \in \bar{y}$. The abstraction set is then chosen based on a cut-off value d supplied by the user: $\mathcal{A}$ will contain (exactly) all the symbols in layers $t > d$.

Intuitively, the problem with this syntactic backward chaining is that it is not discriminative enough between transitions that are actually relevant for violating the error property, and transitions that are not. In our experiments, we observed that, typically, the layers t converge to the entire set of symbols very quickly (in our largest benchmark example, this is the case at $t = 5$); when cutting off very early (at $t = 2$, e. g.), one misses some symbols that are important, and at the same time one includes many symbols that are not important.

Our key idea for improving on these difficulties is to do a more informed relevance analysis. We abstract the problem according to Kupferschmid et al. [5]: we compute an abstract error path with those authors' techniques, and set $\mathcal{A}$ to those symbols that are not affected by any of the transitions contained in the abstract error path. This way, we get a fairly targeted notion of what is relevant for reaching an error and what is not. The abstraction of Kupferschmid et al. [5] does not require any parameters, and hence as a side effect we also get rid of the need to request an input parameter from the user; i. e., our method for choosing $\mathcal{A}$ is fully automatic.

Describing Kupferschmid et al.'s [5] techniques in detail would breach the space limits of this paper and cannot be its purpose. For the sake of self-containedness, the following is a summary of the essential points. Kupferschmid et al.'s abstraction is based on the simplifying assumption that state variables accumulate rather than change, their values. The value $s(v)$ of a variable v in a state s is now a subset rather than an element, of v's domain. If v obtains a new value c, then c is included into $s(v)$ without removing any old values, i. e., the new value subset is defined by $s(v) := s(v) \cup \{c\}$. Hence the value range of each state variable grows monotonically over transitions, and hence Kupferschmid et al. call this the *monotonicity abstraction*.

Of course, the interpretation of formulas, such as transition guards, must be adapted to the new notion of states. This is done by existentially quantifying the state variables in the formula where each quantifier ranges over the value subset assigned to the respective variable in the state. It is easy to see that this abstraction is an over-approximation in the sense that the shortest abstract error path is never longer than the shortest real error path; it may be shorter.

The following example describes a situation where no real error path exists but only an absone. Say we have an integer variable v and one transition with guard $v = 0$ and effect $v := v + 1$. The start state is $v = 0$, and the safety property is $AGv < 2$. Obviously, the safety property is valid, i. e., there is no error path. However, such a path does exist in the abstraction. The abstract start state is $\{0\}$ which after one transition becomes $\{0, 1\}$. Since the transition guard is abstracted to $\exists c \in s(v) : c = 0$, the transition can be applied a second time and we get the state $\{0, 1, 2\}$: the new values obtained for v are 1 (inserting 0 into the effect right hand side) and 2 (inserting 1). The negated safety property, which is abstracted to $\exists c \in s(v) : c \geq 2$, is satisfied in that state.

Kupferschmid et al. develop a method that finds abstract error paths in time that is exponential only in the maximum number of variables of any linear expression over integer variables; i. e., the only exponential parameter is $max\{|V'| \mid ex.\ i, e : i \in I, e \in E_i, (lfn(V') \bowtie c) \in g_e$ or $(v := lfn(V') + c) \in f_e\}$. The method consists of two parts, a forward chaining and a backward chaining step. The forward chaining step simulates the simultaneous execution of all transitions in parallel, starting from the start state. In a layer-wise fashion, this computes for every state variable – i. e., for the location variables $loc_i, i \in I$, as well as the integer variables $v \in V$ and the clock variables $x \in X$ – what the subset of reachable values is. The forward step stops when it reaches a layer where the negation of the safety condition can be true. The backward step then starts at the state variable values falsifying the safety condition; it selects transitions that can be responsible for these values. The guards of these transitions yield new state variable values that must be achieved at an earlier layer. The process is iterated, selecting new transitions to support the new values and so on. The outcome of the process is a sequence $\langle t_1, \ldots, t_n \rangle$ of transitions that leads from the start state to a state falsifying the safety property, when executed under the monotonicity abstraction.

In our method for choosing the abstraction set $\mathcal{A}$, we execute Kupferschmid et al.'s algorithm exactly once to obtain an abstract error path $\bar{t} = \langle t_1, \ldots, t_n \rangle$ for the problem.[4] We then collect all symbols not affected by this path:

$$
\begin{aligned}
\mathcal{A}_0 := & \{i \in I \mid \text{not ex. } e \in \bar{t} \text{ s. t.} e \in E_i\} \cup \\
& \{a \in A \mid \text{not ex. } e \in \bar{t} \text{ s. t.} a_e = a\} \cup \\
& \{x \in X \mid \text{not ex. } e \in \bar{t}, c \text{ s. t.} (x := c) \in f_e, \text{ and} \\
& \quad \text{not ex. } i \in \mathcal{A}_0, e \in E_i, c \text{ s. t.} (x \bowtie c) \in g_e, \text{ and} \\
& \quad \text{not ex. } i \in \mathcal{A}_0, e \in E_i, y, c \text{ s. t.} (x - y \bowtie c) \in g_e\} \cup \\
& \{v \in V \mid \text{not ex. } e \in \bar{t}, lfn(V'), c \text{ s. t.} (v := lfn(V') + c) \in f_e, \text{ and} \\
& \quad \text{not ex. } i \in \mathcal{A}_0, e \in E_i, lfn(V'), c \text{ s. t.} (lfn(V') \bowtie c) \in g_e \text{ and } v \in V'\}.
\end{aligned}
$$

In this notation, $e \in \bar{t}$ is of course a shorthand for asking whether any of the transitions t_i involves e. In words, we keep all automata, actions, clock variables and integer variables that are modified on the path, and we keep all clock and integer variables that are relevant to a guard in an automaton that we keep. We obtain our final abstraction set $\mathcal{A}$ by closing $\mathcal{A}_0$ according to Definition 2.

---

[4] Actually we use a slightly modified version of the described backward chaining procedure, not considering indirect variable dependencies. We found this method to yield better performance, by selecting more relevant variable subsets.

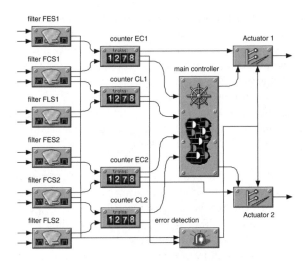

Fig. 1. The Single-tracked Line Segment case study

Kupferschmid et al.'s techniques form an appropriate basis for choosing $\mathcal{A}$ because they are computationally efficient, and they do provide useful information about relevance in the problem. Let us consider an example to illustrate this. Figure 1 illustrates one of our two industrial case studies, called "Single-tracked Line Segment". This study stems from an industrial project partner of the UniForM-project [12]. It concerns the design of a real-time controller for a segment of tracks where trams share a piece of track; each end of the shared piece of track is connected to two other tracks. The property to be checked requires that never both directions are given permission to enter the shared segment simultaneously. That property is not valid because some of the temporal conditions in the control automaton are not strict enough.

Let us consider Figure 1 in some more detail. As one would expect, **Actuator 1** and **Actuator 2** are the two automata in direct control of the signals allowing (signal up) or disallowing (signal down) a tram to enter the shared track. In particular, the safety property expresses that always at most one of those signals is up. The **main controller** automaton contains the (faulty) control logic that governs how the signals are set. The four **counter** automata count how many trains have passed on each of the four tracks that connect to the shared segment. The **error detection** detects inconsistencies between the counts, meaning that a train that should have left the shared segment is actually still inside it. Finally, each **filter** automaton receives an input variable from a sensor, and removes the noise from the signal by turning it into a step function based on a simple threshold test (so as to avoid, e. g., mistaking a passing truck for a tram).

The advantage of Kupferschmid et al.'s abstract error path for this example is that it touches only **Actuator 1**, **Actuator 2**, and the **control unit**. That is, the abstract error path involves exactly those automata that are immediately responsible for the error. Further, the abstract error path involves exactly the variables that are crucial in obtaining the error. The other – irrelevant – variables and automata have only an indirect influence on the error path, and need not be touched to obtain an error under the monotonicity abstraction. On the other hand, consider what happens if we apply Qian and Nymeyer's [8] syntactic backward chaining instead. In the start layer, indexed 0, of the chaining, we have only **Actuator 1** and **Actuator 2**. In the next layer, indexed 1, we correctly get the **control unit** – but we also get **error detection** and all of the **counter** automata. In just one more step, at layer 2, we get every automaton in the whole network. As if that wasn't bad enough, the relevant *variables* involved in producing the error appear much later, some of them in layer 5 only. Hence, based on this information, there is no way of separating the relevant symbols from the irrelevant ones.

5   Empirical Results

We ran experiments on an Intel Xeon 3.06 Ghz system with 4 GByte of RAM. We compare our heuristic to those of Edelkamp et al. [1] and Qian and Nymeyer [8] (both re-implemented), as well as those of Kupferschmid et al. [5], Dräger et al. [6], and Hoffmann et al. [7] (all in the original implementation). We further include results for UPPAAL's breadth-first search, which we abbreviate *BF*, and for UPPAAL's randomised depth-first search, abbreviated *rDF*. We distinguish between *optimal search* and *greedy search*. The former is BF, or A^* with an admissible (lower-bound) heuristic function; the latter is rDF, or greedy best-first search with any (possibly non-admissible) heuristic function. Table 2 shows the results for optimal search, Table 3 shows the results for greedy search. In the figures, our Russian Doll technique is indicated with *RD*. All other techniques are indicated in terms of the respective citations. If a technique requires a parameter setting, then we choose the setting that performs best in terms of total runtime; importantly, this does not compromise the other performance parameters: search space size and memory usage correlate positively with runtime, and error path length behavior does not vary significantly over parameter settings.

The "C_i", $i = 1, \ldots, 9$, examples in the figures come from the Single-tracked Line Segment case study that was explained above. Examples "M_i" and "N_i", $i = 1, \ldots, 4$, come from a study called "Mutual Exclusion". This study models a real-time protocol to ensure mutual exclusion of states in a distributed system via asynchronous communication. The protocol is described in full detail in [13]. The specifications are flawed due to an overly generous time bound. In all of the C_i, M_i, and N_i test beds, the size of the network scales with increasing i.

Consider first Table 2. The results for the C_i examples are striking. While all other techniques suffer from severe scalability issues, we can find the error in even the largest example in basically no time at all (C_2 is somewhat of an outlier). This is due to the quality of the heuristic function, which is clearly indicated in the number of search states explored by UPPAAL (note the direct effect that a smaller number of search states has on the peak memory usage). In the M_i and N_i examples, our technique is less dominant, but still performs better than the other techniques. The only somewhat bad cases are the smaller examples where the overhead for computing the Russian Doll pattern database does not pay off in terms of total runtime. Note that this is benign – what matters are the hard cases. It is remarkable that, consistently, our method explores at least one order of magnitude less search states than any of the others. This clearly indicates that, again,

Table 2. Results for optimal search. Notations: "runtime" is total runtime (including any pre-processes) in seconds; "search space" is the number of states UPPAAL explored before finding an error; "memory" is peak memory usage in MByte; "trace" is the length of the found error path; x e$+y$ means $x \cdot 10^y$

	runtime				search space				memory				trace
	BF	[1]	[5]	[6]	BF	[1]	[5]	[6]	BF	[1]	[5]	[6]	
M_1	0.8	0.7	0.3	0.3	50001	50147	24035	19422	7	9	9	9	48
M_2	3.1	3.3	1.4	1.1	223662	223034	101253	77523	11	14	12	11	51
M_3	3.3	3.3	1.6	1.4	234587	231357	115008	94882	11	14	12	12	51
M_4	13.6	13.8	6.5	6.9	990513	971736	468127	436953	29	33	23	23	54
N_1	5.2	5.6	3.3	2.7	100183	99840	59573	46920	9	11	10	10	50
N_2	25.6	25.7	15.5	12.7	442556	446465	273235	211132	18	21	16	16	53
N_3	26.4	27.0	17.1	13.6	476622	473117	301963	238161	17	20	16	16	53
N_4	120.0	118.3	79.0	68.2	2.0e+6	2.0e+6	1.3e+6	1.1e+6	65	57	40	39	56
C_1	0.3	0.2	0.6	0.1	35325	35768	17570	9784	7	11	10	10	55
C_2	0.9	0.8	1.5	0.4	109583	110593	46945	34644	10	18	13	12	55
C_3	1.2	1.1	1.8	0.5	143013	144199	53081	40078	11	21	14	13	55
C_4	10.8	10.6	14.8	2.9	1.4e+6	1.4e+6	451755	324080	78	124	52	41	56
C_5	114.0	114.2	114.1	21.8	1.2e+7	1.2e+7	3.4e+6	2.4e+6	574	927	329	246	57
C_6	–	–	1211.7	291.5	–	–	3.2e+7	2.4e+7	–	–	2880	2402	57
C_7	–	–	–	–	–	–	–	–	–	–	–	–	57
C_8	–	–	–	–	–	–	–	–	–	–	–	–	57
C_9	–	–	–	–	–	–	–	–	–	–	–	–	58

	runtime			search space			memory			trace
	[7]	[8]	RD	[7]	[8]	RD	[7]	[8]	RD	
M_1	1.4	0.7	4.8	22634	28788	190	9	12	13	48
M_2	2.8	2.9	5.0	94602	121594	4417	12	23	13	51
M_3	3.2	3.1	5.2	121559	131482	11006	12	24	15	51
M_4	9.0	12.8	6.2	466967	543872	41359	24	67	20	54
N_1	4.6	4.9	26.8	46966	61830	345	10	21	21	50
N_2	13.7	27.2	17.7	211935	271912	3811	16	71	21	53
N_3	14.6	30.0	22.4	233609	298208	59062	16	74	33	53
N_4	58.6	154.3	55.5	1.0e+6	1.2e+6	341928	39	305	105	56
C_1	3.5	0.4	1.0	7088	30201	130	10	14	9	55
C_2	3.7	1.0	1.7	15742	95560	89813	11	25	27	55
C_3	3.7	1.4	0.9	15586	127327	197	12	31	9	55
C_4	6.1	12.4	1.0	108603	1.2e+6	1140	23	181	10	56
C_5	13.7	121.5	1.1	733761	1.1e+7	7530	194	1479	11	57
C_6	85.2	–	1.3	7.3e+6	–	39435	745	–	16	57
C_7	–	–	2.1	–	–	149993	–	–	32	57
C_8	–	–	2.2	–	–	158361	–	–	34	57
C_9	–	–	2.1	–	–	127895	–	–	39	58

our approach yields the best quality search information (the relatively high memory usage for N_4 is mostly due to the size of the pattern database).

Consider now Table 3, the data for the greedy searches. The techniques by Kupferschmid et al. [5], Dräger et al. [6], and Hoffmann et al. [7] all perform much better,

Table 3. Results for greedy search. Notations as in Table 2; "K" means thousand.

Exp	runtime				search space				memory				trace			
	rDF	[1]	[5]	[6]	rDF	[1]	[5]	[6]	rDF	[1]	[5]	[6]	rDF	[1]	[5]	[6]
M_1	0.8	0.4	0.0	0.3	29607	31927	5656	21260	7	9	8	9	1072	1349	169	90
M_2	3.1	2.8	0.3	1.0	118341	203051	30743	78117	10	15	10	10	3875	7695	431	102
M_3	2.8	1.6	0.2	1.1	102883	174655	18431	85301	9	12	9	10	3727	5412	231	105
M_4	12.7	7.3	1.2	3.8	543238	579494	122973	287122	22	28	15	16	15K	5819	849	124
N_1	1.9	1.3	0.4	1.2	41218	42931	16335	30970	7	9	9	9	1116	1695	396	110
N_2	9.3	9.5	2.4	5.8	199631	264930	88537	149013	13	17	12	12	4775	9279	990	127
N_3	8.4	4.9	0.6	6.0	195886	134798	28889	158585	12	14	10	12	3938	1656	324	108
N_4	40.9	52.1	4.9	31.6	878706	1.5e+6	226698	785921	39	60	20	32	18K	1986	1199	147
C_1	0.8	0.1	0.1	0.1	25219	19263	2368	2025	7	11	9	10	1056	794	95	149
C_2	1.0	0.4	0.2	0.2	65388	68070	5195	4740	8	15	9	10	875	962	84	198
C_3	1.1	0.6	0.3	0.2	85940	97733	6685	6970	10	19	9	10	760	916	109	198
C_4	8.4	6.1	2.5	0.5	892327	979581	55480	31628	43	96	16	12	1644	2305	142	173
C_5	72.4	69.4	20.8	2.6	8.0e+6	8.8e+6	465796	260088	295	734	68	37	2425	2708	330	268
C_6	–	–	177.4	23.3	–	–	4.5e+6	2.9e+6	–	–	519	303	–	–	490	377
C_7	–	–	–	309.1	–	–	–	2.9e+7	–	–	–	2600	–	–	–	855
C_8	–	–	427.0	293.8	–	–	1.2e+7	2.8e+7	–	–	1266	2608	–	–	433	707
C_9	–	–	875.8	–	–	–	2.0e+7	–	–	–	1946	–	–	–	614	–

Exp	runtime			search space			memory			trace		
	[7]	[8]	RD	[7]	[8]	RD	[7]	[8]	RD	[7]	[8]	RD
M_1	1.4	0.2	4.8	23257	11284	249	9	9	13	51	169	56
M_2	2.4	1.0	4.8	84475	59667	495	12	15	13	53	476	77
M_3	2.5	1.4	4.9	92548	85629	993	12	17	13	56	589	54
M_4	5.6	3.3	5.1	311049	216938	3577	24	32	13	56	419	106
N_1	3.2	0.5	26.5	31593	13902	242	10	11	21	55	159	57
N_2	8.7	3.8	17.7	172531	93467	470	16	28	20	58	624	64
N_3	8.2	5.3	15.4	167350	104104	1787	16	28	19	58	493	71
N_4	39.4	30.7	10.3	975816	422499	10394	39	93	19	61	242	81
C_1	3.2	0.3	0.9	1588	23173	130	10	13	9	159	65	55
C_2	3.5	0.8	1.2	3786	75111	56894	10	21	21	181	77	128
C_3	3.6	1.1	1.0	3846	101049	290	10	26	9	187	75	57
C_4	4.9	8.8	1.1	30741	1.0e+6	1163	14	151	10	241	86	58
C_5	7.1	84.3	1.4	185730	9.1e+6	39837	31	1075	18	423	124	76
C_6	23.6	–	1.7	1.9e+6	–	80878	195	–	25	757	–	65
C_7	204.5	–	6.7	1.8e+7	–	697116	1591	–	129	1064	–	65
C_8	153.5	–	10.4	1.4e+7	–	1.1e+6	1282	–	194	976	–	98
C_9	–	–	20.0	–	–	2.2e+6	–	–	355	–	–	109

compared to the optimal search in Table 2, in terms of runtime, search space size, and peak memory usage. This improvement is bought at the cost of significantly overlong error paths; in most cases, the returned error paths are more than an order of magnitude longer than the shortest possible error path. For rDF and the heuristic functions by Edelkamp et al. [1], the path length increase is even more drastic, by another order of magnitude, and with only a moderate gain in runtime. Qian and Nymeyer's [8] heuristic function yields much improved runtime behavior in M_i and N_i at the cost of significantly overlong error paths; in C_i, greedy search does not make much of a difference.

Finally, consider our RD technique. In M_i and N_i, the search space size performance is drastically improved now beating the other techniques quite convincingly (but not as convincingly in terms of runtime, where [8] is very competitive except in N_4). In C_i, the search spaces become a little larger; it is not clear to us what the reason for that is. The loss in error path quality is relatively minor.

In summary, the empirical results clearly show how superior our Russian Doll heuristic function is, on these examples, in comparison to previous techniques.

6   Related Work

We have already listed the previous methods for generating heuristic functions for directed model checking [3,4,8,5,6,7]. By far the closest relative to our work is the work by Qian and Nymeyer [8] which uses an intuitively similar strategy for generating pattern database heuristics. As we have shown, our improved strategy yields much better heuristic functions, at least in our suite of benchmarks. It remains to be seen whether that is also the case for other problems. It should also be noted that Qian and Nymeyer [8] use their heuristic function in a rather unusual BDD-based iterative deepening A^* procedure, and compare that to a BDD-based breadth-first search. As the authors state themselves, it is not clear in this configuration how much of their empirically observed improvements is due to the heuristic guidance, and how much of it is due to all the other differences between the two search procedures. In our work, we use standard heuristic search algorithms. We finally note that Qian and Nymeyer [8] state as the foremost topic for future work to find better techniques choosing the abstraction; this is exactly what we have done in this paper.[5]

7   Conclusion

We have explored a novel strategy for generating pattern database heuristics for directed model checking. As it turns out, this strategy results in an unprecedented efficiency of detecting error paths, solving within a few seconds, and to optimality, several benchmarks that were previously hardly solvable at all.

Our empirical results must of course be related to the benchmarks on which they were obtained, and it is a priori not clear to what extent they will carry over to other model checking problems. However, there certainly is a non-zero chance that they *will* carry over. This makes the further exploration of this kind of strategy an exciting direction, which we hope will inspire other researchers as well.

Acknowledgements

This work was partly supported by the German Research Council (DFG) as part of the Transregional Collaborative Research Center "Automatic Verification and Analysis of Complex Systems" (SFB/TR 14 AVACS). See http://www.avacs.org/ for more information.

---

[5] We remark on the side that we developed our technique independently from Qian and Nymeyer [8], and only became aware of their work later.

References

1. Leue, S., Edelkamp, S., Lluch Lafuente, A.: Directed Explicit Model Checking with HSF-SPIN. In: Dwyer, M.B. (ed.) SPIN 2001. LNCS, vol. 2057, pp. 57–79. Springer, Heidelberg (2001)
2. Edelkamp, S., Leue, S., Lluch-Lafuente, A.: Directed explicit-state model checking in the validation of communication protocols. STTT 5, 247–267 (2004)
3. Groce, A., Visser, W.: Model checking Java programs using structural heuristics. In: Proc. ISSTA, pp. 12–21. ACM, New York (2002)
4. Nymeyer, A., Qian, K.: Guided Invariant Model Checking Based on Abstraction and Symbolic Pattern Databases. In: Jensen, K., Podelski, A. (eds.) TACAS 2004. LNCS, vol. 2988, pp. 497–511. Springer, Heidelberg (2004)
5. Kupferschmid, S., Hoffmann, J., Dierks, H., Behrmann, G.: Adapting an AI Planning Heuristic for Directed Model Checking. In: Valmari, A. (ed.) SPIN 2006. LNCS, vol. 3925, pp. 35–52. Springer, Heidelberg (2006)
6. Dräger, K., Finkbeiner, B., Podelski, A.: Directed model checking with distance-preserving abstractions. In: Valmari, A. (ed.) SPIN 2006. LNCS, vol. 3925, pp. 19–34. Springer, Heidelberg (2006)
7. Hoffmann, J., Smaus, J.G., Rybalchenko, A., Kupferschmid, S., Podelski, A.: Using predicate abstraction to generate heuristic functions in UPPAAL. In: Edelkamp, S., Lomuscio, A. (eds.) MoChArt IV. LNCS (LNAI), vol. 4428, pp. 51–66. Springer, Heidelberg (2007)
8. Qian, K., Nymeyer, A., Susanto, S.: Abstraction-guided model checking using symbolic ida* and heuristic synthesis. In: Wang, F. (ed.) FORTE 2005. LNCS, vol. 3731, pp. 275–289. Springer, Heidelberg (2005)
9. Culberson, J., Schaeffer, J.: Pattern databases. Comp. Int. 14, 318–334 (1998)
10. Haslum, P., Botea, A., Helmert, M., Bonet, B., Koenig, S.: Domain-independent construction of pattern database heuristics for cost-optimal planning. In: Proc. AAAI (2007)
11. Clarke, E.M., Grumberg, O., Peled, D.A.: Model Checking. MIT Press, Cambridge (2000)
12. Krieg-Brückner, B., Peleska, J., Olderog, E., Baer, A.: The $UniForMWorkbench$, a universal development environment for formal methods. In: Woodcock, J.C.P., Davies, J., Wing, J.M. (eds.) FM 1999. LNCS, vol. 1709, Springer, Heidelberg (1999)
13. Dierks, H.: Comparing Model-Checking and Logical Reasoning for Real-Time Systems. Formal Aspects of Computing 16, 104–120 (2004)
14. Behrmann, G., David, A., Larsen, K.G.: A Tutorial on UPPAAL. In: Bernardo, M., Corradini, F. (eds.) SFM-RT 2004. LNCS, vol. 3185, pp. 200–236. Springer, Heidelberg (2004)
15. Clarke, E.M., Grumberg, O., Long, D.E.: Model Checking and Abstraction. ACM Transactions on Programming Languages and Systems 16, 1512–1542 (1994)
16. Korf, R.E., Felner, A.: Disjoint pattern database heuristics. AIJ 134, 9–22 (2002)

A SAT-Based Approach to Size Change Termination with Global Ranking Functions

Amir M. Ben-Amram[1] and Michael Codish[2]

[1] School of Computer Science, Tel-Aviv Academic College, Israel
[2] Department of Computer Science, Ben-Gurion University, Israel
amirben@mta.ac.il, mcodish@cs.bgu.ac.il

Abstract. We describe a new approach to proving termination with size change graphs. This is the first decision procedure for size change termination (SCT) which makes direct use of global ranking functions. It handles a well-defined and significant subset of SCT instances, designed to be amenable to a SAT-based solution. We have implemented the approach using a state-of-the-art Boolean satisfaction solver. Experimentation indicates that the approach is a viable alternative to the complete SCT decision procedure based on closure computation and local ranking functions. Our approach has the extra benefit of producing an explicit witness to prove termination in the form of a global ranking function.

1 Introduction

Program termination is a cornerstone problem of program verification, as well as being the quintessential example for undecidability. In practice, however, there is a growing conviction that automated termination analysis is viable. This can be explained by the hypothesis that in realistic, correct programs, termination usually follows from reasons that are not very complex. The challenge of termination analysis is to design a useful program abstraction that captures the properties needed to prove termination as often as possible, while making termination checking decidable.

The Size-Change Termination method (SCT) is such an approach. Formally introduced in [17], SCT is a program abstraction where termination is decidable. Briefly, an abstract program is a directed *control-flow graph* (CFG), where each arc is an abstract transition, specified by its source and target locations and annotated by a *size-change graph*. The latter describes how the sizes of program data are affected by the transition. The abstract program terminates if and only if every infinite CFG path implies that a value descends infinitely. We assume that the values described by the size-change graphs are well-founded, so infinite descent is impossible.

The size-change termination method has been successfully applied in a variety of different application areas [18,8,15,24,23,1,19]. A significant factor in the success of the method is that, in line with other recent work [5,10,11,13], it departs from the classic approach of seeking a termination proof in the form of a *global ranking function*—a function that ranks program states so that the rank decreases on every transition. Instead [17] gave an algorithm that takes

C.R. Ramakrishnan and J. Rehof (Eds.): TACAS 2008, LNCS 4963, pp. 218–232, 2008.
© Springer-Verlag Berlin Heidelberg 2008

a local approach, covering all possible CFG cycles and proving termination of each. In [6], the SCT condition is expressed in terms of assigning a *local ranking function* to every possible cycle. That paper shows that it suffices to restrict local ranking functions to a very simple form—namely sums of subsets of the (abstract) program variables. But local ranking functions cannot serve as a witness to termination that can be checked against any transition, in the way a global ranking function can be used.

It is this difference that motivates our interest in global ranking functions: the ranking expression (i.e., the formula that represents the ranking function) is useful as a *certificate*, which can be used to verify the claim that a program terminates. As pointed out in [16], such a setup allows a theorem prover to certify the termination claim while allowing the tool that searches for the termination proof to stay outside the trusted (formally verified) code base. One can also consider applications to proof-carrying code, where again the desire is for the proof to be given as a certificate that is easier to check than to find.

Thus reconciling the SCT method with the global ranking function approach is a theoretical challenge with a practical motivation. Initially, it had not been clear whether there is any constructive way to characterize an SCT termination proof in terms of a global ranking function. A break-through was achieved by Chin Soon Lee [12], who characterized a class of expressions that are sufficient for globally-ranking any terminating SCT program, and showed that the ranking expression can be effectively constructed from the size-change graphs. While this class of expressions is syntactically simple, the ranking expressions themselves can be exponentially large (the upper bound in [12] is triple-exponential). This makes its usage as a certificate difficult.

As Krauss [16] points out, there is a complexity-theoretic argument that precludes the existence of short and simple certificates for size-change termination: the SCT decision problem is PSPACE-complete, and such problems do not have polynomially-verifiable certificates. Ben-Amram [2] gives a more detailed proof, that shows that the assumption "polynomially verifiable" can be replaced with the even humbler "polynomially computable."

Our proposition, presented in this paper, for solving this difficulty is to define a *subset* of SCT instances that is rich enough for practical usage *and* has concise (polynomial) global ranking expressions. Such a set would naturally be in NP, and thus our proposition also gives an answer to a natural theoretical curiosity— namely is there an interesting subset of SCT at the NP level. If a set is in NP, it is amenable for solution strategies not available for PSPACE-complete problems; in particular, it is reducible to SAT, and given the performance of state-of-the art SAT solvers, this is practically significant.

A subset of SCT, decidable in polynomial time and hence called SCP, was presented in [4]. This subset is, however, defined implicitly, by giving an algorithm, also called SCP which can be seen as a heuristic to recognize programs in our class, analogically called SCNP. Thus, SCNP is the natural SCT subset that encompasses the instances handled by SCP. The arguments and examples given in [4] to explain the usefulness of SCP provide initial assurance that SCNP is rich enough. Now, we can also support this claim by ample experimental evidence.

Contributions of this work. We identify a class of expressions that are useful for globally ranking size-change terminating programs: the expressions are concise, they are constructed so that proving the descent in every transition is relatively simple, and they are expressive enough for practical usage of SCT. We define SCNP as the class of SCT instances for which this proof strategy works. We turn this characterization into an effective algorithm using SAT and constraint-solving technology. We have thus created the first tool that not only verifies that an SCT instance terminates, but also produces a ranking expression. To further improve its usefulness for certification, our tool also outputs the *justification*, that is, the argument that links the ranking function to the size-change graphs.

Here are some observations related to comparison between the different SCT algorithms. The standard algorithm for deciding SCT in full is based, as mentioned above, on the local approach and composition closure computation. The SCP algorithm of [4] already handles some examples of the following kinds: (1) instances which need exponentially many local ranking-functions (see [2]), therefore driving the closure algorithm to exponential behavior; and (2) instances where any ranking expression of the form used in [12] must be exponentially big [3]. Thus, our method also handles such examples. We also illustrate where our method outperforms SCP.

The next two sections contain fuller definitions and background facts on SCT and ranking functions. Section 4 describes our class of ranking functions and some related theory, and Sections 5–6 describe the implementation and experiments performed so far.

2   Size Change Termination

This section introduces the SCT abstraction, and reviews the major facts about SCT decision procedure(s). Terminology is not uniform across the related publications and we have made an arbitrary choice. For instance, we use the term *program point* where some references use, e.g., *flow-chart point*, *program location* and *function*, the latter obviously in a functional-programming context.

An abstract program is a set of *abstract transitions*. An abstract transition is a relation on abstract program states. The approach is programming-language independent and focuses solely on abstract states and transitions. A front-end analyzes concrete programs and creates the abstraction for our analysis. Appropriate front ends exist for various programming systems [8,24,23,1,19,16].

Definition 1 (program). *An (abstract) program consists of a finite set P of program points, where every program point p is associated with a fixed list $Arg(p)$ of argument positions; and of a finite set of size-change graphs, defined below, representing possible transitions. The number of argument positions for p is called the arity of p. We sometimes write p/n to denote that p is of arity n.*

Definition 2 (program state). *Let Val be a fixed, infinite well-ordered set. An (abstract) program state is given by associating a value from Val to each argument position of a program point p. The set of all states is St.*

In this paper we write a program state down as a term $p(u_1, \ldots, u_n)$, where n is understood to be the arity of p. The argument positions may represent actual data in the program (of type consistent with Val), but quite often they represent some "size measures" or "norms" associated with the actual data.

Definition 3 (size-change graph). *A size-change graph is formally a triple $g = (p, q, A)$ where p, q are program points and $A \subset Arg(p) \times SizeLabel \times Arg(q)$ is a set of size-change arcs with $SizeLabel = \{\downarrow, \bar{\downarrow}\}$ indicating strict or non-strict descent between an argument of p and an argument of q.*

As an alternative notation, we represent a size-change graph as a constraint logic programming clause $p(\bar{x}) :- \pi; q(\bar{y})$ with $\bar{x} = x_1, \ldots, x_n$, $\bar{y} = y_1, \ldots, y_m$, and π a conjunction of constraints of the form $(x_i > y_j)$ or $(x_i \geq y_j)$. We also write $\pi \models \phi$ to indicate that proposition ϕ (involving values $\bar{x}$ and $\bar{y}$) holds under the assumptions π.

Since the size-change graphs implicitly reveal the set of (relevant) program points, we identify an abstract program with a set $\mathcal{G}$ of size change graphs. The *control-flow graph* (CFG) of the program is the directed (multi-)graph over P underlying $\mathcal{G}$ (namely, every size-change graph corresponds to an arc).

Definition 4 (transitions). *A state transition is a pair (s, s') of states. Let $g = p(\bar{x}) :- \pi; q(\bar{y})$ be a size-change graph. The associated set of transitions is $T_g = \{(p(\bar{x}), q(\bar{y})) \mid \pi\}$. The transition system associated with a set of size-change graphs, $\mathcal{G}$, is $T_{\mathcal{G}} = \bigcup_{g \in \mathcal{G}} T_g$.*

Definition 5 (termination). *Let $\mathcal{G}$ be an SCT instance. A run of $T_{\mathcal{G}}$ is a (finite or infinite) sequence of states $s_0, s_1, s_2 \ldots$ such that for all i, $(s_i, s_{i+1}) \in T_G$. Transition system T_G is uniformly terminating if it has no infinite run.*

An SCT instance $\mathcal{G}$ is positive (or, *satisfies SCT*) if $T_{\mathcal{G}}$ is uniformly terminating. Fortunately, this is not dependent on the specific choice of Val, which justifies considering it as a property of $\mathcal{G}$. This "semantic" definition is not the one given in [17]; indeed, in that paper a "combinatorial" definition is given, in terms of the graphs, and it is a significant result that the given property is equivalent to uniform termination. However, since they are equivalent, we can forego the combinatorial definition, as its details are not used in this work.

It was proved in [17] that the set of positive SCT instances is decidable and its complexity class was determined: it is PSPACE-complete. Decidability is proven in two ways, one of which is direct, i.e., an algorithm that specifically solves this problem. It is based on computing the composition-closure of $\mathcal{G}$, a technique already used by other termination analyzers [18,8]. Such an algorithm is obviously exponential-time. Most current implementations of SCT use this algorithm, but an obvious concern regarding its complexity prompted Lee and Ben-Amram to look for a polynomial-time decidable subset of SCT. A polynomial-time algorithm (SCP, for Size-Change termination in Ptime) that decides such a subset is presented in [4]. In experiments, it performed very well on the benchmark used in that work—a collection of example programs obtained from researchers working on Prolog termination. An interesting part of [4] is an attempt to explicate the capabilities of this algorithm, since it is heuristic and it is not *a priori* obvious why or when it should be successful. The explanation given links the algorithm to specific "size-change patterns"—including lexicographic descent, multiset descent, and dual-multiset descent (the last two terms are defined later in this paper). These observations form the starting point of the current work.

3   Ranking Functions

In this section we introduce ranking functions and describe some known facts regarding SCT and ranking functions.

Definition 6 (quasi-order). *A* quasi-order *over a set D is a binary relation $\succsim \subseteq D \times D$ which is transitive and reflexive. Its* strict part $\succ$ *is defined by $x \succ y \iff x \succsim y \wedge y \not\succsim x$. A* well-quasi-order *means a well-founded one.*

Definition 7 (ranking function). *Let $\mathcal{G}$ be a set of size change graphs. A function ρ which maps program states to a well-quasi-order $(D, \succsim)$ is a (global)* ranking function *for $\mathcal{G}$ if for every graph $g = p(\bar{x}) :- \pi; q(\bar{y}) \in \mathcal{G}$, it holds that $\pi \models \rho(p(\bar{x})) \succ \rho(q(\bar{y}))$.*

The qualifier *global* is used to distinguish this notion of a ranking function from another (local) one (which is not used in this work). When depicting graphs we use solid and dashed lines to respectively indicate strict and nonstrict edges.

Example 1. Consider the following two size-change graphs:

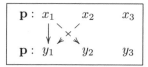 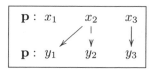

A ranking function for this set is $\rho(x_1, x_2, x_3) = \max\{\langle x_1, 1, x_3\rangle, \langle x_2, 0, x_3\rangle\}$ where tuples are ordered lexicographically.

We remark that lexicographic ordering is used throught this work, and we rely on the well-known fact that if D is well-founded then so is the set of tuples over D of a fixed length, or of a bounded length (when comparing tuples of differing lengths, if one is a prefix of the other, it is considered smaller).

It is obvious that the existence of a ranking function for $\mathcal{G}$ implies termination. This is, in fact, an equivalence (for the other direction, take $\mathcal{T}_{\mathcal{G}}$ as a quasi-order). The ranking technique has been known for a long time and seems to be the natural way to prove termination of transition systems. Even if we know that a system terminates, an explicit ranking function conveys interesting information about the way that computation progresses towards its finish line.

Another view is that a ranking function (given explicitly as some kind of expression) constitutes a *witness*, or *certificate*, to termination. When presented with the expression, one only has to verify that it does decrease on every transition This is conceptually easier than establishing a termination proof from scratch, essentially because it only requires arguing about a single transition at a time. Thus, the argument needed to prove termination, given a ranking function, is logically simpler than the argument necessary for a termination proof using only the SCT graphs, even though this is possible. This simplification is an advantage for users who wish to establish the termination of a program within a theorem-prover [16]. Depending on the form of the ranking function, verifying a certificate may also be easier in a computational-complexity sense (and perhaps a programming sense) than proving termination from the graphs. These considerations are important in "proof-carrying code" scenarios [21].

The SCT criterion was proved in [17] to be decidable, but the algorithms given do not construct a ranking function. The question of whether it is at all possible to obtain an explicit expression for the ranking function (we know that a function exists, once termination is proved!) has only been settled (in the positive) a few years later, in a paper by Chin Soon Lee [12]. The size of the ranking expression in this work is triply-exponential in the worst-case. Recent progress [3] reduces this to a single exponent, but obviously this is still a deterring complexity for practical usage (such as for certification).

However, these works provide an important theoretic underpinning to working with ranking functions for SCT, as they exhibit a class of functions within which all SCT instances can be ranked.

Theorem 1 (Lee 2007). *If $\mathcal{G}$ is SCT, it has a ranking function, effectively constructible from the size-change graphs, of the form: $\rho(s) = \min\{M_1, M_2, \dots\}$ where M_i is $\max\{t_1^i, t_2^i, \dots\}$ and each t_j^i is a tuple of arguments (of the state s) and constants.*

The ranking function in Example 1 has precisely this form (degenerate in that the min operator is unnecessary).

Lee's result indicates a small and yet sufficient set of operators for constructing ranking functions, and also shows that a very limited way of combining them is sufficient. The fact that the expressions are very limited makes the theoretical result even more remarkable. However, it is natural to expect that by narrowing down the class of expressions, we make it more likely that the representation of the ranking function will be big.

In general, we cannot expect *any* reasonable class of expressions to beat the exponential upper bound. This follows from complexity-theoretic considerations, as explained in [2]. However, it is easy to find *instances* where the use of additional operators or expression structures can allow for more concise expressions.

Example 2. The function $\rho(x_1, x_2, \dots, x_n) = \langle \max\{x_1, x_2\}, \dots, \max\{x_{n-1}, x_n\}\rangle$ is of linear size. Expressing it in the form max-of-tuples leads to an expression with $2^{n/2}$ tuples. Thus, simply changing the nesting structure suffices for an exponential improvement in size.

In this work we use several expression constructors that yield concise expressions where, in some cases, the simple forms would lead to exponential size. On the other hand, our class of expressions is not universal. Its specific design is a crucial ingredient in our work and is unveiled in the next section.

4   SCNP: Size-Change Termination NP Subset

This section introduces a class SCNP of size change termination problems. Its definition is derived from a specific form of ranking functions. We *first* define a class of functions; then we define SCNP to include an SCT instance if and only if it has a ranking function of our class. Thus, this definition is *based* on ranking functions and the fact that the resulting subset is NP is an immediate consequence of showing that our ranking functions have polynomial size and that the problem of checking a function against a set of graphs is also in NP.

The building blocks for our construction are four types of well-quasi-orders and certain *level mappings* which are functions mapping program states into these orders. These are defined next.

Definition 8 (multiset extensions). *Let $(D, \succsim)$ be a total order and $(D, \succ)$ its strict part. Let $\wp(D)$ denote the set of multisets of elements of D of at most n elements, where n is fixed by context[1]. The μ-order extension of $(D, \succsim)$, for $\mu \in \{max, min, ms, dms\}$, is the quasi-order $(\wp(D), \succsim^{\mu})$ where:*

1. *(max order) $S \succsim^{max} T$ holds iff $\max(S) \succsim \max(T)$, or T is empty; $S \succ^{max} T$ holds iff $\max(S) \succ \max(T)$, or T is empty while S is not.*
2. *(min order) $S \succsim^{min} T$ holds iff $\min(S) \succsim \min(T)$, or S is empty; $S \succ^{min} T$ holds iff $\min(S) \succ \min(T)$, or T is empty while T is not.*
3. *(multiset order [14]) $S \succ^{ms} T$ holds iff T is obtained by replacing a non-empty sub-multiset $U \subseteq S$ by a (possibly empty) multiset V such that $U \succ^{max} V$; The weak relation $S \succsim^{ms} T$ holds iff $S \succ^{ms} T$ or $S = T$.*
4. *(dual multiset order [4]) $S \succ^{dms} T$ holds iff T is obtained by replacing a sub-multiset $U \subseteq S$ by a non-empty multiset V with $U \succ^{min} V$; The weak relation $S \succsim^{dms} T$ holds iff $S \succ^{dms} T$ or $S = T$.*

Example 3. Let $S = \{4, 3, 3, 0\}$ and $T = \{4, 3, 2, 1, 1\}$. We have $T >^{min} S$, $S \geq^{max} T$ and $T \geq^{max} S$. We have $S >^{ms} T$ because $U = \{3, 0\}$ is replaced by $V = \{2, 1, 1\}$, where all elements are smaller than $\max(U)$. We don't have $S >^{dms} T$, but $T >^{dms} S$.

We give the following well-known facts without proof.

Lemma 1. *When the underlying order is total, so are all the multiset extensions. If $(D, \succ)$ is well-founded, then so is each of the extensions $(D, \succ^{\mu})$.*

Note however that the min/max orders are not partial orders, but rather quasi orders as anti-symmetry does not hold. *Why these four orders?* The motivation lies in previous work with SCT, as mentioned at the end of Section 2.

---

[1] Given an SCT instance $\mathcal{G}$, n is the maximum arity in $\mathcal{G}$.

Definition 9 (level mappings). *Let $\mathcal{G}$ be a set of size change graphs involving N program points; and let M be the sum of arities of all program points. A level mapping is a function f from St to a certain (quasi) ordered set. In this work, level mappings are one of the following:*

Numeric: *f maps each program state $s = p(\bar{u})$ to a natural number $0 \leq f(s) < N$, such that $f(s)$ only depends on the program-point.*

Plain: *f maps a program state $p(\bar{u})$ to a multiset $\{v_1, \ldots, v_k\} \in \wp(Val)$ where $v_1, \ldots, v_k$ are arguments in $\bar{u}$; the selection of argument positions only depends on the program point.*

Tagged: *f maps a program state $p(\bar{u})$ to a multiset $\{(v_1, n_1), \ldots, (v_k, n_k)\} \in \wp(D \times \mathbb{N})$ where $v_1, \ldots, v_k$ are elements of $\bar{u}$ and $n_1, \ldots, n_k$ are natural numbers less than M (called tags). The selection of argument positions as well as the tags is determined by the program point.*

We use a subscripted annotation on f to indicate the order associated with its range and write f_μ with $\mu \in \{max, min, ms, dms\}$ for the multiset orders (both over Val and over Val $\times \mathbb{N}$). We write f_ω for the numeric level mapping, where the order $\succsim^\omega$ is the natural order $\geq$ on integers.

Example 4. The following are plain and tagged level mappings (respectively), assuming a program with program points $p/2$ and $q/3$:

$$f_\mu(s) = \begin{cases} \{u, v\} & \text{if } s = p(u, v) \\ \{u\} & \text{if } s = q(u, v, w) \\ \emptyset & \text{otherwise} \end{cases} \qquad f'_\mu(s) = \begin{cases} \{(u, 0)\} & \text{if } s = p(u, v) \\ \{(u, 1), (w, 0)\} & \text{if } s = q(u, v, w) \\ \emptyset & \text{otherwise} \end{cases}$$

Definition 10 (SCNP). *A set of size change graphs is in SCNP if it has a ranking function which is a tuple of level mappings.*

Example 5. Consider the size change graphs below with the level mappings f_μ and f'_μ (with $\mu = max$) from Example 4.

$$\mathcal{G} = \begin{cases} p(x_1, x_2) :\!\!- \ x_1 > y_1,\ x_2 \geq y_2,\ x_1 \geq y_3; \quad q(y_1, y_2, y_3), \\ q(x_1, x_2, x_3) :\!\!- \ x_1 \geq y_1; \quad p(y_1, y_2) \end{cases}$$

Function $\rho(s) = \langle f'_{max}(s), f_{max}(s)\rangle$ is a ranking function for $\mathcal{G}$; the reader may find it interesting to figure out the justification before reading further.

Definition 11 (orienting graphs). *We say that a level mapping f_μ orients a size-change graph $g = p(\bar{x}) :\!\!- \pi; q(\bar{y})$ if $\pi \models f(p(\bar{x})) \succsim^\mu f(q(\bar{y}))$; it orients g strictly if $\pi \models f(p(\bar{x})) \succ^\mu f(q(\bar{y}))$; and it orients a set $\mathcal{G}$ of size-change graphs if it orients every graph of $\mathcal{G}$, and at least one of them strictly.*

The next lemma is immediate from the definitions.

Lemma 2. *Let $f^1, \ldots, f^m$ be level mappings. The function*

$$\rho(s) = \langle f^1(s), f^2(s), \ldots, f^m(s)\rangle$$

is a (lexicographic) ranking function for $\mathcal{G}$ if and only if for every $g \in \mathcal{G}$, there in an $i \leq m$ such that g is oriented by $f^1, \ldots, f^i$ and strictly oriented by f^i.

Definition 12. *Function* $\rho(s) = \langle f^1(s), f^2(s), \ldots, f^m(s) \rangle$ *is* irredundant *if for all* $i \leq m$, f^i *orients all graphs that are not strictly oriented by* f^j *for some* $j < i$, *and strictly orients at least one of these graphs.*

Observe that an irredundant function is a tuple of length at most $|\mathcal{G}|$. Verifying such a ranking function reduces to the problem of testing whether a graph is (strictly) oriented by a given level mapping. We elaborate on this test for each kind of level mapping. We assume that a level mapping f is given explicitly, by listing the set of argument positions and/or natural number associated with every program point. For the case of numeric level mappings the test is trivial.

Plain level mappings Let f_μ be a plain level mapping and $g = p(\bar{x}) :\!\!- \pi; q(\bar{y})$. It is convenient to view g as a graph (in the way of Definition 3). Thus $\pi \models x \geq y$ is equivalent to g having an arc $x \to y$, while $\pi \models x > y$ if the arc is strict. By g^t we denote the transpose of g (obtained by inverting all the arcs). Let $S \subseteq \bar{x}$ be the set of argument positions selected by $f_\mu(p(\bar{x}))$ and similarly T for $f_\mu(q(\bar{y}))$. The definition of $\succsim^\mu$ indicates precisely what π has to satisfy. We elaborate, assuming that S, T are nonempty.

1. *max order:* for non-strict descent, every $y \in T$ must be "covered" by an $x \in S$ such that $\pi \models x \geq y$. Strict max-descent requires $x > y$.
2. *min order:* Same conditions but on g^t (thus, now T covers S).
3. *multiset order:* for non-strict descent, every $y \in T$ must be "covered" by an $x \in S$ such that $\pi \models x \geq y$. Furthermore each $x \in S$ either covers each related y strictly ($x > y$) or covers at most a single y. Descent is strict if there is some x of the strict kind.
4. *dual multiset order:* Same conditions but on g^t (now T covers S).

Example 6. Consider again $\mathcal{G}$ from Example 5, and f_μ from Example 4. The first SCG (from p to q) is oriented strictly taking $\mu = max$ and $\mu = ms$, but not at all under their duals. The second SCG is oriented weakly for $\mu = min$ and not under any other of the orders.

Tagged level mappings These are just like plain level mappings except that the underlying order is modified by the presence of tags. So to decide whether $\pi \models f(p(\bar{x})) \succ^\mu f(q(\bar{y}))$ where f is a set of tagged arguments, we use the rules given above for the multiset-extension μ, plus the following facts:

$$\pi \models (x, i) \succ (y, j) \iff (\pi \models x \succsim y) \wedge (\pi \models x \succ y \vee i > j)$$
$$\pi \models (x, i) \succsim (y, j) \iff (\pi \models x \succ y) \vee (\pi \models x \succsim y \wedge i \geq j)$$

As an example the reader may want to verify that the function f', defined in Example 4, orients the graphs of Example 5 under *max* ordering, with the second one oriented strictly. This is, of course, used in arguing the correctness of the ranking function in that example.

We are now in position to state the following Theorem.

Theorem 2. *SCNP is in NP.*

Proof. If a ranking function of the desired form exists, then there is an irredundant one of polynomial size. Checking the condition in Lemma 2, according to the rules given above for the different orderings, is clearly polynomial-time.

Since the problem is in NP it is known that it can be reduced to SAT. In fact it is possible to transform a complete problem instance into one big Boolean formula whose satisfying assignment will encode the sought solution. To find the assignment we can make use of an off-the-shelf SAT solver. However, it is far more efficient to make use of the structure of the problem and call the SAT solver several times, on smaller SAT instances.

Our algorithm has the following top-level structure: as long as $\mathcal{G}$ is not empty, find a level mapping f that orients $\mathcal{G}$. Remove the graphs oriented strictly by f, and repeat.

Basically, the instruction "find a level mapping" is performed by trying each of the level-mapping types in turn, so that the smaller NP problems that we reduce to SAT are of the form: given $\mathcal{G}$ and μ, find out if there is a level mapping f_μ that orients it. Numeric level mappings have a special role in this algorithm. Since such a level mapping ignores the argument values we write it as $f(p(\_))$.

Claim. If there is a numeric level mapping f that orients $\mathcal{G}$ and program point q is reachable from p then $f(p(\_)) \geq f(q(\_))$.

This (obvious) property implies that f is constant in every strongly connected component (SCC) of $\mathcal{G}$ (considered as a graph with abstract transitions as arcs). Only inter-component transitions can be strictly oriented by f and in fact all of them can, by assigning f values according to reverse topological order of the SCCs. Now, after deleting the strictly-oriented transitions, SCCs will become disconnected from each other which allows them to be processed separately. We obtain the following revised algorithm.

1. Initialize ρ to the empty tuple.
2. Perform the following steps as long as $\mathcal{G}$ is not empty:
3. Compute the decomposition of $\mathcal{G}$ to strongly connected components (SCC's). If $\mathcal{G}$ has inter-component transitions, define a numeric level mapping f by reverse topological ordering of the SCC's. Extend ρ by f and remove the inter-component transitions.
4. If $\mathcal{G}$ has a non-trivial SCC[2], perform the following for each such component $\mathcal{C}$ in turn: (a) Apply SAT solving, as described in Section 5, to find a level mapping f that orients $\mathcal{C}$. If no level mappings exists, exit with a failure message; and (b) Define the value of f as $\emptyset$ for all program points not in $\mathcal{C}$. Append f to ρ and remove the transitions strictly oriented by f.

We conclude this section by discussing the relations of SCNP, SCT and SCP. Viewing all three as decision problems (sets of instances), we have:

$$\text{SCP} \subset \text{SCNP} \subset \text{SCT}.$$

Arguments for these relations are as follows:

---

[2] That is, an SCC that contains at least one arc.

1. SCNP $\subseteq$ SCT because SCNP is a sound termination condition. The inclusion is strict because there are terminating instances not in SCNP. Here is such an example (from [4]).

   Example 7. $\left\{ \begin{array}{l} p(x,y,z,w) :- \ x \geq x', x \geq y', w > w'; p(x',y',z',w'), \\ p(x,y,z,w) :- \ y > x', y \geq y', z > z'; \ p(x',y',z',w') \end{array} \right\}$

2. SCNP handles some examples not handled by SCP; for instance, Example 1 on page 222 for which $\rho(x_1, x_2, x_3) = \langle \max\{(x_1, 1), (x_2, 0)\}, \max\{x_3\} \rangle$ is a ranking function.
3. Finally, the claim SCP $\subseteq$ SCNP follows from an analysis of the SCP algorithm that cannot be included in this conference paper, however we refer the reader to [4, Section 5] where some ideas of this analysis are already given.

On the point of complexity, it is interesting to observe that the hard cases for the SCT algorithms based on the local-ranking approach are not necessarily hard for our approach based on global ranking functions. In [2], an SCT instance is described, having $n + 1$ arguments and n size-change graphs, that requires 2^n different local ranking functions of the kind discussed in [6]. This means that the closure-based SCT algorithms are driven to exponential behavior. But this instance is handled by SCNP and even SCP.

Finally, we prove that SCNP is complete for NP. Thus solving it with SAT is not an overkill in a complexity-theoretic sense.

Theorem 3. *SCNP is NP-complete.*

Proof. We will prove NP-hardness of a simplified problem—given $\mathcal{G}$ is there any level mapping that orients $\mathcal{G}$? We give a reduction from the well-known *Set Covering* problem SC, defined as follows:

INSTANCE: $\langle n, [S_1, \ldots, S_m], k \rangle$, where each $S_i \subseteq \{1, \ldots, n\}$, and $k \leq n$.
CONDITION: $\{1, \ldots, n\}$ can be covered by k of the sets S_i.
Given an instance of SC, construct size-change graphs as follows. Let $\bar{x} = \langle x_1, \ldots, x_n, x_{n+1}, \ldots, x_{2n-k} \rangle$. We have a single program point $p(\bar{x})$ and graphs $g_i = p(\bar{x}) :- \pi_i; p(\bar{x}')$ for $i = 1, 2$ with:

$$\pi_1 = \{x_i > x'_j \mid j \in S_i\} \cup \{x_i \geq x'_j \mid i \leq n, j > n\}$$
$$\pi_2 = \{x_i \geq x'_{i+1} \mid i < 2n - k\} \cup \{x_{2n-k} \geq x'_1\}.$$

Observe that the CFG is strongly connected, so a numeric level mapping is ruled out. Graph g_2 is easily seen to defeat any multiset based level mapping that does not include all the arguments. Assuming $k < n$, graph g_1 defeats *min* and *dms* ordering, because x_{n+1} is not covered in g_1^t. It is easy to see that g_1 is oriented by *max*, but only weakly (and we cannot use tagging because of g_2). So, to orient g_1 strictly we need the *ms* ordering, and (because of g_2) the set has to include all arguments. Now, arguments x_{n+j} for $j = 1, \ldots, n - k$ can only be covered non-strictly, and so $n - k$ different source arguments are needed to cover them (recall that a source argument can only cover one target argument if it covers it non-strictly). The remaining k arguments among $x_1, \ldots, x_n$ have to cover $x'_1, \ldots, x'_n$ which clearly implies a solution to the Set Covering instance.

This reduction is interesting in that it shows that even if we know the level mapping (in this case, $f_{ms}(p(\bar{x})) = \{x_1, \ldots, x_{2n-k}\}$) it is still NP-hard to verify it, just because of not knowing which arcs of the size-change graph to use. This observation motivates us to report not only the level mapping but also its justification as part of the output of our tool.

5   A SAT Based Implementation

This section is dedicated to our solution of the subproblem—finding an orienting level mapping—with the aid of a SAT solver. We use an approach described in [9], where the problem to be solved is encoded into Boolean and partial order constraints. The latter are propositional statements which contain both propositional variables and atoms of the form $(f > g)$ or $(f = g)$ where f and g are partial order symbols. A satisfying assignment assigns Boolean values to the propositional variables and integer values to the partial order symbols.

Let $\mathcal{G}$ be a set of size change graphs and $\mu \in \{max, min, ms, dms\}$. We construct a propositional formula (with partial order constraints) to determine if there exists a tagged level mapping which μ-orients $\mathcal{G}$. We remark that a plain mapping need not be handled separately: it is a special case of the tagged mapping where all tags are the same. The proposition has the form $\Phi_\mu^{\mathcal{G}} = \varphi^{\mathcal{G}} \wedge \varphi_\mu^{\mathcal{G}}$ where $\varphi^{\mathcal{G}}$ is a representation of $\mathcal{G}$ and $\varphi_\mu^{\mathcal{G}}$ is specific for μ.

Encoding a set of size change graphs. Let $g = p(x_1, \ldots, x_n) :- \pi; q(y_1, \ldots, y_m)$. We create propositional variables e_c^g with c of the form $(p_i > q_j)$ or $(p_i \geq q_j)$. Intuitively, e_c^g represents the fact $\pi \models (x_i, tag_p^i) > (y_j, tag_q^j)$ (or $\geq$). The encoding introduces partial order constraints on the tag values tag_p^i and tag_q^j. We define $\varphi^{\mathcal{G}} = \bigwedge_{g \in \mathcal{G}} \varphi^g$. The following formula encodes graph g. The propositions $\pi \models x_i > y_j$ (or $x_i \geq y_j$) that appear in it are replaced by $\texttt{true}$ or $\texttt{false}$ according to the size-change graph.

$$\varphi^g = \bigwedge_{\substack{1 \leq i \leq n \\ 1 \leq j \leq m}} \left(\begin{array}{l} (e_{x_i > y_j}^g \leftrightarrow (\pi \models x_i > y_j) \vee (\pi \models x_i \geq y_j) \wedge (tag_p^i > tag_q^j)) \\ \wedge (e_{x_i \geq y_j}^g \leftrightarrow (\pi \models x_i > y_j) \vee (\pi \models x_i \geq y_j) \wedge (tag_p^i \geq tag_q^j)) \end{array} \right)$$

Example 8. Let $g = p(x_1, x_2, x_3) :- x_1 > y_1, x_1 \geq y_2; q(y_1, y_2, y_3)$. The encoding is a conjunction of subformulae. Let us consider several of them: The constraint $x_1 > y_1$ contributes the conjuncts $e_{x_1 > y_1}^g$ and $e_{x_1 \geq y_1}^g$; The constraint $x_1 \geq y_2$ contributes the conjuncts $(e_{x_1 > y_2}^g \leftrightarrow tag_p^1 > tag_p^2)$, and $(e_{x_1 \geq y_1}^g \leftrightarrow tag_p^1 \geq tag_p^2)$. The absence of a constraint between x_1 and y_3 contributes $\neg e_{x_1 > y_3}^g$ and $\neg e_{x_1 \geq y_3}^g$.

For the μ specific part of the encoding, the propositional variables $weak_\mu^g$ and $strict_\mu^g$ are interpreted as specifying that graph g is weakly (resp. strictly) oriented by μ respectively. Hence the encoding takes the form:

$$\varphi_\mu^{\mathcal{G}} = \left(\bigwedge_{g \in \mathcal{G}} weak_\mu^g \right) \wedge \left(\bigvee_{g \in \mathcal{G}} strict_\mu^g \right) \wedge \psi_\mu^{\mathcal{G}}$$

The first two conjuncts specify that there exists an f_μ which orients $\mathcal{G}$. The third conjunct $\psi_\mu^{\mathcal{G}}$ constrains variables $weak_\mu^g$ and $strict_\mu^g$ so that they are true exactly when the corresponding graphs are weakly (resp. strictly) oriented by μ. The propositional variables $p_1, \ldots, p_n$ and $q_1, \ldots, q_m$ indicate the argument positions of p and q selected for the level mapping.

Encoding the max set ordering: The following formula encodes the conditions described in Section 4.

$$\psi_{max}^{\mathcal{G}} = \bigwedge_{g=p(\bar{x}) \,:-\, \pi;q(\bar{y})} \left(\begin{array}{l} weak_{max}^g \leftrightarrow \bigwedge_{1 \le j \le m} \left(q_j \to \bigvee_{1 \le i \le n} (p_i \wedge e_{x_i \ge y_j}^g) \right) \wedge \\[3ex] strict_{max}^g \leftrightarrow \bigwedge_{1 \le j \le m} \left(q_j \to \bigvee_{1 \le i \le n} (p_i \wedge e_{x_i > y_j}^g) \right) \wedge \bigvee_{1 \le i \le n} p_i \end{array} \right)$$

Encoding the multiset ordering: We follow the encoding for the multiset ordering described in [22]. The operator $\oplus$ specifies that exactly one of a set of propositional variables is true. For each graph g, propositional variables $\gamma_{i,j}^g$ specify that in size change graph $g = p(\bar{x}) :- \pi; q(\bar{y})$ the ith argument of p/n covers the jth argument of q/m. The propositional variables ε_i^g specify if whatever the ith argument of p/n covers is weak (then it may cover only one) or strict (then it may cover several).

The conjunct for graph g has four parts. The first subformula encodes the conditions for weakly orientation by multiset ordering (see Section 4). The second subformula expresses a strict covering. The third subformula specifies that $\gamma_{i,j}^g$ and ε_i^g agree with their intended meaning. The fourth subformula states that if p_i is selected and ε_i^g indicates weak cover, then position i covers exactly one position j.

$$\psi_{ms}^{\mathcal{G}} = \bigwedge_{g=p(\bar{x}) \,:-\, \pi;q(\bar{y})} \left(\begin{array}{l} weak_{ms}^g \leftrightarrow \bigwedge_{1 \le j \le m} \left(q_j \to \bigvee_{1 \le i \le n} \gamma_{i,j}^g \right) \wedge \\[3ex] strict_{ms}^g \leftrightarrow \bigvee_{1 \le i \le n} (p_i \wedge \neg \varepsilon_i^g) \wedge \\[3ex] \bigwedge_{\substack{1 \le i \le n \\ 1 \le j \le m}} \gamma_{i,j}^g \to p_i \wedge q_j \wedge e_{x_i \ge y_j}^g \wedge (\neg \varepsilon_i^g \leftrightarrow e_{x_i > y_j}^g) \wedge \\[3ex] \bigwedge_{1 \le i \le n} p_i \to \varepsilon_i^g \to \oplus \left\{ \gamma_{i,j}^g \,\Big|\, 1 \le j \le m \right\} \end{array} \right)$$

Encoding the min and dual-multiset orderings: The encodings are obtained through the respective dualities with the max and multiset orderings.

$$\psi_{min}^{\mathcal{G}} = \bigwedge_{g=p(\bar{x}) \,:-\, \pi;q(\bar{y})} \left(\begin{array}{l} weak_{min}^g \leftrightarrow weak_{max}^{g^t} \wedge \\ strict_{min}^g \leftrightarrow strict_{max}^{g^t} \end{array} \right)$$

$$\psi_{dms}^{\mathcal{G}} = \bigwedge_{g=p(\bar{x}) \,:-\, \pi;q(\bar{y})} \left(\begin{array}{l} weak_{dms}^g \leftrightarrow weak_{ms}^{g^t} \wedge \\ strict_{dms}^g \leftrightarrow strict_{ms}^{g^t} \end{array} \right)$$

We have implemented the algorithm in Prolog. After creating the partial order constraints, our program calls the solver described in [9]. This solver transforms the partial order constraint to a CNF which is passed on to the MiniSAT solver for Boolean satisfaction [20] through its Prolog interface described in [7].

6   Experimentation

We have tested our implementation on two benchmark suites. The first is described in [4]. It originates from a logic programming test suite for termination analysis and consists of 123 examples (abstract programs). The second suite originates in a benchmark suite for termination of term rewriting systems (TPDP version 4.0 [25]). It consists of 4062 abstract programs generated when AProVE, a tool to automatically prove termination of term rewriting systems, applied the SCT method based on the embedding order, as described in [24]. The first suite can be obtained via Amir Ben-Amram's web page. The second can be found at http://www.cs.bgu.ac.il/ mcodish/Software/ trs_suite_for_sct.zip

For the first suite, 84 of the 123 examples are SCT positive. All of these are also in SCP and, with no surprises, also in SCNP. The SAT based implementation is much slower than the implementations for SCP and SCT described in [4]. However, analysis times are reasonable (under 3 seconds for the entire suite) and we have the benefit that ranking functions are provided for the SCNP instances.

For the second suite, 3820 of the 4062 examples are in SCT. There is only one example which is SCT but not SCP. In fact, this is Example 7 which was designed expressly to defeat SCP. Here too SCNP agreed with SCP. Again ranking functions are provided for all the verified instances and the entire suite is analyzed in approximately 20 seconds. Our implementation is not optimized and analysis times are only reported to give an idea of their magnitude and show that the use of SAT solving is not prohibitive.

Acknowledgment

We thank Samir Genaim for help with the benchmarking and Peter Schneider-Kamp for harvesting the collection of 4062 sets of size-change graphs. This work was done while Amir Ben-Amram was visiting DIKU, the University of Copenhagen, Denmark; and Michael Codish was visiting the CLIP group at the Technical University of Madrid, supported by a mobility grant (SAB2006-0189) from the Spanish Ministry of Science and Education.

References

1. Avery, J.: Size-change termination and bound analysis. In: Hagiya, M., Wadler, P. (eds.) FLOPS 2006. LNCS, vol. 3945, Springer, Heidelberg (2006)
2. Ben-Amram, A.M.: A complexity tradeoff in ranking-function termination proofs (submitted for publication 2007)
3. Ben-Amram, A.M., Lee, C.S.: Ranking functions for size-change termination II. In: 9th International Workshop on Termination (WST 2007) (July 2007)
4. Ben-Amram, A.M., Lee, C.S.: Size-change analysis in polynomial time. ACM Transactions on Programming Languages and Systems 29(1) (2007)

5. Bruynooghe, M., Codish, M., Gallagher, J.P., Genaim, S., Vanhoof, W.: Termination analysis of logic programs through combination of type-based norms. ACM TOPLAS 29(2) (2007)
6. Codish, M., Lagoon, V., Stuckey, P.J.: Testing for termination with monotonicity constraints. In: Gabbrielli, M., Gupta, G. (eds.) ICLP 2005. LNCS, vol. 3668, pp. 326–340. Springer, Heidelberg (2005)
7. Codish, M., Lagoon, V., Stuckey, P.J.: Logic programming with satisfiability. Theory and Practice of Logic Programming (2007)
8. Codish, M., Taboch, C.: A semantic basis for termination analysis of logic programs. The Journal of Logic Programming 41(1), 103–123 (1999)
9. Codish, M., Lagoon, V., Stuckey, P.J.: Solving partial order constraints for LPO termination. In: Pfenning, F. (ed.) RTA 2006. LNCS, vol. 4098, pp. 4–18. Springer, Heidelberg (2006)
10. Cook, B., Podelski, A., Rybalchenko, A.: Abstraction refinement for termination. In: Hankin, C., Siveroni, I. (eds.) SAS 2005. LNCS, vol. 3672, pp. 87–101. Springer, Heidelberg (2005)
11. Cook, B., Podelski, A., Rybalchenko, A.: Termination proofs for systems code. In: Schwartzbach, M., Ball, T. (eds.) Proc. PLDI, pp. 415–426. ACM Press, New York (2006)
12. Lee, C.S.: Ranking functions for size-change termination (submitted 2007)
13. Dershowitz, N., Lindenstrauss, N., Sagiv, Y., Serebrenik, A.: A general framework for automatic termination analysis of logic programs. Applicable Algebra in Engineering, Communication and Computing 12(1–2), 117–156 (2001)
14. Dershowitz, N., Manna, Z.: Proving termination with multiset orderings. Communications of the ACM 22(8), 465–476 (1979)
15. Jones, N.D., Bohr, N.: Termination analysis of the untyped lambda calculus. In: van Oostrom, V. (ed.) RTA 2004. LNCS, vol. 3091, pp. 1–23. Springer, Heidelberg (2004)
16. Krauss, A.: Certified size-change termination. In: Pfenning, F. (ed.) CADE 2007. LNCS (LNAI), vol. 4603, pp. 460–475. Springer, Heidelberg (2007)
17. Lee, C.S., Jones, N.D., Ben-Amram, A.M.: The size-change principle for program termination. In: Proc. POPL 2001, January 2001, vol. 28, pp. 81–92. ACM Press, New York (2001)
18. Lindenstrauss, N., Sagiv, Y., Serebrenik, A.: Termilog: A system for checking termination of queries to logic programs. In: Grumberg, O. (ed.) CAV 1997. LNCS, vol. 1254, pp. 444–447. Springer, Heidelberg (1997)
19. Manolios, P., Vroon, D.: Termination analysis with calling context graphs. In: Ball, T., Jones, R.B. (eds.) CAV 2006. LNCS, vol. 4144, pp. 401–414. Springer, Heidelberg (2006)
20. MiniSAT solver (Viewed December 2005),
    http://www.cs.chalmers.se/Cs/Research/FormalMethods/MiniSat
21. Necula, G.C.: Proof-carrying code. In: Proc. POPL, pp. 106–119. ACM Press, New York (1997)
22. Schneider-Kamp, P., Thiemann, R., Annov, E., Codish, M., Giesl, J.: Proving termination using recursive path orders and sat solving. In: Konev, B., Wolter, F. (eds.) FroCos 2007. LNCS (LNAI), vol. 4720, pp. 267–282. Springer, Heidelberg (2007)
23. Sereni, D., Jones, N.: Termination analysis of higher-order functional programs. In: Yi, K. (ed.) APLAS 2005. LNCS, vol. 3780, pp. 281–297. Springer, Heidelberg (2005)
24. Thiemann, R., Giesl, J.: The size-change principle and dependency pairs for termination of term rewriting. Applicable Algebra in Engineering, Communication and Computing 16(4), 229–270 (2005)
25. The termination problem data base. http://www.lri.fr/~marche/tpdb/

Efficient Automatic STE Refinement Using Responsibility

Hana Chockler[1], Orna Grumberg[2], and Avi Yadgar[2]

[1] IBM Research
Mount Carmel, Haifa 31905, Israel
hanac@il.ibm.com
[2] Computer Science Department
Technion, Haifa, Israel
{orna,yadgar}@cs.technion.ac.il

Abstract. Symbolic Trajectory Evaluation (STE) is a powerful technique for hardware model checking. It is based on 3-valued symbolic simulation, using $0, 1$, and X ("unknown"). X is used to abstract away values of circuit nodes, thus reducing memory and runtime of STE runs. The abstraction is derived from a given user specification.

An STE run results in "*pass*" (1), if the circuit satisfies the specification, "*fail*" (0) if the circuit falsifies it, and "*unknown*" (X), if the abstraction is too coarse to determine either of the two. In the latter case, refinement is needed: The X values of some of the abstracted inputs should be replaced. The main difficulty is to choose an appropriate subset of these inputs that will help to eliminate the "*unknown*" STE result, while avoiding an unnecessary increase in memory and runtime. The common approach to this problem is to manually choose these inputs.

This work suggests a novel approach to automatic refinement for STE, which is based on the notion of *responsibility*. For each input with X value we compute its *Degree of Responsibility* (DoR) to the "*unknown*" STE result. We then refine those inputs whose DoR is maximal.

We implemented an efficient algorithm, which is linear in the size of the circuit, for computing the approximate DoR of inputs. We used it for refinements for STE on several circuits and specifications. Our experimental results show that DoR is a very useful device for choosing inputs for refinement. In comparison with previous works on automatic refinement, our computation of the refinement set is faster, STE needs fewer refinement iterations and uses less overall memory and time.

1 Introduction

Symbolic Trajectory Evaluation (STE) [13] is a powerful technique for hardware model checking. STE is based on combining 3-valued abstraction with symbolic simulation. It is applied to a circuit M, described as a graph over *nodes* (gates and latches). The specification consists of assertions in a restricted temporal language. An assertions is of the form $A \Longrightarrow C$, where the *antecedent* A expresses constraints on nodes n at different times t, and the *consequent* C expresses requirements that should hold on such nodes (n, t). Abstraction in STE is derived from the specification by initializing all inputs not appearing in A to the X ("unknown") value.

C.R. Ramakrishnan and J. Rehof (Eds.): TACAS 2008, LNCS 4963, pp. 233–248, 2008.

An STE run may result in *"pass"* (1), if the circuit satisfies the specification, *"fail"* (0) if the circuit falsifies it, and *"unknown"* (X), if the abstraction is too coarse to determine either of the two. In the latter case, a refinement is needed: The X values of some of the abstracted inputs should be changed.

The main challenge in this setting is to choose an appropriate subset of these inputs, that will help to eliminate the *"unknown"* STE result. Selecting a "right" set of inputs for refinement is crucial for the success of STE: refining too many inputs may result in memory and time explosion. On the other hand, selecting too few inputs or selecting inputs that do not affect the result of the verification will lead to many iterations with an *"unknown"* STE result.

The common approach to this problem is to manually choose the inputs for refinement. This, however, might be labor-intensive and error-prone. Thus, an automatic refinement is desired.

In this work we suggest a novel approach to automatic refinement for STE, which is based on the notion of *responsibility*. For each input with X value we compute its *Degree of Responsibility* (DoR) to the *"unknown"* STE result. We then refine those inputs whose DoR is maximal.

To understand the notion of responsibility, consider first the following concepts. We say that event B *counterfactually depends* on event A [9] if A and B both hold, and had A not happened then B would not have happened. Halpern and Pearl broadened the notion of causality saying that A is a *cause* of B if there exists some change of the current situation that creates the counterfactual dependence between A and B [8].

As an example, consider the circuit in Figure 1(a). The event "$n = 1$" counterfactually depends on the event "$n_1 = 1$". Next consider the circuit in Figure 1(b). "$n_1 = 0$" is a cause of "$n = 0$". This is because if we change n_2 from 0 to 1, then "$n = 0$" counterfactually depends on "$n_1 = 0$". Similarly, "$n_2 = 0$ is a cause of "$n = 0$".

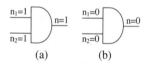

Fig. 1. Cause

The notion of responsibility and of weighted responsibility, introduced in [4], quantifies the change that is needed in order to create the counterfactual dependence. The DoR of A for B is taken to be $1/(k+1)$, where k is the size of the minimal change that creates the counterfactual dependence. For instance, in the example above, the DoR of "$n_1 = 0$" for "$n = 0$" is $1/2$, because the minimal change that creates a counterfactual dependence is of size 1 (changing the value of n_2 from 0 to 1). In this work we use weighted DoR in order to obtain a finer-grain quantification for changes, in the context of STE.

Computing responsibility in circuits is known to be intractable in general [4]. Inspired by the algorithm for read-once formulas in [3], we developed the algorithm *RespSTE* for efficiently computing an *approximate* DoR. Computing the responsibility of the inputs for some output of a circuit involves one traversal of the circuit for each X valued input in the *cone of influence* of the output. The overall complexity is therefore only quadratic in the size of the circuit.

In order to evaluate our algorithm *RespSTE*, we implemented it and used it in conjunction with *Forte*, a BDD based STE tool by Intel [14]. We applied it to several circuits and specifications. We compared our results with the automatic refinement for

STE, suggested in [15]. In all cases, the comparison shows a significant speedup. A significant reduction in BDD nodes is also gained in most of the assertions. In some of the cases, our algorithm needed fewer refinement iterations.

The DoRs we compute gives us a quantitative measure of the importance of each input to the STE "*unknown*" result. By examining these values, we conclude that this quantitative measure is of high quality and is complying with our understanding of the problem as users who are familiar with the models.

When using these results for automatic refinement, the quality of the results is reflected by the number of refinement iterations that were required, and in the number of symbolic variables that were added to the assertion. We point out that even when a non-automatic (manual) refinement is applied, our DoRs can serve as recommended priorities on the candidate inputs for refinement.

Related Work. Abstraction-Refinement takes a major role in model checking [6,10] for reducing the state explosion problem. In [5], it is shown that the abstraction in STE is an abstract interpretation via a Galois connection. In [17], an automatic abstraction-refinement for symbolic simulation is suggested. However, the first automatic refinement for STE has been suggested in [15]. In this refinement scheme, the values of the circuit nodes, as computed by STE, are used in order to trace X paths, and refine the STE assertion by adding symbolic variables to A. While this work is the closest to ours, it is essentially different from using the responsibility concept. We compare our results to this work in Section 5. In [2], an automatic refinement for GSTE is suggested. This method, like [15], traverses the circuit nodes after running STE, and performs a model and an assertion refinement. This method is also essentially different from ours, as it is aimed at solving GSTE problems, where an assertion graph describes the specification, and is used in the refinement process.

SAT based refinements were suggested in [12] and [7]. The method presented in [12] is used for assisting manual refinement. The method presented in [7] takes an automatic CEGAR approach which is applicable only in the suggested SAT based framework. In [1], a method for automatic *abstraction* without refinement is suggested. We believe that our algorithm can complement such a framework.

The rest of the paper is organized as follows. In Section 2 we give the needed background for STE and present the formal definitions of causality and responsibility. Section 3 shows how to define and compute the degrees of responsibility (DoR) in the context of STE refinement. Section 4 describes the abstraction and refinement loop for STE with responsibility. Section 5 presents our experiments and concludes with an evaluation of the results.

2 Preliminaries

2.1 Symbolic Trajectory Evaluation (STE)

A hardware model M is a *circuit*, represented by a directed graph. The graph's nodes $\mathcal{N}$ are input and internal nodes, where internal nodes are latches and combinational gates. A combinational gate represents a Boolean operator. The graph of M may contain cycles, but not combinational cycles. A graph of a circuit is shown in Figure 4(a). Given a directed edge (n_1, n_2), we say that n_1 is an *input* of n_2. We denote by (n, t) the value of node n at time t. The value of a gate (n, t) is the result of applying its operator on the inputs of n at time t. The value of a latch (n, t) is determined by the value of its input at time $t - 1$. The *bounded cone of influence* (BCOI) of a node (n, t) contains all nodes (n', t') with $t' \leq t$ that may influence the value of (n, t), and is defined recursively as follows: the BCOI of a combinational node at time t is the union of the BCOI of its inputs at time t, and the BCOI of a latch at time t is the union of the BCOI of its inputs at time $t - 1$. The BCOI of a node with no inputs is the empty set.

In STE, a node can get a value in a quaternary domain $\mathcal{Q} = \{0, 1, X, \bot\}$. A node whose value cannot be determined by its inputs is given the value X("unknown"). $\bot$ is used to describe an over constrained node. This might occur when there is a contradiction between an external assumption on the circuit and its actual behavior.

A *state* s in M is an assignment of values from $\mathcal{Q}$ to every node, $s : \mathcal{N} \rightarrow \mathcal{Q}$. A *trajectory* π is an infinite series of states, describing a run of M. We denote by $\pi(i), i \in \mathbb{N}$, the state at time i in π, and by $\pi(i)(n), i \in \mathbb{N}, n \in \mathcal{N}$, the value of node n in the state $\pi(i)$. $\pi^i, i \in \mathbb{N}$, denotes the suffix of π starting at time i.

Let $\mathcal{V}$ be a set of *symbolic Boolean variables* over the domain $\{0, 1\}$. A *symbolic expression* over $\mathcal{V}$ is an expression consisting of quaternary operations, applied to $\mathcal{V} \cup \mathcal{Q}$. The truth tables of the quaternary operators are given in Figure 2. A *symbolic state* over $\mathcal{V}$ is a mapping from each node of M to a symbolic expression. A symbolic

AND	X	0	1	$\bot$
X	X	0	X	$\bot$
0	0	0	0	$\bot$
1	X	0	1	$\bot$
$\bot$	$\bot$	$\bot$	$\bot$	$\bot$

OR	X	0	1	$\bot$
X	X	X	1	$\bot$
0	X	0	1	$\bot$
1	1	1	1	$\bot$
$\bot$	$\bot$	$\bot$	$\bot$	$\bot$

NOT	
X	X
0	1
1	0
$\bot$	$\bot$

Fig. 2. Quaternary Operations

state represents a set of states, one for each assignment to $\mathcal{V}$. A *symbolic trajectory* over $\mathcal{V}$ is an infinite series of symbolic states, compatible with the circuit. It represents a set of trajectories, one for each assignment to $\mathcal{V}$. Given a symbolic trajectory π and an assignment ϕ to $\mathcal{V}$, $\phi(\pi)$ denotes the trajectory that is received by applying ϕ to all the symbolic expressions in π.

A *Trajectory Evaluation Logic* (TEL) formula is defined recursively over $\mathcal{V}$ as follows: $f ::= n$ is $p \mid f_1 \wedge f_2 \mid p \rightarrow f \mid \mathbf{N}f$, where $n \in \mathcal{N}$, p is a Boolean expression over $\mathcal{V}$, and $\mathbf{N}$ is the next time operator. The *maximal depth* of a TEL formula f is the maximal time t for which a constraint exists in f on some node n, plus 1.

Given a TEL formula f over $\mathcal{V}$, a symbolic trajectory π over $\mathcal{V}$, and an assignment ϕ to $\mathcal{V}$, we define the satisfaction of f as in [15]:

$$[\phi, \pi \models f] = \bot \leftrightarrow \exists i \geq 0, n \in \mathcal{N} : \phi(\pi)(i)(n) = \bot. \text{ Otherwise:}$$
$$[\phi, \pi \models n \text{ is } p] = 1 \leftrightarrow \phi(\pi)(0)(n) = \phi(p)$$
$$[\phi, \pi \models n \text{ is } p] = 0 \leftrightarrow \phi(\pi)(0)(n) \neq \phi(p) \text{ and } \phi(\pi)(0)(n) \in \{0, 1\}$$
$$[\phi, \pi \models n \text{ is } p] = X \leftrightarrow \phi(\pi)(0)(n) = X \qquad \phi, \pi \models p \rightarrow f \equiv \neg\phi(p) \vee \phi, \pi \models f$$
$$\phi, \pi \models f_1 \wedge f_2 \equiv (\phi, \pi \models f_1 \wedge \phi, \pi \models f_2) \qquad \phi, \pi \models \mathbf{N}f \equiv \phi, \pi^1 \models f$$

Note that given an assignment ϕ to $\mathcal{V}$, $\phi(p)$ is a constant (0 or 1).
We define the truth value of $\pi \models f$ as follows:

$$[\pi \models f] = 0 \leftrightarrow \exists \phi : [\phi, \pi \models f] = 0$$
$$[\pi \models f] = X \leftrightarrow \forall \phi : [\phi, \pi \models f] \neq 0 \text{ and } \exists \phi : [\phi, \pi \models f] = X$$
$$[\pi \models f] = 1 \leftrightarrow \forall \phi : [\phi, \pi \models f] \notin \{0, X\} \text{ and } \exists \phi : [\phi, \pi \models f] = 1$$
$$[\pi \models f] = \bot \leftrightarrow \forall \phi : [\phi, \pi \models f] = \bot$$

This definition creates levels of importance between 0 and X. If there exists an assignment such that $[\phi, \pi \models f] = 0$, the truth value of $\pi \models f$ is 0, even if there are other assignments such that $[\phi, \pi \models f] = X$.

STE assertions are of the form $A \Rightarrow C$, where A (the antecedent) and C (the consequent) are TEL formulae. A expresses constraints on circuit nodes at specific times, and C expresses requirements that should hold on circuit nodes at specific times. We define the truth value of $[M \models A \Rightarrow C]$ as follows:

$[M \models A \Rightarrow C] = 1 \leftrightarrow \forall \pi : [\pi \models A] = 1$ implies $[\pi \models C] = 1$

$[M \models A \Rightarrow C] = \bot \leftrightarrow \forall \pi : [\pi \models A] = \bot$

$[M \models A \Rightarrow C] = 0 \leftrightarrow \exists \pi : [\pi \models A] = 1$ and $[\pi \models C] = 0$

$[M \models A \Rightarrow C] = X \leftrightarrow [M \models A \Rightarrow C] \neq 0$ and $\exists \pi : [\pi \models A] = 1$ and $[\pi \models C] = X$

t	n_1	n_2	n_3	n_4	n_5	n_6
0	X	X	X	0	X	0
1	X	X	0	X	1	X

Fig. 3. Symbolic Simulation

As in [15], an *antecedent failure* is the case where $[M \models A \Rightarrow C] = \bot$. For a node n at time t we say that "(n, t) is X-possible", if there exists a trajectory π and an assignment ϕ such that $\phi(\pi)(t)(n)$ is X. If n at time t is also constrained by C, then we say that it is *undecided*. In that case, $[M \models A \Rightarrow C] = X$. Consider the circuit and STE assertion in Figure 4(a). The table in Figure 3 corresponds to a symbolic simulation of this assertion. n_5 at time 1 is evaluated to 1, and thus the assertion holds.

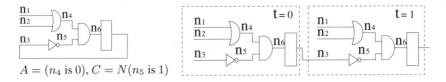

$A = (n_4 \text{ is } 0), C = N(n_5 \text{ is } 1)$

Fig. 4. (a) A circuit M (b) An Unrolling of M to depth 2

2.2   Refinement in STE

A major strength of STE is the use of abstraction. The abstraction is determined by the assignment of the value X to input nodes in M by A. However, if the abstraction is too coarse, then there is not enough information for proving or falsifying the STE assertion. That is, $[M \models A \Rightarrow C] = X$.

The common abstraction and refinement process in STE consists of the following steps: the user writes an STE assertion $A \Rightarrow C$ for M, and receives a result from STE. If $[M \models A \Rightarrow C] = \bot$ (an antecedent failure), then there is a contradiction between A and M, and the user has to write a new assertion. If $[M \models A \Rightarrow C] = 0$, or $[M \models A \Rightarrow C] = 1$, the process ends with the corresponding result. If $[M \models A \Rightarrow C] = X$, a refinement is required. In this case, there is some *X-possible* node (n, t), which is undecided. The user has to manually decide how to refine the specification such that the X truth value will be eliminated.

For automatic refinement, we assume that the STE assertion correctly describes the desired behavior of the model, and that disagreements between the assertion and the model originate from errors in the model. Thus, the refinement should preserve the meaning of the original assertion. Note, that refinement is only performed in cases where an antecedent failure does not occur.

An automatic refinement can be obtained by creating a new antecedent for the STE assertion. The refinement of A should preserve the semantics of $A \Rightarrow C$. Formally, let $A_{new} \Rightarrow C$ denote the refined assertion and let $runs(M)$ denote the set of all concrete trajectories of M. We require that $A_{new} \Rightarrow C$ holds on $runs(M)$ iff $A \Rightarrow C$ holds on $runs(M)$.

Refinement Strategy. In [15], refinement steps add constraints to A by forcing the values of some input nodes at certain times to the value of *fresh symbolic variables*. That is, symbolic variables that are not already in $\mathcal{V}$. By initializing an input (in, t) with a fresh symbolic variable instead of X, the value of (in, t) is accurately represented, and knowledge about its effect on M is added. However, it does not constrain input behavior that was allowed by A, nor does it allow input behavior that was forbidden by A. Thus, the semantics of A is preserved. In [15] it is proven that if $A_{new} \Rightarrow C$ holds in M, then so does $A \Rightarrow C$. Also, if $A_{new} \Rightarrow C$ yields a counterexample ce, then ce is also a counterexample w.r.t $A \Rightarrow C$.

2.3   Causality and Responsibility

In this section, we review the definitions of causality and responsibility. We start with causality. The most intuitive definition of causality is *counterfactual causality*, going back to Hume [9],which is formally defined as follows.

Definition 1 (Counterfactual causality). *We say that an event A is a counterfactual cause of event B if the following conditions hold: (a) both A and B are true, and (b) if we assign A the value false, then B becomes false. We sometimes refer to the dependence of B on A as a counterfactual dependence.*

In this paper, we use a simplified version of the definition of causality from [8]. In order to define causality formally, we start with the definition of causal models (again, due to [8]).

Definition 2 (Causal model). *A causal model M is a tuple $\langle \mathcal{U}, \mathcal{D}, \mathcal{R}, \mathcal{F} \rangle$, where $\mathcal{U}$ is the set of exogenous variables (that is, variables whose value is determined by constraints outside of the model), $\mathcal{D}$ is the set of endogenous variables (that is, variables whose value is determined by the model and the current assignment to $\mathcal{D}$), $\mathcal{R}$ associates with each variable in $\mathcal{U} \cup \mathcal{D}$ a nonempty range of values, and the function $\mathcal{F}$ associates with every variable $Y \in \mathcal{D}$ a function F_Y that describes how the value of Y is determined by the values of all other variables in $\mathcal{U} \cup \mathcal{D}$.*

A context $\vec{d}$ is an assignment for variables in $\mathcal{D}$ (the values of variables in $\mathcal{U}$ are considered constant).

In this paper we restrict our attention to models in which variables do not depend on each other.

A *causal formula* φ is a formula over the set of variables $\mathcal{U} \cup \mathcal{D}$. A causal formula φ is true or false in a causal model given a context $\vec{d}$. We write $(M, \vec{d}) \models \varphi$ if φ is true in M given a context $\vec{d}$. We write $(M, \vec{d}) \models [\vec{Z} \leftarrow \vec{z}]\varphi$ if φ holds in the model M

given the context $\vec{d}$ and the assignment $\vec{z}$ to the variables in the set $\vec{Z} \subset \mathcal{V}$, such that $\vec{z}$ overrides $\vec{d}$ for variables in $\vec{Z}$.

With these definitions in hand, we can give the simplified definition of cause based on the definition in [8]. The main simplification is due to the fact that in our models, variables do not depend on each other, and thus there is no need to explicitly check various cases of mutual dependence between variables.

Definition 3 (Cause). *For a constant y, we say that $Y = y$ is a* cause *of φ in $(M, \vec{d})$ if the following conditions hold:*

AC1. $(M, \vec{d}) \models (Y = y) \wedge \varphi$.

AC2. *There exists a partition $(\vec{Z}, \vec{W})$ of $\mathcal{D}$ with $Y \in \vec{Z}$ and some setting $(y', \vec{w}')$ of the variables in $Y \cup \vec{W}$ such that:*

    (a) $(M, \vec{d}) \models [Y \leftarrow y', \vec{W} \leftarrow \vec{w}']\neg\varphi$. That is, changing $(Y, \vec{W})$ from their original assignment $(y, \vec{w})$ (where $\vec{w} \subset \vec{d}$) to $(y', \vec{w}')$ changes φ from **true** *to* **false**.

    (b) $(M, \vec{d}) \models [Y \leftarrow y, \vec{W} \leftarrow \vec{w}']\varphi$. That is, setting $\vec{W}$ to $\vec{w}'$ should have no effect on φ as long as Y has the value y.

Essentially, Definition 3 says that $Y = y$ is a cause of φ if both $Y = y$ and φ hold in the current context $\vec{d}$, and there exists a change in $\vec{d}$ that creates a counterfactual dependence between $Y = y$ and φ.

The definition of responsibility introduced in [4] refines the "all-or-nothing" concept of causality by measuring the degree of responsibility of $Y = y$ for the truth value of φ in $(M, \vec{d})$. The following definition is due to [4]:

Definition 4 (Responsibility). *Let k be the smallest size of $\vec{W} \subset \mathcal{D}$ such that $\vec{W}$ satisfies the condition* **AC2** *in Definition 3. Then, the* degree of responsibility (DoR) *of $Y = y$ for the value of φ in $(M, \vec{d})$, denoted $dr((M, \vec{d}), Y = y, \varphi)$, is $1/(k+1)$.*

Thus, the degree of responsibility measures the minimal number of changes that have to be made in $\vec{d}$ in order to make $Y = y$ a counterfactual cause of φ. If $Y = y$ is not a cause of φ in $(M, \vec{d})$, then the minimal set $\vec{W}$ in Definition 4 is taken to have cardinality ∞, and thus the degree of responsibility of $Y = y$ is 0. If φ counterfactually depends on $Y = y$, its degree of responsibility is 1. In other cases the degree of responsibility is strictly between 0 and 1. Note that $Y = y$ is a cause of φ iff the degree of responsibility of $Y = y$ for the value of φ is greater than 0.

As we argue in Section 3.1, in our setting it is reasonable to attribute weights to the variables in order to capture the cost of changing their value. Thus, we use the *weighted* version of the definition of the degree of responsibility, also introduced in [4]:

Definition 5 (Weighted responsibility). *Let $wt(Y)$ be the weight of Y and $wt(\vec{W})$ the sum of the weights of variables in the set $\vec{W}$. Then, the* weighted degree of responsibility *of $Y = y$ for φ is $wt(Y)/(k + wt(Y))$, where k is the minimal $wt(\vec{W})$ of a $\vec{W} \subset \mathcal{D}$ for which AC2 holds. This definition agrees with Definition 4 if the weights of all variables are 1.*

Remark 1. We note that in general, there is no connection between the degree of responsibility of $Y = y$ for the value of φ and a probability that φ counterfactually depends on

$Y = y$. Basically, responsibility is concerned with the minimal number of changes in a given context that creates a counterfactual dependence, whereas probability is measured over the space of all possible assignments to variables in $\mathcal{D}$.

3 Responsibility in STE Graphs

In section 4 we will show how to refine STE assertions by using the degree of responsibility (dr) of inputs for *X-possible* nodes. Consider a model circuit M, and an STE assertion $A \Rightarrow C$, such that $[M \models A \Rightarrow C] = X$ and let r be an undecided node. In this section we show how M can be viewed as a causal model, and present an algorithm for computing the degree of responsibility of an input to M for "r is *X-possible*".

3.1 STE Circuits as Causal Models

In order to verify the assertion $A \Rightarrow C$, M has to be simulated k times, where k is the *maximal depth* of A and C. We create a graph by unrolling M k times. Each node $n \in M$ has k instances in the new graph. The ith instance of node n represents node n at time i. In the new graph, the connectivity of the input and gate nodes remains the same. The latches are connected such that the input to a latch at time t are the nodes at time $t - 1$, and the latch is an input to nodes at time t. Due to the new connectivity of the latches, and since M does not have combinational cycles, the unrolled graph is a *DAG*. The leaves of the new graph are k instances of each of the inputs to M, and the initial values of the latches.

We assume that the only nodes assigned by A are leaves. It is straightforward to extend the discussion to internal nodes that are assigned by A, and to nodes that get their value from propagating the assignments of A. Consider the circuit and STE assertion in Figure 4(a). The corresponding unrolling is shown in Figure 4(b). $t = 0$ and $t = 1$ are two instances of the circuit. The inputs to the latch n_3 in $t = 1$ are the nodes of $t = 0$, thus eliminating the cycle of the original circuit. The inputs to the new circuit are the first instance of n_3 (the initial value of the latch), and the two instances of n_1 and n_2. From herein we denote by M the unrolled graph of the circuit.

Regarding M as a *causal model* requires the following definitions: 1) a set of variables and their partition into $\mathcal{U}$ and $\mathcal{D}$, the exogenous and endogenous variables, respectively. 2) $\mathcal{R}$, the range of the endogenous variables. 3) values for the exogenous variables $\mathcal{U}$. 4) a context $\vec{d}$, which is an assignment to the variables in $\mathcal{D}$. 5) $\mathcal{F}$, a function which associates each variable $Y \in D$ with a function F_Y that describes its dependence in all the other variables.

We define the inputs of M to be the variables of the causal model. The inputs that are assigned 1 or 0 by the antecedent A are considered the exogenous variables $\mathcal{U}$, and their values are determined by A. The values of these variables cannot change, and are viewed as part of the model M. The rest of the inputs to M are the endogenous variables $\mathcal{D}$. The range of the variables in $\mathcal{D}$ is $\{0, 1, X\} \cup \mathcal{V}$, where $\mathcal{V}$ is the set of symbolic variables used by A.[1] The context $\vec{d}$ is the current assignment to $\mathcal{D}$, imposed

---

[1] For simplicity of presentation, we do not distinguish between a symbolic variable $v_i \in \mathcal{V}$ and its corresponding element in $\mathcal{R}$.

by the antecedent A. Last, since the variables are inputs to a circuit, their values do not depend on each other. Therefore, the function F associates each variable with the identity function.

Next we have to define a causal formula φ. For an undecided node r, we want to compute the responsibility of the leaves having X values for "r is X-possible". We define the *causal formula* φ to be "r is X-possible". Since the context $\vec{d}$ is imposed by the antecedent A, and Since "r is X-possible" holds under A, we have $(M, \vec{d}) \models \varphi$.

We will compute a weighted degree of responsibility, as described in Definition 5. We choose $wt(n) = 1$ if $\vec{d}(n) \in \mathcal{V}$, and $wt(n) = 2$ if $\vec{d}(n) = X$. Next we explain this choice of weights. For computing the degree of responsibility, we consider changes in the context $\vec{d}$ that replace the assignments to some of the variables in $\mathcal{D}$ from X or $v_i \in \mathcal{V}$ to a Boolean value. When running STE, a symbolic variable may assume either of the Boolean values. On the other hand, a leaf that is assigned X cannot take a Boolean value without changing the antecedent of the STE assertion. Therefore, we consider changing $\vec{d}$ for a variable n such that $\vec{d}(n) \in \mathcal{V}$ to be easier than for a variable n such that $\vec{d}(n) = X$. Thus, our choice of weights takes into account the way in which STE regards X and $v_i \in \mathcal{V}$.

We have shown how an unrolled model M can be viewed as a causal model. Let $I_X(r)$ and $I_V(r)$ be the sets of leaves in $BCOI(r)$, for which A assigns X and symbolic variables, respectively. From herein, for $l \in I_X(r)$, we denote by $dr(M, l, r)$ the degree of responsibility of "l is X" for "r is X-possible". Next we present an algorithm that computes an approximate degree of responsibility of each leaf in $I_X(r)$ for "r is X-possible".

3.2 Computing Degree of Responsibility in Trees

Computing responsibility in circuits is known to be $\text{FP}^{\Sigma_2^P[\log n]}$-complete [2] in general [4], and thus intractable. In order to achieve an efficiently computable approximation, our algorithm is inspired by the algorithm for read-once formulas in [3]. It involves one traversal of the circuit for each $l \in I_X(r)$ and its overall complexity is only quadratic in the size of M. We start by describing an exact algorithm for M which is a tree, and then introduce the changes for M which is a DAG.

We define the following values that are used by our algorithm.

- $c_0(n, M)$: the minimal sum of weights of leaves in $I_X(r) \cup I_V(r)$ that we have to assign 0 or 1 in order to make n evaluate to 0.
- $c_1(n, M)$: the minimal sum of weights of leaves in $I_X(r) \cup I_V(r)$ that we have to assign 0 or 1 in order to make n evaluate to 1.
- $s(n, M, l)$: the minimal sum of weights of leaves in $I_X(r) \cup I_V(r)$ that we have to assign 0 or 1 in order to make "n is X-possible" counterfactually depend on "l is X". If there is no such number, that is, there is no change in the context that causes this dependability, we define $s(n, M, l) = \infty$.

If clear from the context, we omit M from the notation of c_0, c_1 and s.

---

[2] $\text{FP}^{\Sigma_2^P[\log n]}$ is the class of functions computable in polynomial time with $\log n$ queries to oracle in Σ_2.

We would like to compute the degree of responsibility of every leaf $l \in I_X(r)$ for "r is *X-possible*". Therefore, for each $l \in I_X(r)$, our algorithm computes $s(r, l)$. We denote by $A(n)$ the assignment to node n in M, imposed by A. We discuss a model M with AND and NOT operators. Extending the discussion to $OR, NAND$ and NOR operators is straightforward. Given r and $l \in I_X(r)$, our algorithm computes $s(r, l)$ by starting at r, and executing the recursive computation described next. Note that only values that are actually needed for determining $s(r, l)$ are computed.

For a node n, $s(n, l)$ is recursively computed by:

- For n a leaf: if $(n = l)$ then $s(n, l) = 0$, because the value of l counterfactually depends on itself. Otherwise, $s(n, l) = \infty$ since a leaf does not depend on other leaves.
- For $n = n_1 \wedge \ldots \wedge n_m$: W.l.o.g. we assume that l belongs to the subtree of M rooted in n_1 (since M is a tree, l belongs to a subtree of only one input of n). In order to make the value of n counterfactually depend on the value of l, all input to n, except for n_1, should be 1, and the value of n_1 should counterfactually depend on the value of l. Thus, $s(n, l) = s(n_1, l) + \sum_{i=2}^{m} c_1(n_i)$.
- For $n = \neg n_1$: $s(n, l) = s(n_1, l)$, since "n is *X-possible*" iff "n_1 is *X-possible*".

For a node n, $c_0(n)$ and $c_1(n)$ are recursively computed by:

- For n a leaf:
  - If $A(n) = 0$, $c_0(n) = 0$, because no change in the assignments to $I_X(r) \cup I_V(r)$ is required. $c_1(n) = \infty$, because no change in the assignments to $I_X(r) \cup I_V(r)$ will change the value of n.
  - Similarly, if $A(n) = 1$, $c_1(n) = 0$ and $c_0(n) = \infty$.
  - If $A(n) = X$, $c_0(n) = c_1(n) = 2$, because only the value of n has to be changed, and the weight of n is 2.
  - If n is associated with a symbolic variable, $c_0(n) = c_1(n) = 1$, because only the value of n has to be changed, and the weight of n is 1.
- For $n = n_1, \wedge \ldots \wedge n_m$:
  - It is enough to change the value of one of its inputs to 0 in order to change the value of n to 0, thus $c_0(n) = \min_{i \in \{1, \ldots, n\}} c_0(n_i)$.
  - The values of all the inputs of n should be 1 in order for n to be 1, thus $c_1(n) = \sum_{i=1}^{n} c_1(n_i)$.
- For $n = \neg n_1$
  - $c_1(n) = c_0(n_1)$ and $c_0(n) = c_1(n_1)$, as any assignment that gives n_1 the value 0 or 1, gives n the value 1 or 0, respectively.

The computation above directly follows the definitions of c_0, c_1 and s, and thus its proof of correctness is straightforward. For a node r and leaf l, computing the values $c_0(n), c_1(n)$ and $s(n, l)$ for all $n \in BCOI(r)$ is linear in the size of M. Therefore, given r, computing $s(r, l)$ for all $l \in I_X(r)$ is at most quadratic in the size of M. Note that for a node n, the values $c_0(n)$ and $c_1(n)$ do not depend on a particular leaf, and thus are computed only once.

We demonstrate the computations done by our algorithm on the circuit in Figure 5. The antecedent associates l_2, l_4 and l_1, l_3 with symbolic variables and X, respectively. For node out, "out is X-possible" holds. We want to compute $s(out, l_3)$. l_3 is in the subtree of n_2. Therefore, $s(out, l_3) = c_1(n_1) + s(n_2, l_3)$. Since n_1 is an AND gate, $c_1(n_1) = c_1(l_1) + c_1(l_2)$. n_2 is also an AND gate, and therefore $s(n_2, l_3) = c_1(l_4) + s(l_3, l_3)$. The weight of the leaves is according to their assignment. Therefore, $c_1(l_2) = c_1(l_4) = 1$ and $c_1(l_1) = 2$. Additionally, $s(l_3, l_3) = 0$.

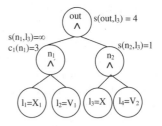

Fig. 5. Computing Responsibility

Finally, the degree of responsibility of "l is X" for "r is X-possible", $dr(M, l, r)$ is $\frac{2}{s(r,l)+2}$. If $s(r, l) = \infty$, then $dr(M, l, r) = 0$, which matches Definition 5. In our example, $dr(M, l_3, out) = \frac{2}{s(out,l_3)+2} = \frac{1}{3}$.

3.3   Computing an Approximate Degree of Responsibility in DAGs

We now introduce a change to the definition of $s(n, l)$, resulting in an efficiently computable approximation of the degree of responsibility in DAGs, as required for STE.

For a DAG M, and a node $n = n_1 \wedge \ldots \wedge n_m$, we no longer assume that l belongs to a subtree of only one input of n. Let $N^S = \{n_i | s(n_i, l) \neq \infty, i \in \{1, \ldots, m\}\}$, and let $N^\infty = \{n_i | s(n_i, l) = \infty, i \in \{1, \ldots, m\}\}$. We define $s(n, l)$ to be:

$$s(n, l) = \sum_{n_i \in N^S} \frac{s(n_i, l)}{|N^S|} + \sum_{n_i \in N^\infty} c_1(n_i)$$

Recall that $dr(M, l, n)$ is inversely proportional to $s(n, l)$. Thus, our new definition gives higher degree of responsibility to leaves that belong to subtrees of multiple inputs of n. Such leaves are likely to be control signals, or otherwise more effective candidates for refinement than other variables.

We demonstrate the effect of this definition on the multiplexer in Figure 6. d_1 and d_2 are the data inputs to the multiplexer, and c is its control input. If $c = 1$, then $out = d_1$, else, $out = d_2$. The value $s(out, d_1)$ is given by $s(out, d_1) = c_0(n_2) + s(n_1, d_1) = 4$. The same computation applies to d_2. On the other hand, c belongs to the subtrees of both n_1 and n_2. Therefore, $s(out, c) = \frac{s(n_1,c)+s(n_2,c)}{2} = 2$. Consequently, $dr(c, out) = \frac{1}{2}$, whereas $dr(d_1, out) = dr(d_2, out) = \frac{1}{3}$.

The rest of the algorithm remains as in Section 3.2. Note that since M is a *DAG*, rather than a tree, not changing the computation of c_0 and c_1 makes it an approximation, as it does not take into account possible dependencies between inputs of nodes.

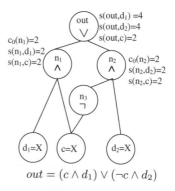

$$out = (c \wedge d_1) \vee (\neg c \wedge d_2)$$

Fig. 6. A multiplexer

4   Applying Responsibility to Automatic Refinement

Refinement of an STE assertion is required when the return value of an STE run is X. In that case, the set of undecided nodes is returned by STE. The goal of the refinement is to add information such that undecided nodes become decided. In this section we show how we employ the concept of responsibility for efficiently refining STE assertions.

The outline of the refinement algorithm follows the discussion in section 2.2: First, a refinement goal r is selected from within the set of undecided nodes. Then, a set of input nodes in $I_X(r)$ is chosen, to be initialized to new symbolic variables.

Choosing a Refinement goal. Our refinement algorithm chooses a single refinement goal on each refinement iteration. This way, the verification process might be stopped early if a constraint over a single node does not hold, without handling the other undecided nodes. Additionally, conceptual relations between the undecided nodes may make them depend on a similar set of inputs. Thus, refinement targeted at one node may be useful for the other nodes as well. For example, all bits of a data vector are typically affected by the same set of control signals.

We would like to add as little symbolic variables as possible. Thus, from within the set of undecided nodes, we choose the nodes with the minimal number of inputs in its BCOI, and among these we choose the one with the minimal number of nodes in its BCOI. If multiple nodes have the minimal number of inputs in their BCOI, we arbitrarily pick one of them. This approach has also been taken in [15].

Choosing Input Nodes. Given a refinement goal r, we have to choose a subset of nodes $I_{ref} \subseteq I_X(r)$ that will be initialized to new symbolic variables, trying to prevent the occurrence of "r is X-possible". We choose the nodes in $I_X(r)$ with the highest degree of responsibility for "r is X-possible", as computed by the algorithm in Section 3.3. These nodes have the most effect on "r is X-possible", and are likely to be the most effective nodes for refinement. Our experimental results support this choice of nodes, as shown in Section 5.

Given the refinement algorithm described above, we construct *RespSTE*, an iterative algorithm for verifying STE assertions: for a model M and an STE assertion $A \Rightarrow C$, while STE returns $[M \models A \Rightarrow C] = X$, RespSTE iteratively chooses a refinement root $r \in M$, computes the degree of responsibility of each leaf $l \in I_X(r)$ for "r is X-possible" and introduces new symbolic variables to A, for all leaves with the highest degree of responsibility. A pseudo code of RespSTE is given in Figure 7.

$RespSTE(M, A, C)$
while $[M \models A \Rightarrow C] = X$ **do**
$\quad r \leftarrow$ choose refinement target
$\quad$ **for all** $l \in I_X(r)$ **do**
$\quad\quad$ compute $dr(r, l)$
$\quad$ **end for**
$\quad max \leftarrow max\{dr(l, r)) | l \in I_X(r)\}$
$\quad I_{ref} \leftarrow \{l | l \in I_X(r), dr(l, r) = max\}$
$\quad \forall l_i \in I_{ref}$, add symbolic variable v_{l_i} to A
end while

Fig. 7. RespSTE

5   Experimental Results

For evaluating our algorithm $RespSTE$, presented in Section 4, we implemented and used it in conjunction with *Forte*, a BDD based STE tool by Intel [14].

For our experiments we used the Content Addressable Memory (*CAM*) module from Intel's GSTE tutorial, and IBM's Calculator 2 design [16]. These models and their specifications are interesting and challenging for model checking. All experiments use dedicated computers with 3.2Ghz Intel Pentium CPU, and 3GB RAM, running Linux operating system.

5.1   Verifying CAM Module

A CAM is a memory module that for each data entry holds a tag entry. Upon receiving an associative read (aread) command, the CAM samples the input "tagin". If a matching tag is found in the CAM, it gives the "hit" output signal the value 1, and outputs the corresponding data entry to "dout". Otherwise, "hit" is given the value 0. The verification of the aread operation using STE is described in [11]. The CAM that we used is shown in Figure 8. It contains 16 entries. Each entry has a data size of 64 bits and a tag size of 8 bits. It contains 1152 latches, 83 inputs and 5064 combinational gates.

We checked the CAM against three assertions. For all the assertions, RespSTE added the smallest number of symbolic variables required for proving or falsifying the assertion. Next we discuss Assertion 1.

Given $\overrightarrow{TAG}$ and $\overrightarrow{A}$, vectors of symbolic variables, Assertion 1 is: (tagin is $\overrightarrow{TAG}$) $\land$ (taddr is $\overrightarrow{A}$)$\land$(twrite is 1)$\land$**N** ((aread is 1)$\land$ (tagin is $\overrightarrow{TAG}$)) $\implies$ **N** (hit is 1). This is to check that if a tag value $\overrightarrow{TAG}$ is written to an address $\overrightarrow{A}$ in the tag memory at time 0, and at time 1 $\overrightarrow{TAG}$ is read, then it should be found

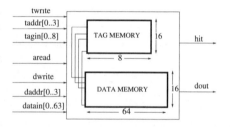

Fig. 8. Content Addressable Memory

in the tag memory, and hit should be 1. If at time 1 there is no write operation to the tag memory (($twrite$, 1) = 0), then $\overrightarrow{TAG}$ should be found in address $\overrightarrow{A}$. If ($twrite$, 1) = 1, $\overrightarrow{TAG}$ should still be found, since it is written again to the tag memory. Therefore, Assertion 1 should pass. However, since twrite and taddr at time 1 are X, the CAM cannot determine whether to write the value of ($tagin$, 1) to the tag memory, and to which tag entry to write it. As a result, the entire tag memory at time 1 is X, causing (hit, 1) to be X. Thus, $[M \models A \Rightarrow C] = X$. In two consecutive refinement iterations, ($twrite$, 1) and ($tadder$, 1) are associated with new symbolic variables, and the assertion passes. The refinement steps of Assertion 1 are presented in Figure 10(a). Each row in the table describes a single refinement iteration, the name of the goal node, and the name and time of the inputs for which symbolic variables were added.

5.2   Verifying Calculator 2

Calculator 2 design [16], shown in Figure 9, is used as a case study design in simulation based verification. It contains 2781 latches, 157 inputs and 56960 combinational gates. The calculator has two internal arithmetic pipelines: one for add/sub and one for shifts. It receives commands from 4 different ports, and outputs the results accordingly. The calculator supports 4 types of commands: add, sub, shift right and shift left. The response is 1 for good, 2 for underflow, overflow or invalid command, 3 for an internal error and 0 for no response. When running the calculator, reset has to be 1 for the first 3 cycles.

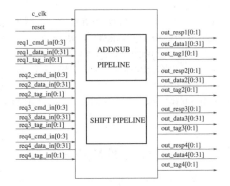

Fig. 9. Calculator

We checked the calculator against four assertions. For all but one of the assertions, RespSTE added the smallest number of symbolic variables required for proving or falsifying the assertion. Next we discuss Assertion 2.

Assertion 2 sets the command sent by a port P_i to add. The msb bits of the sent data are constrained to 0 to avoid an overflow. No constraints are imposed on the commands sent by other ports. The requirement is that the output data for P_i would match the expected data. Assertion 2 fails due to an erroneous specification. The calculator gives priority to the lower indexed ports. Thus, if both ports 1 and 3 send an add command, port 3 does not receive a response at the first possible cycle. Due to the implementation of the priority queue, commands of at least 3 ports have to be definite for falsifying the assertion. $I_X((out\_resp2[0], 7))$ contains cmd, data and tag inputs of all ports at cycles 3 and 4. Out of them, RespSTE added the least number of inputs required for falsifying the assertion. The refinement steps of Assertion 2 are presented in Figure 10(b).

5.3   Evaluation of Results

In [15], an algorithm called *autoSTE* for automatic refinement in STE, is presented. *autoSTE* exploits the results of the STE run, as computed by *Forte*, in order to identify trajectories along which all nodes have the value X. The input nodes of these trajectories are the candidates for refinement. Heuristics are used for choosing subsets of these candidates.

As.	It	Goal	Added Vars
1	1	hit,1	twrite,1
1	2	hit,1	taddr [0:3], 1

(a) CAM

As.	It	Goal	Added Vars
2	1	out_resp2 [0],7	req1_cmd [0:2],3
2	2	out_resp2 [0],7	req1_cmd [3],3
2	3	out_resp2 [0],7	req2_cmd [0:3],3

(b) Calculator 2

Fig. 10. Refinement Steps

We compared our experimental results with those obtained by *autoSTE*. For the sake of comparison, we used in our experiments the same parametric representation of the STE assertions as in [15]. The final results of RespSTE and its comparison with autoSTE are shown in Table 1.

Table 1. Experimental Results. AutoSTE is the algorithm presented in [15]. "Iterations" is the number of refinement iterations that were performed, "Time" is the total runtime in seconds until verification / falsification of the property, "Vars" is the total number of symbolic variables that were added by the refinements, and "BDD Nodes" is the number of BDD nodes used by Forte.

			RespSTE				AutoSTE			
		result	Iterations	Vars	BDD Nodes	Time	Iterations	Vars	BDD Nodes	Time
CAM	1	pass	2	5	3201	2	2	5	4768	3
	2	fail	5	11	30726	5	7	11	57424	20
	3	fail	1	8	14127	3	3	13	29006	17
Calc 2	1	fail	2	5	7735	32	2	2	6241	87
	2	fail	3	8	19717	25	2	8	20134	100
	3	fail	1	8	262201	43	1	8	530733	220
	4	pass	4	16	14005	27	11	16	17323	494

The comparison shows a significant speedup in all of the assertions, and up to $18.5\times$ speedup in the larger ones. A significant reduction in BDD nodes is also gained in most of the assertions. For some of the assertions, RespSTE added less symbolic variables or required less refinement iterations than autoSTE. The overall performance of RespSTE was better than autoSTE even when this was not the case.

Altogether, our experiments demonstrated that using the degree of responsibility as a measure for refinement is a good choice. It provides a quantitative measure of the importance of each input to an undecided node being *X-possible*. By examining these values, we conclude that this quantitative measure reflects the actual importance of the inputs in the model. The results obtained by RespSTE agree with the decisions of a user who is familiar with the circuit. When using these results for automatic refinement, the quality of the results demonstrates itself in the number of refinement iterations that were required, and in the total number of symbolic variables that were added to the antecedent.

Acknowledgements. We thank Rotem Oshman and Rachel Tzoref for the fruitful discussions, and the reviewers for their useful comments.

References

1. Adams, S., Bjork, M., Melham, T., Seger, C.: Automatic Abstraction in Symbolic Trajectory Evaluation. In: FMCAD 2007 (2007)
2. Chen, Y., He, Y., Xie, F., Yang, J.: Automatic Abstraction Refinement for Generalized Symbolic Trajectory Evaluation. In: FMCAD 2007 (2007)
3. Chockler, H., Halpern, J.Y., Kupferman, O.: What causes a system to satisfy a specification? In: ACM TOCL (to appear)
4. Chockler, H., Halpern, J.Y.: Responsibility and blame: a structural-model approach. Journal of Artificial Intelligence Research (JAIR) 22, 93–115 (2004)
5. Chou, C.-T.: The mathematical foundation of symbolic trajectory evaluation. In: Halbwachs, N., Peled, D.A. (eds.) CAV 1999. LNCS, vol. 1633, pp. 196–207. Springer, Heidelberg (1999)

 6. Clarke, E.M., Grumberg, O., Jha, S., Lu, Y., Veith, H.: Counterexample-guided abstraction refinement. In: Emerson, E.A., Sistla, A.P. (eds.) CAV 2000. LNCS, vol. 1855, Springer, Heidelberg (2000)
 7. Grumberg, O., Schuster, A., Yadgar, A.: 3-Valued Circuit SAT for STE with Automatic Refinement. In: Namjoshi, K.S., Yoneda, T., Higashino, T., Okamura, Y. (eds.) ATVA 2007. LNCS, vol. 4762, Springer, Heidelberg (2007)
 8. Halpern, J.Y., Pearl, J.: Causes and explanations: A structural-model approach — part 1: Causes. In: Uncertainty in Artificial Intelligence: Proceedings of the Seventeenth Conference (UAI-2001), pp. 194–202. Morgan Kaufmann, San Francisco (2001)
 9. Hume, D.: A treatise of human nature. John Noon, London (1739)
10. Kurshan, R.P.: Computer-Aided Verification of coordinating processes - the automata theoretic approach (1994)
11. Pandey, M., Raimi, R., Bryant, R.E., Abadir, M.S.: Formal verification of content addressable memories using symbolic trajectory evaluation. DAC 00, 167 (1997)
12. Roorda, J.-W., Claessen, K.: Sat-based assistance in abstraction refinement for symbolic trajectory evaluation. In: Ball, T., Jones, R.B. (eds.) CAV 2006. LNCS, vol. 4144, pp. 175–189. Springer, Heidelberg (2006)
13. Seger, C.-J.H., Bryant, R.E.: Formal verification by symbolic evaluation of partially-ordered trajectories. Formal Methods in System Design 6(2) (1995)
14. Seger, C.-J.H., Jones, R.B., O'Leary, J.W., Melham, T.F., Aagaard, M., Barrett, C., Syme, D.: An industrially effective environment for formal hardware verification. IEEE Trans. on Computer-Aided Design of Integrated Circuits and Systems 24(9) (2005)
15. Tzoref, R., Grumberg, O.: Automatic refinement and vacuity detection for symbolic trajectory evaluation. In: Ball, T., Jones, R.B. (eds.) CAV 2006. LNCS, vol. 4144, pp. 190–204. Springer, Heidelberg (2006)
16. Wile, B., Roesner, W., Goss, J.: Comprehensive Functional Verification: The Complete Industry Cycle. Morgan Kaufmann, San Francisco (2005)
17. Wilson, J.C.: Symbolic Simulation Using Automatic Abstraction of Internal Node Values. PhD thesis, Stanford University, Dept. of Electrical Engineering (2001)

Reasoning Algebraically About P-Solvable Loops

Laura Kovács*

EPFL, Switzerland
laura.kovacs@epfl.ch

Abstract. We present a method for generating polynomial invariants for a sub-family of imperative loops operating on numbers, called the P-solvable loops. The method uses algorithmic combinatorics and algebraic techniques. The approach is shown to be complete for some special cases. By completeness we mean that it generates a set of polynomial invariants from which, under additional assumptions, any polynomial invariant can be derived. These techniques are implemented in a new software package Aligator written in *Mathematica* and successfully tried on many programs implementing interesting algorithms working on numbers.

1   Introduction

This paper discusses an approach for automatically generating polynomial equations as loop invariants by combining advanced techniques from algorithmic combinatorics and polynomial algebra. Polynomial invariants found by an automatic analysis are useful for program verification, as they provide non-trivial valid assertions about the program, and thus significantly simplify the verification task. Finding valid polynomial identities (i. e. invariants) has applications in many classical data flow analysis problems [21], e. g., constant propagation, discovery of symbolic constants, discovery of loop induction variables, etc.

Exploiting the symbolic manipulation capabilities of the computer algebra system *Mathematica*, the approach is implemented in a new software package called Aligator [17]. By using several combinatorial packages developed at RISC, Aligator includes algorithms for solving special classes of recurrence relations (those that are either Gosper-summable or C-finite) and generating polynomial dependencies among algebraic exponential sequences. Using Aligator, a complete set of polynomial invariants is successfully generated for numerous imperative programs working on numbers [17]; some of these examples are presented in this paper.

The key steps of our method for invariant generation are as follows.

(i) Assignment statements from the loop body are extracted. They form a system of *recurrence equations* describing the behavior of those loop variables that are changing at each loop iteration.

---

* The results presented here were obtained at the Research Institute for Symbolic Computation (RISC), Linz, Austria. The work was supported by BMBWK (Austrian Ministry of Education, Science, and Culture), BMWA (Austrian Ministry of Economy and Work) and MEC (Romanian Ministry of Education and Research) in the frame of the e-Austria Timişoara project, and by FWF (Austrian National Science Foundation) - SFB project F1302.

C.R. Ramakrishnan and J. Rehof (Eds.): TACAS 2008, LNCS 4963, pp. 249–264, 2008.

(ii) Methods of algorithmic combinatorics are used to *solve exactly* the recurrence equations, yielding the *closed form* for each loop variable.

(iii) *Algebraic dependencies* among possible exponential sequences of algebraic numbers occurring in the closed forms of the loop variables are derived using algebraic and combinatorial methods.

As a result of these steps, every program variable can be expressed as a polynomial of the initial values of variables (those when the loop is entered), the loop counter, and some new variables, where there are algebraic dependencies among the new variables.

(iv) Loop counters are then eliminated by polynomial methods to derive a finite set of polynomial identities among the program variables as invariants. From this finite set, under additional assumptions when the loop body contains conditionals branches, any polynomial identity that is a loop invariant can be derived.

In our approach to invariant generation, a family of imperative loops, called *P-solvable* (to stand for polynomial-solvable), is identified, for which test conditions in the loop and conditional branches are ignored and the value of each program variable is expressed as a polynomial of the initial values of variables, loop counter, and some new variables where there are algebraic dependencies among the new variables. We show that for such loops, polynomial invariants can be automatically generated. Many non-trivial algorithms working on numbers can be naturally implemented using P-solvable loops.

Further, if the bodies of these loops consist only of assignments whose right hand sides are polynomials of certain shape, then the approach generates a *complete* set of polynomial invariants of the loop from which any other polynomial invariant can be obtained.

Moreover, if the P-solvable loop bodies contain conditional branches as well, under additional assumptions the approach is proved to be also *complete* in generating a set of polynomial invariants of the loop from which any further polynomial invariant can be derived. We could not find any example of a P-solvable loop with conditional branches and assignments for which our approach fails to be complete. We thus conjecture that the imposed constraints cover a large class of imperative programs, and the completeness proof of our approach without the additional assumptions is a challenging task for further research.

The automatically obtained invariant assertions, together with the user-asserted non-polynomial invariant properties, can be subsequently used for proving the partial correctness of programs by generating appropriate verification conditions as first-order logical formulas. This verification process is supported in an imperative verification environment implemented in the *Theorema* system [2].

This paper extends our earlier experimental papers [18, 19] by the completeness and correctness results of the invariant generation algorithm, and by a complete treatment of the affine loops. We omit proofs, they can be found in [17].

The rest of the paper is organized as follows. Section 2 gives a brief overview on related work for invariant generation, followed by Section 3 containing the presentation of some theoretical notions that are used further in the paper. In Section 4 we present our method for polynomial invariant generation and illustrate the algorithm on concrete examples. Section 5 concludes with some ideas for the future work.

2 Related Work

Research into methods for automatically generating loop invariants goes a long way, starting with the works [8,12]. However, success was somewhat limited for cases where only few arithmetic operations (mainly additions) among program variables were involved. Recently, due to the increased computing power of hardware, as well as advances in methods for symbolic manipulation and automated theorem proving, the problem of automated invariant generation is once again getting considerable attention. Particularly, using the abstract interpretation framework [4], many researchers [22, 25, 26, 11] have proposed methods for automatically computing polynomial invariant identities using polynomial ideal theoretic algorithms.

In [22,26], the invariant generation problem is translated to a constraint solving problem. In [26], non-linear (algebraic) invariants are proposed as templates with parameters; constraints on parameters are generated (by forward propagation) and solved using the theory of ideals over polynomial rings. In [22], backward propagation is performed for non-linear programs (programs with non-linear assignments) without branch conditions, by computing a polynomial ideal that represents the weakest precondition for the validity of a *generic polynomial relation* at the target program point. Both approaches need to fix a priori the degree of a generic polynomial template being considered as an invariant. This is also the case in [11] where a method for invariant generation using *quantifier-elimination* [3] is proposed. A *parameterized* invariant formula at any given control point is hypothesized and constraints on parameters are generated by considering all paths through that control point. Solutions of these constraints on parameters are then used to substitute for parameters in a parameterized invariant formula to generate invariants.

A related approach for polynomial invariant generation without any a priori bound on the degree of polynomials is presented in [25]. It is observed that polynomial invariants constitute an ideal. Thus, the problem of finding all polynomial invariants reduces to computing a finite basis of the associated polynomial invariant ideal. This ideal is approximated using a fix-point procedure by computing iteratively the Gröbner bases of a certain polynomial ideal. The fixed point procedure is shown to terminate when the list of (conditional) assignments present in the loop constitutes a *solvable mapping*.

In our work we do not need to fix a priori the degree of a polynomial assertion, and do not use the abstract interpretation framework either. Instead, recurrence relations expressing the value of each program variable at the end of any iteration are formulated and solved exactly. Structural conditions are imposed on recurrence relations so that their closed form solutions can be obtained by advanced symbolic summation techniques. Since these closed form expressions can involve exponentials of algebraic numbers, algebraic dependencies among these exponentials need to be identified, which can be done automatically, unlike [25], where polynomial dependencies could be derived only for a special case of algebraic exponentials, namely, for rationals. Finally, for eliminating the loop counter and the variables standing for the exponential sequences in the loop counter from these closed form solutions expressed as polynomials, a Gröbner basis computation is performed; however, we do not need to perform Gröbner basis computations iteratively. Contrarily to [25] where completeness is always guaranteed, the completeness of our method for loops with conditional branches and assignments is proved only under additional assumptions over ideals of polynomial invariants. It is worth to be mentioned though that these additional constraints cover a wide class of loops, and we could not find any example for which the completeness of our approach is violated.

3   Theoretical Preliminaries

This section contains some definitions and facts about linear recurrences, ideals and algebraic dependencies. For additional details see [5, 7].

In what follows, $\mathbb{N}, \mathbb{Z}, \mathbb{Q}, \mathbb{R}$ denote respectively the set of natural, integer, rational and real numbers. Throughout this paper we assume that $\mathbb{K}$ is a field of characteristic zero (e.g. $\mathbb{Q}, \mathbb{R}$, etc.) and denote by $\bar{\mathbb{K}}$ its algebraic closure. All rings are commutative.

Definition 3.1. Sequences and Recurrences

- A univariate *sequence* in $\mathbb{K}$ is a function $f : \mathbb{N} \to \mathbb{K}$. By $f(n)$ we denote both the value of f at the point n and the whole sequence f itself.
- A *recurrence* for a sequence $f(n)$ is

$$f(n + r) = R(f(n), f(n + 1), \ldots, f(n + r - 1), n) \quad (n \in \mathbb{N}),$$

for some function $R : \mathbb{K}^{r+1} \to \mathbb{K}$, where r is a natural number, called the *order* of the recurrence.

The recurrence equation of $f(n)$ allows the computation of $f(n)$ for any $n \in \mathbb{N}$: first the previous values $f(1), \ldots, f(n - 1)$ are determined, and then $f(n)$ is obtained. A *solution to the recurrence* would be thus more suitable for getting the value of $f(n)$ for any n as a function of the recurrence index n. That is a *closed form* solution of $f(n)$. Since finding closed form expressions of recurrences in the general case is undecidable, it is necessary to distinguish among the type of recurrence equations. In what follows, several classes of recurrences will be briefly presented together with the algorithmic methods for solving them.

Definition 3.2. Gosper-summable and C-finite Recurrences [9, 28]

1. A *Gosper-summable recurrence* f(n) in $\mathbb{K}$ is a recurrence

$$f(n + 1) = f(n) + h(n + 1) \quad (n \in \mathbb{N}), \tag{1}$$

where $h(n)$ is a hypergeometric sequence in $\mathbb{K}$. Namely, $h(n)$ can be a product of factorials, binomials, rational-function terms and exponential expressions in the summation variable n (all these factors can be raised to an integer power).

2. A *C-finite recurrence* f(n) in $\mathbb{K}$ is a (homogeneous) linear recurrence with constant coefficients

$$f(n + r) = a_0 f(n) + a_1 f(n + 1) + \ldots + a_{r-1} f(n + r - 1) \quad (n \in \mathbb{N}), \tag{2}$$

where $r \in \mathbb{N}$ is the *order* of the recurrence, and $a_0, \ldots, a_{r-1}$ are constants from $\mathbb{K}$ with $a_0 \neq 0$. By writing x^i for each $f(n + i)$, $i = 0, \ldots, r$, the corresponding *characteristic polynomial* $c(x)$ of f(n) is

$$c(x) = x^r - a_0 - a_1 x - \cdots - a_{r-1} x^{r-1}.$$

Computation of Closed Forms

(i) The closed-form solution of a Gosper-summable recurrence can be exactly computed [9]; for doing so, we use the recurrence solving package zb [23], implemented in *Mathematica* by the RISC Combinatorics group. For example, given the Gosper-summable recurrence $f(n+1) = f(n) + \frac{1}{2^{n+1}}$, $n \geq 0$, with the initial value $f(0)$, we obtain its closed form $f(n) = f(0) + 2 - 2 * 2^{-n}$.

(ii) A crucial and elementary fact about a C-finite recurrence $f(n)$ in $\mathbb{K}$ is that it always admits a closed form solution [7]. Its closed form is

$$f(n) = p_1(n)\theta_1^n + \cdots + p_s(n)\theta_s^n, \tag{3}$$

where $\theta_1, \ldots, \theta_s \in \bar{\mathbb{K}}$ are the distinct roots of the characteristic polynomial of $f(n)$, and $p_i(n)$ is a polynomial in n whose degree is less than the multiplicity of the root θ_i, $i = 1, \ldots, s$. The closed form (3) of $f(n)$ is called a *C-finite expression*.

An additional nice property of C-finite recurrences is that an *inhomogeneous* linear recurrence with constant coefficients

$$f(n+r) = a_0 f(n) + a_1 f(n+1) + \cdots + a_{r-1}f(n+r-1) + g(n) \quad (n \in \mathbb{N}),$$

where $a_0, \ldots, a_{r-1} \in \mathbb{K}$ and $g(n) \neq 0$ is a C-finite expression in n, can always be transformed into an equivalent (homogenous) C-finite recurrence. Hence, its closed form can always be computed.

For obtaining the closed form solutions of (C-finite) linear recurrences we use the SumCracker package [13], a *Mathematica* implementation by the RISC Combinatorics group. For example, given the linear recurrence $f(n+1) = \frac{1}{2} * f(n) + 1$, $n \geq 0$, with initial value $f(0)$, we obtain its closed form $f(n) = \frac{1}{2^n} * f(0) - \frac{2}{2^n} + 2$.

In this paper we consider the ring $\mathbb{K}[x_1, \ldots, x_m]$ of polynomials in the loop variables $x_1, \ldots, x_m$ with coefficients in $\mathbb{K}$, and perform operations over ideals of $\mathbb{K}[x_1, \ldots, x_m]$. Thus, it is necessary for our approach to effectively compute with ideals. This is possible by using Buchberger's algorithm for Gröbner basis computation [1]. A Gröbner basis is a basis for an ideal with special properties making possible to answer algorithmically questions about ideals, such as ideal membership of a polynomial, equality and inclusion of ideals, etc. A detailed presentation of the Gröbner bases theory can be found in [1].

Definition 3.3. Algebraic Dependencies among Exponential Sequences [14]
Let $\theta_1, \ldots, \theta_s \in \bar{\mathbb{K}}$ be algebraic numbers, and their corresponding exponential sequences $\theta_1^n, \ldots, \theta_s^n$, $n \in \mathbb{N}$.

An *algebraic dependency* (or *algebraic relation*) of these sequences over $\bar{\mathbb{K}}$ is a polynomial $p \in \bar{\mathbb{K}}[x_1, \ldots, x_s]$ in s distinct variables $x_1, \ldots, x_s$, i.e. in as many distinct variables as exponential sequences, such that p vanishes when variables are substituted by the exponential sequences, namely:

$$p(\theta_1^n, \ldots, \theta_s^n) = 0, \quad \forall n \in \mathbb{N}. \tag{4}$$

Note that the multiplicative relations among $\theta_1, \ldots, \theta_s$ imply corresponding relations among $\theta_1^n, \ldots, \theta_s^n$. Further, by results of [14], the ideal $I(\theta_1^n, \ldots, \theta_s^n)$ of algebraic dependencies among the sequences $\theta_1^n, \ldots, \theta_s^n$ is the same as the ideal $I(n, \theta_1^n, \ldots, \theta_s^n)$.

For automatically determining the *ideal* $I(n, \theta_1^n, \ldots, \theta_s^n)$ *of algebraic dependencies* among $\theta_1^n, \ldots, \theta_s^n$ we use the `Dependencies` package [14] implemented in *Mathematica* by the RISC combinatorics group. For example, $\theta_1^{2n} - \theta_2^n = 0$ is an algebraic dependency among the exponential sequences of $\theta_1 = 2$ and $\theta_2 = 4$ and there is no algebraic dependency among the exponential sequences of $\theta_1 = 2$ and $\theta_2 = 3$.

4   Generation of Invariant Polynomial Identities

As observed already by [25], the set of polynomial invariants forms a polynomial ideal. The challenging task is thus to determine the *polynomial invariant ideal*.

The algorithm for polynomial invariant generation presented in this paper combines computer algebra and algorithmic combinatorics in such a way that at the end of the invariant generation process valid polynomial assertions of a *P-solvable loop* are automatically obtained. Moreover, under additional assumptions for loops with conditional branches, our approach is proved to be complete: it returns a *basis* for the polynomial invariant ideal.

In our approach for generating polynomial invariants, test conditions in the loops and conditionals are ignored. This turns the considered loops into *non-deterministic* program fragment.

For any conditional statement $\text{If}[b \text{ Then } S_1 \text{ Else } S_2]$, where S_1 and S_2 are sequences of assignments, we will omit the boolean condition b and write it in the form $\text{If}[\ldots \text{ Then } S_1 \text{ Else } S_2]$ to mean the non-deterministic program $S_1 | S_2$. Likewise, we omit the condition b from a loop $\text{While}[b, S]$, where S is a sequence of assignments, and will write it in the form

$$\text{While}[\ldots, S] \tag{5}$$

to mean the non-deterministic program S^*. A detailed presentation of the syntax and semantics of considered non-deterministic programs can be found in [17].

Ignoring the tests in the conditional branches means that either branch is executed in every possible way, whereas ignoring the test condition of the loop means the loop is executed arbitrarily many nonzero times. We will refer to the loop obtained in this way by dropping the loop condition and all test conditions also as a *P-solvable loop*. In the rest of this paper we will focus on *non-deterministic P-solvable loops with assignments and conditional branches with ignored conditions*, written as below.

$$\text{While}[\ldots, \text{If}[\ldots \text{ Then } S_1]; \ldots; \text{If}[\ldots \text{ Then } S_k]]. \tag{6}$$

The definition of P-solvable loops is available in our earlier conference papers [18, 19]. Informally, an imperative loop is *P-solvable* if the closed form solution of the loop variables are polynomials of the initial values of variables, the loop counter, and some new variables, where there are algebraic dependencies among the new variables. The class of P-solvable loops includes the simple situations when the expressions in the assignment statements are affine mappings, as stated below.

Theorem 4.1. Affine loops are P-solvable

Our experience shows that most practical examples operating on numbers exhibit the P-solvable loop property. Thus, the class of P-solvable loops covers at least a significant part of practical programming.

P-solvable Loops with Assignments Only. We denote by $n \in \mathbb{N}$ the loop counter, by $X = \{x_1, \ldots, x_m\}$ ($m > 1$) the recursively changed loop variables whose initial values (before entering the loop) are denoted by X_0. Our method for automatically deriving a *basis of the polynomial invariant ideal for P-solvable loops with assignments only* is presented in Algorithm 4.1.

Algorithm 4.1 "receives" as input a P-solvable loop with assignments only ($k = 1$ in (6)), and starts first with extracting and solving the recurrence equations of the loop variables. The closed forms of the variables are thus determined (steps 1-3 of Algorithm 4.1). Next, it computes the set A of generators for the ideal of algebraic dependencies among the exponential sequences from the closed form system (step 4 of Algorithm 4.1). Finally, from the ideal I generated by the polynomial system of closed forms and A, the ideal G of *all polynomial relations* among the loop variables is computed by elimination using Gröbner basis w.r.t. a suitable elimination order (steps 5-7 of Algorithm 4.1).

Algorithm 4.1   P-solvable Loops with Assignments Only
Input: Imperative P-solvable loop (5) with only assignment statements S, having its recursively changed variables $X = \{x_1, \ldots, x_m\}$ with initial values X_0
Output: The ideal $G \trianglelefteq \mathbb{K}[X]$ of polynomial invariants among X
Assumption: The recurrence equations of X are of order at least 1, $n \in \mathbb{N}$

  1   Extract the recurrence equations of the loop variables

I. Recurrence Solving.

  2   Identify the type of recurrences and solve them by the methods from page 253
  3   Using the P-solvable loop property, the closed form system is

$$
\begin{cases}
x_1[n] = q_1(n, \theta_1^n, \ldots, \theta_s^n) \\
\vdots \\
x_m[n] = q_m(n, \theta_1^n, \ldots, \theta_s^n)
\end{cases}
\text{, where}
\quad
\begin{array}{l}
\theta_j \in \bar{\mathbb{K}}, \ q_i \in \bar{\mathbb{K}}[n, \theta_1^n, \ldots, \theta_s^n], \\
q_i \text{ are parameterized by } X_0, \\
j = 1, \ldots, s, \ i = 1, \ldots, m
\end{array}
$$

  4   Compute a basis A for the ideal of algebraic dependencies among $n, \theta_1^n, \ldots, \theta_s^n$.

Conform page 253, $\langle A \rangle = I(n, \theta_1^n, \ldots, \theta_s^n)$

  5   Denote $z_0 = n, z_1 = \theta_1^n, \ldots, z_s = \theta_s^n$. Thus $\langle A \rangle \trianglelefteq \bar{\mathbb{K}}[z_0, \ldots, z_s]$ and

$$
\begin{cases}
x_1 = q_1(z_0, z_1, \ldots, z_s) \\
\vdots \\
x_m = q_m(z_0, z_1, \ldots, z_s)
\end{cases}
\text{, where}
\quad
\begin{array}{l}
q_i \in \bar{\mathbb{K}}[z_0, z_1, \ldots, z_s], \ i = 1, \ldots, m, \\
q_i \text{ are parameterized by } X_0.
\end{array}
$$

II. Polynomial Invariant Generation.

6   Consider $I = \langle x_1 - q_1(z_0, \ldots, z_s), \ldots, x_m - q_m(z_0, \ldots, z_s) \rangle + \langle A \rangle$.

$$\text{Thus } I \subset \bar{\mathbb{K}}[z_0, z_1, \ldots, z_s, x_1, \ldots, x_m]$$

7   **return** $G = I \cap \mathbb{K}[x_1, \ldots, x_m]$.

Theorem 4.2. Algorithm 4.1 is correct. Its output G satisfies

1. $G \trianglelefteq \mathbb{K}[x_1, \ldots, x_m]$;
2. every polynomial relation from G is a polynomial invariant among the P-solvable loop variables $x_1, \ldots, x_m$ over $\mathbb{K}[X]$;
3. any polynomial invariant among the P-solvable loop variables $x_1, \ldots, x_m$ over $\mathbb{K}[X]$ can be derived from (the generators of) G.

The restrictions at the various steps of Algorithm 4.1 are crucial. If the recurrences cannot be solved exactly, or their closed forms do not fulfill the P-solvable form, our algorithm fails in generating valid polynomial relations among the loop variables. Thus, Algorithm 4.1 can be applied only to P-solvable loops whose assignment statements describe either Gosper-summable or C-finite recurrences.

Example 4.3. Given the loop

$$\texttt{While}[\ldots, a := a + b; y := y + d/2; b := b/2; d := d/2],$$

its polynomial invariants, by applying Algorithm 4.1 and using `Aligator`, are obtained as follows.

Step 1:
$$\begin{cases} a[n+1] = a[n] + b[n] \\ y[n+1] = y[n] + d[n]/2 \\ b[n+1] = b[n]/2 \\ d[n+1] = d[n]/2 \end{cases}$$

Steps 2,3:
$$\begin{cases} a[n] \underset{Gosper}{=} a[0] + 2 * b[0] - 2 * b[0] * 2^{-n} \\ b[n] \underset{C-\overline{finite}}{=} b[0] * 2^{-n} \\ d[n] \underset{C-\overline{finite}}{=} d[0] * 2^{-n} \\ y[n] \underset{Gosper}{=} y[0] + d[0] - d[0] * 2^{-n} \end{cases}$$

where $a[0], b[0], d[0], y[0]$ denote the initial values of a, b, d, y before the loop.

Steps 4, 5: $z_1 = 2^{-n}, z_2 = 2^{-n}, z_3 = 2^{-n}, z_4 = 2^{-n}$

$$\begin{cases} a = a[0] + 2 * b[0] - 2 * b[0] * z_1 \\ b = b[0] * z_2 \\ d = d[0] * z_3 \\ y = y[0] + d[0] - d[0] * z_4 \end{cases} \quad \text{with} \quad \begin{cases} z_1 - z_4 = 0 \\ z_2 - z_4 = 0 \\ z_3 - z_4 = 0 \end{cases}$$

algebraic dependencies:

Steps 6, 7: The Gröbner basis computation with $z_1 \succ z_2 \succ z_3 \succ z_4 \succ a \succ b \succ d \succ y$ yields:
$G = \langle d + y - d[0] - y[0], y\, b[0] + b\, d[0] - b[0]d[0] - b[0]y[0], a + 2b - a[0] - 2b[0] \rangle$.

Based on Theorems 4.1 and 4.2, we finally state the theorem below.

Theorem 4.4. The ideal of polynomial invariants for an affine loop is algorithmically computable by Algorithm 4.1.

P-solvable Loops with Conditionals and Assignments. We consider a generalization of Algorithm 4.1. for P-solvable loops with conditional branches and assignments.

The starting point of our approach is to do first program transformations (see Theorem 4.5). Namely, transform the P-solvable loop with conditional branches, i.e. outer loop, into nested P-solvable loops with assignments only, i.e. inner loops. Further, we apply steps of Algorithm 4.1 to reason about the inner loops such that at the end we derive polynomial invariants of the outer loop. Moreover, under the additional assumptions introduced in Theorem 4.12, we prove that our approach is complete. Namely, it returns a basis for the polynomial invariant ideal for some special cases of P-solvable loops with conditional branches and assignments. It is worth to be mentioned that the imposed assumptions cover a wide class of imperative programs (see [17] for concrete examples). Moreover, we could not yet find any example of a P-solvable loop for which the completeness of our approach is violated.

Theorem 4.5. Let us consider the following two loops:

$$\texttt{While}[b, s_0; \texttt{If}[b_1 \texttt{ Then } s_1 \texttt{ Else } \ldots \texttt{ If}[b_{k-1} \texttt{ Then } s_{k-1} \texttt{ Else } s_k]\ldots]; s_{k+1}] \quad (7)$$

and

$$\begin{aligned} &\texttt{While}[b, \\ &\texttt{While}[b \wedge b_1', \ s_0; s_1; s_{k+1}]; \\ &\ldots \\ &\texttt{While}[b \wedge \neg b_1' \wedge \cdots \wedge \neg b_{k-1}', \ s_0; s_k; s_{k+1}]], \end{aligned} \quad (8)$$

where s_0, s_1, $\ldots$, s_k, s_{k+1} are sequences of assignments, and $b_i' = \mathrm{wp}(s_0, b_i)$ is the weakest precondition of s_0 with postcondition b_i, $i = 1, \ldots, k-1$.

Then any formula I is an invariant of the first loop if and only if it is an invariant of the second loop and all of its inner loops.

Since in our approach for invariant generation tests are ignored in the loop and conditional branches, the loop (7) can be equivalently written as (6), by denoting $S_i = s_0; s_i; s_{k+1}$. Further, using our notation for basic non-deterministic programs mentioned on page 254, the outer loop (8) can be written as $(S_1|S_2|\ldots|S_k)^*$. Based on Theorem 4.5, an imperative loop having $k \geq 1$ *conditional branches and assignment statements only* is called *P-solvable* if the inner loops obtained after performing the transformation rule from Theorem 4.5 are P-solvable.

Example 4.6. Consider the loop implementing Wensley's algorithm for real division [27].

$$\begin{aligned} &\texttt{While}[(d \geq Tol), \\ &\quad \texttt{If}[(P < a + b) \\ &\quad\quad \texttt{Then } b := b/2; d := d/2 \\ &\quad\quad \texttt{Else } a := a + b; y := y + d/2; b := b/2; d := d/2]]. \end{aligned} \quad (9)$$

After applying Theorem 4.5 and omitting all test conditions, the obtained nested loop system is as follows.

$$\begin{aligned} &\texttt{While}[\ldots, \\ S_1: \quad &\texttt{While}[\ldots, b := b/2; d := d/2]; \\ S_2: \quad &\texttt{While}[\ldots, a := a + b; y := y + d/2; b := b/2; d := d/2]]. \end{aligned}$$

What remains is to determine the relation between the polynomial invariants of the P-solvable loop (7) and the polynomial identities of the inner loops from (8). For doing so, the main steps of our algorithm are as follows.

(i) Firstly, we determine the ideal of polynomial relations for an *arbitrary iteration* of the outer loop (8) (see Theorem 4.8).
(ii) Finally, from the ideal of polynomial relations after the *first* iteration of the outer loop (8), we keep only the *polynomial invariants* for the P-solvable loop (7) (see Theorem 4.10).

> Moreover, under the *additional assumptions* of Theorem 4.12, the polynomial invariants thus obtained form a *basis for the polynomial invariant ideal* of the P-solvable loop (7).

In more detail, we proceed as follows. (i) In the general case of a P-solvable loop (7) with a nested conditional statement having $k \geq 1$ conditional branches, by applying Theorem 4.5, we obtain an outer loop (8) with k P-solvable inner loops $S_1, \ldots, S_k$. Thus an *arbitrary iteration* of the outer loop is described by an arbitrary sequence of the k P-solvable loops. Since the tests are ignored, for any iteration of the outer loop we have $k!$ possible sequences of inner P-solvable loops.

Let us denote the set of permutations of length k over $\{1, \ldots, k\}$ by $\mathfrak{S}_k$. Consider a permutation $W = (w_1, \ldots, w_k) \in \mathfrak{S}_k$ and a sequence of numbers $J = \{j_1, \ldots, j_k\} \in \mathbb{N}^k$. Then we write $S_W^J = S_{w_1}^{j_1}; S_{w_2}^{j_2}; \ldots; S_{w_k}^{j_k}$ to denote an *arbitrary iteration of the outer loop*, i.e. an arbitrary sequence of the k inner loops. By S_i^j we mean the sequence of assignments $\underbrace{S_i; \ldots; S_i}_{j \text{ times}}$.

Using steps 1-4 of Algorithm 4.1, for each P-solvable inner loop $S_{w_i}^{j_i}$ from S_W^J we obtain their system of closed forms together with their ideal of algebraic dependencies among the exponential sequences (steps 1-4 of Algorithm 4.2). Further, the system of closed forms of loop variables after S_W^J is obtained by *merging* the closed forms of its inner loops. Merging is based on the fact that the initial values of the loop variables corresponding to the inner loop $S_{w_{i+1}}^{j_{i+1}}$ are given by the final values of the loop variables after $S_{w_i}^{j_i}$ (step 5 of Algorithm 4.2). In [17] we showed that merging of closed forms of P-solvable inner loops yields a polynomial closed form system as well.

We can now compute the ideal of valid polynomial relations among the loop variables X with initial values X_0 corresponding to the sequence of assignments $\underbrace{S_{w_1}; \ldots; S_{w_1}}_{j_1 \text{ times}};$ $\underbrace{S_{w_2}; \ldots; S_{w_2}}_{j_2 \text{ times}}; \ldots \ldots; \underbrace{S_{w_k}; \ldots; S_{w_k}}_{j_k \text{ times}}$. Using notation introduced on page 254, we thus compute the ideal of valid polynomial relations after $S_{w_1}^*; \ldots; S_{w_k}^*$. This is presented in Algorithm 4.2.

Algorithm 4.2   Polynomial Relations of a P-solvable Loop Sequence
Input: k P-solvable inner loops $S_{w_1}, \ldots, S_{w_k}$
Output: The ideal $G \trianglelefteq \mathbb{K}[X]$ of polynomial relations among X with initial values X_0 after $S_{w_1}^*; \ldots; S_{w_k}^*$
Assumption: S_{w_i} are sequences of assignments, $w_i \in \{1, \ldots, k\}, j_i \in \mathbb{N}, k \geq 1$

1 **for** each $S_{w_i}^{j_i}$, $i = 1, \ldots, k$ **do**

2   Apply steps 1-3 of Algorithm 4.1 for determining the closed form of $S_{w_i}^{j_i}$

3   Compute the ideal A_{w_i} of algebraic dependencies for $S_{w_i}^{j_i}$

4 **endfor**

5 Compute the merged closed form of $S_{w_1}^{j_1}; \ldots; S_{w_k}^{j_k}$:

$$
\begin{cases}
x_1[j_1, \ldots, j_k] = f_1(j_1, \theta_{w_11}^{j_1}, \ldots, \theta_{w_1s}^{j_1}, \cdots \cdots, j_k, \theta_{w_k1}^{j_k}, \ldots, \theta_{w_ks}^{j_k}) \\
\vdots \\
x_m[j_1, \ldots, j_k] = f_m(j_1, \theta_{w_11}^{j_1}, \ldots, \theta_{w_1s}^{j_1}, \cdots \cdots, j_k, \theta_{w_k1}^{j_k}, \ldots, \theta_{w_ks}^{j_k})
\end{cases} \text{, where}
$$

$f_l \in \bar{\mathbb{K}}[z_{10}, \ldots, z_{1s}, \cdots \cdots, z_{k0}, \ldots, z_{ks}],$
the variables $z_{i0}, \ldots, z_{is}$ are standing for the C-finite sequences $j_i, \theta_{w_i1}^{j_i}, \ldots, \theta_{w_is}^{j_i}$,
the coefficients of f_l are given by the initial values before $S_{w_1}^{j_1}; \ldots; S_{w_k}^{j_k}$

6 $A_* = \displaystyle\sum_{i=1}^{k} A_{w_i}$

7 $I = \langle x_1 - f_1, \ldots, x_m - f_m \rangle + A_* \subset \bar{\mathbb{K}}[z_{10}, \cdots \cdots, z_{ks}, x_1, \ldots, x_m]$

8 **return** $G = I \cap \mathbb{K}[x_1, \ldots, x_m]$.

Elimination of $z_{10}, \ldots, z_{ks}$ at step 8 is performed by Gröbner basis computation of I w.r.t. an elimination order $\succ$ such that $z_{10} \succ \cdots \cdots \succ z_{ks} \succ x_1 \cdots \succ x_m$.

Example 4.7. For Example 4.6, the steps of Algorithm 4.2 are presented below.

Steps 1-4. Similarly to Example 4.3, the closed form systems of the inner loops S_1 and S_2 are as follows.

Inner loop S_1:

$j_1 \in \mathbb{N}$

$z_{11} = 2^{-j_1}, z_{12} = 2^{-j_1}$

$$
\begin{cases}
a[j_1] & = & a[0_1] \\
b[j_1] & _{C-\overline{finite}} & b[0_1] * z_{11} \\
d[j_1] & _{C-\overline{finite}} & d[0_1] * z_{12} \\
y[j_1] & = & y[0_1]
\end{cases}
$$

Inner loop S_2:

$j_2 \in \mathbb{N}$

$z_{21} = 2^{-j_2}, z_{22} = 2^{-j_2}, z_{23} = 2^{-j_2}, z_{24} = 2^{-j_2}$

$$
\begin{cases}
a[j_2] & _{\overline{Gosper}} & a[0_2] + 2 * b[0_2] - 2 * b[0_2] * z_{21} \\
b[j_2] & _{C-\overline{finite}} & b[0_2] * z_{22} \\
d[j_2] & _{C-\overline{finite}} & d[0_2] * z_{23} \\
y[j_2] & _{\overline{Gosper}} & y[0_2] + d[0_2] - d[0_2] * z_{24},
\end{cases}
$$

with the computed algebraic dependencies

$$
\{ z_{11} - z_{12} = 0 \qquad \text{and} \qquad \begin{cases} z_{21} - z_{24} = 0 \\ z_{22} - z_{24} = 0 \\ z_{23} - z_{24} = 0, \end{cases}
$$

where $X_{01} = \{a[0_1], b[0_1], d[0_1], y[0_1]\}$ and $X_{02} = \{a[0_2], b[0_2], d[0_2], y[0_2]\}$ are respectively the initial values of a, b, d, y before entering the inner loops S_1 and S_2.

Steps 5-6. For the inner loop sequence $S_1^{j_1}; S_2^{j}$ the initial values X_{02} are given by the values $a[j_1], b[j_1], d[j_1], y[j_1]$ after $S_1^{j_1}$. Hence, the merged closed form of $S_1^{j_1}; S_2^{j_2}$ is given below. For simplicity, let us rename the initial values X_{01} to respectively $X_0 = \{a[0], b[0], d[0], y[0]\}$.

$$\begin{cases} a[j_1, j_2] = a[0] + 2 * b[0] * z_{11} - 2b[0] * z_{21} * z_{11} \\ b[j_1, j_2] = b[0] * z_{22} * z_{11} \\ d[j_1, j_2] = d[0] * z_{12} * z_{23} \\ y[j_1, j_2] = y[0] + d[0] * z_{12} - d[0] * z_{24} * z_{12}, \end{cases} \tag{10}$$

with the already computed algebraic dependencies

$$A_* = \langle z_{11} - z_{12}, z_{21} - z_{24}, z_{22} - z_{24}, z_{23} - z_{24} \rangle. \tag{11}$$

Steps 7, 8. From (10) and (11), by eliminating $z_{11}, z_{12}, z_{21}, z_{22}, z_{23}, z_{24}$, we obtain the ideal of polynomial relations for $S_1^{j_1}; S_2^{j_2}$, as below.

$$G = \langle\, -b[0] * d + b * d[0], a * d[0] - a[0] * d[0] - 2 * b[0] * y + 2 * b[0] * y[0],$$
$$a * d - a[0] * d - 2 * b * y + 2 * b * y[0] \rangle.$$

In order to get all polynomial relations among the loop variables X with initial values X_0 corresponding to an arbitrary iteration of the outer loop (8), we need to apply Algorithm 4.2 on each possible sequence of k inner loops that are in a number of $k!$. This way, for each sequence of k inner loops we get the ideal of their polynomial relations among the loop variables X with initial values X_0 (step 3 of Algorithm 4.3). Using ideal theoretic results, by taking the *intersection* of all these ideals, we derive *the ideal of polynomial relations among the loop variables X with initial values X_0 that are valid after any sequence of k P-solvable inner loops* (step 4 of Algorithm 4.3). The intersection ideal thus obtained is the ideal of polynomial relations among the loop variables X with initial values X_0 *after an arbitrary iteration of the outer loop* (8). This can be algorithmically computed as follows.

Algorithm 4.3   Polynomial Relations for an Iteration of (8)
Input: P-solvable loop (8) with P-solvable inner loops $S_1, \ldots, S_k$
Output: The ideal $PI \subset \mathbb{K}[X]$ of the polynomial relations among X with initial values X_0 corresponding to an arbitrary iteration of (8)
Assumption: X_0 are the initial values of X before the arbitrary iteration of (8)

1   $PI = $ Algorithm 4.2$\big(S_1, \ldots, S_k\big)$
2   **for** each $W \in \mathfrak{S}_k \setminus \{(1, \ldots, k)\}$ **do**
3       $G = $ Algorithm 4.2$\big(S_{w_1}, \ldots, S_{w_k}\big)$
4       $PI = PI \cap G$
5   **endfor**
6   **return** PI.

Theorem 4.8. Algorithm 4.3 is correct. It returns the generators for the ideal PI of polynomial relations among the loop variables X with initial values X_0 after a possible iteration of the outer loop (8).

Example 4.9. Similarly to Example 4.7, we compute the ideal of polynomial relations for $S_2^{j_2}; S_1^{j_1}$ for Example 4.6. Further, we take the intersection of the ideals of polynomial relations for $S_1^{j_1}; S_2^{j_2}$ and $S_2^{j_2}; S_1^{j_1}$. We thus obtain

$$PI = \langle\, -b[0] * d + b * d[0], a * d[0] - a[0] * d[0] - 2 * b[0] * y + 2 * b[0] * y[0],$$
$$a * d - a[0] * d - 2 * b * y + 2 * b * y[0] \rangle.$$

(ii) What remains is to identify the relationship between the polynomial invariants among the loop variables X of the *outer loop* and the computed polynomial relations using Algorithm 4.3 for *an arbitrary iteration of the outer loop*. For doing so, we proceed as follows.

1. Note that the initial values X_0 of the loop variables X at the entry point of the outer loop are also the initial values of the loop variables X before the *first* iteration of the outer loop (8). We thus firstly compute by Algorithm 4.3 the ideal of all polynomial relations among the loop variables X with initial values X_0 corresponding to the *first* iteration of the outer loop (8). We denote this ideal by PI_1.

2. Next, from (the generators of) PI_1 we keep only the set GI of polynomial relations that are invariants among the loop variables X with initial values X_0: they are preserved by any iteration of the outer loop (8) starting in a state in which the initial values of the loop variables X are X_0. By correctness of Theorem 4.5, the polynomials from GI thus obtained are invariants among the loop variables X with initial values X_0 of the P-solvable loop (7) (see Theorem 4.10).

Finally, we can now formulate our algorithm for polynomial invariant generation for P-solvable loops with conditional branches and assignments.

Algorithm 4.4   P-solvable Loops with Non-deterministic Conditionals
Input: P-solvable loop (7) with $k \geq 1$ conditional branches and assignments
Output: Polynomial invariants of (7) among X with initial values X_0

1 Apply Theorem 4.5, yielding a nested loop (8) with k P-solvable inner loops $S_1, \ldots, S_k$
2 Apply Algorithm 4.3 for computing the ideal PI_1 of polynomial relations among X after the first iteration of the outer loop (8)
3 From PI_1 keep the set GI of those polynomials whose conjunction is preserved by each $S_1, \ldots, S_k$:

$$GI = \{p \in PI_1 \mid wp(S_i, p(X) = 0) \in \langle GI \rangle, i = 1, \ldots, k\} \subset PI_1, \text{ where}$$
$wp(S_i, p(X) = 0)$ is the weakest precondition of S_i with postcondition $p(X) = 0$

4 <u>*return*</u> GI.

Theorem 4.10. Algorithm 4.4 is correct. It returns polynomial invariants among the loop variables X with initial values X_0 of the P-solvable loop (7).

Example 4.11. From Example 4.9 we already have the set PI_1 for Example 4.6. By applying step 3 of Algorithm 4.4, the set of polynomial invariants for Example 4.6 is

$$GI = \{b[0] * d + b * d[0], a * d[0] - a[0] * d[0] - 2 * b[0] * y + 2 * b[0] * y[0],$$
$$a * d - a[0] * d - 2 * b * y + 2 * b * y[0]\}.$$

In what follows, we state under which additional assumptions Algorithm 4.4 returns a basis of the polynomial invariant ideal. We fix some further notation.

- J_* the polynomial invariant ideal among X with initial values X_0 of the P-solvable loop (7).
- J_W denotes the ideal of polynomial relations among X with initial values X_0 after S_W^J.
- For all $i = 1, \ldots, k$ and $j \in \mathbb{N}$, we denote by $J_{W,i}$ the ideal of polynomial relations among X with initial values X_0 after $S_W^J; S_i^j$.

For proving completeness of our method, we impose structural conditions on the ideal of polynomial relations among X with initial values X_0 corresponding to sequences of k and $k + 1$ inner loops, as presented below.

Theorem 4.12. Let $\mathfrak{a}_k = \bigcap_{W \in \mathfrak{S}_k} J_W, \mathfrak{a}_{k+1} = \bigcap_{\substack{W \in \mathfrak{S}_k \\ i=1,\ldots,k}} J_{W,i}$. Let GI be as in Algorithm 4.4.

1. If $\mathfrak{a}_k = \mathfrak{a}_{k+1}$ then $J_* = \mathfrak{a}_k$.
2. If $\langle GI \rangle = \mathfrak{a}_k \cap \mathfrak{a}_{k+1}$ then $J_* = \mathfrak{a}_k \cap \mathfrak{a}_{k+1}$.
3. If $\langle GI \rangle = \mathfrak{a}_k$ then $J_* = \mathfrak{a}_k$.

Example 4.13. From Examples 4.9 and 4.11 we obtain $GI = PI_1$. By Theorem 4.12 we thus derive $GI = J_*$, yielding the completeness of Algorithm 4.4 for Example 4.6.

Further Examples. We have successfully tested our method on a number of interesting number theoretic examples [17], some of them being listed in the table below. The first column of the table contains the name of the example, the second and third columns specify the applied combinatorial methods and the number of generated polynomial invariants for the corresponding example, whereas the fourth column shows the timing (in seconds) needed by the implementation on a Pentium 4, 1.6GHz processor with 512 Mb RAM. The fifth columns shows whether our method was complete.

5 Conclusion

A framework for generating loop invariants for a family of imperative programs operating on numbers. We give several methods for invariant generation and prove a number of new results showing soundness, and also sometimes completeness of these methods. These results use non-trivial mathematics based on combining combinatorics, algebraic relations and logic. Moreover, the framework is implemented as a *Mathematica* package, called `Aligator`, and used further for imperative program verification in the *Theorema* system. A collection of examples successfully worked out using the framework is presented in [17].

So far, the focus has been on generating polynomial equations as loop invariants. We believe that it should be possible to identify and generate polynomial inequalities in addition to polynomial equations, as invariants as well. We have been investigating the manipulation of pre- and postconditions, and other annotations of programs, if available, along with conditions in loops and conditional statements, as well as the simple

Example	Comb. Methods	Nr.Poly.	(sec)	Compl.
P-solvable loops with assignments only				
Division [6]	Gosper	1	0.08	yes
Integer square root [15]	Gosper	2	0.09	yes
Integer square root [16]	Gosper	2	0.09	yes
Integer cubic root [16]	Gosper	2	0.15	yes
Fibonacci [17]	Generating functions, Alg.Dependencies	1	0.73	yes
Sum of powers n^5 [24]	Gosper	1	0.07	yes
P-solvable loops with conditional branches and assignments				
Wensley's Algorithm [27]	Gosper, C-finite, Alg.Dependencies	2	0.48	yes
LCM-GCD computation [6]	Gosper	1	0.33	yes
Extended GCD [16]	Gosper	5	2.65	yes
Fermat's factorization [16]	Gosper	1	0.32	yes
Square root [29]	Gosper, C-finite, Alg.Dependencies	1	1.28	yes
Binary Product [16]	Gosper, C-finite, Alg.Dependencies	1	0.47	yes
Binary Product [25]	Gosper, C-finite, Alg.Dependencies	1	9.6	yes
Binary Division [10]				
1st Loop	C-finite, Alg. Dependencies	2	0.10	yes
2nd Loop	C-finite, Gosper, Alg.Dependencies	1	0.72	yes
Square root [6]				
1st Loop	C-finite, Alg. Dependencies	2	0.15	yes
2nd Loop	Gosper, C-finite, Alg. Dependencies	1	8.7	yes
Hardware Integer Division [20]				
1st Loop	C-finite, Alg. Dependencies	3	0.19	yes
2nd Loop	Gosper, C-finite, Alg.Dependencies	3	0.64	yes
Hardware Integer Division [26]				
1st Loop	C-finite, Alg. Dependencies	3	0.17	yes
2nd Loop	Gosper, C-finite, Alg.Dependencies	3	0.81	yes
Factoring Large Numbers [16]	C-finite, Gosper	1	14.4	yes

fact that no loop is executed less than 0 times. Quantifier elimination methods on theories, including the theory of real closed fields, should be helpful. We are also interested in generalizing the framework to programs on nonnumeric data structures.

Acknowledgements. The author wishes to thank Tudor Jebelean, Andrei Voronkov, Deepak Kapur and Manuel Kauers for their help and comments.

References

1. Buchberger, B.: Gröbner-Bases: An Algorithmic Method in Polynomial Ideal Theory. In: Multidimensional Systems Theory - Progress, Directions and Open Problems in Multidimensional Systems, pp. 184–232 (1985)

2. Buchberger, B., Craciun, A., Jebelean, T., Kovacs, L., Kutsia, T., Nakagawa, K., Piroi, F., Popov, N., Robu, J., Rosenkranz, M., Windsteiger, W.: Theorema: Towards Computer-Aided Mathematical Theory Exploration. Journal of Applied Logic 4(4), 470–504 (2006)

3. Collins, G.E.: Quantifier Elimination for the Elementary Theory of Real Closed Fields by Cylindrical Algebraic Decomposition. In: Brakhage, H. (ed.) GI-Fachtagung 1975. LNCS, vol. 33, pp. 134–183. Springer, Heidelberg (1975)

4. Cousot, P., Halbwachs, N.: Automatic Discovery of Linear Restraints among Variables of a Program. In: ACM SIGPLAN-SIGACT Symposium on Principles of Programming Languages, pp. 84–97 (1978)

5. Cox, D., Little, J., O'Shea, D.: Ideal, Varieties, and Algorithms. An Introduction to Computational Algebraic Geometry and Commutative Algebra, 2nd edn. Springer, Heidelberg (1998)

6. Dijkstra, E.W.: A Discipline of Programming. Prentice-Hall, Englewood Cliffs (1976)
7. Everest, G., van der Poorten, A., Shparlinski, I., Ward, T.: Recurrence Sequences. Mathematical Surveys and Monographs, American Mathematical Society, 104 (2003)
8. German, S.M., Wegbreit, B.: A Synthesizer of Inductive Assertions. IEEE Transactions on Software Engineering 1, 68–75 (1975)
9. Gosper, R.W.: Decision Procedures for Indefinite Hypergeometric Summation. Journal of Symbolic Computation 75, 40–42 (1978)
10. Kaldewaij, A.: Programming. The Derivation of Algorithms. Prentince-Hall, Englewood Cliffs (1990)
11. Kapur, D.: A Quantifier Elimination based Heuristic for Automatically Generating Inductive Assertions for Programs. Journal of Systems Science and Complexity 19(3), 307–330 (2006)
12. Karr, M.: Affine Relationships Among Variables of Programs. Acta Informatica 6, 133–151 (1976)
13. Kauers, M.: SumCracker: A Package for Manipulating Symbolic Sums and Related Objects. Journal of Symbolic Computation 41, 1039–1057 (2006)
14. Kauers, M., Zimmermann, B.: Computing the Algebraic Relations of C-finite Sequences and Multisequences. Technical Report 2006-24, SFB F013 (2006)
15. Kirchner, M.: Program Verification with the Mathematical Software System Theorema. Technical Report 99-16, RISC-Linz, Austria, Diplomaarbeit (1999)
16. Knuth, D.E.: The Art of Computer Programming, 3rd edn. vol. 2. Addison-Wesley, Reading (1998)
17. Kovács, L.: Automated Invariant Generation by Algebraic Techniques for Imperative Program Verification in Theorema. PhD thesis, RISC, Johannes Kepler University Linz (2007)
18. Kovács, L., Jebelean, T.: Finding Polynomial Invariants for Imperative Loops in the Theorema System. In: Proc. of Verify 2006, FLoC 2006, pp. 52–67 (2006)
19. Kovács, L., Popov, N., Jebelean, T.: Combining Logic and Algebraic Techniques for Program Verification in Theorema. In: Proc. of ISOLA 2006 (2006)
20. Manna, Z.: Mathematical Theory of Computation. McGraw-Hill Inc, New York (1974)
21. Müller-Olm, M., Seidl, H., Petter, M.: Interprocedurally Analyzing Polynomial Identities. In: Durand, B., Thomas, W. (eds.) STACS 2006. LNCS, vol. 3884, pp. 50–67. Springer, Heidelberg (2006)
22. Müller-Olm, M., Seidl, H.: Polynomial Constants Are Decidable. In: Hermenegildo, M.V., Puebla, G. (eds.) SAS 2002. LNCS, vol. 2477, pp. 4–19. Springer, Heidelberg (2002)
23. Paule, P., Schorn, M.: A Mathematica Version of Zeilberger's Algorithm for Proving Binomial Coefficient Identities. Journal of Symbolic Computation 20(5-6), 673–698 (1995)
24. Petter, M.: Berechnung von polynomiellen Invarianten. Master's thesis, Technical University München, Germany (2004)
25. Rodriguez-Carbonell, E., Kapur, D.: Generating All Polynomial Invariants in Simple Loops. J. of Symbolic Computation 42(4), 443–476 (2007)
26. Sankaranaryanan, S., Sipma, H.B., Manna, Z.: Non-Linear Loop Invariant Generation using Gröbner Bases. In: Proc. of POPL 2004 (2004)
27. Wegbreit, B.: The Synthesis of Loop Predicates. Communication of the ACM 2(17), 102–112 (1974)
28. Zeilberger, D.: A Holonomic System Approach to Special Functions. Journal of Computational and Applied Mathematics 32, 321–368 (1990)
29. Zuse, K.: The Computer - My Life. Springer, Heidelberg (1993)

On Local Reasoning in Verification

Carsten Ihlemann, Swen Jacobs, and Viorica Sofronie-Stokkermans

Max-Planck-Institut für Informatik, Campus E1 4, Saarbrücken, Germany
{ihlemann,sjacobs,sofronie}@mpi-inf.mpg.de

Abstract. We present a general framework which allows to identify complex theories important in verification for which efficient reasoning methods exist. The framework we present is based on a general notion of locality. We show that locality considerations allow us to obtain parameterized decidability and complexity results for many (combinations of) theories important in verification in general and in the verification of parametric systems in particular. We give numerous examples; in particular we show that several theories of data structures studied in the verification literature are local extensions of a base theory. The general framework we use allows us to identify situations in which some of the syntactical restrictions imposed in previous papers can be relaxed.

1 Introduction

Many problems in verification can be reduced to proving the satisfiability of conjunctions of literals in a background theory (which can be a standard theory, the extension of a theory with additional functions – free, monotone, or recursively defined – or a combination of theories). It is very important to identify situations where the search space can be controlled without losing completeness. Solutions to this problem were proposed in proof theory, algebra and verification: In [8,11], McAllester and Givan studied the proof-theoretical notion of "local inference systems" – where for proving/disproving a goal only ground instances of the inference rules are needed which contain ground terms which appear in the goal to be proved. In universal algebra, Burris [3] established a link between PTIME decidability of the uniform word problem in quasi-varieties of algebras and embeddability of partial into total models. A link to the notion of locality was established by Ganzinger [5]. In the verification literature, locality properties were investigated in the context of reasoning in pointer data structures by McPeak, Necula [12] and in the study of fragments of the theory of arrays by Bradley, Manna and Sipma [1] and Ghilardi, Nicolini, Ranise and Zucchelli [7]. The applications in verification usually require reasoning in complex domains. In [6,13] we study *local extensions of theories* and show that in such extensions proof tasks can be reduced, hierarchically, to proof tasks in the base theory.

The main contributions of this paper can be described as follows:

(1) We introduce generalized notions of locality and stable locality and show that theories important in verification (e.g. the theory of arrays in [1] and the theory of pointer structures in [12]) satisfy such locality conditions.

C.R. Ramakrishnan and J. Rehof (Eds.): TACAS 2008, LNCS 4963, pp. 265–281, 2008.
© Springer-Verlag Berlin Heidelberg 2008

(2) We present a general framework which allows to identify local theories important in verification. This allows us to also handle fragments which do not satisfy all syntactical restrictions imposed in previous papers. In particular, the axiom sets which we consider may contain alternations of quantifiers.
(3) We use these results to give new examples of local theories of data types.
(4) We discuss the experiments we made with an implementation.

The paper is structured as follows. We start (Sect. 1.1 and 1.2) by discussing the application domains we consider and illustrating our main idea. Section 2 contains basic definitions. In Sect. 3 local extensions are defined, results on hierarchical reasoning, parameterized decidability and complexity results, and possibilities of recognizing local extensions are summarized. Section 4 contains a large number of examples, ranging from extensions with monotonicity, injectivity and (guarded) boundedness properties to theories of data structures (pointers, arrays). A general framework for recognizing locality in verification is presented in Sect. 5. We describe our implementation and some experiments in Sect. 6.

1.1   Application Domains

The application domains we consider are mainly related to the verification of parametric systems (parametric either w.r.t. the number of subsystems involved, or w.r.t. some data used to describe the states and their updates).

We model systems using transition constraint systems $T = (V, \Sigma, \mathsf{Init}, \mathsf{Update})$ which specify: the variables (V) and function symbols (Σ) whose values change over time; a formula Init specifying the properties of initial states; a formula Update with variables in $V \cup V'$ and function symbols in $\Sigma \cup \Sigma'$ (where V' and Σ' are copies of V resp. Σ, denoting the variables resp. functions after the transition) which specifies the relationship between the values of variables x and function symbols f before a transition and their values (x', f') after the transition. Such descriptions can be obtained from system specifications (for an example cf. [4]). With every specification, a *background theory* $\mathcal{T}_S$ – describing the data types used in the specification and their properties – is associated. The verification problems we consider are *invariant checking* and *bounded model checking*.

Invariant checking. We can check whether a formula Ψ is an inductive invariant of a transition constraint system $T = (V, \Sigma, \mathsf{Init}, \mathsf{Update})$ in two steps: (1) prove that $\mathcal{T}_S, \mathsf{Init} \models \Psi$; (2) prove that $\mathcal{T}_S, \Psi, \mathsf{Update} \models \Psi'$, where Ψ' results from Ψ by replacing each $x \in V$ by x' and each $f \in \Sigma$ by f'. Failure to prove (2) means that Ψ is not an invariant, or Ψ is not inductive w.r.t. T.[1]

Bounded model checking. We check whether, for a fixed k, unsafe states are reachable in at most k steps. Formally, we check whether:

$$\mathcal{T}_S \wedge \mathsf{Init}_0 \wedge \bigwedge_{i=1}^{j} \mathsf{Update}_i \wedge \neg \Psi_j \models \bot \quad \text{for all } 0 \leq j \leq k,$$

---

[1] Proving that Ψ is an invariant of the system in general requires to find a stronger formula Γ (i.e., $\mathcal{T}_S \models \Gamma \to \Psi$) and prove that Γ is an inductive invariant.

where Update_i is obtained from Update by replacing all variables $x \in V$ by x_i and any $f \in \Sigma$ by f_i, and all $x' \in V'$, $f' \in \Sigma'$ by x_{i+1}, f_{i+1}; Init_0 is Init with x_0 replacing $x \in V$ and f_0 replacing $f \in \Sigma$; Ψ_i is obtained from Ψ similarly.

We are interested in checking whether a safety property (expressed by a suitable formula) is an invariant, or holds for paths of bounded length, *for given instances of the parameters*, or *under given constraints on parameters*. We aim at identifying situations in which decision procedures exist. We will show that this is often the case, by investigating locality phenomena in verification. As a by-product, this will allow us to consider problems more general than usual tasks in verification, namely to *derive constraints between parameters* which guarantee safety. These constraints may also be used to solve optimization problems (maximize/minimize some of the parameters) such that safety is guaranteed.

1.2   Illustration

We illustrate the problems as well as our solution on the following example.[2] Consider a parametric number m of processes. The priorities associated with the processes (non-negative real numbers) are stored in an array p. The states of the processes – enabled (1) or disabled (0) are stored in an array a. At each step only the process with maximal priority is enabled, its priority is set to x and the priorities of the waiting processes are increased by y. This can be expressed with the following set of axioms which we denote by $\mathsf{Update}(a, p, a', p')$

$$\forall i(1 \le i \le m \wedge \ (\forall j(1 \le j \le m \wedge j \ne i \rightarrow p(i) > p(j))) \longrightarrow a'(i) = 1)$$
$$\forall i(1 \le i \le m \wedge \ (\forall j(1 \le j \le m \wedge j \ne i \rightarrow p(i) > p(j))) \longrightarrow p'(i) = x)$$
$$\forall i(1 \le i \le m \wedge \neg(\forall j(1 \le j \le m \wedge j \ne i \rightarrow p(i) > p(j))) \longrightarrow a'(i) = 0)$$
$$\forall i(1 \le i \le m \wedge \neg(\forall j(1 \le j \le m \wedge j \ne i \rightarrow p(i) > p(j))) \longrightarrow p'(i) = p(i)+y)$$

where x and y are considered to be parameters. We may need to check whether if at the beginning the priority list is injective, i.e. formula $(\mathsf{Inj})(p)$ holds:

$$\mathsf{Inj}(p) \quad \forall i, j(1 \le i \le m \wedge 1 \le j \le m \wedge i \ne j \rightarrow p(i) \ne p(j))$$

then it remains injective after the update, i.e. check the satisfiability of:

$$(\mathbb{Z} \cup \mathbb{R}_+ \cup \{0, 1\}) \wedge \mathsf{Inj}(p) \wedge \mathsf{Update}(a, p, a', p') \wedge 1 \le c \le m \wedge 1 \le d \le m \wedge c \ne d \wedge p'(c) = p'(d).$$

We may need to check satisfiability of the formula under certain assumptions on the values of x and y (for instance if $x = 0$ and $y = 1$), or to determine constraints on x and y for which the formula is (un)satisfiable.

Problem. The problem above is a satisfiability problem for a formula with (alternations of) quantifiers in a combination of theories. SMT provers heuristically compute ground instances of the problems, and return unsatisfiable if a contradiction is found, and unknown if no contradiction can be derived from these instances. It is important to find a set of ground instances which are sufficient for deriving a contradiction if one exists. [1] presents a fragment of the theory

---

[2] All the examples in this paper will address invariant checking only. Bounded model checking problems can be handled in a similar way.

of arrays for which this is possible. The formula above does not belong to this fragment: $\mathsf{Inj}(p)$ contains the premise $i \neq j$; $\mathsf{Update}(a, p, a', p')$ contains $\forall\exists$ axioms.

Idea. Let $\mathcal{T}_0$ be the many-sorted combination of the theory of integers (for indices), of real numbers (priorities), and $\{0, 1\}$ (enabled/disabled). We consider:

(i) The extension $\mathcal{T}_1$ of $\mathcal{T}_0$ with the functions $a : \mathbb{Z} \to \{0, 1\}$ (a free function) and $p : \mathbb{Z} \to \mathbb{R}_+$ satisfying $\mathsf{Inj}(p)$;

(ii) The extension $\mathcal{T}_2$ of $\mathcal{T}_1$ with the functions $a' : \mathbb{Z} \to \{0, 1\}$, $p' : \mathbb{Z} \to \mathbb{R}_+$ satisfying the update axioms $\mathsf{Update}(a, p, a', p')$.

We show that both extensions have a locality property which allows us to use determined instances of the axioms without loss of completeness; the satisfiability problem w.r.t. $\mathcal{T}_2$ can be hierarchically reduced to a satisfiability problem w.r.t. $\mathcal{T}_1$ and then to a satisfiability problem w.r.t. $\mathcal{T}_0$. The purpose of this paper is to show that we can do this in a systematic way in a large number of situations.

2   Preliminaries

We assume known standard definitions from first-order logic. (Logical) theories can be regarded as collections of formulae (i.e. can be described as the consequences of a set of axioms), as collections of models (the set of all models of a set of axioms, or concrete models such as $\mathbb{Z}$ or $\mathbb{R}$), or both. If $\mathcal{T}$ is a theory and ϕ, ψ are formulae, we say that $\mathcal{T} \wedge \phi \models \psi$ (written also $\phi \models_{\mathcal{T}} \psi$) if ψ is true in all models of $\mathcal{T}$ which satisfy ϕ. If $\mathcal{T} \wedge \phi \models \perp$ (where $\perp$ is false), there are no models of $\mathcal{T}$ which satisfy ϕ, i.e. ϕ is unsatisfiable w.r.t. $\mathcal{T}$. For the verification tasks mentioned above, efficient reasoning in certain theories, which depend on the specification of the systems under consideration, is extremely important.

Local theory extensions. We consider extensions $\mathcal{T}_0 \cup \mathcal{K}$ of a theory $\mathcal{T}_0$ with new sorts and new function symbols (called *extension functions*) satisfying a set $\mathcal{K}$ of (universally quantified) clauses. An extension $\mathcal{T}_0 \subseteq \mathcal{T}_0 \cup \mathcal{K}$ is *local* if satisfiability of a set G of clauses w.r.t. $\mathcal{T}_0 \cup \mathcal{K}$ only depends on $\mathcal{T}_0$ and those instances $\mathcal{K}[G]$ of $\mathcal{K}$ in which the terms starting with *extension functions* are in the set $\mathsf{st}(\mathcal{K}, G)$ of ground terms which already occur in G or $\mathcal{K}$ [13]. A weaker locality notion, namely *stable locality*, exists; it allows to restrict the search to the instances $\mathcal{K}^{[G]}$ of $\mathcal{K}$ in which the variables below extension functions are instantiated with Σ_0-terms generated from $\mathsf{st}(\mathcal{K}, G)$. These generalize the notion of *local theories* introduced by [8,11,9] resp. of locality and stable locality studied in [5]. In such extensions hierarchical reasoning is possible (cf. also Sect. 3.1).

Partial and total models. Local and stably local theory extensions can be recognized by proving embeddability of partial into total models [13,16]. Let $\Pi = (S, \Sigma, \mathsf{Pred})$ be an S-sorted signature where Σ is a set of function symbols and Pred a set of predicate symbols. In a *partial Π-structure* the function symbols may be partial (for definitions cf. [2]). If A is a partial structure and $\beta : X \to \mathcal{A}$ is a valuation we say that $(A, \beta) \models_w (\neg)P(t_1, \ldots, t_n)$ iff (a) $\beta(t_i)$ are all defined and their values are in the relationship $(\neg)P_A$; or (b) at least one of $\beta(t_i)$ is undefined.

This holds in particular for the equality relation. (A, β) *weakly satisfies a clause* C (notation: $(A, \beta) \models_w C$) if it satisfies at least one literal in C. A is a *weak partial model* of a set of clauses $\mathcal{K}$ if $(A, \beta) \models_w C$ for every valuation β and every clause C in $\mathcal{K}$. *(Evans) partial models* are defined similarly, with the following difference: $(A, \beta) \models t \approx s$ iff (a) $\beta(t)$ and $\beta(s)$ are both defined and equal; or (b) $\beta(s)$ is defined, $t = f(t_1, \ldots, t_n)$ and $\beta(t_i)$ is undefined for at least one of the direct subterms of t; or (c) both $\beta(s)$ and $\beta(t)$ are undefined.

3   Locality

As seen in Section 1.2, the axioms occurring in applications may contain alternations of quantifiers. To address this, we study the notion of *extended (stable) locality* (cf. also [13]). Let $\mathcal{T}_0$ be a theory with signature $\Pi_0 = (S_0, \Sigma_0, \mathsf{Pred})$, where S_0 is a set of sorts, Σ_0 a set of function symbols, and Pred a set of predicate symbols. We consider extensions $\mathcal{T}_1$ of $\mathcal{T}_0$ with new sorts and function symbols (i.e. with signature $\Pi = (S_0 \cup S_1, \Sigma_0 \cup \Sigma_1, \mathsf{Pred}))$, satisfying a set $\mathcal{K}$ of axioms of the form $(\Phi(x_1, \ldots, x_n) \vee C(x_1, \ldots, x_n))$, where $\Phi(x_1, \ldots, x_n)$ is an *arbitrary first-order formula* in the base signature Π_0 with free variables $x_1, \ldots, x_n$, and $C(x_1, \ldots, x_n)$ is a *clause* in the signature Π. The free variables $x_1, \ldots, x_n$ of such an axiom are considered to be universally quantified. We are interested in disproving closed formulae Σ in the extension Π^c of Π with new constants Σ_c.

Example 1. *Consider the example in Sect. 1.2. In modeling this problem we start from the disjoint combination $\mathcal{T}_0$ of integers, reals and Booleans with signature $\Pi_0 = (S_0, \Sigma_0, \mathsf{Pred})$, where $S_0 = \{\mathsf{int}, \mathsf{real}, \mathsf{bool}\}$ and Σ_0, Pred consist of the (many-sorted) combination of the signatures of the corresponding theories. In a first step, $\mathcal{T}_0$ is extended to $\mathcal{T}_1 = \mathcal{T}_0 \cup \mathsf{Inj}(p)$, with signature $\Pi_1 = (S_0, \Sigma_0 \cup \{a, p\}, \mathsf{Pred})$. $\mathsf{Inj}(p)$ is a clause. In a second step, $\mathcal{T}_1$ is extended to a theory $\mathcal{T}_2 = \mathcal{T}_1 \cup \mathsf{Update}(a, p, a', p')$ with signature $(S_0, \Sigma_0 \cup \{a, p\} \cup \{a', p'\}, \mathsf{Pred})$. The axioms in $\mathsf{Update}(a, p, a', p')$ are of the form $\phi(i) \vee C(i)$ and $\neg \phi(i) \vee D(i)$, where $\phi(i) = \forall j (1 \leq j \leq m \wedge j \neq i \rightarrow p(i) > p(j))$. (Thus it can be seen that the first two axioms in $\mathsf{Update}(a, p, a', p')$ contain a $\forall \exists$ quantifier alternation.)*

We can extend the notion of locality accordingly. We study extensions $\mathcal{T}_0 \subseteq \mathcal{T}_0 \cup \mathcal{K}$ as above satisfying the locality and stable locality conditions (ELoc, ESLoc):

(ELoc)   For every formula $\Gamma = \Gamma_0 \cup G$, where Γ_0 is a Π_0^c-sentence and G is a finite set of ground Π^c-clauses, $\mathcal{T}_1 \cup \Gamma \models \bot$ iff $\mathcal{T}_0 \cup \mathcal{K}[\Gamma] \cup \Gamma$ has no weak partial model in which all terms in $\mathsf{st}(\mathcal{K}, G)$ are defined.

Here $\mathcal{K}[\Gamma]$ consists of all instances of $\mathcal{K}$ in which the terms starting with extension functions are in the set $\mathsf{st}(\mathcal{K}, G)$ (defined in Sect. 2).

(ESLoc)   For every formula $\Gamma = \Gamma_0 \cup G$, where Γ_0 is a Π_0^c-sentence and G is a finite set of ground Π^c-clauses, $\mathcal{T}_1 \cup \Gamma \models \bot$ iff $\mathcal{T}_0 \cup \mathcal{K}^{[\Gamma]} \cup \Gamma$ has no partial model in which all terms in $\mathsf{st}(\mathcal{K}, G)$ are defined.

Here $\mathcal{K}^{[\Gamma]}$ consists of all instances of $\mathcal{K}$ in which the variables below a Σ_1-symbol are instantiated with Σ_0-terms generated from $\mathsf{st}(\mathcal{K}, G)$.

The problem with (ESLoc) is that the number of instances in $\mathcal{K}^{[\Gamma]}$ is finite only if the number of Σ_0-terms generated from $\mathsf{st}(\mathcal{K}, G)$ can be guaranteed to be finite, i.e. when $\Sigma_0 = \emptyset$ (in which case the size of $\mathcal{K}^{[\Gamma]}$ is polynomial in the size of $\mathsf{st}(\mathcal{K}, G)$) or when only finitely many non-equivalent Σ_0-terms (modulo $\mathcal{T}_0$) can be generated from a finite set of generators (then the size of $\mathcal{K}^{[\Gamma]}$ is polynomial in the number of such non-equivalent terms). To overcome these problems, we identify a family of conditions in between locality and stable locality.

Let Ψ be a function associating with a set $\mathcal{K}$ of axioms and a set of ground terms T a set $\Psi_{\mathcal{K}}(T)$ of ground terms such that (i) all ground subterms in $\mathcal{K}$ and T are in $\Psi_{\mathcal{K}}(T)$; (ii) for all sets of ground terms T, T' if $T \subseteq T'$ then $\Psi_{\mathcal{K}}(T) \subseteq \Psi_{\mathcal{K}}(T')$; (iii) Ψ is a closure operation, i.e. for all sets of ground terms T, $\Psi_{\mathcal{K}}(\Psi_{\mathcal{K}}(T)) \subseteq \Psi_{\mathcal{K}}(T)$; (iv) Ψ is compatible with any map h between constants, i.e. for any map $h : C \to C$, $\Psi_{\mathcal{K}}(\overline{h}(T)) = \overline{h}(\Psi_{\mathcal{K}}(T))$, where $\overline{h}$ is the unique extension of h to terms. Let $\mathcal{K}[\Psi_{\mathcal{K}}(G)]$ be the set of instances of $\mathcal{K}$ in which the extension terms are in $\Psi_{\mathcal{K}}(\mathsf{st}(\mathcal{K}, G))$, which here will be denoted by $\Psi_{\mathcal{K}}(G)$. We say that an extension $\mathcal{T}_0 \subseteq \mathcal{T}_0 \cup \mathcal{K}$ is Ψ-local if it satisfies condition (ELoc$^{\Psi}$):

(ELoc$^{\Psi}$)   for every formula $\Gamma = \Gamma_0 \cup G$, where Γ_0 is a Π_0^c-sentence and G a finite set of ground Π^c-clauses, $\mathcal{T}_1 \cup \Gamma \models \perp$ iff $\mathcal{T}_0 \cup \mathcal{K}[\Psi_{\mathcal{K}}(G)] \cup \Gamma$ has no weak partial model in which all terms in $\Psi_{\mathcal{K}}(G)$ are defined.

If $\mathcal{K}$ consists of clauses and only satisfiability of sets G of ground clauses is considered we obtain a condition (Loc$^{\Psi}$) extending the notion (Loc) of locality in [13]. Ψ-stable locality (ESLoc$^{\Psi}$) can be defined replacing $\mathcal{K}[\Psi_{\mathcal{K}}(G)]$ by $\mathcal{K}^{[\Psi_{\mathcal{K}}(G)]}$.

3.1   Hierarchical Reasoning in Local Theory Extensions

Let $\mathcal{T}_0 \subseteq \mathcal{T}_1 = \mathcal{T}_0 \cup \mathcal{K}$ be a theory extension satisfying condition (E(S)Loc) or (E(S)Loc$^{\Psi}$). To check the satisfiability w.r.t. $\mathcal{T}_1$ of a formula $\Gamma = \Gamma_0 \cup G$, where Γ_0 is a Π_0^c-sentence and G is a set of ground Π^c-clauses, we proceed as follows:

Step 1: By the locality assumption, $\mathcal{T}_1 \cup \Gamma_0 \cup G$ is satisfiable iff $\mathcal{T}_0 \cup \mathcal{K}*[G] \cup \Gamma_0 \cup G$ has a (weak) partial model with corresponding properties, where, depending on the type of locality, $\mathcal{K}*[G]$ is $\mathcal{K}[G], \mathcal{K}^{[G]}, \mathcal{K}[\Psi_{\mathcal{K}}(G)]$ or $\mathcal{K}^{[\Psi_{\mathcal{K}}(G)]}$.

Step 2: Purification. We purify $\mathcal{K}*[G] \cup G$ by introducing, in a bottom-up manner, new constants c_t (from a set Σ_c of constants) for subterms $t = f(g_1, \dots, g_n)$ with $f \in \Sigma_1$, g_i ground $\Sigma_0 \cup \Sigma_c$-terms, together with their definitions $c_t \approx t$. The set of formulae thus obtained has the form $\mathcal{K}_0 \cup G_0 \cup \Gamma_0 \cup D$, where D consists of definitions of the form $f(g_1, \dots, g_n) \approx c$, where $f \in \Sigma_1$, c is a constant, $g_1, \dots, g_n$ are ground $\Sigma_0 \cup \Sigma_c$-terms, and $\mathcal{K}_0, G_0, \Gamma_0$ are Π_0^c-formulae.

Step 3: Reduction to testing satisfiability in $\mathcal{T}_0$. We reduce the problem to testing satisfiability in $\mathcal{T}_0$ by replacing D with the following set of clauses:

$$N_0 = \{ \bigwedge_{i=1}^{n} c_i \approx d_i \to c = d \mid f(c_1, \dots, c_n) \approx c, f(d_1, \dots, d_n) \approx d \in D \}.$$

This yields a sound and complete hierarchical reduction to a satisfiability problem in the base theory $\mathcal{T}_0$ (for (E(S)Loc$^{\Psi}$) the proof is similar to that in [13]):

Theorem 1. *Let $\mathcal{K}$ and $\Gamma = \Gamma_0 \wedge G$ be as specified above. Assume that $\mathcal{T}_0 \subseteq \mathcal{T}_0 \cup \mathcal{K}$ satisfies condition* (E(S)Loc) *or* (E(S)Loc$^{\Psi}$). *Let $\mathcal{K}_0 \cup G_0 \cup \Gamma_0 \cup D$ be obtained from $\mathcal{K} * [G] \cup \Gamma_0 \cup G$ by purification, as explained above. The following are equivalent:*

(1) $\mathcal{T}_0 \cup \mathcal{K} * [G] \cup \Gamma_0 \cup G$ has a partial model with all terms in $\mathsf{st}(\mathcal{K}, G)$ defined.
(2) $\mathcal{T}_0 \cup \mathcal{K}_0 \cup G_0 \cup \Gamma_0 \cup D$ has a partial model with all extension terms in D defined.
(3) $\mathcal{T}_0 \cup \mathcal{K}_0 \cup G_0 \cup \Gamma_0 \cup N_0$ has a (total) model.

Alternatively, if $\mathcal{K}$ consists only of clauses and all variables occur below an extension function and if Γ is a set of ground clauses then $\mathcal{K} * [G] \wedge \Gamma$ consists of ground clauses, so locality also allows us to reduce reasoning in $\mathcal{T}_1$ to reasoning in an extension of $\mathcal{T}_0$ with free function symbols; an SMT procedure can be used. If Γ_0 contains quantifiers or $\mathcal{K} * [G]$ contains free variables it is problematic to use SMT provers without loss of completeness.

3.2 Decidability, Parameterized Complexity

Assume that $\mathcal{K}$ consists of axioms of the form $\overline{C} = (\Phi_C(\overline{x}) \vee C(\overline{x}))$, where $\Phi_C(\overline{x})$ is in a fragment (class of formulae) $\mathcal{F}$ of $\mathcal{T}_0$ and $C(\overline{x})$ is a Π-clause, and $\Gamma = \Gamma_0 \wedge G$, where Γ_0 is a formula in $\mathcal{F}$ without free variables, and G is a set of ground Π^c-clauses, both containing constants in Σ_c.

Theorem 2. *Assume that the theory extension $\mathcal{T}_0 \subseteq \mathcal{T}_1$ satisfies* (E(S)Loc), *or* (E(S)Loc$^{\Psi}$). *Satisfiability of goals $\Gamma_0 \cup G$ as above w.r.t. $\mathcal{T}_1$ is decidable provided $\mathcal{K} * [G]$ is finite and $\mathcal{K}_0 \cup G_0 \cup \Gamma_0 \cup N_0$ belongs to a decidable fragment of $\mathcal{T}_0$.*

Locality allows us to obtain parameterized decidability and complexity results:

Case 1: If for each $\overline{C} = \Phi_C(\overline{x}) \vee C(\overline{x}) \in \mathcal{K}$ all free variables occur below some extension symbol, then $\mathcal{K} * [G]$ contains only formulae of the form $\Phi_C(\overline{g}) \vee C(\overline{g})$, where $\overline{g}$ consists of ground Σ_0-terms, so $\mathcal{K}_0 \cup G_0 \cup \Gamma_0 \cup N_0 \in \mathcal{F}_g$, the class obtained by instantiating all free variables of formulae in $\mathcal{F}$ with ground Σ_0-terms.

Decidability and complexity: If checking satisfiability for the class $\mathcal{F}_g$ w.r.t. $\mathcal{T}_0$ is decidable, then checking satisfiability of goals of the form above w.r.t. $\mathcal{T}_1$ is decidable. Assume that the complexity of a decision procedure for the fragment $\mathcal{F}_g$ of $\mathcal{T}_0$ is $g(n)$ for an input of size n. Let m be the size of $\mathcal{K}_0 \cup G_0 \cup \Gamma_0 \cup N_0$. Then the complexity of proving satisfiability of $\Gamma_0 \cup G$ w.r.t. $\mathcal{T}_1$ is of order $g(m)$.

(i) For local extensions, $\mathcal{K} * [G] = \mathcal{K}[G]$; the size m of $\mathcal{K}_0 \cup G_0 \cup \Gamma_0 \cup N_0$ is of order $|G|^k$ for some $2 \leq k \in \mathbb{Z}$ for a fixed $\mathcal{K}$ (at least quadratic because of N_0).
(ii) For stably local extensions, the size of $\mathcal{K} * [G] = \mathcal{K}^{[G]}$ is polynomial in the size s of the model of $\mathcal{T}_0$ freely generated by $|\mathsf{st}(\mathcal{K}, G)|$ generators.

Similarly for Ψ-(stably) local extensions (with $\mathsf{st}(\mathcal{K}, G)$ replaced by $\Psi_\mathcal{K}(G)$).

Case 2: If not all free variables in $\mathcal{K}$ occur below an extension symbol, then the instances in $\mathcal{K} * [G]$ contain free variables, so $\mathcal{K}_0 \cup G_0 \cup \Gamma_0 \cup N_0$ is in the universal closure $\forall \mathcal{F}$ of $\mathcal{F}$. The decidability and complexity remarks above here apply relative to the complexity of checking satisfiability of formulae in the fragment $\forall \mathcal{F}$ of $\mathcal{T}_0$ with constants in Σ_c (regarded as existentially quantified variables).

3.3   Recognizing Generalized Locality

Theory extensions $\mathcal{T}_0 \subseteq \mathcal{T}_1$ satisfying (E(S)Loc), (E(S)Loc$^\Psi$) can be recognized by showing that certain partial models of $\mathcal{T}_1$ can be completed to total models. We consider the following completability conditions:

(Comp$_w$) Every weak partial model A of $\mathcal{T}_1$ with totally defined Σ_0-functions and extension functions with a finite definition domain weakly embeds into a total model B of $\mathcal{T}_1$ s.t. $A_{|\Pi_0}$ and $B_{|\Pi_0}$ are isomorphic.

(Comp$_w^\Psi$) Every weak partial model A of $\mathcal{T}_1$ with totally defined Σ_0-functions and such that $\{f(a_1, \ldots, a_n) \mid a_i \in A, f \in \Sigma_1, f_A(a_1, \ldots, a_n) \text{ defined}\}$ is finite and closed under $\Psi_\mathcal{K}$ weakly embeds into a total model B of $\mathcal{T}_1$ s.t. $A_{|\Pi_0}$ and $B_{|\Pi_0}$ are elementarily equivalent.

Conditions (Comp), (Comp$^\Psi$) can be defined by replacing "weak partial model" with "Evans partial model". Assume Ψ satisfies conditions (i)–(iv) in Sect.3:

Theorem 3. *(1) If all terms of $\mathcal{K}$ starting with a Σ_1-function are flat and linear and the extension $\mathcal{T}_0 \subseteq \mathcal{T}_1$ satisfies (Comp$_w$) (resp. (Comp$_w^\Psi$)) then it satisfies (ELoc) [13] (resp. (ELoc$^\Psi$)).*
(2) If $\mathcal{T}_0$ is a universal theory and the extension $\mathcal{T}_0 \subseteq \mathcal{T}_1$ satisfies (Comp) (resp. (Comp$^\Psi$)) then it satisfies (ESLoc) [13] (resp. (ESLoc$^\Psi$)).

Theorem 3 allows us to identify many examples of local extensions (see Sect. 4). A combination of extensions of a theory $\mathcal{T}_0$ which satisfy condition Comp (Comp$_w$) also satisfies condition Comp (Comp$_w$) and hence also condition ESLoc (ELoc).

Theorem 4 ([15]). *Let $\mathcal{T}_0$ be a first order theory with signature $\Pi_0 = (\Sigma_0, \mathsf{Pred})$ and (for $i \in \{1, 2\}$) $\mathcal{T}_i = \mathcal{T}_0 \cup \mathcal{K}_i$ be an extension of $\mathcal{T}_0$ with signature $\Pi_i = (\Sigma_0 \cup \Sigma_i, \mathsf{Pred})$. Assume that both extensions $\mathcal{T}_0 \subseteq \mathcal{T}_1$ and $\mathcal{T}_0 \subseteq \mathcal{T}_2$ satisfy condition (Comp$_w$), and that $\Sigma_1 \cap \Sigma_2 = \emptyset$. Then the extension $\mathcal{T}_0 \subseteq \mathcal{T} = \mathcal{T}_0 \cup \mathcal{K}_1 \cup \mathcal{K}_2$ satisfies condition (Comp$_w$). If, additionally, in $\mathcal{K}_i$ all terms starting with a function symbol in Σ_i are flat and linear, for $i = 1, 2$, then the extension is local.*

4   Examples

4.1   Extensions with Free, (Strictly) Monotone, Injective Functions

Any extension $\mathcal{T}_0 \cup \mathsf{Free}(\Sigma)$ of a theory $\mathcal{T}_0$ with a set Σ of *free function symbols* satisfies condition (Comp$_w$). We also consider monotonicity/antitonicity conditions[3] for an n-ary function f w.r.t. a subset I of its arguments:

$$\mathsf{Mon}^\sigma(f) \qquad \bigwedge_{i \in I} x_i \leq_i^{\sigma_i} y_i \wedge \bigwedge_{i \notin I} x_i = y_i \rightarrow f(x_1, .., x_n) \leq f(y_1, .., y_n),$$

where for $i \in I$, $\sigma_i \in \{-, +\}$, and for $i \notin I$, $\sigma_i = 0$, and $\leq^+ = \leq$ and $\leq^- = \geq$.

---

[3] If $I = \{1, \ldots, n\}$ we speak of monotonicity in all arguments; we denote $\mathsf{Mon}^I(f)$ by $\mathsf{Mon}(f)$. If $I = \emptyset$, $\mathsf{Mon}^\emptyset(f)$ is equivalent to the congruence axiom for f.

We showed [13,16] that the extensions of any (possibly many-sorted) theory whose models are posets with functions satisfying the axioms $\mathsf{Mon}^\sigma(f)$ satisfy condition ($\mathsf{Comp_w}$) if the codomains of the functions have a bounded semilattice reduct or are totally ordered. In particular, any extension of the theory of reals, rationals or integers with functions satisfying $\mathsf{Mon}^\sigma(f)$ into an numeric domain (reals, rationals, integers or a subset thereof) is local, since ($\mathsf{Comp_w}$) holds.

Example 2. The sortedness property $\mathsf{Sorted}(a)$ of the array a can be expressed as a monotonicity axiom: $\forall i, j (1 \leq i \leq j \leq m \to a(i) \leq a(j))$. An extension of the theory of integers with a function a of arity $\mathsf{i} \to \mathsf{e}$ satisfying $\mathsf{Sorted}(a)$ (where e is a new or old sort and the theory of sort e is totally ordered) is local.

Consider now the following conditions:
$$\mathsf{SMon}(f)\quad \forall i, j(i < j \to f(i) < f(j)) \quad \text{and} \quad \mathsf{Inj}(f)\quad \forall i, j(i \neq j \to f(i) \neq f(j))$$

Theorem 5. *Assume that in all models of $\mathcal{T}_0$ the support of sort i has an underlying strict total order relation $<$. Let $\mathcal{T}_1 = \mathcal{T}_0 \cup \mathsf{SMon}(f)$, where f is a new function of arity $\mathsf{i} \to \mathsf{e}$ (e may be a new or an old sort), in all models of $\mathcal{T}_1$ the support of sort e has an underlying strict total order $<$, and there exist injective order-preserving maps from any interval of the support of sort i to any interval of the support e. Then the extension $\mathcal{T}_0 \subseteq \mathcal{T}_1$ satisfies ($\mathsf{Comp_w}$), hence it is local.*

Example 3. Let $\mathcal{T}_0$ be the (many-sorted) combination of $\mathcal{T}_0^\mathsf{i}$ (the theory of linear integer arithmetic, sort i) and $\mathcal{T}_0^\mathsf{num}$ (the theory of real numbers, sort num). The extension $\mathcal{T}_1$ of $\mathcal{T}_0$ with a function f of arity $\mathsf{i} \to \mathsf{num}$ satisfying $\mathsf{SMon}(f)$ is local.

Theorem 6. *A theory extension $\mathcal{T}_0 \subseteq \mathcal{T}_1 = \mathcal{T}_0 \cup \mathsf{Inj}(f)$ with a function f of arity $\mathsf{i} \to \mathsf{e}$ satisfying $\mathsf{Inj}(f)$ is local provided that in all models of $\mathcal{T}_1$ the cardinality of the support of sort i is lower or equal to the cardinality of the support of sort e.*

4.2   Extensions with Definitions and Boundedness Conditions

Let $\mathcal{T}_0$ be a theory containing a binary predicate $\leq$ which is reflexive, and $f \notin \Sigma_0$.

Guarded boundedness. Let $m \in \mathbb{N}$. For $1 \leq i \leq m$ let $t_i(x_1, \ldots, x_n)$ and $s_i(x_1, \ldots, x_n)$ be terms in the signature Π_0 with variables among $x_1, \ldots, x_n$, and let $\phi_i(x_1, \ldots, x_n)$, $i \in \{1, \ldots, m\}$ be Π_0-formulae with free variables among $x_1, \ldots, x_n$, such that (i) for every $i \neq j$, $\phi_i \wedge \phi_j \models_{\mathcal{T}_0} \bot$, and (ii) for every i, $\mathcal{T}_0 \models \forall \overline{x}(\phi_i(\overline{x}) \to s_i(\overline{x}) \leq t_i(\overline{x}))$. Let $\mathsf{GBound}(f) = \bigwedge_{i=1}^m \mathsf{GBound}^{\phi_i}(f)$, where:
$$\mathsf{GBound}^{\phi_i}(f)\quad \forall \overline{x}(\phi_i(\overline{x}) \to s_i(\overline{x}) \leq f(\overline{x}) \leq t_i(\overline{x})).$$
The extension $\mathcal{T}_0 \subseteq \mathcal{T}_0 \cup \mathsf{GBound}(f)$ is local.

Boundedness for (strictly) monotone and injective functions. Any extension of a theory for which $\leq$ is a partial order (or at least reflexive) with functions satisfying $\mathsf{Mon}^\sigma(f)$ and boundedness $\mathsf{Bound}^t(f)$ conditions is local [14,16].
$$\mathsf{Bound}^t(f)\quad \forall x_1, \ldots, x_n(f(x_1, \ldots, x_n) \leq t(x_1, \ldots, x_n))$$
where $t(x_1, \ldots, x_n)$ is a Π_0-term with variables among $x_1, \ldots, x_n$ whose associated function has the same monotonicity as f in any model. Similar results hold for strictly monotone/injective functions (under the conditions in Thm. 5, 6).

4.3 Pointer Data Structures à la McPeak and Necula

In [12], McPeak and Necula investigate reasoning in pointer data structures. The language used has sorts p (pointer) and s (scalar). Sets Σ_p and Σ_s of pointer resp. scalar fields are modeled by functions of sort $p \rightarrow p$ and $p \rightarrow s$, respectively. A constant null of sort p exists. The only predicate of sort p is equality; predicates of sort s can have any arity. The axioms considered in [12] are of the form

$$\forall p \quad \mathcal{E} \vee \mathcal{C} \tag{1}$$

where $\mathcal{E}$ contains disjunctions of pointer equalities and $\mathcal{C}$ contains scalar constraints (sets of both positive and negative literals). It is assumed that for all terms $f_1(f_2(\dots f_n(p)))$ occurring in the body of an axiom, the axiom also contains the disjunction $p = \text{null} \vee f_n(p) = \text{null} \vee \cdots \vee f_2(\dots f_n(p)) = \text{null}$.[4] Examples of axioms (for doubly linked data structures with priorities) considered there are:

$$\forall p \quad p \neq \text{null} \wedge \text{next}(p) \neq \text{null} \rightarrow \text{prev}(\text{next}(p)) = p \tag{2}$$
$$\forall p \quad p \neq \text{null} \wedge \text{prev}(p) \neq \text{null} \rightarrow \text{next}(\text{prev}(p)) = p \tag{3}$$
$$\forall p \quad p \neq \text{null} \wedge \text{next}(p) \neq \text{null} \rightarrow \text{priority}(p) \geq \text{priority}(\text{next}(p)) \tag{4}$$

(the first two axioms state that prev is a left inverse for next, the third axiom is a monotonicity condition on the function priority). Let $\Psi_\mathcal{K}(T) = \text{st}(\mathcal{K}) \cup T \cup \{f(t) \mid t \in \text{st}(\mathcal{K}) \cup T, f \in \Sigma_s\}$ for any set of ground terms T.

Theorem 7. *Let $\mathcal{T}_0$ be a Π_0-theory, where $S_0 = \{s\}$, and $\mathcal{T}_1 = \mathcal{T}_0 \cup \mathcal{K}$ be the extension of $\mathcal{T}_0$ with signature $\Pi = (\{p, s\}, \Sigma, \text{Pred})$ – where $\Sigma = \Sigma_p \cup \Sigma_s \cup \Sigma_0$, and $\mathcal{K}$ is a set of axioms $\forall p(\mathcal{E} \vee \mathcal{C})$ of type (1). Then every partial model A of $\mathcal{K}$ with total Σ_0 functions such that the definition domain of A is closed under $\Psi_\mathcal{K}$ (i.e. if $f \in \Sigma_s$ and the p-term t is defined in A then $f(t)$ is defined in A) weakly embeds into a total model of $\mathcal{K}$. Hence $\mathcal{T}_0 \subseteq \mathcal{T}_1$ is a Ψ-stably local extension.*

Ψ-stable locality is not harmful in this case, since all universally quantified variables in the axioms in $\mathcal{K}$ are of sort p, and the number of instances of these variables with subterms in $\Psi_\mathcal{K}(G)$ which need to be considered is polynomial in the size of $\text{st}(\mathcal{K}, G)$ (no operations with output sort s generate such terms).

4.4 The Theory of Arrays à la Bradley, Manna and Sipma

In [1] the *array property fragment* is studied, a fragment of the theory of arrays with Presburger arithmetic as index theory and parametric element theories. Consider the extension of the combination $\mathcal{T}_0$ of the index and element theories with functions read, write and axioms:

$$\text{read}(\text{write}(a, i, e), i) = e \qquad j \neq i \rightarrow \text{read}(\text{write}(a, i, e), j) = \text{read}(a, j).$$

The array property fragment is defined as follows[5]:

---

[4] This has the rôle of excluding null pointer errors.

[5] The considerations below are for arrays of dimension 1, the general case is similar.

An *index guard* is a positive Boolean combination of atoms of the form $t \leq u$ or $t = u$ where t and u are either a variable of index sort or a ground term (of index sort) constructed from (Skolem) constants and integer numbers using addition and multiplication with integers. A formula of the form $(\forall i)(\varphi_I(i) \rightarrow \varphi_V(i))$ is an *array property* if φ_I is an index guard and if any universally quantified variable of index sort i only occurs in a direct array read $\mathsf{read}(a, x)$ in φ_V. Array reads may not be nested. The *array property fragment* consists of all existentially-closed Boolean combinations of array property formulae and quantifier-free formulae.

The decision procedure proposed in [1] decides satisfiability of formulae in negation normal form in the array property fragment in the following steps.

1. Replace all existentially quantified array variables with Skolem constants; replace all terms of the form $\mathsf{read}(a, i)$ with $a(i)$; eliminate all terms of the form $\mathsf{write}(a, i, e)$ by replacing the formula $\phi(\mathsf{write}(a, i, e))$ with the conjunction of the formula $\phi(b)$ (obtained by introducing a fresh array name b for $\mathsf{write}(a, i, e)$) with $(b(i) = e) \wedge \forall j(j \leq i - 1 \vee i + 1 \leq j \rightarrow b(j) = a(j))$.[6]
2. Existentially quantified index variables are replaced with Skolem constants.
3. Universal quantification over index variables is replaced by conjunction of suitably chosen instances of the variables.

For determining the set of ground instances to be used in Step 3, the authors prove that certain partial "minimal" models can be completed to total ones.

Theorem 8 (cf. also [1]). *Let $\mathcal{K}$ be the clause part and G the ground part (after the transformation steps (1)–(3)), and $\mathcal{I}$ be the set of index terms defined in [1]. Let $\Psi_{\mathcal{K}}(G) = \{f(i_1, \ldots, i_n) \mid f$ array name $, i_1, \ldots, i_n \in \mathcal{I}\}$. Every partial model of $\mathcal{T}_0 \cup \mathcal{K}[\Psi_{\mathcal{K}}(G)] \cup G$ in which all terms in $\Psi_{\mathcal{K}}(G)$ are defined can be transformed into a (total) model of $\mathcal{T}_0 \cup \mathcal{K} \cup G$. This criterion entails (ELoc^Ψ).*

5   A General Framework for Obtaining Locality Results

In Section 4 we identified a large number of theory extensions which can be proved to be local and arise in a natural way in invariant checking and bounded model checking. We distinguish several aspects:

- Programs usually handle complex data structures; it may be necessary to reason about various data types such as lists, arrays, records, etc. We presented classes of such theories for which locality properties hold. Theorem 4 identifies cases in which locality is preserved when combining theories.
- The transition constraint systems we consider define updates of the values of variables and functions which are guarded by formulae which describe a partition of the state space, and therefore define local theory extensions.
- In invariant checking and bounded model checking, the paths to be verified (consisting of successive updates) can be used to identify *chains of extensions* to be considered in the deduction process. These extensions are often (combinations) of various extensions with guarded boundedness conditions.

---

[6] Note that, by the definition of array property formulae, if a term $\mathsf{write}(a, i, e)$ occurs in the array property fragment then i is an existentially quantified index variable.

Thus, results in Sect. 4.2 and 3.3 allow us to extend the classes of theories from verification for which instantiation-based complete decision procedures exist.

Extensions of the fragment of Necula and McPeak. We are interested in pointer structures which can be changed during execution of a program (a cell of a list can be removed, or a new subtree added into a tree structure). The general remarks above also apply for such situations.

Theorem 9. *Assume that the update axioms* $\mathsf{Update}(\Sigma, \Sigma')$ *describe how the values of the Σ-functions change, depending on a finite set $\{\phi_i \mid i \in I\}$ of mutually exclusive conditions, expressed as formulae over the base signature and the Σ-functions (axioms of type (5) below represent precise ways of defining the updated functions, whereas axioms of type (6) represent boundedness properties on the updated scalar fields, assuming the scalar domains are partially ordered):*

$$\forall \overline{x}(\phi_i(\overline{x}) \rightarrow f_i'(\overline{x}){=}s_i(\overline{x})) \quad i \in I, \ \text{where} \ \phi_i(\overline{x}) \wedge \phi_j(\overline{x}) \models_{\mathcal{T}_0} \bot \ \text{for} \ i{\neq}j \quad (5)$$

$$\forall \overline{x}(\phi_i(\overline{x}) \rightarrow t_i(\overline{x}){\leq}f_i'(\overline{x}){\leq}s_i(\overline{x})) \quad i \in I, \ \text{where} \ \phi_i(\overline{x}) \wedge \phi_j(\overline{x}) \models_{\mathcal{T}_0} \bot \ \text{for} \ i{\neq}j \quad (6)$$

where s_i, t_i are terms over the signature Σ such that $\mathcal{T}_0 \models \forall \overline{x}(\phi_i(\overline{x}){\rightarrow}t_i(\overline{x}){\leq}s_i(\overline{x}))$ for all $i \in I$. They define local theory extensions. This holds for any extensions of disjoint combinations of various pointer structures with such update axioms.

Example 4. Consider the following algorithm for inserting an element c with priority field $c.\mathsf{prio} = x$ into a doubly-linked list sorted w.r.t. the priority fields.

$c.\mathsf{prio} = x, c.\mathsf{next} = \mathsf{null}$
for all $p \neq c$ **do**
if $p.\mathsf{prio} \leq x$ **then if** $p.\mathsf{prev} = \mathsf{null}$ **then** $c.\mathsf{next}' = p$, **endif**; $p.\mathsf{next}' = p.\mathsf{next}$
$\quad\quad p.\mathsf{prio} > x$ **then**   **case** $p.\mathsf{next} = \mathsf{null}$ **then** $p.\mathsf{next}' := c, c.\mathsf{next}' = \mathsf{null}$
$\quad\quad\quad\quad\quad\quad\quad\quad\quad p.\mathsf{next} \neq \mathsf{null} \wedge p.\mathsf{next} > x$ **then** $p.\mathsf{next}' = p.\mathsf{next}$
$\quad\quad\quad\quad\quad\quad\quad\quad\quad p.\mathsf{next} \neq \mathsf{null} \wedge p.\mathsf{next} \leq x$ **then** $p.\mathsf{next}' = c, c.\mathsf{next}' = p.\mathsf{next}$

The update rules $\mathsf{Update}(\mathsf{next}, \mathsf{next}')$ can be read from the program above:

$\forall p(p{\neq}\mathsf{null} \wedge p{\neq}c \wedge \mathsf{prio}(p){\leq}x \wedge (\mathsf{prev}(p) = \mathsf{null}) \rightarrow \mathsf{next}'(c){=}p \wedge \mathsf{next}'(p){=}\mathsf{next}(p))$
$\forall p(p{\neq}\mathsf{null} \wedge p{\neq}c \wedge \mathsf{prio}(p){\leq}x \wedge (\mathsf{prev}(p) \neq \mathsf{null}) \rightarrow \mathsf{next}'(p){=}\mathsf{next}(p))$
$\forall p(p{\neq}\mathsf{null} \wedge p{\neq}c \wedge \mathsf{prio}(p){>}x \wedge \mathsf{next}(p){=}\mathsf{null} \rightarrow \mathsf{next}'(p){=}c \wedge \mathsf{next}'(c){=}\mathsf{null})$
$\forall p(p{\neq}\mathsf{null} \wedge p{\neq}c \wedge \mathsf{prio}(p){>}x \wedge \mathsf{next}(p){\neq}\mathsf{null} \wedge \mathsf{prio}(\mathsf{next}(p)){>}x \rightarrow \mathsf{next}'(p){=}\mathsf{next}(p))$
$\forall p(p{\neq}\mathsf{null} \wedge p{\neq}c \wedge \mathsf{prio}(p){>}x \wedge \mathsf{next}(p){\neq}\mathsf{null} \wedge \mathsf{prio}(\mathsf{next}(p)){\leq}x \rightarrow \mathsf{next}'(p){=}c \wedge \mathsf{next}'(c){=}\mathsf{next}(p))$

We prove that if the list is sorted, it remains so after insertion, i.e. the formula:

$$d \neq \mathsf{null} \wedge \mathsf{next}'(d) \neq \mathsf{null} \wedge \neg \mathsf{prio}(d) \geq \mathsf{prio}(\mathsf{next}'(d))$$

is unsatisfiable in the extension $\mathcal{T}_1 = \mathcal{T}_0 \cup \mathsf{Update}(\mathsf{next}, \mathsf{next}')$ of the theory $\mathcal{T}_0$ of doubly linked lists with a monotone field prio. $\mathcal{T}_0$ is axiomatized by the axioms $\mathcal{K} = \{(2), (3), (4)\}$ in Sect. 4. The update rules are guarded boundedness axioms, so the extension $\mathcal{T}_0 \subseteq \mathcal{T}_1$ is local. Hence, the satisfiability task above w.r.t. $\mathcal{T}_1$ can be reduced to a satisfiability task w.r.t. $\mathcal{T}_0$ as follows:

Update_0	$d\neq\text{null} \wedge d\neq c \wedge \text{prio}(d)\leq x \wedge \text{prev}(d)=\text{null} \rightarrow c_1=d$
	$d\neq\text{null} \wedge d\neq c \wedge \text{prio}(d)\leq x \wedge \text{prev}(d)=\text{null} \rightarrow d_1=\text{next}(d)$
	$d\neq\text{null} \wedge d\neq c \wedge \text{prio}(d)\leq x \wedge \text{prev}(d)\neq\text{null} \rightarrow d_1=\text{next}(d)$
	$d\neq\text{null} \wedge d\neq c \wedge \text{prio}(d)>x \wedge \text{next}(d)=\text{null} \rightarrow d_1=c \wedge c_1=\text{null}$
	$d\neq\text{null} \wedge d\neq c \wedge \text{prio}(d)>x \wedge \text{next}(d)\neq\text{null} \wedge \text{prio}(\text{next}(d))<x \rightarrow d_1=\text{next}(d)$
	$d\neq\text{null} \wedge d\neq c \wedge \text{prio}(d)>x \wedge \text{next}(d)\neq\text{null} \wedge \text{prio}(\text{next}(d))\leq x \rightarrow d_1=c$
	$d\neq\text{null} \wedge d\neq c \wedge \text{prio}(d)>x \wedge \text{next}(d)\neq\text{null} \wedge \text{prio}(\text{next}(d))\leq x \rightarrow c_1=\text{next}(d)$
G_0	$d \neq \text{null} \wedge \text{next}'(d) \neq \text{null} \wedge \neg\text{prio}(d) \geq \text{priority}(\text{next}'(d))$
N_0	$d=c \rightarrow d_1=c_1 \qquad$ (corresponds to $\text{Def}: \text{next}'(d)=d_1 \wedge \text{next}'(c)=c_1$)

To check the satisfiability of $G' = \text{Update}_0 \wedge G_0 \wedge N_0$ w.r.t. $\mathcal{T}_0$ we use the Ψ-stable locality of the theory defined by the axioms $\mathcal{K} = \{(2),(3),(4)\}$ of doubly linked lists with decreasing priorities in Sect. 4 or the instantiation method in [12].

Extending the array property fragment. Let $\mathcal{T}_0$ be the array property fragment in [1] (set of arrays Σ_0). There are several ways of extending $\mathcal{T}_0$:

Theorem 10. *Let $\mathcal{T}_1=\mathcal{T}_0\cup\mathcal{K}$ be an extension of $\mathcal{T}_0$ with new arrays in a set Σ_1.*

(1) If $\mathcal{K}$ consists of guarded boundedness axioms, or guarded definitions (cf. Sect.4.2) for the Σ_1-function symbols, then the extension $\mathcal{T}_0 \subseteq \mathcal{T}_1$ is local. [7]
(2) If $\mathcal{K}$ consists of injectivity or (strict) monotonicity (and possibly boundedness axioms) for the function symbols in Σ_1 then the extension $\mathcal{T}_0 \subseteq \mathcal{T}_1$ is local if the assumptions about the element theory specified in Sect. 4.1 hold.
(3) Any combination of extensions of $\mathcal{T}_0$ as those mentioned in (1),(2) with disjoint sets of new array constants leads to a local extension of $\mathcal{T}_0$.

If the guards ϕ_i of the axioms in $\mathcal{K}$ are clauses then the result of the hierarchical reasoning method in Thm. 1 is a formula in $\mathcal{T}_0$, hence satisfiability of ground clauses w.r.t. $\mathcal{T}_0 \cup \mathcal{K}$ is decidable. Similarly for chains of extensions. The same holds for testing satisfiability of goals $\Gamma_0 \cup G$ where Γ_0 and $(\mathcal{K}[G])_0$ belong to the array property fragment. For general guards and chains of extensions decidability depends on the form of the formulae obtained by hierarchical reduction(s).

Example 5. The example presented in Section 1.2 illustrates the extension of the fragment in [1] we consider. The task is to check the unsatisfiability of the formula $\quad G = (1 \leq c \leq m \wedge 1 \leq d \leq m \wedge c \neq d \wedge p'(c) = p'(d)) \quad$ in the extension of the many sorted combination $\mathcal{T}_0$ of $\mathbb{Z}, \mathbb{R}_+, \{0,1\}$ with the axioms $\forall i, j(1 \leq i \leq m \wedge 1 \leq j \leq m \wedge i \neq j \rightarrow p(i) \neq p(j)) \wedge \text{Update}(a,p,a',p')$.
The extension can be expressed as a chain: $\mathcal{T}_0 \subseteq \mathcal{T}_1 = \mathcal{T}_0 \cup \text{Inj}(p) \subseteq \mathcal{T}_2 = \mathcal{T}_1 \cup \text{Update}(a,p,a',p')$. By the locality of the second extension (with guarded boundedness axioms) we obtain the following reduction of the task of proving $\mathcal{T}_2 \wedge G \models \perp$ to a satisfiability problem w.r.t. $\mathcal{T}_1$. We take into account only the instances of $\text{Update}(a,p,a',p')$ which contain ground terms occurring in G. This means that the axioms containing a' do not need to be considered. After purification and skolemization of the existentially quantified variables we obtain:

---
[7] An example are definitions of new arrays by writing x at a (constant) index c, axiomatized by $\{\forall i(i \neq c \rightarrow a'(i) = a(i)), \quad \forall i(i = c \rightarrow a'(i) = x)\}$.

Update$_0$	$1 \leq c \leq m \wedge (1 \leq k_c \leq m \wedge k_c{\neq}c \rightarrow p(c){>}p(k_c)) \rightarrow c_1{=}x$
	$1 \leq d \leq m \wedge (1 \leq k_d \leq m \wedge k_d{\neq}d \rightarrow p(d){>}p(k_d)) \rightarrow d_1{=}x$
	$\forall j(1 \leq j \leq m \wedge j{\neq}c \rightarrow p(c){>}p(j)) \vee (1 \leq c \leq m \rightarrow c_1{=}p(c){+}y)$
	$\forall j(1 \leq j \leq m \wedge j{\neq}d \rightarrow p(d){>}p(j)) \vee (1 \leq d \leq m \rightarrow d_1{=}p(d){+}y)$
G_0	$1 \leq c \leq m \wedge 1 \leq d \leq m \wedge c \neq d \wedge c_1 = d_1$
N_0	$c = d \rightarrow c_1 = d_1$ (corresponds to Def : $p'(c) = c_1 \wedge p'(d) = d_1$)

We reduced the problem to checking satisfiability of $G_1 = $ Update$_0 \wedge G_0 \wedge N_0$ (which contains universal quantifiers) w.r.t. $\mathcal{T}_1$. Let $G_1 = G_g \wedge G_\forall$, where G_g is the ground part of G and $G_\forall$ the part of G containing universally quantified variables. We now have to check whether $\mathcal{T}_0 \wedge \mathsf{Inj}(p) \wedge G_\forall \wedge G_g \models \perp$. Note that extensions of injectivity axioms and boundedness are local, and thus $\mathcal{T}_0 \subseteq \mathcal{T}_0 \wedge \mathsf{Inj} \wedge G_\forall$ is a local extension. This makes the following reduction possible:

Inj$_0$	$1{\leq}i{\neq}j{\leq}m \rightarrow p(i){\neq}p(j)$	where i, j are instan-
$G_{\forall 0}$	$(1{\leq}j{\leq}m \wedge j{\neq}c \rightarrow c_2{>}p(j)) \vee (1{\leq}c{\leq}m \rightarrow c_1{=}c_2{+}y)$	tiated with c, d, k_c, k_d
	$(1{\leq}j{\leq}m \wedge j{\neq}d \rightarrow d_2{>}p(j)) \vee (1 \leq d \leq m \rightarrow d_1{=}d_2{+}y)$	+ purification
G_g	$1{\leq}c{\leq}m \wedge (1{\leq}k_c{\leq}m \wedge k_c{\neq}c \rightarrow c_2{>}c_3) \rightarrow c_1{=}x$	$c{=}d \rightarrow c_1{=}d_1$
	$1{\leq}d{\leq}m \wedge (1{\leq}k_d{\leq}m \wedge k_d{\neq}d \rightarrow d_2{>}d_3) \rightarrow d_1{=}x$	
	$1{\leq}c{\leq}m \wedge 1{\leq}d{\leq}m \wedge c{\neq}d \wedge c_1{=}d_1$	
N_0'	$c{=}d \rightarrow c_2{=}d_2,\ c{=}k_c \rightarrow c_2{=}c_3,\ c{=}k_d \rightarrow c_2{=}d_3,\ d{=}k_c \rightarrow d_2{=}c_3,\ d{=}k_d \rightarrow d_2{=}d_3,$	
	$k_c{=}k_d \rightarrow c_3{=}d_3$ (corr. to Def$_1$: $p(c){=}c_2 \wedge p(d){=}d_2 \wedge p(k_c){=}c_3 \wedge p(k_d){=}d_3$)	

We can use a prover for a combination of integers and reals to determine whether the conjunction of formulae above is satisfiable or symbolic computation packages performing quantifier elimination over the combined theory to derive constraints between x and y which guarantee injectivity after update.

6   Experiments

We have implemented the approach for hierarchical reasoning in local theory extensions described in [13], cf. also Sect. 3.1. The tool we devised allows us to reduce satisfiability problems in an extended theory to a base theory for which we can then use existing solvers. It takes as input the axioms of the theory extension, the ground goal and the list of extension function symbols. Chains of extensions are handled by having a list of axiom sets, and correspondingly a list of lists of extension function symbols. We follow the steps in Sect. 3.1: the input is analyzed for ground subterms with extension symbols at the root. After instantiating the axioms w.r.t. these terms, the instances are purified (so the extension symbols are removed). The resulting formula is either given to a prover for a base theory, or taken as goal for another reduction (if we have a chain of extensions). Currently, we can produce base theory output for Yices, Mathsat, CVC and Redlog, but other solvers can be integrated easily. We ran tests on various examples, including different versions of a train controller example [10,4], an array version of the insertion algorithm, and reasoning in theories of lists. Test results and comparisons can be found in [17] (which contains preliminary versions of some of the results in this paper, in an extended form). Runtimes range from 0.047s to 0.183s for various versions of the train controller example resp. to 0.4s for array examples (including an example from [1]). While Yices can also be used successfully directly for unsatisfiable formulae, this does not hold if we change the input problem to a formula which is satisfiable w.r.t. the extended theory. In this case, Yices returns "unknown" after a 300 second timeout. After the reduction with our tool, Yices (applied to the problem for the base theory) returns "satisfiable" in fractions of a second, and even a model for this problem that can easily be lifted to a model in the extended theory for the initial set of clauses[8]. Even more information can be obtained using the quantifier elimination facilities offered e.g. by Redlog for determining *constraints between the parameters* of the problems which guarantee safety.

We are working towards extending the tool support to stable locality, as well as for extensions with clauses containing proper first-order formulae.

7   Conclusions

We presented a general framework – based on a general notion of locality – which allows to identify complex theories important in verification for which efficient (hierarchical and modular) reasoning methods exist. We showed that locality considerations allow us to obtain parameterized decidability and complexity results for many (combinations of) theories important in verification (of parametric systems). We showed that many theories of data structures studied in the verification literature are local extensions of a base theory. The list of theories we considered is not exhaustive. (Due to space limitations we did not discuss the theory of arrays studied in [7], whose main ingredient is the existence of undefined values in arrays and properties (e.g. injectivity) are guarded by definedness conditions. The main result in [7] can be seen as a locality result as the arguments used are based on the possibility of completing partial to total models.) The general framework we use allows us to identify situations in which some of the syntactical restrictions imposed in previous papers can be relaxed.

The deduction tasks we considered here are typical for invariant checking and bounded model checking. The next step would be to integrate these methods into verification tools based on abstraction/refinement. Our work on hierarchical interpolation in local extensions [14] can be extended to many of the theories of data structures described in this paper. This is the topic of a future paper.

Acknowledgments. We thank Aaron Bradley for helpful comments made on a preliminary version of this paper. This work was partly supported by the German Research Council (DFG) as part of the Transregional Collaborative Research Center "Automatic Verification and Analysis of Complex Systems" (SFB/TR 14 AVACS). See www.avacs.org for more information.

---

[8] The lifting is straightforward, given the output of our tool, but is not automated at the moment.

References

1. Bradley, A.R., Manna, Z., Sipma, H.B.: What's decidable about arrays? In: Emerson, E.A., Namjoshi, K.S. (eds.) VMCAI 2006. LNCS, vol. 3855, pp. 427–442. Springer, Heidelberg (2006)
2. Burmeister, P.: A Model Theoretic Oriented Approach to Partial Algebras: Introduction to Theory and Application of Partial Algebras, Part I. In: Mathematical Research, vol. 31, Akademie-Verlag, Berlin (1986)
3. Burris, S.: Polynomial time uniform word problems. Mathematical Logic Quarterly 41, 173–182 (1995)
4. Faber, J., Jacobs, S., Sofronie-Stokkermans, V.: Verifying CSP-OZ-DC specifications with complex data types and timing parameters. In: Davies, J., Gibbons, J. (eds.) IFM 2007. LNCS, vol. 4591, pp. 233–252. Springer, Heidelberg (2007)
5. Ganzinger, H.: Relating semantic and proof-theoretic concepts for polynomial time decidability of uniform word problems. In: Proc. 16th IEEE Symposium on Logic in Computer Science (LICS 2001), pp. 81–92. IEEE Computer Society Press, Los Alamitos (2001)
6. Ganzinger, H., Sofronie-Stokkermans, V., Waldmann, U.: Modular proof systems for partial functions with Evans equality. Information and Computation 204(10), 1453–1492 (2006)
7. Ghilardi, S., Nicolini, E., Ranise, S., Zucchelli, D.: Deciding extensions of the theory of arrays by integrating decision procedures and instantiation strategies. In: Fisher, M., van der Hoek, W., Konev, B., Lisitsa, A. (eds.) JELIA 2006. LNCS (LNAI), vol. 4160, pp. 177–189. Springer, Heidelberg (2006)
8. Givan, R., McAllester, D.: New results on local inference relations. In: Principles of Knowledge Representation and Reasoning: Proceedings of the Third International Conference (KR 1992), pp. 403–412. Morgan Kaufmann, San Francisco (1992)
9. Givan, R., McAllester, D.A.: Polynomial-time computation via local inference relations. ACM Transactions on Computational Logic 3(4), 521–541 (2002)
10. Jacobs, S., Sofronie-Stokkermans, V.: Applications of hierarchical reasoning in the verification of complex systems. Electronic Notes in Theoretical Computer Science 174(8), 39–54 (2007)
11. McAllester, D.: Automatic recognition of tractability in inference relations. Journal of the Association for Computing Machinery 40(2), 284–303 (1993)
12. McPeak, S., Necula, G.C.: Data structure specifications via local equality axioms. In: Etessami, K., Rajamani, S.K. (eds.) CAV 2005. LNCS, vol. 3576, pp. 476–490. Springer, Heidelberg (2005)
13. Sofronie-Stokkermans, V.: Hierarchic reasoning in local theory extensions. In: Nieuwenhuis, R. (ed.) CADE 2005. LNCS (LNAI), vol. 3632, pp. 219–234. Springer, Heidelberg (2005)
14. Sofronie-Stokkermans, V.: Interpolation in local theory extensions. In: Furbach, U., Shankar, N. (eds.) IJCAR 2006. LNCS (LNAI), vol. 4130, pp. 235–250. Springer, Heidelberg (2006)
15. Sofronie-Stokkermans, V.: Hierarchical and modular reasoning in complex theories: The case of local theory extensions. In: Konev, B., Wolter, F. (eds.) FroCos 2007. LNCS (LNAI), vol. 4720, pp. 47–71. Springer, Heidelberg (2007)

16. Sofronie-Stokkermans, V., Ihlemann, C.: Automated reasoning in some local extensions of ordered structures. In: Proc. of ISMVL-2007, IEEE Computer Society Press, Los Alamitos (2007), http://dx.doi.org/10.1109/ISMVL.2007.10
17. Sofronie-Stokkermans, V., Ihlemann, C., Jacobs, S.: Local theory extensions, hierarchical reasoning and applications to verification. In: Dagstuhl Seminar Proceedings 07401,, http://drops.dagstuhl.de/opus/volltexte/2007/1250

Interprocedural Analysis of Concurrent Programs Under a Context Bound*

Akash Lal[1,**], Tayssir Touili[2], Nicholas Kidd[1], and Thomas Reps[1,3]

[1] University of Wisconsin, Madison, WI, USA
{akash,kidd,reps}@cs.wisc.edu
[2] LIAFA; CNRS & University of Paris 7, Paris, France
touili@liafa.jussieu.fr
[3] GrammaTech, Inc., Ithaca, NY, USA

Abstract. Analysis of recursive programs in the presence of concurrency and shared memory is undecidable. In previous work, Qadeer and Rehof [23] showed that context-bounded analysis is decidable for recursive programs under a finite-state abstraction of program data. In this paper, we show that context-bounded analysis is decidable for certain families of infinite-state abstractions, and also provide a new symbolic algorithm for the finite-state case.

1 Introduction

This paper considers the analysis of concurrent programs with shared-memory and interleaving semantics. Such an analysis for recursive programs is, in general, undecidable, even with a finite-state abstraction of data (e.g., Boolean Programs [1]). As a consequence, to deal with concurrency soundly (i.e., capture all concurrent behaviors), some analyses give up precise handling of procedure call/return semantics. Alternatively, tools use inlining to unfold multi-procedure programs into single-procedure ones. This approach cannot handle recursive programs, and can cause an exponential blowup in size for non-recursive ones.

A different way to sidestep the undecidability issue is to limit the amount of concurrency by bounding the number of *context switches*, where a context switch is defined as the transfer of control from one thread to another. Such an approach is not sound because it does not capture all of the behaviors of a program; however, it has proven to be useful in tools for bug-finding because many bugs can be found after a few context switches [24,23,20]. For example, KISS [24] is a verification tool that analyzes programs for only up to two context switches; it was able to find a number of bugs in device drivers. We call the analysis of recursive, concurrent programs under a context bound *context-bounded analysis* (CBA). CBA does not impose any bound on the execution length between context switches. Thus, even under a context bound, the analysis still has to consider the possibility that the next switch takes place in any one of the

---

* Supported by NSF under grants CCF-0540955 and CCF-0524051.
** Supported by a Microsoft Research Graduate Fellowship.

C.R. Ramakrishnan and J. Rehof (Eds.): TACAS 2008, LNCS 4963, pp. 282–298, 2008.

(possibly infinite) states that may be reached after a context switch. Because of this, CBA still considers an infinite number of interleavings.

Qadeer and Rehof [23] showed that CBA is decidable for recursive programs under a finite-state abstraction of data. This paper shows that CBA is decidable for certain families of infinite-state abstractions, and also provides a new symbolic algorithm for the finite-state case. We give conditions on the abstractions under which CBA can be solved precisely, along with a new algorithm for CBA. In addition to the usual conditions required for precise interprocedural analysis of sequential programs, we require the existence of a *tensor product* (see §6). We show that these conditions are satisfied by a class of abstractions, thus giving precise algorithms for CBA with those abstractions. These include finite-state abstractions, such as the ones used for verification of Boolean programs, as well as infinite-state abstractions, such as affine-relation analysis [19].

Our results are achieved using techniques that are quite different from the ones used in the Qadeer and Rehof (QR) algorithm [23]. In particular, to explore all possible interleavings, the QR algorithm crucially relies on the finiteness of the data abstraction because it enumerates all reachable (abstract) data states at a context switch. Our algorithm is based on *weighted transducers* (weighted automata that read input and write output) and requires no such enumeration in the case of finite-state data abstractions, which also makes it capable of handling infinite-state abstractions.

The contributions of this paper can be summarized as follows:

- We give sufficient conditions under which CBA is decidable for infinite-state abstractions, along with an algorithm. Our result proves that CBA can be decided for affine-relation analysis, i.e., we can precisely find all affine relationships between program variables that hold in a concurrent program (under the context bound).
- We show that the reachability relation of a weighted pushdown system (WPDS) can be encoded using a weighted transducer (§5), which generalizes a previous result for (unweighted) PDSs [8]. We use WPDSs to model each thread of the concurrent program, and the transducers can be understood as summarizing the (sequential) execution of a thread.
- We give precise algorithms for composing weighted transducers (§6), when tensor products exist for the weights. This generalizes previous work on manipulating weighted automata and transducers [17,18].

The remainder of the paper is organized as follows. §2 introduces some terminology and notation. §3 sketches an alternative to the QR algorithm for finite-state abstractions; the rest of the paper generalizes the algorithm to infinite-state abstractions. §4 gives background on WPDSs. §5 gives an efficient construction of transducers for WPDSs. §6 shows how weighted transducers can be composed. §7 discusses related work. Additional material can be found in [16].

2   Terminology and Notation

A context-bounded analysis (CBA) considers a set of concurrent threads that communicate via global variables. Synchronization is easily implementable using global variables as locks. Analysis of such models is undecidable [25], i.e., it is not possible, in general, to determine whether or not a given configuration is reachable. Let n be the number of threads and let $t_1, t_2, \cdots, t_n$ denote the threads. We do not consider dynamic creation of threads in our model. (Dynamic creation of up to n threads can be encoded in the model [23].)

Let G be the set of global states (valuations of global variables) and L_i be the set of local states of t_i. Then the state space of the entire program consists of the global state paired with local states of each of the threads, i.e., the set of states is $G \times L_1 \times \cdots \times L_n$. Let the transition relation of thread t_i, which is a relation on $G \times L_i$, be denoted by $\Rightarrow_{t_i}$. If $(g, l_i) \Rightarrow_{t_i} (g', l'_i)$, the transition $(g, l_1, \cdots, l_i, \cdots, l_n) \Rightarrow_{t_i}^c (g', l_1 \cdots, l'_i, \cdots, l_n)$ is a valid transition for the concurrent program.

The execution of a concurrent program proceeds in a sequence of *execution contexts*. In an execution context, one thread has control and it executes a finite number of steps. The execution context changes at a *context switch* and control is passed to a different thread. The CBA problem is to find the set of reachable states of the concurrent program under a bound on the number of context switches. Formally, let k be the bound on the number of context switches; thus, there are $k + 1$ execution contexts. Let $\Rightarrow^c$ be $(\cup_{i=1}^{n}(\Rightarrow_{t_i}^c)^*)$, the transition relation that describes the effect of one execution context; we wish to find the reachable states in the transition relation given by $(\Rightarrow^c)^{k+1}$.

Definition 1. *A **pushdown system** (PDS) is a triple $\mathcal{P} = (P, \Gamma, \Delta)$, where P is a finite set of states or control locations, Γ is a finite set of stack symbols, and $\Delta \subseteq P \times \Gamma \times P \times \Gamma^*$ is a finite set of rules. A **configuration** of $\mathcal{P}$ is a pair $\langle p, u \rangle$ where $p \in P$ and $u \in \Gamma^*$. A rule $r \in \Delta$ is written as $\langle p, \gamma \rangle \hookrightarrow \langle p', u \rangle$, where $p, p' \in P$, $\gamma \in \Gamma$ and $u \in \Gamma^*$. These rules define a transition relation $\Rightarrow$ on configurations of $\mathcal{P}$ as follows: If $r = \langle p, \gamma \rangle \hookrightarrow \langle p', u' \rangle$, then $\langle p, \gamma u \rangle \Rightarrow \langle p', u'u \rangle$ for all $u \in \Gamma^*$. The reflexive transitive closure of $\Rightarrow$ is denoted by $\Rightarrow^*$. For a set of configurations C, we define $pre^*(C) = \{c' \mid \exists c \in C : c' \Rightarrow^* c\}$ and $post^*(C) = \{c' \mid \exists c \in C : c \Rightarrow^* c'\}$, which are just backward and forward reachability under the transition relation $\Rightarrow$.*

Without loss of generality, we restrict the pushdown rules to have at most two stack symbols on the right-hand side [28].

PDSs can encode recursive programs with a finite-state data abstraction [28]: the data values get tracked by the PDS state, and recursion gets handled by the PDS stack. In this case, a PDS configuration represents a program state (current data values and stack). For sequential programs, the problem of interest is to find the set of all reachable configurations, starting from a given set of configurations. This can then be used, for example, for assertion checking (i.e., determining if a given assertion can ever fail) or to find the set of all data values that may arise at a program point (for dataflow analysis). Because the number of configurations of a PDS is unbounded, it is useful to use finite automata to describe regular sets of configurations.

Definition 2. *If* $\mathcal{P} = (P, \Gamma, \Delta)$ *is a PDS then a* $\mathcal{P}$-**automaton** *is a finite automaton* $(Q, \Gamma, \rightarrow, P, F)$, *where* $Q \supseteq P$ *is a finite set of states,* $\rightarrow \subseteq Q \times \Gamma \times Q$ *is the transition relation,* P *is the set of initial states, and* F *is the set of final states. We say that a configuration* $\langle p, u \rangle$ *is accepted by a* $\mathcal{P}$-*automaton if it can accept* u *when started in the state* p. *A set of configurations is* **regular** *if it is the language of some* $\mathcal{P}$-*automaton.*

For a regular set of configurations C, both $post^*(C)$ and $pre^*(C)$ are also regular [2,7,11]. The algorithms for computing $post^*$ and pre^*, called *poststar* and *prestar*, respectively, take a $\mathcal{P}$-automaton $\mathcal{A}$ as input, and if C is the set of configurations accepted by $\mathcal{A}$, produce $\mathcal{P}$-automata $\mathcal{A}_{post^*}$ and $\mathcal{A}_{pre^*}$ that accept the sets $post^*(C)$ and $pre^*(C)$, respectively [2,10,11].

3 A New Approach Using Thread Summarization

Between consecutive context switches only one thread is executing, and a concurrent program acts like a sequential program. However, a recursive thread can reach an infinite number of states before the next context switch, because it has an unbounded stack. A CBA must consider the possibility that a context switch occurs at any of these states.

The QR algorithm works under the assumption that the set G is finite. It uses a PDS to encode each thread (using a finite-state data abstraction). The algorithm follows a computation tree, each node of which represents a set of states $\{g\} \times S_1 \times \cdots S_n$ of the concurrent program, where $S_i \subseteq L_i$, i.e., the set of states represented by each node has the same global state. The root of the tree represents the set of initial states, and nodes at the ith level represent all states reachable after $i - 1$ context switches.

At each node, including the root, the computation tree branches: For each choice of thread t_j that receives control, a new set of states is obtained by running *poststar* on the PDS for thread t_j, starting with the node's (unique) global state and local states of t_j. The local states of t_h, $h \neq j$, are held fixed. The resulting set is split according to the reachable global states, to create multiple new nodes (maintaining the invariant that each node only represents a single global state). This process is repeated until the computation tree is completely built for $k + 1$ levels, giving all reachable states in k or fewer context switches. The "splitting" of nodes depending on reachable global states causes branching of the computation tree proportional to the size of G at each level.

Another drawback of the QR algorithm is its use of *poststar* to compute the forward reachable states of a given thread. *Poststar* represents a function that maps a starting set of configurations to a set of reachable configurations. Hence, *poststar* needs to be re-executed if the starting set changes. The discovery of new starting sets forces the QR algorithm to make multiple calls on *poststar* (for a given thread) to compute different sets of forward reachable states.

A similar problem arises in interprocedural analysis of sequential programs: a procedure can be called from multiple places with multiple different input values. Instead of reanalyzing a procedure for each input value, a more efficient approach is to analyze each procedure independently of the calling context to create a *summary*. The summary describes the effect of executing the procedure in any calling context, in terms of a *relation* between inputs and outputs.

Our first step is to develop a new algorithm—based on a suitable form of summary relation for threads—for the case of unweighted PDSs. The motivation is to develop an algorithm that avoids enumerating all global states at a context switch, and then use that algorithm as the starting point for a generalization that handles infinite-state abstractions. A difficulty that we face, however, is that each summary relation must relate starting sets of configurations to reachable sets of configurations. Because both of these sets can be infinite, we need summary relations to be representable symbolically.

Our approach to generalizing the QR algorithm (for both finite-state and infinite-state data abstractions) is based on the following observation:

Observation 1. *One can construct an appropriate summary of a thread's behavior using a finite-state transducer (an automaton with input and output tapes).*

Definition 3. *A **finite-state transducer** τ is a tuple $(Q, \Sigma_i, \Sigma_o, \lambda, I, F)$, where Q is a finite set of states, Σ_i and Σ_o are input and output alphabets, $\lambda \subseteq Q \times (\Sigma_i \cup \{\varepsilon\}) \times (\Sigma_o \cup \{\varepsilon\}) \times Q$ is the transition relation, $I \subseteq Q$ is the set of initial states, and $F \subseteq Q$ is the set of final states. If $(q_1, a, b, q_2) \in \lambda$, written as $q_1 \xrightarrow{a/b} q_2$, we say that the transducer can go from state q_1 to q_2 on input a, and outputs the symbol b. For state $q \in I$, the transducer accepts string $\sigma_i \in \Sigma_i^*$ with output $\sigma_o \in \Sigma_o^*$ if there is a path from q to a final state that takes input σ_i and outputs σ_o. The **language** of the transducer $\mathcal{L}(\tau)$ is the relation $\{(\sigma_i, \sigma_o) \in \Sigma_i^* \times \Sigma_o^* \mid$ the transducer can output string σ_o when the input is $\sigma_i\}$.*

In the case of finite-state abstractions, and each thread represented as some PDS $\mathcal{P}$, one can construct a transducer $\tau_{\mathcal{P}}$ whose language equals $\Rightarrow^*$, the transitive closure of $\mathcal{P}$'s transition relation: The transducer accepts a pair (c_1, c_2) if a thread, when started in state c_1, can reach state c_2. The advantage of using transducers is that they are closed under relational composition:

Lemma 1. *Given transducers τ_1 and τ_2 with input and output alphabet Σ, one can construct a transducer $(\tau_1; \tau_2)$ such that $\mathcal{L}(\tau_1; \tau_2) = \mathcal{L}(\tau_1); \mathcal{L}(\tau_2)$, where the latter ";" denotes composition of relations. Similarly, if $\mathcal{A}$ is an automaton with alphabet Σ, one can construct an automaton $\tau_1(\mathcal{A})$ such that its language is the image of $\mathcal{L}(\mathcal{A})$ under $\mathcal{L}(\tau_1)$, i.e., the set $\{u \in \Sigma^* \mid \exists u' \in \mathcal{L}(\mathcal{A}), (u', u) \in \mathcal{L}(\tau_1)\}$.*

Both of these constructions are carried out in a manner similar to intersection of automata [13]. One can also take the union of transducers (union of their languages) in a manner similar to union of automata.

In the case of CBA with a finite-state data abstraction, each thread is represented using a PDS. We construct a transducer τ_{t_i} for the transition relation $\Rightarrow_{t_i}^*$. By extending τ_{t_i} to perform the identity transformation on stack symbols of threads other than t_i (using transitions of the form $p \xrightarrow{\gamma/\gamma} q$), we obtain a transducer $\tau_{t_i}^c$ for $(\Rightarrow_{t_i}^c)^*$. Next, a union of these transducers gives τ^c, which represents $\Rightarrow^c$. Performing the composition of τ^c k times with itself gives us a transducer τ that represents $(\Rightarrow^c)^{k+1}$. If an automaton $\mathcal{A}$ captures the set of starting states of the concurrent program, $\tau(\mathcal{A})$ gives a single automaton for the set of all reachable states in the program (under the context bound).

The rest of the paper generalizes this approach to infinite-state abstractions by going from PDSs to WPDSs. This requires the construction (§5) and composition (§6) of weighted transducers.

4   Weighted Pushdown Systems (WPDSs)

A WPDS is a PDS augmented with weights drawn from a *bounded idempotent semiring* [27,4]. Such semirings are powerful enough to encode finite-state data abstractions, as used in bitvector dataflow analysis, Boolean program verification [1], and the IFDS dataflow-analysis framework [26], as well as infinite-state data abstractions, such as linear-constant propagation and affine-relation analysis [19]. We review some of this here; see also [27].

Weights encode the effect that each statement (or PDS rule) has on the data state of the program. They can be thought of as abstract transformers that specify how the abstract state changes when a statement is executed.

Definition 4. *A* **bounded idempotent semiring** *(or "weight domain") is a tuple $(D, \oplus, \otimes, \overline{0}, \overline{1})$, where D is a set of* **weights**, *$\overline{0}, \overline{1} \in D$, and $\oplus$ (combine) and $\otimes$ (extend) are binary operators on D such that*

1. *$(D, \oplus)$ is a commutative monoid with $\overline{0}$ as its neutral element, and where $\oplus$ is idempotent. $(D, \otimes)$ is a monoid with the neutral element $\overline{1}$.*
2. *$\otimes$ distributes over $\oplus$, i.e., for all $a, b, c \in D$ we have*
   $$a \otimes (b \oplus c) = (a \otimes b) \oplus (a \otimes c) \text{ and } (a \oplus b) \otimes c = (a \otimes c) \oplus (b \otimes c).$$
3. *$\overline{0}$ is an annihilator with respect to $\otimes$, i.e., for all $a \in D$, $a \otimes \overline{0} = \overline{0} = \overline{0} \otimes a$.*
4. *In the partial order $\sqsubseteq$ defined by $\forall a, b \in D$, $a \sqsubseteq b$ iff $a \oplus b = a$, there are no infinite descending chains.*

The *height* of a weight domain is defined to be the length of the longest descending chain in the domain. In this paper, we assume the height to be bounded for ease of discussing complexity results, but WPDSs, and the algorithms in this paper, can also be used in certain cases when the height is unbounded (as long as there are no infinite descending chains). $O_s(.)$ denotes the time bound in terms of semiring operations.

Often, weights are data transformers: extend is composition; combine is *meet*; $\overline{0}$ is the transformer for an infeasible path; and $\overline{1}$ is the identity transformer.

Definition 5. *A* **weighted pushdown system** *is a triple $\mathcal{W} = (\mathcal{P}, \mathcal{S}, f)$ where $\mathcal{P} = (P, \Gamma, \Delta)$ is a pushdown system, $\mathcal{S} = (D, \oplus, \otimes, \overline{0}, \overline{1})$ is a bounded idempotent semiring and $f : \Delta \to D$ is a map that assigns a weight to each rule of $\mathcal{P}$.*

Let $\sigma \in \Delta^*$ be a sequence of rules. Using f, we can associate a value to σ, i.e., if $\sigma = [r_1, \ldots, r_k]$, then we define $v(\sigma) \stackrel{\text{def}}{=} f(r_1) \otimes \ldots \otimes f(r_k)$. Moreover, for any two configurations c and c' of $\mathcal{P}$, we use $path(c, c')$ to denote the set of all rule sequences that transform c into c'. If $\sigma \in path(c, c')$, then we say $c \Rightarrow^\sigma c'$. Reachability problems on PDSs are generalized to WPDSs as follows:

Definition 6. *Let $\mathcal{W} = (\mathcal{P}, \mathcal{S}, f)$ be a WPDS, where $\mathcal{P} = (P, \Gamma, \Delta)$, and let $S, T \subseteq P \times \Gamma^*$ be regular sets of configurations. Then the* ***meet-over-all-valid-paths*** *value $\mathrm{MOVP}(S, T)$ is defined as $\bigoplus \{v(\sigma) \mid s \Rightarrow^\sigma t, s \in S, t \in T\}$.*

A PDS is simply a WPDS with the *Boolean weight domain* $(\{\bar{0}, \bar{1}\}, \oplus, \otimes, \bar{0}, \bar{1})$ and weight assignment $f(r) = \bar{1}$ for all rules $r \in \Delta$. In this case, $\mathrm{MOVP}(S, T) = \bar{1}$ iff there is a path from a configuration in S to a configuration in T, i.e., $post^*(S) \cap T$ and $S \cap pre^*(T)$ are non-empty.

One way of modeling programs as WPDSs is as follows: the PDS models the control flow of the program and the weight domain models transformers for an abstraction of the program's data. Examples are given in [16].

4.1   Solving for the MOVP Value

There are two algorithms for solving for MOVP values, called *prestar* and *poststar* (by analogy with the algorithms for PDSs) [27]. Their input is an automaton that accepts the set of initial configurations. Their output is a *weighted automaton*:

Definition 7. *Given a WPDS $\mathcal{W} = (\mathcal{P}, \mathcal{S}, f)$, a $\mathcal{W}$-**automaton** $\mathcal{A}$ is a $\mathcal{P}$-automaton, where each transition in the automaton is labeled with a weight. The weight of a path in the automaton is obtained by taking an extend of the weights on the transitions in the path in either a forward or backward direction. The automaton is said to accept a configuration $c = \langle p, u \rangle$ with weight $w = \mathcal{A}(c)$ if w is the combine of weights of all accepting paths for u starting from state p in $\mathcal{A}$. We call the automaton a **backward $\mathcal{W}$-automaton** if the weight of a path is read backwards, and a **forward $\mathcal{W}$-automaton** otherwise.*

Let $\mathcal{A}$ be an unweighted automaton and $\mathcal{L}(\mathcal{A})$ be the set of configurations accepted by it. Then there is an algorithm $prestar(\mathcal{A})$ that produces a forward weighted automaton $\mathcal{A}_{pre^*}$ as output, such that $\mathcal{A}_{pre^*}(c) = \mathrm{MOVP}(\{c\}, \mathcal{L}(\mathcal{A}))$, and an algorithm $poststar(\mathcal{A})$ produces a backward weighted automaton $\mathcal{A}_{post^*}$ as output, such that $\mathcal{A}_{post^*}(c) = \mathrm{MOVP}(\mathcal{L}(\mathcal{A}), \{c\})$ [27]. For a weighted automaton $\mathcal{A}'$, we define $\mathcal{A}'(C) = \bigoplus \{\mathcal{A}'(c) \mid c \in C\}$. The values of $\mathcal{A}'(c)$ and $\mathcal{A}'(C)$ can be computed by the algorithms presented in [27].

Lemma 2. *[27] Given a WPDS with PDS $\mathcal{P} = (P, \Gamma, \Delta)$, if $\mathcal{A} = (Q, \Gamma, \rightarrow, P, F)$ is a $\mathcal{P}$-automaton, $poststar(\mathcal{A})$ produces an automaton with at most $|Q| + |\Delta|$ states and runs in time $O_s(|P||\Delta|(|Q_0| + |\Delta|)H + |P||\lambda_0|H)$, where $Q_0 = Q \backslash P$, $\lambda_0 \subseteq \rightarrow$ is the set of all transitions leading from states in Q_0, and H is the height of the weight domain.*

4.2   CBA Problem Definition

Definition 8. *A **weighted relation** on a set S, weighted with semiring $(D, \oplus, \otimes, \bar{0}, \bar{1})$, is a function from $(S \times S)$ to D. The composition of two weighted* *relations R_1 and R_2 is defined as $(R_1; R_2)(s_1, s_3) = \oplus\{w_1 \otimes w_2 \mid \exists s_2 \in S : w_1 = R_1(s_1, s_2), w_2 = R_2(s_2, s_3)\}$. The union of the two weighted relations is defined as $(R_1 \cup R_2)(s_1, s_2) = R_1(s_1, s_2) \oplus R_2(s_1, s_2)$. The identity relation is the function that maps each pair (s, s) to $\bar{1}$ and others to $\bar{0}$. The reflexive-transitive closure is defined in terms of these operations, as before.*

The transition relation of a WPDS is a weighted relation over the set of PDS configurations. For configurations c_1 and c_2, if $r_1, \cdots, r_m$ are all the rules such that $c_1 \Rightarrow^{r_i} c_2$, then $(c_1, c_2, \oplus_i f(r_i))$ is in the weighted relation of the WPDS. In a slight abuse of notation, we use $\Rightarrow$ and its variants for the weighted transition relation of a WPDS. Note that the weighted relation $\Rightarrow^*$ maps a configuration pair (c_1, c_2) to $\text{MOVP}(\{c_1\}, \{c_2\})$.

The CBA problem is defined as in §2, except that all relations are weighted. Each thread is modeled as a WPDS. Given the weighted relation $(\Rightarrow^c)^{k+1}$ as R, the set of initial states S and a set of final states T (of the concurrent program), we want to be able to compute the weight $R(S, T) = \oplus\{R(s, t) \mid s \in S, t \in T\}$. This captures the net transformation on the data state between S and T: it is the combine over the weights of all paths involving at most k context switches that go from a state in S to a state in T. Our results from §5 and §6 allow us to compute this value when S and T are regular.

5   Weighted Transducers

In this section, we show how to construct a weighted transducer for the weighted relation $\Rightarrow^*$ of a WPDS. We defer the definition of a weighted transducer to a little later in this section (Defn. 9). Our solution uses the following observation about paths in a PDS's transition relation. Every path $\sigma \in \Delta^*$ that starts from a configuration $\langle p_1, \gamma_1 \gamma_2 \cdots \gamma_n \rangle$ can be decomposed as $\sigma = \sigma_1 \sigma_2 \cdots \sigma_k \sigma_{k+1}$ (see Fig. 1) such that $\langle p_i, \gamma_i \rangle \Rightarrow^{\sigma_i} \langle p_{i+1}, \varepsilon \rangle$ for $1 \le i \le k$, and $\langle p_{k+1}, \gamma_{k+1} \rangle \Rightarrow^{\sigma_{k+1}} \langle p_{k+2}, u_1 u_2 \cdots u_j \rangle$: every path has zero or more *pop phases* $(\sigma_1, \sigma_2, \cdots, \sigma_k)$ followed by a single *growth phase* (σ_{k+1}):

1. **Pop-phase:** A path such that the net effect of the pushes and pops performed along the path is to take $\langle p, \gamma u \rangle$ to $\langle p', u \rangle$, without looking at $u \in \Gamma^*$. Equivalently, it can take $\langle p, \gamma \rangle$ to $\langle p', \varepsilon \rangle$.
2. **Growth-phase:** A path such that the net effect of the pushes and pops performed along the path is to take $\langle p, \gamma u \rangle$ to $\langle p', u'u \rangle$ with $u' \in \Gamma^+$, without looking at $u \in \Gamma^*$. Equivalently, it can take $\langle p, \gamma \rangle$ to $\langle p', u' \rangle$.

Intuitively, this holds because for a path to look at γ_2, it must pop off γ_1. If it does not pop off γ_1, then the path is in a growth phase starting from γ_1. Otherwise, the path just completed a pop phase. We construct the transducer for a WPDS by computing the net transformation (weight) implied by these phases. First, we define two procedures:

$$\langle p_1, \gamma_1\ \gamma_2\ \gamma_3 \cdots \gamma_n \rangle \Rightarrow^{\sigma_1} \quad \langle p_2, \gamma_2\ \gamma_3 \cdots \gamma_{k+1}\ \gamma_{k+2} \cdots \gamma_n \rangle$$
$$\Rightarrow^{\sigma_2} \quad \langle p_3, \gamma_3 \cdots \gamma_{k+1}\ \gamma_{k+2} \cdots \gamma_n \rangle$$
$$\cdots$$
$$\Rightarrow^{\sigma_k} \quad \langle p_{k+1}, \gamma_{k+1}\ \gamma_{k+2} \cdots \gamma_n \rangle$$
$$\Rightarrow^{\sigma_{k+1}} \langle p_{k+2}, u_1\ u_2 \cdots u_j\ \gamma_{k+2} \cdots \gamma_n \rangle$$

Fig. 1. A path in the PDS's transition relation; $u_i \in \Gamma, j \geq 1, k < n$

1. $pop : P \times \Gamma \times P \to D$ is defined as follows:
$$pop(p, \gamma, p') = \bigoplus \{v(\sigma) \mid \langle p, \gamma \rangle \Rightarrow^\sigma \langle p', \varepsilon \rangle\}$$
2. $grow : P \times \Gamma \to ((P \times \Gamma^+) \to D)$ is defined as follows:
$$grow(p, \gamma)(p', u) = \bigoplus \{v(\sigma) \mid \langle p, \gamma \rangle \Rightarrow^\sigma \langle p', u \rangle\}$$

Note that $grow(p, \gamma) = poststar(\langle p, \gamma \rangle)$, where the latter is interpreted as a function from configurations to weights. The following lemmas give efficient algorithms for computing the above procedures. Proofs are given in [16].

Lemma 3. *Let $\mathcal{A} = (P, \Gamma, \emptyset, P, P)$ be a $\mathcal{P}$-automaton that represents the set of configurations $C = \{\langle p, \varepsilon \rangle \mid p \in P\}$. Let $\mathcal{A}_{pop}$ be the forward weighted-automaton obtained by running prestar on $\mathcal{A}$. Then $pop(p, \gamma, p')$ is the weight on the transition (p, γ, p') in $\mathcal{A}_{pop}$. We can generate $\mathcal{A}_{pop}$ in time $O_s(|P|^2|\Delta|H)$, and it has at most $|P|$ states.*

Lemma 4. *Let $\mathcal{A}_F = (Q, \Gamma, \to, P, F)$ be a $\mathcal{P}$-automaton, where $Q = P \cup \{q_{p,\gamma} \mid p \in P, \gamma \in \Gamma\}$ and $p \xrightarrow{\gamma} q_{p,\gamma}$ for each $p \in P, \gamma \in \Gamma$. Then $\mathcal{A}_{\{q_{p,\gamma}\}}$ represents the configuration $\langle p, \gamma \rangle$. Let $\mathcal{A}$ be this automaton where we leave the set of final states undefined. Let $\mathcal{A}_{grow}$ be the backward weighted-automaton obtained from running poststar on $\mathcal{A}$ (poststar does not need to know the final states). If we restrict the final states in $\mathcal{A}_{grow}$ to be just $q_{p,\gamma}$, we obtain a backward weighted-automaton $\mathcal{A}_{p,\gamma} = poststar(\langle p, \gamma \rangle) = grow(p, \gamma)$. We can compute $\mathcal{A}_{grow}$ in time $O_s(|P||\Delta|(|P||\Gamma| + |\Delta|)H)$, and it has at most $|P||\Gamma| + |\Delta|$ states.*

The advantage of the construction presented in Lemma 4 is that it just requires a single *poststar* query to compute all of the $\mathcal{A}_{p,\gamma}$, instead of one query for each $p \in P$ and $\gamma \in \Gamma$. Because the standard *poststar* algorithm builds an automaton that is larger than the input automaton (Lemma 2), $\mathcal{A}_{grow}$ has many fewer states than those in all of the individual $\mathcal{A}_{p,\gamma}$ automata put together.

The idea behind our approach is to use $\mathcal{A}_{pop}$ to simulate the first phase where the PDS pops off stack symbols. With reference to Fig. 1, the transducer consumes $\gamma_1 \cdots \gamma_k$ from the input tape. When the transducer (non-deterministically) decides to switch over to the growth phase, and is in state p_{k+1} in $\mathcal{A}_{pop}$ with γ_{k+1} being the next symbol in the input, it passes control to $\mathcal{A}_{p_{k+1},\gamma_{k+1}}$ to start generating the output $u_1 \cdots u_j$. Then it moves into an accept phase where it copies the untouched part of the input stack $(\gamma_{k+2} \cdots \gamma_n)$ to the output.

Note that $\mathcal{A}_{pop}$ is a forward-weighted automaton, whereas $\mathcal{A}_{grow}$ is a backward-weighted automaton. Therefore, when we mix them together to build a transducer, we must allow it to switch directions for computing the weight of a path.

Consider Fig. 1; a PDS rule sequence consumes the input configuration from left to right (in the pop phase), but produces the output stack configuration u from right to left (as it pushes symbols on the stack). Because we need the transducer to output $u_1 \cdots u_j$ from left to right, we need to switch directions for computing the weight of a path. For this, we define *partitioned* transducers.

Definition 9. *A **partitioned weighted finite-state transducer** τ is a tuple $(Q, \{Q_i\}_{i=1}^2, \mathcal{S}, \Sigma_i, \Sigma_o, \lambda, I, F)$ where Q is a finite set of states, $\{Q_1, Q_2\}$ is a partition of Q, $\mathcal{S} = (D, \oplus, \otimes, \overline{0}, \overline{1})$ is a bounded idempotent semiring, Σ_i and Σ_o are input and output alphabets, $\lambda \subseteq Q \times D \times (\Sigma_i \cup \{\varepsilon\}) \times (\Sigma_o \cup \{\varepsilon\}) \times Q$ is the transition relation, $I \subseteq Q_1$ is the set of initial states, and $F \subseteq Q_2$ is the set of final states. We restrict the transitions that cross the state partition: if $(q, w, a, b, q') \in \lambda$ and $q \in Q_l, q' \in Q_k$ and $l \neq k$, then $l = 1, k = 2$ and $w = \overline{1}$. Given a state $q \in I$, the transducer accepts a string $\sigma_i \in \Sigma_i^*$ with output $\sigma_o \in \Sigma_o^*$ if there is a path from state q to a final state that takes input σ_i and outputs σ_o.*

For a path η that goes through states $q_1, \cdots, q_m$, such that the weight of the ith transition is w_i, and all states q_i are in Q_j for some j, then the weight of this path $v(\eta)$ is $w_1 \otimes w_2 \otimes \cdots \otimes w_m$ if $j = 1$ and $w_m \otimes w_{m-1} \otimes \cdots \otimes w_1$ if $j = 2$, i.e., the state partition determines the direction in which we perform extend. For a path η that crosses partitions, i.e., $\eta = \eta_1 \eta_2$ such that each η_j is a path entirely inside Q_j, then $v(\eta) = v(\eta_1) \otimes v(\eta_2)$.

In this paper, we refer to partitioned weighted transducers as weighted transducers, or simply transducers when there is no possibility of confusion. Note that when the extend operator is commutative, as in the case of the Boolean semiring used for encoding PDSs as WPDSs, the partitioning is unnecessary.

Theorem 1. *We can compute a transducer $\tau_{\mathcal{W}}$ such that if $\tau_{\mathcal{W}}$ is given input $(p\ u)$, $p \in P, u \in \Gamma^*$, then the combine over the values of all paths in $\tau_{\mathcal{W}}$ that output the string $(p'\ u')$ is precisely $\mathrm{MOVP}(\{\langle p, u \rangle\}, \{\langle p', u' \rangle\})$. Moreover, this transducer can be constructed in time $O_s(|P||\Delta|(|P||\Gamma| + |\Delta|)H)$, has at most $|P|^2|\Gamma| + |P||\Delta|$ states and at most $|P|^2|\Delta|^2$ transitions.*

Usually the WPDSs used for modeling programs have $|P| = 1$ and $|\Gamma| < |\Delta|$. In that case, constructing a transducer has similar complexity and size as running a single *poststar* query; see [16].

6   Composing Weighted Transducers

Composition of unweighted transducers is straightforward, but this is not the case with weighted transducers. The requirement here is to take two weighted transducers, say τ_1 and τ_2, and create another one, say τ_3, such that $\mathcal{L}(\tau_3) = \mathcal{L}(\tau_1); \mathcal{L}(\tau_2)$. The difficulty is that this requires composition of weighted languages (see Defn. 8). We begin with a slightly simpler problem on weighted automata. The machinery that we develop for this problem will be used for composing weighted transducers.

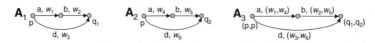

Fig. 2. Forward-weighted automata with final states q_1, q_2, and (q_1, q_2), respectively

6.1   The Sequential Product of Two Weighted Automata

Given forward-weighted automata $\mathcal{A}_1$ and $\mathcal{A}_2$, we define their sequential product as another weighted automaton $\mathcal{A}_3$ such that for any configuration c, $\mathcal{A}_3(c) = \mathcal{A}_1(c) \otimes \mathcal{A}_2(c)$. More generally, we want the following identity for any regular set of configurations C: $\mathcal{A}_3(C) = \bigoplus \{\mathcal{A}_3(c) \mid c \in C\} = \bigoplus \{\mathcal{A}_1(c) \otimes \mathcal{A}_2(c) \mid c \in C\}$. (In this section, we assume that configurations consist of just the stack and $|P| = 1$.) This problem is the special case of transducer composition when a transducer only has transitions of the form (γ/γ). For the Boolean weight domain, it reduces to unweighted automaton intersection.

To take the sequential product of weighted automata, we start with the algorithm for intersecting unweighted automata. This is done by taking transitions (q_1, γ, q_2) and (q_1', γ, q_2') in the respective automata to produce $((q_1, q_1'), \gamma, (q_2, q_2'))$ in the new automaton. We would like to do the same with weighted transitions: given weights of the matching transitions, we want to compute a weight for the created transition. In Fig. 2, intersecting automata $\mathcal{A}_1$ and $\mathcal{A}_2$ produces $\mathcal{A}_3$ (ignore the weights for now). Automaton $\mathcal{A}_3$ should accept (a b) with weight $\mathcal{A}_1(\text{a b}) \otimes \mathcal{A}_2(\text{a b}) = w_1 \otimes w_2 \otimes w_4 \otimes w_5$.

One way of achieving this is to pair the weights while intersecting (as shown in $\mathcal{A}_3$ in Fig. 2). Matching the transitions with weights w_1 and w_4 produces a transition with weight (w_1, w_4). For reading off weights, we need to define operations on paired weights. Define extend on pairs $(\otimes_p)$ to be componentwise extend $(\otimes)$. Then $\mathcal{A}_3(\text{a b}) = (w_1, w_4) \otimes_p (w_2, w_5) = (w_1 \otimes w_2, w_4 \otimes w_5)$. Taking an extend of the two components produces the desired answer. Thus, this $\mathcal{A}_3$ together with a read out operation in the end (that maps a weight pair to a weight) is a first attempt at constructing the sequential product of $\mathcal{A}_1$ and $\mathcal{A}_2$.

Because the number of accepting paths in an automaton may be infinite, one also needs a combine $(\oplus_p)$ on paired weights. The natural attempt is to define it componentwise. However, this is not precise. For example, if $C = \{c_1, c_2\}$ then $\mathcal{A}_3(C)$ should be $(\mathcal{A}_1(c_1) \otimes \mathcal{A}_2(c_1)) \oplus (\mathcal{A}_1(c_2) \otimes \mathcal{A}_2(c_2))$. However, using componentwise combine, we would get $\mathcal{A}_3(C) = \mathcal{A}_3(c_1) \oplus_p \mathcal{A}_3(c_2) = (\mathcal{A}_1(c_1) \oplus \mathcal{A}_1(c_2), \mathcal{A}_2(c_1) \oplus \mathcal{A}_2(c_2))$. Applying the read-out operation (extend of the components) gives four terms $\bigoplus \{(\mathcal{A}_1(c_i) \otimes \mathcal{A}_2(c_j)) \mid 1 \leq i, j \leq 2\}$, which includes cross terms like $\mathcal{A}_1(c_1) \otimes \mathcal{A}_2(c_2)$. The same problem arises also for a single configuration c if $\mathcal{A}_3$ has multiple accepting paths for it.

Under certain circumstances there is an alternative to pairing that lets us compute precisely the desired sequential product of weighted automata:

Definition 10. *The nth sequentializable tensor product (n-STP) of a weight domain $\mathcal{S} = (D, \oplus, \otimes, \bar{0}, \bar{1})$ is defined as another weight domain $\mathcal{S}_t =*

$(D_t, \oplus_t, \otimes_t, \overline{0}_t, \overline{1}_t)$ with operations $\odot : D^n \to D_t$ (called the tensor operation) and $DeTensor : D_t \to D$ such that for all $w_j, w'_j \in D$ and $t_1, t_2 \in D_t$,

1. $\odot(w_1, w_2, \cdots, w_n) \otimes_t \odot(w'_1, w'_2, \cdots, w'_n) = \odot(w_1 \otimes w'_1, w_2 \otimes w'_2, \cdots, w_n \otimes w'_n)$
2. $DeTensor(\odot(w_1, w_2, \cdots, w_n)) = (w_1 \otimes w_2 \otimes \cdots \otimes w_n)$ and
3. $DeTensor(t_1 \oplus_t t_2) = DeTensor(t_1) \oplus DeTensor(t_2)$.

When $n = 2$, we write the tensor operator as an infix operator. Note that because of the first condition in the above definition, $\overline{1}_t = \odot(\overline{1}, \cdots, \overline{1})$ and $\overline{0}_t = \odot(\overline{0}, \cdots, \overline{0})$. Intuitively, one may think of the tensor product of i weights as a kind of generalized i-tuple of those weights. The first condition above implies that extend of tensor products must be carried out componentwise. The $DeTensor$ operation is the "read-out" operation that puts together a tensor product by taking extend of its components. The third condition distinguishes the tensor product from a simple tupling operation. It enforces that the $DeTensor$ operation distributes over the combine of the tensored domain, which pairing does not satisfy.

If a 2-STP exists for a weight domain, then we can take the product of weighted automata for that domain: if $\mathcal{A}_1$ and $\mathcal{A}_2$ are the two input automata, then for each transition (p_1, γ, q_1) with weight w_1 in $\mathcal{A}_1$, and transition (p_2, γ, q_2) with weight w_2 in $\mathcal{A}_2$, add the transition $((p_1, p_2), \gamma, (q_1, q_2))$ with weight $(w_1 \odot w_2)$ to $\mathcal{A}_3$. The resulting automaton satisfies the property: $DeTensor(\mathcal{A}_3(c)) = \mathcal{A}_1(c) \otimes \mathcal{A}_2(c)$, and more generally, $DeTensor(\mathcal{A}_3(C)) = \bigoplus\{\mathcal{A}_1(c) \otimes \mathcal{A}_2(c) \mid c \in C\}$. (A proof is given in [16].) Thus, with the application of the $DeTensor$ operation, $\mathcal{A}_3$ behaves like the desired automaton for the product of $\mathcal{A}_1$ and $\mathcal{A}_2$. A similar construction and proof hold for taking the product of n automata at the same time, when an n-STP exists.

Before generalizing to composition of transducers, we show that n-STP exists, for all n, for a class of weight domains. This class includes the one needed to perform affine-relation analysis [16].

6.2   Sequentializable Tensor Product

We say that a weight domain is commutative if its extend is commutative. STP is easy to construct for commutative domains (tensor is extend, and $DeTensor$ is identity), but such domains are not useful for encoding abstractions for CBA. Under a commutative extend, interference from other threads can have no effect on the execution of a thread. However, such domains still play an important role in constructing STPs. We show that STPs can be constructed for *matrix domains* built on top of a commutative domain.

Definition 11. Let $\mathcal{S}_c = (D_c, \oplus_c, \otimes_c, \overline{0}_c, \overline{1}_c)$ be a commutative weight domain. Then a **matrix weight domain** on $\mathcal{S}_c$ of order n is a weight domain $\mathcal{S} = (D, \oplus, \otimes, \overline{0}, \overline{1})$ such that D is the set of $n \times n$ matrices with elements from D_c; $\oplus$ is element-wise $\oplus_c$; $\otimes$ is matrix multiplication; $\overline{0}$ is the matrix in which all elements are $\overline{0}_c$; $\overline{1}$ is the matrix with $\overline{1}_c$ on the diagonal and $\overline{0}_c$ elsewhere.

$\mathcal{S}$ is a bounded idempotent semiring even if $\mathcal{S}_c$ is not commutative.

The advantage of looking at weights as matrices is that it gives us essential structure to manipulate for constructing the STP. We need the following operation on matrices: the *Kronecker product* [29] of two matrices A and B, of sizes $n_1 \times n_2$ and $n_3 \times n_4$, respectively, is the matrix C of size $(n_1 \ n_3) \times (n_2 \ n_4)$ such that $C(i,j) = A(i \operatorname{div} n_3, j \operatorname{div} n_4) \otimes B(i \mod n_3, j \mod n_4)$, where matrix indices start from zero. It is much easier to understand this definition pictorially (writing $A(i,j)$ as a_{ij}):

$$C = \begin{pmatrix} a_{11}B & \cdots & a_{1n_2}B \\ \vdots & \ddots & \vdots \\ a_{n_1 1}B & \cdots & a_{n_1 n_2}B \end{pmatrix}$$

The Kronecker product, written as $\odot$, is an associative operation. Moreover, for matrices A, B, C, D with elements that have commutative multiplication, $(A \odot B) \otimes (C \odot D) = (A \otimes C) \odot (B \otimes D)$ [29].

Note that the Kronecker product has all pairwise products of elements from the original matrices. One can come up with *projection* matrices p_i (with just $\bar{1}$ and $\bar{0}$ entries) such that $p_i \otimes m \otimes p_j$ selects the (i,j) entry of m (zeros out other entries). Using these matrices in conjunction with *permutation* matrices (that can permute rows and columns and change the size of a matrix), one can compute the product of two matrices from their Kronecker product: there are fixed matrices e_i, e_j and an expression $\theta_m = \bigoplus_{i,j}(e_i \otimes m \otimes e_j)$, such that $\theta_{m_1 \odot m_2} = m_1 \otimes m_2$. This can be generalized to multiple matrices to get an expression θ_m of the same form as above, such that $\theta_{m_1 \odot \cdots \odot m_n} = m_1 \otimes \cdots \otimes m_n$. The advantage of having an expression of this form is that $\theta_{m_1 \oplus m_2} = \theta_{m_1} \oplus \theta_{m_2}$ (because matrix multiplication distributes over their addition, or combine).

Theorem 2. *A n-STP exists on matrix domains for all n. If $\mathcal{S}$ is a matrix domain of order r, then its n-STP is a matrix domain of order r^n with the following operations: the tensor product of weights is defined as their Kronecker product, and the DeTensor operation is defined as $\lambda m.\theta_m$.*

The necessary properties for the tensor operation follow from those for Kronecker product (this is where we need commutativity of the underlying semiring) and the expression θ_m. This also implies that the tensor operation is associative and one can build weights in the nth STP from a weight in the $(n-1)^{\text{th}}$ STP and the original matrix weight domain by taking the Kronecker product. It follows that the sequential product of n automata can be built from that of the first $(n-1)$ automata and the last automaton. The same holds for composing n transducers. Therefore, for CBA, the context-bound can be increased incrementally, and the transducer constructed for $(\Rightarrow^c)^k$ can be used to construct one for $(\Rightarrow^c)^{k+1}$.

6.3   Composing Transducers

Unweighted transducer composition proceeds in a similar fashion to automaton intersection: for transitions $(q_1, \gamma_1/\gamma_2, q_2)$ and $(q'_1, \gamma_2/\gamma_3, q'_2)$ in the respective transducers, add $((q_1, q'_1), \gamma_1/\gamma_3, (q_2, q'_2))$ to the new transducer.

If our weighted transducers were unidirectional (completely forwards or completely backwards) then composing them would be the same as taking the product of weighted automata: the weights on matching transitions would get tensored together. However, our transducers are partitioned, and have both a forwards component and a backwards component. To handle the partitioning, we need additional operations on weights.

Definition 12. *Let $\mathcal{S} = (D, \oplus, \otimes, \overline{0}, \overline{1})$ be a weight domain. Then a **transpose** operation on this domain is defined as $(.)^T : D \to D$ such that for all $w_1, w_2 \in D$, $w_1^T \otimes w_2^T = (w_2 \otimes w_1)^T$ and it is its self-inverse: $(w_1^T)^T = w_1$. An n-**transposable STP** (TSTP) on $\mathcal{S}$ is defined as an n-STP along with another de-tensor operation: $TDeTensor : D^n \to D$ such that $TDeTensor(\odot(w_1, w_2, \cdots, w_n)) = w_1 \otimes w_2^T \otimes w_3 \otimes w_4^T \otimes \cdots w_n'$, where $w_n' = w_n$ if n is odd and w_n^T if n is even.*

TSTPs always exist for matrix domains: the transpose operation is the matrix-transpose operation, and the *TDeTensor* operation can be defined using an expression similar to that for *DeTensor*. We can use TSTPs to remove the partitioning. Let τ be a partitioned weighted transducer on $\mathcal{S}$, for which a transpose exists, as well as a 2-TSTP. The partitioning on the states of τ naturally defines a partitioning on its transitions as well (a transition is said to belong to the partition of its source state). Replace weights w_1 in the first (forwards) partition with $(w_1 \odot \overline{1})$, and weights w_2 in the second (backwards) partition with $(\overline{1} \odot w_2^T)$. This gives a completely forwards transducer τ' (without any partitioning). The invariant is that for any sets of configurations S and T, $\tau(S, T)$, which is the combine over all weights with which the transducer accepts $(s, t), s \in S, t \in T$, equals $TDeTensor(\tau'(S, T))$.

This can be extended to compose partitioned weighted transducers. Composing n transducers requires a $2n$-TSTP: each transducer is converted to a non-partitioned one over the 2-TSTP domain; input/output labels are matched just as for unweighted transducers; and the weights are tensored together.

Theorem 3. *Given n weighted transducers $\tau_1, \cdots, \tau_n$ on a weight domain with $2n$-TSTP, the above construction produces a weighted transducer τ such that for any sets of configurations S and T, $TDeTensor(\tau(S, T)) = R(S, T)$, where R is the weighted composition of $\mathcal{L}(\tau_1), \cdots, \mathcal{L}(\tau_n)$.*

By composing the weighted languages of transducers, we can construct a weighted transducer τ for $(\Rightarrow^c)^{k+1}$. If automaton $\mathcal{A}_S$ represents the set of starting states of a program, $\tau(\mathcal{A}_S)$ provides a weighted automaton $\mathcal{A}$ describing all reachable states (under the context bound), i.e., the weight $\mathcal{A}(t)$ gives the net transformation in data state in going from S to t ($\overline{0}$ if t is not reachable).

7   Related Work

Reachability analysis of concurrent recursive programs has also been considered in [4,22,9]. These consider the problem by computing overapproximations of the execution paths of the program, whereas here we compute underapproximations of the reachable configurations. Analysis under restricted communication policies (in contrast to shared memory) has also been considered [6,14]. The basic technique of Qadeer and Rehof has been generalized to handle more abstractions in [5,3], however, these also require enumeration of states at a context switch, and cannot handle infinite-state abstractions like affine-relation analysis.

The goal of partial-order reduction techniques [12] for concurrent programs is to avoid explicit enumeration of all interleavings. Our work is in similar spirit, however, we use symbolic techniques to avoid explicitly considering all interleavings. In the QR algorithm, only the stack was kept symbolic using automata, and we extended that approach to keep both stack and data symbolic.

Constructing transducers. As mentioned in the introduction, a transducer construction for PDSs was given earlier by Caucal [8]. However, the construction was given for prefix-rewriting systems in general and is not accompanied by a complexity result, except for the fact that it runs in polynomial time. Our construction for PDSs, obtained as a special case of the construction given in §5, is quite efficient. The technique, however, seems to be related. Caucal constructed the transducer by exploiting the fact that the language of the transducer is a union of the relations $(pre^*(\langle p, \gamma \rangle), post^*(\langle p, \gamma \rangle))$ for all $p \in P$ and $\gamma \in \Gamma$, with an identity relation appended onto them to accept the untouched part of the stack. This is similar to our decomposition of PDS paths (see Fig. 1). Construction of a transducer for WPDSs has not been considered before. This was crucial for developing an algorithm for CBA with infinite-state data abstractions.

Composing transducers. There is a large body of work on weighted automata and weighted transducers in the speech-recognition community [17,18]. However, the weights in their applications usually satisfy many more properties than those of a semiring, including (i) the existence of an inverse, and (ii) commutativity of extend. We refrain from making such assumptions.

The sequential product of weighted automata on semirings was also considered in [15]. However, that algorithm handles only the special case of taking one product of a forwards automaton with a backwards one. It cannot take the product of three or more automata. The techniques in this paper are for taking the product any number of times (provided STPs exist).

Tensor products have been used previously in program analysis for combining abstractions [21]. We use them in a different context and for a different purpose. In particular, previous work has used them for combining abstractions that are performed in *lock-step*; in contrast, we use them to stitch together the data state *before* a context switch with the data state *after* a context switch.

References

1. Ball, T., Majumdar, R., Millstein, T., Rajamani, S.K.: Automatic predicate abstraction of C programs. In: PLDI (2001)
2. Bouajjani, A., Esparza, J., Maler, O.: Reachability analysis of pushdown automata: Application to model checking. In: Mazurkiewicz, A., Winkowski, J. (eds.) CONCUR 1997. LNCS, vol. 1243, Springer, Heidelberg (1997)

3. Bouajjani, A., Esparza, J., Schwoon, S., Strejcek, J.: Reachability analysis of multithreaded software with asynchronous communication. In: Ramanujam, R., Sen, S. (eds.) FSTTCS 2005. LNCS, vol. 3821, pp. 348–359. Springer, Heidelberg (2005)
4. Bouajjani, A., Esparza, J., Touili, T.: A generic approach to the static analysis of concurrent programs with procedures. In: POPL (2003)
5. Bouajjani, A., Fratani, S., Qadeer, S.: Context-bounded analysis of multithreaded programs with dynamic linked structures. In: Damm, W., Hermanns, H. (eds.) CAV 2007. LNCS, vol. 4590, pp. 207–220. Springer, Heidelberg (2007)
6. Bouajjani, A., Müller-Olm, M., Touili, T.: Regular symbolic analysis of dynamic networks of pushdown systems. In: Abadi, M., de Alfaro, L. (eds.) CONCUR 2005. LNCS, vol. 3653, pp. 473–487. Springer, Heidelberg (2005)
7. Büchi, J.R.: Finite Automata, their Algebras and Grammars. Springer, New York(1988)
8. Caucal, D.: On the regular structure of prefix rewriting. TCS 106(1), 61–86 (1992)
9. Chaki, S., Clarke, E.M., Kidd, N., Reps, T.W., Touili, T.: Verifying concurrent message-passing C programs with recursive calls. In: Hermanns, H., Palsberg, J. (eds.) TACAS 2006. LNCS, vol. 3920, pp. 334–349. Springer, Heidelberg (2006)
10. Esparza, J., Hansel, D., Rossmanith, P., Schwoon, S.: Efficient algorithms for model checking pushdown systems. In: Emerson, E.A., Sistla, A.P. (eds.) CAV 2000. LNCS, vol. 1855, Springer, Heidelberg (2000)
11. Finkel, A., Willems, B., Wolper, P.: A direct symbolic approach to model checking pushdown systems. Electronic Notes in Theoretical Comp. Sci. 9 (1997)
12. Godefroid, P.: Partial-Order Methods for the Verification of Concurrent Systems. LNCS, vol. 1032. Springer, Heidelberg (1996)
13. Hopcroft, J., Ullman, J.: Introduction to Automata Theory, Languages, and Computation. Addison-Wesley, Reading (1979)
14. Kahlon, V., Gupta, A.: On the analysis of interacting pushdown systems. In: POPL (2007)
15. Lal, A., Kidd, N., Reps, T., Touili, T.: Abstract error projection. In: Riis Nielson, H., Filé, G. (eds.) SAS 2007. LNCS, vol. 4634, pp. 200–217. Springer, Heidelberg (2007)
16. Lal, A., Touili, T., Kidd, N., Reps, T.: Interprocedural analysis of concurrent programs under a context bound. TR-1598, University of Wisconsin (July 2007)
17. Mohri, M., Pereira, F., Riley, M.: Weighted automata in text and speech processing. In: ECAI (1996)
18. Mohri, M., Pereira, F., Riley, M.: The design principles of a weighted finite-state transducer library. In: Watanabe, O., Hagiya, M., Ito, T., van Leeuwen, J., Mosses, P.D. (eds.) TCS 2000. LNCS, vol. 1872, Springer, Heidelberg (2000)
19. Müller-Olm, M., Seidl, H.: Precise interprocedural analysis through linear algebra. In: POPL (2004)
20. Musuvathi, M., Qadeer, S.: Iterative context bounding for systematic testing of multithreaded programs. In: PLDI (2007)
21. Nielson, F., Nielson, H.R., Hankin, C.: Principles of Program Analysis. Springer, Heidelberg (1999)
22. Patin, G., Sighireanu, M., Touili, T.: Spade: Verification of multithreaded dynamic and recursive programs. In: Damm, W., Hermanns, H. (eds.) CAV 2007. LNCS, vol. 4590, Springer, Heidelberg (2007)
23. Qadeer, S., Rehof, J.: Context-bounded model checking of concurrent software. In: Halbwachs, N., Zuck, L.D. (eds.) TACAS 2005. LNCS, vol. 3440, pp. 93–107. Springer, Heidelberg (2005)

24. Qadeer, S., Wu, D.: KISS: Keep it simple and sequential. In: PLDI (2004)
25. Ramalingam, G.: Context-sensitive synchronization-sensitive analysis is undecidable. In: TOPLAS (2000)
26. Reps, T., Horwitz, S., Sagiv, M.: Precise interprocedural dataflow analysis via graph reachability. In: POPL (1995)
27. Reps, T., Schwoon, S., Jha, S., Melski, D.: Weighted pushdown systems and their application to interprocedural dataflow analysis. In: SCP, vol. 58 (2005)
28. Schwoon, S.: Model-Checking Pushdown Systems. PhD thesis, Technical Univ. of Munich, Munich, Germany (July 2002)
29. Wikipedia. Kronecker product, http://en.wikipedia.org/wiki/Kronecker_product

Context-Bounded Analysis of Concurrent Queue Systems[*]

Salvatore La Torre[1], P. Madhusudan[2], and Gennaro Parlato[1,2]

[1] Università degli Studi di Salerno, Italy
[2] University of Illinois at Urbana-Champaign, USA

Abstract. We show that the bounded context-switching reachability problem for concurrent finite systems communicating using unbounded FIFO queues is decidable, where in each context a process reads from only one queue (but is allowed to write onto all other queues). Our result also holds when individual processes are finite-state recursive programs provided a process dequeues messages only when its local stack is empty. We then proceed to classify architectures that admit a decidable (unbounded context switching) reachability problem, using the decidability of bounded context switching. We show that the precise class of decidable architectures for recursive programs are the forest architectures, while the decidable architectures for non-recursive programs are those that do not have an undirected cycle.

1 Introduction

Networks of concurrent processes communicating via message queues form a very natural and useful model for several classes of systems with inherent parallelism. Two natural classes of systems can be modeled using such a framework: asynchronous programs on a multi-core computer and distributed programs communicating on a network.

In parallel programming languages for multi-core or even single-processor systems (e.g., Java, web service design), *asynchronous programming* or *event-driven programming* is a common idiom that programming languages provide [19,7,13]. In order to obtain higher performance and low latency, programs are equipped with the ability to issue tasks using *asynchronous* calls that immediately return, but are processed later, either in parallel with the calling module or perhaps much later, depending on when processors and other resources such as I/O become free. Asynchronous calls are also found in event-driven programs where a program can register *callback* functions that are associated to particular events (such as a new connection arriving on a socket), and are called when the event occurs. Programs typically call several other functions asynchronously so that they do not get blocked waiting for them to return. The tasks issued by a system are typically handled using queues, and we can build faithful models of these systems as networks of processes communicating via queues.

---

[*] The first and third authors were partially supported by the MIUR grants ex-60% 2006 and 2007 Università degli Studi di Salerno.

C.R. Ramakrishnan and J. Rehof (Eds.): TACAS 2008, LNCS 4963, pp. 299–314, 2008.

Distributed systems communicating via FIFO message channels also form a natural example of networks of processes communicating via queues. Motivated by the verification problem of distributed communication protocols, the model-checking problem for these systems has been studied extensively, where each process in the system is modeled using a finite-state transition system [1,15,10].

In this paper, we study the reachability problem for finite-state processes (and finite-state recursive processes) communicating via FIFO queues. We follow the paradigm of *abstraction*, where we assume that each program has been abstracted (using, for example, predicates) or modeled as a finite-state process, and algorithmically subject to model-checking.

The main barrier to model-check queue systems is that the FIFO message queues give an infinite state-space that is intractable: even reachability of two processes communicating via queues with each other is *undecidable*. There have been several ways to tackle the undecidability in this framework. One line of attack has been to weaken the power of queues by assuming that messages can get arbitrarily lost in queues; this leads to a decidable reachability problem [1] that is appealing in the distributed protocol domain as messages indeed can get lost, but is less natural in the event-driven programming domain as enlisted tasks seldom get lost.

Another technique is to ignore the FIFO order of messages and model the queue as a bag of messages, where any element of the bag can be delivered at any time [18,11]. When the number of kinds of messages is bounded, this amounts to keeping track of how many messages of each kind are present in the bag, which can be tracked using counters. Using the fact that counter systems without a zero-check admit a decidable reachability problem, model-checking of these systems can be proved decidable. In the realm of event-driven programming the assumption of modeling pending tasks as a bag is appealing because of the nondeterministic nature of scheduling.

In this paper, we do not destroy the contents of queues nor destroy the FIFO order, but model queues accurately. To curb undecidability, we show that the *bounded context-switching reachability problem* is decidable. More precisely, a *context* of a queueing network is defined as an (arbitrarily long) evolution of one process that is allowed to dequeue messages from (only) one queue and enqueue messages on all its outgoing message queues. The bounded context-switching reachability problem asks whether a global control state is reachable through a run that switches contexts at most k times, for a fixed value k.

Bounded context switching for recursive concurrent (non-queueing) programs was introduced in [16] in order to find a meaningful way to explore initial parts of executions using algorithmic techniques. The intuition is that many errors manifest themselves even with a short number of context-switches, and hence a model-checker that explores thoroughly the states reached within a few context-switches can prove effective in finding bugs. Bounded context-switching for non-queueing programs have exhibited good coverage of state-spaces [14] and are an appealing restriction for otherwise intractable verification problems of concurrent programs.

We show the decidability of bounded context switching reachability for queueing finite-state programs, which in addition can have a finite *shared memory*. We show that the problem is also decidable for *recursive programs*, wherein each process has a local call-stack that it can manipulate on its moves, provided each process is *well-queueing*. A set of programs is well-queueing if each process dequeues messages only when its local stack is empty. This model allows us to capture general event-driven programs that have recursive synchronous calls, and the well-queueing assumption is natural as the most prevalent programs dequeue a task and execute it to completion before dequeuing the next task (see [18,5] for similar restrictions). We show both the above decidability results by a reduction to the bounded phase reachability of multistack machines, which was recently proven by us to be decidable [12].

We also study the *unbounded context-switching* reachability problem for queue systems by classifying the architectures that admit decidable reachability problems. An architecture is a set of process sites and queues connecting certain pairs of process sites. For the class of recursive programs, we show that the only architectures with a decidable reachability problem are the directed forest architectures. This decidability result is shown using the *bounded context switching decidability* result. We find this surprising: the decidability of bounded context switching (including the notion of a context) stems from a technical result on bounded phase multistack automata, which were defined with no queues in mind, and yet proves to be sufficient to capture all decidable queueing architectures.

Turning to non-recursive architectures, we again provide an exact characterization: the precise class of decidable architectures are those whose underlying *undirected* graph is a forest. The decidability for this result uses a simple idea that queues in architectures can be reversed, and the proof of decidability of tree architectures is considerably simpler as we can build a global finite-state machine simulating the network with bounded-length message queues.

The paper is organized as follows. The next section defines networks of processes communicating via queues, and the reachability and bounded context switching reachability problems. Section 3 establishes our results on bounded context switching reachability of queue systems using multi-stack pushdown automata. Section 4 encompasses our results on the exact class of decidable architectures for recursive and non-recursive programs, and Section 5 ends with some conclusions.

Related Work. The idea of context-bounded analysis for concurrent systems was introduced in [16] where it was shown that it yields a decidable reachability problem for shared memory recursive Boolean programs, and is a generalization of the KISS framework proposed by Shaz Qadeer [17]. The last two years has seen an increasing interest in context-bounded analysis for otherwise intractable systems, including context-bounded analysis for asynchronous dynamic pushdown networks [2], for systems with bounded visible heaps [3], and for a more general notion of context-switching for recursive Boolean programs [12]. A recent paper [14] shows experimentally that a few number of context-switches achieves large coverage of state-space in multithreaded programs.

Message-passing queue systems has been a well-studied problem over the last two decades, and several restrictions based on automata-theoretic analysis have been proposed to verify such systems. These include systems with lossy channels [1], and several restricted models of queue systems, such as systems with a single queue [10], systems where message queues contain only one kind of message [15], half-duplex (and quasi-duplex) systems where only one queue can be active and contain messages at any point [4], and reversal bounded multicounter machines connected via a single queue [9].

Finally, asynchronous programs have been shown to have a decidable reachability problem when at any point only a single recursive process runs, enqueuing tasks onto a bag of tasks, where enqueuing of tasks can only be performed when the local stack is empty [18]. In a recent paper, an under and over approximation scheme based on bounding the counters representing messages has been proposed, and implemented, to solve dataflow analysis problems for asynchronous programs [11].

2   Queue Systems

In this section, we define networks of shared-memory processes communicating via unbounded FIFO queues. The number of processes will be bounded, and the state of each process will be modeled using a global finite-state control that models the control locations of the processes, the local variables, and the global shared memory they access. The global finite-state control can be either a non-recursive program, or a recursive program modeled by each process having its own call-stack that it can push and pop from.

We model any number of queues using which the processes can communicate; each queue has a unique sending process and a unique receiving process. There will be a finite message alphabet, but each queue has an unbounded capacity to store messages. Processes hence communicate either using the shared-memory (which carries only a bounded amount of information) or through queues (which carry unbounded information).

An *architecture* is a structure $(P, Q, Sender, Receiver)$ where P is a finite set of processes, Q is a finite set of queues, and $Sender: Q \to P$ and $Receiver: Q \to P$ are two functions that assign a unique *sender* process and *receiver* process for each queue in Q, respectively. We assume that the sender of a queue cannot be its receiver as well: i.e. for every $q \in Q$, $Sender(q) \neq Receiver(q)$.

We refer to processes in P using notations such as p, p', p_i, $\widehat{p}$, etc., and queues using q, q', etc.

Recursive Programs Communicating Via Queues

Let Π be a finite message alphabet. Consider an architecture $\mathcal{A}=(P, Q, Sender, Receiver)$. An *action of a process* $p \in P$ (over Π) is of one of the following forms:

- $p\colon send(q, m)$ where $m \in \Pi$, $q \in Q$, and $Sender(q) = p$.

    – $p\!: recv(q, m)$ where $m \in \Pi$, $q \in Q$, and $Receiver(q) = p$.
    – $p\!: int$ or $p\!: call$ or $p\!: ret$.

Intuitively, a "$p\!: int$" action is an internal action of process p that does not manipulate queues, "$p\!: send(q, m)$" is an action where process p enqueues the message m on queue q (the receiver is predetermined as the receiver process for the queue), and "$p\!: recv(q, m)$" corresponds to the action where p receives and dequeues the message m from queue q.

    The *stack actions* are those of the form $p\!: call$ or $p\!: ret$. The stack action $p\!: call$ corresponds to a *local call of a procedure* in process p, where the process pushes onto its local stack some data (the valuation of its local variables) and moves to a new state. The stack action $p\!: ret$ corresponds to a return from a procedure where the local stack is popped and the process moves to a new state that depends on the current state and the data popped from the stack.

    Let Act_p denote the set of actions of p, and let $Act = \bigcup_{p \in P} Act_p$ denote the set of all actions. Let $Calls$ denote the set of call actions $\{p\!: call \mid p \in P\}$ and $Rets$ denote the set of return actions $\{p\!: ret \mid p \in P\}$.

Definition 1. *A recursive queueing concurrent program (RQCP) over an architecture $(P, Q, Sender, Receiver)$ is a structure $(S, s_0, \Pi, \Gamma, \{T_p\}_{p\in P})$, where S is a finite set of states, $s_0 \in S$ is an initial state, Π is a finite message alphabet, and Γ is a finite stack alphabet. If Act_p is the set of actions of process p on the message alphabet Π, then T_p is a set of* transitions:
$$T_p \subseteq (S \times (Act_p \setminus \{p\!: call, p\!: ret\}) \times S) \cup (S \times \{p\!: call\} \times S \times \Gamma)$$
$$\cup\, (S \times \{p\!: ret\} \times \Gamma \times S).$$

The size of an RQCP as above is the size of the tuple representation.
A *configuration* of an RQCP $R = (S, s_0, \Pi, \Gamma, \{T_p\}_{p\in P})$ is a tuple $(s, \{\sigma_p\}_{p\in P}, \{\mu_q\}_{q\in Q})$ where $s \in S$, for each $p \in P$, $\sigma_p \in \Gamma^*$ is the content of the local stack of p, and for each queue $q \in Q$, $\mu_q \in \Pi^*$ is the content of q.[1]

    Transitions between configurations are defined as follows:
$$(s, \{\sigma_p\}_{p\in P}, \{\mu_q\}_{q\in Q}) \xrightarrow{act} (s', \{\sigma'_p\}_{p\in P}, \{\mu'_q\}_{q\in Q}) \text{ if}$$

[Internal] $act = \widehat{p}\!: int$ and there is a transition $(s, \widehat{p}\!: int, s') \in T_{\widehat{p}}$ such that
    – for every $q \in Q$, $\mu'_q = \mu_q$, and
    – for every $p \in P$, $\sigma'_p = \sigma_p$.
[Send] $act = \widehat{p}\!: send(\widehat{q}, m)$ and there is a transition
    $(s, \widehat{p}\!: send(\widehat{q}, m), s') \in T_{\widehat{p}}$ such that
    – $\mu'_{\widehat{q}} = m.\mu_{\widehat{q}}$, and for every $q \neq \widehat{q}$, $\mu'_q = \mu_q$
    – for every $p \in P$, $\sigma'_p = \sigma_p$.
[Receive] $act = \widehat{p}\!: recv(\widehat{q}, m)$ and there is a transition
    $(s, \widehat{p}\!: recv(\widehat{q}, m), s') \in T_{\widehat{p}}$ such that
    – $\mu_{\widehat{q}} = \mu'_{\widehat{q}}.m$ and for every $q \neq \widehat{q}$, $\mu'_q = \mu_q$
    – for every $p \in P$, $\sigma'_p = \sigma_p$.

---

[1] The top of the stack of p is at the beginning of σ_p, and the last message enqueued onto q is at the beginning of μ_q, by convention.

[Call] $act = \widehat{p}\colon call$ and there is a transition $(s, \widehat{p}\colon call, s', \gamma) \in T_{\widehat{p}}$ such that
- $\sigma'_{\widehat{p}} = \gamma\sigma_{\widehat{p}}$, and for every $p \neq \widehat{p}$, $\sigma'_p = \sigma_p$,
- for every $q \in Q$, $\mu'_q = \mu_q$.

[Return] $act = \widehat{p}\colon ret$ and there is a transition $(s, \widehat{p}\colon ret, \gamma, s') \in T_{\widehat{p}}$ such that
- $\sigma_{\widehat{p}} = \gamma\sigma'_{\widehat{p}}$ and for every $p \neq \widehat{p}$, $\sigma'_p = \sigma_p$,
- for every $q \in Q$, $\mu'_q = \mu_q$.

A *run* of an RQCP is a sequence of transitions $c_0 \xrightarrow{act_1} c_1 \xrightarrow{act_2} c_2 \dots \xrightarrow{act_n} c_n$ with $c_0 = (s, \{\sigma_p\}_{p \in P}, \{\mu_q\}_{q \in Q})$, where $s = s_0$ is the initial state, $\sigma_p = \epsilon$ for each $p \in P$ (initial stacks are empty), and $\mu_q = \epsilon$ for each $q \in Q$ (initial queues are empty). A state $\widehat{s}$ is said to be *reachable* if there is a run $c_0 \xrightarrow{act_1} c_1 \xrightarrow{act_2} c_2 \dots \xrightarrow{act_n} c_n$ such that $c_n = (\widehat{s}, \{\sigma_p\}_{p \in P}, \{\mu_q\}_{q \in Q})$.

The *reachability problem* for recursive programs communicating via queues is to determine, given an RQCP $(S, s_0, \Pi, \Gamma, \{T_p\}_{p \in P})$ and a set of target states $T \subseteq S$, whether any $\widehat{s} \in T$ is reachable.

Non-recursive programs communicating via queues

A non-recursive queueing concurrent program (QCP) over the processes P, message alphabet Π, and queues Q is an RQCP $(S, s_0, \Pi, \Gamma, \{T_p\}_{p \in P})$ in which there are no transitions on calls and returns (i.e. there is no transition on an action of the form $p\colon call$ or $p\colon ret$ in T_p). Consequently, we remove the stack alphabet Γ from its description, and its configurations do not involve the local stacks of each process. A QCP hence is of the form $(S, s_0, \Pi, \{T_p\}_{p \in P})$ where $T_p \subseteq (S \times (Act_p \setminus \{p\colon call, p\colon ret\}) \times S)$, a configuration of a QCP is of the form $(s, \{\mu_q\}_{q \in Q})$, and the semantics of transitions on configurations are the appropriately simplified versions of the rules for internal, send, and receive actions described above. The reachability problem is analogously defined.

Bounded context switching

It is well-known that the reachability problem for even non-recursive queueing concurrent programs is undecidable (see Lemma 8 later). The undecidability result holds even for a very simple architecture with only two processes p and p', and two queues, one from p to p' and the other from p' to p.

Since reachability is undecidable for queue systems, we study bounded context-switching of queue systems. Intuitively, a context of a queueing system is a sequence of moves where only one process evolves, dequeuing at most one queue q (but possibly enqueuing messages on any number of queues that it can write to). The bounded-context switching reachability problem for an RQCP (or QCP) is the problem of finding whether a target set of states is reachable by some run that switches contexts at most k times, for an a priori fixed bound k.

Formally, for any $p \in P$, $q \in Q$ such that $Receiver(q) = p$, let

$Act_{p,q} = \{p\colon int, p\colon call, p\colon ret\} \cup \{p\colon send(q', m) \mid q' \in Q, Sender(q') = p, m \in \Pi\}$
$\qquad \cup \{p\colon recv(q, m) \mid m \in \Pi\}$

denote the set of actions of p with dequeue actions acting only on queue q. A run $c_0 \xrightarrow{act_1} c_1 \xrightarrow{act_2} \dots \xrightarrow{act_n} c_n$ has at most k context switches if the cardinality of the set $\{i \mid act_i \in Act_{p,q}, act_{i+1} \notin Act_{p,q}, p \in P, q \in Q\}$ is bounded by k.

The bounded context-switching reachability problem is to determine, given an RQCP (or QCP), a target set of states T, and a bound $k \in \mathbb{N}$, whether any state in T is reachable on a run that has at most k context switches.

Well-queueing processes

An RQCP is said to be *well-queueing* if every process p dequeues a message from a queue only when its local stack is empty. Formally, an RQCP is well-queueing if there is no run of the form $c_0 \xrightarrow{act_1} c_1 \xrightarrow{act_2} \ldots c_{n-1} \xrightarrow{act_n} c_n$ where $c_{n-1} = (s, \{\sigma_p\}_{p\in P}, \{\mu_q\}_{q\in Q})$, $act_{n-1} = p\colon recv(q,m)$ and $\sigma_p \neq \epsilon$.

3   The Bounded Context-Switching Reachability Problem

In this section, we recall multi-stack pushdown systems and show that bounded context-switching reachability for both non-recursive and well-queueing recursive concurrent programs can be decided via a reduction to bounded phase reachability for multi-stack pushdown systems [12].

Multi-stack Pushdown Systems

A multi-stack pushdown system is the natural extension of standard pushdown system with multiple stacks. Formally, a *multi-stack pushdown system* (MSPS) is $M = (S, s_0, St, \Gamma, \Delta)$ where S is a finite set of states, $s_0 \in S$ is the initial state, St is a finite set of stacks, Γ is the stack alphabet and $\Delta = \Delta_{int} \cup \Delta_{push} \cup \Delta_{pop}$ is the transition relation with $\Delta_{int} \subseteq S \times S$, $\Delta_{push} \subseteq S \times St \times \Gamma \times S$, and $\Delta_{pop} \subseteq S \times St \times \Gamma \times S$.

A *configuration* c of an MSPS M is a tuple $\langle s, \{\sigma_{st}\}_{st\in St}\rangle$, where $s \in S$ is the current control state of M, and for every $st \in St$, $\sigma_{st} \in \Gamma^*$ denotes the content of stack st (we assume that the leftmost symbol of st is the top of the stack). The *initial configuration* of M is $\langle s_0, \{\sigma_{st}\}_{st\in St}\rangle$, where for every $st \in St$, $\sigma_{st} = \epsilon$ denoting that each stack is empty. The semantics of M is given by defining the transition relation induced by Δ on the set of configurations of M. We write $\langle s, \{\sigma_{st}\}_{st\in St}\rangle \xrightarrow{\delta} \langle s', \{\sigma'_{st}\}_{st\in St}\rangle$ iff one of the following cases holds: (unless it is differently specified, we assume that $\sigma_{st} = \sigma'_{st}$ for every $st \in St$)

[Internal move] δ is $(s, s') \in \Delta_{int}$.
[Push onto stack $\widehat{st}$] δ is $(s, \widehat{st}, a, s') \in \Delta_{push}$ and $\sigma'_{\widehat{st}} = a.\sigma_{\widehat{st}}$.
[Pop from stack $\widehat{st}$] δ is $(s, \widehat{st}, a, s') \in \Delta_{pop}$ and $\sigma_{\widehat{st}} = a.\sigma'_{\widehat{st}}$.

A *run* of an MSPS M is a sequence of transitions $c_0 \xrightarrow{\delta_1} c_1 \xrightarrow{\delta_2} c_2 \ldots \xrightarrow{\delta_n} c_n$. A state $\widehat{s} \in S$ is reachable if there exists a run $c_0 \xrightarrow{\delta_1} c_1 \xrightarrow{\delta_2} c_2 \ldots \xrightarrow{\delta_n} c_n$ such that c_0 is the initial configuration, and c_n is a configuration of the form $\langle \widehat{s}, \{\sigma_{st}\}_{st\in St}\rangle$.

A *phase* of a run is a portion of the run in which the pop moves are all from the same stack. For a positive integer k, a *k-phase* run is a run that is composed of at most k phases. Formally, an M run $c_0 \xrightarrow{\delta_1} c_1 \xrightarrow{\delta_2} c_2 \ldots \xrightarrow{\delta_n} c_n$ is k-phase if we can split the sequence $\delta_1 \ldots \delta_n$ into $\alpha_1 \ldots \alpha_k$ such that: for each $i = 1, \ldots, k$, there is a stack $st \in St$ such that each rule $\delta \in \Delta_{pop}$ within α_i is of the form (s, st, a, s'). Therefore, in a k-phase run the stack from which we pop symbols is changed at most $k - 1$ times (*phase-switches*). A state $\widehat{s}$ is k-phase reachable if it is reachable on a k-phase run. The *bounded phase reachability problem* is the problem of determining whether, given an MSPS M, a set of states T, and a positive integer k, there is a state of T that is reachable on a k-phase run.

Theorem 1. *[12] The bounded phase reachability problem for* MSPS*s is decidable. Moreover, the problem can be solved in time exponential in the number of states and double exponential in the number of phases.*

Decidability of Bounded Context-Switching Reachability

We start showing that context-switching reachability for QCPs is decidable.

Theorem 2. *The bounded context-switching reachability problem for non-recursive queuing concurrent programs is decidable. Moreover, the problem can be solved in time double exponential in the number of context-switches, and exponential in the size of the program.*

Proof. We reduce the reachability problem up to k context switches for QCPs to the reachability problem up to $2k + 1$ phases for MSPSs. Fix a QCP A over an architecture $(P, Q, Sender, Receiver)$ and let S be the set of states of A. We construct an MSPS M which simulates A by keeping track of the state of A in its control state, and stores the contents of each queue q in a stack st_q, and has an additional work stack st.

Let us denote a context with $(\widehat{p}, \widehat{q})$, where $\widehat{p}$ is the active process dequeuing from q in the context. Fix a run of A and let $(\widehat{p}, \widehat{q})$ be the context at a particular point in the run. M is defined such that the following invariant is preserved: the content of any queue $q \neq \widehat{q}$ is stored in st_q with the rear at the top, stack $st_{\widehat{q}}$ is empty and the content of queue $\widehat{q}$ is stored in st with the front at the top.

An internal move of A is simulated by an internal move of M; sending a message m to a queue $q \neq \widehat{q}$ corresponds to push m onto stack st_q; receiving a message m from $\widehat{q}$ corresponds to pop m from the work stack st. Consequently, in one context, there are no phase switches in the simulating machine M. On switching context from $(\widehat{p}, \widehat{q})$ to $(\widehat{p}', \widehat{q}')$, M moves the content of st onto stack $st_{\widehat{q}}$ and then the content of stack $st_{\widehat{q}'}$ onto st. Observe that the first of these two tasks does not cause a change of phase in the run on M since st is the stack which is popped while simulating the context $(\widehat{p}, \widehat{q})$. The second task requires popping from a new stack and thus causes a change of phase.

We can design the described MSPS M such that it has states polynomial in $|S|$. Therefore, reachability in A within k context-switches reduces to reachability within $2k + 1$ phases in M ($k + 1$ phases are required for the $k + 1$ contexts and k additional phases for context switching). The stated complexity bound thus follows form Theorem 1. □

The construction sketched in the above proof can be adapted to show the decidability of bounded context-switching reachability for well-queueing RQCPs:

Theorem 3. *The bounded context-switching reachability problem for well-queueing recursive concurrent programs is decidable. Moreover, the problem can be solved in time double exponential in the number of context-switches, and exponential in the size of the program.*

Proof. Let R be a well-queueing RQCP. We will simulate R using an MSPS as in the proof of Theorem 2. The MSPS will have one stack st_q for every queue q, and an extra work stack st, as before, but in addition it will have one stack st_p for every process p.

When the current context is $(\widehat{p}, \widehat{q})$, we will maintain the invariant that the local stack of all processes p $(p \neq \widehat{p})$ in the RQCP is stored in the reverse order in stack st_p, and the queue contents of each queue q $(q \neq \widehat{q})$ are stored in the stack st_q as before; the stacks $st_{\widehat{p}}$ and $st_{\widehat{q}}$ will be empty and the stack st will have the content of queue $\widehat{q}$ and on top of it the content of the local stack of $\widehat{p}$. Internal moves and enqueuing operations are performed as before, and calls and returns are performed by pushing and popping the work-stack. When process $\widehat{p}$ dequeues from queue $\widehat{q}$, its local stack must be empty (by the well-queueing assumption), and hence the next message to be dequeued from q will be at the top of the stack st, and can hence be popped. When the context switches from $(\widehat{p}, \widehat{q})$ to $(\widehat{p}', \widehat{q}')$, we transfer the top portion of stack st onto stack $st_{\widehat{p}}$ and the bottom portion onto the stack $st_{\widehat{q}}$, and then transfer the contents of stack $st_{\widehat{q}'}$ to st followed by the contents of stack $st_{\widehat{p}'}$ to st. This requires two extra phases and maintains the invariant. The complexity follows from Theorem 1.   □

The Well-Queueing Assumption and the Notion of Context

Reachability for recursive queueing concurrent programs that are not well-queueing is complex and even the simplest of architectures has an undecidable bounded context-switching reachability problem:

Theorem 4. *The bounded context-switching reachability problem for RQCPs (which need not be well-queueing) is undecidable for the architecture containing two processes p and p' with a single queue connecting p to p'. The undecidability re-* *sult holds even if we restrict to runs with at most a* single *context switch.*

Also relaxing the requirement that in each context a process can dequeue at most from one queue immediately leads to undecidability.

Theorem 5. *The bounded context-switching reachability problem for QCPs (hence for well-queueing RQCPs) where a process can dequeue from more than one queue in each context is undecidable. The undecidability result holds even if we restrict to runs with just one context switch and allow processes to dequeue from at most two queues in each context.*

4   Unbounded Context-Switching: Decidable Architectures

In this section, we study the class of architectures for which *unbounded* context-switching reachability (or simply reachability) is decidable. Our goal is to give exact characterizations of decidable architectures for the framework where individual processes are non-recursive, as well as the framework where individual processes are recursive. We restrict ourselves to studying the reachability problem for programs that have *no shared memory* and are *well-queueing*. As we show later in this section (Section 4.3), programs with shared memory and recursive programs that are not well-queueing are undecidable even for the simplest of architectures. We prove that for recursive well-queueing concurrent programs with no shared memory, the class of decidable architectures is precisely the class of directed forest architectures.For the non-recursive queueing concurrent programs with no shared memory, we show that the class of decidable architectures is precisely the polyforest architectures (a polyforest is a set of disjoint polytrees; a polytree is an architecture whose underlying undirected graph is a tree).

Processes with no shared memory: A recursive queueing concurrent program $(S, s_0, \Pi, \Gamma, \{T_p\}_{p \in P})$ is said to have *no shared memory* if its state space is the product of local state-spaces and each move of a process depends only on its local state, and updates only its local state. In other words, $S = \Pi_{p \in P} S_p$, where S_p is a finite set of *local* states of process p, and there is a *local* transition relation LT_p (for each $p \in P$) where

$$LT_p \subseteq (S_p \times (Act_p \setminus \{p{:}\, call, p{:}\, ret\}) \times S_p) \cup (S_p \times \{p{:}\, call\} \times S_p \times \Gamma)$$
$$\cup (S_p \times \{p{:}\, ret\} \times \Gamma \times S_p)$$

such that for all $p \in P$ and $s, s' \in S$:

- for every $a \in (Act_p \setminus \{p{:}\, call, p{:}\, ret\})$,
  $(s, a, s') \in T_p$ iff $((s[p], a, s'[p]) \in LT_p$ and $s'[p'] = s[p']$ for every $p \neq p')$;
- for every $\gamma \in \Gamma$, $(s, p{:}\, call, s', \gamma) \in T_p$ iff
  $((s[p], p{:}\, call, s'[p], \gamma) \in LT_p$ and $s'[p'] = s[p']$ for every $p \neq p')$;
- for every $\gamma \in \Gamma$, $(s, p{:}\, ret, \gamma, s') \in T_p$ iff
  $((s[p], p{:}\, call, \gamma, s'[p]) \in LT_p$ and $s'[p'] = s[p']$ for every $p \neq p')$.

In fact, for RQCPs with no shared memory, we can assume that the RQCP is presented in terms of its local transition relations, and model it as a tuple $(\{S_p\}_{p \in P}, s_0, \Pi, \Gamma, \{LT_p\}_{p \in P})$ where $s_0 \in \Pi_{p \in P} S_p$. The *size* of an RQCP with no shared memory will be in terms of this representation: i.e. the size of this tuple. Note that this size is possibly exponentially smaller than the size of the RQCP with the global transition relations. The complexity results in this section will refer to the size of RQCPs with no shared memory measured with the local transition relations.

The graph of an architecture: We will characterize decidable architectures based on properties of the underlying graphs. The *graph of an architecture* $\mathcal{A}=(P, Q, Sender, Receiver)$ is $G=(V, E)$ where $V=P$ and E is the set of labeled edges $E=\{(p, q, p') \mid Sender(q) = p, Receiver(q) = p', q \in Q, \; p, p' \in P\}$.

4.1   Decidable Architectures for Recursive Programs

We now show that the only architectures that admit a decidable reachability problem for well-queueing recursive concurrent programs (with no shared memory) are the class of directed forest architectures.

An architecture is said to be a *directed tree architecture* if its graph is a rooted tree, i.e. there is a root process p_0, every other process p is reachable from p_0 using directed edges, and there is no undirected cycle in the graph. An architecture is said to be a *directed forest architecture* if its graph is the disjoint union of rooted trees. The main theorem of this section is:

Theorem 6. *An architecture admits a decidable reachability problem for well-queueing RQCPs with no shared memory iff it is a directed forest architecture. Moreover, the reachability problem is decidable in time doubly exponential in the number of processes and singly exponential in the size of the RQCP.*

The above theorem is proved using Lemma 1 and Lemma 3 below.

The decidability result is obtained using the decidability of bounded context-switching reachability established in the previous section. Intuitively, given a directed tree architecture, any execution of the processes is equivalent to a run where the root process first runs, enqueuing messages to its children, and then its children run (one after another) dequeuing messages from the incoming queue 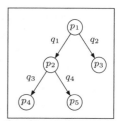 and writing to their children, and so on. For example, for the directed tree architecture shown on the right, any reachable state of the system can be reached by a run that has 4 context switches: in the first context p_1 runs enqueuing messages on q_1 and q_2, then p_2 runs dequeuing messages from q_1 and enqueuing messages in q_3 and q_4, and then in three contexts, p_3, p_4 and p_5 run, one after the other, dequeuing messages from their incoming queues.

Lemma 1. *The reachability problem for well-queueing RQCPs with no shared memory is decidable for all directed forest architectures, and is decidable in time doubly exponential in the number of processes, and singly exponential in the size of the RQCP.*

Proof. On directed tree architectures, unbounded reachability reduces to bounded context-switching reachability, where each process in the tree runs at most once, processing messages from its only incoming queue and writing to its outgoing queues. Directed forest architectures can be analyzed by executing its component directed trees one after another. Note that the fact that in a tree there is at most one incoming edge to a node is crucial; and so is the assumption that there is no shared memory. Hence, given an RQCP M with no shared memory over a directed forest architecture, we can reduce it to the problem of reachability within n contexts (where n is the number of processes) of a new RQCP M' (with shared memory); furthermore, the number of states of M' is linearly proportional to the local states of M. The lemma now follows from Theorem 3.   □

Let us now show that all other architectures are undecidable for well-queueing RQCPs with no shared memory. First, we establish that three architectures are undecidable:

Lemma 2. *The following architectures are undecidable for all well-queueing recursive concurrent programs with no shared memory:*

- *the architecture consisting of three processes p_1, p_2 and p_3, with a queue from p_1 to p_3, and another from p_2 to p_3;*
- *the two-process cyclic architecture consisting two processes p_1 and p_2, with two queues, one from p_1 to p_2, and the other from p_2 to p_1;*

- *the architecture with processes p_1 and p_2, with two queues from p_1 to p_2.*

The above lemma can be extended to show that any architecture embedding any of the above architectures is undecidable:

Lemma 3. *Any architecture that has (a) a process with two incoming queues, or (b) a set of processes forming a cycle, or (c) has two distinct paths from one process to another, is undecidable for well-queueing RQCPs with no shared memory. Consequently, any architecture that is not a directed forest is undecidable for recursive well-queueing concurrent programs with no shared memory.*

Lemma 1 and Lemma 3 establish Theorem 6.

4.2   Decidable Architectures for Non-recursive programs

We now turn to the classification of architectures that admit a decidable reachability problem for non-recursive queueing programs with no shared memory. A directed graph is a polytree if it does not have any undirected cycles, i.e. the undirected graph corresponding to it is a tree. A polyforest is a disjoint union of polytrees. An architecture is a polytree (or a polyforest) if its graph is a 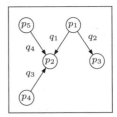 polytree (or polyforest). We show that the class of decidable architectures for non-recursive programs is precisely the polyforest architectures. For example, the architecture depicted on the right is a polytree architecture, but not a directed tree architecture; hence it admits decidable reachability for non-recursive programs but not for well-queueing recursive programs.

Theorem 7. *The class of architectures that admit a decidable reachability problem for QCPs with no shared memory are precisely the polyforest architectures.*

We prove the above theorem using Lemma 7 and Lemma 9 below.

First, we can reduce the reachability problem to the reachability problem on empty queues (where a state is deemed reachable only if it is reachable with all queues emptied). Any QCP can be transformed so that any individual process, for any of its outgoing queues, stops sending messages (throwing away future messages sent on this queue) and instead sends a special symbol on the queues signaling that this is the last message that will be received by the recipient. All processes must receive these last messages before they reach the target states.

Lemma 4. *The reachability problem for QCPs (or even RQCPs) on any architecture is polynomial time reducible to the reachability problem on empty queues for QCPs (or RQCPs, respectively) on the same architecture.*

Now, we show a crucial lemma: for non-recursive programs the direction of a queue in an architecture does not matter for decidability. Intuitively, consider two architectures that are exactly the same except for a queue q which connects p_1 to p_2 in A_1, and connects p_2 to p_1 in A_2 instead. Then, reachability on empty queues for a QCP on A_1 can be transformed to reachability on empty queues for a corresponding program over A_2 by letting p_1 receive in A_2 the messages from p_2 which it would have instead sent to p_2 in A_1: the program at p_1 simply dequeues from q whenever the original program at p_1 enqueued onto q; similarly process p_2 enqueues onto q whenever the original program at p_2 dequeued q.[2]

Lemma 5. *Let A_1 and A_2 be two architectures whose underlying undirected graphs are isomorphic. Then, reachability on empty queues for QCPs with no shared memory on A_1 can be effectively (and in polynomial time) reduced to reachability on empty queues for QCPs with no shared memory on A_2.*

We now show that reachability on all directed-forest architectures is decidable, which, combined with the above lemmas will show that all polyforest architectures are decidable. While this already follows from our result for recursive programs on directed forest architectures, we can give a much simpler proof for non-recursive architectures. Essentially, a QCP with no shared memory on a directed tree architecture can be simulated by a *finite-state* process that keeps track of the global state of each process and synchronizes processes on sending/receiving messages. Since a process lower in a tree can never enable or disable a transition in a process higher in the tree, and since there is no shared memory, we can argue that this finite-state process will discover all reachable states. The argument easily extends to directed forest architectures, and it easy to see that it results in a PSPACE decision procedure. The problem is PSPACE-hard as even reachability of synchronizing finite-state machines is PSPACE-hard [6].

---

[2] The reader may wonder why this transformation cannot work recursive programs; it does indeed work. However, it may make a well-queueing program non well-queueing!

Lemma 6. *The reachability problem for QCPs with no shared memory over directed forest architectures is PSPACE-complete.*

Combining the above with Lemmas 4 and 5, we establish the upper bounds:

Lemma 7. *The reachability problem for QCPs with no shared memory over polyforest architectures is decidable and is PSPACE-complete.*

Let us now show that all but the polyforest architectures are undecidable.

Lemma 8. *The reachability problem for QCPs with no shared memory over the architecture consisting of two processes, p_1 and p_2, with one queue from p_1 to p_2, and the other from p_2 to p_1, is undecidable.*

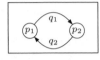

The above proof can be extended to show that any architecture with a directed cycle is undecidable. Combining this with Lemmas 4 and 5 we get that all architectures whose graphs have an undirected cycle are undecidable.

Lemma 9. *The reachability problem for QCPs with no shared memory over any architecture that is not a polyforest architecture is undecidable.*

4.3   The Well-Queueing Assumption and Absence of Shared Memory

This section has dealt with *well-queueing* processes communicating with each other through unbounded queues and *without any shared memory*. Reachability in shared-memory concurrent queue systems is more complex and even the simplest of architectures is undecidable:

Theorem 8. *The reachability problem for QCPs (and hence well-queueing RQCPs) is undecidable for the architecture containing two processes p and p' with a single queue connecting p to p' (depicted on the right). For well-queueing RQCPs, the*

undecidability result holds even if there are two processes and no queues.

Similarly, recursive queueing concurrent programs that are not well-queueing are complex too and even the simplest of architectures is undecidable:

Theorem 9. *The reachability problem for RQCPs with no shared memory (which need not be well-queueing) is undecidable for the architecture containing two processes p and p' with a single queue connecting p to p'.*

Consequently, the classification of decidable architectures is interesting only under the assumptions of no shared memory and well-queueing.

5   Conclusions

We have shown that bounded context-switching reachability is decidable for queueing non-recursive programs and well-queueing recursive programs. Using this result, we have precisely characterized the architectures that admit a decidable reachability problem for both recursive and non-recursive programs. Our contribution is theoretical, but addresses an important problem involving a model that can capture both asynchronous programs as well as distributed communicating processes.

The most important future direction we see is in designing *approximate* analysis for queue systems based on the theory we have presented that will work well on domain-specific applications. Two recent papers give us hope: in [18], the authors addressed the reachability problem for asynchronous programs communicating via unbounded *bags* of messages using counter systems, and a year later, a convergent under- and over-approximation of counter contents led to a practical implementation of dataflow analysis for asynchronous programs [11]. A similar scheme for queue systems would be interesting and useful.

References

1. Abdulla, P., Jonsson, B.: Verifying programs with unreliable channels. In: LICS, pp. 160–170. IEEE Computer Society, Los Alamitos (1993)
2. Bouajjani, A., Esparza, J., Schwoon, S., Strejcek, J.: Reachability analysis of multithreaded software with asynchronous communication. In: Ramanujam, R., Sen, S. (eds.) FSTTCS 2005. LNCS, vol. 3821, pp. 348–359. Springer, Heidelberg (2005)
3. Bouajjani, A., Fratani, S., Qadeer, S.: Context-bounded analysis of multithreaded programs with dynamic linked structures. In: Damm, W., Hermanns, H. (eds.) CAV 2007. LNCS, vol. 4590, pp. 207–220. Springer, Heidelberg (2007)
4. Cécé, G., Finkel, A.: Programs with quasi-stable channels are effectively recognizable (extended abstract). In: Grumberg, O. (ed.) CAV 1997. LNCS, vol. 1254, pp. 304–315. Springer, Heidelberg (1997)
5. Chadha, R., Viswanathan, M.: Decidability results for well-structured transition systems with auxiliary storage. In: Caires, L., Vasconcelos, V.T. (eds.) CONCUR. LNCS, vol. 4703, Springer, Heidelberg (2007)
6. Cheng, A., Esparza, J., Palsberg, J.: Complexity Results for 1-Safe Nets. Theor. Comput. Sci. 147(1-2), 117–136 (1995)
7. Gay, D., Levis, P., von Behren, J.R., Welsh, M., Brewer, E.A., Culler, D.E.: The Nesc language: A holistic approach to networked embedded systems. In: PLDI, pp. 1–11. ACM Press, New York (2003)
8. Hopcroft, J.E., Ullman, J.D.: Introduction to Automata Theory, Languages, and Computation. Addison-Wesley, Reading (1979)
9. Ibarra, O.H.: Verification in queue-connected multicounter machines. Int. J. Found. Comput. Sci. 13(1), 115–127 (2002)
10. Ibarra, O.H., Dang, Z., San Pietro, P.: Verification in loosely synchronous queue-connected discrete timed automata. Theor. Comput. Sci. 290(3), 1713–1735 (2003)
11. Jhala, R., Majumdar, R.: Interprocedural analysis of asynchronous programs. In: POPL, pp. 339–350. ACM Press, New York (2007)

12. La Torre, S., Madhusudan, P., Parlato, G.: A robust class of context-sensitive languages. In: LICS, pp. 161–170. IEEE Computer Society Press, Los Alamitos (2007)
13. Libasync, http://pdos.csail.mit.edu/6.824-2004/async/.
14. Musuvathi, M., Qadeer, S.: Iterative context bounding for systematic testing of multithreaded programs. In: PLDI, pp. 446–455. ACM, New York (2007)
15. Peng, W., Purushothaman, S.: Analysis of a class of communicating finite state machines. Acta Inf. 29(6/7), 499–522 (1992)
16. Qadeer, S., Rehof, J.: Context-bounded model checking of concurrent software. In: Halbwachs, N., Zuck, L.D. (eds.) TACAS 2005. LNCS, vol. 3440, pp. 93–107. Springer, Heidelberg (2005)
17. Qadeer, S., Wu, D.: Kiss: keep it simple and sequential. In: PLDI, pp. 14–24. ACM, New York (2004)
18. Sen, K., Viswanathan, M.: Model checking multithreaded programs with asynchronous atomic methods. In: Ball, T., Jones, R.B. (eds.) CAV 2006. LNCS, vol. 4144, pp. 300–314. Springer, Heidelberg (2006)
19. Zeldovich, N., Yip, A., Dabek, F., Morris, R., Mazières, D., Kaashoek, M.F.: Multiprocessor support for event-driven programs. In: USENIX (2003)

On Verifying Fault Tolerance of Distributed Protocols

Dana Fisman[1,2], Orna Kupferman[1], and Yoad Lustig[1]

[1] School of Computer Science and Engineering, Hebrew University, Jerusalem 91904, Israel
[2] IBM Haifa Research Lab, Haifa University Campus, Haifa 31905, Israel
{danafi,orna,yoadl}@cs.huji.ac.il

Abstract. Distributed systems are composed of processes connected in some network. Distributed systems may suffer from faults: processes may stop, be interrupted, or be maliciously attacked. Fault-tolerant protocols are designed to be resistant to faults. Proving the resistance of protocols to faults is a very challenging problem, as it combines the parameterized setting that distributed systems are based-on, with the need to consider a hostile environment that produces the faults. Considering all the possible fault scenarios for a protocol is very difficult. Thus, reasoning about fault-tolerance protocols utterly needs formal methods.

In this paper we describe a framework for verifying the fault tolerance of (synchronous or asynchronous) distributed protocols. In addition to the description of the protocol and the desired behavior, the user provides the fault type (e.g., fail-stop, Byzantine) and its distribution (e.g., at most half of the processes are faulty). Our framework is based on augmenting the description of the configurations of the system by a mask describing which processes are faulty. We focus on regular model checking and show how it is possible to compile the input for the model-checking problem to one that takes the faults and their distribution into an account, and perform regular model-checking on the compiled input. We demonstrate the effectiveness of our framework and argue for its generality.

1 Introduction

Distributed systems are composed of processes connected in some network [25,30]. In a typical setting, the processes are isomorphic, in the sense that they execute the same protocol up to renaming. Thus, the systems are *parameterized* by the number of processes, and a protocol is correct if it is correct for any number of processes.

With the implementation of distributed protocols, it has been realized that the model of computation that basic protocols assume is often unrealistic. In reality, the processes and the communication between them may suffer from *faults*: messages may be omitted, processes may stop, may be interrupted, and may be maliciously attacked, causing them not to follow their protocol. For example, in the *fail-stop* fault, processes may fail before completing the execution of their code [29]. Even a simple task like broadcasting a message from a sender process to all other processes becomes difficult in the presence of such faults. Indeed, the sender may fail after sending the message to only a subset of the other processes, resulting in disagreement about the content of the message among processes that have not failed.

The realization of faults has led to the development of *fault-tolerant protocols*, which are designated to be resistant to faults. For example, for the broadcasting task, a protocol

C.R. Ramakrishnan and J. Rehof (Eds.): TACAS 2008, LNCS 4963, pp. 315–331, 2008.

of n rounds (n is the number of processes) in which the sender broadcasts the message in the first round and every process that has received the message for the first time in the same round broadcasts it to all other processes in the next round, ensures that all processes that have not failed agree on the content of the message [14].

Proving the resistance of protocols to faults is a very challenging problem, as it combines the multi-process setting that distributed protocols are based-on, with the need to consider a hostile environment that produces the faults. Considering all the possible fault scenarios for a protocol is very difficult. This is reflected in the very complicated manual proofs that new protocols are accompanied with, and in the unfortunate fact that it is not rare that errors escape these manual proofs [12,7,19]. Thus, verification of fault-tolerance protocols utterly needs formal methods.

Current applications of model checking to reasoning about fault-tolerant distributed protocols are very elementary [5]. For example, [27] reports an error in the Byzantine self-stabilizing protocol of [13]. The error has been detected using the model checker SMV for the case $n = 4$. Likewise, a corrected version of the protocol has been proven correct in SMV for the case $n = 4$ [26]. While these works clearly demonstrate the necessity and effectiveness of model checking, there is no general methodology for reasoning about fault-tolerant protocols. Moreover, these works ignore the unbounded state-space that the parameterized setting involves; proving that a protocol is correct for the case $n = 4$ does not guarantee the protocol is correct for any number of processes. Thus, formal reasoning about distributed protocols, which is so utterly needed, requires the development and application of parameterized verification methods.

The parameterized setting is, in general, undecidable [4]. There has been extensive research in the last decade on finding settings for which the problem is decidable (c.f., [17]) and on developing methods that are sound but incomplete. Efforts in this direction include induction, network invariants, abstraction, and more [18,24,20].

A direction that has received a lot of attention is that of *regular model checking* [23,3]. In regular model checking, we describe configurations of the system as well as transitions between configurations by regular languages. In more details, in a *regular description of a protocol*, letters in the alphabet Σ describe states of the underlying processes, and a configuration of the system corresponds to a word in Σ^*. The protocol is then given by a regular language $I \subseteq \Sigma^*$ describing the possible initial configurations, and a regular language $R \subseteq (\Sigma \times \Sigma)^*$ describing the transition relation (a letter $[\sigma, \sigma']$ describes the current (σ) and next (σ') state of a certain process). For example, if each process may either have a token or not have it, then a letter in $\Sigma = \{N, T\}$ describes a state of each process, $I = T \cdot N^*$ describes a set of configurations in which only the leftmost process has the token, and $R = ([T, T] + [N, N] + [T, N] \cdot [N, T])^*$ describes a set of transitions in which processes either maintain their state or participate in a pass of a token from a process to its right. In this example all processes make a step simultaneously, thus they represent a synchronous distributed systems. However, we can also represent asynchronous systems using a regular description by coding a transition in which only one process can make a step at each time unit. It is sometimes more convenient to describe the protocol in a monadic second order logic over finite words (FMSO) [23], which is as expressive as regular expressions [11,16]. Then, a formula over Σ

describes the initial configurations, and a formula over $\Sigma \cup \Sigma'$ describes the transitions, with Σ' referring to the letters in the successor state.

A weakness of regular model checking is that not all protocols have a regular description. Moreover, even when a regular description exists, reasoning about it may diverge. The good news is that many interesting protocols do have a regular description. Also, various *acceleration*, *abstraction*, and *symmetry-reduction* techniques are successfully combined with regular model checking and lead the model-checking algorithm into termination [10,1,28,9,8]. Regular model checking has successfully been applied for the verification of a variety of protocols, including ones involving systems with queues, counters, and dynamic linked data structures [10,1]. In particular, termination of regular model checking is guaranteed for systems in which the set of reachable configurations is regular [22].

In this paper we suggest a methodology for reasoning about the fault tolerance of (synchronous or asynchronous) distributed protocols.[1] In addition to the description of the protocol, the user provides the following parameters:

1. *Fault type*: The user can specify the type of faults with which he wishes to challenge the protocol. We support faults like *fail-stop* (processes halt before completing the execution of the code), *Byzantine* (processes do not follow their code, and we also allow variants of Byzantine faults, like *omission* and *timing* faults), and *transient* (the state of the faulty processes is perturbed for a finite duration) faults. The methodology is compositional in the sense that the faults can be combined. For example, the user can check *self-stabilization* (resistance to transient faults) of a protocol in the presence of Byzantine faults.

2. *Fault distribution:* The user can specify the distribution of the faulty processes. The distribution is specified as a bound on the number of the sound/faulty processes, or on their ratio (e.g., a strict minority of the processes are faulty).[2] In fact, as explained shortly, we support all fault distributions that can be specified by a context-free language (CFG).

3. *Desired behavior:* The user specifies the desired property in LTL(FMSO) — an extension of LTL in which the propositional layer is replaced by a second-order layer describing the unbounded configurations [2]. We show how, using LTL(FMSO), the user can specify both properties of the global setting (e.g., all processes eventually agree on the content of the message) or properties that refer to the underlying processes (e.g., every sound process that tries to enter the critical section, eventually enters it).

Our methodology is based on augmenting the description of the configurations of the system by a *mask* describing which processes are faulty. We describe our methodology in the framework of regular model checking. Technically, we replace the alphabet Σ

---

[1] A different approach to reasoning about fault-tolerant systems is taken in [6]. There, following the classification of faults in [5], faults are modeled by transitions that perturb the state of the system. The problem studied in [6] is that of closed-system *synthesis*. Thus, this work is orthogonal to ours and, in particular, it does not address the parametric setting.

[2] Proving the correctness of a system, one is typically interested in an upper bound on the faulty processes and/or a lower bound on the sound processes. Refuting the correctness of a system, one is typically interested in an upper bound on the sound processes and/or a lower bound on the faulty processes.

by the alphabet $\Sigma \times \{S, F\}$, in which each letter describes not only the state of the corresponding process but also whether it is sound (S) or faulty (F). We then compile the languages $I \subseteq \Sigma^*$ of the initial configurations into a language $I' \subseteq (\Sigma \times \{S, F\})^*$, and compile the language $R \subseteq (\Sigma \times \Sigma)^*$ of transitions into a language $R' \subseteq ((\Sigma \times \{S, F\}) \times (\Sigma \times \{S, F\}))^*$. The type of the fault is reflected in the way faulty processes behave in I' and R'. The compilation is automatic and is done on top of the FMSO description of the underlying process. We can determine the distribution of the faults by restricting I' to configurations whose projection on $\{S, F\}$ belongs to a language that describes the desired distribution. Here, we may use either a regular language (say, for bounding the number of faulty processes by a constant) or a context-free language (say, for bounding the ratio of the faulty processes).[3]

We demonstrate the application of our methodology in a toy example of a token-ring-based mutual-exclusion protocol. Application of our methodology to a real example of the reliable broadcasting protocol of [14] can be found in the full version of the paper.

2   Preliminaries

2.1   Regular Description of a Protocol

A *regular description of a protocol* is a tuple $P = \langle \Sigma, I, R \rangle$, where Σ is an alphabet, each letter of which describes a possible state of one process. Intuitively, each configuration of a system composed of processes that follow the protocol P is a word $w \in \Sigma^*$. The length of w is the number of underlying processes, with the first letter describing the state of the first process, the second letter describing the state of the second process, and so on. Accordingly, $I \subseteq \Sigma^*$ is a regular language describing the initial configuration of the system for any number of processes, and $R \subseteq (\Sigma \times \Sigma)^*$ is a regular language describing its transition relation. Given two words over Σ of same length, say $w = \sigma_1 \cdot \sigma_2 \cdots \sigma_n$ and $w' = \sigma'_1 \cdot \sigma'_2 \cdots \sigma'_n$, we use $[w, w'] \in R$ to abbreviate $[\sigma_1, \sigma'_1] \cdot [\sigma_2, \sigma'_2] \cdots [\sigma_n, \sigma'_n] \in R$. A *computation* of the system is a sequence $w_0, w_1, w_2, \ldots$ of words over Σ such that $w_0 \in I$, and for every $i \geq 0$, we have $[w_i, w_{i+1}] \in R$.

For a regular language $L \subseteq \Sigma^*$, let $pre_R(L) = \{w : \exists w' \in L \text{ such that } [w, w'] \in R\}$ and $post_R(L) = \{w : \exists w' \in L \text{ such that } [w', w] \in R\}$ be the pre- and post-images of L, respectively. We use pre_R^* and $post_R^*$ to denote the transitive closure of pre_R and $post_R$, respectively. Thus, if L describes a set of configurations, then $pre_R^*(L)$ is the set of configurations that can reach a configuration in L, and dually for $post_R^*(L)$.

Example 1. Consider the Token-Ring protocol described below. Each process has a boolean variable *token_is_mine* indicating whether it holds the token. The process may be in one of the three locations ℓ_0, ℓ_1, and ℓ_2. Location ℓ_2 is a critical section.

---

[3] The restriction of I' can be done after the fixed-point computation that model checking involves is completed. This enables us to proceed with both forward and backward model checking. This is also why we do not sacrifice decidability in the richer context-free setting.

A process that enters ℓ_2 exits it (and returns to ℓ_0) in the next transition. Location ℓ_1 is a trying section. A process in ℓ_1 waits for the token, and once it has it, it moves to the critical section in the next transition. Location ℓ_0 is the non-

---
Protocol 1. Token-Ring
---
boolean *token_is_mine*
repeat
  ℓ_0 : **if** *token_is_mine* **then**
  pass_token_to_right();
      goto $\{\ell_0, \ell_1\}$;
  ℓ_1 : **await** *token_is_mine*;
  ℓ_2 : *critical*;
until forever ;
---

critical section. A process in ℓ_0 may either stay in ℓ_0 or proceed to ℓ_1. In addition, if the process has the token, it passes it to the process to its right.

We now present a regular description of the token-ring protocol. Let $\Sigma_{loc} = \{\ell_0, \ell_1, \ell_2\}$ and $\Sigma_{tok} = \{N, T\}$. A state of a process is a letter in $\Sigma = \Sigma_{loc} \times \Sigma_{tok}$, describing both the location of the process and the value of *token_is_mine*. For example, the letter $\langle \ell_2, T \rangle$ indicates a process in location ℓ_2 that has the token. For simplicity, we use the letters $0T, 1T, 2T, 0N, 1N$, and $2N$ to describe the letters in Σ.

The initial configuration of a system in which all processes are in location ℓ_0 and the token is owned by one[4] process is given by $0T \cdot 0N^*$. In order to describe the transition relation, we distinguish between three types of actions a process may be involved at during a transition. Each action corresponds to a letter $[\sigma, \sigma'] \in \Sigma \times \Sigma$, where σ describes the current state of the process and σ' describes the next state.

- The process does *not* pass or receive the token. These actions correspond to the letters $S_N = \{[0N, 0N], [0N, 1N], [1N, 1N], [2N, 0N], [1T, 2T], [2T, 0T]\}$.
- The process has the token in location ℓ_0, in which case it *passes* it to the right. These actions correspond to the letters $S_P = \{[0T, 0N], [0T, 1N]\}$.
- The process does not have the token and *receives* it from the left. These actions correspond to the letters $S_R = \{[0N, 0T], [0N, 1T], [1N, 1T], [2N, 0T]\}$.

The transition function R then allows all processes to proceed with actions in S_N and allows adjacent processes to proceed with S_P (the left process) and S_R (the right process) simultaneously. Accordingly,[5] $R = (S_N + S_P \cdot S_R)^* + (S_R \cdot (S_N + S_P \cdot S_R)^* \cdot S_P)$.

Note that R indeed reflects the protocol. In particular, the transition function is defined also for processes that are in the critical section without the token, and for configurations in which there is more than a single token. Indeed, for different initial configurations, such transitions may be taken.[6]

---

[4] Since we use words to model a ring architecture, we arbitrarily set the token owner to be the leftmost process. Nevertheless, the transitions are defined so that the so called rightmost process has this leftmost process as its neighbor to the right.

[5] The second term corresponds to the rightmost process closing the ring.

[6] We note that the common description of token-passing protocols in the regular model-checking literature allows only a single pass to take place in a transition. In a transition in our model, all processes proceed together and any number of tokens may be passed simultaneously (yet a process cannot receive and pass a token at the same transition).

2.2 FMSO and LTL(FMSO)

In Section 2.1, we used regular expressions in order to specify configurations of the distributed system. In this section we present *finitary monadic second order logic* (FMSO) [11,16,31] – an alternative formalism for specifying regular languages. Describing configurations of a parameterized system by a monadic second order logic is suggested in [23], where the logic used is FS1S. A similar direction was taken in [2], where LTL is augmented with MSO. We choose to work with FMSO, which unifies both approaches.

FMSO formulas are interpreted over finite words over Σ. Formulas are defined with respect to a set $\mathbb{F}$ of first-order variables ranging over positions in the word, and a set $\mathbb{S}$ of second-order variables ranging over sets of positions in the word. Let us emphasize to readers who are familiar with temporal logic that the variables in $\mathbb{F}$ and $\mathbb{S}$ do not point to points in time (or sets of such points) — an FMSO formula describes a configuration of the system at a single time point, and the variables in $\mathbb{F}$ and $\mathbb{S}$ point to positions (or sets of positions) in the configuration, namely to identity of processes in the parameterized system.

In our application, the alphabet Σ describes a state of a process, and a word of length n describes a configuration consisting of n processes. Typically, $\Sigma = \Sigma_1 \times \cdots \times \Sigma_k$ is the product of *underlying alphabets*, each describing a propositional aspect of a state of a process. For example, in Example 1, we had $\Sigma = \Sigma_{loc} \times \Sigma_{tok}$. We refer to the set $\{\Sigma_1, \ldots, \Sigma_k\}$ as the *signature* of Σ and refer to the set $\Sigma_1 \cup \cdots \cup \Sigma_k$ as the set of *underlying letters*. An advantage of FMSO is that it enables convenient reference to the underlying letters. Given a word in Σ^*, a position term $p \in \mathbb{F}$ points to a letter in Σ, and preceding it by an underlying alphabet points to an underlying letter. For example, the letter term $\Sigma_{tok}[p]$ is evaluated to the status of the token of the process in position p. Thus, if p is evaluated to 3, then the letter term $\Sigma_{tok}[p]$, when interpreted over the word $\langle \ell_0, T \rangle, \langle \ell_0, N \rangle, \langle \ell_0, N \rangle, \langle \ell_0, N \rangle$, is evaluated to N – the projection on $\{N, T\}$ of the third letter. We now describe the syntax and the semantics of FMSO formally.

Syntax. Let $\mathbb{F}, \mathbb{S}$ be sets of variables as above, and let $\Sigma = \Sigma_1 \times \cdots \times \Sigma_k$. Terms and formulas of FMSO are defined inductively as follows.

- A *position (first order) term* is of the form $0, i, p \oplus 1$, or $p \ominus 1$, for $i \in \mathbb{F}$ and a position term p.
- A *letter term* is of the form τ or $x[p]$, for $\tau \in \Sigma_1 \cup \cdots \cup \Sigma_k$, a position term p, and x an underlying alphabet in $\{\Sigma_1, \ldots, \Sigma_k\}$.
- A *formula* is of the form $a_1 = a_2, p_1 \le p_2, I_1 \subseteq I_2, p \in I, \neg \varphi, \varphi \vee \psi, \exists i \varphi$, or $\exists I \varphi$, for letter terms a_1 and a_2, position terms p, p_1 and p_2, formulas φ and ψ, $i \in \mathbb{F}$, and $I_1, I_2, I \in \mathbb{S}$.

Writing formulas, we use the standard abbreviations $=, <, \ne, \wedge, \rightarrow$, and $\forall$. In addition, we use $\Sigma[p] = \langle \sigma_1, \ldots, \sigma_k \rangle$ as an abbreviation for $\Sigma_1[p] = \sigma_1 \wedge \ldots \wedge \Sigma_k[p] = \sigma_k$. An FMSO formula is *closed* if all the occurrences of variables in $\mathbb{F}$ and $\mathbb{S}$ are in a scope of a quantifier.

Semantics. For an integer $n \in \mathbb{N}$, let $\mathbb{Z}_n$ denote the set $\{0, 1, \ldots, n-1\}$. We define the semantics of an FMSO formula with respect to a tuple $\mathcal{I} = \langle n, \mathcal{I}_F, \mathcal{I}_S, \mathcal{I}_\Sigma \rangle$, where $n \in \mathbb{N}$ is the length of the word that $\mathcal{I}$ models, $\mathcal{I}_F : \mathbb{F} \rightarrow \mathbb{Z}_n$ assigns the first-order variables with locations in $\mathbb{Z}_n$, $\mathcal{I}_S : \mathbb{S} \to 2^{\mathbb{Z}_n}$ assigns the second-order variable with subsets of $\mathbb{Z}_n$, and $\mathcal{I}_\Sigma : \mathbb{Z}_n \to \Sigma$ is the word that $\mathcal{I}$ models. Given a letter $\sigma \in \Sigma$ and an underlying alphabet $x \in \{\Sigma_1, \ldots, \Sigma_k\}$, we denote the projection of σ on x by $\sigma_{|x}$.

Position terms are evaluated with respect to n and $\mathcal{I}_F$ as follows: $[\![0]\!] = 0$, $[\![i]\!] = \mathcal{I}_F(i)$, $[\![p \oplus 1]\!] = ([\![p]\!] + 1) \bmod n$, and $[\![p \ominus 1]\!] = ([\![p]\!] - 1) \bmod n$. Letter terms are evaluated with respect to $\mathcal{I}_\Sigma$ as follows: $[\![\tau]\!] = \tau$ and $[\![x[p]]\!] = \mathcal{I}_\Sigma(p)_{|x}$. Satisfaction of formulas is defined as follows:

$\mathcal{I} \models a_1 = a_2$ iff $[\![a_1]\!] = [\![a_2]\!]$ $\mathcal{I} \models \neg\varphi$ iff $\mathcal{I} \not\models \varphi$

$\mathcal{I} \models p_1 \leq p_2$ iff $[\![p_1]\!] \leq [\![p_2]\!]$ $\mathcal{I} \models \varphi \vee \psi$ iff $\mathcal{I} \models \varphi$ or $\mathcal{I} \models \psi$

$\mathcal{I} \models I_1 \subseteq I_2$ iff $\mathcal{I}_S(I_1) \subseteq \mathcal{I}_S(I_2)$ $\mathcal{I} \models \exists i\varphi$ iff $\exists m \in \mathbb{Z}_n$ s.t. $\mathcal{I}[i \mapsto m] \models \varphi$

$\mathcal{I} \models p_1 \in I$ iff $[\![p_1]\!] \in \mathcal{I}_S(I)$ $\mathcal{I} \models \exists I\varphi$ iff $\exists S \subseteq \mathbb{Z}_n$ s.t. $\mathcal{I}[I \mapsto S] \models \varphi$,

where $\mathcal{I}[i \mapsto m]$ is obtained from $\mathcal{I}$ by letting $\mathcal{I}_F(i)$ be m, and similarly for $\mathcal{I}[I \mapsto S]$.

LTL(FMSO). The logic LTL is traditionally defined over computations in which each point in time can be characterized by a propositional formula. In the parameterized setting, each point in time is an unbounded configuration, and can be characterized by an FMSO formula. The logic LTL(FMSO) is an extension of LTL in which the propositional layer is replaced by FMSO. Thus, the FMSO formulas are used to describe a configuration of the computation at a given instance of time, and the LTL operators are used to reason about the on-going behavior of the system. The internal FMSO formulas may contain a free variable whose quantification is external to the temporal operators. A regular model-checking procedure for LTL(FMSO) is described in [2]. The syntax and semantics of LTL(FMSO) are given in the full version of the paper. Here, we give some examples.

Example 2. Consider the token-ring protocol given in Example 1. We use LTL(FMSO) in order to specify its desired properties:

- Mutual exclusion (there is always at most one process in the critical section):
  $\Box(\forall i, j : (i \neq j) \to \neg(\Sigma_{loc}[i] = \ell_2 \wedge \Sigma_{loc}[j] = \ell_2))$.
- Non-starvation (whenever a process tries to enter the critical section, it eventually does): $\Box\forall i : (\Sigma_{loc}[i] = \ell_1 \to \Diamond(\Sigma_{loc}[i] = \ell_2))$.

2.3 An FMSO-Based Description of a Protocol

In this section we explain how FMSO can be used to define protocols and the parameterized system they induce. A similar description appears in [23].[7] There, however, formulas describe the parameterized system whereas here formulas describe an underlying process parameterized by its identity. An FMSO description of the parameterized system is then automatically derived from the description of its underlying process. The ability to describe a single process is fundamental to our method since the input to our application carries information on how a fault affects a single process rather than how it affects the parameterized system (In Remark 5, we elaborate on the significance of this ability further).

A *protocol parameterized by* $i \in \mathbb{F}$ is a tuple $P[i] := \langle \Sigma, \Theta[i], \Delta[i] \rangle$, where $\Sigma = \Sigma_1 \times \cdots \times \Sigma_k$ is the alphabet, $\Theta[i]$ is an FMSO formula that specifies the initial state of

---

[7] The monadic second order used in [23] is FS1S (rather than FMSO).

the process i, and $\Delta[i]$ is an FMSO formula over $\Sigma \cup \Sigma'$ where Σ' is a primed version of the alphabet Σ. The formula $\Delta[i]$ relates the current configuration (over the alphabet Σ) with the successor configuration (over the alphabet Σ'). The only free variable in the formulas $\Theta[i]$ and $\Delta[i]$ is i. Note that the formulas may refer to the current as well as the successor state of other processes, but this reference is either relativized by i (say, to $i \oplus 1$) or is universal or existential.[8]

The *parameterized system induced by* $P[i]$ is given by $P = \langle \Sigma, \Theta, \Delta \rangle$, where the initial configuration is $\Theta = \forall i \Theta[i]$, and the transition relation is $\Delta = \forall i \Delta[i]$. Thus, as expected, each process starts in an initial state, and in each point in time, all processes simultaneously proceed according to the protocol. Note that, as in the regular description of a protocol, this does not prevent us from describing asynchronous systems. Asynchronous systems can be modeled by adding to $\Delta[i]$ a disjunct of the form $\Sigma[i]=\Sigma'[i]$ that allows a process to remain in its state.

Example 3. Consider the Token-Ring protocol discussed in Example 1. We can provide an FMSO description of the protocol $P[i] := \langle \Sigma, \Theta[i], \Delta[i] \rangle$ as follows. The alphabet is $\Sigma = \Sigma_{loc} \times \Sigma_{tok}$. The initial state stipulates that the control location is ℓ_0 and the token is owned by the process iff its identity is 1. Thus $\Theta[i] := (\Sigma_{loc}[i]=\ell_0) \wedge ((i= 1 \wedge \Sigma_{tok}[i]=T) \vee (i \neq 1 \wedge \Sigma_{tok}[i]=N))$. Following the regular description given in Example 1, we define three transitions $\delta_N[i]$, $\delta_P[i]$, and $\delta_R[i]$, where $\delta_N[i]$ corresponds to the case where the process does not pass or receive the token, $\delta_P[i]$ corresponds to the case where the process passes the token and $\delta_R[i]$ corresponds to the case where the process receives the token. Since a token may pass from a process to its right neighbor, the overall transition relation is then $\Delta[i] := \delta_N[i] \vee (\delta_P[i] \wedge \delta_R[i \oplus 1]) \vee (\delta_R[i] \wedge \delta_P[i \ominus 1])$.

The transitions $\delta_N[i]$, $\delta_P[i]$, and $\delta_R[i]$ are defined as follows:

- $\delta_N[i] := (\Sigma_{tok}[i]=\Sigma'_{tok}[i]) \wedge (\Sigma_{loc}[i]=\ell_0 \rightarrow (\Sigma'_{loc}[i]=\ell_0 \vee \Sigma'_{loc}[i]=\ell_1)) \wedge (\Sigma[i]= \langle \ell_1, N \rangle \rightarrow \Sigma'[i]=\langle \ell_1, N \rangle) \wedge (\Sigma[i]=\langle \ell_1, T \rangle \rightarrow \Sigma'[i]=\langle \ell_2, T \rangle) \wedge (\Sigma_{loc}[i]=\ell_2 \rightarrow \Sigma'_{loc}[i]=\ell_0)$.

- $\delta_P[i] := (\Sigma_{tok}[i]=T \wedge \Sigma'_{tok}[i]=N) \wedge (\Sigma_{loc}[i]=\ell_0 \wedge (\Sigma'_{loc}[i]=\ell_0 \vee \Sigma'_{loc}[i]=\ell_1))$.

- $\delta_R[i] := (\Sigma_{tok}[i]=N \wedge \Sigma'_{tok}[i]=T) \wedge (\Sigma_{loc}[i]=\ell_0 \rightarrow (\Sigma'_{loc}[i]=\ell_0 \vee \Sigma'_{loc}[i]= \ell_1)) \wedge (\Sigma_{loc}[i]=\ell_1 \rightarrow \Sigma'_{loc}[i]=\ell_1) \wedge (\Sigma_{loc}[i]=\ell_2 \rightarrow \Sigma'_{loc}[i]=\ell_0)$.

3   Verifying Resistance to Faults

In this section we describe our methodology for verifying the resistance of distributed protocols to faults. The idea behind our methodology is as follows.

- Recall that each process is defined with respect to a set of underlying alphabets. We add to this set the underlying alphabet $\Sigma_f = \{S, F\}$. Doing so, each process i may be either sound ($\Sigma_f[i] = S$) or faulty ($\Sigma_f[i] = F$).

---

[8] The ability of process i to refer to other processes may seem to give it a power to force another process into doing something. However, in the induced parameterized system all processes take a transition simultaneously. Thus, there should be an agreement between what the other process does and what process i stipulates it does.

- Given a protocol $P[i]$ parameterized by $i \in \mathbb{F}$, we automatically modify $P[i]$ to include also transitions that correspond to a faulty behavior. The modification depends on the type of fault, and is described in Section 3.2. A process follows the new transitions iff it is faulty. Transitions may not change the classification to faulty and sound.[9]
- Given the modified protocol, we (automatically, see Section 2.3) generate from it a parameterized system. Note that each of the processes in the parameterized system may be either faulty or sound, and that this classification is indicated in Σ_f. By translating the FMSO formulas to regular expressions, we obtain a regular description $\tilde{P} = \langle \Sigma \times \Sigma_f, I, R \rangle$ of the system. For some types of faults, we need to exclude from $\tilde{P}$ computations that do not satisfy some fairness conditions. Rather than augmenting $\tilde{P}$ with a fairness constraint, we associate with it an LTL(FMSO) formula ψ_{fair} that we later use as an assumption in the specification.[10]
- Given a fault distribution in terms of an upper/lower bound on the faulty/sound processes or an upper/lower bound on the ratio between the faulty and sound processes, we translate it into a CFG language $D \subseteq \Sigma_f^*$. A configuration of $\tilde{P}$ agrees with the fault distribution if its projection on Σ_f is in D. The translation is automatic (see Section 3.3). The user may also describe D directly. For a language $L \subseteq (\Sigma \times \Sigma_f)^*$ and a language $D \subseteq \Sigma_f^*$, let $agree(L, D)$ denote the subset of L whose projection on Σ_f agrees with D. Formally, $[\sigma_1, \sigma_1'] \cdots [\sigma_n, \sigma_n'] \in agree(L, D)$ iff $[\sigma_1, \sigma_1'] \cdots [\sigma_n, \sigma_n'] \in L$ and $\sigma_1' \cdots \sigma_n' \in D$.
- It is left to check $\tilde{P}$ with fault distribution D with respect to the desired LTL(FMSO) property ψ. We proceed with the regular model-checking algorithm of [2], applied to $\psi_{fair} \rightarrow \psi$. Whenever a computation of the algorithm refers to the language I of initial configurations, we refer instead to $agree(I, D)$. It is possible to restrict I to configurations that agree with D at various steps in the model-checking procedure. Also, restricting I can be replaced by restricting fixed-points calculated during the computation. As detailed in Section 3.4, this flexibility has helpful practical implication.

Remark 1. While the methodology is presented for the general parametric setting, its idea can be applied also for a bounded finite number of processes. In particular, it is easy to adapt existing BDD based model checkers to apply for this case. Needless to say, some simple technical updates must be made, such as replacing FMSO with the model-checker language, and providing the fault distribution in a way suitable for BDD. Note also that when the number of processes is bounded but big, the parametric setting may still be advantageous.

We now provide the details of our methodology, starting by reviewing types of faults.

3.1 Types of Faults

The theory of fault-tolerant distributed systems studies a large variety of types of faults. We consider here the most common types. As we explain in Section 3.2, our method is versatile and one should be able to apply it to more types.

---

[9] As we show in Section 3.2 this does not prohibit us from modeling *fail-stop* and *transient* failures.

[10] One could also consider protocols with fairness constraints [28]. We found the description via LTL(FMSO) simpler.

• **Fail-stop.** A process that suffers from a *fail-stop* failure halts before the termination of its protocol. Such a process has a well-defined failure-mode operating characteristics, and indeed the idea behind fail-stop faults is to minimize the effect of failures – the faulty process halts in response to a failure, and it often does so in a detectable manner and before the effect of the failure becomes visible [29].

• **Byzantine.** In general, a *Byzantine* process is not committed to the protocol. Thus, it can take arbitrary transitions, changing its state and the values of variables it shares. The fact the process is Byzantine is undetectable. Byzantine faults are the most general type of faults and model a wide variety of problems ranging from hardware failures (causing unexpected system behavior) to malicious attack of hackers on the system. One often consider variants of Byzantine faults, like *timing faults* (the process does follow the protocol, but there are arbitrary delays between the execution of successive statements) and *omission faults* (the messages sent by and/or to the process do not get to their destination. The process might or might not be aware of the fact that the transmission went wrong).

• **Transient.** A *transient* fault occurs when a process suffers from a temporal failure, say part of its memory is corrupted. Technically, transient faults are similar to Byzantine faults, only that the duration of the Byzantine behavior is bounded. In addition, the fault may be restricted to specific elements of the process (memory, clock, etc.). Protocols that tolerant transient faults are often termed *self-stabilizing*, as they recover from faults in the prefix of the computation.

3.2 Generating the Faulty Protocol

Let $P[i] := \langle \Sigma, \Theta[i], \Delta[i] \rangle$ be a protocol parameterized by position variable i. For each type of fault discussed in section 3.1, we show how to construct a process $\widetilde{P}[i] := \langle \widetilde{\Sigma}, \widetilde{\Theta}[i], \widetilde{\Delta}[i] \rangle$ in which the process may be either sound or faulty. In the latter case, the process may exhibit a faulty behavior of the corresponding type.

For all types of faults, the signature of $\widetilde{\Sigma}$ consists of the signature of Σ and contains, in addition, the underlying alphabet $\Sigma_f = \{S, F\}$ (and possibly more underlying alphabets, according to the specific fault). Recall that the classification of processes to sound and faulty may not change. Accordingly, for all types of faults, the transition formula $\widetilde{\Delta}[i]$ is of the form $\Delta_f[i] \wedge (\Sigma_f[i] = \Sigma'_f[i])$, where $\Delta_f[i]$ is a modification of $\Delta[i]$ that depends on the specific fault. Below we describe the compilation of $\Delta[i]$ into $\Delta_f[i]$ for the various faults. Also, for some faults, we also generate an LTL(FMSO) formula ψ_{fair} that serves as a fairness condition for the faulty system. Unless we state differently, $\psi_{fair} = \mathbf{true}$, thus no fairness is required.

Fail-stop faults.   Recall that Σ_f classifies the processes to sound and faulty. In the fail-stop fault, the faulty processes start their execution as sound processes, but may halt before the completion of the protocol. In order to model fail-stop faults, we add to the signature the underlying alphabet $\Sigma_t = \{A, H\}$, which indicates whether a faulty process is still alive (A) or has already halted (H). Sound processes and faulty, yet alive, processes should satisfy the original initial formula, thus $\widetilde{\Theta}[i] := (\Sigma_f[i]=S \vee \Sigma_t[i]= A) \rightarrow \Theta[i]$. The transition formula $\Delta_f[i]$ makes sure that (1) only a faulty process may halt (2) once a process halts, it cannot become alive, (3) the state of a process that halts does not change, and (4) processes that are sound or alive respect $\Delta[i]$. Formally, $\Delta_f[i] = [(\Sigma_t[i]{=}\text{H}) \rightarrow (\Sigma_f[i]{=}\text{F} \wedge \Sigma_t'[i]{=}\text{H})] \wedge [(\Sigma_t[i]{=}\text{H}) \rightarrow \Sigma[i]{=}\Sigma'[i]] \wedge [(\Sigma_t[i]{=}\text{A}) \rightarrow \Delta[i]]$.

Remark 2. Recall that fail-stop faults are detectable. Detectability can be modeled by making Σ_t observable to the other processes (either by putting it in a shared memory, or by letting the failing processes broadcast a failure notification before they halt). Thus, the original protocol, which is likely to be designed towards fail-stop faults, already has Σ_t in its signature, and the transitions in $\Delta[i]$ may refer to it.

Byzantine faults. Under a Byzantine failure, no assumption is made on the behavior of a faulty processes. A Byzantine process may start in an arbitrary configuration (which may or may not be valid for a sound process) and in each time unit it can transit to any other (valid/invalid) configuration . Accordingly, in $\widetilde{P}[i]$, the requirement to respect $\Theta[i]$ and $\Delta[i]$ is restricted to sound processes. Formally, $\widetilde{\Theta}[i] := (\Sigma_f[i]{=}\text{S}) \rightarrow \Theta[i]$ and $\Delta_f[i] := (\Sigma_f[i]{=}\text{S}) \rightarrow \Delta[i]$. In the full version of the paper we expand on **timing** and **omission faults**.

Transient faults. A process i affected by a transient fault need not respect $\Theta[i]$ and $\Delta[i]$. Unlike a Byzantine fault, however, the duration of the fault is finite. Thus, at some point, the process recovers and proceeds (from the arbitrary state it has reached in its perturbed behavior) according to Δ_i. In order to model transient faults, we add to the signature the underlying alphabet $\Sigma_t = \{\text{P}, \text{R}\}$, which indicates whether a faulty process is still perturbing (P) or has already recovered (R). Only faulty processes may perturb, and perturbed processes need not satisfy the initial formula.[11] Thus, $\widetilde{\Theta}[i] := (\Sigma_t[i]{=}\text{P} \rightarrow \Sigma_f[i]{=}\text{F}) \wedge (\Sigma_f[i]{=}\text{S} \rightarrow \Sigma_t[i]{=}\text{R}) \wedge (\Sigma_t[i]{=}\text{R} \rightarrow \Theta[i])$. In addition, perturbed processes need not satisfy the transition formula, and a recovered process cannot perturb again. Thus, $\Delta_f[i] := (\Sigma_t[i]{=}\text{R}) \rightarrow (\Delta[i] \wedge \Sigma_t'[i]{=}\text{R})$. Finally, to ensure that a process can perturb only during a finite prefix of the computation, we add the assumption formula $\psi_{fair} = \forall i(\Diamond\Box \ \Sigma_t[i]{=}\text{R})$.

Remark 3. Transient faults are often associated with specific components of the process. For example, it may be known that certain areas in the memory of the protocol may be temporarily corrupted. Accordingly, rather than letting the affected processes ignore $\Theta[i]$ and $\Delta[i]$, we let them satisfy the projection of $\Theta[i]$ and $\Delta[i]$ on the underlying alphabets in the signature that have not been affected.

Remark 4. An approach that is taken in the distributed-algorithm community is to reason about the self-stabilization of a protocol by reasoning about the protocol when starting from an arbitrary initial configuration (or, per Remark 3, from a set of allowed initial configurations that extends the original set). Such a reasoning can be easily done in our model by leaving $P[i]$ as is, except for $\Theta[i]$.

---

[11] We could give up Σ_t and model a recovery by modifying the F indication in Σ_f to S. The reason we do use Σ_t is practical: as we explain in Section 3.4, by keeping F and S fixed, we can sample the fault distribution at any time in the computation, which enables us to proceed with both forward and backward model checking.

Remark 5. It is easy to see that the computation of faulty processes need not respect the original protocol. Note, however, that sound processes may also follow computations that were not possible for them in the original protocol although they are obeying the protocol. For example, if the transition of process i is of the form $\alpha \vee (\Sigma[i \oplus 1] = \sigma \wedge \alpha')$, for some formulas α and α', and process $i + 1$, when respecting the protocol, never satisfies $\Sigma[i \oplus 1] = \sigma$, then process i always proceeds with α. In a faulty system, however, process $i + 1$ may satisfy $\Sigma[i \oplus 1] = \sigma$, letting process i, which is sound, to proceed with either α or α'. By compiling $P[i]$ rather than the parameterized system P we make sure that such scenarios do not escape the resulting faulty parameterized system. Another reason to compile underlying processes is practical: one of the heuristics that are applied to regular-model checking is symmetry reduction. Keeping the protocol of all (either sound or faulty) processes identical, reasoning about the compiled system can apply these reductions.

3.3   Handling Fault Distributions

The specification of fault-tolerance includes assumptions about the distribution of faults (e.g., a strict minority of the processes are faulty). We model a fault distribution by a language over $\{S, F\}$. To ease the work of the specification engineer, we suggest a simple and readable formalism in which common distributions can be specified. Formally, a *distribution bound* is a word $\gamma \in \{U, L\} \times \{S, F\} \times (\mathbb{N} \cup (\mathbb{N} \times \mathbb{N}))$. The first letter indicates whether γ imposes an upper (U) or lower (L) bound, the second letter indicates whether the bound refers to the sound or faulty processes, and the third indicates whether it is a constant bound $k \in \mathbb{N}$ or a ratio bound $\frac{k_1}{k_2}$, for $k_1, k_2 \in \mathbb{N}$. For example, $\gamma = \langle U, F, k \rangle$ (resp. $\langle L, S, k \rangle$) checks tolerance for a parameterized system with at most k faulty (at least k sound) processes, and $\gamma = \langle U, F, k_1, k_2 \rangle$ checks tolerance for a parameterized system in which at most $\frac{k_1}{k_2}$ of the processes are faulty. Given a distribution bound, we generate a language over $\{S, F\}$ that describes it. For a word w over $\{S, F\}$ and a letter $\sigma \in \{S, F\}$, let $\#(\sigma, w)$ denote the number of occurrences of σ in w. Then (other bounds are isomorphic to the ones below),

- $\langle U, F, k \rangle$ induces the regular language $S^* \cdot ((F + S) \cdot S^*)^k$
- $\langle L, S, k \rangle$ induces the regular language $F^* \cdot (S \cdot F^*)^k \cdot (F + S)^*$
- $\langle U, F, k_1, k_2 \rangle$ induces the context-free language $\{w \mid k_1 \#(F, w) \leq (k_2 - k_1)\#(S, w)\}$.

The user may also provide the distribution language directly, thus describing richer types of distributions, like $(S + F)^* \cdot F^k \cdot (S + F)^*$ (there exists a neighborhood of k faulty processes), $(S^{k-1} \cdot (S + F))^*$ (only every other k processes may be faulty), etc. Such distribution languages are particularly appropriate in architectures like rings, where the position of the process in the word describing the configuration is important. Also, a conjunction of bounds may be obtained by intersecting the corresponding (at most one context-free) languages.

We are now ready to model check the system with the faults according to the fault distribution in D. We first formalize properties of the compilation that are useful in the model-checking procedure. For simplicity, we assume that the alphabet of the compiled system is $\Sigma \times \Sigma_f$ (when its alphabet contains additional underlying alphabets, we project them in an existential manner). Theorem 1 below states that it is possible to augment the description of a protocol by a mask describing the faulty systems, and that reasoning about the augmented description can be done in both a backward and forward manner. The correctness of the theorem follows from the fact that the Σ_f component of the augmented protocol, which describes the mask, is fixed throughout the execution of the protocol. Let $w = \sigma_1 \cdot \sigma_2 \cdots \sigma_n$ and $w' = \sigma_1' \cdot \sigma_2' \cdots \sigma_n'$ be two words of the same length over the alphabets Σ and Σ', respectively. We use $w \otimes w'$ to denote the word over $\Sigma \times \Sigma'$ obtained by merging the letters of w and w'. That is, $w \otimes w' = (\sigma_1, \sigma_1') \cdot (\sigma_2, \sigma_2') \cdots (\sigma_n, \sigma_n')$.

Theorem 1. *Consider an* FMSO *description* $P[i]$ *over* Σ *of a protocol parameterized by position variable* i, *a type* β *of a fault, and a distribution language* $D \subseteq \Sigma_f^*$. *Let* P *be the parameterized system induced by* $P[i]$ *and let* $\widetilde{P}$ *and* ψ_{fair} *be the parameterized system over* $\Sigma \times \Sigma_f$ *to which* $P[i]$ *is compiled.*

1. $w_0, w_1, w_2 \ldots$ *is a computation of the system* P *when suffering from a fault of type* β *with fault distribution* D *iff there is a word* $d \in D$ *such that* $w_0 \otimes d, w_1 \otimes d, w_2 \otimes d \ldots$ *is a computation of* $\widetilde{P}$ *that satisfies* ψ_{fair}.
2. *Let* $\widetilde{R}$ *be the transition relation of* $\widetilde{P}$. *For a set* $S \subseteq (\Sigma \times \Sigma_f)^*$, *we have* $pre_{\widetilde{R}}^*(agree(S, D)) = agree(pre_{\widetilde{R}}^*(S), D)$ *and* $post_{\widetilde{R}}^*(agree(S, D)) = agree$ $(post_{\widetilde{R}}^*(S), D)$.

3.4 Model Checking the Faulty System

We now describe how we adjust the LTL(FMSO) regular model-checking algorithm of [2] to consider the distribution language. Let us first review the procedure in [2].

Given an LTL(FMSO) specification ψ, it is possible to extend the translation of LTL formulas to Büchi automata [32] and generate from ψ a Büchi transducer $\mathcal{A}_\psi$ (automaton over $\Sigma \times \Sigma$, in the terminology of [2]) that accepts exactly all the models of ψ. The transducer consists of three regular languages: initial configurations $I_\psi \subseteq \Sigma^*$, transitions $R_\psi \subseteq (\Sigma \times \Sigma)^*$, and acceptance condition $\alpha \subseteq \Sigma^*$. Let $\mathcal{A}_{\neg\psi} = \langle \Sigma, I_{\neg\psi}, R_{\neg\psi}, \alpha_{\neg\psi} \rangle$ be the Büchi transducer for an LTL(FMSO) formula $\neg\psi$. A parameterized system $P = \langle \Sigma, I, R \rangle$ then violates ψ if the product of P with $\mathcal{A}_{\neg\psi}$, namely the Büchi transducer $\langle \Sigma, I \cap I_{\neg\psi}, R \cap R_{\neg\psi}, \alpha_{\neg\psi} \rangle$, has a fair computation. It is shown in [28,2] how bad-cycle detection algorithms can be lifted to the regular setting.

Let $\mathcal{S} = \langle \Sigma \times \Sigma_f, I, R, \alpha \rangle$ be the product of the regular description of the faulty protocol with a Büchi transducer $\mathcal{A}_{\neg(\psi_{fair} \to \psi)}$ for $\neg(\psi_{fair} \to \psi)$, and let $D \subseteq \Sigma_f^*$ be the distribution language with respect to which the protocol is checked. By Theorem 1 (1), the system P tolerates the fault with distribution D iff $\mathcal{S}$ does not contain a computation that visits α infinitely often and whose projection on Σ_f is in D.

Thus, searching for bad cycles in $\mathcal{S}$, we should restrict attention to computations whose projection on Σ_f is in D. By Theorem 1 (2), we can sample the projection of the computation on Σ_f at any point, and can also do it after the computations of fixed-points converge. Accordingly, for forward model checking, we can start with I and restrict to computations that agree with D after the calculations of $post^*$. Likewise, for backward model checking, we can start with α and restrict to computations that agree with D

after the calculations of pre^*. Note that, as observed in [21], it is possible to conduct backward/forward model checking in which the last step uses a context-free rather than a regular language. This is possible due to the fact that context free languages are closed under intersection with regular languages and the emptiness of a context free language is decidable. Therefore, we can use a context-free language for ratio bounds.

Remark 6. The compilation of $P[i]$ to $\widetilde{P}[i]$ is easy to describe when $P[i]$ is given in FMSO. The model-checking algorithm, however, requires the translation of the FMSO formulas to automata or regular expressions. In general, the translation is non-elementary. The blow-up, however, is caused by nested negations, which are not typical in our setting, and is quite rare in practice [15]. For many faults, we can do the compilation on top of the regular description of the protocol and circumvent FMSO. In some cases, however, such as the one described in Remark 5, going through FMSO is much simpler.

Remark 7. It is sometimes desirable to check a protocol with respect to a combination of faults (for example, whether it is self-stabilized in the presence of a Byzantine fault). It is easy to see that our method is compositional, in the sense that the compilations described in Section 3.2 can be applied on top of each other, each with its distribution of faults (at most one distribution, however, can induce a context-free language). Also, by relating the underlying alphabets that specify the mask for the faulty processes in each type fault, it is possible to relate the faulty processes in the different faults (for example, the processes that suffer from the transient faults are necessarily different from these that suffer from the Byzantine fault).

Remark 8. The user may use the methodology in a *query mode*, in which the bound in the fault distribution is not specified. Thus, the bound is of the form $\{L, U\} \times \{S, F\} \times \{?\}$, and the user asks for the maximal/minimal number m of faulty/sound processes with which the property holds/is violated. Since the language D plays a role only in the last step of the model-checking procedure, an algorithm that does a binary search for m can reuse the result of the fixed-point computation that the steps that are independent of D have calculated, and only project it iteratively on different distribution languages. A similar approach can be used for ratio bounds.

We now demonstrate the application of our methodology for the verification of the token-ring protocol presented in Example 1. In the full version of the paper we consider a more impressive application, to the reliable broadcasting protocol of [14].

Example 4. Consider the token-ring protocol given in Example 1. We would like to verify whether it satisfies the mutual-exclusion and non-starvation properties specified in Example 2, in the presence of fail-stop, and Byzantine faults.

We start with fail-stop faults. We first follow the compilation described in Section 3.2 and compile the protocol $P[i]$ that is described in Example 3 to a protocol $\widetilde{P}[i]$ that takes the fail-stop faults into an account. Recall that $P[i]$ is over $\Sigma = \{\ell_0, \ell_1, \ell_2\} \times \{N, T\}$ and $\widetilde{P}[i]$ is over $\widetilde{\Sigma} = \Sigma \times \{A, H\} \times \{S, F\}$. For $S_{loc} \subseteq \{\ell_0, \ell_1, \ell_2\}$, $S_{tok} \subseteq \{N, T\}$, $S_t \subseteq \{A, H\}$, and $S_f \subseteq \{S, F\}$, we use $[S_{loc}, S_{tok}, S_l, S_f]$ to abbreviate the regular expression that is the union of all letters $\langle s_{loc}, s_{toc}, s_t, s_f \rangle \in S_{loc} \times S_{toc} \times S_t \times S_f$.

When $S_{loc} = \Sigma_{loc}$, we replace S_{loc} by $\_$. When S_{loc} is a singleton $\{s_{loc}\}$, we simply write s_{loc}, and similarly for the other underlying alphabets.

Since mutual exclusion is a safety property, the model-checking procedure is simple, and we only have to check whether the set of reachable states (per a given distribution language) intersects the language L_{bad} of configurations that violate the property (the language is generated automatically from the Büchi transducer for the negation of the formula, and it is extended to the alphabet $\widetilde{\Sigma}$). Formally, $L_{bad} := \widetilde{\Sigma}^* \cdot [\ell_2, \_, \_, \_] \cdot \widetilde{\Sigma}^* \cdot [\ell_2, \_, \_, \_] \cdot \widetilde{\Sigma}^*$.

Using acceleration methods such as in [28,22], we can calculate the set L_{reach} of reachable configurations of $\tilde{P}$. $L_{reach} = [\{\ell_0, \ell_1\}, N, \_, \_]^* \cdot [\_, T, \_, \_] \cdot [\{\ell_0, \ell_1\}, N, \_, \_]^*$.

It is easy to see that the intersection of L_{bad} and L_{reach} is empty, regardless of the distribution bound. Thus, even if all processes are faulty, mutual exclusion holds.

As for non-starvation, the product of $\tilde{P}$ with the Büchi transducer for the negation of the property is not empty even for the distribution bound $\langle U, \mathrm{F}, 1 \rangle$. Indeed, the computation that begins in the configuration $\langle \ell_0, T, \mathrm{H}, \mathrm{F} \rangle \cdot \langle \ell_0, N, \mathrm{A}, \mathrm{S} \rangle^*$, and then loops forever in the configuration $\langle \ell_0, T, \mathrm{H}, \mathrm{F} \rangle \cdot \langle \ell_1, N, \mathrm{A}, \mathrm{S} \rangle^*$, is a computation of $\tilde{P}$ that is accepted by the Büchi transducer. Also, all the configurations along it belong to the distribution language $\mathrm{S}^* \cdot (\mathrm{S} + \mathrm{F}) \cdot \mathrm{S}^*$ that is induced by $\langle U, \mathrm{F}, 1 \rangle$. Note that the computation corresponds to the case the first process fail-stops as soon as the execution of the protocol begins, causing the token not to be passed at all.

Let us now move to Byzantine faults. Since a Byzantine process can produce or destroy tokens as he sees fit, the protocol is not resistant to Byzantine faults, even with a single Byzantine process. Recall that when modelling Byzantine faults, we have $\widetilde{\Sigma} = \Sigma_{loc} \times \Sigma_{tok} \times \{\mathrm{S}, \mathrm{F}\}$. The protocol $\tilde{P}$ contains the computation that begins with the configuration $\langle \ell_0, T, \mathrm{F} \rangle \cdot \langle \ell_0, N, \mathrm{S} \rangle^*$, then moves to $\langle \ell_1, T, \mathrm{F} \rangle \cdot \langle \ell_1, T, \mathrm{S} \rangle \cdot \langle \ell_0, N, \mathrm{S} \rangle^*$, and then moves to $\langle \ell_2, T, \mathrm{F} \rangle \cdot \langle \ell_2, T, \mathrm{S} \rangle \cdot \langle \ell_0, N, \mathrm{S} \rangle^*$. Clearly, the third configuration intersects the language of bad configurations. Thus, mutual exclusion does not hold. Intuitively, the computation corresponds to the faulty process passing the token to the right but keeping a copy of the token to itself. The protocol also contains the computation that begins with the configuration $\langle \ell_0, T, \mathrm{F} \rangle \cdot \langle \ell_0, N, \mathrm{S} \rangle^*$, and then loops forever in the configuration $\langle \ell_0, N, \mathrm{F} \rangle \cdot \langle \ell_1, N, \mathrm{S} \rangle^*$. This computation is accepted by the Büchi transducer for the negation of the non-starvation property. Intuitively, it corresponds to a scenario where the faulty process destroys the token. Also, both computations are consistent with the fault distribution $\langle U, \mathrm{F}, 1 \rangle$. Thus, the properties do not hold in the presence of even a single Byzantine process.

Finally, in timing faults, the set of reachable states is similar to the set of reachable states in the original protocol (lifted by the new underlying alphabets), thus mutual exclusion holds. Non-starvation holds too, as the computations in the product that do violate the property are not fair.

4 Discussion

State-of-the-art work on verifying fault tolerance of distributed systems is restricted to the non-parametric setting. This is true both in work studying specific protocols, as [27,26], which model-check protocols for the case of four processes; as well as in work describing a general methodology, as [6], which studies synthesis of distributed systems with a bounded number of processes.

The idea behind our methodology is simple: it is possible to augment the description of a process by an indication of whether the process is faulty or sound, it is possible to let the process proceed with both indications (in case it is sounds it follows the original protocol, in case it is faulty it follows a modified protocol that is automatically generated according to the type of fault), and it is possible to use a symbolic description of the fault distribution in order to control the number or the fraction of the faulty processes. The methodology is generic in the sense that it can be applied to both synchronous and asynchronous systems, considering a large variety of faults, and taking into account a large variety of distribution faults (any distribution that can be specified by a context-free language).

We demonstrated our methodology in the framework of regular model checking (augmented to support a context-free language describing the fault-distribution). We are optimistic about the application of the methodology in other approaches that address the parameterized setting. In particular, in the approach of *network invariants* [33], one tries to find a system I such that (1) I abstracts P or $P \| P$ and (2) I abstracts $I \| P$. Our initial results in this front show that assuming the composition is symmetric, it is possible to replace P in the above conditions by finite compositions of P with faulty versions of it. For example, in order to prove resistance to c faults, one can replace P by a composition of P with c faulty versions of it; likewise in order to prove the resistance to a $\frac{k_1}{k_2}$ fraction of faulty processes, one can replace P by a combination of k_1 instances of P with $k_2 - k_1$ instances of a faulty version of P. Our future research aims at generalizing these ideas further.

Acknowledgment. We thank Danny Dolev and Ezra Hoch for many helpful discussions on distributed systems and fault-tolerant protocols.

References

1. Abdulla, P.A., d'Orso, J., Jonsson, B., Nilsson, M.: Algorithmic improvements in regular model checking. In: Hunt Jr., W.A., Somenzi, F. (eds.) CAV 2003. LNCS, vol. 2725, pp. 236–248. Springer, Heidelberg (2003)

2. Abdulla, P.A., Jonsson, B., Nilsson, M., d'Orso, J., Saksena, M.: Regular model checking for LTL(MSO). In: Alur, R., Peled, D.A. (eds.) CAV 2004. LNCS, vol. 3114, pp. 348–360. Springer, Heidelberg (2004)

3. Abdulla, P.A., Jonsson, B., Nilsson, M., d'Orso, J., Saksena, M.: A survey of regular model checking. In: Gardner, P., Yoshida, N. (eds.) CONCUR 2004. LNCS, vol. 3170, pp. 35–48. Springer, Heidelberg (2004)

4. Apt, K., Kozen, D.: Limits for automatic verification of finite-state concurrent systems. Information Processing Letters 22(6), 307–309 (1986)

5. Arora, A., Gouda, M.G.: Closure and convergence: A foundation of fault-tolerant computing. Software Engineering 19(11), 1015–1027 (1993)

6. Attie, P.C., Arora, A., Emerson, E.A.: Synthesis of fault-tolerant concurrent programs. ACM TOPLAS 26, 128–185 (2004)

7. Awerbuch, B.: Optimal distributed algorithms for minimum weight spanning tree, counting, leader election and related problems. In: Proc. 19th STOC, pp. 230–240 (1987)

8. Baier, C., Bertrand, N., Schnoebelen, P.: On computing fixpoints in well-structured regular model checking, with applications to lossy channel systems. In: Hermann, M., Voronkov, A. (eds.) LPAR 2006. LNCS (LNAI), vol. 4246, pp. 347–361. Springer, Heidelberg (2006)
9. Bardin, S., Finkel, A., Leroux, J., Schnoebelen, P.: Flat acceleration in symbolic model checking. In: Peled, D.A., Tsay, Y.-K. (eds.) ATVA 2005. LNCS, vol. 3707, pp. 474–488. Springer, Heidelberg (2005)
10. Bouajjani, A., Habermehl, P., Vojnar, T.: Abstract regular model checking. In: Alur, R., Peled, D.A. (eds.) CAV 2004. LNCS, vol. 3114, pp. 372–386. Springer, Heidelberg (2004)
11. Büchi, J.R.: Weak second-order arithmetic and finite automata. Zeit. Math. Logik und Grundl. Math. 6, 66–92 (1960)
12. Keneddey Space Center. NASA space shuttle launch archive, mission STS-1 (1981) http://science.ksc.nasa.gov/shuttle/missions/sts-1/mission-sts-1.html
13. Daliot, A., Dolev, D., Parnas, H.: Linear time byzantine self-stabilizing clock synchronization. In: Proc. of 7th PODC, pp. 7–19 (2003)
14. Dolev, D., Strong, H.R.: Authenticated algorithms for byzantine agreement. SIAM Journal on Computing 12, 656–666 (1983)
15. Elgaard, J., Klarlund, N., Möller, A.: Mona 1.x: new techniques for WS1S and WS2S. In: Y. Vardi, M. (ed.) CAV 1998. LNCS, vol. 1427, pp. 516–520. Springer, Heidelberg (1998)
16. Elgot, C.: Decision problems of finite-automata design and related arithmetics. Trans. Amer. Math. Soc. 98, 21–51 (1961)
17. Emerson, E.A., Kahlon, V.: Reducing model checking of the many to the few. In: Proc. 17th CAD, pp. 236–255 (2000)
18. Emerson, E.A., Namjoshi, K.S.: On reasoning about rings. IJFCS 14(4), 527–550 (2003)
19. Faloutsos, M., Molle, M.: Optimal distributed algorithm for minimum spanning trees revisited. In: Proc. 14th PODC, pp. 231–237 (1995)
20. Fang, Y., Piterman, N., Pnueli, A., Zuck, L.: Liveness with invisible ranking. STTT 8(3), 261–279 (2004)
21. Fisman, D., Pnueli, A.: Beyond regular model checking. In: Hariharan, R., Mukund, M., Vinay, V. (eds.) FSTTCS 2001. LNCS, vol. 2245, Springer, Heidelberg (2001)
22. Habermehl, P., Vojnar, T.: Regular model checking using inference of regular languages. ENTCS 138(3), 21–36 (2005)
23. Kesten, Y., Maler, O., Marcus, M., Pnueli, A., Shahar, E.: Symbolic model checking with rich assertional languages. TCS 256, 93–112 (2001)
24. Lesens, D., Halbwachs, N., Raymond, P.: Automatic verification of parameterized linear networks of processes. In: Proc. 24th POPL, pp. 346–357 (1997)
25. Lynch, N.A.: Distributed Algorithms. Morgan Kaufmann, San Francisco (1996)
26. Malekpour, M.R.: A byzantine fault-tolerant self-stabilization synchronization protocol for distributed clock synchronization systems. TR NASA/TM-2006-214322, NASA STI (2006)
27. Malekpour, M.R., Sinimiceanu, R.: Comments on the byzantine self-stabilization synchronization protocol: counterexamples. TR NASA/TM-2006-213951, NASA STI, (2006)
28. Pnueli, A., Shahar, E.: Liveness and acceleration in parameterized verification. In: Proc. 12th CAV, pp. 328–343 (2000)
29. Schlichting, R.D., Schneider, F.B.: Fail-stop processors: An approach to designing fault-tolerant computing systems. Computer Systems 1(3), 222–238 (1983)
30. Tanenbaum, A., van Steen, M.: Distributed Systems: Principles and Paradigms. Prentice Hall, Englewood Cliffs (2007)
31. Thomas, W.: Automata on infinite objects. Handbook of Theoretical Computer Science, 133–191 (1990)
32. Vardi, M.Y., Wolper, P.: Reasoning about infinite computations. I&C 115(1), 1–37 (1994)
33. Wolper, P., Lovinfosse, V.: Verifying properties of large sets of processes with network invariants. In: Proc. Automatic verification methods for finite state systems, pp. 68–80 (1990)

The Real-Time Maude Tool

Peter Csaba Ölveczky[1] and José Meseguer[2]

[1] Department of Informatics, University of Oslo
`peterol@ifi.uio.no`
[2] Department of Computer Science, University of Illinois at Urbana-Champaign
`meseguer@cs.uiuc.edu`

Abstract. Real-Time Maude is a rewriting-logic-based tool supporting the formal specification and analysis of real-time systems. Our tool emphasizes expressiveness and ease of specification over algorithmic decidability of key properties, and provides a spectrum of analysis methods, including symbolic simulation, and unbounded and time-bounded reachability analysis and LTL model checking. Real-Time Maude has proved well suited to analyze both correctness and performance of large and complex real-time systems, including state-of-the-art schedulers, network protocols, and wireless sensor network algorithms.

1 Introduction

Real-Time Maude is a high-performance tool that extends the rewriting logic-based Maude system [1] to support the formal specification and analysis of real-time systems. The characteristic features of Real-Time Maude are:

- Its specification formalism emphasizes generality and expressiveness, yet is simple and intuitive.
- Real-Time Maude is particularly suitable for specifying distributed real-time systems in an object-oriented style, and provides advanced object-oriented features such as inheritance and dynamic object creation and deletion.
- It does not build in a fixed communication model; instead, the user has the flexibility to easily define the appropriate communication model.
- It supports a range of analysis methods, including symbolic simulation and unbounded and time-bounded reachability analysis and LTL model checking.

Real-Time Maude is particularly useful for specifying and analyzing advanced distributed object-based systems with novel forms of communications and/or complex and unbounded data types. Such systems are typically beyond the pale of timed-automaton-based tools, as well as formal tools and simulation tools that are based on a fixed model of communication. One example of an application domain with new forms of communications for which Real-Time Maude has proved useful is the rapidly emerging field of *wireless sensor networks*.

Real-Time Maude is implemented in Maude [1] as an extension of Full Maude. Since most commands are executed by translating them into Maude commands [2], Real-Time Maude's performance is in essence the good one of Maude.

C.R. Ramakrishnan and J. Rehof (Eds.): TACAS 2008, LNCS 4963, pp. 332–336, 2008.
© Springer-Verlag Berlin Heidelberg 2008

The tool is available at `http://www.ifi.uio.no/RealTimeMaude`. The paper [2] describes in detail the semantic foundations of our tool. The enhancements in the tool and its applications since our previous tool paper [3] include: (i) development of conditions that guarantee soundness and completeness of Real-Time Maude analysis for many applications (Section 3); (ii) important new applications (Section 4); and (iii) improved support for object-oriented features such as subclasses, attributes, etc., in search and model checking commands.

2   Specification and Analysis in Real-Time Maude

A Real-Time Maude specification is a tuple (Σ, E, IR, TR), where

-   (Σ, E) is a theory in *membership equational logic* [4], with Σ a signature and E a terminating and confluent set of conditional equations and membership axioms. (Σ, E) specifies the system's state space as an algebraic data type.
-   IR is a set of *conditional instantaneous rewrite rules* specifying the system's *instantaneous* (i.e., zero-time) local transition patterns.
-   TR is a set of *tick rewrite rules* which model the time elapse in the system and have the form

    `{t} => {t'} in time` τ `if` *cond*

    where τ is a term denoting the *duration* of the rule, t and t' are terms, and `{_}` is an operator encapsulating the global state, so that the form of the tick rules ensures that time advances uniformly in all parts of the system. Intuitively, the tick rule says that it takes time $\sigma(\tau)$ to go from state $\{\sigma(t)\}$ to state $\{\sigma(t')\}$ for any substitution σ of the variables in t, t', and τ that satisfies the condition *cond*.

Real-Time Maude is particularly well suited to specify real-time systems in an object-oriented way. The state of a system is then represented by a term that has the structure of a *multiset* of objects and messages (with *delays*).

To cover the entire time domain (which can be either discrete or dense), tick rules typically have the form `{t} => {t'} in time` X `if` $X \leq u \wedge$ *cond*, for X a variable not occurring in t. To execute such rules, Real-Time Maude offers a choice of heuristic-based *time sampling strategies*, so that only *some* moments in time are visited. The choice of such strategies includes:

-   Advancing time by a fixed amount Δ in each application of a tick rule.
-   The *maximal* strategy, that advances time to the next moment when some action must be taken. That is, time is advanced by u time units in the above tick rule. This corresponds to *event-driven simulation*.

Real-Time Maude offers a spectrum of analysis commands, including:

-   *Timed rewriting* that simulates *one* behavior of the system, possibly up to a time limit, from an initial state.

- Explicit-state breadth-first *search* for *reachability analysis*. This command analyzes all possible behaviors of the system, relative to the selected time sampling strategy, to check whether a state matching a *pattern* and satisfying a *condition* can be reached from the initial state. Paths leading to the (un)desired state can be exhibited. Search may be limited to search only for states reachable from the initial state in a desired time interval.
- Explicit-state *linear temporal logic (LTL) model checking*. Although our tool does not support model checking of *metric* LTL properties, it offers model checking of "clocked" properties that involve both the states and the *durations* in which the states can be reached. Model checking may be unbounded, or consider only behaviors up to a given duration. Since, relative to a time sampling strategy, the number of states reachable from an initial state in a finite time interval should be finite, time-bounded LTL model checking is possible also when an infinite number of states can be reached *without* a time bound. Our tool gives a counterexample if a formula does not hold.
- Finding the *shortest* and the *longest* time it takes to reach a state pattern.

3 Soundness and Completeness of the Analysis

The behaviors obtained by applying the tick rules according to a time sampling strategy is a subset of all possible behaviors in a system. Therefore, Real-Time Maude search and model checking analyses are *sound* in the sense that any counterexample to the validity of an invariant or LTL property found by such analysis is a valid counterexample in the system. However, Real-Time Maude analyses are in general *incomplete* for dense time, since there is no guarantee that the selected time sampling strategy covers all interesting behaviors.

In [5] we investigate under what circumstances *maximal time sampling* analyses are *sound and complete*. For object-oriented systems, we give a set of simple and easily checkable conditions for completeness of such analyses. These conditions are satisfied by useful classes of systems encountered in practice, including the large and complex AER/NCA and OGDC case studies mentioned below, that fall outside the class of dense-time systems for which well known decision procedures exist. For such systems, *time-bounded* search and model checking relative to the maximal time sampling strategy become sound and complete decision procedures for the satisfaction of, respectively, invariants and LTL properties *not including the next operator* $\bigcirc$. For discrete time, our results justify using maximal time sampling instead of visiting each time instant, which can drastically reduce the state space to make search and model checking analyses feasible.

4 Some Real-Time Maude Applications

The following is a sample of advanced Real-Time Maude applications in which the tool has been useful both as a simulation tool and as a model checking tool. Other Real-Time Maude applications include: time-sensitive cryptographic protocols [6], parts of a multicast protocol developed by IETF [7], other state-of-the-art wireless sensor network algorithms [8], and power management algorithms for multimedia systems [9].

The AER/NCA Active Network Protocol Suite [10]. AER/NCA is a suite of active network protocols that aim to make network multicast scalable, fault-tolerant, and congestion-avoidant. The definition of the protocol mandated that aspects such as the capacity, speed, and propagation delay of each link, as well as the size of the packets, be modeled. Thanks to the ease with which we could experiment with different values of such parameters, we could use Real-Time Maude simulation and model checking to discover: (i) all flaws known by the protocol developers that we were not told about; and (ii) non-trivial design errors that were *not* known by the protocol developers, and that were not found during traditional network simulation and testing.

A Modification of the CASH Scheduling Algorithm [11]. The CASH algorithm is a sophisticated state-of-the-art scheduling algorithm with advanced features for reusing unused execution budgets. Because the number of elements in the queue of unused resources can grow beyond any bound, the CASH algorithm poses challenges to its formal specification and analysis. Using search, we found subtle behaviors in the proposed modification of CASH that lead to missed deadlines. Furthermore, by using a pseudo-random function, we could generate tasks with "random" arrival and execution times, and used rewriting to perform "Monte-Carlo simulations." Extensive such simulation indicated that it is unlikely that the missed deadline could be found by simulation alone.

The OGDC Wireless Sensor Network Algorithm [12]. OGDC is a sophisticated algorithm for wireless sensor networks that tries to maintain sensing coverage of an area for as long as possible. Wireless sensor networks pose many challenges to their modeling and analysis, including novel communication forms (area broadcast with delays for OGDC), treatment of geometrical areas, and the need to analyze both correctness and performance. The OGDC developers used the ns-2 simulator to show that OGDC outperforms other coverage algorithms.

To the best of our knowledge, the Real-Time Maude analysis of OGDC was the first formal analysis of an advanced wireless sensor network algorithm. Using a pseudo-random function to place sensor nodes in pseudo-random locations, we performed a series of simulations of OGDC with up to 800 sensor nodes. The Real-Time Maude simulations gave performance figures quite similar to the ns-2 simulations when we did *not* consider transmission delays. Since the OGDC developers told us that they probably did not include delays in their simulations, this indicates that the Real-Time Maude simulations provided fairly accurate performance estimates of OGDC. Nevertheless, since the definition of the OGDC algorithm does take transmission delays into account, such delays should be modeled. Real-Time Maude simulations *with delays* showed that then the performance of OGDC is more than twice as bad as in the ns-2 simulations. We could also point to a flaw in OGDC that explains this difference in performance.

These facts seem to indicate that Real-Time Maude simulations provide more reliable performance estimates for OGDC than the network simulation tool ns-2.

Embedded Car Software. Real-Time Maude has been used by a Japanese research institute to find several time-dependent bugs in embedded car software used by major car makers. The time sampling approach of Real-time Maude was crucial to detect the bugs, which could not be found by the usual model-checking tools employed in industry.

References

1. Clavel, M., Durán, F., Eker, S., Lincoln, P., Martí-Oliet, N., Meseguer, J., Talcott, C.: All About Maude - A High-Performance Logical Framework. LNCS, vol. 4350. Springer, Heidelberg (2007)
2. Ölveczky, P.C., Meseguer, J.: Semantics and pragmatics of Real-Time Maude. Higher-Order and Symbolic Computation 20(1-2), 161–196 (2007)
3. Ölveczky, P.C., Meseguer, J.: Specification and analysis of real-time systems using Real-Time Maude. In: Wermelinger, M., Margaria-Steffen, T. (eds.) FASE 2004. LNCS, vol. 2984, pp. 354–358. Springer, Heidelberg (2004)
4. Meseguer, J.: Membership algebra as a logical framework for equational specification. In: Parisi-Presicce, F. (ed.) WADT 1997. LNCS, vol. 1376, Springer, Heidelberg (1998)
5. Ölveczky, P.C., Meseguer, J.: Abstraction and completeness for Real-Time Maude. Electronic Notes in Theoretical Computer Science 176(4), 5–27 (2007)
6. Ölveczky, P.C., Grimeland, M.: Formal analysis of time-dependent cryptographic protocols in Real-Time Maude. In: IPDPS 2007, IEEE, Los Alamitos (2007)
7. Lien, E.: Formal modelling and analysis of the NORM multicast protocol using Real-Time Maude. Master's thesis, Dept. of Linguistics, University of Oslo (2004)
8. Katelman, M., Meseguer, J., Hou, J.: Formal modeling, analysis, and debugging of a wireless sensor network protocol with Real-Time Maude and statistical model checking. Technical report, Dept. of Computer Science, University of Illinois at Urbana-Champaign (In preparation, 2008)
9. Kim, M., Dutt, N., Venkatasubramanian, N.: Policy construction and validation for energy minimization in cross layered systems: A formal method approach. In: IEEE RTAS 2006 (2006)
10. Ölveczky, P.C., Meseguer, J., Talcott, C.L.: Specification and analysis of the AER/NCA active network protocol suite in Real-Time Maude. Formal Methods in System Design 29, 253–293 (2006)
11. Ölveczky, P.C., Caccamo, M.: Formal simulation and analysis of the CASH scheduling algorithm in Real-Time Maude. In: Baresi, L., Heckel, R. (eds.) FASE 2006. LNCS, vol. 3922, pp. 357–372. Springer, Heidelberg (2006)
12. Ölveczky, P.C., Thorvaldsen, S.: Formal modeling and analysis of the OGDC wireless sensor network algorithm in Real-Time Maude. In: Bonsangue, M.M., Johnsen, E.B. (eds.) FMOODS 2007. LNCS, vol. 4468, pp. 122–140. Springer, Heidelberg (2007)

Z3: An Efficient SMT Solver

Leonardo de Moura and Nikolaj Bjørner

Microsoft Research, One Microsoft Way, Redmond, WA, 98074, USA
{leonardo,nbjorner}@microsoft.com

Abstract. Satisfiability Modulo Theories (SMT) problem is a *decision problem* for logical first order formulas with respect to combinations of background theories such as: arithmetic, bit-vectors, arrays, and uninterpreted functions. Z3 is a new and efficient SMT Solver freely available from Microsoft Research. It is used in various software verification and analysis applications.

1 Introduction

Satisfiability modulo theories (SMT) generalizes boolean satisfiability (SAT) by adding equality reasoning, arithmetic, fixed-size bit-vectors, arrays, quantifiers, and other useful first-order theories. An SMT solver is a tool for deciding the satisfiability (or dually the validity) of formulas in these theories. SMT solvers enable applications such as extended static checking, predicate abstraction, test case generation, and bounded model checking over infinite domains, to mention a few.

Z3 is a new SMT solver from Microsoft Research. It is targeted at solving problems that arise in software verification and software analysis. Consequently, it integrates support for a variety of theories. A prototype of Z3 participated in SMT-COMP'07, where it won 4 first places, and 7 second places. Z3 uses novel algorithms for quantifier instantiation [4] and theory combination [5]. The first external release of Z3 was in September 2007. More information, including instructions for downloading and installing the tool, is available at the Z3 web page: http://research.microsoft.com/projects/z3.

Currently, Z3 is used in Spec#/Boogie [2,7], Pex [13], HAVOC [11], Vigilante [3], a verifying C compiler (VCC), and Yogi [10]. It is being integrated with other projects, including SLAM/SDV [1].

2 Clients

Before describing the inner workings of Z3, two selected uses are briefly described. Front-ends interact with Z3 by using either a textual format or a binary API. Three textual input-formats are supported: The SMT-LIB [12] format, the Simplify [8] format, and a low-level native format in the spirit of the DIMACS format for propositional SAT formulas. One can also call Z3 procedurally by using either an ANSI C API, an API for the .NET managed common language runtime, or an OCaml API.

C.R. Ramakrishnan and J. Rehof (Eds.): TACAS 2008, LNCS 4963, pp. 337–340, 2008.
© Springer-Verlag Berlin Heidelberg 2008

Spec#/Boogie3. generates logical verification conditions from a Spec# program (an extension of C#). Internally, it uses Z3 to analyze the verification conditions, to prove the correctness of programs, or to find errors on them. The formulas produced by Spec#/Boogie contain universal quantifiers, and also use linear integer arithmetic. Spec# replaced the Simplify theorem prover by Z3 as the default reasoning engine in May 2007, resulting in substantial performance improvements during theorem proving.

Pex. (Program EXploration) is an intelligent assistant to the programmer. By automatically generating unit tests, it allows to find bugs early. In addition, it suggests to the programmer how to fix the bugs. Pex learns the program behavior from the execution traces, and Z3 is used to produce new test cases with different behavior. The result is a minimal test suite with maximal code coverage. The formulas produced by Pex contains fixed-sized bit-vectors, tuples, arrays, and quantifiers.

3   System Architecture

Z3 integrates a modern DPLL-based SAT solver, a *core theory solver* that handles equalities and uninterpreted functions, *satellite solvers* (for arithmetic, arrays, etc.), and an *E-matching abstract machine* (for quantifiers). Z3 is implemented in C++. A schematic overview of Z3 is shown in the following figure.

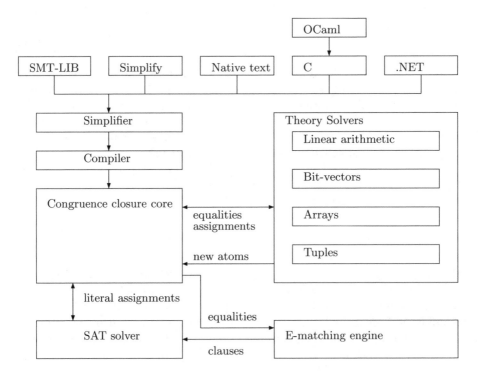

Simplifier. Input formulas are first processed using an incomplete, but efficient simplification. The simplifier applies standard algebraic reduction rules, such as $p \wedge \mathtt{true} \mapsto p$, but also performs limited contextual simplification, as it identifies equational definitions within a context and reduces the remaining formula using the definition, so for instance $x = 4 \wedge q(x) \mapsto x = 4 \wedge q(4)$. The trivially satisfiable conjunct $x = 4$ is not compiled into the core, but kept aside in the case the client requires a model to evaluate x.

Compiler. The simplified abstract syntax tree representation of the formula is converted into a different data-structure comprising of a set of clauses and congruence-closure nodes.

Congruence Closure Core. The congruence closure core receives truth assignments to atoms from the SAT solver. Atoms range over equalities and theory specific atomic formulas, such as arithmetical inequalities. Equalities asserted by the SAT solver are propagated by the congruence closure core using a data structure that we will call an E-graph following [8]. Nodes in the E-graph may point to one or more theory solvers. When two nodes are merged, the set of theory solver references are merged, and the merge is propagated as an equality to the theory solvers in the intersection of the two sets of solver references. The core also propagates the effects of the theory solvers, such as inferred equalities that are produced and atoms assigned to `true` or `false`. The theory solvers may also produce fresh atoms in the case of non-convex theories. These atoms are subsequently owned and assigned by the SAT solver.

Theory Combination. Traditional methods for combining theory solvers rely on capabilities of the solvers to produce all implied equalities or a pre-processing step that introduces additional literals into the search space. Z3 uses a new theory combination method that incrementally reconciles models maintained by each theory [5].

SAT Solver. Boolean case splits are controlled using a state-of-the art SAT solver. The SAT solver integrates standard search pruning methods, such as two-watch literals for efficient Boolean constraint propagation, lemma learning using conflict clauses, phase caching for guiding case splits, and performs non-chronological backtracking.

Deleting clauses. Quantifier instantiation has a side-effect of producing new clauses containing new atoms into the search space. Z3 garbage collects clauses, together with their atoms and terms, that were useless in closing branches. Conflict clauses, and literals used in them, are on the other hand not deleted, so quantifier instantiations that were useful in producing conflicts are retained as a side-effect.

Relevancy propagation. DPLL(T) based solvers assign a Boolean value to potentially all atoms appearing in a goal. In practice, several of these atoms are *don't cares*. Z3 ignores these atoms for expensive theories, such as bit-vectors, and inference rules, such as quantifier instantiation. The algorithm used for discriminating relevant atoms from don't cares is described in [6].

Quantifier instantiation using E-matching. Z3 uses a well known approach for quantifier reasoning that works over an E-graph to instantiate quantified variables. Z3 uses new algorithms that identify matches on E-graphs incrementally and efficiently. Experimental results show substantial performance improvements over existing state-of-the-art SMT solvers [4].

Theory Solvers. Z3 uses a linear arithmetic solver based on the algorithm used in Yices [9]. The array theory uses lazy instantiation of array axioms. The fixed-sized bit-vectors theory applies bit-blasting to all bit-vector operations, but equality.

Model generation. Z3 has the ability to produce models as part of the output. Models assign values to the constants in the input and generate partial function graphs for predicates and function symbols.

4   Conclusion

Z3 is being used in several projects at Microsoft since February 2007. Its main applications are extended static checking, test case generation, and predicate abstraction.

References

1. Ball, T., Rajamani, S.K.: The SLAM project: debugging system software via static analysis. SIGPLAN Not. 37(1), 1–3 (2002)
2. Barnett, M., Leino, K.R.M., Schulte, W.: The Spec# programming system: An overview. In: Barthe, G., Burdy, L., Huisman, M., Lanet, J.-L., Muntean, T. (eds.) CASSIS 2004. LNCS, vol. 3362, pp. 49–69. Springer, Heidelberg (2005)
3. Costa, M., Crowcroft, J., Castro, M., Rowstron, A.I.T., Zhou, L., Zhang, L., Barham, P.: Vigilante: end-to-end containment of internet worms. In: Herbert, A., Birman, K.P. (eds.) SOSP, pp. 133–147. ACM Press, New York (2005)
4. Bjørner, N.S., de Moura, L.: Efficient E-Matching for SMT Solvers. In: Pfenning, F. (ed.) CADE 2007. LNCS (LNAI), vol. 4603, pp. 183–198. Springer, Heidelberg (2007)
5. de Moura, L., Bjørner, N.: Model-based Theory Combination. In: SMT 2007 (2007)
6. de Moura, L., and Bjørner, N.: Relevancy Propagation. Technical Report MSR-TR-2007-140, Microsoft Research (2007)
7. DeLine, R., Leino, K.R.M.: BoogiePL: A typed procedural language for checking object-oriented programs. Technical Report 2005-70, Microsoft Research (2005)
8. Detlefs, D., Nelson, G., Saxe, J.B.: Simplify: a theorem prover for program checking. J. ACM 52(3), 365–473 (2005)
9. Dutertre, B., de Moura, L.: A Fast Linear-Arithmetic Solver for DPLL(T). In: Ball, T., Jones, R.B. (eds.) CAV 2006. LNCS, vol. 4144, pp. 81–94. Springer, Heidelberg (2006)
10. Gulavani, B.S., Henzinger, T.A., Kannan, Y., Nori, A.V., Rajamani, S.K.: Synergy: a new algorithm for property checking. In: Young, M., Devanbu, P.T. (eds.) SIGSOFT FSE, pp. 117–127. ACM, New York (2006)
11. Lahiri, S.K., Qadeer, S.: Back to the Future: Revisiting Precise Program Verification using SMT Solvers. In: POPL 2008 (2008)
12. Ranise, S., Tinelli, C.: The Satisfiability Modulo Theories Library (SMT-LIB) (2006), http://www.SMT-LIB.org
13. Tillmann, N., Schulte, W.: Unit Tests Reloaded: Parameterized Unit Testing with Symbolic Execution. IEEE software 23, 38–47 (2006)

Computation and Visualisation of Phase Portraits for Model Checking SPDIs

Gordon Pace[1] and Gerardo Schneider[2]

[1] Dept. of Computer Science, University of Malta, Msida, Malta
gordon.pace@um.edu.mt
[2] Dept. of Informatics, University of Oslo — PO Box 1080 Blindern, N-0316 Oslo,
Norway
gerardo@ifi.uio.no

1 Introduction and Background

Hybrid systems combining discrete and continuous dynamics arise as mathematical models of various artificial and natural systems, and as an approximation to complex continuous systems. Reachability analysis has been the principal research question in the verification of hybrid systems, even though it is a well-known result that most non-trivial subclasses of hybrid systems reachability and most verification problems are undecidable [1]. Nonetheless, various decidable subclasses have been identified, including polygonal hybrid systems (SPDIs) [2]. SPDIs can be used, for instance, in the analysis of approximations of non-linear differential equations in two-dimensions.

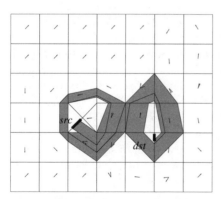

Fig. 1. Reachability on SPDI

Qualitative analysis of hybrid systems is an alternative but rather neglected research direction [3,4,5,6]. Typical qualitative questions include: "Are there 'sink' regions which one can never leave once they have been entered?"; "Which are the basins of attraction of such regions?"; "Are there regions in which every point in the region is reachable from any other point in the same region without leaving it?". Answering such questions usually implies giving a collection of objects characterising such sets, which provide useful information about the qualitative behaviour of the hybrid system. We call the set of all such objects the *phase portrait* of the system.

Defining and constructing phase portraits of hybrid systems has been directly addressed for SPDIs in [7,8]. In this paper we present a tool implementing the generation of phase portraits for SPDIs following the latter papers, and we show how these can be used to optimise the reachability analysis, in some cases even giving an immediate answer, as exposed in [9].

C.R. Ramakrishnan and J. Rehof (Eds.): TACAS 2008, LNCS 4963, pp. 341–345, 2008.
© Springer-Verlag Berlin Heidelberg 2008

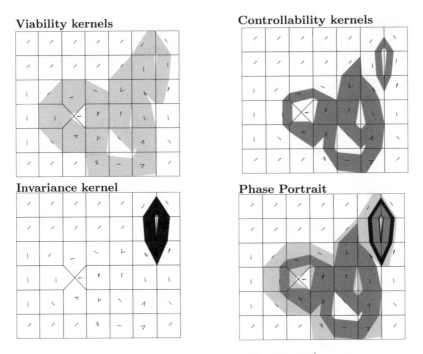

Fig. 2. Example generated by SPeeDI$^+$

An *SPDI* (Fig. 1) consists of a finite partition $\mathbb{P}$ of the plane (into convex polygonal areas), such that, each $P \in \mathbb{P}$ is associated to a pair of vectors $\mathbf{a}_P$ and $\mathbf{b}_P$ (shown as arrows in the polygons in the figure). The SPDI behaviour is defined by the differential inclusion $\dot{\mathbf{x}} \in \angle_{\mathbf{a}_P}^{\mathbf{b}_P}$ for $\mathbf{x} \in P$, where $\angle_{\mathbf{a}}^{\mathbf{b}}$ denotes the angle on the plane between the vectors $\mathbf{a}$ and $\mathbf{b}$. In [2] it has been proved that edge-to-edge and polygon-to-polygon reachability is decidable by exploiting the topological properties of the plane. The information gathered for computing reachability turns out to be useful for computing certain phase portrait objects of SPDIs. Given a cycle on a SPDI, we can speak about a number of kernels pertaining to that cycle [7,8]. The *viability* kernel is the largest set of points in the cycle which may loop forever within the cycle. The *controllability* kernel is the largest set of strongly connected points in the cycle. The *invariant kernel* is the largest set of points in a loop such that each point must keep rotating within the set forever.

Kernels are not only interesting as a mathematical curiosity but are crucial in model checking. The invariance kernel, for instance, has been used to prove termination in a breadth-first search algorithm for model checking SPDIs [10]. It is also of interest since it is much cheaper than reachability analysis, and one can use the kernels to abstract and reduce the size of SPDIs [9].

2   SPeeDI$^+$

The tool-set SPeeDI [11] is a collection of utilities to manipulate and reason mechanically about SPDIs, implemented in Haskell including:

Visualisation aids: Graphical representations of SPDIs, including simulation of trajectories and signatures within it.

Information gathering: SPeeDI calculates edge-to-edge successor function composition and enlist signatures going from one edge to another.

Reachability analysis: SPeeDI allows the user to verify a system by checking reachability between restricted edges. It also enables the use of signatures (abstract paths through an SPDI), to enable exploration of feasible paths in an SPDI.

Trace generation: Whenever reachability analysis succeeds, SPeeDI generates an abstract signature as a witness. Since a signature embodies a collection of concrete paths through the SPDI, SPeeDI also provides tools to generate concrete paths from abstract signatures.

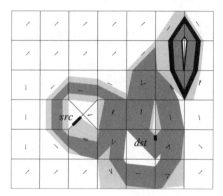

Fig. 3. Immediate answer using the kernels

Despite the fact that lazy functional languages have a rather bad reputation regarding performance, the performance we obtained was more than adequate for our examples.

In this paper we present SPeeDI$^+$, which extends our earlier tool SPeeDI, enabling the computation and analysis of three important phase portrait objects of an SPDI, namely viability, controllability and invariance kernels. Fig. 2 shows all the kernels for the SPDI depicted in Fig. 1. The top left figure shows the union of the viability kernels of ten (overlapping) loops present in the given SPDI. Similarly, the top right figure depicts the controllability kernels and the bottom left show the unique invariance kernel. Note that some loops do not have a controllability kernel. The bottom right figure shows the complete phase portrait — all the kernels of the SPDI. The execution time for obtaining all the kernels in this example is instantaneous.

3   Applications and Discussion

SPeeDI$^+$ implements the algorithms published in [7,8] based on the analysis of qualitative behaviours generated by a discrete dynamical system characterised by positive affine Poincaré maps. Currently there are no other tools specifically for SPDI analysis. Tools for generic hybrid systems, such as HyTech, are more generic, but are subsequently only semi-algorithms and less efficient than SPeeDI$^+$. See [11] for a direct comparison.

We use the kernels computed with SPeeDI$^+$ for optimising the reachability analysis, in some cases giving an immediate answer without exploring the state space. For example, the reachability question answered by the path given in Fig. 1 (and generated using the reachability analysis in SPeeDI) can be answered immediately just by observing the phase portrait picture (without performing reachability analysis) as can be seen in Fig. 3. Using a property of viability kernels, we know that there is a trajectory starting in the initial interval which will reach a point in the controllability kernel of the same cycle. Furthermore, by definition of the controllability kernel, the final interval (on another controllability kernel which intersects the first) is then reachable from the initial point.

As already noted, we can also use the kernels to abstract and reduce the state-space of a given SPDI. For example, when verifying reachability between two edges both lying within an invariance kernel, we can reduce the SPDI by discarding all regions outside the kernel, since by definition of the invariance kernel they can play no role in the reachability analysis, as it is not possible to leave the kernel. Similarly viability and controllability kernels can be used to decompose a reachability question to smaller ones by splitting the state space using the outline of these kernels as boundaries, and performing model checking on the smaller spaces independentaly. The theoretical results concerning state-space reduction and optimisation using kernels (and semi-separatrices) have been presented in [9], while the results showning how kernels can also be used to decompose reachability questions thus effectively giving a parallel algorithm for SPDI reachability has been presented in [12].

References

1. Henzinger, T., Kopke, P., Puri, A., Varaiya, P.: What's decidable about hybrid automata? In: STOC 1995, pp. 373–382. ACM Press, New York (1995)
2. Asarin, E., Schneider, G., Yovine, S.: On the decidability of the reachability problem for planar differential inclusions. In: Di Benedetto, M.D., Sangiovanni-Vincentelli, A.L. (eds.) HSCC 2001. LNCS, vol. 2034, pp. 89–104. Springer, Heidelberg (2001)
3. Aubin, J.P., Lygeros, J., Quincampoix, M., Sastry, S., Seube, N.: Viability and invariance kernels of impulse differential inclusions. In: Conference on Decision and Control. IEEE, vol. 40, pp. 340–345 (2001)
4. Aubin, J.P.: The substratum of impulse and hybrid control systems. In: Di Benedetto, M.D., Sangiovanni-Vincentelli, A.L. (eds.) HSCC 2001. LNCS, vol. 2034, pp. 105–118. Springer, Heidelberg (2001)
5. Deshpande, A., Varaiya, P.: Viable control of hybrid systems. In: Antsaklis, P.J., Kohn, W., Nerode, A., Sastry, S.S. (eds.) HS 1994. LNCS, vol. 999, pp. 128–147. Springer, Heidelberg (1995)
6. Kourjanski, M., Varaiya, P.: Stability of hybrid systems. In: Alur, R., Sontag, E.D., Henzinger, T.A. (eds.) HS 1995. LNCS, vol. 1066, pp. 413–423. Springer, Heidelberg (1996)
7. Asarin, E., Schneider, G., Yovine, S.: Towards computing phase portraits of polygonal differential inclusions. In: Tomlin, C.J., Greenstreet, M.R. (eds.) HSCC 2002. LNCS, vol. 2289, pp. 49–61. Springer, Heidelberg (2002)
8. Schneider, G.: Computing invariance kernels of polygonal hybrid systems. Nordic Journal of Computing 11, 194–210 (2004)
9. Pace, G., Schneider, G.: Static analysis for state-space reduction of polygonal hybrid systems. In: Asarin, E., Bouyer, P. (eds.) FORMATS 2006. LNCS, vol. 4202, pp. 306–321. Springer, Heidelberg (2006)

10. Pace, G., Schneider, G.: Model checking polygonal differential inclusions using invariance kernels. In: Steffen, B., Levi, G. (eds.) VMCAI 2004. LNCS, vol. 2937, pp. 110–121. Springer, Heidelberg (2004)
11. Asarin, E., Pace, G., Schneider, G., Yovine, S.: SPeeDI: a verification tool for polygonal hybrid systems. In: Brinksma, E., Larsen, K.G. (eds.) CAV 2002. LNCS, vol. 2404, pp. 354–358. Springer, Heidelberg (2002)
12. Pace, G., Schneider, G.: A compositional algorithm for parallel model checking of polygonal hybrid systems. In: Barkaoui, K., Cavalcanti, A., Cerone, A. (eds.) ICTAC 2006. LNCS, vol. 4281, pp. 168–182. Springer, Heidelberg (2006)

GOAL Extended: Towards a Research Tool for Omega Automata and Temporal Logic*

Yih-Kuen Tsay, Yu-Fang Chen, Ming-Hsien Tsai, Wen-Chin Chan,
and Chi-Jian Luo

Department of Information Management, National Taiwan University, Taiwan

Abstract. This paper reports extensions to the GOAL tool that enable it to become a research tool for omega automata and temporal logic. The extensions include an expanded collection of translation, simplification, and complementation algorithms, a command-line mode which makes GOAL functions accessible by programs, and utility functions for such common tasks as file format conversion, random formulae generation, and statistics collection.

1 Introduction

GOAL (http://goal.im.ntu.edu.tw) is a graphical interactive tool for defining and manipulating ω-automata, in particular Büchi automata, and temporal logic formulae. It was first formally introduced in [20]. Two most useful and distinctive functions of GOAL are (1) translation of quantified propositional linear temporal logic (QPTL) formulae into equivalent Büchi automata and (2) equivalence test between two Büchi automata or between a Büchi automaton and a QPTL formula. With these and other utility functions, the GOAL tool may be used for educational purposes and for supplementing automata-theoretic model checkers such as SPIN [8]. For example, the user may use GOAL to prepare a Büchi automaton diagram that is checked to be correct in that it is equivalent to another larger reference Büchi automaton or some easier-to-understand QPTL formula.

In this paper, we report extensions to GOAL that enable it to become a research tool for ω-automata and temporal logic. We have at present focused on Büchi automata and PTL (which subsumes LTL). The extensions and their usage for supporting research are described in the next section. Table 1 summarizes the major algorithms implemented in GOAL. Though the number of supported functions does not actually increase, a larger collection of algorithms are very useful for various research purposes. In addition, several utility functions have been implemented for common tasks in experimentation such as (1) collecting statistic data and (2) generating random automata and temporal formulae. These functions allow researchers to test correctness of their translation

---

* This work was partially supported by the iCAST project sponsored by the National Science Council, Taiwan, under the Grant No. NSC96-3114-P-001-002-Y.

C.R. Ramakrishnan and J. Rehof (Eds.): TACAS 2008, LNCS 4963, pp. 346–350, 2008.

Table 1. Major algorithms in GOAL. An * indicates that the algorithm had already been implemented in earlier versions of GOAL [20].

Translation	Complementation
Tableau*, Inc. Tableau [9], Temp. Tester [10],	Safra*, WAPA [18], WAA [11], Piterman [13]
GPVW [5], GPVW+ [5], LTL2AUT [1],	**Simplification**
LTL2AUT+ [19], LTL2BA [3], PLTL2BA [4]	Simulation*, Pruning fair sets [15]

algorithm, collect comparison data, and, with GOAL's graphical interface, visually observe and manipulate automata generated from their algorithm. The extensions also enhance the original roles of GOAL as a learning/teaching tool and as a supplementary model-checking tool.

2   The Extensions for Supporting Research

In this section, we detail the extensions to GOAL and explain how they may be used for supporting research.

- **Translation Algorithms:** In addition to the Tableau algorithm [12], we have now implemented eight translation algorithms. Four (Tableau, Incremental Tableau, Temporal Tester, and PLTL2BA) of the nine algorithms originally support past operators. We have extended three more (GPVW, LTL2AUT, and LTL2AUT+) to allow past operators. All these nine algorithms are further extended to support quantification on propositions.

  As an illustration of usage, Table 2 summarizes the results of translating the following two equivalent formulae into generalized Büchi automata by seven algorithms:

  1. $\neg(\Diamond p \rightarrow (\neg p \, \mathcal{U} \, (q \wedge \neg p \wedge \bigcirc(\neg p \, \mathcal{U} \, r))))$
  2. $\neg\Box(p \rightarrow (\Diamond(r \wedge \ominus \Diamond q)))$

  Each formula is the negation of a formula stating that p must be triggered by q and r with q occurring strictly before r. The first formula with only future operators is taken from the Spec Patterns respository [16].

- **Complementation and Simplification Algorithms:** In addition to Safra's construction, GOAL now has another three complementation algorithms, including complementation via weak alternating parity automata (WAPA) [18], complementation via weak alternating automata (WAA) [11], and Piterman's construction [13]. Cross-checking greatly increases our confidence in the correctness of the different complementation algorithms, which are difficult, and hence the correctness of the language containment and equivalence tests. GOAL applies simplification algorithms to the input automata before an equivalence test, and this substantially enhances the performance. Besides the simulation-based method in [15], we have also implemented simplification heuristics based on pruning fair sets in the same work.

Table 2. Comparison of seven translation algorithms without and with simplification. The column acc indicates the number of acceptance sets.

No.	Tableau			Extended GPVW			GPVW+			Extended LTL2AUT			Extended LTL2AUT+			LTL2BA			PLTL2BA		
	st	tran	acc	st	tran	acc	st	tran	acc	st	tran	acc	st	tran	acc	st	tran	acc	st	tran	acc
1.	65	550	3	72	456	1	49	288	1	22	84	1	21	105	1	8	30	1	33	118	1
2.	49	396	1	13	55	1	-	-	-	9	23	1	8	17	1	-	-	-	15	38	1
1.	14	68	3	14	58	1	13	52	1	13	46	1	8	27	1	8	30	1	14	41	1
2.	10	26	1	7	21	1	-	-	-	5	10	1	5	10	1	-	-	-	10	23	1

- **The Command-Line Mode:** This mode makes most of the GOAL functions accessible by programs or shell scripts. It therefore provides an interface between GOAL and external tools. Sample shell scripts that compare translation algorithms and output the results as text files are provided. They can be easily adapted to handle other different tasks.
- **Utility Functions:** Utility functions are available for collecting statistic data (numbers of states, transitions, and acceptance sets) and for generating random automata and random temporal formulae. Outputs from external automata tools MoDeLLa [14] and LTL2Buchi [6] may also be converted to the GOAL File Format (GFF, which is an XML file format designed to cover all ω-automata) for further processing by GOAL.

We now describe a typical use case for the above functions, namely **checking correctness of a translation algorithm**. This task can be performed with high confidence by comparing the results of the algorithm under test with (1) those of a large number of different translation algorithms, (2) those of a reference algorithm, or (3) a set of reference answers, consisting of pairs of formulae and their equivalent Büchi automata.

We assume a reference algorithm. To carry out the correctness checking process, generate an adequate number of random temporal formulae and then apply the following procedure repeatedly for each formula f:

1. Use the reference algorithm to generate two automata A_f and $A_{\neg f}$ that are equivalent to f and $\neg f$ respectively.
2. Use the algorithm under test to translate f into an automaton B.
3. Test if both $A_{\neg f} \cap B$ and $A_f \cap \overline{B}$ are empty.

If all the emptiness tests succeed, then the algorithm should be correct. Otherwise, GOAL will produce counterexamples which can be run interactively on the automata to "see" what the problem might be. We developed our translation algorithms in this manner. GOAL helped us to find some subtle bugs and possible room for improvement.

3   Performance Evaluation and an Example Experiment

We present an experiment that, on the one hand, evaluates the performance of GOAL and, on the other, demonstrates experimental comparative studies

Table 3. Comparison of complementation algorithms without and with simplification. Only successful runs are accounted in the accumulated States, Transitions, and Time.

	States	Transitions	Time	Timeout
$\neg f$ to BA	1629	6906	51.0s	0
Safra	2461	11721	175.7s	6
Simplification+Safra	2077	9707	$22.1s + 114.8s$	5
WAPA	89196	4902278	6346.3s	51
Simplification+WAPA	8828	425248	$14.0s + 202.9s$	27
WAA	2920	27870	3629.4s	51
Simplification+WAA	1886	17740	$14.1s + 167.3s$	27
Piterman	1816	8314	224.5s	5
Simplification+Piterman	1531	6916	$23.4s + 442.4s$	3

that may be conducted with GOAL. The experiment was run on an Intel Xeon 3.2GHz machine with 2GB of memory allocated to the Java Virtual Machine.

In the experiment, we compared the four complementation algorithms implemented in GOAL without and with simplification. Note that the performance of a complementation algorithm dictates the performance of the equivalence test function it supports. We generated 300 random PTL formulae with a length of 5 and translated them into Büchi automata as inputs using the LTL2AUT algorithm. None of the 300 formulae are valid or unsatisfiable. The average size of the input automata is about 5.4. We set a timeout of 10 minutes. From this experiment, we found that (1) Safra's and Piterman's algorithms perform much better than complementation via WAPA and complementation via WAA and (2) simplification can significantly speed up the complementation task, especially complementation via WAPA and complementation via WAA.

4   Remarks

The extension of GOAL will continue to include a few more complementation algorithms, for example [2]. Another effort will be to include even more translation algorithms, in particular those that utilize intermediary automata with acceptance conditions on transitions such as [17] and those that do simplification while constructing automata on-the-fly [7]. The fact that Safra's and Piterman's algorithms in average work better than complementation via WAPA and complementation via WAA is also worthy of further investigation.

Acknowledgment. We thank Susan H. Rodger at Duke University for granting us the permission to use and modify the JFLAP source code.

References

1. Daniele, M., Giunchiglia, F., Vardi, M.Y.: Improved automata generation for linear temporal logic. In: Halbwachs, N., Peled, D.A. (eds.) CAV 1999. LNCS, vol. 1633, pp. 249–260. Springer, Heidelberg (1999)

2. Friedgut, E., Kupferman, O., Vardi, M.Y.: Büchi complementation made tighter. In: Wang, F. (ed.) ATVA 2004. LNCS, vol. 3299, pp. 64–78. Springer, Heidelberg (2004)
3. Gastin, P., Oddoux, D.: Fast LTL to Büchi automata translations. In: Berry, G., Comon, H., Finkel, A. (eds.) CAV 2001. LNCS, vol. 2102, pp. 53–65. Springer, Heidelberg (2001)
4. Gastin, P., Oddoux, D.: LTL with past and two-way very-weak alternating automata. In: Rovan, B., Vojtáš, P. (eds.) MFCS 2003. LNCS, vol. 2747, pp. 439–448. Springer, Heidelberg (2003)
5. Gerth, R., Peled, D., Vardi, M.Y., Wolper, P.: Simple on-the-fly automatic verification of linear temporal logic. In: PSTV 1995, pp. 3–18. Chapman & Hall, Boca Raton (1995)
6. Giannakopoulou, D., Lerda, F.: From states to transitions: Improving translation of LTL formulae to Büchi automata. In: Peled, D.A., Vardi, M.Y. (eds.) FORTE 2002. LNCS, vol. 2529, pp. 308–326. Springer, Heidelberg (2002)
7. Hammer, M., Knapp, A., Merz, S.: Truly on-the-fly LTL model checking. In: Halbwachs, N., Zuck, L.D. (eds.) TACAS 2005. LNCS, vol. 3440, pp. 191–205. Springer, Heidelberg (2005)
8. Holzmann, G.J.: The SPIN Model Checker: Primer and Reference Manual. Addison-Wesley, Reading (2003)
9. Kesten, Y., Manna, Z., McGuire, H., Pnueli, A.: A decision algorithm for full propositional temporal logic. In: Courcoubetis, C. (ed.) CAV 1993. LNCS, vol. 697, pp. 97–109. Springer, Heidelberg (1993)
10. Kesten, Y., Pnueli, A.: Verification by augmented finitary abstraction. In: Information and Computation, vol. 163, pp. 203–243 (2000)
11. Kupferman, O., Vardi, M.Y.: Weak alternating automata are not that weak. ACM Transactions on Computational Logic 2(3), 408–429 (2001)
12. Manna, Z., Pnueli, A.: Temporal Verification of Reactive Systems: Safty. Springer, Heidelberg (1995)
13. Piterman, N.: From nondeterministic Büchi and Streett automata to deterministic parity automata. In: LICS 2006, pp. 255–264. IEEE Computer Society, Los Alamitos (2006)
14. Sebastiani, R., Tonetta, S.: More deterministic vs. smaller Büchi automata for efficient LTL model checking. In: Geist, D., Tronci, E. (eds.) CHARME 2003. LNCS, vol. 2860, pp. 126–140. Springer, Heidelberg (2003)
15. Somenzi, F., Bloem, R.: Efficient Büchi automata from LTL formulae. In: Emerson, E.A., Sistla, A.P. (eds.) CAV 2000. LNCS, vol. 1855, pp. 248–263. Springer, Heidelberg (2000)
16. The Spec Patterns repository, http://patterns.projects.cis.ksu.edu/
17. Tauriainen, H.: Automata and Linear Temporal Logic: Translations with Transition-based Acceptance. PhD thesis, Helsinki University of Technology (2006)
18. Thomas, W.: Complementation of Büchi automata revisited. In: Jewels are Forever, Contributions on Theoretical Computer Science in Honor of Arto Salomaa (1998)
19. Tsai, M.-H., Chan, W.-C., Tsay, Y.-K., Luo, C.-J.: Full PTL to Büchi automata translation for on-the-fly model checking. Manuscript (2007)
20. Tsay, Y.-K., Chen, Y.-F., Tsai, M.-H., Wu, K.-N., Chan, W.-C.: GOAL: A graphical tool for manipulating Büchi automata and temporal formulae. In: Grumberg, O., Huth, M. (eds.) TACAS 2007. LNCS, vol. 4424, pp. 466–471. Springer, Heidelberg (2007)

RWset: Attacking Path Explosion in Constraint-Based Test Generation

Peter Boonstoppel, Cristian Cadar, and Dawson Engler

Computer Systems Laboratory, Stanford University

Abstract. Recent work has used variations of symbolic execution to automatically generate high-coverage test inputs [3, 4, 7, 8, 14]. Such tools have demonstrated their ability to find very subtle errors. However, one challenge they all face is how to effectively handle the exponential number of paths in checked code. This paper presents a new technique for reducing the number of traversed code paths by discarding those that must have side-effects identical to some previously explored path. Our results on a mix of open source applications and device drivers show that this (sound) optimization reduces the numbers of paths traversed by several orders of magnitude, often achieving program coverage far out of reach for a standard constraint-based execution system.

1 Introduction

Software testing is well-recognized as both a crucial part of software development and, because of the weakness of current testing techniques, a perennial problem as well. Manual testing is labor intensive and its results often closer to embarrassing than impressive. Random testing is easily applied, but also often gets poor coverage. Even a single equality conditional can derail it: satisfying a 32-bit equality in a branch condition requires correctly guessing one value out of four billion possibilities. Correctly getting a sequence of such conditions is hopeless. Recent work has attacked these problems using *constraint-based execution* (a variant of *symbolic execution*) to automatically generate high-coverage test inputs [3, 4, 7, 8, 14].

At a high-level, these tools use variations on the following idea. Instead of running code on manually or randomly constructed input, they run it on symbolic input that is initially allowed to take any value. They substitute program variables with symbolic values and replace concrete program operations with ones that manipulate symbolic values. When program execution branches based on a symbolic value, the system (conceptually) follows both branches at once, maintaining a set of constraints called the *path constraint* which must hold on execution of that path. When a path terminates or hits a bug, a test case can be generated by solving the current path constraint to obtain concrete input values. Assuming deterministic code, feeding this concrete input to an uninstrumented version of the checked code will cause it to follow the same path and hit the same bug.

C.R. Ramakrishnan and J. Rehof (Eds.): TACAS 2008, LNCS 4963, pp. 351–366, 2008.

A significant scalability challenge for these tools is how to handle the exponential number of paths in the code. Recent work has tried to address this scalability challenge in a variety of ways: by using heuristics to guide path exploration [4]; caching function summaries for later use by higher-level functions [7]; or combining symbolic execution with random testing [13].

This paper presents a largely complementary technique that prunes redundant paths by tracking the memory locations read and written by the checked code, in order to determine when the remainder of a particular execution is capable of exploring new behaviors. This technique, which we call *read-write set* (RWset) analysis, dramatically reduces the number of paths explored by discarding those that will produce the same effects as some previously explored path.

RWset analysis employs two main ideas. First, an execution that reaches a program point in the same state as some previous execution will produce the same subsequent effects and can be pruned. Second, this idea can be greatly amplified by exploiting the fact that two states that only differ in program values that are not subsequently read will produce the same subsequent effects and can be treated as being identical. Consequently, the second execution is redundant and can also be pruned.

We measure the effectiveness of our RWset implementation by applying it to server, library, and device driver code. Our results show that RWset analysis is effective in discarding redundant paths, often reducing the number of paths traversed by several orders of magnitude and achieving coverage out-of-reach for the base version of the system, which easily gets stuck continuously revisiting provably redundant states.

The paper is structured as follows. Section 2 gives an overview of RWset analysis using several small examples, while Section 3 discusses the implementation more thoroughly. Section 4 measures the efficiency of our implementation. Finally, Section 5 discusses related work and Section 6 concludes.

2   Overview

This section gives a general overview of RWset analysis. To make the paper self-contained, we first briefly describe how constraint-based execution works in the context of our tool, EXE. (For the purpose of this paper, one can view other constraint-based execution tools as roughly equivalent; RWset analysis can be implemented in any of them.) We subsequently describe the main idea behind RWset analysis and then discuss some of the refinements employed to maximize the number of redundant paths detected.

2.1   Constraint-Based Execution

EXE lets users explicitly mark which memory locations should be treated as holding *symbolic data*, whose values are initially entirely unconstrained. EXE instruments the user program so that it can track these symbolic values. When the program runs, at each statement EXE checks if all inputs to that statement have exactly one value, i.e. they are *concrete* rather than symbolic. In such

	Path Constraints	
	Path 1	Path 2
1: x = read_sym_input();	$\{x = *\}$	
2: if(x == 1234)	$\swarrow$ *fork* $\searrow$	
3: printf("foo");	$\{x = 1234\}$	
4: else printf("bar");		$\{x \neq 1234\}$
5: ...	$\{x = 1234\}$	$\{x \neq 1234\}$

Fig. 1. Contrived example to illustrate constraint-based execution. The code has two paths, both of which will be followed. The first path (lines 1,2,3,5) ends with the constraint that $x = 1234$. The second (lines 1,2,3,4) with the constraint that $x \neq 1234$.

cases, the statement executes exactly as it would in the uninstrumented code. Otherwise, EXE adds the effects of the statement as a constraint to the current path. For example, given the statement $i = x + y$, if x and y have the values $x = 4$ and $y = 5$, EXE executes the statement and assigns the 9 to i. If not, it adds the path constraint that $i = x + y$.

When execution reaches a symbolic branch condition, EXE uses the STP constraint solver [5] to check if the current path constraints make either branch direction infeasible, and, if so, follows the other. If it cannot prove that one direction is infeasible, EXE (conceptually) forks execution and follows both paths, adding the appropriate branch constraint on each path.

To illustrate these points, consider the contrived code in Figure 1, where the call to read_sym_input() marks x as an unconstrained symbolic value. This code has two feasible paths, both of which EXE will explore, and generates two concrete test cases to exercise each path. The steps followed by EXE are as follows:

Line 1: EXE adds the path constraint $x = *$, i.e. x is unconstrained.
Line 2: Since both branches are possible, EXE forks execution: on the true path it adds the constraint $x = 1234$ and on the false path the constraint $x \neq 1234$.
Line 3, 5: Assume that EXE follows the true path first. When it terminates or hits an error, EXE solves the path constraints for concrete values. In this case it will generate $x = 1234$. If the code is deterministic, rerunning the program on this value will cause the same path (lines 1,2,3,5,...) to execute.
Line 4, 5: Similarly, the false path is followed and generates more test cases.

In order to handle real code, EXE tracks all constraints with bit-level accuracy. EXE supports pointers, arrays, unions, bit-fields, casts, and aggressive bit-operations such as shifting, masking, and byte swapping. The interested reader can refer to [4] for details.

2.2 Scalability Challenge: Discarding Redundant Paths

While constraint-based execution can automatically explore program paths, the number of distinct paths increases exponentially with the number of conditional statements traversed. In all but the smallest programs, this typically leads to an essentially inexhaustible set of paths to explore. However, not all paths are equal; very often multiple paths produce the same *effects*, and there is no reason to explore more than one such path. The effects of an execution path can be defined in any way desired, depending on the needs of the testing process. One common definition, which we also use in this paper, defines the effects of an execution path to be the basic blocks it executes.

The basic idea behind RWset analysis is to truncate exploration of a path as soon as we can determine that its continued execution will produce effects that we have seen before. In particular, we stop exploring a path as soon as we can determine that its suffix will execute exactly the same as the suffix of a previously explored path. Note that truncating a path explored by EXE results in a large gain, as the number of new paths spawned from a path can be exponential in the number of symbolic branch conditions encountered in its suffix. In real code, this truncation can easily be the difference between doing useful work and getting uselessly stuck revisiting that same program point in equivalent states, as illustrated in one of the contrived examples presented later in this section, but also as suggested by our experiments in Section 4.

The RWset algorithm is sound – relative to the base system – with respect to the effects that we observe in the program (in our particular implementation with respect to the basic branch coverage achieved in the program), as the RWset analysis only discards execution paths that are proven to generate the same effects as some previously explored path (e.g., that are proven to cover the very same basic blocks). The soundness guarantee is relative to the base system, because the RWset technique only discards redundant paths; if, for example, the base symbolic execution tool misses a non-redundant path due to imprecision in its analysis, then the RWset version of the same system will miss that path too.

In order to determine when we can stop executing a path, we apply the simple observation that deterministic code applied to the same input in the same internal state must compute the same result. For simplicity, assume for now that the *state* of a program is just the current set of path constraints (we discuss details concerning program states in the next section). If a path arrives at a program point in the same state as a previous instance, the system generates a test case, and then halts execution. We call such an event a *cache hit*. We generate a test case on a cache hit so that the prefix of the path (which so far has been unique) will be tested.

The attentive reader will note that, as discussed so far, such a cache hit will actually be fairly rare — the only reason a different path would execute is because of a branch, which would add the corresponding branch condition on one path and its negation on the other (e.g., $x = 1234$ and $x \neq 1234$), preventing most subsequent cache hits. We greatly increase the applicability of the basic idea by exploiting the following refinement: a value not subsequently read by the program can be dropped from the state, as it cannot affect any subsequent computation.

	Constraint Cache No refinement	Live vars	Refined cache
1: x = read_sym_input();	$\{x = *\}$	$\{x\}$	$\{x = *\}$
2: if(x == 1234)	$\{x = *\}$	$\{\}$	$\{\}$
3: printf("foo");	$\{x = 1234\}$	$\{\}$	$\{\}$
4: else printf("bar");	$\{x \neq 1234\}$	$\{\}$	$\{\}$
5: ...	$\{x = 1234\}, \{x \neq 1234\}$	$\{\}$	$\{\}$ *HIT!*

Fig. 2. Constraint cache example using code from Figure 1 both with and without refinement. The constraint cache is used to truncate paths that reach a program point with the same constraints as some previous path. "Live vars" denotes the set of all variables read by code after a program point given a set of path constraints. Refinement considers two constraint sets equal if all constraints (transitively) involving live variables are equal.

As the program executes, a *constraint cache* records all the states with which each program point was reached. When we get a cache hit (i.e., a path reaches a program point with the same constraint set as some previous path) we stop executing the path. We illustrate how RWset analysis works on the simple code example in Figure 1, both without and with the refinement discussed above. As shown in Figure 2, the initially empty constraint cache gets populated by the two code paths as follows. At line 1, EXE checks if the path constraint $\{x = *\}$ is already in the cache. Since this is not the case, the constraint set is added to this program point and execution continues. When line 2 is reached, EXE forks execution, adding the constraint $x = 1234$ on the first path, and $x \neq 1234$ on the second. Subsequently, the current constraint set for each path is added to the constraint cache: $\{x = 1234\}$ at line 3, and $\{x \neq 1234\}$ at line 4. Finally, when both paths reach line 5, they add their current constraint sets to the constraint cache.

Note that when the second path reaches line 5 with constraint set $\{x \neq 1234\}$, there is no cache hit, since the only constraint set already in the cache at this point is $\{x = 1234\}$. However, if we assume that the code from line 5 onward does not read x again (x is a *dead variable*), we can drop all the constraints involving x, thus changing the picture dramatically.

More precisely, before adding the constraint set to the cache, we intersect it with the current set of *live variables* (details on how liveness is computed in our frameworks are described in § 3.2). Since x is not read after line 2 it is not in the set of live variables, and at lines 2, 3, 4 and 5 we add the empty set to the constraint cache. In particular, when path 1 reaches line 5, it adds the empty set to the cache. Then, when path 2 reaches line 5 too, its constraint set is also the empty set, and thus the system gets a cache hit at this point, and stops executing path 2. As discussed earlier, when pruning path 2, EXE generates a test case to cover path 2's unique prefix – if we did not generate a test case, we would not have a test case that exercises the printf call at line 4. Note that pruning a path can save significant work since the number of paths the pruned path would otherwise spawn can increase exponentially with the number of symbolic branches hit by the path's suffix.

As positive as it is to truncate paths spawned at if-statements, it is even better to truncate loops. As an example, consider a common style of event processing loop that shows up frequently in device drivers and networking applications where the code spins in an infinite loop, reading data and then processing it:

```
while(1) {
    x = read_data();   // x is symbolic.
    process(x);
}
```

Here, a naive constraint-based execution system will never terminate, since it will keep reading new symbolic data and generating new paths. A widely-used hack for handling such loops is to traverse them a fixed number of times. Unfortunately, such blind truncation can easily miss interesting paths. In contrast, as long as the loop has a finite number of states (or more precisely, as long as it is observed in a finite number of ways), RWset analysis will automatically determine when the loop reaches a fixed point and terminate it afterwards. Note that while the code above is contrived, the problem is very real: handling such loops in device drivers and networking applications was a primary motivation to build RWset analysis in EXE.

As an even more common pattern, consider the case of a loop that uses a symbolic variable as a loop bound, as in the following code where we assume the constraint that $n < 10$:

```
...
1: for(i = 0; i < n; i++)
2:    foo();
3: ...no reads of i, n...
```

When running this loop, EXE will spawn ten new executions, one for every feasible loop exit, each with different constraints on n (that is, $NOT(0 < n)$, $NOT(1 < n)$, etc). If there are no subsequent reads of i or n, then RWset analysis will prune all but one of these ten new executions, thus saving an enormous amount of subsequent work.

3   Key Implementation Details

This section discusses some key implementation details that are critical in making the approach scale to real applications. To make the exposition clearer, Table 1 groups the terms used by this section for ease of reference.

3.1   Program States

This section discusses state representation issues.

Handling mixed symbolic and concrete execution. If execution happened entirely symbolically, path constraints would provide a complete description of the current program state and would be the only thing stored in the constraint

Table 1. Terminology

Term	Definition
Program point (§ 3.1)	A context-sensitive MD4 hash of the program counter and callstack.
Path constraints (§ 2.1)	All constraints accumulated on a given path thus far.
Writeset (§ 3.1)	The set of concrete values written to concrete memory locations by a given path thus far.
Readset (§ 3.2)	All locations read after a program point given a program state.
Program state (§ 3.1)	A program point plus its writeset and path constraints Two program paths with identical program states must produce identical subsequent effects.

cache. However, for efficiency, we want to do as many things concretely as possible. While conceptually concrete values can be viewed as equality constraints (e.g., if variable x has the value 4, this could be represented by the constraint $x = 4$), it is more efficient to separate the symbolic and concrete cases. Thus, a program state includes both the current path constraints (the symbolic state) and the values of all concrete memory locations (the concrete state).

Because the concrete state can be huge, we do not record it directly but instead only track the set of values written along the path — i.e., the path's difference from the initial concrete state all paths begin in. We call this set the *writeset*. When a concrete value x is assigned to a memory location v, we add the pair (v, x) to the writeset. We reduce spurious differences between writesets by removing a memory location from a writeset in two cases. First, when it is deallocated (by function call return or explicit heap deallocation) since we know these elements cannot be read later (a separate component of EXE catches use-after-free errors). Note that we only remove these values from the writeset, not from the path constraints, since deallocating a variable should have no impact on previously formulated constraints. To make this point clearer, assume we add the constraint that $x < y$ and then deallocate y; the constraint $x < y$ should definitely remain. The second, implementation-specific removal happens whenever an operation makes a formerly concrete memory location symbolic: it this case we remove the concrete location from the writeset, since it will now appear in the path constraints. The simplest example of such an operation is assigning a symbolic value to a concrete location.

Callsite-aware caching. The state must also include some context-sensitive notion of the current program point. Otherwise, the constraint cache entries for a function generated from other callsites can cause us to falsely think we can prune execution. Truncating path exploration when we get a cache hit is only sound if the entire path suffix after the current program point is identical to some previously explored one. This is only guaranteed when the current call will return to the same callsites that generated the cache entry. For example, consider a program that has calls to both of the following functions:

```
a() {              b() {
   c();               c();
}                  }
```

Assume the tool first follows a path that calls a, which will then call c, populating c's constraint cache. Subsequently, it follows a path that calls b and, hence, c. If we ignore context, we may (incorrectly) get a cache hit in c on an entry added by a, and stop execution, despite the fact that returning to the call in b can produce a very different result with the current constraints than returning to the call in a. Our implementation handles this problem by associating a secure MD4 hash of the current callstack with each constraint cache entry. Other approaches are also possible.

Granularity. Our cache tracks values at the byte level. One extreme would be to track the values associated with each bit. While this adds more precision, it was not clear the increase in bookkeeping was worth it. We could also choose a more coarse-grained approach, such as tracking constraints at the variable or memory object level, which would decrease the amount of bookkeeping, but unfortunately would miss many redundant paths, since often only some parts of a memory object are dead, but not the entire object. We picked byte-level granularity because it seems to be the right trade-off between memory consumption and precision, and because it's a straightforward match of C's view of memory.

3.2   Live Variables

We call the set of locations read after a program point the *readset* at that program point; any value in the program state not in this set can be discarded. Thus, the more precise (smaller) we can make the readset, the more irrelevant parts of the current state we can discard and the more likely we are to get cache hits and prune an exponential number of redundant paths.

One approach to computing the readset would be to use a static live variable analysis. Unfortunately, doing so would be incredibly imprecise — for example, often the heap contains most of the program state, which such an analysis typically gives up on. Instead, we compute the locations dynamically, which turns out to be both cheap and very accurate. The basic algorithm is as follows. At a given program point, we do a complete depth-first (DFS) traversal of all paths after that point. The union of all values read by these paths is the readset for that program point, and any part of the current state not observed by this readset can be discarded. As a simple but effective optimization, as we propagate the readset backwards up each path, we remove from it all locations that are deallocated or overwritten. For example, a read of z will be removed from the readset if we hit an assignment to z.

The reader may be concerned about whether this algorithm is sound when the DFS traversal does not achieve full branch coverage, such as when some path constraints make some branches infeasible. For example, assume we traverse the following code with the constraint that $x \neq 12$:

```
       ...
       // after DFS from this point, the readset will be {x}
1:  if(x == 12)
2:     if(y == 34)     // constraint x!=12 makes this branch unreachable
3:        printf("hello\n");
       ... no further reads of x or y ...
```

In this case, we will never execute the branch at line 2, so y will not be in the readset, and will be discarded from the current program state. Will this cause us to discard states that could reach line 2? The answer is no: since x is in the readset, the only states that will be discarded at line 2 are those that have an equivalent set of constraints on x, i.e, those for which $x \neq 12$. But these states don't satisfy the branch at line 1 and so will not execute the branch at line 2 either. Recursively applying this argument can easily be used to formally prove that the dynamic algorithm is sound even when it does not explore all branches.

3.3 Symbolic Memory References

Symbolic memory references complicate both readset and writeset construction. Assume we have an array reference a[i] where i is symbolic. If the only constraint on i is that it is in-bounds, a[i] can refer to any location in a. Even if the constraints on i limit it to a narrow range, the cost of precisely determining this range (via expensive constraint solver interactions) often means that we must accept imprecision. For reads, this imprecision inflates the readset in two ways. First, we must conservatively assume a[i] can reference any location in a unless we can prove otherwise. Thus, a single reference can pull all of a into the readset. Second, when propagating the readset back up a path, when we hit an assignment to a[i] we cannot remove any element from the readset unless we can prove a[i] overwrites it. As a result, in our implementation, assignments to arrays at symbolic offsets (indices) do not filter the readset at all.

Similarly, such assignments identically prevent removing elements from the writeset. Recall that assigning a symbolic value to x causes x to be removed from the writeset and added as a path constraint instead. However, when we assign to a[i] we can only remove an element from the writeset if we can prove that a[i] must overwrite it.

3.4 State Refinement

Given a program state and a readset, we remove irrelevant parts of the program state as follows:

1 Concrete state: Keep the locations in the intersection of the readset and writeset.

2 Symbolic state: Keep the transitive closure of all constraints that overlap with the readset. For example, if the readset is $\{x\}$ and the current path constraint is: $\{x < y, y < 10, z < w\}$, our transitive closure would be $\{x < y, y < 10\}$. Note that taking the intersection instead of the transitive closure, would produce constraint sets that allow solutions illegal in the original path constraint.

3.5 Abstraction Issues

For space reasons, we have currently taken a very literal view of what the program state is, what reads and writes are, what is considered a cache hit, and what the effects of a path are. One can, of course, profitably vary all of these, depending on the requirements of the testing process. We consider two first-order decisions.

First, what effects of computation are we interested in? The literal view is everything. We can also consider things more abstractly. For example, one may consider only the effects that affect branch coverage, or those that expose bugs in the program. Deciding what effects to focus on determines what reads (or writes) we must consider: if a read cannot affect the given metric, then the read can be ignored. For example, if we are aiming for branch coverage, we can ignore all reads not involved in an eventual control dependency.

Second, what is a cache hit? Thus far we have assumed two states are equal if they match exactly. We can however, improve on this definition. One sound improvement is to notice that two sets of constraints are equal if they would cause the same effect. For example, if one path has $x < 10$ and another $x < 20$ and the only subsequent use of x is a branch comparison $x < 30$, then we could consider these two constraints to be equal since they both satisfy the condition.

3.6 Summary

We now summarize the basic RWset implementation in EXE. We represent the symbolic state by the current path constraint, the concrete state by the writeset, and the program point by the callstack and program counter. Each context-sensitive program point records all previous states it has been visited in, and associates with each of these entries the complete set of reads (observations) done by all subsequent paths when reached in this state (the readset). We determine if we have already seen a state by comparing it against each of these entries after first intersecting it with the entry's associated readset. If we get a hit, we generate a test case (to exercise the path up to this point) and terminate further exploration of this path. Otherwise we continue.

4 Evaluation

This section evaluates the effectiveness of RWset analysis on real code, using a mix of server and library code and operating system device drivers. The results show that the technique gives an order of magnitude reduction in the number of tests needed to reach the same number of branches, and often achieves branch coverage out-of-reach for the base version of EXE. All experiments were performed on a dual-core 3.2 GHz Intel Pentium D machine with 2 GB of RAM, and 2048 KB of cache.

4.1 Server and Library Code

Our first experiments measure the improvement given by RWset analysis on five medium-sized open-source benchmarks previously used to evaluate the base

Table 2. Number of tests in RWset mode necessary to achieve the same coverage as in the base system

| | Base | | RWset |
	Branches	Tests	% tests needed
tcpdump	123	2175	11.4%
bpf	171	6333	16.2%
expat	472	677	31.1%
udhcpd	166	225	49.7%
pcre	1268	26,596	72.2%

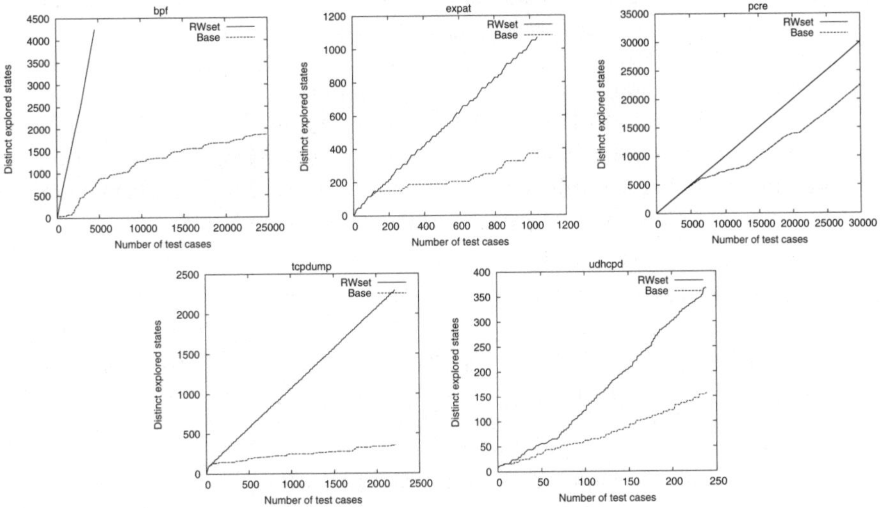

Fig. 3. Distinct explored states over number of test cases for the base system versus the RWset version for the server and library code benchmarks. With the exception of PCRE, the base system without RWset wastes much of it time exploring provably redundant states.

version of EXE [4]: **bpf**, the Berkeley Packet Filter; **udhcpd**, a DHCPD server; **expat**, an XML parser library; **tcpdump**, a tool for printing out headers of network packets matching a boolean expression; and **pcre**, the Perl Compatible Regular Expression library.

We ran each of these benchmarks for roughly 30 minutes each with the base version of EXE, and recorded: (1) the (maximum) branch coverage achieved, and (2) how many test cases were necessary to achieve this coverage (note that sometimes we generate more than this number of test cases in 30 minutes, but the extra tests don't hit any new branches). The one exception was PCRE, which we ran longer until it generated 30,000 test cases in order to have a meaningful comparison between the base and RWset versions. The second column of Table 2 gives the number of branches hit by these runs and the third column gives the number of test cases.

We then reran each benchmark using the RWset version of EXE and recorded the number of test cases necessary to achieve the same coverage as the base version did in half an hour. The last column of Table 2 gives the percentage of test cases needed for the RWset version to match the coverage from the base run. As the table shows, the improvement can be substantial: tcpdump only needs 11.4% the number of test cases to get equivalent coverage (249 vs 2175 tests) and bpf needs 16%. In fact, with the exception of pcre, all benchmarks need less than half the number of test cases with the RWset version.

We also measured the number of distinct states visited by the RWset version relative to the base. The graphs, shown in Figure 3, indicate that without RWset analysis the system wastes enormous resources constantly revisiting redundant states, thus generating many irrelevant test cases.

Finally, we measured the runtime overhead of our RWset implementation by running an EXE version that performs all computations RWset requires (constructing readsets and writesets, checking for cache hits), but without pruning any paths. Thus, this version generates exactly the same tests as the base version of EXE, while paying the full cost of RWset analysis. Our measurements show that for all benchmarks the average overhead is at most 4.38%.

4.2   Device Drivers

We also checked OS-level code by applying EXE to three Minix device drivers. Minix 3 [16, 10], is an open source, Unix-like, microkernel-based operating system, with a kernel of under 4000 lines of code, and almost all functionality – including device drives – running in user space. [1]

Drivers make up the bulk of modern operating systems and are notoriously buggy [1, 15]. Drivers are an interesting case for systems such as EXE because, while drivers ostensibly require a physical version of the device they are intended to drive, they only interact with the device through memory-mapped I/O, which mechanically looks like a memory array with special read and write semantics. Thus, we can effectively test a driver by marking this array as symbolic and running the driver inside our symbolic environment.

The Minix driver interface makes this approach easy to apply. Minix drivers are built as standalone processes that use a small message-passing interface to communicate with the rest of the system. Their organization mirrors that of many network servers: a main dispatch loop that waits for incoming messages from other processes, the kernel or the hardware (the kernel translates hardware interrupts into messages as well) and processes the incoming requests. Thus, applying EXE to these drivers was relatively easy: for each read the driver does, we just return a symbolic message.

We made two modifications to the driver code. First, we performed simple "downscaling," such as reducing data buffer sizes, which only required changing

---

[1] We have a lot of experience checking Linux drivers but switched to Minix because of the first author's affiliation with the Minix group. We do not expect our results to change for Linux.

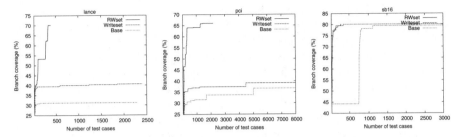

Fig. 4. Branch coverage (in percentage) over the number of test cases generated for the device drivers, comparing the base version of EXE and the RWset version with and without the use of readsets. In the first two cases, the full RWset system quickly gets branch coverage dramatically beyond that of the base system or writeset alone.

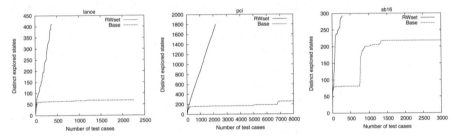

Fig. 5. Distinct explored states over number of test cases generated for the device drivers, comparing the base and the RWset versions of EXE. As with the server experiments, RWset typically both explores many more distinct states than the base system and does so very quickly.

a few constant values in header files. Second, we fixed the number of iterations in the dispatch loop and limited the search depth (expressed in number of symbolic branches). These latter changes were needed in order to do a better comparison between the base and the RWset versions of EXE. Without them, the base version gets stuck in infinite cycles. As a result of these changes, our experiments *underestimate* the improvement given by the RWset technique.

We run each device driver for one hour in three modes. As before, we use the base and the RWset versions of EXE. In addition, we also measure the effectiveness of using the readset to filter irrelevant state details by disabling this step and only pruning paths when states are exactly equal (*writeset*).

We statically counted the total number of branches in each driver (using a compiler pass) and then, for the three runs, recorded the branches hit by each generated test case. Figure 4 uses this data to plot the cumulative percentage of code branches covered by the given number of test cases. As the figure shows: (1) the RWset version outperforms the base version and (2) a lot of this improvement comes from the readset filtering. For `lance` and `pci`, the base version keeps visiting the same branches, and cannot achieve more than 40% branch coverage in the first hour. In the case of `sb16`, the base version does not fare as poorly, although it still doesn't achieve as much coverage as the RWset version.

Figure 4.2 shows the number of distinct states visited by the base and the RWset versions of EXE. The most striking feature of the graph is how quickly the base version gets stuck, repeatedly visiting states that are provably the same and thus generating large numbers of redundant test cases.

While testing these device drivers, we also checked for bugs. Unsurprisingly, the bug count improves with the amount of branch coverage achieved. While we only looked for simple low-level errors (such as `assert()` failures, null pointer dereferences, buffer overflows and out-of-bounds errors) the RWset version still found thirteen unique, confirmed bugs. On the other hand, the base version of EXE missed all but four of these.

5   Related Work

The idea for RWset was inspired by two bug-finding systems the authors were involved with [9, 18]. The first system [9] statically found bugs by pushing user-written compiler extensions down all paths in a checked program. For scalability, it tracked the internal state of these checkers and stopped exploring paths when a basic block was revisited in the same state. We reused this caching idea to do path truncation dynamically. In retrospect, adding a variation of the readset calculation presented in this paper would have likely made a big improvement in this static system since it would allow it to discard many more paths in a simple way, and transparently scale up with the power of any underlying path-sensitivity added to the system. The second system [18] provided the idea of using read and write sets when computing state equivalence. It dynamically computed such information in terms of the disk blocks a file system repair program read and wrote as a way to determine when crashing and restarting such a program during repair would compute identical results to not crashing. The use of read and write sets let it save enormous amounts of work, leading us to try a similar approach for memory (rather than disk) in our more general checking context.

Recent work on constraint-based execution tools have approached the path explosion problem in a variety of ways. Two methods that use heuristics to guide path exploration are [4] (which attempts to explore paths that hit less-often executed statements) and [13] (which combines symbolic execution with random testing). We view these techniques as largely complementary to the RWset analysis: one can use RWset analysis to discard irrelevant paths and then use these techniques to prioritize the residue.

Another approach, which like RWset analysis uses a static analysis-inspired technique to attack path explosion, tests code compositionally by reusing function summaries [7]. Roughly speaking, it does a bottom-up analysis that records the result of analyzing a function at a given callsite and, if it encounters another call to the same function with the same inputs, reuses the result of this analysis. If we regard program suffixes as functions taking as arguments the current state of the program, then [7] becomes equivalent to our RWSet technique without the readset refinement. We believe the function summary approach could also use a variation of readsets to prune out irrelevant details, and thus both get more summary hits and remove unneeded path constraints.

More generally, the idea of pruning equivalent states is an old one and has shown up in many different situations. A context closely related to ours is the use of state caching in explicit state model checking (e.g., [17]), which tracks the states generated by an abstract model of a system and does not explore the successors of an already-seen state. State caching is often improved through dead variable elimination. In most systems, this is accomplished by running a standard static live variable analysis before model checking begins, as in SPIN and Bebop [11, 2]. In [12], the system uses runtime information to eliminate infeasible paths at various points in the program in order to improve the results of the static live variable analysis. While such pruning helps, we expect the significant imprecision inherent to a static live variable forces this approach to miss many pruning opportunities. However, comparing the two techniques is hard as the benchmarks used in [12] seem to be on the order of a hundred lines of code or less, with at most three loops per program.

We note that while in hindsight it may appear clear that state caching is worth applying to constraint-based tools, the context seems different enough that, while all authors of such tools that we talked to complained about the path explosion problem, no one suggested using a state-caching approach.

A final model checking technique related to RWset analysis is *partial order reduction* [6], which skips redundant states by exploiting the fact that if two actions are independent then the order in which they occur does not matter. The two approaches should work well together: partial order reduction is a "horizontal" approach that eliminates path interleavings, while the RWset technique is a "vertical" one that truncates the remaining paths.

6   Conclusion

While constraint-based execution is a promising approach for automatically generating test cases to cover all program paths, it faces significant scalability challenges for checking large applications. This paper introduces RWset analysis, a technique for detecting and pruning large numbers of redundant paths. RWset analysis tracks all the reads and writes performed by the checked program and uses this information to truncate a path as soon as it determines that the path will execute equivalently to some previously explored one.

We measured the effectiveness of our RWset implementation by applying it to server, library, and device driver code. Our results show that RWset analysis can reduce the tests needed to reach a given number of branches by an order of magnitude, and often achieves branch coverage out-of-reach for the base version of the system, which easily gets stuck revisiting provably redundant states.

References

[1] Ball, T., Bounimova, E., Cook, B., Levin, V., Lichtenberg, J., McGarvey, C., Ondrusek, B., Rajamani, S.K., Ustuner, A.: Thorough static analysis of device drivers. In: EuroSys (April 2006)

[2] Ball, T., Rajamani, S.K.: Bebop: A symbolic model checker for boolean programs. In: Havelund, K., Penix, J., Visser, W. (eds.) SPIN 2000. LNCS, vol. 1885, Springer, Heidelberg (2000)

[3] Cadar, C., Engler, D.: Execution generated test cases: How to make systems code crash itself. In: Godefroid, P. (ed.) SPIN 2005. LNCS, vol. 3639, pp. 2–23. Springer, Heidelberg (2005)

[4] Cadar, C., Ganesh, V., Pawlowski, P., Dill, D., Engler, D.: EXE: Automatically generating inputs of death. In: Proceedings of the 13th ACM Conference on Computer and Communications Security (October-November 2006)

[5] Ganesh, V., Dill, D.L.: A decision procedure for bit-vectors and arrays. In: Damm, W., Hermanns, H. (eds.) CAV 2007. LNCS, vol. 4590, pp. 519–531. Springer, Heidelberg (2007)

[6] Godefroid, P.: Partial-Order Methods for the Verification of Concurrent Systems. LNCS, vol. 1032. Springer, New York (1996)

[7] Godefroid, P.: Compositional dynamic test generation. In: Proceedings of the 34th Symposium on Principles of Programming Languages (POPL 2007) (January 2007)

[8] Godefroid, P., Klarlund, N., Sen, K.: DART: Directed automated random testing. In: Proceedings of the Conference on Programming Language Design and Implementation (PLDI), Chicago, IL USA, ACM Press, New York (June 2005)

[9] Hallem, S., Chelf, B., Xie, Y., Engler, D.: A system and language for building system-specific, static analyses (2002)

[10] Herder, J.N.: Towards a true microkernel operating system. Master's thesis, Vrije Universiteit Amsterdam (2005)

[11] Holzmann, G.J.: The engineering of a model checker: The Gnu i-protocol case study revisited (1999)

[12] Lewis, M., Jones, M.: A dead variable analysis for explicit model checking. In: In Proceedings of the ACM SIGPLAN 2006 Workshop on Partial Evaluation and Program (2006)

[13] Majumdar, R., Sen, K.: Hybrid concolic testing. In: Proceedings of the 29th International Conference on Software Engineering (ICSE 2007) (May 2007)

[14] Sen, K., Marinov, D., Agha, G.: CUTE: A concolic unit testing engine for C. In: In 5th joint meeting of the European Software Engineering Conference and ACM SIGSOFT Symposium on the Foundations of Software Engineering (ESEC/FSE 2005) (September 2005)

[15] Swift, M.M., Annamalai, M., Bershad, B.N., Levy, H.M.: Recovering device drivers. In: OSDI, pp. 1–16 (December 2004)

[16] Tanenbaum, A.S., Woodhull, A.S.: Operating Systems Design and Implementation, 3rd edn. Prentice Hall, Englewood Cliffs (2006)

[17] Stern, U., Dill, D.L.: Improved Probabilistic Verification by Hash Compaction. In: Camurati, P.E., Eveking, H. (eds.) CHARME 1995. LNCS, vol. 987, pp. 206–224. Springer, Heidelberg (1995)

[18] Yang, J., Twohey, P., Engler, D., Musuvathi, M.: Using model checking to find serious file system errors (December 2004)

Demand-Driven Compositional
Symbolic Execution

Saswat Anand[1,*], Patrice Godefroid[2], and Nikolai Tillmann[2]

[1] Georgia Institute of Technology,
saswat@cc.gatech.edu
[2] Microsoft Research,
{pg,nikolait}@microsoft.com

Abstract. We discuss how to perform symbolic execution of large programs in a manner that is both compositional (hence more scalable) and demand-driven. Compositional symbolic execution means finding feasible interprocedural program paths by composing symbolic executions of feasible intraprocedural paths. By demand-driven, we mean that as few intraprocedural paths as possible are symbolically executed in order to form an interprocedural path leading to a specific target branch or statement of interest (like an assertion). A key originality of this work is that our demand-driven compositional interprocedural symbolic execution is performed entirely using first-order logic formulas solved with an off-the-shelf SMT (Satisfiability-Modulo-Theories) solver – no procedure in-lining or custom algorithm is required for the interprocedural part. This allows a uniform and elegant way of summarizing procedures at various levels of detail and of composing those using logic formulas.

We have implemented a prototype of this novel symbolic execution technique as an extension of Pex, a general automatic testing framework for .NET applications. Preliminary experimental results are encouraging. For instance, our prototype was able to generate tests triggering assertion violations in programs with large numbers of program paths that were beyond the scope of non-compositional test generation.

1 Introduction

Given a sequential program P with input parameters $\overrightarrow{I}$, the *test generation problem* consists in generating automatically a set of input values to exercise as many program statements as possible. There are essentially two approaches to solve this problem. *Static* test generation [15,22,7] consists in analyzing the program P statically, using symbolic execution techniques to attempt to compute inputs to drive P along specific paths or branches, but without ever executing the program. In contrast, *dynamic test generation* [16,11,5] consists in executing the program, typically starting with some random inputs, while simultaneously performing a symbolic execution to collect symbolic constraints on inputs obtained from predicates in branch statements along the execution, and then using a constraint solver to infer variants of the previous inputs in order to steer program

---

* The work of this author was done mostly while visiting Microsoft Research.

C.R. Ramakrishnan and J. Rehof (Eds.): TACAS 2008, LNCS 4963, pp. 367–381, 2008.
© Springer-Verlag Berlin Heidelberg 2008

executions along alternative program paths. Since dynamic test generation extends static test generation with additional runtime information, it can be more powerful [11,10], and is therefore used as the basis of this work.

As recently pointed out [10], automatic test generation (whether static or dynamic) does not scale to large programs with many feasible program paths, *unless* test generation is performed *compositionally*. Inspired by interprocedural static analysis, compositional test generation consists in encoding test results of lower-level functions with test *summaries*, expressed using preconditions over function inputs and postconditions over function outputs, and then re-using those summaries when testing higher-level functions. In contrast with traditional interprocedural static analysis, the framework introduced in [10] involves detailed summaries where function preconditions and postconditions are represented using logic formulas, and the interprocedural analysis (test generation) is performed using an automated theorem prover. A key component of this approach is thus *compositional symbolic execution*: how to find feasible interprocedural program paths by composing symbolic executions of feasible intraprocedural paths, represented as logic "summaries".

In this paper, we develop compositional symbolic execution further. We present a detailed formalization of how to generate first-order logic formulas with uninterpreted functions in order to represent function summaries and allow compositional symbolic execution using a SMT (Satisfiability-Modulo-Theories) solver. Our formalization generalizes the one of [10] as it allows incomplete summaries (which correspond to only a subset of all paths of a function) to be expanded *lazily* on a *demand-driven* basis, instead of being expanded in the fixed "innermost-first" order described in [10]. With demand-driven symbolic execution, as few intraprocedural paths as possible are symbolically executed in order to form an interprocedural path leading to a specific target branch or statement of interest (like an assertion). This increased flexibility also allows test generation to adapt dynamically, as more statements get covered, in order to focus on those program statements that are still uncovered. In practice, real-life software applications are very complex, and allowing the search to be demand-driven is often key to reach a specific target in a reasonable time. It is also useful for selective regression testing aimed at generating tests targeted to cover new code embedded in old code.

We have implemented a prototype of demand-driven compositional symbolic execution as an extension of Pex [20], a general automatic testing framework for .NET applications. Preliminary experimental results are encouraging. For instance, our prototype implementation was able to generate tests triggering assertion violations in programs with large numbers of program paths that were beyond the scope of non-compositional test generation.

2   Background

We assume we are given a sequential program P with input parameters $\overrightarrow{I}$. *Symbolic execution* of P means symbolically exploring the tree $\mathcal{T}$ defined by the *execution paths* of the program when considering all possible value assignments to input parameters. For each execution path ρ, i.e., a sequence of statements executed by the program, a *path constraint* ϕ_ρ is constructed that characterizes the input assignments for which the program executes along ρ. Each variable appearing in ϕ_ρ is thus a program input, while each constraint is expressed in some theory T decided by a constraint solver (for instance, including linear arithmetic, bit-vector operations, etc.). A constraint solver is an automated theorem prover which also returns a satisfying assignment for all variables appearing in formulas it can prove satisfiable. All program paths can be enumerated by a search algorithm that explores all possible branches at conditional statements. The paths ρ for which ϕ_ρ is satisfiable are *feasible* and are the only ones that can be executed by the actual program. The solutions to ϕ_ρ exactly characterize the inputs that drive the program through ρ. Assuming that the constraint solver used to check the satisfiability of all formulas ϕ_ρ is sound and complete, this use of symbolic execution for programs with finitely many paths amounts to program verification.

In practice, symbolic execution of large programs is bound to be imprecise due to complex program statements (pointer manipulations, floating-point operations, etc.) and calls to operating-system and library functions that are hard or impossible to reason about symbolically with good enough precision at a reasonable cost. Whenever precise symbolic execution is not possible during dynamic test generation, concrete values can be used to simplify constraints and carry on with a simplified, partial symbolic execution [11].

Systematically executing symbolically *all* feasible program paths does not scale to large programs. Indeed, the number of feasible paths can be exponential in the program size, or even infinite in presence of loops with unbounded number of iterations. This *path explosion* can be alleviated by performing symbolic execution *compositionally* [10].

Let us assume the program P consists of a set of functions. In what follows, we use the generic term of *function* to denote any part of the program P whose observed behaviors are summarized; obviously, any other kinds of program fragments such as arbitrary program blocks or object methods can be treated as "functions" as done in this paper. To simplify the presentation, we assume that the functions in P do not perform recursive calls, and that all the executions of P terminate. (These assumptions do not prevent P from possibly having infinitely many executions paths, as is the case if P contains a loop whose number of iterations may depend on some unbounded input.)

In compositional symbolic execution [10], a function summary ϕ_f for a function f is defined as a formula in propositional logic whose propositions are constraints expressed in some theory T. ϕ_f can be derived by successive iterations and defined as a disjunction of formulas ϕ_w of the form $\phi_w = pre_w \wedge post_w$, where pre_w is a conjunction of constraints on the inputs of f while $post_w$ is a conjunction of constraints on the outputs of f. ϕ_w can be computed from the path constraint corresponding to the execution path w as described later. An input to a function f is any value that can be read by f in some of its executions, while an output of f is any value written by f in some of its executions

```
int abs(int x){                    int testAbs(int p, int q){
  if(x > 0) return x;                int m = abs(p);
  else if(x == 0)                    int n = abs(q);
         return 100;                 if(m > n && p > 0)
  else return −x;                        assert false;  //target
}                                  }
```

Fig. 1. Example program

and later read by P after f returns. To simplify the presentation, we assume in what follows that each function takes a fixed number of arguments as inputs and returns a single value.

3 Motivating Example and Overview

To illustrate the motivation for *demand-driven* compositional symbolic execution, consider the simple program in Fig. 1, which consists of a top-level function testAbs which calls another function abs. Intraprocedural execution trees for each function are shown in Fig. 2. Each node in such trees represents the execution of a program statement such that a path from the root of the tree to a leaf corresponds to an intraprocedural path. Each such path can be identified by its leaf node. Edges in execution trees are labeled with constraints expressed in terms of the function inputs. The conjunction of constraints labeling the edges of a path represents its associated path constraint as defined earlier. For example, Fig. 2(a) shows the (partial) execution tree of function abs, shown in Fig. 1, after the execution of abs with a single input x=1. In what follows, we call a node *dangling* if it represents a path that has not been exercised yet. For example, after executing the abs with input x=1, any path on which the input is less than or equal to 0 is not exercised. In Fig. 2(a), the sole dangling node is denoted by a circle.

The demand-driven compositional symbolic execution we develop in this work has two key properties: given a specific target to cover, it tries to (1) explore as few paths as possible (called *lazy exploration*) and to (2) avoid exploring paths that can be guaranteed not to cover the target (called *relevant exploration*). We now illustrate these two features.

Lazy Exploration. Assume that we first run the program of Fig. 1 by executing the function testAbs with p=1 and q=1. This first execution will exercise the then branch of the first conditional statement in abs (node 3), as well as the else branch of the conditional statement in testAbs (node 10). The execution trees of abs and testAbs resulting from this execution are shown in Fig. 2(a) and (c), respectively. Suppose we want to generate a test input to cover node 11, corresponding to the assertion in testAbs. The search ordering described in [10] is not target-driven and would attempt to next exercise the unexplored paths in the innermost, lower-level function abs. In contrast, the more flexible formalization introduced in the next section allows us to check whether a combination of currently-known fully-explored intraprocedural paths are sufficient to generate

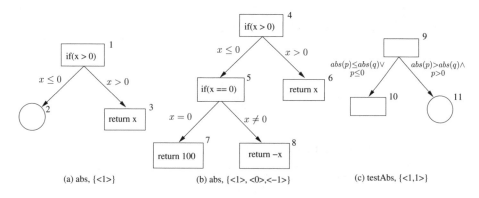

Fig. 2. Execution trees for the functions `abs` and `testAbs` from Fig. 1. Each execution tree represents paths exercised by a set of test inputs shown as vectors inside the curly braces.

a new test input covering the target node. In this example, this is the case as the assertion can be reached in `testAbs` without exploring new paths in `abs`, for instance with values p=2 and q=1.

Relevant Exploration. Now, assume we first execute the program with inputs p=0 and q=1. Suppose our target is again node 11 corresponding to the assert statement. From the condition guarding the assert statement, observe that any combination of input values for p and q where p has a non-positive value has no chance to cover the target. As we will see, our proposed algorithm is able to infer such information automatically from the previous execution with inputs p=0 and q=1, and will thus prune automatically the entire sub-search tree where p is not greater than 0.

4   Demand-Driven Compositional Symbolic Execution

4.1   Main Algorithm

Algorithm 1 outlines our test-generation algorithm. Given a program P, Algorithm 1 iteratively computes a set of test inputs to cover all reachable statements in P. The algorithm starts with an empty set of intraprocedural execution trees, and a random program input. It performs two steps in sequence until all reachable nodes in the program have been explored. (1) Function `Execute` executes the program with some test input, both normally and symbolically. During symbolic execution of the specific path exercised by the test input, new nodes and edges with constraint labels are added to the intraprocedural execution trees of the individual program functions being executed, while dangling nodes, used as place-holders along this specific path in previous executions, become regular nodes. (2) `ChooseDanglingNode` chooses a dangling node as the next target to be covered, using any heuristic (search strategy). If there is no dangling node

---

input : Program P
output: A set of test inputs

exTrees ← emptyExTree ;
input ← RandomInput();
repeat
    if input ≠ emptyModel **then**
        exTrees ← Execute(P, input, exTrees);
        OutputTest(input);
    else
        RemoveDanglingNode(n);
    end
    n ← ChooseDanglingNode(exTrees);
    if n ≠ nil **then**
        input ← FindTestInput(exTrees, n);
    end
until n = nil ;
return;

Algorithm 1. Test-input generation algorithm

remaining, the algorithm terminates. Otherwise, `FindTestInput` computes a test input to cover the target, as will be described next.

4.2 Compositional Symbolic Execution

In compositional symbolic execution, the condition under which a node in a function can be reached from the program's entry point is the conjunction of (1) the condition under which the function's entry node can be reached, referred to as *calling context*; and (2) the condition under which the node can be reached within its function, referred to as the *local (intraprocedural) path constraint*.

Local (Intraprocedural) Path Constraint. The local path constraint of a node n in the intraprocedural execution tree $\mathcal{T}_f$ of function f is defined as the path constraint of the path w from the entry node of f to the statement represented by n. The local path constraint of node n, represented by $localpc(n)$, is expressed in terms of the input parameter symbols $\overrightarrow{\mathcal{P}_f}$ of f and represents a precondition $pre(w)$ for execution of the path w [10]. It is defined as follows.

$$localpc(n) := lpc_n \wedge \bigwedge_{\text{for each } g(\overrightarrow{a}) \text{ appearing in } lpc_n} D_g(\overrightarrow{a})$$

where lpc_n is the conjunction of constraints appearing on the edges of the path w from the root of $\mathcal{T}_f$ to n, and each definition predicate $D_g(\overrightarrow{a})$ represents the (possibly partial) summary currently available for function g, called from f with $\overrightarrow{a}$ as arguments, and mentioned in lpc_n. Definition predicates are formally defined as follows.

Definition predicate. When function f calls function g during symbolic execution, we treat the return value of the function call to g as a (fresh) symbolic input to f. We represent the return value by the expression $g(\overrightarrow{a})$, where $\overrightarrow{a}$ are the arguments expressed in terms of $\overrightarrow{\mathcal{P}_f}$. If the return value is used in a conditional statement of f, then $g(\overrightarrow{a})$ appears in the path constraint. The function symbol g will be treated as an uninterpreted function symbol by the constraint solver, and we restrict possible interpretations by an axiom of the form $\forall x.\ g(x) = E[x]$, where $E[x]$ is an expression that may involve the bound variable x. As an example, for the abs function in Fig. 1, abs can be defined as follows (where ITE denotes the If-Then-Else construct):

$$\forall x.\ abs(x) = ITE(x > 0, x, ITE(x = 0, 100, -x))$$

However, return values on some paths of a function may be currently unknown since paths are explored incrementally and on-demand. In those cases, we cannot use the above encoding directly. We could use a special *undefined* value that represents the result of an unexercised path, and lift all operations accordingly. Instead, we use a *definition-predicate* D_g for each function symbol that represents the return value of a function call. We define this predicate with the axiom δ_g as follows.

$$\delta_g := \forall \overrightarrow{\mathcal{P}_g}.\ D_g(\overrightarrow{\mathcal{P}_g}) \Leftrightarrow \bigvee_{\text{leaf } l \text{ in } \mathcal{T}_g} localpc(l) \wedge ret(l)$$

where

$$ret(l) := \begin{cases} \mathcal{G}_l & \text{if } l \text{ is a dangling node} \\ g(\overrightarrow{\mathcal{P}_g}) = Ret_g(l) & \text{otherwise} \end{cases}$$

In the above definition, $Ret_g(l)$ represents the return value of g, which is an expression in terms of $\overrightarrow{\mathcal{P}_g}$, on the fully-explored intraprocedural path represented by l. For each dangling node d, $\mathcal{G}_d$ represents an auxiliary boolean variable that uniquely corresponds to d; we use these boolean variables in Sec. 4.3 to control the search by specifying whether the exploration of a new execution path through a dangling node is permissible.

For the example shown in Fig. 1, suppose we execute testAbs with $\mathsf{p} = 1$ and $\mathsf{q} = 1$. The execution trees for abs and testAbs obtained from this input are shown in Fig. 2(a) and (c) respectively. Now, the local path constraint of the node n, labeled 11 in the figure, will be as follows.

$$localpc(n) := abs(p) > abs(q) \wedge p > 0 \wedge D_{abs}(p) \wedge D_{abs}(q)$$

With the above input, since only the path where $x > 0$ has been explored in abs, there is a dangling node d, labeled 2, which represents the (unexplored) else branch of the conditional statement. The definition predicate D_{abs} is then defined by the following axiom.

$$\delta_{abs} := \forall x.\ D_{abs}(x) \Leftrightarrow ITE(x > 0, abs(x) = x, \mathcal{G}_d)$$

If all the paths of abs had been explored (as shown in Fig. 2(b)), its definition-predicate axiom would instead be as follows.

$$\delta_{abs} := \forall x.\ D_{abs}(x) \Leftrightarrow (x \leq 0 \wedge x = 0 \wedge abs(x) = 100)$$
$$\vee (x \leq 0 \wedge x \neq 0 \wedge abs(x) = -x)$$
$$\vee (x > 0 \wedge abs(x) = x)$$
$$= \forall x.\ D_{abs}(x) \Leftrightarrow ITE(x \leq 0, ITE(x = 0, abs(x) = 100, abs(x) = -x),$$
$$abs(x) = x)$$

Note that, with the specific innermost-first search order used in [10] for incrementally computing summaries, dangling and target nodes are always in the current innermost function in the call stack and the above formalization of partial summaries can then be simplified. In contrast, the formalization presented here is more general as it allows dangling nodes and target nodes to be located anywhere in the program.

Calling-context Predicate. The calling-context predicate associated with a function f describes under which conditions, and with which arguments, f can be reached. The calling-context predicate of function f, written as $C_f(\overrightarrow{a})$, evaluates to true iff on some program path f can be called with arguments $\overrightarrow{a}$. $C_f(\overrightarrow{a})$ is defined by the *calling-context axiom* γ_f as follows.

$$\gamma_f := \begin{cases} \forall \overrightarrow{a}.\ C_f(\overrightarrow{a}) \Leftrightarrow \overrightarrow{a} = \overrightarrow{I} & \text{if } f \text{ is entry function of program } P \\ \forall \overrightarrow{a}.\ C_f(\overrightarrow{a}) \Leftrightarrow \bigvee_{\substack{\text{for each} \\ \text{function } g \text{ in } P}} C_f^g(\overrightarrow{a}) & \text{otherwise} \end{cases}$$

with

$$C_f^g(\overrightarrow{a}) := \exists \overrightarrow{P_g}.\ C_g(\overrightarrow{P_g}) \wedge (knownC_f^g(\overrightarrow{a}) \vee unknownC^g)$$

where

$$knownC_f^g(\overrightarrow{a}) := \bigvee_{m \in callsites(\mathcal{T}_g, f)} \overrightarrow{a} = args(m) \wedge localpc(m)$$
$$unknownC^g := \bigvee_{\text{dangling node } d \text{ in } \mathcal{T}_g} localpc(d) \wedge \mathcal{G}_d$$

We distinguish two cases in γ_f. First, if f is the entry function of the program P, then the arguments of f are the program inputs $\overrightarrow{I}$. Otherwise, $C_f(\overrightarrow{a})$ is true iff f can be called from some function g with arguments $\overrightarrow{a}$. $C_f^g(\overrightarrow{a})$ represents the condition under which g may call f with arguments $\overrightarrow{a}$. $C_f^g(\overrightarrow{a})$ in turn evaluates to true iff (1) g itself can be called with arguments $\overrightarrow{P_g}$; and either (2.a) f can be called from g in a *known* call site denoted by $m \in callsites(\mathcal{T}_g, f)$ with arguments $\overrightarrow{a} = args(m)$, where $args(m)$ denote the arguments (in terms of $\overrightarrow{P_g}$) passed to call at m; or (2.b) f *might* be called (with unknown arguments) on a path in g, represented by a dangling node d, that has not been explored so far. In either case, the local path constraint $localpc(m)$ leading to the known call site m or $localpc(d)$ leading to a possible call site d, respectively, is appended as a condition necessary to reach the respective call site.

Consider again the program shown in Fig. 1 with `testAbs` as the top-level entry function. The calling-context predicate for `testAbs` is then defined by the following axiom.

$$\gamma_{testAbs} := \forall p, q. \ C_{testAbs}(p, q) \Leftrightarrow p = \overrightarrow{I}(0) \wedge q = \overrightarrow{I}(1).$$

For the function `abs`, the definition of the calling-context predicate is more complicated because `abs` can be called twice in `testAbs`. Suppose the execution trees of `abs` and `testAbs` are as shown in Fig. 2(b) and (c) respectively. For both known call-sites of `abs` in `testAbs`, where p and q are passed as arguments, $localpc$ evaluates to $true$. And, there is one unknown call-site, which is represented by the dangling node d (labeled 11). For d, we have $localpc(d) := abs(p) > abs(q) \wedge p > 0 \wedge D_{abs}(p) \wedge D_{abs}(q)$. Now, $C_{abs}(a)$ is defined by the axiom γ_{abs} as follows.

$$\gamma_{abs} := \forall a. \ C_{abs}(a) \Leftrightarrow C_{abs}^{testAbs}(a)$$
$$C_{abs}^{testAbs}(a) := \exists p, q. \ C_{testAbs}(p, q) \wedge (a = p \vee a = q$$
$$\vee (abs(p) > abs(q) \wedge p > 0 \wedge D_{abs}(p) \wedge D_{abs}(q) \wedge \mathcal{G}_d))$$

Note that an existential quantification is used in C_f^g to limit the scope of parameter symbols $\mathcal{P}_g$ to specific call-sites. However, this existential quantification can be eliminated by skolemization since it always appears within the scope of the universal quantifier in the definition of γ_f.

Also note that the formalization proposed in [10] does not require calling-context predicates because it only supports a fixed inner-most ordering in which intraprocedural paths are explored. Since we relax here the restriction on the exploration ordering so that paths can be explored in any order on-demand, calling-context predicates become necessary.

Interprocedural path constraint. Given a node n in the intraprocedural execution tree $\mathcal{T}_f$ of a function f, path constraints of interprocedural paths leading to n are represented by Ψ_n, which is defined recursively as follows:

$$\Psi_n = localpc(n) \wedge C_f(\overrightarrow{\mathcal{P}_f}) \wedge \bigwedge_{C_g(\overrightarrow{a}) \ \text{appears in} \ \Psi_n} \gamma_g \wedge \bigwedge_{g(\overrightarrow{a}) \ \text{appears in} \ \Psi_n} \delta_g$$

Ψ_n represents the disjunction of path constraints of all interprocedural paths to target n that can be formed by joining intraprocedural paths, represented by execution trees of different functions. (Disjunctions arise from the definitions of γ_g and δ_g.) An intraprocedural path p in $\mathcal{T}_f$ can be *joined* with an intraprocedural path q in $\mathcal{T}_g$, if either (1) p ends at a leaf node (possibly a dangling node) in $\mathcal{T}_f$, and q starts at a node in $\mathcal{T}_g$ corresponding to a call-site of f in g; or, (2) p ends at a node representing a call-site of g in f and q starts at the entry-node of $\mathcal{T}_g$; or, (3) p ends at a dangling node, and q starts from the entry-node of $\mathcal{T}_g$, where g is any arbitrary function.

With compositional symbolic execution, the size of an interprocedural path constraint is linear in the sum of the sizes of the execution trees $\mathcal{T}_f$ [10].

Examples. As our first example, suppose the execution trees for `abs` and `testAbs` are as shown in Fig. 2(b) and (c), respectively. If the target is the node labeled 11, then the interprocedural path constraint is as follows.

$abs(p) > abs(q) \wedge p > 0 \wedge D_{abs}(p) \wedge D_{abs}(q) \wedge p > 0 \wedge C_{testAbs}(p, q)$
$\bigwedge \forall x.\ D_{abs}(x) \Leftrightarrow ITE(x \leq 0, ITE(x = 0, abs(x) = 100, abs(x) = -x), abs(x) = x)$
$\bigwedge \forall p, q.\ C_{testAbs}(p, q) \Leftrightarrow p = \overrightarrow{I}(0) \wedge q = \overrightarrow{I}(1)$

As another example, suppose the execution trees for `abs` and `testAbs` are again as shown in Fig. 2(b) and (c), respectively. Now if the target is node labeled 2, the path constraint is as follows (where $\mathcal{G}_{11}$ represents the unique boolean variable corresponding to the dangling node labeled 11):

$x \leq 0 \wedge C_{abs}(x)$
$\bigwedge \forall x.\ D_{abs}(x) \Leftrightarrow ITE(x \leq 0, ITE(x = 0, abs(x) = 100, abs(x) = -x), abs(x) = x)$
$\bigwedge \forall a.\ C_{abs}(a) \Leftrightarrow \exists p, q.\ C_{testAbs}(p, q) \wedge (a = p \vee a = q$
$\qquad\qquad\qquad \vee (abs(p) > abs(q) \wedge p > 0 \wedge D_{abs}(p) \wedge D_{abs}(q) \wedge \mathcal{G}_{11}))$
$\bigwedge \forall p, q.\ C_{testAbs}(p, q) \Leftrightarrow p = \overrightarrow{I}(0) \wedge q = \overrightarrow{I}(1)$

4.3 Demand-Driven Symbolic Execution

In compositional symbolic execution, interprocedural paths are formed by combining intraprocedural paths. To allow compositional symbolic execution to be demand-driven, we allow in this work (unlike [10]) interprocedural paths to be formed by combining intraprocedural paths that end in dangling nodes. We call an interprocedural path *partially-explored* iff it goes through one or more dangling nodes; otherwise we call the path *fully-explored*. Note that a fully-explored path may end at, but not go through, a dangling node.

Algorithm 2 is used to find a feasible, interprocedural path from the entry of the program to a target node using demand-driven compositional symbolic execution. The algorithm corresponds to the subroutine `FindTestInput` in Algorithm 1. It takes as input a set of intraprocedural execution trees exTrees, and a dangling node n in one of these execution trees, which is the target to cover. It returns either (1) a designated value emptyModel representing the fact that the target node is unreachable, or (2) program inputs $\overrightarrow{I}$ that exercises a path that may cover the target. The algorithm calls an SMT solver by invoking the function `FindModel($\Psi$)`, which returns a model for the path constraint Ψ if it is satisfiable, or returns emptyModel otherwise. $G(\Psi)$ represents the set of all boolean flags that appear in the path constraint Ψ, each of which uniquely corresponds to a dangling node in exTrees. The algorithm first computes the interprocedural path constraint for the target node n in exTrees as presented in Sec. 4.2. Then it performs two steps, referred to as *lazy exploration* and *relevant exploration* in what follows.

---

input : Set of execution trees exTrees, target node n to be covered
output: Program inputs that *may* cover n, or emptyModel if the target is
        unreachable

$\Psi_n \leftarrow$ InterprocPC(n,exTrees);
input $\leftarrow$ FindModel($\Psi_n \wedge \bigwedge\limits_{\mathcal{G}_d \in G(\Psi_n) \wedge d \neq n} \mathcal{G}_d = false$);
if input = emptyModel **then**
    input $\leftarrow$ FindModel(Ψ_n);
end
return input ;

Algorithm 2. Demand-driven, compositional FindTestInput algorithm

Lazy Exploration. In this step, the algorithm checks if it is possible to form a feasible, fully-explored, interprocedural path to n by combining only (fully-explored) intraprocedural paths in exTrees. To do so, it computes a constraint that represents the disjunction of the path constraints of all such paths and checks its satisfiability. The new constraint is formed by conjoining Ψ_n with equations that set all variables but $\mathcal{G}_n$ in $G(\Psi_n)$ to $false$ so that all intraprocedural paths that end at a dangling node other than n are made infeasible. If the augmented constraint is satisfiable, FindModel returns a program test input that is guaranteed to cover the target (provided symbolic execution has perfect precision). Otherwise, we need to explore new partially-explored intraprocedural paths, which is done in the next step.

Relevant Exploration. We say that a partially-explored, interprocedural path is *relevant* if it ends at the target. In other words, such a path starts at the program entry, goes through one or more dangling nodes, finally taking the path from the root node of $\mathcal{T}_f$ to the target node n, where $\mathcal{T}_f$ represents the execution tree of function f where n is located. In this second step, the algorithm checks if a feasible relevant path can be formed by combining all (both fully-explored and partially-explored) intraprocedural paths in exTrees. To do so, the algorithm checks satisfiability of Ψ_n with a second call to FindModel. If Ψ_n is unsatisfiable, the algorithm returns emptyModel representing unreachability of the target. Otherwise, it returns a program input that *might* exercise a path to the target. This time, the boolean variables in $G(\Psi_n)$ are not constrained to any specific value as is done in the previous step. As a result, the constraint solver assigns $true$ to a boolean variable if the path to the corresponding dangling node is used to form the interprocedural path to the target. Such a relevant path is not guaranteed to reach the target, since the program's behavior at dangling nodes, which may appear on a relevant path, is currently unknown.

The following theorems characterize the correctness of the above algorithms. These theorems hold *assuming symbolic execution has perfect precision*, i.e., that constraint generation and solving is both sound and complete for all program statements. (Proofs are omitted due to space limitations.)

Theorem (Relative Completeness). If Algorithm 2 returns emptyModel, then the target n is unreachable.

Theorem (Progress). If Algorithm 2 returns a program input $\vec{I}$ (different from emptyModel), then the execution of the program with $\vec{I}$ exercises a new intraprocedural path (i.e., at least one dangling node is removed from exTrees).

Theorem (Termination). If the program has a finite number of paths, Algorithm 1 terminates.

5   Preliminary Experiments

We have implemented a prototype of demand-driven compositional symbolic execution in Pex [20], a general automatic testing framework for .NET programs. Pex generates test inputs for parameterized unit tests [21] by performing a variation of dynamic [11] test generation using the SMT constraint solver Z3 [8]. Pex' goal is to analyze as many feasible execution paths of a given .NET program as possible in a given amount of time. During the search, Pex picks the next target node using a scheduling algorithm that is fair between all dangling nodes. Pex is a comprehensive testing tool and framework, which has been used within Microsoft on several .NET applications and contributed to finding many bugs (including several security-critical ones) in released software and software still under development at Microsoft.

We present experiments with three programs written in C# using both non-compositional and demand-driven compositional symbolic execution. These experiments were conducted on a 3.4 GHz Pentium 4 with 2 GB memory.

HWM is program that takes a string as input, and an assertion fails if the input string contains all of the four substrings: "Hello", "world", "at", "Microsoft!". Although it is a simple program, it has hundreds of millions of feasible whole-program paths. The program has a main method that calls contains(s,t) four times in succession. contains(s,t) checks if string s contains substring t. contains(s,t) calls containsAt(s,i,t) that checks if s contains t starting from index i in s.

Parser is a parser for a subset of a Pascal-like language. The program takes a string as input, and successfully parses it if it represents a syntactically valid program in the language. An assertion is violated if parsing is successful. A valid program starts with the keyword "program" followed by an arbitrary string representing program name. Furthermore, the body of the program starts with keyword "begin" and end with keyword "end". And the body may optionally include function definitions.

IncDec is a program that takes an integer as argument. It increments it several times and then decrements until a certain condition specified as an assertion is satisfied.

The table in Fig. 3 presents results of experiments. The three first columns represent the total number of executions, the total time taken over all executions,

Benchmark	No. of Executions		Time in sec		time per execution		Exception found	
	new	old	new	old	new	old	new	old
HWM	37	maxed	65	705	1.75	0.02	yes	no
Parser	144	maxed	71	338	0.49	0.01	yes	yes
IncDec	74	1207	14	43	0.18	0.03	yes	yes

Fig. 3. Comparison between new (demand-driven, compositional) and old (non-compositional) symbolic execution techniques

and the time taken per execution. (Execution time includes time taken by the constraint solver.) The last column shows whether the respective technique was able to generate an input that violates the assertion contained in each program. In the column showing the number of executions, "maxed" denotes that non-compositional symbolic execution hits an upper bound of 20,000 executions; in those cases, total execution time represents the time taken to reach the upper bound.

We make the following observations from the table in Fig. 3. (1) The number of executions required with demand-driven compositional symbolic execution is often several orders of magnitude smaller compared to non-compositional symbolic execution. (2) The improvement in total time cannot be measured as non-compositional symbolic execution technique hits the upper bound on the number of execution in two of the three cases. (3) The time taken for each execution increases when the symbolic execution is demand-driven and compositional, as the formulas generated are more complicated and the constraint solver needs more time to solve those, although most can be solved in seconds. (4) In the case of HWM, only the search with demand-driven compositional symbolic execution is able to find the assertion violation, whereas the non-compositional search is lost in search-space due to path explosion. The other two examples have fewer execution paths, and the fair search heuristics implemented in Pex are able to find the assertion violations, even with non-compositional searches.

6   Other Related Work

Interprocedural *static* analysis always involves some form of summarization [19]. Summaries are usually defined either at some fixed-level of abstraction, e.g., for points-to analysis [17], or as abstractions of intraprocedural pre and postconditions, e.g., projections onto a set of predicates [3,23]. Even when a SAT solver is used for a precise intraprocedural analysis [6,23,2], the interprocedural part of the analysis itself is carried out either using some custom fixpoint computation algorithm [4,23] or by in-lining functions [6,2], the latter leading to combinatorial explosion.

In contrast with prior work on interprocedural static analysis, we represent function summaries as uninterpreted functions with arbitrary pre/postconditions represented as logic formulas, and we use an SMT solver to carry out the interprocedural part of the analysis. Of course, the constraint solver may need to in-line summaries during its search for a model satisfying a whole-program path constraint, but it will do so lazily, only if necessary, and while memoizing new induced facts in order to avoid re-inferring those later, hence simulating the effect of caching previously-considered calling contexts and new summaries inferred by transitivity, as in compositional algorithms for hierarchical finite-state machine verification [1].

How to perform *abstract* symbolic execution with simplified summary representations [14,2,12] in *static* program analysis is orthogonal to the demand-driven and compositionality issues addressed in our paper.

The use of automatically-generated software stubs [11] for abstracting (over-approximating) lower-level functions during dynamic test generation [18,9] is also mostly orthogonal to our approach. However, the practicality of this idea is questionable because anticipating side-effects of stubbed functions accurately is problematic. In contrast, our approach is compositional while being grounded in testing and concrete execution, thus without ever generating false alarms.

Demand-driven dynamic test generation for single procedures has previously been discussed in [16,13]. This prior work is based on dataflow analysis, does not use logic and automated theorem proving, and does not discuss interprocedural analysis. As discussed earlier, our work extends the compositional test generation framework introduced in [10] by precisely formalizing how to implement it using first-order logic formulas with uninterpreted functions and a SMT solver, and by allowing it to be demand-driven.

7 Conclusion

This paper presents an automatic and efficient symbolic execution technique for test-input generation, which is both demand-driven and compositional. By demand-driven, we mean that, given a target to cover, the technique aims to explore as few program paths as possible (called lazy exploration), and avoid exploring paths that can be guaranteed not to cover the target (called relevant exploration). By compositional, we mean that, instead of enumerating all interprocedural paths one-by-one, the technique finds feasible, interprocedural paths by combining intraprocedural paths. Because the technique is demand-driven, it can be very efficient when the goal is to cover a particular location in the program (e.g., an assertion). And, due to its compositionality, it can alleviate the path-explosion problem, which severely limits the scalability of automatic test-input generation. We have implemented a prototype of the proposed technique on top of Microsoft's Pex test-generation tool. Preliminary experimental results are promising. Currently, we are extending our prototype to handle implementation issues such as summarizing side-effects through the heap. Future work includes applying the technique to a larger set of programs to further assess its effectiveness.

Acknowledgments. We thank Jonathan 'Peli' de Halleux, one of the Pex developers, Nikolaj Bjørner and Leonardo de Moura for the Z3 SMT constraint solver and their support, and the anonymous reviewers for helpful comments.

References

1. Alur, R., Yannakakis, M.: Model Checking of Hierarchical State Machines. In: Vaudenay, S. (ed.) FSE 1998. LNCS, vol. 1372, pp. 175–188. Springer, Heidelberg (1998)
2. Babic, D., Hu, A.J.: Structural Abstraction of Software Verification Conditions. In: Damm, W., Hermanns, H. (eds.) CAV 2007. LNCS, vol. 4590, Springer, Heidelberg (2007)
3. Ball, T., Majumdar, R., Millstein, T., Rajamani, S.: Automatic Predicate Abstraction of C Programs. In: Proceedings of PLDI 2001 (2001)
4. Bush, W.R., Pincus, J.D., Sielaff, D.J.: A static analyzer for finding dynamic programming errors. Software Practice and Experience 30(7), 775–802 (2000)
5. Cadar, C., Ganesh, V., Pawlowski, P.M., Dill, D.L., Engler, D.R.: EXE: Automatically Generating Inputs of Death. In: ACM CCS (2006)
6. Clarke, E., Kroening, D., Lerda, F.: A Tool for Checking ANSI-C Programs. In: Jensen, K., Podelski, A. (eds.) TACAS 2004. LNCS, vol. 2988, Springer, Heidelberg (2004)
7. Csallner, C., Smaragdakis, Y.: Check'n Crash: Combining Static Checking and Testing. In: Inverardi, P., Jazayeri, M. (eds.) ICSE 2005. LNCS, vol. 4309, Springer, Heidelberg (2006)
8. de Moura, L., Bjørner, N.: Z3, 2007. Web page: http://research.microsoft.com/projects/Z3
9. Engler, D., Dunbar, D.: Under-constrained execution: making automatic code destruction easy and scalable. In: Proceedings of ISSTA 2007 (2007)
10. Godefroid, P.: Compositional Dynamic Test Generation. In: POPL 2007, pp. 47–54 (January 2007)
11. Godefroid, P., Klarlund, N., Sen, K.: DART: Directed Automated Random Testing. In: PLDI 2005, Chicago, pp. 213–223 (June 2005)
12. Gopan, D., Reps, T.: Low-level Library Analysis and Summarization. In: Damm, W., Hermanns, H. (eds.) CAV 2007. LNCS, vol. 4590, pp. 68–81. Springer, Heidelberg (2007)
13. Gupta, N., Mathur, A.P., Soffa, M.L.: Generating Test Data for Branch Coverage. In: Proceedings of ASE 2000, pp. 219–227 (September 2000)
14. Khurshid, S., Suen, Y.L.: Generalizing Symbolic Execution to Library Classes. In: PASTE 2005, Lisbon (September 2005)
15. King, J.C.: Symbolic Execution and Program Testing. Journal of the ACM 19(7), 385–394 (1976)
16. Korel, B.: A Dynamic Approach of Test Data Generation. In: ICSM, pp. 311–317 (November 1990)
17. Livshits, V.B., Lam, M.: Tracking Pointers with Path and Context Sensitivity for Bug Detection in C Programs. In: Johansson, T. (ed.) FSE 2003. LNCS, vol. 2887, Springer, Heidelberg (2003)
18. Majumdar, R., Sen, K.: Latest: Lazy dynamic test input generation. Technical report, UC Berkeley (2007)
19. Reps, T., Horwitz, S., Sagiv, M.: Precise interprocedural dataflow analysis via graph reachability. In: Proceedings of POPL 1995, pp. 49–61 (1995)
20. Tillmann, N., de Halleux, J.: Pex (2007), http://research.microsoft.com/Pex
21. Tillmann, N., Schulte, W.: Parameterized unit tests. In: ESEC-FSE 2005, pp. 253–262. ACM, New York (2005)
22. Visser, W., Pasareanu, C., Khurshid, S.: Test Input Generation with Java PathFinder. In: ISSTA 2004, Boston (July 2004)
23. Xie, Y., Aiken, A.: Scalable Error Detection Using Boolean Satisfiability. In: Proceedings of POPL 2005 (2005)

Peephole Partial Order Reduction

Chao Wang[1], Zijiang Yang[2], Vineet Kahlon[1], and Aarti Gupta[1]

[1] NEC Laboratories America, Princeton, NJ
{chaowang,kahlon,agupta}@nec-labs.com
[2] Western Michigan University, Kalamazoo, MI
zijiang.yang@wmich.edu

Abstract. We present a symbolic dynamic partial order reduction (POR) method for model checking concurrent software. We introduce the notion of guarded independent transitions, i.e., transitions that can be considered as independent in certain (but not necessarily all) execution paths. These can be exploited by using a new peephole reduction method. A symbolic formulation of the proposed peephole reduction adds concise constraints to allow automatic pruning of redundant interleavings in an SMT/SAT solver based search. Our new method does not directly correspond to any explicit-state algorithm in the literature, e.g., those based on persistent sets. For two threads, our symbolic method guarantees the removal of all redundant interleavings (better than the smallest persistent-set based methods). To our knowledge, this type of reduction has not been achieved by other symbolic methods.

1 Introduction

Verifying concurrent programs is hard due to the large number of interleavings of transitions from different threads. In explicit-state model checking, partial order reduction (POR) techniques [7, 17, 20] have been be used to exploit the equivalence of interleavings of independent transitions to reduce the search state space. Since computing the precise dependence relation may be as hard as verification itself, existing POR methods often use a conservative static analysis to compute an approximation. Dynamic partial order reduction [6] and Cartesian partial order reduction [11] lift the need of applying static analysis *a priori* by detecting collision (data dependency) on-the-fly. These methods in general can achieve more reduction due to the more accurate collision detection. However, applying these POR methods (which were designed for explicit-state algorithms) to symbolic model checking is not an easy task.

A major strength of SAT-based symbolic methods [2] is that *property dependent* and *data dependent* search space reduction is automatically exploited inside modern SAT or SMT (Satisfiability Modulo Theory) solvers, through the addition of conflict clauses and non-chronological backtracking. Symbolic methods are often more efficient in reasoning about variables with large domains. However, combining classic POR methods (e.g., those based on persistent-sets [8]) with symbolic algorithms has proven to be difficult [1, 15, 10, 3, 13]. The difficulty arises from the fact that symbolic methods typically manipulate a large *set of states* implicitly as opposed to manipulating states individually. Capturing and exploiting transitions that are dynamically independent with respect to a *set of states* is much harder than it is for individual states.

C.R. Ramakrishnan and J. Rehof (Eds.): TACAS 2008, LNCS 4963, pp. 382–396, 2008.

```
┌──────────────────┐   ┌──────────────────┐
│ T₁               │   │ T₂               │
│                  │   │                  │
│    i = foo() ;   │   │    j = bar() ;   │
│                  │   │                  │
│    ...           │   │    ...           │
│ A   a[i] = 10 ;  │   │ α   a[j] = 50 ;  │
│ B   a[i] = a[i]+20;│  │ β   a[j] = a[j]+100;│
│ C   *p = a[j] ;  │   │ γ   *q = a[i] ;  │
│                  │   │                  │
└──────────────────┘   └──────────────────┘
```

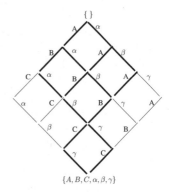

Fig. 1. t_A, t_B are independent with t_α, t_β when $i \neq j$; t_C is independent with t_γ when $(p \neq q)$.

Fig. 2. The lattice of interleavings

For example, in Fig. 1 there are two concurrent threads accessing a global array $a[\ ]$. The two pointers p and q may be aliased. Statically, transitions t_A, t_B in thread T_1 are dependent with t_α, t_β in T_2. Therefore, POR methods relying on a static analysis may be ineffective. Note that when $i \neq j$ holds in some executions, t_A, t_B and t_α, t_β become independent, meaning that the two sequences $t_A; t_B; t_\alpha; t_\beta; t_C; t_\gamma$; and $t_\alpha; t_\beta; t_A; t_B; t_C; t_\gamma$; are equivalent. However, none of the existing symbolic partial order reduction methods [1, 15, 10, 3, 13] takes advantage of such information[1]. Among explicit-state POR methods, dynamic partial order reduction [6] and Cartesian partial order reduction [11] are able to achieve some reduction by detecting conflicts on-the-fly; in any individual state s, the values of i and j (as well as p and q) are fully determined, making it much easier to detect conflicts. However, it is not clear how to directly apply these techniques to symbolic model checking, where conflict detection is performed with respect to a set of states.

Missing out these kind of partial-order reductions can be costly, since the symbolic model checker needs to exhaustively search among the reduced set of execution sequences. The number of valid interleavings (sequences) can be large even for moderate sized programs. For the running example, we can capture all possible interleavings using a lattice structure (Fig. 2). Let $Q = \{t_A, t_B, t_C, t_\alpha, t_\beta, t_\gamma\}$ be the set of transitions from both threads. Each vertex in the figure represents a distinct subset of Q, consisting of the executed transitions up to that point. The top vertex is $\{\ \}$ and the bottom vertex is $\{t_A, t_B, t_C, t_\alpha, t_\beta, t_\gamma\}$. A path from top to bottom denotes a unique interleaving. For example, the left-most path corresponds to $t_A; t_B; t_C; t_\alpha; t_\beta; t_\gamma$. The set of vertices forms a powerset 2^Q.

In this paper, we present a new *peephole partial order reduction* method to exploit the dynamic independence of transitions. To this end, we introduce a new notion of independence relation called *guarded independence relation (GIR)*. It is an extension of

---

[1] The method in [13] can reduce equivalent interleavings if we replace `i=foo()` and `j=bar()` with `i=1` and `j=2`, but not in the general case.

the classic (conditional) independence relation [14, 8]: instead of defining independence with respect to either a single state or for all global states, we define the GIR relation R_G with respect to a predicate over programs variables. Each $\langle t_1, t_2, c_G \rangle \in R_G$ corresponds to a pair of transitions t_1, t_2 that are independent iff c_G holds. A major advantage of GIR is that it can be accurately computed by a simple traversal of the program structure. We further propose a peephole reduction which concisely captures the guarded independent transitions as constraints over a fixed number of adjacent transitions to restrict the satisfiability formula during symbolic search (e.g., in bounded model checking). The added constraints allow the underlying SAT/SMT solver to prune search space automatically. Adding these GIR constraints requires identification of a pattern in a fixed sized time window only.

The basic observation exploited by various POR methods is that different execution sequences may correspond to the same equivalence class. According to Mazurkiewicz's trace theory [16], two sequences are equivalent if they can be obtained from each other by successively permuting adjacent independent transitions. In this sense, our peephole POR method has the same goal as the classic POR methods[7, 17, 20, 6, 11]; however, it does not directly correspond to any existing method. In particular, it is not a symbolic implementation of any of these explicit-state methods. For a system with two threads, our method can guarantee optimality in reduction; that is, all redundant interleavings are removed (proof is in Section 3.2). To our knowledge, there has not been such guarantee among existing POR methods. We also show an example on which our method achieves strictly more reduction than any persistent-set based method. Finally, the proposed encoding scheme is well suited for symbolic search using SAT/SMT solvers.

To summarize, our main contributions are: (1) the notion of guarded independence relation, which accurately captures independence between a pair of transitions in terms of predicates on states; (2) a peephole partial order reduction that adds local constraints based on the guarded independence relation, along with a symbolic formulation; (3) the guarantee of removing all redundant interleavings for systems with two threads. This kind of reduction has not been achieved by previous symbolic methods [1, 15, 10, 3, 13].

2 Guarded Independence Relation

In this section, we review the classic notion [14, 8] of independent transitions, and then present the new notion of guarded independence relation.

Let T_i $(1 \le i \le N)$ be a thread with the set $trans_i$ of transitions. Let $trans = \bigcup_{i=1}^{N} trans_i$ be the set of all transitions. Let V_i be the set of local variables in thread T_i, and V_{global} be the set of global variables. For $t_1 \in trans_i$, we denote the thread index by tid_{t_1}, and denote the enabling condition by en_{t_1}. If t_1 is a transition in T_i from control location loc_1 to loc_2 and is guarded by $cond$, then en_{t_1} is defined as $(pc_i = loc_1) \wedge cond$. Here $pc_i \in V_i$ is a special variable representing the thread program counter. Let S be the set of global states of the system. A state $s \in S$ is a valuation of all local and global variables. For two states $s, s' \in S$, $s \xrightarrow{t_1} s'$ denotes a state transition by applying t_1, and $s \xRightarrow{t_i...t_j} s'$ denotes a sequence of state transitions.

2.1   Independence Relation

Definition 1 (Independence Relation [14, 8]). $R \subseteq trans \times trans$ *is an independence relation iff for each* $\langle t_1, t_2 \rangle \in R$ *the following two properties hold for all* $s \in S$:

1. *if* t_1 *is enabled in s and s* $\xrightarrow{t_1}$ *s', then* t_2 *is enabled in s iff* t_2 *is enabled in s'; and*
2. *if* t_1, t_2 *are enabled in s, there is a unique state s' such that* $s \xRightarrow{t_1 t_2} s'$ *and* $s \xRightarrow{t_2 t_1} s'$.

In other words, independent transitions can neither disable nor enable each other, and enabled independent transitions commute. As pointed out in [7], the definition has been mainly of semantic use since it is not practical to check the above two properties for all states to determine which transitions are independent. Instead, traditionally collision detection often uses conservative but easy-to-check sufficient conditions. For instance, the following properties [7] have been used in practice to compute independent transitions:

1. the set of threads that are active for t_1 is disjoint from the set of threads that are active for t_2, and
2. the set of objects that are accessed by t_1 is disjoint from the set of objects that are accessed by t_2.

Note that some independent transitions may be conservatively classified as dependent, like t_1:$a[i] = e_1$ and t_2:$a[j] = e_2$ when $i \neq j$, since it is not clear statically if $a[i]$ and $a[j]$ refer to the same element. This can in turn lead to a coarser persistent set.

In the *conditional* dependence relation [14, 8], two transitions are defined as independent with respect to a state $s \in S$ (as opposed to for all $s \in S$). This extension is geared towards explicit-state model checking, in which persistent sets are computed for individual states. A persistent set at state s is a subset of the enabled transitions that need to be traversed in adaptive search. A transition is added to the persistent set if it has any conflict with a future operation of another thread. The main difficulty in persistent set computation lies in detecting future collision with enough precision. Although it is not practical to compute the conditional dependence relation for each state in S for collision detection purposes, there are explicit-state methods (e.g., [6, 11]) to exploit such dynamically independent transitions. However, these classic definitions of independence are not well suited for symbolic search.

2.2   Guarded Independence Relation

Definition 2. *Two transitions* t_1, t_2 *are guarded independent with respect to a condition* c_G *iff* c_G *implies that the following properties hold:*

1. *if* t_1 *is enabled in s and s* $\xrightarrow{t_1}$ *s', then* t_2 *is enabled in s iff* t_2 *is enabled in s'; and*
2. *if* t_1, t_2 *are enabled in s, there is a unique state s' such that* $s \xRightarrow{t_1 t_2} s'$ *and* $s \xRightarrow{t_2 t_1} s'$.

This can be considered as an extension of the *conditional* dependence relation; instead of defining $\langle t_1, t_2, s \rangle$ with respect to a state $s \in S$, we define $\langle t_1, t_2, c_G \rangle$ with respect to a predicate over local and global program variables. The independence relation is valid for all states in which c_G holds, i.e., it is valid with respect to a (potentially large) set of states. Unlike the previous definitions, when computing GIR, we are able to apply the two properties in Definition 2 precisely.

The guard c_G can be efficiently computed by a traversal of the structure of the program. For a transition t, we use $V_{RD}(t)$ to denote the set of variables read by t, and $V_{WR}(t)$ to denote the set of variables written by t. We define the *potential conflict set* between t_1 and t_2 from different threads to be

$$\mathcal{C}_{t_1,t_2} = V_{RD}(t_1) \cap V_{WR}(t_2) \cup V_{RD}(t_2) \cap V_{WR}(t_1) \cup V_{WR}(t_1) \cap V_{WR}(t_2) .$$

In our running example, $\mathcal{C}_{t_A,t_\alpha} = \{a[i], a[j]\}$. For a C-like program, we list the different scenarios under which we compute the guarded independence relation R_G:

1. when $\mathcal{C}_{t_1,t_2} = \emptyset$, add $\langle t_1, t_2, true \rangle$ to R_G;
2. when $\mathcal{C}_{t_1,t_2} = \{a[i], a[j]\}$, add $\langle t_1, t_2, i \neq j \rangle$ to R_G;
3. when $\mathcal{C}_{t_1,t_2} = \{*p_i, *p_j\}$, add $\langle t_1, t_2, p_i \neq p_j \rangle$ to R_G;
4. when $\mathcal{C}_{t_1,t_2} = \{x\}$, consider the following cases:

   a. **RD-WR:** if $x \in V_{RD}(t_1)$ and the assignment $x := e$ appears in t_2, add $\langle t_1, t_2, x = e \rangle$ to R_G;
   b. **WR-WR:** if $x := e_1$ appears in t_1 and $x := e_2$ appears in t_2, add $\langle t_1, t_2, e_1 = e_2 \rangle$ to R_G;
   c. **WR-C:** if x appears in the condition *cond* of a branching statement t_1, such as if(cond), and $x := e$ appears in t_2, add $\langle t_1, t_2, cond = cond[x \rightarrow e] \rangle$ to R_G, in which $cond[x \rightarrow e]$ denotes the replacement of x with e.

Overall the computational complexity is $O(|trans|^2)$, where $|trans|$ is the number of transitions. If desired, the set of rules can be easily extended to handle a richer set of language constructs.

Rules 1,2, and 3 correspond to standard semantics of a program. Pattern 4(a) states that two read/write operations to the same variable are guarded independent if the write operation does not change its value. Pattern 4(b) states that two write operations to the same variable are guarded independent if their newly assigned values are the same. In these two cases, c_G may evaluate to true more frequently than one may think, especially when these variables have small ranges and when they are used for branching purposes. If b is a Boolean variable, then $b := e_1$ and $b := e_2$ independent in two of the four possible cases. Pattern 4(c) is a special case of 4(a): clearly $x = e$ implies $cond = cond[x \rightarrow e]$; however, there are cases when $x \neq e$ but $cond = cond[x \rightarrow e]$. For example, let if$(x < 10)$ be a transition in thread 1 and $x := e$ be in thread 2. They are guarded independent if $(x < 10) = (e < 10)$, even if x changes after the assignment. Multiple patterns can appear in the same pair of transitions. In such cases, c_G is a conjunction or disjunction of individual conditions. For example, consider t_1:if(a[i]>5) and t_2:a[j]:=x. Here c_G is defined as $i \neq j \vee ((a[i] > 5) = (x > 5))$.

In symbolic search based on SMT/SAT solvers, the guarded independence relation can be compactly encoded as symbolic constraints in the problem formulation, as described in the next section. These constraints facilitate automatic pruning of the search space.

3   Peephole Partial Order Reduction

After reviewing the basics of SMT/SAT based bounded model checking in Section 3.1, we will present our new partial order reduction method in Section 3.2.

3.1   Bounded Model Checking (BMC)

Given a multi-threaded program and a reachability property, BMC can check the property on all execution paths of the program up to a fixed depth K. For each step $0 \leq k \leq K$, BMC builds a formula Ψ such that Ψ is satisfiable iff there exists a length-k execution that violates the property. The formula is denoted $\Psi = \Phi \wedge \Phi_{prop}$, where Φ represents all possible executions of the program up to k steps and Φ_{prop} is the constraint indicating violation of the property. (For more information about Φ_{prop}, refer to [2].) In the following, we focus on the formulation of Φ.

Let $V = V_{global} \cup \bigcup V_i$, where V_{global} are global variables and V_i are local variables in T_i. For every local (global) program variable, we add a state variable to V_i (V_{global}). Array and pointer accesses need special handling. For an array access $a[i]$, we add separate variables for the index i and for the content $a[i]$. Similarly, for a pointer access $*p$, we assign separate state variables for $(*p)$ and p. We add a pc_i variable for each thread T_i to represent its current program counter. To model nondeterminism in the scheduler, we add a variable sel whose domain is the set of thread indices $\{1, 2, \ldots, N\}$. A transition in T_i is executed only when $sel = i$.

At every time frame we add fresh copies of the set of state variables. Let $v^i \in V^i$ denote the copy of $v \in V$ at the i-th time frame. To represent all possible length-k interleavings, we first encode the transition relations of individual threads and the scheduler, and unfold the composed system exactly k time frames.

$$\Phi := I(V^0) \wedge \bigwedge_{i=0}^{k} \left(SCH(V^i) \wedge \bigwedge_{j=1}^{N} TR_j(V^i, V^{i+1}) \right)$$

where $I(V^0)$ represents the set of initial states, SCH represents the constraint on the scheduler, and TR_j represents the transition of thread T_j. Without any partial order reduction, $SCH(V^i) := true$, which means that sel takes arbitrary values at every step. This default SCH considers all possible interleavings. Partial order reduction can be implemented by adding constraints to SCH to remove redundant interleavings.

We now consider the formulation of TR_j. Let $VS_j = V_{global} \cup V_j$ denote the set of variables visible to T_j. At the i-th time frame, for each $t \in trans_j$ (a transition between control locations loc_1 and loc_2), we create tr_t^i. If t is an assignment $v := e$, then $tr_t^i :=$

$$pc_j^i = loc_1 \wedge pc_j^{i+1} = loc_2 \wedge v^{i+1} = e^i \wedge (VS_j^{i+1} \setminus v^{i+1}) = (VS_j^i \setminus v^i) .$$

If t is a branching statement[2] $assume(c)$, as in `if(c)`, then $tr_t^i :=$

$$pc_j^i = loc_1 \wedge pc_j^{i+1} = loc_2 \wedge c^i \wedge VS_j^{i+1} = VS_j^i.$$

---

[2] We assume that there is a preprocessing phase in which the program is simplified to have only assignments and branching statements, as in tools like FSoft [12].

Overall, TR_j^i is defined as follows:

$$TR_j^i := \left(sel^i = j \wedge \bigvee_{t \in trans_j} tr_t^i \right) \vee \left(sel^i \neq j \wedge V_j^{i+1} = V_j^i \right)$$

The second term says that if T_j is not selected, variables in V_j do not change values.

3.2 Peephole Partial Order Reduction

SCH initially consists of all possible interleavings of threads. If multiple length-k sequences are in the same equivalence class, only one representative needs to be checked for property violation. To facilitate such reduction, we add constraints for each pair of guarded independent transitions to restrict the scheduler.

For each $\langle t_1, t_2, c_G \rangle \in R_G$ such that $tid_{t_1} < tid_{t_2}$, we conjoin the following constraint to SCH,

$$en_{t_1}(V^k) \wedge en_{t_2}(V^k) \wedge c_G(V^k) \rightarrow \neg(sel^k = tid_{t_2} \wedge sel^{k+1} = tid_{t_1})$$

Here, $en_{t_1}(V^k)$ and $en_{t_2}(V^k)$ are the enabling conditions for t_1 and t_2 at the k-th time frame. The above constraint says that, if independent transitions t_1 and t_2 are enabled, sequences starting with both $t_1; \ldots$ and $t_2; \ldots$ are allowed to be explored. However, among the sequences starting with $t_2; \ldots$, we forbid $t_2; t_1; \ldots$ through the addition of constraint $\neg(sel^k = tid_{t_2} \wedge sel^{k+1} = tid_{t_1})$. In essence, the above constraint enforces a fixed order on the priority of scheduling two independent transitions t_1, t_2. We always prefer sequences in which two *adjacent* independent transitions t_1, t_2 are scheduled in their thread index order, i.e., t_1 ahead of t_2 if $tid_{t_1} < tid_{t_2}$. The alternative sequences are removed, as illustrated in Fig. 3.

In the running example, the new $SCH(V^k)$ is

$$\begin{pmatrix} pc_1^k = A \wedge pc_2^k = \alpha \wedge (i^k \neq j^k) \end{pmatrix} \rightarrow \neg(sel^k = 2 \wedge sel^{k+1} = 1)) \wedge$$
$$\begin{pmatrix} pc_1^k = A \wedge pc_2^k = \beta \wedge (i^k \neq j^k) \end{pmatrix} \rightarrow \neg(sel^k = 2 \wedge sel^{k+1} = 1)) \wedge$$
$$\begin{pmatrix} pc_1^k = B \wedge pc_2^k = \alpha \wedge (i^k \neq j^k) \end{pmatrix} \rightarrow \neg(sel^k = 2 \wedge sel^{k+1} = 1)) \wedge$$
$$\begin{pmatrix} pc_1^k = B \wedge pc_2^k = \beta \wedge (i^k \neq j^k) \end{pmatrix} \rightarrow \neg(sel^k = 2 \wedge sel^{k+1} = 1)) \wedge$$
$$\begin{pmatrix} pc_1^k = C \wedge pc_2^k = \gamma \wedge (i^k \neq j^k \wedge p^k \neq q^k) \end{pmatrix} \rightarrow \neg(sel^k = 2 \wedge sel^{k+1} = 1))$$

When $i \neq j$, the above constraint removes sequences containing $t_\alpha; t_A; \ldots$.

Theorem 1. *All interleavings removed by the peephole reduction are redundant.*

Proof. Let $\pi = \pi_0 \pi_1 \ldots$ be a valid sequence that is forbidden by the peephole reduction. Then there exists at least one index k in π such that c_G holds, π_k and π_{k+1} are independent. By swapping the two adjacent independent transitions, we produce another sequence π' such that $\pi_k' = \pi_{k+1}$, $\pi_{k+1}' = \pi_k$, and $\pi_i' = \pi_i$ for all $i \neq k$ and $i \neq k+1$. π' is (Mazurkiewicz) equivalent to π. (1) If π' is not forbidden by the peephole reduction, π is redundant and we have a proof. (2) If π' is also forbidden, then there exists an index k in π' such that π_k', π_{k+1}' are guarded independent—because otherwise π' cannot be removed by the peephole reduction. Due to the finiteness of the sequence, if we continue the *find-and-swap* process, eventually we will find a sequence π'' that is not forbidden by the peephole reduction. In this case π is redundant (equivalent to π'') and we complete the proof.   □

Theorem 2. *For two threads, the peephole reduction removes all the redundant interleavings.*

Proof. We prove by contradiction. Assume π, π' are two remaining sequences and they are (Mazurkiewicz) equivalent. By definition, π and π' have the same set of transitions; π' is a permutation of π. Let π_j in π be the first transition from T_2 that is swapped to be π'_i in π' (where $i < j$). Then π and π' share a common prefix up to i (Fig. 4). Furthermore, all transitions $\pi_i, \ldots, \pi_{j-1}$ in π belong to T_1. This is because if any of them belongs to T_2, it would not be possible to move π_j ahead of π' – the order of transitions from the same thread cannot be changed. Therefore, there are only two cases regarding π_{j-1} from T_1 and π_j from T_2: (1) if they are dependent, swapping them produces a non-equivalent sequences; (2) if they are independent, the fact that π_j appears after π_{j-1} in π means that $tid_{\pi_j} > tid_{\pi_{j-1}}$. This implies that $tid_{\pi_j} > tid_{\pi_i}$, and π' would have been removed. Since both cases contradict the assumption, the assumption is not correct.   □

For more than two threads, the proposed peephole reduction does not always guarantee the removal of all redundant interleavings. For example, let transitions t_A, t_α, t_x belong to threads T_1, T_2, T_3, respectively. Assume that t_A and t_x are dependent, but t_α is guarded independent with both t_A and t_x. When the guard is true, the following two interleavings are equivalent,

$$t_x; t_A; t_\alpha; \ldots$$
$$t_\alpha; t_x; t_A; \ldots$$

Both sequences conform to the GIR constraints, since the segment $(t_A; t_\alpha;)$ conforms to $tid_{t_A} < tid_{t_\alpha}$ and the segment $(t_\alpha; t_x;)$ conforms to $tid_{t_\alpha} < tid_{t_x}$. The three transitions can be grouped into two independent sets: $\{t_A, t_x\}$ and $\{t_\alpha\}$. The non-optimality arises from the fact that there is not an order of the two sets in which the pairwise independent

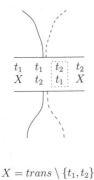

$X = trans \setminus \{t_1, t_2\}$

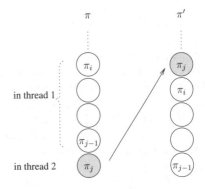

in thread 1

in thread 2

Fig. 3. We remove only redundant interleavings

Fig. 4. For two threads, we remove all redundant interleavings

transitions are ordered in a way consistent with the ordered thread indices[3] . If we arrange the threads in a different order, t_A, t_x, t_α are in T_1, T_2, T_3, then the sequence $t_\alpha; \underline{t_x; t_A};\ldots$ would be removed by our reduction. Extending the peephole reduction to guarantee the removal of all redundant interleavings in the more general cases may be possible. However, any such extension is likely to be more expensive than the peephole reduction proposed here. In practice, there is a tradeoff between the encoding overhead and the amount of achievable reduction.

3.3 Comparison with Persistent-Set Based Methods

The peephole reduction add only local constraints, i.e., constraints over a fixed number of adjacent time steps. The reduction relies on whether two transitions t_1, t_2 are *locally* (guarded) independent, for which the precise information is available (Section 2.2). This is in contrast to persistent set based methods relying on detecting *future* conflicts (for which precise information in general is expensive to compute). Persistent set based methods were designed to be used in adaptive search during explicit-state model checking. Depending on the order in which transitions are picked during persistent set computation, there can be more than one persistent set. Some persistent sets achieve more reduction than others. In practice, computing the smallest persistent set at each step of the adaptive search can be costly. The following example shows that even if the smallest persistent sets were available at each step of the adaptive search (in a hypothetical algorithm), there would still be redundant interleavings.

Fig. 5 is derived from the running example by assuming $i = 1$, $j = 2$, and $p \neq q$. Since t_A has a collision with a future transition of thread T_2 (transition t_γ), and similarly t_α has a collision with t_C, the smallest persistent set at the starting point is $PS(s) = \{t_A, t_\alpha\}$. This allows both $t_A;\ldots$ and $t_\alpha;\ldots$ to be explored. In the reduced lattice in Fig. 5, there are many redundant sequences (paths over solid thick lines). In fact, the only reduction is achieved by the persistent set $PS(s') = \{C\}$, which is a strict subset of the enabled set $\{C, \gamma\}$.

In our peephole POR method, since t_A and t_α are independent and $tid_{t_A} < tid_{t_\alpha}$, we remove the sequences starting with $\underline{t_\alpha; t_A};\ldots$ but allow the sequences starting with $t_\alpha; t_\beta;\ldots$. As shown by the reduced lattice in Fig. 6, the following adjacent transitions are forbidden: (t_α, t_A), $(t_\beta; t_A)$, $(t_\alpha; t_B)$, $(t_\beta; t_B)$, and $(t_\gamma; t_C)$. The forbidden combinations of adjacent independent transitions are depicted by dotted arrows. The last dotted arrow in Fig. 6 deserves more explanation: our method forbids t_C only when t_γ is the previous transition, but allows t_C to execute if the previous transition is t_B (both t_C and t_B are from T_1). Note that there is no redundant interleaving.

This example suggests that the benefit of *peephole reduction* is separate from the benefit of accurate *guarded independence relation*. In this example, both the persistent set method and the peephole reduction can use the most precise independence relation, yet our method can forbid more interleavings. Therefore, the advantages of our approach in general come from two distinct sources: the peephole reduction and the accurate guarded independence relation.

---

[3] There are eight distinct scenarios of the pairwise dependency of $\langle t_A, t_\alpha, t_x \rangle$, each of which corresponds to six interleavings. The proposed reduction removes all the redundant sequences except one.

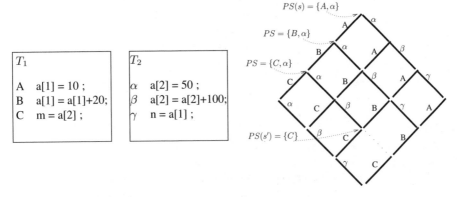

T_1

A   a[1] = 10 ;
B   a[1] = a[1]+20;
C   m = a[2] ;

T_2

α a[2] = 50 ;
β a[2] = a[2]+100;
γ n = a[1] ;

Fig. 5. Smallest persistent-sets do not remove all redundant interleavings

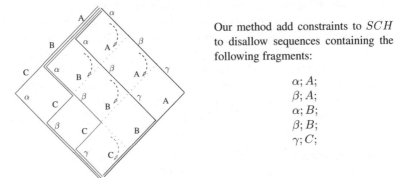

Our method add constraints to SCH to disallow sequences containing the following fragments:

$\alpha; A;$
$\beta; A;$
$\alpha; B;$
$\beta; B;$
$\gamma; C;$

Fig. 6. Our method removes all the redundant interleavings

Persistent set computation looks only into *current* and *future* transitions of other threads. The methods based on sleep set [9] also consider *past* transitions when computing reduction. Our peephole POR method differs from sleep sets in two aspects: First, the peephole reduction guarantees the optimality for two threads. Second, the encoding in peephole reduction is *memoryless* in that there is no need to store information about past transitions (and to carry the information around) explicitly.

4   Reducing the Overhead of GIR Constraints

For the symbolic formulation outlined in the previous section, the number of GIR constraints added is linear in the number of guarded independent transition pairs (which can be quadratic in the number of transitions). These constraints need to be added at each time frame, which may pose a significant overhead for the SMT/SAT solver. On the other hand, missing out these reductions can be costly, since the model checker needs to explore all allowed execution sequences, which can be many. In practice, there is a tradeoff between the encoding overhead and the amount of achievable reduction. Having said that, there are techniques to reduce the encoding overhead in practical settings.

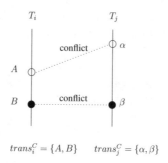

$$trans_i^C = \{A, B\} \qquad trans_j^C = \{\alpha, \beta\}$$

Fig. 7. Using dependent transitions to simplify encoding

First, if a cheap static analysis can be used to figure out statically independent transitions, based on which high quality persistent sets can be computed, then it should be used before proceeding to the more advanced reduction. In principle, one can reserve peephole reduction to transitions that are not statically independent (or those that cannot be easily identified statically). Furthermore, when programs have clearly specified synchronization disciplines, e.g., all shared variables are protected by locks, transaction based methods [18, 19, 5] can be used to reduce the search space. These methods are orthogonal to our peephole reduction, and in principle transactions can be exploited along with our proposed reduction techniques. In addition to these conventional techniques, we present the following simplifications.

Merging GIR Constraints. If transition $t_1 \in trans_i$ is guarded independent with respect to all transitions $t_2 \in trans_j$, we do not need to add constraints separately for all $\langle t_1, t_2 \rangle$ pairs. Instead, we merge all these GIR constraints as

$$en_{t_1}(V^k) \wedge c_G(V^k) \rightarrow \neg(sel^k = j \wedge sel^{k+1} = i) \ .$$

As a simple case, this simplification can be applied when t_1 is a local transition (independent with all other threads). In this case, the effect captured is similar to that obtained from detecting transactions. However, the above rule is not restricted only to such simple cases. As a more general case, consider N dining philosophers in which all transitions in one philosopher (thread) are visible to two adjacent philosophers (threads). There is no local transition *per se*. However, for any two non-adjacent philosophers, a transition t_1 in the i-th philosopher is always independent with all transitions in the j-th philosopher. Therefore the above simplification can be applied.

Encoding Dependent Transitions. For loosely coupled threads, the number of independent transition pairs are significantly larger than the number of *dependent transition pairs* (conflicts). In such cases, we can use an alternative encoding scheme. Instead of adding a constraint for every independent transition pair, we focus on dependent transition pairs. For threads T_i and T_j ($i < j$), we use $trans_i^C \subseteq trans_i$ and $trans_j^C \subseteq trans_j$ to denote the subsets of transitions that *may be guarded dependent*[4] with the other thread. By definition, $\forall t_1 \in (trans_i \setminus trans_i^C)$ and $\forall t_2 \in (trans_j \setminus trans_j^C)$,

---

[4] In $\langle t_1, t_2, c_G \rangle$, if c_G is not constant true, then t_1 and t_2 *may be dependent*.

t_1 and t_2 are always independent. This is illustrated in Fig. 7. To encode the GIR constraints, first, we define $enable_{T_i}$ for thread T_i as follows,

$$enable_{T_i} := \bigvee_{t \in (trans_i \setminus trans_i^C)} en_t \ .$$

Then, we summarize constraints for the *always independent* transition pairs.

$$enable_{T_i}(V^k) \wedge enable_{T_j}(V^k) \rightarrow \neg(sel^k = j \wedge sel^{k+1} = i) \ .$$

Finally, some transitions in $trans_i^C$ and $trans_j^C$ may still be independent from each other. For each $t_1 \in trans_i^C$ and $t_2 \in trans_j^C$, if $\langle t_1, t_2, c_G \rangle \in R_G$, we add the GIR constraint as in Section 3.2. As an example, if two threads are completely independent, only one constraint needs to be added to SCH.

5   Experiments

We have implemented the new methods in an SMT-based bounded model checker using the Yices SMT solver [4]. Yices is capable of deciding satisfiability formulae with a combination of theories including propositional logic, integer linear arithmetic, and arrays. We performed experiments with three variants of the peephole reduction, and a baseline BMC algorithm with no POR. The three variants represent different tradeoffs between the encoding overhead and the amount of achievable reduction. The first one is *static POR*, in which constraints are added only for statically independent transitions. The second one is *simple PPOR*, which adds constraints also for guarded independent transitions covered by GIR cases 1-3 (in Section 2.2). The third one is *full PPOR*, which adds constraints for all guarded independent transitions covered by GIR cases 1-4. Our experiments were conducted on a workstation with 2.8 GHz Xeon processor and 4GB memory running Red Hat Linux 7.2.

Parameterized Examples. The first set of examples are parameterized versions of *dining philosopher* and *indexer*. For dining philosopher, we used a version that guarantees the absence of deadlocks. Each philosopher (thread) has its own local state variables, and threads communicate through a shared array of chop-sticks. When accessing the global array, threads may have conflicts (data dependency). The first property (pa) we checked is whether all philosophers can eat simultaneously (the answer is no). The second property (pb) is whether it is possible to reach a state in which all philosophers have eaten at least once (the answer is yes). For the *indexer* example, we used the version from [6]. In this example, concurrent threads manipulate a shared hash table. Each thread needs to write four distinct values into the hash table. An atomic compare-and-swap instruction is used to check if a hash entry is available; if so, it writes the value; otherwise, the thread changes the hash key before retry. The property we checked is whether it is possible to reach a state in which all threads have completed. This example is interesting because there is no collision in accessing the hash table with up to 11 threads. However, such information cannot be detected by a static analysis.

For dining philosopher, with 2 threads we set the unrolling depths to 15,30,...,120, and compared the runtime of the four methods as well as the number of backtracks of

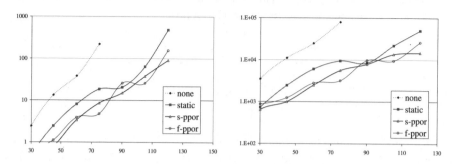

Fig. 8. Comparing runtime (left) and the number of backtracks in the SMT solver (right); performed on two philosophers with the property *pa*

Table 1. Comparing the performance of four symbolic partial order reduction techniques

Test Program			Total CPU Time (s)				#Conflicts (k)				#Decisions (k)			
name	steps	sat	none	static	s-ppor	f-ppor	none	static	s-ppor	f-ppor	none	static	s-ppor	f-ppor
phil2-pa	15	no	0.3	0.1	0.1	0.1	0.5	0.1	0.1	0.9	1.1	0.6	0.6	0.4
phil3-pa	22	no	27	6	1.2	0.7	17	5	2	1	23	8	4	1
phil4-pa	29	no	69	50	26	28	39	28	13	13	54	41	21	20
phil2-pb	15	yes	0.1	0.1	0.1	0.1	0.1	0.1	0.1	0.1	0.5	0.6	0.4	0.3
phil3-pb	22	yes	1.7	0.8	0.4	1.4	2	1.1	0.4	1.0	3	2	1	3
phil4-pb	29	yes	19	17	1.5	2.9	12	9	1	2	17	15	4	5
indexer2	10	no	0.3	0.2	0.1	0.1	0.3	0.3	0.1	0.1	1	1	1	1
indexer3	15	no	31	23	0.4	0.3	14	14	0.4	0.3	183	183	1	1
indexer4	20	no	T/O	1791	1.2	1.7	-	344	1	1	-	395	2	2
indexer5	25	no	T/O	T/O	5.1	6.6	-	-	2	2	-	-	6	6
indexer2	11	yes	3	2	0.4	0.7	1.5	1.5	0.3	0.6	54	54	15	33
indexer3	16	yes	22	17	4	3	5	5	1	1	163	163	77	127
indexer4	21	yes	179	177	12	6	283	283	3	2	432	432	181	139
indexer5	26	yes	T/O	T/O	38	35	-	-	4	4	-	-	579	427

the SMT solver. The results are given in Fig. 8. The x-axis is the unrolling depths. The y-axis are the BMC runtime in seconds (left figure), and the number of backtracks (right figure). The y-axis is in logarithmic scale. The number of decisions of the SMT solver looks similar to the runtime curves; we omit it for brevity. These results show that both *simple PPOR* and *full PPOR* have shown significant performance improvement over *static*. Due to its larger encoding overhead, the runtime of *full PPOR* is less consistent and is sometimes inferior to *simple PPOR*.

We also set the number of threads to 2, 3, 4 for both dining philosopher and indexer examples and compared the four methods. In these experiments the BMC unrolling depths are chosen to be large enough (larger than the estimated reachable diameters [2]), so that the verification results are conclusive. The detailed results are given in Table 1. In Table 1, Columns 1-3 show the name of the examples, the number of BMC unrolling steps, and whether the property is true or not. Columns 4-7 report the runtime of the four methods. Columns 8-11 and Columns 12-15 report the number of backtracks and the number of decisions of the SMT solver.

The Daisy Example. The second set of examples come from a much larger concurrent program called Daisy. Daisy has been used before as a benchmark for verifying concurrent programs. The version we used is written in C and has been verified previously in [13]. The parsing and encoding of these examples were performed automatically. Note that in [13] there already exists a state-of-the-art symbolic POR method based on persistent sets, advanced static analysis techniques, and the exploitation of nested locks. Our peephole POR method was implemented on top of these techniques. The two properties we checked are data race conditions (both are reachable).

For comparison purposes, we implemented the peephole reduction on the same SAT-based BMC procedure as in [13]. Compared with the previous method, our peephole POR method can significantly reduce the BMC runtime in detecting these data races. In particular, for the first property, the new method was able to find a counterexample of length 132 and reduced the BMC runtime from 519 seconds to 374 seconds. For the second property, the new method was able to find a counterexample of length 136 and reduced the BMC runtime from 1540 seconds to 998 seconds.

6   Conclusions

We have presented a peephole partial order reduction method for model checking concurrent systems, based on a new notion of guarded independence relation between transitions. We have presented a concise symbolic encoding of local dynamically independent transition pairs which is well suited for using SMT/SAT solvers to find property violations. We have shown that the new peephole POR method can achieve significantly more reduction compared to other existing methods. For a system with two concurrent threads, our method guarantees the removal of all redundant interleavings. For future work, we plan to investigate additional techniques for simplifying the GIR constraints.

References

[1] Alur, R., Brayton, R.K., Henzinger, T.A., Qadeer, S., Rajamani, S.K.: Partial-order reduction in symbolic state-space exploration. Formal Methods in System Design 18(2), 97–116 (2001)

[2] Biere, A., Cimatti, A., Clarke, E., Zhu, Y.: Symbolic model checking without BDDs. In: Cleaveland, W.R. (ed.) TACAS 1999. LNCS, vol. 1579, Springer, Heidelberg (1999)

[3] Cook, B., Kroening, D., Sharygina, N.: Symbolic model checking for asynchronous boolean programs. In: Godefroid, P. (ed.) SPIN 2005. LNCS, vol. 3639, pp. 75–90. Springer, Heidelberg (2005)

[4] Dutertre, B., de Moura, L.: A fast linear-arithmetic solver for dpll(t). In: Ball, T., Jones, R.B. (eds.) CAV 2006. LNCS, vol. 4144, pp. 81–94. Springer, Heidelberg (2006)

[5] Dwyer, M.B., Hatcliff, J., Robby, Ranganath., V.P.: Exploiting object escape and locking information in partial-order reductions for concurrent object-oriented programs. Formal Methods in System Design 25(2-3), 199–240 (2004)

[6] Flanagan, C., Godefroid, P.: Dynamic partial-order reduction for model checking software. In: Principles of programming languages (POPL 2005), pp. 110–121 (2005)

[7] Godefroid, P.: Partial-Order Methods for the Verification of Concurrent Systems. LNCS, vol. 1032. Springer, Heidelberg (1996)

[8] Godefroid, P., Pirottin, D.: Refining dependencies improves partial-order verification methods. In: Courcoubetis, C. (ed.) CAV 1993. LNCS, vol. 697, pp. 438–449. Springer, Heidelberg (1993)

[9] Godefroid, P., Wolper, P.: Using partial orders for the efficient verification of deadlock freedom and safety properties. Formal Methods in System Design 2(2), 149–164 (1993)

[10] Grumberg, O., Lerda, F., Strichman, O., Theobald, M.: Proof-guided underapproximation-widening for multi-process systems. In: Principles of programming languages (POPL 2005), pp. 122–131 (2005)

[11] Gueta, G., Flanagan, C., Yahav, E., Sagiv, M.: Cartesian partial-order reduction. In: Bošnački, D., Edelkamp, S. (eds.) SPIN 2007. LNCS, vol. 4595, pp. 95–112. Springer, Heidelberg (2007)

[12] Ivančić, F., Shlyakhter, I., Gupta, A., Ganai, M.K., Kahlon, V., Wang, C., Yang, Z.: Model checking C program using F-Soft. In: International Conference on Computer Design, October 2005, pp. 297–308 (2005)

[13] Kahlon, V., Gupta, A., Sinha, N.: Symbolic model checking of concurrent programs using partial orders and on-the-fly transactions. In: Ball, T., Jones, R.B. (eds.) CAV 2006. LNCS, vol. 4144, pp. 286–299. Springer, Heidelberg (2006)

[14] Katz, S., Peled, D.: Defining conditional independence using collapses. Theor. Comput. Sci. 101(2), 337–359 (1992)

[15] Lerda, F., Sinha, N., Theobald, M.: Symbolic model checking of software. Electr. Notes Theor. Comput. Sci. 89(3) (2003)

[16] Mazurkiewicz, A.W.: Trace theory. In: Brauer, W., Reisig, W., Rozenberg, G. (eds.) APN 1986. LNCS, vol. 255, pp. 279–324. Springer, Heidelberg (1987)

[17] Peled, D.: All from one, one for all: on model checking using representatives. In: Courcoubetis, C. (ed.) CAV 1993. LNCS, vol. 697, pp. 409–423. Springer, Heidelberg (1993)

[18] Stoller, S.D.: Model-checking multi-threaded distributed java programs. International Journal on Software Tools for Technology Transfer 4(1), 71–91 (2002)

[19] Stoller, S.D., Cohen, E.: Optimistic synchronization-based state-space reduction. In: Garavel, H., Hatcliff, J. (eds.) TACAS 2003. LNCS, vol. 2619, pp. 489–504. Springer, Heidelberg (2003)

[20] Valmari, A.: Stubborn sets for reduced state space generation. In: Rozenberg, G. (ed.) APN 1990. LNCS, vol. 483, pp. 491–515. Springer, Heidelberg (1991)

Efficient Interpolant Generation
in Satisfiability Modulo Theories*

Alessandro Cimatti[1], Alberto Griggio[2], and Roberto Sebastiani[2]

[1] FBK-IRST, Povo, Trento, Italy
cimatti@fbk.eu
[2] DISI, Università di Trento, Italy
{griggio,rseba}@disi.unitn.it

Abstract. The problem of computing Craig Interpolants for propositional (SAT) formulas has recently received a lot of interest, mainly for its applications in formal verification. However, propositional logic is often not expressive enough for representing many interesting verification problems, which can be more naturally addressed in the framework of Satisfiability Modulo Theories, SMT.

Although some works have addressed the topic of generating interpolants in SMT, the techniques and tools that are currently available have some limitations, and their performace still does not exploit the full power of current state-of-the-art SMT solvers.

In this paper we try to close this gap. We present several techniques for interpolant generation in SMT which overcome the limitations of the current generators mentioned above, and which take full advantage of state-of-the-art SMT technology. These novel techniques can lead to substantial performance improvements wrt. the currently available tools.

We support our claims with an extensive experimental evaluation of our implementation of the proposed techniques in the MathSAT SMT solver.

1 Introduction

Since the seminal paper of McMillan [19], interpolation has been recognized to be a substantial tool for verification in the case of boolean systems [7, 17, 18]. The tremendous improvements of Satisfiability Modulo Theory (SMT) solvers in the recent years have enabled the lifting of SAT-based verification algorithms to the non-boolean case [2, 1], and made it practical the implementation of other approaches such as CEGAR [21].

However, the research on interpolation for SMT has not kept the pace of the SMT solvers. In fact, the current approaches to producing interpolants for SMT [20,30,27,16, 15] all suffer from a number of limitations. Some of the approaches are severely limited in terms of their expressiveness. For instance, the tool described in [27] can only deal with conjunctions of literals, whilst the recent work described in [16] can not deal with many useful theories. Furthermore, very few tools are available [27,20], and these tools do not seem to scale particularly well. More than to naïve implementation, this appears to be due to the underlying algorithms, that substantially deviate from or ignore choices

---

* This work has been partly supported by ORCHID, a project sponsored by Provincia Autonoma di Trento, and by a grant from Intel Corporation.

C.R. Ramakrishnan and J. Rehof (Eds.): TACAS 2008, LNCS 4963, pp. 397–412, 2008.

common in state-of-the-art SMT. For instance, in the domain of linear arithmetic over the rationals ($\mathcal{LA}(\mathbb{Q})$), strict inequalities are encoded in [20] as the conjunction of a weak inequality and a disequality; although sound, this choice destroys the structure of the constraints, requires additional splitting, and ultimately results in a larger search space. Similarly, the fragment of Difference Logic ($\mathcal{DL}(\mathbb{Q})$) is dealt with by means of a general-purpose algorithm for full $\mathcal{LA}(\mathbb{Q})$, rather than one of the well-known and much faster specialized algorithms. An even more fundamental example is the fact that state-of-the-art SMT reasoners use dedicated algorithms for Linear Arithmetic [10].

In this paper, we tackle the problem of generating interpolants within a state of the art SMT solver. We present a fully general approach that can generate interpolants for the most effective algorithms in SMT, most notably the algorithm for deciding $\mathcal{LA}(\mathbb{Q})$ presented in [10] and those for $\mathcal{DL}(\mathbb{Q})$ in [9, 23]. Our approach is also applicable to the combination of theories, based on the Delayed Theory Combination (DTC) method [5, 6], as an alternative to the traditional Nelson-Oppen method.

We carried out an extensive experimental evaluation on a wide range of benchmarks. The proposed techniques substantially advance the state of the art: our interpolator can deal with problems that can not be expressed in other solvers; furthermore, a comparison on problems that can be dealt with by other tools shows dramatic improvements in performance, often by orders of magnitude.

The paper is structured as follows. In §2 we present some background on interpolation in SMT. In §3 and §4 we show how to efficiently interpolate $\mathcal{LA}(\mathbb{Q})$ and the subcase of $\mathcal{DL}(\mathbb{Q})$. In §5 we discuss interpolation for combined theories. In §6 we analyze the experimental evaluation, whilst in §7 we draw some conclusions. For lack of space, we omit the proofs of the theorems. They can be found in the extended technical report [8].

2   Background

2.1   Satisfiability Modulo Theory – SMT

Our setting is standard first order logic. A 0-ary function symbol is called a *constant*. A *term* is a first-order term built out of function symbols and variables. A *linear term* is either a linear combination $c_1x_1 + \ldots + c_nx_n + c$, where c and c_i are numeric constants and x_i are variables. When doing arithmetic on terms, simplifications are performed where needed. We write $t_1 \equiv t_2$ when the two terms t_1 and t_2 are syntactically identical. If $t_1, \ldots, t_n$ are terms and p is a predicate symbol, then $p(t_1, \ldots, t_n)$ is an *atom*. A *literal* is either an atom or its negation. A *(quantifier-free) formula* ϕ is an arbitrary boolean combination of atoms. We use the standard notions of theory, satisfiability, validity, logical consequence. We consider only theories with equality. We call *Satisfiability Modulo (the) Theory* $\mathcal{T}$, SMT($\mathcal{T}$), the problem of deciding the satisfiability of quantifier-free formulas wrt. a background theory $\mathcal{T}$. [1]

We denote formulas with ϕ, ψ, A, B, C, I, variables with x, y, z, and numeric constants with a, b, c, l, u. Given a theory $\mathcal{T}$, we write $\phi \models_\mathcal{T} \psi$ (or simply $\phi \models \psi$) to denote

---

[1] The general definition of SMT deals also with quantified formulas. Nevertheless, in this paper we restrict our interest to quantifier-free formulas.

that the formula ψ is a logical consequence of ϕ in the theory $\mathcal{T}$. With $\phi \preceq \psi$ we denote that all uninterpreted (in $\mathcal{T}$) symbols of ϕ appear in ψ. Without loss of generality, we also assume that the formulas are in Conjunctive Normal Form (CNF). If C is a clause, $C \downarrow B$ is the clause obtained by removing all the literals whose atoms do not occur in B, and $C \setminus B$ that obtained by removing all the literals whose atoms do occur in B. With a little abuse of notation, we might sometimes denote conjunctions of literals $l_1 \wedge \ldots \wedge l_n$ as sets $\{l_1, \ldots, l_n\}$ and vice versa. If $\eta \equiv \{l_1, \ldots, l_n\}$, we might write $\neg\eta$ to mean $\neg l_1 \vee \ldots \vee \neg l_n$.

We call $\mathcal{T}$-solver a procedure that decides the consistency of a conjunction of literals in $\mathcal{T}$. If $S \equiv \{l_1, \ldots, l_n\}$ is a set of literals in $\mathcal{T}$, we call *($\mathcal{T}$)-conflict set* any subset η of S which is inconsistent in $\mathcal{T}$. [2] We call $\neg\eta$ a $\mathcal{T}$-lemma (notice that $\neg\eta$ is a $\mathcal{T}$-valid clause). Given a set of clauses $S \equiv \{C_1, \ldots, C_n\}$ and a clause C, we call a *resolution proof* that $\bigwedge_i C_i \models_\mathcal{T} C$ a DAG $\mathcal{P}$ such that:

1. C is the root of $\mathcal{P}$;
2. the leaves of $\mathcal{P}$ are either elements of S or $\mathcal{T}$-lemmas;
3. each non-leaf node C' has two parents C_{p_1} and C_{p_2} such that $C_{p_1} \equiv p \vee \phi_1$, $C_{p_2} \equiv \neg p \vee \phi_2$, and $C' \equiv \phi_1 \vee \phi_2$. The atom p is called the *pivot* of C_{p_1} and C_{p_2}.

If C is the empty clause (denoted with $\perp$), then $\mathcal{P}$ is a *resolution proof of unsatisfiability* for $\bigwedge_i C_i$.

A standard technique for solving the SMT($\mathcal{T}$) problem is to integrate a DPLL-based SAT solver and a $\mathcal{T}$-solver in a *lazy* manner (see, e.g., [28] for a detailed description). DPLL is used as an enumerator of truth assignments for the propositional abstraction of the input formula. At each step, the set of $\mathcal{T}$-literals S corresponding to the current assignment is sent to the $\mathcal{T}$-solver to be checked for consistency in $\mathcal{T}$. If S is inconsistent, the $\mathcal{T}$-solver returns a conflict set η, and the corresponding $\mathcal{T}$-lemma $\neg\eta$ is added as a blocking clause in DPLL, and used to drive the backjump mechanism. With a small modification of the embedded DPLL engine, a lazy SMT solver can also be used to generate a resolution proof of unsatisfiability.

2.2 Interpolation in SMT

We consider the SMT($\mathcal{T}$) problem for some background theory $\mathcal{T}$. Given an ordered pair (A, B) of formulas such that $A \wedge B \models_\mathcal{T} \perp$, a *Craig interpolant* (simply "interpolant" hereafter) is a formula I s.t.:

a) $A \models_\mathcal{T} I$,
b) $I \wedge B \models_\mathcal{T} \perp$,
c) $I \preceq A$ and $I \preceq B$.

The use of interpolation in formal verification has been introduced by McMillan in [19] for purely-propositional formulas, and it was subsequently extended to handle SMT($\mathcal{EUF} \cup \mathcal{LA}(\mathbb{Q})$) formulas in [20], $\mathcal{EUF}$ being the theory of equality and uninterpreted functions. The technique is based on earlier work by Pudlák [25], where

---

[2] In the next sections, as we are in an SMT($\mathcal{T}$) context, we often omit specifying "in the theory $\mathcal{T}$" when speaking of consistency, validity, etc.

two interpolant-generation algorithms are described: one for computing interpolants for propositional formulas from resolution proofs of unsatisfiability, and one for generating interpolants for conjunctions of (weak) linear inequalities in $\mathcal{LA}(\mathbb{Q})$. An interpolant for (A, B) is constructed from a resolution proof of unsatisfiability of $A \wedge B$, generated as outlined in §2.1. The algorithm can be described as follows:

Algorithm 1. Interpolant generation for SMT$(\mathcal{T})$

1. Generate a proof of unsatisfiability $\mathcal{P}$ for $A \wedge B$.
2. For every $\mathcal{T}$-lemma $\neg\eta$ occurring in $\mathcal{P}$, generate an interpolant $I_{\neg\eta}$ for $(\eta \setminus B, \eta \downarrow B)$.
3. For every input clause C in $\mathcal{P}$, set $I_C \equiv C \downarrow B$ if $C \in A$, and $I_C \equiv \top$ if $C \in B$.
4. For every inner node C of $\mathcal{P}$ obtained by resolution from $C_1 \equiv p \vee \phi_1$ and $C_2 \equiv \neg p \vee \phi_2$, set $I_C \equiv I_{C_1} \vee I_{C_2}$ if p does not occur in B, and $I_C \equiv I_{C_1} \wedge I_{C_2}$ otherwise.
5. Output $I_\perp$ as an interpolant for (A, B).

Notice that Step 2. of the algorithm is the only part which depends on the theory $\mathcal{T}$, so that the problem of interpolant generation in SMT$(\mathcal{T})$ reduces to that of finding interpolants for $\mathcal{T}$-lemmas. To this extent, in [20] McMillan gives a set of rules for constructing interpolants for $\mathcal{T}$-lemmas in the theory of $\mathcal{EUF}$, that of weak linear inequalities $(0 \leq t)$ in $\mathcal{LA}(\mathbb{Q})$, and their combination. Linear equalities $(0 = t)$ can be reduced to conjunctions $(0 \leq t) \wedge (0 \leq -t)$ of inequalities. Thanks to the combination of theories, also strict linear inequalities $(0 < t)$ can be handled in $\mathcal{EUF} \cup \mathcal{LA}(\mathbb{Q})$ by replacing them with the conjunction $(0 \leq t) \wedge (0 \neq t)$,[3] but this solution can be very inefficient. The combination $\mathcal{EUF} \cup \mathcal{LA}(\mathbb{Q})$ can also be used to compute interpolants for other theories, such as those of lists, arrays, sets and multisets [15].

In [20], interpolants in the combined theory $\mathcal{EUF} \cup \mathcal{LA}(\mathbb{Q})$ are obtained by means of ad-hoc combination rules. The work in [30], instead, presents a method for generating interpolants for $\mathcal{T}_1 \cup \mathcal{T}_2$ using the interpolant-generation procedures of $\mathcal{T}_1$ and $\mathcal{T}_2$ as black-boxes, using the Nelson-Oppen approach [22].

Also the method of [27] allows to compute interpolants in $\mathcal{EUF} \cup \mathcal{LA}(\mathbb{Q})$. Its peculiarity is that it is not based on unsatisfiability proofs. Instead, it generates interpolants in $\mathcal{LA}(\mathbb{Q})$ by solving a system of constraints using an off-the-shelf Linear Programming (LP) solver. The method allows both weak and strict inequalities. Extension to uninterpreted functions is achieved by means of reduction to $\mathcal{LA}(\mathbb{Q})$ using a hierarchical calculus. The algorithm works only with conjunctions of atoms, although in principle it could be integrated in Algorithm 1 to generate interpolants for $\mathcal{T}$-lemmas in $\mathcal{LA}(\mathbb{Q})$. As an alternative, the authors show in [27] how to generate interpolants for formulas that are in Disjunctive Normal Form (DNF).

Another different approach is explored in [16]. There, the authors use the *eager* SMT approach to encode the original SMT problem into an equisatisfiable propositional problem, for which a propositional proof of unsatisfiability is generated. This proof is later "lifted" to the original theory, and used to generate an interpolant in a way

---

[3] The details are not given in [20]. One possible way of doing this is to rewrite $(0 \neq t)$ as $(y = t) \wedge (z = 0) \wedge (z \neq y)$, z and y being fresh variables.

$$\text{HYP} \ \frac{}{\Gamma \vdash \phi} \ \phi \in \Gamma \quad \text{LEQEQ} \ \frac{\Gamma \vdash 0 = t}{\Gamma \vdash 0 \leq t} \quad \text{COMB} \ \frac{\Gamma \vdash 0 \leq t_1 \qquad \Gamma \vdash 0 \leq t_2}{\Gamma \vdash 0 \leq c_1 t_1 + c_2 t_2} \ c_1, c_2 > 0$$

Fig. 1. Proof rules for $\mathcal{LA}(\mathbb{Q})$ (without strict inequalities)

similar to Algorithm 1. At the moment, the approach is however limited to the theory of equality only (without uninterpreted functions).

All the above techniques construct *one* interpolant for (A, B). In general, however, interpolants are not unique. In particular, some of them can be better than others, depending on the particular application domain. In [12], it is shown how to manipulate proofs in order to obtain stronger interpolants. In [13, 14], instead, a technique to restrict the language used in interpolants is presented and shown to be useful in preventing divergence of techniques based on predicate abstraction.

3   Interpolation for Linear Arithmetic with a State-of-the-Art Solver

Traditionally, SMT solvers used some kind of incremental simplex algorithm [29] as $\mathcal{T}$-solver for the $\mathcal{LA}(\mathbb{Q})$ theory. Recently, Dutertre and de Moura [10] have proposed a new simplex-based algorithm, specifically designed for integration in a lazy SMT solver. The algorithm is extremely efficient and was shown to significantly outperform (often by orders of magnitude) the traditional ones. It has now been integrated in several SMT solvers, including ARGOLIB, CVC3, MATHSAT, YICES, and Z3. Remarkably, this algorithm allows for handling also strict inequalities.

In this Section, we show how to exploit this algorithm to efficiently generate interpolants for $\mathcal{LA}(\mathbb{Q})$ formulas. In §3.1 we begin by considering the case in which the input atoms are only equalities and non-strict inequalities. In this case, we only need to show how to generate a proof of unsatisfiability, since then we can use the interpolation rules defined in [20]. Then, in §3.2 we show how to generate interpolants for problems containing also strict inequalities and disequalities.

3.1   Interpolation with Non-strict Inequalities

Similarly to [20], we use the proof rules of Figure 1: HYP for introducing hypotheses, LEQEQ for deriving inequalities from equalities, and COMB for performing linear combinations.[4] As in [20], we consider an atom "$0 \leq c$", c being a negative numerical constant, as a synonym of $\perp$.

The original Dutertre-de Moura algorithm. In its original formulation, the Dutertre-de Moura algorithm assumes that the variables x_i are partitioned a priori in two sets, hereafter denoted as $\hat{\mathcal{B}}$ ("initially basic") and $\hat{\mathcal{N}}$ ("initially non-basic"), and that the algorithm receives as inputs two kinds of atomic formulas:[5]

---

[4] In [20] the LEQEQ rule is not used in $\mathcal{LA}(\mathbb{Q})$, because the input is assumed to consist only of inequalities.

[5] Notationally, we use the hat symbol ˆ to denote the initial value of the generic symbol.

- a set of *equations* eq_i, one for each $x_i \in \hat{\mathcal{B}}$, of the form $\sum_{x_j \in \hat{\mathcal{N}}} \hat{a}_{ij} x_j + \hat{a}_{ii} x_i = 0$
  s.t. all $\hat{a}_{ij}$'s are numerical constants;
- *elementary atoms* of the form $x_j \geq l_j$ or $x_j \leq u_j$ s.t. l_j, u_j are numerical constants.

The initial equations eq_i are then used to build a tableau T:

$$\{x_i = \sum_{x_j \in \mathcal{N}} a_{ij} x_j \mid x_i \in \mathcal{B}\}, \tag{1}$$

where $\mathcal{B}$ ("basic"), $\mathcal{N}$ ("non-basic") and a_{ij} are such that initially $\mathcal{B} \equiv \hat{\mathcal{B}}$, $\mathcal{N} \equiv \hat{\mathcal{N}}$ and $a_{ij} \equiv -\hat{a}_{ij}/\hat{a}_{ii}$.

In order to decide the satisfiability of the input problem, the algorithm performs manipulations of the tableau that change the sets $\mathcal{B}$ and $\mathcal{N}$ and the values of the coefficients a_{ij}, always keeping the tableau T in (1) equivalent to its initial version. An inconsistency is detected when it is not possible to satisfy all the bounds on the variables introduced by the elementary atoms: as the algorithm ensures that the bounds on the variables in $\mathcal{N}$ are always satisfied, then there is a variable $x_i \in \mathcal{B}$ such that the inconsistency is caused either by the elementary atom $x_i \geq l_i$ or by the atom $x_i \leq u_i$ [10]. In the first case, [6] a conflict set η is generated as follows:

$$\eta = \{x_j \leq u_j | x_j \in \mathcal{N}^+\} \cup \{x_j \geq l_j | x_j \in \mathcal{N}^-\} \cup \{x_i \geq l_i\}, \tag{2}$$

where $x_i = \sum_{x_j \in \mathcal{N}} a_{ij} x_j$ is the row of the current version of the tableau T (1) corresponding to x_i, $\mathcal{N}^+$ is $\{x_j \in \mathcal{N} | a_{ij} > 0\}$ and $\mathcal{N}^-$ is $\{x_j \in \mathcal{N} | a_{ij} < 0\}$.

Notice that η is a conflict set in the sense that it is made inconsistent by (some of) the equations in the tableau T (1), i.e. $T \cup \eta \models_{\mathcal{LA}(\mathbb{Q})} \bot$.

In order to handle problems that are not in the above form, a satisfiability-preserving preprocessing step is applied upfront, before invoking the algorithm.

Our variant. In our variant of the algorithm, instead, the input is an arbitrary set of inequalities $l_k \leq \sum_h \hat{a}_{kh} y_h$ or $u_k \geq \sum_h \hat{a}_{kh} y_h$, and the preprocessing step is applied internally. In particular, we introduce a "slack" variable s_k for each distinct term $\sum_h \hat{a}_{kh} y_h$ occurring in the input inequalities. Then, we replace such term with s_k (thus obtaining $l_k \leq s_k$ or $u_k \geq s_k$) and add an equation $s_k = \sum_h \hat{a}_{kh} y_h$. Notice that we introduce a slack variable even for "elementary" inequalities ($l_k \leq y_k$). With this transformation, the initial tableau T (1) is:

$$\{s_k = \sum_h \hat{a}_{kh} y_h\}_k, \tag{3}$$

s.t. $\hat{\mathcal{B}}$ is made of all the slack variables s_k's, $\hat{\mathcal{N}}$ is made of all the original variables y_h's, and the elementary atoms contain only slack variables s_k's.

In our variant, we can use η to generate a conflict set η', thanks to the following lemma.

Lemma 1. *In the set η of (2), x_i and all the x_j's are slack variables introduced by our preprocessing step. Moreover, the set $\eta' \equiv \eta_{\mathcal{N}^+} \cup \eta_{\mathcal{N}^-} \cup \eta_i$ is a conflict set, where*

---

[6] Here we do not consider the second case $x_i \leq u_i$ as it is analogous to the first one.

$$\eta_{\mathcal{N}^+} \equiv \{u_k \geq \textstyle\sum_h \hat{a}_{kh}\, y_h | s_k \equiv x_j \text{ and } x_j \in \mathcal{N}^+\},$$
$$\eta_{\mathcal{N}^-} \equiv \{l_k \leq \textstyle\sum_h \hat{a}_{kh}\, y_h | s_k \equiv x_j \text{ and } x_j \in \mathcal{N}^-\},$$
$$\eta_i \equiv \{l_k \leq \textstyle\sum_h \hat{a}_{kh}\, y_h | s_k \equiv x_i\}.$$

We construct a proof of inconsistency as follows. From the set η of (2) we build a conflict set η' by replacing each elementary atom in it with the corresponding original atom, as shown in Lemma 1. Using the HYP rule, we introduce all the atoms in $\eta_{\mathcal{N}^+}$, and combine them with repeated applications of the COMB rule: if $u_k \geq \sum_h \hat{a}_{kh}\, y_h$ is the atom corresponding to s_k, we use as coefficient for the COMB the a_{ij} (in the i-th row of the current tableau) such that $s_k \equiv x_j$. Then, we introduce each of the atoms in $\eta_{\mathcal{N}^-}$ with HYP, and add them to the previous combination, again using COMB. In this case, the coefficient to use is $-a_{ij}$. Finally, we introduce the atom in η_i and add it to the combination with coefficient 1.

Lemma 2. *The result of the linear combination described above is the atom $0 \leq c$, such that c is a numerical constant strictly lower than zero.*

Besides the case just described (and its dual when the inconsistency is due to an elementary atom $x_i \leq u_i$), another case in which an inconsistency can be detected is when two contradictory atoms are asserted: $l_k \leq \sum_h \hat{a}_{kh}\, y_h$ and $u_k \geq \sum_h \hat{a}_{kh}\, y_h$, with $l_k > u_k$. In this case, the proof is simply the combination of the two atoms with coefficient 1.

The extension for handling also equalities like $b_k = \sum_h \hat{a}_{kh}\, y_h$ is straightforward: we simply introduce two elementary atoms $b_k \leq s_k$ and $b_k \geq s_k$ and, in the construction of the proof, we use the LEQEQ rule to introduce the proper inequality.

Finally, notice that the current implementation in MATHSAT (see §6) is slightly different from what presented here, and significantly more efficient. In practice, η, η' are not constructed in sequence; rather, they are built simultaneously. Moreover, some optimizations are applied to eliminate some slack variables when they are not needed.

3.2 Interpolation with Strict Inequalities and Disequalities

Another benefit of the Dutertre-de Moura algorithm is that it can handle strict inequalities directly. Its method is based on the following lemma.

Lemma 3 (Lemma 1 in [10]). *A set of linear arithmetic atoms Γ containing strict inequalities $S = \{0 < p_1, \ldots, 0 < p_n\}$ is satisfiable iff there exists a rational number $\varepsilon > 0$ such that $\Gamma_\varepsilon = (\Gamma \cup S_\varepsilon) \setminus S$ is satisfiable, where $S_\varepsilon = \{\varepsilon \leq p_1, \ldots, \varepsilon \leq p_n\}$.*

The idea of [10] is that of treating the *infinitesimal parameter* ε symbolically instead of explicitly computing its value. Strict bounds $(x < b)$ are replaced with weak ones $(x \leq b - \varepsilon)$, and the operations on bounds are adjusted to take ε into account.

We use the same idea also for computing interpolants. We transform every atom $(0 < t_i)$ occurring in the proof of unsatisfiability into $(0 \leq t_i - \varepsilon)$. Then we compute an interpolant I_ε in the usual way. As a consequence of the rules of [20], I_ε is always a single atom. As shown by the following lemma, if I_ε contains ε, then it must be in the form $(0 \leq t - c\varepsilon)$ with $c > 0$, and we can rewrite I_ε into $(0 < t)$.

Lemma 4 (Interpolation with strict inequalities). *Let* Γ, S, Γ_ε *and* S_ε *be defined as in Lemma 3. Let* Γ *be partitioned into* A *and* B, *and let* A_ε *and* B_ε *be obtained from* A *and* B *by replacing atoms in* S *with the corresponding ones in* S_ε. *Let* I_ε *be an interpolant for* $(A_\varepsilon, B_\varepsilon)$. *Then:*

- *If* $\varepsilon \npreceq I_\varepsilon$, *then* I_ε *is an interpolant for* (A, B).
- *If* $\varepsilon \preceq I_\varepsilon$, *then* $I_\varepsilon \equiv (0 \le t - c\varepsilon)$ *for some* $c > 0$, *and* $I \equiv (0 < t)$ *is an interpolant for* (A, B).

Thanks to Lemma 4, we can handle also negated equalities $(0 \ne t)$ directly. Suppose our set S of input atoms (partitioned into A and B) is the union of a set S' of equalities and inequalities (both weak and strict) and a set $S^{\ne}$ of disequalities, and suppose that S' is consistent. (If not so, an interpolant can be computed from S'.) Since $\mathcal{LA}(\mathbb{Q})$ is convex, S is inconsistent iff exists $(0 \ne t) \in S^{\ne}$ such that $S' \cup \{(0 \ne t)\}$ is inconsistent, that is, such that both $S' \cup \{(0 < t)\}$ and $S' \cup \{(0 > t)\}$ are inconsistent.

Therefore, we pick one element $(0 \ne t)$ of $S^{\ne}$ at a time, and check the satisfiability of $S' \cup \{(0 < t)\}$ and $S' \cup \{(0 > t)\}$. If both are inconsistent, from the two proofs we can generate two interpolants I^- and I^+. We combine I^+ and I^- to obtain an interpolant I for (A, B): if $(0 \ne t) \in A$, then I is $I^+ \vee I^-$; if $(0 \ne t) \in B$, then I is $I^+ \wedge I^-$, as shown by the following lemma.

Lemma 5 (Interpolation for negated equalities). *Let* A *and* B *two conjunctions of* $\mathcal{LA}(\mathbb{Q})$ *atoms, and let* $n \equiv (0 \ne t)$ *be one such atom. Let* $g \equiv (0 < t)$ *and* $l \equiv (0 > t)$. *If* $n \in A$, *then let* $A^+ \equiv A \setminus \{n\} \cup \{g\}$, $A^- \equiv A \setminus \{n\} \cup \{l\}$, *and* $B^+ \equiv B^- \equiv B$. *If* $n \in B$, *then let* $A^+ \equiv A^- \equiv A$, $B^+ \equiv B \setminus \{n\} \cup \{g\}$, *and* $B^- \equiv B \setminus \{n\} \cup \{l\}$. *Assume that* $A^+ \wedge B^+ \models_{\mathcal{LA}(\mathbb{Q})} \bot$ *and that* $A^- \wedge B^- \models_{\mathcal{LA}(\mathbb{Q})} \bot$, *and let* I^+ *and* I^- *be two interpolants for* (A^+, B^+) *and* (A^-, B^-) *respectively, and let*

$$I \equiv \begin{cases} I^+ \vee I^- & \text{if } n \in A \\ I^+ \wedge I^- & \text{if } n \in B. \end{cases}$$

Then I *is an interpolant for* (A, B).

4   Graph-Based Interpolation for Difference Logic

Several interesting verification problems can be encoded using only a subset of $\mathcal{LA}(\mathbb{Q})$, the theory of Difference Logic ($\mathcal{DL}(\mathbb{Q})$), in which all atoms are inequalities of the form $(0 \le y - x + c)$, where x and y are variables and c is a numerical constant. Equalities can be handled as conjunctions of inequalities. Here we do not consider the case when we also have strict inequalities $(0 < y - x + c)$, because in $\mathcal{DL}(\mathbb{Q})$ they can be handled in a way which is similar to that described in §3.2 for $\mathcal{LA}(\mathbb{Q})$. Moreover, we believe that our method may be extended straightforwardly to $\mathcal{DL}(\mathbb{Z})$ because the graph-based algorithm described in this section applies also to $\mathcal{DL}(\mathbb{Z})$; in $\mathcal{DL}(\mathbb{Z})$ a strict inequality $(0 < y - x + c)$ can be safely rewritten a priori into the inequality $(0 \le y - x + c - 1)$.

$\mathcal{DL}(\mathbb{Q})$ is simpler than full linear arithmetic. Many SMT solvers use dedicated, graph-based algorithms for checking the consistency of a set of $\mathcal{DL}(\mathbb{Q})$ atoms [9, 23]. Intuitively, a set S of $\mathcal{DL}(\mathbb{Q})$ atoms induces a graph whose vertexes are the variables of the atoms, and there exists an edge $x \xrightarrow{c} y$ for every $(0 \leq y - x + c) \in S$. S is inconsistent if and only if the induced graph has a cycle of negative weight.

We now extend the graph-based approach to generate interpolants. Consider the interpolation problem (A, B) where A and B are sets of inequalities as above, and let C be (the set of atoms in) a negative cycle in the graph corresponding to $A \cup B$.

If $C \subseteq A$, then A is inconsistent, in which case the interpolant is $\bot$. Similarly, when $C \subseteq B$, the interpolant is $\top$. If neither of these occurs, then the edges in the cycle can be partitioned in subsets of A and B. We call maximal A-paths of C a path $x_1 \xrightarrow{c_1} \ldots \xrightarrow{c_{n-1}} x_n$ such that (I) $x_i \xrightarrow{c_i} x_{i+1} \in A$, and (II) C contains $x' \xrightarrow{c'} x_1$ and $x_n \xrightarrow{c''} x''$ that are in B. Clearly, the end-point variables x_1, x_n of the maximal A-path are such $x_1, x_n \preceq A$ and $x_1, x_n \preceq B$.

Let the *summary constraint* of a maximal A-path $x_1 \xrightarrow{c_1} \ldots \xrightarrow{c_{n-1}} x_n$ be the inequality $0 \leq x_n - x_1 + \sum_{i=1}^{n-1} c_i$. We claim that the conjunction of summary constraints of the A-paths of C is an interpolant. In fact, using the rules for $\mathcal{LA}(\mathbb{Q})$ it is easy to see that a maximal A-path entails its summary constraint. Hence, A entails the conjunction of the summary constraints of maximal A-paths. Then, we notice that the conjunction of the summary constraints is inconsistent with B. In fact, the weight of a maximal A-path and the weight of its summary constraint are the same. Thus the cycle obtained from C by replacing each maximal A-path with the corresponding summary constraint is also a negative cycle. Finally, we notice that every variable x occurring in the conjunction of the summary constraints is an end-point variable, and thus $x \preceq A$ and $x \preceq B$.

A final remark is in order. In principle, to generate a proof of unsatisfiability for a conjunction of $\mathcal{DL}(\mathbb{Q})$ atoms, the same rules used for $\mathcal{LA}(\mathbb{Q})$ [20] could be used. However, the interpolants generated from such proofs are in general not $\mathcal{DL}(\mathbb{Q})$ formulas anymore and, if computed starting from the same inconsistent set C, they are either identical or weaker than those generated with our method. In fact, due to the interpolation rules in [20], it is easy to see that the interpolant obtained is in the form $(0 \leq \sum_i t_i)$ s.t. $\bigwedge_i (0 \leq t_i)$ is the interpolant generated with our method.

Example 1. Consider the following sets of $\mathcal{DL}(\mathbb{Q})$ atoms:

$$A = \{(0 \leq x_1 - x_2 + 1), (0 \leq x_2 - x_3), (0 \leq x_4 - x_5 - 1)\}$$
$$B = \{(0 \leq x_5 - x_1), (0 \leq x_3 - x_4 - 1)\}.$$

corresponding to the negative cycle on the right. It is straightforward to see from the graph that the resulting interpolant is $(0 \leq x_1 - x_3 + 1) \wedge (0 \leq x_4 - x_5 - 1)$, because the first conjunct is the summary constraint of the first two conjuncts in A.

Applying instead the rules of Figure 1, the proof of unsatisfiability is:

By using the interpolation rules for $\mathcal{LA}(\mathbb{Q})$ (see [20]), the interpolant we obtain is $(0 \leq x_1 - x_3 + x_4 - x_5)$, which is not in $\mathcal{DL}(\mathbb{Q})$, and is weaker than that computed above.

5   Computing Interpolants for Combined Theories Via DTC

One of the typical approaches to the SMT problem in combined theories, $SMT(\mathcal{T}_1 \cup \mathcal{T}_2)$, is that of combining the solvers for $\mathcal{T}_1$ and for $\mathcal{T}_2$ with the Nelson-Oppen (NO) integration schema [22].

The NO framework works for combinations of *stably-infinite* and *signature-disjoint* theories $\mathcal{T}_i$ with equality. Moreover, it requires the input formula to be *pure* (i.e., s.t. all the atoms contain only symbols in one theory): if not, a *purification* step is performed, which might introduce some additional variables but preserves satisfiability. In this setting, the two decision procedures for $\mathcal{T}_1$ and $\mathcal{T}_2$ cooperate by exchanging (disjunctions of) implied *interface equalities*, that is, equalities between variables appearing in atoms of different theories (*interface variables*).

The work in [30] gives a method for generating an interpolant for a pair (A, B) of $\mathcal{T}_1 \cup \mathcal{T}_2$-formulas using the NO schema. Besides the requirements on $\mathcal{T}_1$ and $\mathcal{T}_2$ needed to use NO, it requires also that $\mathcal{T}_1$ and $\mathcal{T}_2$ are *equality-interpolating*. A theory $\mathcal{T}$ is said to be equality-interpolating when for all pairs of formulas (A, B) in $\mathcal{T}$ and for all equalities $x_a = x_b$ such that (i) $x_a \npreceq B$ and $x_b \npreceq A$ (i.e. $x_a = x_b$ is an *AB-mixed equality*), and (ii) $A \wedge B \models_\mathcal{T} x_a = x_b$, there exists a term t such that $A \wedge B \models_\mathcal{T} x_a = t \wedge t = x_b$, $t \preceq A$ and $t \preceq B$. E.g., both $\mathcal{EUF}$ and $\mathcal{LA}(\mathbb{Q})$ are equality-interpolating.

Recently, an alternative approach for combining theories in SMT has been proposed, called Delayed Theory Combination (DTC) [5, 6]. With DTC, the solvers for $\mathcal{T}_1$ and $\mathcal{T}_2$ do not communicate directly. The integration is performed by the SAT solver, by augmenting the boolean search space with up to all the possible interface equalities. DTC has several advantages wrt. NO, both in terms of ease of implementation and in reduction of search space [5, 6], so that many current SMT tools implement variants of DTC. In this Section, we give a method for generating interpolants for a pair of $\mathcal{T}_1 \cup \mathcal{T}_2$-formulas (A, B) when $\mathcal{T}_1$ and $\mathcal{T}_2$ are combined using DTC. As in [30], we assume that A and B have been purified using disjoint sets of auxiliary variables.

5.1   Combination without AB-Mixed Interface Equalities

Let Eq be the set of all interface equalities introduced by DTC. We first consider the case in which Eq does not contain AB-mixed equalities. That is, Eq can be partitioned into two sets $(Eq \setminus B) \equiv \{(x = y) | (x = y) \preceq A \text{ and } (x = y) \npreceq B\}$ and $(Eq \downarrow B) \equiv \{(x = y) | (x = y) \preceq B\}$. In this restricted case, nothing special needs to be done, despite the fact that the interface equalities in Eq do not occur neither in A nor in B, but might be introduced in the resolution proof $\mathcal{P}$ by $\mathcal{T}$-lemmas. This is because —as observed in [20]— as long as for an atom p either $p \preceq A$ or $p \preceq B$ holds, it is possible to consider it part of A (resp. of B) simply by assuming the tautology clause $p \vee \neg p$ to be part of A (resp. of B). Therefore, we can treat the interface equalities in $(Eq \setminus B)$ as if they appeared in A, and those in $(Eq \downarrow B)$ as if they appeared in B.

5.2   Combination with AB-Mixed Interface Equalities

We can handle the case in which some of the equalities in Eq are AB-mixed under the hypothesis that $\mathcal{T}_1$ and $\mathcal{T}_2$ are equality-interpolating. Currently, we also require that $\mathcal{T}_1$ and $\mathcal{T}_2$ are convex, although the extension of the approach to non-convex theories is part of ongoing work.

The idea is similar to that used in [30] in the case of NO: using the fact that the $\mathcal{T}_i$'s are equality-interpolating, we reduce this case to the previous one by "splitting" every AB-mixed interface equality $(x_a = x_b)$ into the conjunction of two parts $(x_a = t) \wedge (t = x_b)$, such that $(x_a = t) \preceq A$ and $(t = x_b) \preceq B$. The main difference is that we do this *a posteriori*, after the construction of the resolution proof of unsatisfiability $\mathcal{P}$. This makes it possible to compute different interpolants for different partitions of the input problem into an A-part and a B-part *from the same proof $\mathcal{P}$*. Besides the advantage in performance of not having to recompute the proof every time, this is particularly important in some application domains like abstraction refinement [11], where the relation between interpolants obtained from the same proof tree is exploited to prove some properties of the refinement procedure. [7] To do this, we traverse $\mathcal{P}$ and split every AB-mixed equality in it, performing also the necessary manipulations to ensure that the modified DAG is still a resolution proof of unsatisfiability (according to the definition in §2.2). As long as this requirement is met, our technique is independent from the exact procedure implementing it. In the rest of this Section, we describe the algorithm that we have implemented, for the combination $\mathcal{EUF} \cup \mathcal{LA}(\mathbb{Q})$. Due to lack of space, we can not describe it in detail, rather we only provide the main intuitions.

First, we control the branching and learning heuristics of the SMT solver to ensure that the generated resolution proof of unsatisfiability $\mathcal{P}$ has a property that we call *locality wrt. interface equalities*. We say that $\mathcal{P}$ is local wrt. interface equalities (ie -local) if the interface equalities occur only in subproofs $\mathcal{P}_i^{\text{ie}}$ of $\mathcal{P}$, in which both the root and the leaves are $\mathcal{T}_1 \cup \mathcal{T}_2$-valid, the leaves of $\mathcal{P}_i^{\text{ie}}$ are also leaves of $\mathcal{P}$, the root of $\mathcal{P}_i^{\text{ie}}$ does not contain any interface equality, and in $\mathcal{P}_i^{\text{ie}}$ all the pivots are interface equalities. In order to generate ie -local proofs, we adopt a variant of the DTC Strategy 1 of [6]. We never select an interface equality for case splitting if there is some other unassigned atom, and we always assign false to interface equalities first. Moreover, when splitting on interface equalities, we restrict both the backjumping and the learning procedures of the DPLL engine as follows. Let d be the depth in the DPLL tree at which the first interface equality is selected for case splitting. If during the exploration of the current DPLL branch we have to backjump above d, then we generate by resolution a conflict clause that does not contain any interface equality, and "deactivate" all the $\mathcal{T}$-lemmas containing some interface equality, so that they can not be used elsewhere in the search tree. Only when we start splitting on interface equalities again, we can re-activate such $\mathcal{T}$-lemmas.

---

[7] In particular, the following relation: $I_{A,B\cup C}(\mathcal{P}) \wedge C \implies I_{A\cup C,B}(\mathcal{P})$ (where $I_{A,B}(\mathcal{P})$ is an interpolant for (A, B) generated from the proof $\mathcal{P}$) is used to show that for every spurious counterexample found, the interpolation-based refinement procedure is able to rule-out the counterexample in the refined abstraction [11]. It is possible to show that a similar relation holds also for $I_{A,B\cup C}(\mathcal{P}_1)$ and $I_{A\cup C,B}(\mathcal{P}_2)$, when $\mathcal{P}_1$ and $\mathcal{P}_2$ are obtained from the same $\mathcal{P}$ by splitting AB-mixed interface equalities with the technique described here. However, for lack of space we can not include such proof.

The idea of the Strategy just described is that of "emulating" the NO combination of the two $\mathcal{T}_i$-solvers. The conflict clause generated by resolution plays the role of the $\mathcal{T}$-lemma generated by the NO-based $\mathcal{T}_1 \cup \mathcal{T}_2$ solver, and the $\mathcal{T}$-lemmas containing positive interface equalities are used for exchanging implied equalities. The difference is that the combination is performed by the DPLL engine, and encoded directly in the ie-local subproofs $\mathcal{P}_i^{ie}$ of $\mathcal{P}$.

Since AB-mixed equalities can only occur in $\mathcal{P}_i^{ie}$ subproofs, we can handle the rest of $\mathcal{P}$ in the usual way. Therefore, we now describe only how to manipulate the $\mathcal{P}_i^{ie}$'s such that all the AB-mixed equalities are split.

In order accomplish this task, we exploit the following fact: since we are considering only convex theories, all the $\mathcal{T}_i$-lemmas generated by the $\mathcal{T}_i$-solvers contain at most one positive interface equality $(x = y)$.[8] Let $C \equiv (x = y) \vee \neg\eta$ be one such $\mathcal{T}_i$-lemma. Then $\eta \models_{\mathcal{T}_i} (x = y)$. Since $\mathcal{T}_i$ is equality-interpolating, if $(x = y)$ is AB-mixed, we can split C into $C_1 \equiv (x = t) \vee \neg\eta$ and $C_2 \equiv (t = y) \vee \neg\eta$. (E.g. by using the algorithms given in [30] for $\mathcal{EUF}$ and $\mathcal{LA}(\mathbb{Q})$.) Then, we replace every occurrence of $\neg(x = y)$ in the leaves of $\mathcal{P}_i^{ie}$ with the disjunction $\neg(x = t) \vee \neg(t = y)$. Finally, we replace the subproof

$$\frac{(x = y) \vee \neg\eta \qquad \neg(x = y) \vee \phi}{\neg\eta \vee \phi} \quad \text{with} \quad \frac{\dfrac{(x = t) \vee \neg\eta \qquad \neg(x = t) \vee \neg(t = y) \vee \phi}{\neg\eta \vee \neg(t = y) \vee \phi} \qquad (t = y) \vee \neg\eta}{\neg\eta \vee \phi}.$$

If this is done recursively, starting from $\mathcal{T}_i$-lemmas $\neg\eta \vee (x = y)$ such that $\neg\eta$ contains no negated AB-mixed equality, then the procedure terminates and the new proof $\mathcal{P}_i^{ie}{}'$ contains no AB-mixed equality.

Finally, we wish to remark that what just described is only one possible way of splitting AB-mixed equalities in $\mathcal{P}$. In particular, the restrictions on the branching and learning heuristics needed to generate ie-local proofs might have a negative impact in the performance of the SMT solver. In fact, we are currently investigating some alternative strategies.

6   Experimental Evaluation

The techniques presented in previous sections have been implemented within MATH-SAT 4 [4] (Hereafter, we will refer to such implementation as MATHSAT-ITP). MATH-SAT is an SMT solver supporting a wide range of theories and their combinations. In the last SMT solvers competition (SMT-COMP'07), it has proved to be competitive with the other state-of-the-art solvers. In this Section, we experimentally evaluate our approach.

6.1   Description of the Benchmark Sets

We have performed our experiments on two different sets of benchmarks. The first is obtained by running the BLAST software model checker [11] on some Windows

---

[8] There is a further technical condition that must be satisfied by the $\mathcal{T}_i$-solvers, i.e. they must not generate conflict sets containing redundant disequalities. This is true for all the $\mathcal{T}_i$-solvers on $\mathcal{EUF}$, $\mathcal{DL}(\mathbb{Q})$ and $\mathcal{LA}(\mathbb{Q})$ implemented in MATHSAT.

Family	# of problems	MATHSAT-ITP	FOCI	CLP-PROVER
kbfiltr.i	64	0.16	0.36	1.47
diskperf.i	119	0.33	0.78	3.08
floppy.i	235	0.73	1.64	5.91
cdaudio.i	130	0.35	1.07	2.98

Fig. 2. Comparison of execution times of MATHSAT-ITP, FOCI and CLP-PROVER on problems generated by BLAST

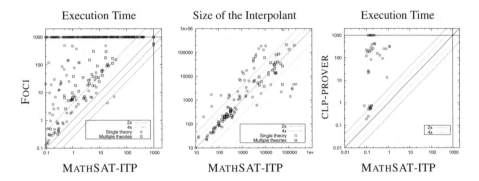

Fig. 3. Comparison of MATHSAT-ITP and FOCI on SMT-LIB instances: execution time (left), and size of the interpolant (right). In the left plot, points on the horizontal and vertical lines are timeouts/failures.

Fig. 4. Comparison of MATH-SAT-ITP and CLP-PROVER on conjunctions of $\mathcal{LA}(\mathbb{Q})$ atoms

device drivers; these are similar to those used in [27]. This is one of the most important applications of interpolation in formal verification, namely abstraction refinement in the context of CEGAR. The problem represents an abstract counterexample trace, and consists of a conjunction of atoms. In this setting, the interpolant generator is called very frequently, each time with a relatively simple input problem.

The second set of benchmarks originates from the SMT-LIB [26], and is composed of a subset of the unsatisfiable problems used in the 2007 SMT solvers competition (http://www.smtcomp.org). The instances have been converted to CNF and then split in two consistent parts of approximately the same size. The set consists of problems of varying difficulty and with a nontrivial boolean structure.

The experiments have been performed on a 3GHz Intel Xeon machine with 4GB of RAM running Linux. All the tools were run with a timeout of 600 seconds and a memory limit of 900 MB.

6.2 Comparison with the State-of-the-Art Tools Available

In this section, we compare with the only other interpolant generators which are available: FOCI [20, 13] and CLP-PROVER [27]. Other natural candidates for comparison would have been ZAP [3] and LIFTER [16]; however, it was not possible to obtain them from the authors.

The comparison had to be adapted to the limitations of FOCI and CLP-PROVER. In fact, the current version of FOCI does not handle the full $\mathcal{LA}(\mathbb{Q})$, but only the $\mathcal{DL}(\mathbb{Q})$ fragment[9]. We also notice that the interpolants it generates are not always $\mathcal{DL}(\mathbb{Q})$ formulas. (See, e.g., Example 1 of Section 4.) CLP-PROVER, on the other hand, does handle the full $\mathcal{LA}(\mathbb{Q})$, but it accepts only conjunctions of atoms, rather than formulas with arbitrary boolean structure. These limitations made it impossible to compare all the three tools on all the instances of our benchmark sets. Therefore, we perform the following comparisons:

– We compare all the three solvers on the problems generated by BLAST;
– We compare MATHSAT-ITP with FOCI on SMT-LIB instances in the theories of $\mathcal{EUF}$, $\mathcal{DL}(\mathbb{Q})$ and their combination. In this case, we compare both the execution times and the sizes of the generated interpolants (in terms of number of nodes in the DAG representation of the formula). For computing interpolants in $\mathcal{EUF}$, we apply the algorithm of [20], using an extension of the algorithm of [24] to generate $\mathcal{EUF}$ proof trees. The combination $\mathcal{EUF} \cup \mathcal{DL}(\mathbb{Q})$ is handled with the technique described in §5;
– We compare MATHSAT-ITP and CLP-PROVER on $\mathcal{LA}(\mathbb{Q})$ problems consisting of conjunctions of atoms. These problems are single branches of the search trees explored by MATHSAT for some $\mathcal{LA}(\mathbb{Q})$ instances in the SMT-LIB. We have collected several problems that took more than 0.1 seconds to MATHSAT to solve, and then randomly picked 50 of them. In this case, we do not compare the sizes of the interpolants as they are always atomic formulas.

The results are collected in Figures 2, 3 and 4. We can observe the following facts:

– Interpolation problems generated by BLAST are trivial for all the tools. In fact, we even had some difficulties in measuring the execution times reliably. Despite this, MATHSAT-ITP seems to be a little faster than the others.
– For problems with a nontrivial boolean structure, MATHSAT-ITP outperforms FOCI in terms of execution time. This is true even for problems in the combined theory $\mathcal{EUF} \cup \mathcal{DL}(\mathbb{Q})$, despite the fact that the current implementation is still preliminary.
– In terms of size of the generated interpolants, the gap between MATHSAT-ITP and FOCI is smaller on average. However, the right plot of Figure 3 (which considers only instances for which both tools were able to generate an interpolant) shows that there are more cases in which MATHSAT-ITP produces a smaller interpolant.
– On conjunctions of $\mathcal{LA}(\mathbb{Q})$ atoms, MATHSAT-ITP outperforms CLP-PROVER, sometimes by more than two orders of magnitude.

7   Conclusions

In this paper, we have shown how to efficiently build interpolants using state-of-the-art SMT solvers. Our methods encompass a wide range of theories (including $\mathcal{EUF}$,

---

[9] For example, it fails to detect the $\mathcal{LA}(\mathbb{Q})$-unsatisfiability of the following problem: $(0 \leq y - x + w) \wedge (0 \leq x - z - w) \wedge (0 \leq z - y - 1)$.

difference logic, and linear arithmetic), and their combination (based on the Delayed Theory Combination schema). A thorough experimental evaluation shows that the proposed methods are vastly superior to the state of the art interpolants, both in terms of expressiveness, and in terms of efficiency.

In the future, we plan to investigate the following issues. First, we will improve the implementation of the interpolation method for combined theories, that is currently rather naïve, and limited to the case of convex theories. Second, we will investigate interpolation with other rules, in particular Ackermann's expansion. Finally, we will integrate our interpolator within a CEGAR loop based on decision procedures, such as BLAST or the new version of NuSMV. In fact, such an integration raises interesting problems related to controlling the structure of the generated interpolants [13, 14], e.g. in order to limit the number or the size of constants occurring in the proof.

References

1. Audemard, G., Bozzano, M., Cimatti, A., Sebastiani, R.: Verifying industrial hybrid systems with mathsat. Electr. Notes Theor. Comput. Sci. 119(2) (2005)
2. Audemard, G., Cimatti, A., Kornilowicz, A., Sebastiani, R.: Bounded model checking for timed systems. In: Peled, D.A., Vardi, M.Y. (eds.) FORTE 2002. LNCS, vol. 2529, Springer, Heidelberg (2002)
3. Ball, T., Lahiri, S.K., Musuvathi, M.: Zap: Automated theorem proving for software analysis. In: Sutcliffe, G., Voronkov, A. (eds.) LPAR 2005. LNCS (LNAI), vol. 3835, Springer, Heidelberg (2005)
4. Bozzano, M., Bruttomesso, R., Cimatti, A., Junttila, T., Rossum, P., Schulz, S., Sebastiani, R.: MathSAT: A Tight Integration of SAT and Mathematical Decision Procedure. Journal of Automated Reasoning 35(1-3) (October 2005)
5. Bozzano, M., Bruttomesso, R., Cimatti, A., Junttila, T., van Rossum, P., Ranise, S., Sebastiani, R.: Efficient Theory Combination via Boolean Search. Information and Computation 204(10) (2006)
6. Bruttomesso, R., Cimatti, A., Franzén, A., Griggio, A., Sebastiani, R.: Delayed Theory Combination vs. Nelson-Oppen for Satisfiability Modulo Theories: A Comparative Analysis. In: Hermann, M., Voronkov, A. (eds.) LPAR 2006. LNCS (LNAI), vol. 4246, Springer, Heidelberg (2006)
7. Cabodi, G., Murciano, M., Nocco, S., Quer, S.: Stepping forward with interpolants in unbounded model checking. In: Proc. ICCAD 2006, ACM, New York (2006)
8. Cimatti, A., Griggio, A., Sebastiani, R.: Efficient Interpolant Generation in Satisfiability Modulo Theories. Technical Report DIT-07-075, DISI - University of Trento (2007)
9. Cotton, S., Maler, O.: Fast and Flexible Difference Constraint Propagation for DPLL(T). In: Biere, A., Gomes, C.P. (eds.) SAT 2006. LNCS, vol. 4121, pp. 170–183. Springer, Heidelberg (2006)
10. Dutertre, B., de Moura, L.: A Fast Linear-Arithmetic Solver for DPLL(T). In: Ball, T., Jones, R.B. (eds.) CAV 2006. LNCS, vol. 4144, pp. 81–94. Springer, Heidelberg (2006)
11. Henzinger, T.A., Jhala, R., Majumdar, R., McMillan, K.L.: Abstractions from proofs. In: Jones, N.D., Leroy, X. (eds.) POPL, ACM, New York (2004)
12. Jhala, R., McMillan, K.: Interpolant-based transition relation approximation. In: Etessami, K., Rajamani, S.K. (eds.) CAV 2005. LNCS, vol. 3576, pp. 39–51. Springer, Heidelberg (2005)

13. Jhala, R., McMillan, K.L.: A Practical and Complete Approach to Predicate Refinement. In: Hermanns, H., Palsberg, J. (eds.) TACAS 2006. LNCS, vol. 3920, Springer, Heidelberg (2006)
14. Jhala, R., McMillan, K.L.: Array Abstractions from Proofs. In: Damm, W., Hermanns, H. (eds.) CAV 2007. LNCS, vol. 4590, Springer, Heidelberg (2007)
15. Kapur, D., Majumdar, R., Zarba, C.G.: Interpolation for data structures. In: Young, M., Devanbu, P.T. (eds.) SIGSOFT FSE, ACM, New York (2006)
16. Kroening, D., Weissenbacher, G.: Lifting Propositional Interpolants to the Word-Level. In: FMCAD, USA, pp. 85–89. IEEE Computer Society, Los Alamitos, CA, USA (2007)
17. Li, B., Somenzi, F.: Efficient Abstraction Refinement in Interpolation-Based Unbounded Model Checking. In: Hermanns, H., Palsberg, J. (eds.) TACAS 2006. LNCS, vol. 3920, pp. 227–241. Springer, Heidelberg (2006)
18. Marques-Silva, J.: Interpolant Learning and Reuse in SAT-Based Model Checking. Electr. Notes Theor. Comput. Sci. 174(3), 31–43 (2007)
19. McMillan, K.: Interpolation and SAT-based model checking. In: Proc. CAV (2003)
20. McMillan, K.L.: An interpolating theorem prover. Theor. Comput. Sci. 345(1) (2005)
21. McMillan, K.L.: Lazy Abstraction with Interpolants. In: Ball, T., Jones, R.B. (eds.) CAV 2006. LNCS, vol. 4144, pp. 123–136. Springer, Heidelberg (2006)
22. Nelson, G., Oppen, D.: Simplification by Cooperating Decision Procedures. ACM Trans. on Programming Languages and Systems 1(2) (1979)
23. Nieuwenhuis, R., Oliveras, A.: DPLL(T) with Exhaustive Theory Propagation and Its Application to Difference Logic. In: Etessami, K., Rajamani, S.K. (eds.) CAV 2005. LNCS, vol. 3576, Springer, Heidelberg (2005)
24. Nieuwenhuis, R., Oliveras, A.: Fast Congruence Closure and Extensions. Inf. Comput. 2005(4), 557–580 (2007)
25. Pudlák, P.: Lower bounds for resolution and cutting planes proofs and monotone computations. J. of Symb. Logic 62(3) (1997)
26. Ranise, S., Tinelli, C.: The Satisfiability Modulo Theories Library (SMT-LIB) (2006), http://www.SMT-LIB.org
27. Rybalchenko, A., Sofronie-Stokkermans, V.: Constraint Solving for Interpolation. In: VMCAI. LNCS, Springer, Heidelberg (2007)
28. Sebastiani, R.: Lazy Satisfiability Modulo Theories. Journal on Satisfiability, Boolean Modeling and Computation, J.SAT 3 (2007)
29. Vanderbei, R.J.: Linear Programming: Foundations and Extensions. Springer, Heidelberg (2001)
30. Yorsh, G., Musuvathi, M.: A combination method for generating interpolants. In: Nieuwenhuis, R. (ed.) CADE 2005. LNCS (LNAI), vol. 3632, pp. 353–368. Springer, Heidelberg (2005)

Quantified Invariant Generation Using an Interpolating Saturation Prover

K.L. McMillan

Cadence Berkeley Labs

Abstract. Interpolating provers have a variety of applications in verification, including invariant generation and abstraction refinement. Here, we extended these methods to produce universally quantified interpolants and invariants, allowing the verification of programs manipulating arrays and heap data structures. We show how a paramodulation-based saturation prover, such as SPASS, can be modified in a simple way to produce a first-order interpolating prover that is complete for universally quantified interpolants. Using a partial axiomatization of the theory of arrays with transitive closure, we show that the method can verify properties of simple programs manipulating arrays and linked lists.

1 Introduction

An interpolating prover derives an interpolant for a pair (or in general a sequence) of logical formulas from a proof of unsatisfiability of those formulas. An interpolant for a pair of formulas (A, B) is a formula over their common vocabulary that is implied by A and inconsistent with B. Interpolating provers have been used to generate inductive invariants for proving properties of sequential circuits [7] and sequential programs [9], as well as abstraction refinement [4]. However, their use so far has been limited to propositional logic (with a Boolean satisfiability solver) or quantifier-free first-order logic for fixed theories (with a ground decision procedure) [8]. While effective, these methods are strongly limited in their ability to handle programs manipulating arrays and heap data structures because these generally require quantified invariants.

In this paper, we show how to modify a paramodulation-based prover for first order logic (FOL) with equality to produce an interpolating prover. This prover is complete for generation of universally quantified interpolants (though the input formulas may be in full FOL). Because it is a full first order prover, it allows us to introduce various theories that may be useful for expressing invariants by axiomatizing them. For example, we show that an incomplete axiomatization of FO(TC), the first-order theory of transitive closure, allows us to verify properties of simple heap-manipulating programs.

The primary problem that we must solve in making a practical interpolating prover is *divergence* of the interpolants. That is, we generate inductive invariants from the interpolants obtained by refuting unwindings of the program of increasing length. If these interpolants diverge with increasing unwinding length (for

C.R. Ramakrishnan and J. Rehof (Eds.): TACAS 2008, LNCS 4963, pp. 413–427, 2008.
© Springer-Verlag Berlin Heidelberg 2008

example by exhibiting increasing numeric constants or function nesting depth or number of quantifiers) then this approach fails. This problem was solved for quantifier-free case (for certain theories) in [5]. Here, we solve the problem in a different way, by bounding the clause language of the saturation prover. We show that the method is complete for universally quantified invariant generation, that is, if there is an inductive invariant proving a given property, we are guaranteed to find one eventually.

We also show experimentally, by modifying the SPASS prover [14] that the method does in fact converge for some simple example programs manipulating arrays and linked lists.

Related work. Indexed predicate abstraction [6] is a method that can generate the strongest universally quantified inductive invariant of a program over a fixed set of atomic predicates. However, some of these atomic predicates typically must be provided manually, as effective selection algorithms are lacking. Moreover, the forward image operator in this method is problematic, requiring in the worst case an exponential number of calls to a decision oracle for first-order logic. The method presented here does not require an image operator or a decision oracle. It may, however, provide a useful heuristic for indexed predicate refinement.

Since the method presented here can handle FO(TC), it is comparable in power to canonical heap abstraction [12]. The abstract states in this method (with reachability predicates) can be expressed as formulas in FO(TC). The difference between the methods is therefore mainly a matter of efficiency, which remains to be determined. However, the interpolation method has the advantage that it does not require the user to provide instrumentation predicates manually. It could be that interpolation in FO(TC) will be a useful approach for automated refinement in the canonical abstraction method.

Finally, the method can also be compared to parameterized invariant generation methods such as [13]. The main advantage of interpolation is that it can synthesize the Boolean structure of the invariant, and it can handle heap properties using transitive closure that cannot be handled by parameterized methods. On the other hand, the arithmetic reasoning ability of the present approach is limited compared to these methods.

2 Background: Paramodulation Calculus

Paramodulation [11] is the method of choice for proving first order formulas with equality. We begin by describing the basic principles of saturation provers based on paramodulation. This is necessarily a quick review. The material in this section is derived from an excellent article by Niewenhuis and Rubio [10], to which the reader is referred for greater depth.

Preliminaries. Let Σ be a countable vocabulary of function and predicate symbols, with associated arities. Function symbols with arity zero will be called constants. We assume that Σ contains at least one constant. We will use meta-variables f, g, h to represent function symbols, a, b, c to represent constants, and

P, Q to represent predicate symbols. We will also distinguish a finite subset Σ_I of Σ as *interpreted* symbols. In particular, we assume that Σ_I contains the binary predicate symbol $\simeq$, representing equality. Let $\mathcal{V}$ be a countable set of variables, distinct from Σ. We will use U, V to represent variables. The set of terms $\mathcal{T}$ is the least set such that $\mathcal{V} \subseteq \mathcal{T}$ and for every function symbol f of arity k, and terms $t_1 \ldots t_k \in \mathcal{T}^k$, we have $f(t_1, \ldots, t_k) \in \mathcal{T}$. We will use s, t (and sometimes l, r) to represent terms. The vocabulary of a term or formula ϕ, denoted $L(\phi)$ is the set of uninterpreted symbols occurring in ϕ. If S is a vocabulary, we let $\mathcal{T}(S)$ denote the set of terms t such that $L(t) \subseteq S$. Similarly, $\mathcal{L}(S)$ is the set of first-order formulas ϕ such that $L(\phi) \subseteq S$. We will also write $\mathcal{L}(\phi)$ for $\mathcal{L}(L(\phi))$.

An *atom* is $P(t_1, \ldots, t_k)$, where P is a k-ary predicate symbol and $t_1, \ldots, t_k$ are terms. A *literal* is an atom or its negation. A *clause* is a disjunction of literals in which the variables are implicitly universally quantified. Following tradition, we will write clauses in the form $\Gamma \rightarrow \Delta$, where Γ is the multiset of negative literals in the clause, and Δ is the multiset of positive literals. Also following tradition, we will write a formula multiset as list of formulas and formula multisets. Thus, if Γ is a multiset of formulas and ϕ a formula, then Γ, ϕ represents $\Gamma \cup \{\phi\}$.

A substitution σ is a map from variables to terms. For any term of formula ϕ, we write $\phi\sigma$ to indicate the simultaneous substitution in ϕ of $\sigma(U)$ for all free occurrences of U, for all variables U in the domain of σ. A formula or term is said to be *ground* if it contains no variables. A substitution is ground if all terms in its range are ground. The *ground instances* of a clause C are all the clauses $C\sigma$, where σ is a ground substitution over the variables in C. A *position* p is a finite sequence of natural numbers, representing a syntactic position in a term or formula. If ϕ is a formula or term, then $\phi|_p$ represents the subformula or subterm of ϕ at position p. Thus, $\phi|_\epsilon$ is ϕ itself, $\phi|_i$ is the i-th argument of ϕ, $\phi|_{ij}$ is the j-th argument of the i-th argument, and so on. The notation $\phi[\psi]_p$ means ϕ with ψ substituted in position p.

Paramodulation with constrained clauses. Paramodulation provers use the concept of a *reduction order* to reduce that amount of deduction that is required for completeness. For our purposes, a reduction order $\succ$ is a total, well-founded order on ground terms that is *monotonic* and has the *subterm property*. Monotonicity means that whenever $\psi_1 \succ \psi_2$, we have $\phi[\psi_1]_p \succ \phi[\psi_2]_p$. The subterm property says that $\phi \succ \phi|_p$ for all $p \neq \epsilon$. A reduction order can be extended to finite multisets of formulas. Given two multisets S and S', we say $S \succ S'$ if $S(\phi) > S'(\phi)$, where ϕ is the maximal formula such that $S(\phi) \neq S'(\phi)$. This allows us to totally order the ground clauses with respect to $\succ$.

We will be concerned here with refutation systems that take a set of clauses, and try to prove that the set is unsatisfiable by deriving the empty clause (equivalent to false). For purposes of refutation, a clause with variables is logically equivalent to the set of its ground instances (this is a consequence of Herbrand's theorem). Thus, it is useful to think of a clause with variables as simply a pattern abbreviating a countable set of ground clauses. To describe the operation of a paramodulation prover, it is useful to introduce the notion of a *constrained clause.* This is written in form $C \mid T$ where C is a clause, and T is a constraint. The constraint is usually a conjunction of constraints of the form $s = t$ or $s > t$, where s and t are terms or atoms. For a given ground substitution σ, $s = t$ means $s\sigma$ and $t\sigma$ are the syntactically equal, and $s > t$ means $s\sigma \succ t\sigma$. The interpretation of $C \mid T$ is the set of all ground instances $C\sigma$ of C such that $T\sigma$ is true. For example, $P(U, V) \mid U > a$ means that P holds of all pairs of ground terms U, V, such that $U \succ a$. Note that a clause with an unsatisfiable constraint is by definition equivalent to true and an empty clause with a satisfiable constraint is equivalent to false.

An *inference* is the derivation of a constrained clause (the *conclusion*) from a multiset of constrained clauses (the *premises*) and is written in this form:

$$\frac{C_1 \mid T_1 \ldots C_n \mid T_n}{D \mid T}$$

An *inference rule* is a pattern that finitely describes a set of valid inferences. For example, here is the rule for resolution:

$$\frac{\Gamma \to \Delta, \phi \mid T_1 \quad \Gamma', \phi' \to \Delta' \mid T_2}{\Gamma, \Gamma' \to \Delta, \Delta' \mid \phi = \phi' \wedge T_1 \wedge T_2}$$

Note that because of the constraint $\phi = \phi'$ in the conclusion, every ground instance of this inference is valid. Most resolution provers eliminate the constraint $\phi = \phi'$ by substituting with σ, the most general unifier of ϕ and ϕ', yielding $(\Gamma, \Gamma' \to \Delta, \Delta')\sigma \mid (T_1 \wedge T_2)\sigma$. If ϕ and ϕ' cannot be unified, the conclusion's constraint is unsatisfiable, and the inference is discarded. In the sequel, we will omit the constraints on the premises and take it as implied that these constraints are inherited by the conclusion.

For refutation in the theory of equality, most modern provers use a superposition calculus (since resolution, though complete, is very inefficient for this purpose). This is based on substitution of equals for equals. Here is an example of a superposition inference:

$$\frac{P \to f(x) = y \quad Q \to x = z}{P, Q \to f(z) = y}$$

We say we have performed superposition *with* $x = z$, *into* $f(x) = y$. This approach can generate an enormous number of inferences. However, we can reduce this chaos by using *ordered superposition*. That is, we only need to perform the above inference if x and $f(x)$ are *maximal* terms in their respective clauses, with respect to $\succ$. Intuitively, we are always rewriting downward in the order. The inference rules for ordered superposition are as follows:

superposition right: $\quad \dfrac{\Gamma \to \Delta, s \simeq t \quad \Gamma' \to \Delta', l \simeq r}{\Gamma, \Gamma' \to \Delta, \Delta', s[r]_p \simeq t \mid s|_p = l \wedge OC}$

superposition left: $\quad \dfrac{\Gamma, s \simeq t \to \Delta \quad \Gamma' \to \Delta', l \simeq r}{\Gamma, \Gamma', s[r]_p \simeq t \to \Delta, \Delta' \mid s|_p = l \wedge OC}$

$$\text{equality resolution: } \frac{\Gamma, s \simeq t \to \Delta}{\Gamma \to \Delta \mid s = t \land OC}$$

$$\text{equality factoring: } \frac{\Gamma \to s \simeq t, s' \simeq t', \Delta}{\Gamma, t \simeq t' \to s = t', \Delta \mid s = s' \land OC}$$

The equality resolution rule enforces reflexivity of equality, while the equality factoring rule eliminates redundant equalities. In each rule, OC is an ordering constraint. These constraints are not necessary, but they reduce the number of possible inferences greatly without sacrificing completeness. From our point of view, the only thing we need to know about OC is that it implies in the superposition rules that s and l are maximal terms in their respective clauses. Details can be found in [10].

We will call this system of inference rules $\mathcal{I}_\succ$, where $\succ$ is the reduction ordering used in the ordering constraints. Given any unsatisfiable set of "well-constrained clauses", $\mathcal{I}_\succ$ can derive false. The notion of "well-constrained" is too technical to present here (see [10]). We note only that clauses with constraints of the form $a < U$ are well-constrained, which is all the we require for present purposes. To be more precise, we have:

Theorem 1 ([10]). *For any reduction order $\succ$, system $\mathcal{I}_\succ$ is complete for refutation of well-constrained clause sets with equality.*

Note that this system handles only equality predicates. However, we can in principle translate any other predicate symbol P into a function symbol, such that $P(x, y, \ldots)$ is equivalent to $P(x, y, \ldots) = t$, where t is a symbol representing "true". Thus in principle, equality predicates are sufficient. In practice, provers typically retain arbitrary predicate symbols and also implement resolution.

Redundancy and saturation. A saturation prover has inference rules that deduce new clauses, and also *reduction rules* that delete redundant clauses. The prover is said to reach *saturation* when any new inference from existing clauses can be deleted by the reduction rules.

Relative to a set S of derived clauses and a reduction order $\succ$, a clause C is said to be *redundant* when it is entailed by clauses in S that are less than C. A more general notion is redundancy of inferences. An inference I is said to be redundant when its conclusion is entailed by clauses in S less than the maximal clause in its premises (for all ground instances satisfying its constraint). Intuitively, by deleting a redundant inference, we "postpone" the deduction of its conclusion (or lesser clauses entailing it). However cannot postpone its derivation infinitely, since the reduction order is well-founded.

A saturation prover starts with a set of "usable" clauses U, and an empty set of "worked off" clauses W. At each iteration of its main loop, it removes a clause G from U, called the *given clause*. Reduction rules are applied to G (possibly adding derived clauses to U). If G is not deleted, all possible inferences using G and some set of clauses from W are then generated, and G is added to W. If U becomes empty, then W is saturated.

The main results about saturation provers that are of interest here are the following:

1. If the set of inference rules is complete, and if only redundant inferences are deleted, and if the selection of given clauses is fair, then the saturation prover is complete for refutation.
2. Moreover, if any clause C is entailed by the original clauses, then eventually it is entailed by clauses in W that are less than C in the reduction order.

To express rules for deleting redundant inferences, we will introduce a notation for *replacement rules*. These have the form $I \xrightarrow{S} J$, where I is an inference, S is a clause set and J is a set of (sound) inferences. The intuitive meaning of a replacement is that, if clauses S are proved, adding inferences J makes inference I redundant. As an example, if $Q \succ a \succ b \succ P$, the following is a valid replacement:

$$\frac{P \quad P \to Q(a)}{Q(a)} \quad \xrightarrow{a=b} \quad \frac{P \to Q(a) \quad a = b}{P \to Q(b)}$$

That is, since $P \to Q(a)$ is greater than P, $P \to Q(b)$ and $a = b$, and these imply $Q(a)$, we have a valid replacement. For each given clause G, the prover checks whether I, the inference that produced G, can be deleted and replaced by other inferences J, using a replacement rule. Since this adds only valid inferences and deletes only redundant ones, both soundness and completeness are preserved.

3   Interpolants from Superposition Proofs

Given a pair of formulas (A, B), such that $A \wedge B$ is inconsistent, an *interpolant* for (A, B) is a formula $\hat{A}$ with the following properties:

- A implies $\hat{A}$,
- $\hat{A} \wedge B$ is unsatisfiable, and
- $\hat{A} \subseteq \mathcal{L}(A) \cap \mathcal{L}(B)$.

The Craig interpolation lemma [3] states that an interpolant always exists for inconsistent formulas in FOL.

We now show how to use a saturation prover to generate universally quantified interpolants from arbitrary formulas in FOL. The approach is based on generating local proofs:

Definition 1. *An inference is* local *for a pair of formulas (A, B) when its premises and conclusions are either all in $\mathcal{L}(A)$ or all in $\mathcal{L}(B)$. A proof is local for (A, B) when all its inferences are local.*

From a *local* refutation proof of A, B, we can derive an interpolant for the pair in linear time [5]. This interpolant is a Boolean combination of the formulas in the proof.

Unfortunately, it is easily shown that the superposition calculus described above is not complete if we restrict it to local proofs. Consider the case where A consist of the clauses $Q(f(a))$ and $\neg Q(f(b))$, while B contains $f(V) = c$ and $b, c \in L(B)$. An interpolant for (A, B) is $f(a) \not\simeq f(b)$. However, no local superposition inferences are possible for these clauses. To solve this problem, we show that by choosing the precedence order appropriately and adding a replacement rule, we can force all the inferences to be local without sacrificing completeness, so long as A and B have an interpolant in $\mathcal{L}_\forall$. This yields a complete procedure for generating universally quantified interpolants.

Definition 2. *A reduction order $\succ$ is* oriented *for a pair of formula sets (A, B) when, for all terms or formulas ϕ_1, ϕ_2 over $L(A, B)$, if $\phi_1 \notin \mathcal{L}(B)$ and $\phi_2 \in \mathcal{L}(B)$, then $\phi_1 \succ \phi_2$.*

Intuitively, as we descend the order, we eliminate the symbols that occur only in A. One way to construct an oriented reduction order is to use the standard RPOS (recursive path ordering with status), setting the precedence order so that the symbols in $L(A) \setminus L(B)$ precede all the symbols in $L(B)$.

Now let us consider again our example of of incompleteness of local superposition. In this example, although no local superposition inferences are possible, we can make the non-local inference $Q(f(a)), f(V) \simeq c \vdash Q(c)$. We can then make the following *replacement*:

$$\frac{Q(f(a)) \quad f(V) \simeq c}{Q(c)} \quad \rightarrow \quad \frac{Q(f(a))}{f(a) \simeq U \rightarrow Q(U) \mid f(a) > U}$$

where U is a fresh variable. This replacement is valid for the following reasons. First, the right-hand inference is sound (that is, if Q holds of $f(a)$, then Q holds of any U equal to $f(a)$). Second, the conclusion on the right, $f(a) \simeq U \rightarrow Q(U) \mid f(a) > U$, when resolved with $f(V) \simeq c$, gives us $Q(c)$. Thus, the conclusion on the left is implied by proved clauses. Moreover, those clauses are both less than $Q(f(a))$ in the reduction order, given the constraint $f(a) > U$. That is, the conclusion on the left is implied by derived clauses less than its maximal premise. This means that adding the right inference makes the left one redundant.

We can now continue to construct a fully local refutation for our example problem, using replacements of this type:

1. $\rightarrow Q(f(a))$ (hypothesis from A)
2. $\rightarrow f(V) \simeq c$ (hypothesis from B)
3. $f(a) \simeq U \rightarrow Q(U)$ (superposition in 1 with 2, with replacement)
4. $Q(f(b)) \rightarrow$ (hypothesis from A)
5. $f(b) \simeq U, Q(U) \rightarrow$ (superposition in 4 with 2, with replacement)
6. $f(a) \simeq U, f(b) \simeq U \rightarrow$ (resolution of 3 and 5)
7. $f(b) \simeq c \rightarrow$ (resolution of 6 and 2)
8. $\rightarrow$ (resolution of 7 and 2)

Notice that the replacement allowed us to postpone the superposition steps until only symbols from B remained. For this reason, we will refer to this type of replacement as "procrastination". The procrastination rule for deletion of superposition right inferences can be stated as follows:

$$\frac{\Gamma \rightarrow \Delta, s \simeq t \quad \Gamma' \rightarrow \Delta', l \simeq r}{\Gamma, \Gamma' \rightarrow \Delta, \Delta', s[r]_p \simeq t \mid s|_p = l \wedge OC} \quad \overset{*}{\rightarrow} \quad \frac{\Gamma \rightarrow \Delta, s \simeq t}{s|_p \simeq U, \Gamma \rightarrow \Delta, s[U]_p \simeq t \mid s|_p > U}$$

where OC is the ordering constraint of the superposition right rule. The asterisk is to indicate that this rule is to be applied when p is *not* ϵ, the top position. This means that l is a strict subterm of s, and thus $s > l$.

Now we argue that this rule is valid. Call the left inference L and the right inference R. It is easily verified that R is sound. Now let LA_1, LA_2, LS, RA, RS stand respectively for the premises and conclusion of the left and right inferences. Since OC implies that $l > r$, we have $RS, LA_2 \models LS$, which we can prove by resolution. Finally, we need to show that $LA_1 \succ LA_2$ and $LA_1 \succ RS$. The former is guaranteed by the asterisk (that is, since $s > l$, and l is a maximal term in LA_1, we have $LA_1 \succ LA_2$). The latter is guaranteed by the constraint $s|_p > U$, which implies $s > s|_p > U$, and, by monotonicity, $s > s[U]_p$. Thus, procrastination right is a valid replacement.

The rule replacing superposition left inferences is similar:

$$\frac{\Gamma, s \simeq t \to \Delta \quad \Gamma' \to \Delta', l \simeq r}{\Gamma, \Gamma', s[r]_p \simeq t \to \Delta, \Delta' \mid s|_p = l \wedge OC} \quad \overset{*}{\to} \quad \frac{\Gamma, s \simeq t \to \Delta}{s|_p \simeq U, \Gamma, s[U]_p \simeq t \to \Delta \mid s|_p > U}$$

The argument for validity is similar to that for procrastination right. Since the procrastination rules are valid replacements, meaning that they only generate sound inferences and delete redundant ones, we have immediately that:

Lemma 1. *System $\mathcal{I}_\succ$ with procrastination is complete for refutation for well-constrained clause sets.*

We now observe that, for pairs (A, B) with universally quantified interpolants, we require only local ground instances of B clauses for refutation completeness.

To be more precise, if C is a clause, let $C \mid L(B)$ stand for the set of ground instances $C\sigma$ of C where the range of σ is contained in $\mathcal{T}(B)$. That is, we constrain the values of the variables in C to be terms over $L(B)$. If our reduction ordering is oriented for (A, B), then $C \mid L(B)$ can be expressed as $C \mid a > U \wedge a > V \cdots$ where a is the least ground term not in $L(B)$, and $U, V, \ldots$ are the variables occurring in C. Thus, $C \mid L(B)$ is well-constrained. Finally, if S is a clause set, then let $S \mid L(B)$ stand for the set of $C \mid L(B)$ for C in S.

Lemma 2. *Let A and B be clause sets. If there is an interpolant for (A, B) in $\mathcal{L}_\forall$, then A and $B|L(B)$ are inconsistent.*

We are now ready to prove the key lemma that will allow us to build an interpolating prover. We show that on interpolation problems, superposition with procrastination makes only local deductions:

Lemma 3. *Let A and B be clause sets, and $\succ$ be a reduction order oriented for (A, B). Then system $\mathcal{I}_\succ$ with procrastination, applied to A and $B \mid L(B)$ generates only inferences local for (A, B).*

The above lemma holds only for provers that rigorously propagate the ordering constraints from one inference to the next. However, in practice this is not necessary to obtain a local proof. If we test the ordering constraints for satisfiability but do not propagate them, the worst outcome is that unnecessary deductions will be made. We can simply throw away the resulting non-local deductions, since we know by the above lemma that they are not required for completeness.

Since saturation with procrastination is complete and generates local proofs for interpolation problems, we can use it to build an interpolation algorithm:

Algorithm 1
   Input: A pair of equality clause sets (A, B) having an interpolant in $\mathcal{L}_\forall$.
   Output: An interpolant for (A, B)
   1) Choose a reduction order $\succ$ oriented for (A, B).
   2) Apply system $\mathcal{I}_\succ$ with procrastination to $A, B \mid L(B)$.
   3) If the prover generates a refutation P local for (A, B), then
   4)   Derive an interpolant for (A, B) from P and output the result,
   5) Else (if the prover saturates) abort.

Theorem 2. *Algorithm 1 is correct and terminating.*

To allow us to speak of interpolants of program unwindings, we generalize the notion of interpolant from pairs to finite sequences of formulas. That is, an interpolant for a sequence of formulas $A_1, \ldots, A_n$ is a sequence $\hat{A}_1, \ldots \hat{A}_{n-1}$ such that:

- A_1 implies $\hat{A}_1$
- for all $1 \leq i < n$, $\hat{A}_i \wedge A_i$ implies $\hat{A}_{i+1}$
- $A_n \wedge \hat{A}_{n-1}$ implies false.
- for all $1 \leq i < n$, $\hat{A}_i \in (\mathcal{L}(A_1 \ldots A_i) \cap \mathcal{L}(A_{i+1} \ldots A_n))$.

We can think of the interpolant for a sequence of formulas as being structured refutation of that sequence.

Though we do not prove it here, we can generalize Algorithm 1 to generate interpolants for sequences, replacing (A, B) with the sequence $A_1 \ldots A_n$. We say that a proof is local for $A_1 \ldots A_n$ when every inference is local to some A_i, and a reduction order $\succ$ is oriented for $A_1 \ldots A_n$ when it is oriented for all the pairs $(\{A_1 \ldots A_i\}, \{A_{i+1} \ldots A_n\})$. Finally, instead of $A, B \mid L(B)$, we refute $A_1, A_2 \mid L(A_2 \ldots A_n), \ldots, A_n \mid L(A_n)$. The result is a local refutation for $A_1 \ldots A_n$, from which we can derive an interpolant sequence in linear time in the proof size and n.

4   Invariant Generation

Now we come to the question of generating invariants with interpolants. The intuition behind this approach is the following. Suppose we wish to prove the correctness of a single-loop while program. For example, we might want to prove:

$$\{i = 0\} \ \textbf{while} \ i < N \ \textbf{do} \ a[i]:=0; \ i{+}{+} \ \textbf{od} \ \{\forall (0 \leq j < N) a[j] = 0\}$$

where $i{+}{+}$ is a shorthand for $i:=i + 1$. To do this, we might try unwinding the loop n times and proving the resulting in-line program. If we are lucky, the resulting Floyd/Hoare proof will contain an inductive invariant for the loop. For example, for $n = 2$, we might have:

$$\{i = 0\} \quad [i < N]; \; a[i]:=0; \; i{+}{+} \quad \{\forall(0 \le j < i)a[j] = 0\}$$
$$[i < N]; \; a[i]:=0; \; i{+}{+} \quad \{\forall(0 \le j < N)a[j] = 0\}$$

where $[\phi]$ denotes a guard. Note that the middle assertion of this proof is an inductive assertion for the loop, which we can verify with a suitable first-order prover. On the other hand, if we are unlucky, we might obtain:

$$\{i = 0\} \quad [i < N]; \; a[i]:=0; \; i{+}{+} \quad \{i = 1 \wedge a[0] = 0\}$$
$$[i < N]; \; a[i]:=0; \; i{+}{+} \quad \{\forall(0 \le j < N)a[j] = 0\}$$

This is also a valid proof, but the intermediate assertion is useless for generating an inductive invariant. If we unwind the loop further, we might obtain $i = 2 \wedge a[0] = 0 \wedge a[1] = 0$, and so on, producing a diverging series of non-inductive formulas.

As we will see, the Floyd/Hoare proofs for the unwindings can be produced by interpolation. The trick is to prevent the interpolant formulas from diverging as we unwind the loops further. We will show that by bounding the behavior of the prover appropriately, we can prevent divergence and guarantee to eventually produce an inductive invariant if one exists in $\mathcal{L}_\forall$.

Transition systems, unfoldings and interpolants. We will use first-order formulas to characterize the transition behavior of a system, using the usual device of primed symbols to represent the next state of the system. That is, a set of uninterpreted function and constant symbols S represents the system state. A state of the system is an interpretation of S. For every symbol $s \in S$, we let the symbol s' represent the value of s one time unit in the future. Moreover, we think of s with n primes added as representing the value of s at n time units in the future. For any formula or term ϕ, we will use the notation ϕ' to represent the result of adding one prime to all the occurrence of state symbols in ϕ (meaning ϕ at the next time), and $\phi^{\langle n \rangle}$ to denote the addition of n primes to all occurrence of state symbols in ϕ (meaning ϕ at n time units in the future).

A *state formula* is a formula in $\mathcal{L}(S)$ (which may also include various interpreted symbols, such as $\simeq$ and $+$). A *transition formula* is a formula in $\mathcal{L}(S \cup S')$. A *safety transition system* M is a triple (I, T, P), where state formula I represents the initial states, transition formula T represents the set of transitions, and and state formula P represents the set of safe states. A *safety invariant* for M is a state formula ϕ such that $I \models \phi$ and $\phi, T \models \phi'$ and $\phi \models P$. That is, a safety invariant is an inductive invariant of the system that proves that all reachable states satisfy P.

We will say that an *invariant generator* $\mathcal{G}$ is a procedure that takes a safety transition system M as input and outputs a sequence of formulas. For a given language $L \subseteq \mathcal{L}(S)$, we say that $\mathcal{G}$ is *complete for invariant generation* in L when, for every M that has a safety invariant in L, $\mathcal{G}$ eventually outputs a safety invariant for M. If we have a complete invariant generation procedure, then we have an complete procedure to verify safety transition systems that have safety invariants in $\mathcal{L}_\forall$: we use a complete first-order prover to attempt to prove correctness of each invariant candidate in the sequence, in an interleaved manner.

Of course, there is a trivial complete invariant generator that simply outputs all of the formulas in L in order of their Gödel numbers. Our purpose here is to construct a *practical* invariant generator that uses proofs about finite behaviors to focus the invariant candidates on relevant facts, and thus in a heuristic sense tends to produce valid invariants quickly. In particular, we will be concerned with the language $\mathcal{L}_\forall(S)$ of universally quantified state formulas. We will describe a simple safety invariant generator based on our interpolation algorithm that is complete for invariant generation in $\mathcal{L}_\forall(S)$. It prevents divergence by bounding the language of the prover.

The algorithm is based on *unfolding* the transition system in the style of Bounded Model Checking [1]. For $k \geq 0$, the k-step unfolding of M (denoted $\mathcal{U}_k(M)$) is the following sequence of formulas:

$$\mathcal{U}_k(M) = I, T, T^{\langle 1 \rangle}, \ldots, T^{\langle k-1 \rangle}, \neg P^{\langle k \rangle}$$

This formulas characterizes the set of runs of the transition system of exactly k steps that end in an unsafe state. The system M is safe when $\mathcal{U}_k(M)$ is unsatisfiable for all $k \geq 0$. For simplicity, we will assume that $\neg P \wedge T \rightarrow \neg P'$. That is, once the safety condition is false, it remains false. This can easily be arranged by, for example, adding one state bit that remembers when the property has been false in the past.

To generate invariant candidates, we will make use of a *bounded* saturation prover to refute unfoldings. Given a language L, a saturation prover bounded by L simply throws away all derived clauses not in L (after attempting reductions). For example, the SPASS prover [14] implements bounding by W_k, the set of clauses with k symbols or fewer (*i.e.*, clauses of "weight" up to k). In the sequel, we will assume that $L_1, L_2, \ldots$ is a sequence of finite languages such that $L_1 \subset L_2 \subset \cdots$ and $\bigcup_i L_i$ is the set of all clauses. For example, the sequence $W_1, W_2, \ldots$ meets these criterion. Note that for any finite L, a saturation prover bounded by L must terminate on any input, since the number of clauses it can generate is bounded.

Now let $\succ$ be RPOS for some precedence order oriented for $S, S', S'', \ldots$ and let $\dot\succ$ be a reduction order such that the set of terms less than any given term t over a finite vocabulary is finite. For example, we could say that $t \dot\succ s$ when the weight of s is less than the weight of t or the weights are equal and $t \succ s$. Let $SPB(L)$ stand for a saturation prover using the union of systems $\mathcal{I}_\succ$ and $\mathcal{I}_{\dot\succ}$ with procrastination, restricted to local deductions and bounded by L. For any system M with a universally quantified safety invariant, a fixed language L_m suffices to refute unfoldings of any length using this prover:

Lemma 4. *Let M be a safety transition system with a safety invariant in $\mathcal{L}_\forall$. There exists an integer m, such that for every $k \geq 0$, $SPB(L_m)$ refutes $\mathcal{U}_k(M)$.*

Our invariant generation algorithm is as follows (where $\text{unp}(\phi)$ is ϕ with primes removed):

Algorithm 2

> *Input: A system $M = (I, T, P)$ having a safety invariant in $\mathcal{L}_\forall$.*
> *Output: A sequence of formulas containing a safety invariant for M.*
> *1) Let $i = 1$ and $k = 1$*
> *2) Repeat:*
> *3)   Apply Algorithm 1 using prover $SPB(L_i)$ to $\mathcal{U}_k(M)$.*
> *4)   If the algorithm returns an interpolant $\hat{A}$, then*
> *5)   For $j = 1$ to $k + 1$, output $\bigvee_{l=1\ldots j} \text{unp}(\hat{A}_l)$*
> *6)   Increase k.*
> *7)   Else (if Algorithm 1 aborts) increase i*

Theorem 3. *Algorithm 2 eventually outputs a safety invariant for M.*

It is worth noting that this algorithm achieves completeness despite the fact that the prover is not "complete for consequence generation" as is required in [5]. The generated invariant candidates can be checked for inductiveness using any complete first-order prover. Since this prover may not terminate in the negative case, we must interleave these checks, rather than executing them sequentially. This is a fairly naïve approach to generating invariants from interpolants. We could also use, for example, the method of [7] or the lazy abstraction method [9]. Both of these methods would require a decision oracle for first-order logic. However, in practice we could use saturation of the (unbounded) prover as an indication of unsatisfiability and accept a possibility of non-termination.

5   Implementation and Experiments

The interpolation algorithm has been implemented by modifying the SPASS prover. This is an efficient saturation prover that implements superposition with a variety of reduction rules. SPASS was modified in several ways:

1. The procrastination rules were added.
2. The input formulas are numbered in sequence, and a precedence order is constructed that is oriented for that sequence.
3. Non-local inferences (after replacement) are discarded.

Moreover, it is also allowed to define a background theory by specifying additional interpreted function and predicate symbols and providing axioms for the theory. The background axioms may contain only interpreted symbols. Thus, use of the axioms does not affect locality of the proofs. When computing interpolants from proofs, the axioms in the proof are replaced with true, since they are tautologies of the theory.

The bound mechanism of SPASS was also modified to allow bounds other than weight (number of symbols) and nesting depth. In particular, we implemented a bounding scheme in which L_i allows all clauses with at most nesting depth i and at most i variables. This is a finite set of clauses (modulo subsumption).

For the experiments, we axiomatized three theories: the natural numbers with zero, successor and $<$, the theory of arrays with select and store, and transitive closure of arrays, with a reachability predicate. These axioms are necessarily incomplete. However, we found them adequate to prove properties of some simple programs manipulating arrays and linked lists. For each example program an assertion was specified. The the loops were manually unwound n times, for increasing values of n, and translated into static single-assignment (SSA) form in the manner of the CBMC tool [2]. These unwindings were then verified using the modified prover, increasing the bound i until a refutation was found for violation of the assertion. Then the interpolants were tested to see if they contain inductive invariants for the loops that prove the assertions.

Table 5 shows the results obtained. For each example, the table gives a brief description of the program, the assertion, the number of loop unwindings, the bound language required, and the run time of the prover in seconds.

Table 1. Results of invariant generation experiments

name	description	assertion	unwindings	bound	time (s)
array_set	set all array elements to 0	all elements zero	3	L_1	0.01
array_test	set all array elements to 0 then test all elements	all tests OK	3	L_1	0.01
ll_safe	create a linked list then traverse it	memory safety	3	L_1	0.04
ll_acyc	create a linked list	list acyclic	3	L_1	0.02
ll_delete	delete an acyclic list	memory safety	2	L_1	0.01
ll_delmid	delete any element of acyclic list	result acyclic	2	L_1	0.02
ll_rev	reverse an acyclic list	result acyclic	3	L_1	0.02

As an example, here is the (somewhat simplified) inductive invariant generated for example list_acyc. This is a loop in which newly allocated elements are added to the beginning of a list by modifying their link field:

```
and( reachable(link,x,nil),
     forall([U], or(U = nil, not(reachable(link,x,U)), alloc(U))))
```

This says that x (the list head) can reach nil (the list terminator) via the link field, and every cell reachable from x via the link field is allocated. The former condition guarantees that the list is acyclic, while the latter implies that in the future a cell already in the list will not be appended to the head, creating a cycle. This shows one advantage of using interpolants for invariant generation relative to parametric invariant generation techniques such as [13]. That is, the interpolator is able to synthesize Boolean combinations without requiring the user to provide a template. Moreover, it can handle theories other than arithmetic, such as reachability. Using the interpolating superposition prover and lazy abstraction, the IMPACT software model checker [9] can automatically verify all of the above examples.

The linked list examples in the table could be handled easily by canonical heap abstraction methods [12]. However, using interpolation, we are not required to provide the instrumentation predicates that define the abstraction. This may be a significant advantage in scaling to larger programs. In the quantifier-free case at least, the ability of the interpolating prover to focus invariant generation on relevant facts has proved to be a significant advantage [7,4,9].

While the example programs we used are very simple, experience shows that even very simple programs can produce divergence in infinite-state verification techniques such as predicate abstraction [5]. Our results give some reason to believe that the divergence problem can be controlled.

6   Conclusion and Future Work

We have shown that, by a small modification of a paramodulation-based saturation prover, we can obtain an interpolating prover that is complete for universally quantified interpolants. This was done by constraining the reduction order and adding a reduction rule in order to obtain local proofs. We also solved the problem of divergence in interpolant-based invariant generation by bounding the language of the prover and gradually relaxing the bound. Some experiments verifying simple programs show that, in fact, divergence can be avoided, and termination can be achieved with shallow unwindings.

The next obvious task is to study the scaling behavior of the approach using a program verification system such as IMPACT [9], to determine whether the prover is capable of focusing on just the facts relevant to proving shallow properties of large programs. In addition, the are a number of possible extensions. The SPASS prover has the ability to split cases on ground atoms and to backtrack. However, it may still be much less efficient than a modern DPLL satisfiability solver. It might be useful to integrate it with an efficient DPLL solver in the style of "SAT modulo theories" (SMT) for greater efficiency. Moreover, it would be useful to integrate it with some ground arithmetic procedure (though again, the divergence problem would have to be solved).

Finally, it would be possible to use an interpolant generator for universally quantified interpolants as a predicate refinement heuristic for indexed predicate abstraction [6] much in the same way that this is done for ordinary predicate abstraction in [4]. Having an effective refinement heuristic might make the indexed predicate abstraction technique more practical.

References

1. Biere, A., Cimatti, A., Clarke, E.M., Zhu, Y.: Symbolic model checking without BDDs. In: Cleaveland, W.R. (ed.) TACAS 1999. LNCS, vol. 1579, Springer, Heidelberg (1999)
2. Clarke, E., Kroening, D., Lerda, F.: A tool for checking ANSI-C programs. In: Jensen, K., Podelski, A. (eds.) TACAS 2004. LNCS, vol. 2988, pp. 168–176. Springer, Heidelberg (2004)
3. Craig, W.: Three uses of the Herbrand-Gentzen theorem in relating model theory and proof theory. J. Symbolic Logic 22(3), 269–285 (1957)
4. Henzinger, T.A., Jhala, R., Majumdar, R., McMillan, K.L.: Abstractions from proofs. In: POPL, pp. 232–244. ACM, New York (2004)
5. Jhala, R., McMillan, K.L.: A practical and complete approach to predicate refinement. In: Hermanns, H., Palsberg, J. (eds.) TACAS 2006. LNCS, vol. 3920, pp. 459–473. Springer, Heidelberg (2006)
6. Lahiri, S.K., Bryant, R.E.: Constructing quantified invariants via predicate abstraction. In: Steffen, B., Levi, G. (eds.) VMCAI 2004. LNCS, vol. 2937, pp. 267–281. Springer, Heidelberg (2004)
7. McMillan, K.L.: Interpolation and SAT-based model checking. In: Hunt Jr., W.A., Somenzi, F. (eds.) CAV 2003. LNCS, vol. 2725, pp. 1–13. Springer, Heidelberg (2003)
8. McMillan, K.L.: An interpolating theorem prover. Theor. Comput. Sci. 345(1), 101–121 (2005)
9. McMillan, K.L.: Lazy abstraction with interpolants. In: Ball, T., Jones, R.B. (eds.) CAV 2006. LNCS, vol. 4144, pp. 123–136. Springer, Heidelberg (2006)
10. Nieuwenhuis, R., Rubio, A.: Paramodulation-based theorem proving. In: Robinson, A., Voronkov, A. (eds.) Handbook of Automated Reasoning, vol. I, ch. 7, pp. 371–443. Elsevier Science, Amsterdam (2001)
11. Robinson, G.A., Wos, L.T.: Paramodulation and theorem proving in first order theories with equality. Machine Intelligence 4, 135–150 (1969)
12. Sagiv, S., Reps, T.W., Wilhelm, R.: Parametric shape analysis via 3-valued logic. In: POPL, pp. 105–118. ACM, New York (1999)
13. Sankaranarayanan, S., Sipma, H.B., Manna, Z.: Constraint-based linear-relations analysis. In: Giacobazzi, R. (ed.) SAS 2004. LNCS, vol. 3148, pp. 53–68. Springer, Heidelberg (2004)
14. Weidenbach, C., Schmidt, R.A., Hillenbrand, T., Rusev, R., Topic, D.: System description: SPASS version 3.0. In: Pfenning, F. (ed.) CADE 2007. LNCS (LNAI), vol. 4603, pp. 514–520. Springer, Heidelberg (2007)

Accelerating Interpolation-Based Model-Checking

Nicolas Caniart, Emmanuel Fleury, Jérôme Leroux, and Marc Zeitoun

LaBRI, Université Bordeaux - CNRS UMR 5800,
351 cours de la Libération, F-33405 Talence CEDEX France
{caniart,fleury,leroux,mz}@labri.fr

Abstract. *Interpolation-based model-checking* and *acceleration* techniques have been widely proved successful and efficient for reachability checking. Surprisingly, these two techniques have never been combined to strengthen each other. Intuitively, acceleration provides under-approximation of the reachability set by computing the exact effect of some control-flow cycles and combining them with other transitions. On the other hand, interpolation-based model-checking is refining an over-approximation of the reachable states based on spurious error-traces. The goal of this paper is to combine acceleration techniques with interpolation-based model-checking at the refinement stage. Our method, called *"interpolant acceleration"*, helps to refine the abstraction, ruling out not only a single spurious error-trace but a possibly infinite set of error-traces obtained by any unrolling of its cycles. Interpolant acceleration is also proved to strictly enlarge the set of transformations that can be usually handled by acceleration techniques.

1 Introduction

Counterexample-guided abstraction refinement (CEGAR) paradigm [6] makes it possible to perform efficient verification of real-life software. In this approach (see Fig.1), an initial coarse predicate abstraction [10] of the concrete model is first derived and explored by a model-checker for reachability of error states. If no error path is found, the system is said to be 'safe'. If an abstract error-trace is found, it is checked against the concrete model. When

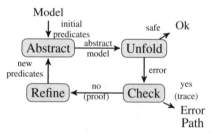

Fig. 1. Interpolant-based Model-Checking

the error also exists in the concrete model, the system is said to be *'unsafe'* and a concrete error path is provided to the operator. Finally, when the error is found to be spurious, a proof of the spuriousness of the trace is used to build a refinement of the abstraction.

Interpolation-based model-checking [14, 15] is a CEGAR framework where checking the error-trace is performed using decision procedures for various logics and refinement is produced by computing an interpolant, which provides a set of predicates needed to invalidate the considered spurious error-trace in the abstraction. Interpolation-based model-checking technique has been proved robust and efficient but, as other

C.R. Ramakrishnan and J. Rehof (Eds.): TACAS 2008, LNCS 4963, pp. 428–442, 2008.

CEGAR frameworks, cannot easily handle numerous cycles or infinite behaviors which tend to generate a lot (possibly an infinity) of predicates, while another, better chosen predicate could have captured the whole behavior of the cycle at once. Recently, a '*lazy*' [12] approach of this method has been introduced [16], allowing it to deal with infinite systems. Still, the interpolation-based model-checking technique suffers from a lack of good strategies to efficiently handle infinite behaviors of the input model. As an illustration, consider the example shown on Fig. 2 taken from [13], and well-known in the CEGAR framework [11]. On such a (correct) program, an interpolant-based model-checker might never stop while deriving the predicates to refine the abstraction because an infinity of values of i will have to be checked.

```
void foo(int i, int j) {
   x = i; y = j;
   while (x != 0)
      { x--; y--; }
   if (i == j)
      assert (y == 0);
}
```

Fig. 2. An example of CEGAR divergence (C code and Control-Flow Automaton (CFA))

On the other hand, *acceleration techniques* [3, 5, 1] make it possible to check for reachability of infinite systems thanks to a symbolic representation of configurations. Basically, given some suitable control-flow cycle σ fulfilling some properties and a set of states X, acceleration tries to compute the infinite union of all $\sigma^n(X)$. Such a set is called the σ^*-*acceleration set*. It captures the reachable states from X through any unrolling of the cycle σ. Acceleration model-checking is usually performed by adding meta-transitions σ^* to the original model in order to create 'shortcuts' allowing to explore arbitrary iterations of a cycle in one single step, and thus computing the reachable states even for infinite sequences of transitions. For example, systems such as the one presented in Fig. 2 are quite easy to accelerate. Unfortunately, acceleration techniques do not scale up to large systems and termination cannot be ensured.

Intuitively, interpolant-based model-checking focuses on large and simple systems (large number of states, few predicates), where acceleration techniques focus more on small and complex systems. Therefore, our idea is to combine interpolation-based model-checking and acceleration techniques. Interpolation-based model-checking offers a quite helpful automatic abstraction/refinement scheme which can discard unnecessary parts of the system, helping the acceleration technique to deal with smaller chunks to accelerate. Similarly, the acceleration technique can help the interpolation-based model-checking to deal with complex behaviors. We propose here three ways to combine them together:

– **Static Acceleration:** one simply performs static-analysis on the abstract model to detect interesting cycles and adding the corresponding meta-transitions σ^* to the model. This method is quite simple but probably also extremely inefficient because we possibly have to deal with large systems at this stage of the CEGAR for which acceleration would not scale.

- **On-the-fly Acceleration:** While exploring and thus unfolding the abstract model, paths can be processed on-the-fly to detect control loops and check for their conformance to acceleration requirements. Acceleration can then be used to fasten the state-space exploration. This simple method is expected to have a better efficiency as it does not require exhaustive cycle detection. Still, its complexity overhead can be high since many cycles might be found during the unfolding. Heuristics can at last be added to decide whether it is relevant or not to compute an acceleration.
- **Interpolant Acceleration:** Last but not least, we believe this method to be the most promising one, though it can only be applied to lazy interpolant-based model-checking and not to any CEGAR scheme as the previous ones. It takes place at the refining stage, just after identifying an error-trace as '*spurious*' and when computing an interpolant for this trace. Suppose that some suitable cycles σ are found to be such that any unrolling of them are also proved to be spurious. Then, computing the σ^*-acceleration and extracting the interpolant will capture an enlarged set of spurious counter-examples, thus yielding a better abstraction refinement.

We focus here on "*interpolant acceleration*" which reveals to be both theoretically interesting and with room for improvements. We first extend the notion of *interpolant on a path* [16] with the notion of *error-pattern* and *accelerated interpolant* and prove that if an error-pattern is spurious, then there is an accelerated interpolant that will witness every error-trace matching the error-pattern (section 2). We then identify two classes of computable accelerated interpolants: *Presburger* accelerated interpolants (section 4) and *poly-bounded* ones (sections 5 and 6). The first one makes it possible to assess the spuriousness for error-patterns labeled by Presburger transformations, using standard acceleration techniques. The second one allows us to compute interpolants for error-patterns labeled by transformations whose iteration has polynomial, and not only linear, behaviors (*i.e.* which are of the form $x' = Mx + v$ where $v \in \mathbb{Z}^n$ and $M \in \mathcal{M}_n(\mathbb{Z})$ is such that the coefficients of its ℓ-th power are bounded by a polynomial in ℓ). Our proof is constructive and can be translated into a (non-optimized) algorithm.

Our work is related to the framework recently presented in [2]. The approach of [2] is to extract "*path programs*", which are sub-graphs of the program leading to errors. In our framework, we aim at capturing a characteristic unfolding of the program leading to the error trace. Where *path programs* can be extremely complex and difficult to exploit for acceleration techniques, *error patterns* tend to be simpler in the way loops interleave and easier to process. On the other hand, *path programs* can capture much more behaviors than *error patterns*.

The remainder of the paper is organized as follows: in Section 2 we recall the notion of interpolant, introduce '*accelerated interpolant*' and relate it to set separability. We recall basics on linear algebra and characterize the class of transformations that our method can handle in Section 3. In Section 4, we rephrase the problem of computing an accelerated interpolant for Presburger sets in more suitable terms. We then reduce this latter problem in Section 5. Finally, using these intermediate results, Section 6 describes how to compute an accelerated interpolant for our class of linear transformations and two Presburger definable sets, one of which is finite. At last, we show that the finiteness condition for one of the Presburger sets cannot be dropped.

2   Introducing Accelerated Interpolants

The need for *interpolants* in the CEGAR loop of *interpolation-based model-checking* arises during the refinement step. More precisely, if we assume the input program of the CEGAR loop to be given as a *control-flow automaton* [12] (CFA), an abstraction of this one will be unfolded and explored to find an *error-trace*. In case one is found, the algorithm tries to checks if it witnesses a real error-path or appears as a side effect of a too coarse abstraction. In the latter case the trace is said *spurious*. Finally, if proved spurious, abstraction is refined to rule out the spurious error-trace thanks to the computation of an interpolant capturing this trace.

Formally a *CFA* is a tuple $G = (Q, q_{ini}, q_{err}, \mathbb{D}, T)$ where Q is the finite set of *control-states*, $q_{ini} \in Q$ is the *initial state*, $q_{err} \in Q$ is the *error state*, $\mathbb{D}$ is a possibly infinite set representing the data domain, and T is a finite set of transitions $t = (q, r_t, q')$ with $q, q' \in Q$ and $r_t \subseteq \mathbb{D} \times \mathbb{D}$. Intuitively, the binary relations over $\mathbb{D} \times \mathbb{D}$ can be used either to encode guards, or to encode updates (see for instance Example 4.2). A *trace* $\pi = t_0 \cdots t_k$ is a word of transitions $t_i \in T$ such that there exist $q_0, \ldots, q_{k+1} \in Q$ and $r_0, \ldots, r_k \subseteq \mathbb{D} \times \mathbb{D}$ with $t_i = (q_i, r_i, q_{i+1})$ for $0 \le i \le k$. Such a trace is also denoted $\pi = q_0 \xrightarrow{r_0} q_1 \cdots \xrightarrow{r_k} q_{k+1}$, or just $q_0 \xrightarrow{r_\pi} q_{k+1}$ with $r_\pi = r_0 \cdots r_k$ [1]. It is called an *error-trace* if $q_0 = q_{ini}$ and $q_{k+1} = q_{err}$. It is a *cycle* if $q_{k+1} = q_0$. We denote by $r^* = \bigcup_{\ell \in \mathbb{N}} r^\ell$ the reflexive and transitive closure of a binary relation $r \subseteq \mathbb{D} \times \mathbb{D}$ where r^ℓ denotes the ℓ-th power of r.

Semantically, a CFA defines a *labeled transition system* given by the set of *configurations* $Q \times \mathbb{D}$ and the binary relations $\xrightarrow{r}$ over the set of configurations by $(q, d) \xrightarrow{r} (q', d')$ if $q \xrightarrow{r} q'$ and $(d, d') \in r$. A *path* is an alternating sequence of configurations and binary relations $(q_0, d_0) \xrightarrow{r_0} (q_1, d_1) \cdots \xrightarrow{r_k} (q_{k+1}, d_{k+1})$. A *concretization* of a trace $q_0 \xrightarrow{r_0} q_1 \cdots \xrightarrow{r_k} q_{k+1}$ is a path of the form $(q_0, d_0) \xrightarrow{r_0} (q_1, d_1) \cdots \xrightarrow{r_k} (q_{k+1}, d_{k+1})$, unambiguously abusing the $\xrightarrow{r_k}$ notation, for the sake of simplicity.

Definition 2.1. *An error-trace is said* spurious *if it does not have a concretization.*

By definition, the existence of a concretization is sufficient to certify that an error-trace is not spurious. Let us now recall why a sequence of sets $X_0, \ldots, X_k$ called an *interpolant* can certify that an error-trace *is* spurious. Let introduce few notations, given $X, X' \subseteq \mathbb{D}$ and $r \subseteq \mathbb{D} \times \mathbb{D}$, let $\mathrm{post}_r(X) = \{d' \mid \exists d\, (d, d') \in r \land d \in X\}$ and $\mathrm{wpre}_r(X') = \{d \mid \forall d'\, (d, d') \in r \Rightarrow d' \in X'\}$. Recall that $(\mathrm{post}_r(), \mathrm{wpre}_r())$ forms a *Galois connection*, since clearly $\mathrm{post}_r(X) \subseteq X'$ iff $X \subseteq \mathrm{wpre}_r(X')$. If these inclusions hold true, we write $X \xrightarrow{r} X'$. Moreover if $X = X'$ then X is called an r-invariant.

Definition 2.2. *A sequence* $X_0, \ldots, X_{k+1}$ *of subsets of $\mathbb{D}$ is called an* interpolant *for a decomposition* $\pi_0, \ldots, \pi_k$ *of an error-trace* $\pi = \pi_0 \ldots \pi_k$ *if:*

$$\mathbb{D} = X_0 \xrightarrow{r_{\pi_0}} X_1 \cdots X_k \xrightarrow{r_{\pi_k}} X_{k+1} = \varnothing$$

Thus, the existence of an interpolant witnesses the spuriousness of an error-trace. Conversely, we would like to establish that if an error-trace is spurious, then there exists an interpolant. This immediately follows from [7, Propositions 1&2].

---

[1]   By convention r_π is the identity binary relation if π is the empty word of T^*.

Proposition 2.3 ([7, Propositions 1&2]). *An error-trace $\pi_0 \cdots \pi_k$ is spurious if and only if there exists an interpolant $(X_i)_{0 \le i \le k+1}$. In this case $(\mathrm{post}_{r_{\pi_0} \ldots r_{\pi_{i-1}}}(\mathbb{D}))_{0 \le i \le k+1}$ and $(\mathrm{wpre}_{r_{\pi_i} \ldots r_{\pi_k}}(\varnothing))_{0 \le i \le k+1}$ are interpolants and we have:*

$$\forall 0 \le i \le k+1 \quad \mathrm{post}_{r_{\pi_0} \ldots r_{\pi_{i-1}}}(\mathbb{D}) \subseteq X_i \subseteq \mathrm{wpre}_{r_{\pi_i} \ldots r_{\pi_k}}(\varnothing).$$

Thus, an error-trace is spurious iff one can find an interpolant witnessing its spuriousness. Unfortunately, using this property, the classical CEGAR scheme may only discard error-traces one by one. Consider the case where a trace contains cycles forming *error-patterns*. We would like then to discard *every* error-traces matching a pattern *at once* (whatever is the number of iterations along each cycle). That is, we would like to prove that an error-pattern is spurious, not only a single error-trace. More formally:

Definition 2.4. *An* error-pattern *is an sequence* $(\pi_0, \theta_1, \pi_1, \ldots, \theta_k, \pi_k)$ *where each* π_i *is a trace and each* θ_i *is a cycle, of the following form:*

Note that, by extension, an error-pattern $(\pi_0, \theta_1, \pi_1 \ldots, \theta_k, \pi_k)$ is said *spurious* if all error-traces in $\pi_0 \theta_1^* \pi_1 \ldots \theta_k^* \pi_k$ are spurious.

Definition 2.5 (Accelerated Interpolant). *A sequence* $X_0, \ldots, X_{k+1}$ *of subsets of* $\mathbb{D}$ *is called an* accelerated interpolant *for an error-pattern* $(\pi_0, \theta_1, \pi_1, \ldots, \theta_k, \pi_k)$ *if:*

That is, in order for an interpolant $X_0, \ldots, X_{k+1}$ for $(\pi_0, \pi_1, \ldots, \pi_k)$ to be an accelerated interpolant for the error-pattern $(\pi_0, \theta_1, \pi_1, \ldots, \theta_k, \pi_k)$, we require in addition that each X_i is an r_{θ_i}-invariant, for $1 \le i \le k$. Once again, it is easy to check that accelerated interpolants characterize spurious error-patterns.

Lemma 2.6. *Let* $(\pi_0, \theta_1, \pi_1, \ldots, \theta_k, \pi_k)$ *be an error-pattern,* $r_{\theta_0} = r_{\theta_{k+1}}$ *be the identity relation on* $\mathbb{D}$, *and* $p_i, s_i \subseteq \mathbb{D} \times \mathbb{D}$ *defined by* $p_i = r_{\theta_0}^* r_{\pi_0} r_{\theta_1}^* \cdots r_{\pi_{i-1}} r_{\theta_i}^*$, $s_i = r_{\theta_i}^* r_{\pi_i} \cdots r_{\theta_k}^* r_{\pi_k}$. *The error-pattern is spurious if and only if there exists an accelerated interpolant* $(X_i)_{0 \le i \le k+1}$. *Moreover, in this case both* $(\mathrm{post}_{p_i}(\mathbb{D}))_{0 \le i \le k+1}$ *and* $(\mathrm{wpre}_{s_i}(\varnothing))_{0 \le i \le k+1}$ *are accelerated interpolants such that:*

$$\forall 0 \le i \le k+1 \quad \mathrm{post}_{p_i}(\mathbb{D}) \subseteq X_i \subseteq \mathrm{wpre}_{s_i}(\varnothing).$$

Corollary 2.7. *An error-pattern is spurious iff there exists an accelerated interpolant.*

We now investigate the computation of accelerated interpolants for error-patterns containing one single cycle. We show that the accelerated interpolation problem for such an error-pattern (π_0, θ, π_1) reduces to a separation problem.

Definition 2.8. *Given a binary relation r, a set X is called a r-separator for a pair of sets (E, F) if $X \xrightarrow{r} X$, $E \subseteq X$ and $X \cap F = \varnothing$. If such a set exists, (E, F) is said r-separable.*

In fact, observe that $(\mathbb{D}, X, \varnothing)$ is an accelerated interpolant for (π_0, θ, π_1) iff X is an r_θ-separator for (E, F) where $E = \mathrm{post}_{r_{\pi_0}}(\mathbb{D})$ and $F = \mathrm{wpre}_{r_{\pi_1}}(\varnothing)$.

We have shown that if an error-pattern is spurious, then there exist an interpolant that will witness it spuriousness. But, to find an interpolant for a given a error-pattern, we need to be able to compute or approximate the relations $r_{\theta_i}^*$. Considering the fact that the set of error-traces matching a pattern may be infinite, it is obvious that this is not possible in general. This is the question addressed in the next sections.

3   Some Notes on Linear Algebra

The method we present in the next sections computes accelerated interpolants for an error-pattern with one single cycle θ whose associated binary relation is $x \; r_\theta \; y$ if and only if $y = Mx + v$, where $v \in \mathbb{Z}^n$ and $M \in \mathcal{M}_n(\mathbb{Z})$ is such that the coefficients of its ℓ-th power are bounded by a polynomial in ℓ. In this section, we first briefly recall some material about matrices, and then characterize these integer matrices whose ℓ-th power is polynomially bounded in ℓ.

Considering $\mathbb{K} \in \{\mathbb{C}, \mathbb{R}, \mathbb{Q}, \mathbb{Z}\}$, we denote by $\mathcal{M}_n(\mathbb{K})$ the set of n-dim *square matrices* with coefficients in $\mathbb{K}$. The n-dim *identity matrix* and the *zero matrix* are respectively denoted by I_n and 0_n. The *inverse* of an *invertible matrix* P is denoted by P^{-1}. The matrix M^ℓ, where $\ell \in \mathbb{N}$, denotes the ℓ-th power of M. The multiplicative monoid $\{M^\ell \mid \ell \in \mathbb{N}\}$ is denoted by M^*. Given $S \subseteq \mathbb{K}^n$, we let $MS = \{Mx \mid x \in S\}$ and $M^*S = \bigcup_{\ell=0}^\infty M^\ell S$. Two matrices M_1, M_2 *commute* if $M_1 M_2 = M_2 M_1$. An n-dim matrix Δ is said *diagonal* if $\Delta_{ij} = 0$ whenever $i \neq j$. A matrix D is said *diagonalizable* if there exists a diagonal matrix $\Delta \in \mathcal{M}_n(\mathbb{C})$ and an invertible matrix $P \in \mathcal{M}_n(\mathbb{C})$ such that $D = P\Delta P^{-1}$. A matrix N is said *nilpotent* if there exists $\ell \in \mathbb{N} \setminus \{0\}$ such that $N^\ell = 0_n$. Remember that $N^n = 0_n$. A set $S \subseteq \mathbb{K}^n$ is called an M-*invariant* if $MS \subseteq S$. An M-invariant S is called an M-*attractor* for a vector $x \in \mathbb{K}^n$ if there exists $\ell_0 \in \mathbb{N}$ such that $M^{\ell_0}x \in S$. Observe that $M^\ell x \in S$ for any $\ell \geq \ell_0$ since S is an M-invariant.

Let $L_m(X) = \frac{1}{!m}X \cdots (X - m + 1)$ be the m-th *Lagrange polynomial*. The *binomial theorem* states that for every pair (M_1, M_2) of commuting matrices and for every $\ell \in \mathbb{N}$:

$$(M_1 + M_2)^\ell = \sum_{m=0}^\ell L_m(\ell) M_1^{\ell-m} M_2^m$$

Observe that a matrix $M \in \mathcal{M}_n(\mathbb{Z})$ generates a finite monoid M^* if and only if the coefficients of M^ℓ are bounded independently of ℓ. And the finiteness of M^* is decidable in polynomial time [3]. We are going to show that the Dunford decomposition algorithmically characterizes the set of matrices $M \in \mathcal{M}_n(\mathbb{Z})$ such that the coefficients of M^ℓ are *polynomially bounded* in ℓ. Recall that the *Dunford decomposition theorem* proves that any matrix M can be uniquely decomposed into a pair (D, N) of commuting matrices of $\mathcal{M}_n(\mathbb{C})$ such that $M = D + N$, where D is diagonalizable and N is nilpotent. Moreover if $M \in \mathcal{M}_n(\mathbb{Q})$ then $D, N \in \mathcal{M}_n(\mathbb{Q})$ are effectively computable in polynomial time[2]. In particular, we can decide in polynomial time if a matrix $M \in \mathcal{M}_n(\mathbb{Q})$ is diagonalizable. In fact, a matrix M is diagonalizable if and only if its Dunford decomposition (D, N) satisfies $D = M$ and $N = 0_n$.

A matrix M is *poly-bounded* if all the coefficients of M^ℓ are polynomially bounded in ℓ.

Proposition 3.1. *A matrix $M \in \mathcal{M}_n(\mathbb{Z})$ is poly-bounded if and only if the Dunford decomposition (D, N) of M is such that D^* is finite.*

---

[2] A possible algorithm consists in computing $P = \chi_M / \gcd(\chi_M, \chi_M')$, where χ_M denotes the characteristic polynomial of M, and the sequence defined by $D_0 = M$, and $D_{k+1} = D_k - P(D_k) \circ (P'(D_k))^{-1}$, which is well-defined and stabilizes to D after $O(\log n)$ iterations.

Example 3.2. Below is a poly-bounded matrix, and the transition system it encodes.

$$M = \begin{pmatrix} 1\,1\,0 \\ 0\,1\,1 \\ 0\,0\,1 \end{pmatrix} \text{ is poly-bounded as } M^\ell = \begin{pmatrix} 1\ \ell\ \frac{\ell(\ell-1)}{2} \\ 0\ 1\ \ \ell \\ 0\ 0\ \ \ 1 \end{pmatrix} \qquad \begin{aligned} x_1' &= x_1 + x_2 \\ x_2' &= x_2 + x_3 \\ x_3' &= x_3 \end{aligned}$$

4   Presburger Accelerated Interpolants

In this section, we focus on the expressive power of the Presburger logic for effectively computing accelerated interpolants.

Presburger logic [17] is a first-order additive arithmetic theory over the integers. This decidable logic is used in a large range of applications such as compiler optimization, program analysis and model-checking. A set $Z \subseteq \mathbb{Z}^n$ that can be encoded by a formula $\phi(\boldsymbol{x})$ in this logic is called a *Presburger set*. In this paper, we use two geometrical characterizations of the Presburger sets respectively based on *linear sets* and *linear constraints*. A *linear set* Z is a set of the form $Z = \boldsymbol{a} + P^*$ where $\boldsymbol{a} \in \mathbb{Z}^n$, P is a finite subset of $\mathbb{Z}^n$ and P^* denotes the set of finite sums $\sum_{i=1}^{k} \boldsymbol{p_i}$ with $\boldsymbol{p_1}, \ldots, \boldsymbol{p_k} \in P$ and $k \in \mathbb{N}$. Recall that a set is Presburger if and only if it is equal to a finite union of linear sets [9]. A *linear constraint* is either an inequality constraint $\langle \boldsymbol{\alpha}, \boldsymbol{x} \rangle \leq c$ or a modular constraint $\langle \boldsymbol{\alpha}, \boldsymbol{x} \rangle \equiv_b c$ where $\boldsymbol{\alpha} \in \mathbb{Z}^n$, $b \in \mathbb{N} \setminus \{0\}$, $c \in \mathbb{Z}$ and where $\langle \boldsymbol{\alpha}, \boldsymbol{x} \rangle = \sum_{i=1}^{n} \alpha_i x_i$ denotes the *dot product* of $\boldsymbol{\alpha}$ and $\boldsymbol{x}$, and $\equiv_b$ denotes the *equivalence binary relation* over $\mathbb{Z}$ satisfying $z_1 \equiv_b z_2$ if and only if b divides $z_1 - z_2$. A *quantification elimination* shows that a set $Z \subseteq \mathbb{Z}^n$ is Presburger if and only if it can be encoded by a propositional formula of linear constraints (*i.e.*, a quantifier-free Presburger formula).

A CFA $G = (Q, q_{ini}, q_{err}, \mathbb{Z}^n, T)$ is said *Presburger* if $\boldsymbol{x}\ r_t\ \boldsymbol{x}'$ is encoded by a Presburger formula $\phi_t(\boldsymbol{x}, \boldsymbol{x}')$ for any transition $t \in T$. We say that an interpolant (resp. accelerated interpolant) $X_0, \ldots, X_{k+1}$ is *Presburger* if the sets $X_0, \ldots, X_{k+1}$ are Presburger. Since Presburger logic is decidable, observe that the spuriousness problem for error-traces of Presburger CFA is decidable and that we can effectively compute a Presburger interpolant.

Concerning the computation of Presburger accelerated interpolants, observe that the reachability problem for *Minsky machines* can be reduced to the spuriousness problem of an error-pattern of the form (π_0, θ, π_1) where π_0 intuitively initialized the Minsky machine, π_1 tests if the final state is reached and θ encodes the one step reachability relation of the Machine. This reduction shows that the spuriousness problem for error-patterns of Presburger CFA is undecidable. However, observe that if there exists a Presburger accelerated interpolant, such an interpolant can be effectively computed with an enumerative approach. In fact, the set of Presburger accelerated interpolants is recursively enumerable since it is sufficient to fairly enumerate the sequences of Presburger formulas $\phi_0(\boldsymbol{x}), \ldots, \phi_{k+1}(\boldsymbol{x})$ and checks if such a sequence effectively encodes an accelerated interpolant. Therefore, the spuriousness problem for error-patterns of Presburger CFA is undecidable. Note that when a Presburger accelerated interpolant exists, it can effectively be computed.

Naturally, such an enumerative algorithm has no practical interest. This explains why we focus on error-pattern classes admitting Presburger accelerated interpolants based on a non enumerative algorithm. Acceleration techniques provide such a class.

The following theorem shows that if θ is a control-flow cycle such that $\boldsymbol{x}\ r_\theta\ \boldsymbol{y}$ iff $\boldsymbol{y} = M\boldsymbol{x} + \boldsymbol{v}$ where $\boldsymbol{v} \in \mathbb{Z}^n$ and $M \in \mathcal{M}_n(\mathbb{Z})$ has a finite monoid M^*, then we can effectively compute a Presburger formula encoding the binary relation r_θ^*. Thus, if the cycles of an error-pattern satisfy the finite monoid condition, we can effectively decide the spuriousness, and in this case we can effectively compute a Presburger accelerated interpolant. Observe that the obtained interpolant does not use the fact that r_θ^* can be approximated, whereas the definition of accelerated interpolants does not require a precise computation of this relation.

Proposition 4.1 (Acceleration [4, 8]). *A binary relation r over $\mathbb{Z}^n$ such that $\boldsymbol{x}\ r\ \boldsymbol{y}$ if and only if $\boldsymbol{y} = M\boldsymbol{x} + \boldsymbol{v}$ where $\boldsymbol{v} \in \mathbb{Z}^n$ and $M \in \mathcal{M}_n(\mathbb{Z})$ satisfies r^* is Presburger if and only if M^* is finite. Moreover, in this case we can compute a Presburger formula $\phi(\boldsymbol{x}, \boldsymbol{y})$ encoding $\boldsymbol{x}\ r^*\ \boldsymbol{y}$.*

Here is an example of spurious error-pattern with no Presburger accelerated interpolant.

Example 4.2. Let $n = 2$ and consider the CFA G_1 depicted in Fig 3. Intuitively, t_{ini} reset two integer variables x_1 and x_2, t_1 and t_2 are two deterministic loops such that r_{t_2} performs the inverse of r_{t_1}, t does not modify the variables, and t_{err} tests if $x_1 = 0$ and $x_2 > 0$. More formally $G_1 = (Q, q_{ini}, q_{err}, \mathbb{Z}^2, T)$ where $Q = \{q_{ini}, q_1, q_2, q_{err}\}$ and where $T = \{t_{ini}, t_1, t, t_2, t_{err}\}$ is defined by :

$$
\begin{array}{lllll}
t_{ini} = (\ q_{ini}\ ,\ r_{ini}\ ,\ q_1\ ) & \text{with } (\boldsymbol{x}, \boldsymbol{x}') \in r_{ini} & \text{iff } x_1' = 0 \wedge x_2' = 0 \\
t_1 = (\ q_1\ ,\ r_1\ ,\ q_1\ ) & \text{with } (\boldsymbol{x}, \boldsymbol{x}') \in r_1 & \text{iff } x_1' = x_1 + 1 \wedge x_2' = x_2 + x_1 \\
t = (\ q_1\ ,\ r\ ,\ q_2\ ) & \text{with } (\boldsymbol{x}, \boldsymbol{x}') \in r & \text{iff } x_1' = x_1 \wedge x_2' = x_2 \\
t_2 = (\ q_2\ ,\ r_2\ ,\ q_2\ ) & \text{with } (\boldsymbol{x}, \boldsymbol{x}') \in r_2 & \text{iff } x_1 = x_1' + 1 \wedge x_2 = x_2' + x_1' \\
t_{err} = (\ q_2\ ,\ r_{err}\ ,\ q_{err}\ ) & \text{with } (\boldsymbol{x}, \boldsymbol{x}') \in r_{err} & \text{iff } x_1 = 0 \wedge x_2 > 0
\end{array}
$$

Observe that $(\mathbb{Z}^2, X, X, \varnothing)$ where $X = \{\boldsymbol{x} \in \mathbb{Z}^2 \mid x_2 = \frac{x_1(x_1-1)}{2}\}$ is an accelerated interpolant for the error-pattern $(t_{ini}, t_1, t, t_2, t_{err})$. In particular this error-pattern is spurious. Unfortunately X is not a Presburger set. Actually, the following lemma shows that it is hopeless to try computing a Presburger accelerated interpolant.

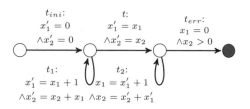

Fig. 3. The CFA G_1

Lemma 4.3. *There does not exist a Presburger accelerated interpolant for the spurious error-pattern $(t_{ini}, t_1, t, t_2, t_{err})$.*

Proof. Let us consider an accelerated interpolant $(\mathbb{Z}^2, X_1, X_2, \varnothing)$ for the spurious error-pattern $(t_{ini}, t_1, t, t_2, t_{err})$ and assume by contradiction that X_1 is a Presburger set. By replacing X_1 by $X_1 \cap \mathbb{N}^2$, we can assume without loss of generality that $X_1 \subseteq \mathbb{N}^2$. Let us consider a Presburger formula $\phi_1(\boldsymbol{x})$ encoding X_1. An immediate induction proves that $\text{post}_{r_{ini}r_1^*}(\mathbb{Z}^2)$ is equal to $X' = \{\boldsymbol{x} \in \mathbb{N}^2 \mid x_2 = \frac{x_1(x_1-1)}{2}\}$. As $(\mathbb{Z}^2, X_1, X_2, \varnothing)$ is an interpolant, we deduce that $X' \subseteq X_1$. Note that if $X_1 \cap \{\boldsymbol{x} \in \mathbb{N}^2 \mid x_2 > \frac{x_1(x_1-1)}{2}\}$ is empty then X' is encoded by the Presburger formula $\phi'(\boldsymbol{x}') := \phi_1(\boldsymbol{x}') \wedge \forall x_2 \phi_1(x_1', x_2) \implies x_2 \leq x_2'$. As X' is not a Presburger set we deduce that this intersection is not empty. Thus, there exists $x \in X_1$ such that $x_2 > \frac{x_1(x_1-1)}{2}$. Now, just observe that $\text{post}_{rr_2^{x_2} r_{err}}(\{x\})$ shows that $\text{post}_{rr_2^* r_{err}}(X_1) \neq \varnothing$ which is in contradiction with the fact that $(\mathbb{Z}^2, X_1, X_2, \varnothing)$ is an accelerated interpolant. □

5 Half-Space Attractors

In this section we provide an algorithm for solving the following convergence decision problem: given the *half-space*

$$H(\alpha, c) = \{x \in \mathbb{R}^n \mid \langle \alpha, x \rangle \geq c\}$$

with $\alpha \in \mathbb{Z}^n$ and $c \in \mathbb{Z}$, and a matrix $M \in \mathcal{M}_n(\mathbb{R})$ such that $N = M - I_n$ is nilpotent, decide whether a vector $x \in \mathbb{Z}^n$ satisfies $M^\ell x \in H(\alpha, c)$ for some $\ell \in \mathbb{N}$. This algorithm will be crucial for computing accelerated interpolants, in the next section.

We first show that the following two sets can be decomposed into an effectively computable Boolean combination of half-spaces:

$$E_-(\alpha, c) = \{x \in \mathbb{R}^n \mid \exists \ell_0 \in \mathbb{N}, \forall \ell \geq \ell_0, M^\ell x \notin H(\alpha, c)\},$$
$$E_+(\alpha, c) = \{x \in \mathbb{R}^n \mid \exists \ell_0 \in \mathbb{N}, \forall \ell \geq \ell_0, M^\ell x \in H(\alpha, c)\}.$$

It is clear that $E_-(\alpha, c)$ and $E_+(\alpha, c)$ are disjoint (the decomposition proof will show in addition that $\mathbb{R}^n = E_-(\alpha, c) \cup E_+(\alpha, c)$). Recall that $L_m(X)$ denotes the Lagrange polynomial. Since $N^n = 0_n$ and $L_m(\ell) = 0$ for any $m > \ell$, the binomial theorem applied to the commutative matrices I_n and N yields:

$$\langle \alpha, M^\ell x \rangle = \sum_{m=0}^{n-1} L_m(\ell) \langle \alpha, N^m x \rangle \tag{1}$$

We introduce the sets $Z_k(\alpha)$ for $k \in \mathbb{Z}$. First, $Z_0(\alpha) = \{x \in \mathbb{R}^n \mid \bigwedge_{j \geq 1} \langle \alpha, N^j x \rangle = 0\}$ and, for $\varepsilon \in \{-1, +1\}$ and $m \in \mathbb{N} \setminus \{0\}$:

$$Z_{\varepsilon.m}(\alpha) = \{x \in \mathbb{R}^n \mid \varepsilon.\langle \alpha, N^m x \rangle > 0 \wedge \bigwedge_{j > m} \langle \alpha, N^j x \rangle = 0\}.$$

Clearly, the $Z_k(\alpha)$ are pairwise disjoint, $Z_k(\alpha) = \varnothing$ if $|k| \geq n$, and $\bigcup_{k \in \mathbb{Z}} Z_k(\alpha) = \mathbb{R}^n$.

Lemma 5.1. *Let $\alpha, x \in \mathbb{R}^n$. We have:*

$$\lim_{\ell \to +\infty} \langle \alpha, M^\ell x \rangle = \begin{cases} +\infty & \text{if } x \in \bigcup_{k \geq 1} Z_k(\alpha), \\ \langle \alpha, x \rangle & \text{if } x \in Z_0(\alpha), \\ -\infty & \text{if } x \in \bigcup_{k \leq -1} Z_k(\alpha). \end{cases}$$

From the previous lemma, we deduce the expression of $E_-(\alpha, c)$ and $E_+(\alpha, c)$:

$$E_-(\alpha, c) = (Z_0(\alpha) \setminus H(\alpha, c)) \cup \bigcup_{k \leq -1} Z_k(\alpha), \tag{2}$$

$$E_+(\alpha, c) = (Z_0(\alpha) \cap H(\alpha, c)) \cup \bigcup_{k \geq 1} Z_k(\alpha). \tag{3}$$

Naturally, if $x \in E_+(\alpha, c)$ we can conclude that there exists $\ell \in \mathbb{N}$ such that $M^\ell x \in H(\alpha, c)$. On the other hand, if $x \in E_-(\alpha, c)$ we cannot conclude that $M^\ell x \notin H(\alpha, c)$ for all $\ell \in \mathbb{N}$. We are going to characterize a set $X_-(\alpha, c)$ with an empty intersection with $H(\alpha, c)$ that is an M-attractor for any vector $x \in E_-(\alpha, c)$. Thus, if $x \in E_-(\alpha, c)$, it suffices to compute the beginning of the sequence $M^\ell x$ until we discover ℓ such that $M^\ell x$ is in $H(\alpha, c)$ or $X_-(\alpha, c)$. In the first case there must be an ℓ such that $M^\ell x \in H(\alpha, c)$ and in the second case we can tell that $M^\ell x \notin H(\alpha, c)$ for every $\ell \in \mathbb{N}$. The situation is show in Fig. 4.

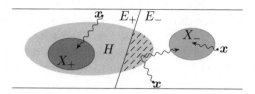

Fig. 4. Likely trajectories of $M^\ell x$, omitting (α, c)

We define the two sets $X_-(\alpha, c)$ and $X_+(\alpha, c)$ as follows:

$$X_-(\alpha, c) = \{x \notin H(\alpha, c) \mid \bigwedge_{j \geq 1} \langle \alpha, N^j x \rangle \leq 0\},$$

$$X_+(\alpha, c) = \{x \in H(\alpha, c) \mid \bigwedge_{j \geq 1} \langle \alpha, N^j x \rangle \geq 0\}.$$

Proposition 5.2. (a) $X_-(\alpha, c)$ *is an M-attractor for every* $x \in E_-(\alpha, c)$, *and* (b) $X_+(\alpha, c)$ *is an M-attractor for every* $x \in E_+(\alpha, c)$.

Proof. We only prove (a) since (b) is symmetrical.

We first show that $X_-(\alpha, c)$ is an M-invariant. Consider $x \in X_-(\alpha, c)$. Since $M = I_n + N$, we have $\langle \alpha, Mx \rangle = \langle \alpha, x \rangle + \langle \alpha, Nx \rangle$. From $x \notin H(\alpha, c)$, we get $\langle \alpha, x \rangle < c$ and since $x \in X_-(\alpha, c)$, we deduce $\langle \alpha, Nx \rangle \leq 0$. Therefore $\langle \alpha, Mx \rangle < c$ and we have proved that $Mx \notin H(\alpha, c)$. Moreover, given $j \geq 1$, observe that $\langle \alpha, N^j Mx \rangle = \langle \alpha, N^j x \rangle + \langle \alpha, N^{j+1} x \rangle$. From $x \in X_-(\alpha, c)$ we get $\langle \alpha, N^j x \rangle \leq 0$ and $\langle \alpha, N^{j+1} x \rangle \leq 0$. We deduce that $\langle \alpha, N^j Mx \rangle \leq 0$ for any $j \geq 1$. We have proved that $X_-(\alpha, c)$ is an M-invariant.

It remains to show that for $x \in E_-(\alpha, c)$, there exists ℓ such that $M^\ell x \in X_-(\alpha, c)$. We use the expression (2) of $E_-(\alpha, c)$. The case $x \in Z_0(\alpha) \setminus H(\alpha, c)$ is immediate since it implies $x \in X_-(\alpha, c)$. Thus, we can assume that there exists $m \in \mathbb{N} \setminus \{0\}$ such that $x \in Z_{-m}(\alpha)$. By Lemma 5.1, there exists ℓ_0 such that $\langle \alpha, M^\ell x \rangle < c$ for any $\ell \geq \ell_0$. Let $j \geq 1$ and let us prove that there exists $\ell_j \in \mathbb{N}$ such that $\langle \alpha, N^j M^\ell x \rangle \leq 0$ for any $\ell \geq \ell_j$. Since M and N commute, we deduce that $\langle \alpha, N^j M^\ell x \rangle = \langle \alpha, M^\ell N^j x \rangle$. From equation (1) we get:

$$\langle \alpha, M^\ell N^j x \rangle = \sum_{i=0}^{n-1} L_i(\ell) \langle \alpha, N^{i+j} x \rangle$$

Thus $\ell \mapsto \langle \alpha, N^j M^\ell x \rangle$ is a polynomial in ℓ. If this polynomial is equal to zero then $\langle \alpha, N^j M^\ell x \rangle \leq 0$ for any $\ell \geq 0$. Otherwise, we get $j \leq m$ by definition of $Z_{-m}(\alpha)$, and the leading coefficient of this polynomial is equal to $\frac{\langle \alpha, N^m x \rangle}{!(m-j)}$. Now $\langle \alpha, N^m x \rangle < 0$ again by definition of $Z_{-m}(\alpha)$, and we deduce that $\lim_{\ell \to +\infty} \langle \alpha, N^j M^\ell x \rangle = -\infty$.

Therefore there exists $\ell_j \in \mathbb{N}$ such that $\langle \boldsymbol{\alpha}, N^j M^\ell \boldsymbol{x} \rangle \leq 0$ for all $\ell \geq \ell_j$. Now, just observe that $M^\ell \boldsymbol{x} \in X_-(\boldsymbol{\alpha}, c)$ if $\ell = \max\{\ell_0, \dots, \ell_{n-1}\}$. $\square$

6 Computing Presburger Accelerated Interpolants

This section focus on the computation of a Presburger r-separator for a pair (E, F) of r-separable Presburger sets. Observe that this is equivalent to the Presburger accelerated interpolation problem for a spurious error-pattern with a unique cycle. We assume that the relation r satisfies $\boldsymbol{x} \, r \, \boldsymbol{y}$ iff $\boldsymbol{y} = M\boldsymbol{x} + \boldsymbol{v}$ where $\boldsymbol{v} \in \mathbb{Z}^n$ and $M \in \mathcal{M}_n(\mathbb{Z})$ is a poly-bounded matrix. Note that this condition strictly extend the finite monoid M^* condition required in acceleration techniques (see Theorem 4.1). We prove that if (E, F) is r-separable, then there exists a constructible Presburger r-separator for (E, F).

Remark 6.1. The unique cycle restriction is motivated by Example 4.2. In fact, this example exhibits a spurious error-pattern $(t_{ini}, t_1, t, t_2, t_{err})$ such that the cycles t_1 and t_2 satisfy the condition presented above. However, let us recall that this error-pattern does not admit a Presburger accelerated interpolant.

In the sequel, the Presburger sets E and F are decomposed into sets (E_i, F_j) following the half-space attractors introduced in the previous section. Note that a Presburger r-separator for (E, F) can be obtained as a combination of the Presburger r-separators for (E_i, F_j) thanks to the following straightforward Lemma 6.2.

Lemma 6.2 (Stability by union)

(a) If X_i r-separates (E_i, F) for $1 \leq i \leq p$, then $\bigcup_{i=1}^{p} X_i$ r-separates $(\bigcup_{i=1}^{p} E_i, F)$.

(b) If X_j r-separates (E, F_j) for $1 \leq j \leq m$, then $\bigcap_{j=1}^{m} X_j$ r-separates $(E, \bigcup_{j=1}^{m} F_j)$.

Now, we reduce the r-separability problem to the uniform case $\boldsymbol{v} = \boldsymbol{0}$. As expected, this reduction is obtained by adding an extra component that remains equal to 1. More precisely, consider the pair (E', F') of Presburger sets defined by $E' = E \times \{1\}$ and $F' = F \times \{1\}$ and the binary relation r' over $\mathbb{Z}^{n+1}$ defined by $((\boldsymbol{x}, x_{n+1}), (\boldsymbol{y}, y_{n+1})) \in r'$ iff $\boldsymbol{y} = M\boldsymbol{x} + \boldsymbol{v}x_{n+1}$ and $y_{n+1} = x_{n+1}$. Note that the matrix $M' = [[M \, \boldsymbol{v}][0, 1]] \in \mathcal{M}_{n+1}(\mathbb{Z})$ is poly-bounded. Moreover (E, F) is r-separable if and only if (E', F') is r'-separable. From a Presburger r'-separator X' of (E', F') we deduce a Presburger r-separator for (E, F) by considering $X = \{\boldsymbol{x} \in \mathbb{Z}^n \mid (\boldsymbol{x}, 1) \in X'\}$. Note that under the condition $\boldsymbol{v} = \boldsymbol{0}$, a pair (E, F) of sets is r-separable if and only if $M^*E \cap F = \varnothing$ and a set X is a r-separator if and only if X is an M-invariant such that $E \subseteq X$ and $X \cap F = \varnothing$. Such a pair (E, F) is said M-*separable* and X is called a M-*separator*.

Next, the M-separability problem is reduced to a poly-bounded matrix $M = I_n + N$ where $N \in \mathcal{M}_n(\mathbb{Z})$ is a nilpotent matrix.

Lemma 6.3. *Let $M \in \mathcal{M}_n(\mathbb{Z})$ be a poly-bounded matrix. Let (D, N) be the Dunford decomposition of M. There exists an integer $d \in \mathbb{N} \setminus \{0\}$ such that the matrix $D' = D^d$ satisfies $D'D' = D'$. In this case $N' = M^d - D'$ is a nilpotent matrix of $\mathcal{M}_n(\mathbb{Z})$ and $M' = I_n + N'$ satisfies $M^{d\ell}M^{dn} = (M')^\ell M^{dn}$ for any ℓ.*

A pair (E, F) *is* M-*separable if and only if* (E', F') *with* $E' = \bigcup_{\ell=0}^{d-1} M^{dn+\ell} E$ *and* $F' = F$ *is* M'-*separable. Moreover, given an* M'-*separator* X' *for* (E', F'), *the following set* X *is an* M-*separator for* (E, F).

$$X = E \cup \ldots \cup M^{dn-1} E \cup \left(\bigcap_{\ell=0}^{d-1} \{ \boldsymbol{x} \in M^{dn} \mathbb{Z}^n \mid M^\ell \boldsymbol{x} \in X' \} \right)$$

Finally, denoting by $b > 0$ an integer extracted from the modular constraints defining the Presburger set F, the following lemma shows that by replacing $(I_n + N)$ by one of its powers $I_n + N' = (I_n + N)^d$, we can assume that $M \equiv_b I_n$.

Lemma 6.4. *For any matrix* $M \in \mathcal{M}_n(\mathbb{Z})$ *such that* $M = I_n + N$ *and for any integer* $d > 0$ *we have* $M^d = I_n + N'$ *where* N' *is a nilpotent matrix. Moreover, for any integer* $b > 0$ *there exists an integer* $d > 0$ *such that* $M^d \equiv_b I_n$.

A pair (E, F) *is* M-*separable if and only if the pair* (E', F') *with* $E' = \bigcup_{\ell=0}^{d-1} M^\ell E$ *and* $F' = F$ *is* M^d-*separable. Moreover, given an* M^d-*separator for* (E', F'), *the following set* X *is an* M-*separator for* (E, F).

$$X = \bigcap_{\ell=0}^{d-1} \{ \boldsymbol{x} \in \mathbb{Z}^n \mid M^\ell \boldsymbol{x} \in X' \}$$

We can now provide the proof of our main Presburger separability theorem.

Theorem 6.5. *Let* r *be a binary relation over* $\mathbb{Z}^n$ *such that* $\boldsymbol{x} \; r \; \boldsymbol{y}$ *iff* $\boldsymbol{y} = M\boldsymbol{x} + \boldsymbol{v}$ *where* $\boldsymbol{v} \in \mathbb{Z}^n$ *and* $M \in \mathcal{M}_n(\mathbb{Z})$ *be poly-bounded. A pair* (E, F) *of Presburger sets, with either* E *or* F *finite, is* r-*separable if and only if it is Presburger* r-*separable. Moreover in this case we can effectively compute a Presburger* r-*separator.*

Proof. We have previously provided the reduction to the uniform case $\boldsymbol{v} = 0$. Let (E, F) be a pair of r-separable Presburger sets. Recall that this condition is equivalent to $M^* E \cap F = \varnothing$. From the reduction given in Lemma 6.3, we can assume that $M = (I_n + N)$ where $N \in \mathcal{M}_n(\mathbb{Z})$ is nilpotent. We have to find a Presburger r-separator X for (E, F) i.e., an M-invariant X such that $E \subseteq X$ and $X \cap F = \varnothing$.

Since the condition $M^* E \cap F = \varnothing$ is equivalent to $(M^{-1})^* F \cap E = \varnothing$, and since by hypothesis, either E or F is finite, it suffices by symmetry to handle the case where E is finite. Since F is a Presburger set, it is defined by a propositional formula of linear constraints, and one can effectively compute an integer $b \in \mathbb{N} \setminus \{0\}$ and an expression $F = \bigcup_{j=1}^m (C_j \cap \bigcap_{i=1}^{q_j} H(\boldsymbol{\alpha}_{i,j}, c_{i,j}))$, where for all $\boldsymbol{x} \in C_j$, $\boldsymbol{x} \equiv_b \boldsymbol{y}$ implies $\boldsymbol{y} \in C_j$. By the reduction given in Lemma 6.4 one can assume that $M\boldsymbol{x} \equiv_b \boldsymbol{x}$ for all $\boldsymbol{x} \in \mathbb{Z}^n$. Notice that this implies that both C_j and $\mathbb{Z}^n \setminus C_j$ are M-invariant. By Lemma 6.2 (b), one can assume without loss of generality that F is of the form $C \cap \bigcap_{i=1}^q H(\boldsymbol{\alpha}_i, c_i)$.

Let $\boldsymbol{x} \in E$. Assume that $\boldsymbol{x} \in \bigcap_{i=1}^q E_+(\boldsymbol{\alpha}_i, c_i) \cap C$. Then $M^* \boldsymbol{x} \cap X_+(\boldsymbol{\alpha}_i, c_i) \neq \varnothing$ for $1 \leq i \leq q$ by Proposition 5.2(b). Since $X_+(\boldsymbol{\alpha}_i, c_i)$ is M-invariant, one would have $M^* \boldsymbol{x} \cap \bigcap_{i=1}^r X_+(\boldsymbol{\alpha}_i, c_i) \neq \varnothing$. Since $X_+(\boldsymbol{\alpha}_i, c_i) \subseteq H(\boldsymbol{\alpha}_i, c_i)$, and since $\boldsymbol{x}$ also belongs to C which is M-invariant, one would finally get $M^* \boldsymbol{x} \cap F \neq \varnothing$, contradicting the hypothesis $M^* E \cap F = \varnothing$. Therefore, $E \subseteq \bigcup_{i=1}^q E_-(\boldsymbol{\alpha}_i, c_i) \cup (\mathbb{Z}^n \setminus C)$, so that

$$E = \left[\bigcup_{i=1}^q E_-(\boldsymbol{\alpha}_i, c_i) \cap C \cap E \right] \cup [(\mathbb{Z}^n \setminus C) \cap E] \tag{4}$$

Again by Lemma 6.2 (a), it suffices to treat two cases

$$(a) \quad E \subseteq E_-(\alpha_i, c_i) \cap C, \text{ and} \qquad (b) \quad E \subseteq \mathbb{Z}^n \setminus C.$$

In case (a), Proposition 5.2 shows that for every $x \in E$ there exists ℓ such that $M^\ell x \in X_-(\alpha_i, c_i)$. Since E is finite and $X_-(\alpha_i, c_i)$ is an invariant, there exists ℓ such that $M^\ell E \subseteq X_-(\alpha_i, c_i)$. Furthermore, one can compute such an integer ℓ, just by computing successive images of E by M. Therefore, $X = \{M^k E \mid k \le \ell\} \cup X_-(\alpha_i, c_i)$ is an M-separator for (E, F).

In case (b), where $E \subseteq \mathbb{Z}^n \setminus C$, it suffices to choose $X = \mathbb{Z}^n \setminus C$, which is a Presburger M-invariant set such that $E \subseteq X$ and $X \cap F = \varnothing$.   □

We finally prove that finiteness of either E or F is necessary to entail r-separability.

Proposition 6.6. *Consider $E = (1, 1)\mathbb{N}$ and $F = \{x \in \mathbb{Z}^2 \mid x_2 < x_1 \wedge x_1 < 0\}$. Let $r \subseteq \mathbb{Z}^2 \times \mathbb{Z}^2$ defined by $x \, r \, y$ if $y_1 = x_1 + x_2 - 2$ and $y_2 = x_2 - 2$. Then, the pair (E, F) is r-separable, but it is not Presburger r-separable.*

Proof. Computing $r^\ell E = -(\ell(\ell+1), 2\ell) + (\ell+1, 1)\mathbb{N}$ shows that $r^* E \cap F = \varnothing$, whence $r^* E$ is an r-separator for (E, F). Assume by contradiction that there is a Presburger r-separator X for (E, F). For $t \in \mathbb{Z}$ and $t \ge -1$, let $D_t = (t, t) + (t, -1)\mathbb{N}$. This linear set is located on the line $(\Delta_t) : x_1 + t x_2 = t + t^2$. Figure 6 (a) depicts the set E, its successive images under r, and F. Figure 6 (b) displays the sets D_t and the lines Δ_t. An easy computation gives $(t, t) + k(t, -1) = r^k(t+k, t+k) \in r^* E$, so $\bigcup_{t \ge -1} D_t \subseteq r^* E$.

Let $R_t \subseteq \mathbb{Z}^2$ be the set of points between Δ_{t-1} and Δ_t in the half space $x_1 \ge x_2$.

$$R_t = \{(x_1, x_2) \mid x_1 + t x_2 < t + t^2, \quad x_1 + (t-1)x_2 > (t-1) + (t-1)^2, \text{ and } x_1 \ge x_2\}.$$

This is a Presburger set, and $F = R_0$. One easily checks that $r R_t \subseteq R_{t-1}$. We claim that there exists t such that $\varnothing \ne R_t \cap X$. This will yield the contradiction, since then $\varnothing \ne r(R_t \cap X) \subseteq r(R_t) \cap r(X) \subseteq R_{t-1} \cap X$, and by induction, $\varnothing \ne R_0 \cap X = F \cap X$, contradicting the assumption that X is an r-separator for (E, F).

Choose an expression of the Presburger set X as a finite union of linear sets, and let $N \in \mathbb{N}$ be greater than all the norms of the periods appearing in this expression. Then, every point of X but a finite number is at distance at most N of another element of X. Choose $x \in D_N \subseteq X$, with x_1 large enough so that the distance from x to both D_{N-1}

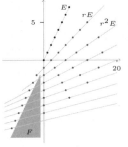

(a) $r^* E$ as an infinite union of $r^\ell E$

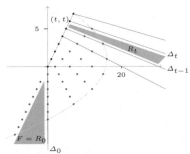

(b) $r^* E$ as an infinite union of D_t

and D_{N+1} is greater than N. There are infinitely many such x, since D_N is neither parallel to D_{N-1} nor to D_{N+1}. Now, any two points of $\Delta_N \cap \mathbb{Z}^2$ are at distance at least N. By the choice of x and the definition of N, there must be an element in $X \cap R_N$ or $X \cap R_{N+1}$. This proves the claim and concludes the proof of the proposition.   □

7   Conclusion and Further Work

The main idea of this paper is to combine *interpolation-based model-checking*, which works well on large and simple systems, and *acceleration techniques*, which prefers small and complex ones. We explored a track to combine them, named *interpolant acceleration*. in which we see a fair trade-off between the lack of scalability of acceleration, by applying it locally, and CEGAR inability to deal with of infinite behaviors. We also strongly believe this paper to open a new field of investigation, and to offer interesting research perspectives for future work.

We introduced the notion of *error-pattern* and *accelerated interpolant*. We identified two classes of computable accelerated interpolants: 'Presburger' accelerated interpolants and 'poly-bounded' accelerated interpolants. The second one allows to compute interpolants for error-patterns labeled by transformations which strictly enlarge usual classes used in acceleration techniques. This method is applicable for programs with a finite set of initializations or with a finite set of errors, and this condition is necessary due to Proposition 6.6. It would be interesting to extend the class of transformations, and to find finer conditions for such interpolants to be computable. One can extract straight from our constructive proof a rough algorithm. We would like to make it explicit, to compute its theoretical complexity, and to test how it behaves in practice.

Indeed, we would like to find efficient algorithms to compute accelerated interpolants as the one we provide here through the proof is brute-force. One possible track is to compute them from symbolic (*e.g.* automata based) set representations, and then build an effective implementation of a CEGAR loop using accelerated interpolants. Next, the full potential of accelerated interpolants in the refinement remains to be explored. From a more theoretical point of view, there are also many possible extensions: among others, we would like to be able to handle transitions with explicit guards, or check for some extensions of the class of transformations for which we can compute accelerated interpolants. A full study of these classes would allow us to clearly delimit what is the frontier between programs that can be handled by accelerated interpolants and others. Finally, another track would be to investigate the influence of some structural properties of the CFA (*e.g.* nested cycles) and how to deal with spurious error-traces whose proof does not hold after some unrolling.

References

[1] Bardin, S., Finkel, A., Leroux, J., Schnoebelen, P.: Flat Acceleration in Symbolic Model-Checking. In: Peled, D.A., Tsay, Y.-K. (eds.) ATVA 2005. LNCS, vol. 3707, pp. 474–488. Springer, Heidelberg (2005)

[2] Beyer, D., Henzinger, T.A., Majumdar, R., Rybalchenko, A.: Path Invariants. In: Proc. of the ACM SIGPLAN 2007 Conference on Programming Language Design and Implementation (PLDI 2007), pp. 300–309. ACM Press, New York (2007)

[3] Boigelot, B.: Symbolic Methods for Exploring Infinite State Spaces. PhD thesis, Faculté des Sciences Appliquées de l'Université de Liège (1999)

[4] Boigelot, B.: On Iterating Linear Transformations Over Recognizable Sets of Integers. Theoret. Comput. Sci. 309(1-3), 413–468 (2003)

[5] Bouajjani, A., Jonsson, B., Nilsson, M., Touili, T.: Regular Model-Checking. In: Emerson, E.A., Sistla, A.P. (eds.) CAV 2000. LNCS, vol. 1855, pp. 403–418. Springer, Heidelberg (2000)

[6] Clarke, E.M., Grumberg, O., Jha, S., Lu, Y., Veith, H.: CounterExample-Guided Abstraction Refinement for Symbolic Model Checking. J. ACM 50(5), 752–794 (2003)

[7] Esparza, J., Schwoon, S., Kiefer, S.: Abstraction Refinement with Craig Interpolation and Symbolic Pushdown Systems. In: Hermanns, H., Palsberg, J. (eds.) TACAS 2006. LNCS, vol. 3920, pp. 489–503. Springer, Heidelberg (2006)

[8] Finkel, A., Leroux, J.: How to Compose Presburger-Accelerations: Applications to Broadcast Protocols. In: Agrawal, M., Seth, A.K. (eds.) FSTTCS 2002. LNCS, vol. 2556, pp. 145–156. Springer, Heidelberg (2002)

[9] Ginsburg, S., Spanier, E.H.: Semigroups, Presburger Formulas and Languages. Pacific Journal of Mathematics 16(2), 285–296 (1966)

[10] Graf, S., Saïdi, H.: Construction of Abstract State Graphs with PVS. In: Grumberg, O. (ed.) CAV 1997. LNCS, vol. 1254, pp. 72–83. Springer, Heidelberg (1997)

[11] Gulavani, B., Henzinger, T.A., Kannan, Y., Nori, A., Rajamani, S.K.: Synergy: A New Algorithm for Property Checking. In: FSE 2006, pp. 117–127. ACM Press, New York (2006)

[12] Henzinger, T.A., Jhala, R., Majumbar, R., Sutre, G.: Lazy Abstraction. In: Proc. of 29th Symp. on Principles of Programming Languages (POPL 2002), pp. 58–70 (2002)

[13] Jhala, R., McMillan, K.L.: A Practical and Complete Approach to Predicate Refinement. In: Hermanns, H., Palsberg, J. (eds.) TACAS 2006. LNCS, vol. 3920, pp. 459–473. Springer, Heidelberg (2006)

[14] McMillan, K.L.: Interpolation and SAT-Based Model Checking. In: Hunt Jr., W.A., Somenzi, F. (eds.) CAV 2003. LNCS, vol. 2725, pp. 1–13. Springer, Heidelberg (2003)

[15] McMillan, K.L.: An Interpolating Theorem Prover. Journal of Theoritical Computer Science 345(1), 101–121 (2005)

[16] McMillan, K.L.: Lazy Abstraction with Interpolants. In: Ball, T., Jones, R.B. (eds.) CAV 2006. LNCS, vol. 4144, pp. 123–136. Springer, Heidelberg (2006)

[17] Presburger, M.: Über die Vollständigkeit eines gewissen Systems der Arithmetik ganzer Zahlen, in welchem die Addition als einzige Operation hervortritt. In: Comptes Rendus du 1er congrès de Mathématiciens des Pays Slaves, pp. 92–101 (1929)

Automatically Refining Abstract Interpretations

Bhargav S. Gulavani[1], Supratik Chakraborty[1], Aditya V. Nori[2], and Sriram K. Rajamani[2]

[1] IIT Bombay
[2] Microsoft Research India

Abstract. Abstract interpretation techniques prove properties of programs by computing abstract fixpoints. All such analyses suffer from the possibility of false errors. We present three techniques to automatically refine such abstract interpretations to reduce false errors: (1) a new operator called *interpolated widen*, which automatically recovers precision lost due to widen, (2) a new way to handle disjunctions that arise due to refinement, and (3) a new refinement algorithm, which refines abstract interpretations that use the join operator to merge abstract states at join points. We have implemented our techniques in a tool DAGGER. Our experimental results show our techniques are effective and that their combination is even more effective than any one of them in isolation. We also show that DAGGER is able to prove properties of C programs that are beyond current abstraction-refinement tools, such as SLAM [4], BLAST [15], ARMC [19], and our earlier tool [12].

1 Introduction

Abstract interpretation [7] is a general technique to compute sound fixpoints for programs. Such fixpoint computations have to lose precision in order to guarantee termination. However, precision losses can lead to false errors. Over the past few years, counterexample driven refinement has been successfully used to automatically refine *predicate abstractions* (a special kind of abstract interpretation) to reduce false errors [4, 15, 19]. This has spurred significant research in counterexample guided discovery of "relevant" predicates [14, 17, 8, 20, 5]. A natural question to ask therefore is whether counterexample guided automatic refinement can be applied to any abstract interpretation. A first attempt in this direction was made in [12] where widen was refined by convex hull in the polyhedra domain. This was subsequently improved upon in [22] where widen was refined using extrapolation. This paper improves the earlier efforts in three significant ways that combine to give enhanced accuracy and efficiency. First, we propose an interpolated widen operator that refines widen using interpolants. Second, we propose a new algorithm to implicitly handle disjunctions that occur during refinement. Finally, we propose a new algorithm to refine abstract interpretations that use the join operator to merge abstract states at program locations where conditional branches merge. We have built a tool DAGGER that implements these ideas. Our empirical results show that DAGGER outperforms

C.R. Ramakrishnan and J. Rehof (Eds.): TACAS 2008, LNCS 4963, pp. 443–458, 2008.

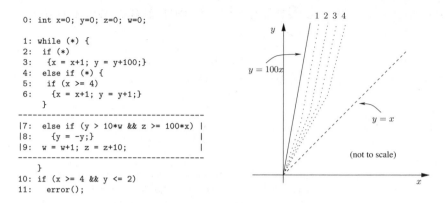

```
0: int x=0; y=0; z=0; w=0;

1: while (*) {
2:   if (*)
3:     {x = x+1; y = y+100;}
4:   else if (*) {
5:     if (x >= 4)
6:       {x = x+1; y = y+1;}
     }
------------------------------------------
|7:   else if (y > 10*w && z >= 100*x) |
|8:     {y = -y;}                       |
|9:   w = w+1; z = z+10;                |
------------------------------------------
   }
10: if (x >= 4 && y <= 2)
11:   error();
```

Fig. 1. Example program

a number of available tools on a range of benchmarks, and is able to prove array-bounds properties of several programs that are beyond the reach of current abstraction-refinement tools such as SLAM [4], BLAST [15], ARMC [19], and our earlier tool [12].

The widen operator is typically used in abstract interpreters to generate invariants by generalizing from multiple symbolic executions. However, widen is unaware of the target property that needs to be verified, and may result in approximations too coarse to prove the property. Interpolants offer a complementary generalization capability by providing succinct reasons for spuriousness of counterexamples. However, interpolants are generated with respect to specific counterexample traces, and are not guaranteed to be fixpoints with respect to all executions. By combining the strengths of interpolants and widen in an effective way, *interpolated widen* gives benefits of both.

To illustrate the benefit of using interpolants in conjunction with invariants obtained by widening, consider the program in Figure 1 (ignore the boxed code for now). The error at line 11 is unreachable. The inductive loop invariant $x \leq y \leq 100x$ suffices to prove unreachability of the error. However, if we refine widen using convex hull as in [12], we obtain the weaker invariant $100x \geq y$ that does not help in proving the program correct. The polyhedra obtained after the ith such refinement iteration is indicated in Figure 1 by the region between the line $y = 100x$ and the ith dotted boundary. This dotted boundary is then discarded in subsequent widen operations, and the abstract fixpoint intersects the error. Therefore the refinement of widen to convex hull continues ad infinitum, giving the imprecise invariant $100x \geq y$. Note that the extrapolation technique for polyhedra given in [22] will also face a similar problem. In contrast, an interpolant generation technique [17] can compute the interpolant $y \geq x$ easily by analyzing a counterexample. By using this in conjunction with the invariant obtained by widen, we obtain the stronger invariant $x \leq y \leq 100x$, which is strong enough to prove that the error at line 11 is unreachable.

In the above example, $y \geq x$ is itself a strong enough loop invariant to prove unreachability of the error. It may therefore appear that interpolation based techniques perform better than widen based techniques. However, interpolation alone does not work in all cases. To illustrate this, consider the same example including the boxed code (lines 7-9). In this program line 8 is unreachable. The inductive invariant required for proving the error unreachable is now $(x \leq y \leq 100x) \wedge (z = 10w)$. There is no obvious reason why interpolation techniques like [17, 20] will choose $100x \geq y$ as part of an interpolant among the many possible interpolants during counterexample analysis. Experiments show that ARMC, which uses a sophisticated interpolation algorithm [20], does not terminate on this example in 2000s. STING [21] does not generate invariants strong enough to prove the error unreachable either. The refinement engine of BLAST is equipped to generate only difference and bounds predicates, hence it fails to prove the program correct. Since the coefficient 100 in the required predicate $100x \geq y$ is large, recursively enumerating interpolants, as suggested in [17], is also unlikely to work well. Widen based techniques like [12] can easily generate invariants like $100x \geq y$ and $z = 10w$, but not $x \leq y$, which can be easily generated by interpolant based techniques. Thus, by combining invariants obtained by widen with interpolants obtained during counterexample analysis, we obtain the right inductive invariant needed to prove the property. Further, our empirical results (see Section 4) show that interpolated widen is better than superficially combining widen and interpolation, i.e., by first computing invariants using widen, and then using them to strengthen the transition relation in interpolation based predicate abstraction frameworks, as suggested in [16].

Refining widen using specific operations in polyhedral abstract domains has been used earlier [12, 22]. While the widen up-to operator of [22] does not guarantee elimination of spurious counterexamples, the intuition behind widen up-to and extrapolation are useful. In [13] Halbwachs et al. introduced the widen up-to operator to improve the precision of widen with pre-computed (static) thresholds. The use of dynamically computed interpolants to refine widen is an original contribution of our work, and can be viewed as a generalization of the widen up-to operators of [13, 22]. Since interpolants provide succinct reasons for spuriousness of counterexamples (by referring only to common variables between a pair of formulas being interpolated), we enjoy the benefits of ideas in [12,22] while potentially using simpler/fewer predicates. Unlike [12, 22], we can also leverage independent advances in widening [10, 3] and interpolation techniques [17, 20, 5] in a simple framework. In [16], predicate abstraction based analysis is improved by using weak invariants discovered by widen in an initial pass. However, potentially stronger invariants that may be discovered by widen after few iterations of refinement are not considered. In contrast, our analysis based on interpolated widen can benefit from such stronger invariants discovered later, especially if sophisticated widening techniques [3, 10, 2] are used.

In addition to widen, if the join operator in an abstract domain loses precision, we need disjunctions to recover precision losses that are necessary to prove a property. However, this makes us work over a powerset domain, where operations like interpolation and widen are expensive. We propose a technique that implicitly uses disjunctions to recover precision as appropriate, while ensuring that interpolation and widen are applied only on base abstract domain (and not powerset domain) elements. This contrasts with other approaches [12, 22] that use similar base abstract domains but must use powerset widening.

In programs with conditional branches, the tree-based exploration used in our earlier work [12] can result in traversing an exponential (in size of program) number of paths. This can be avoided in abstract interpretation by using join operations when different branches of conditional statements merge, in addition to performing widen operations at loopheads. This is indeed a DAG-based exploration. Therefore, an interesting question to ask is: *can we perform counterexample driven automatic refinement with a DAG-based exploration?* In this paper, we propose a refinement algorithm that achieves this and also gives progress guarantees. Counterexample-DAG based predicate abstraction has been used earlier for programs with finite domain variables [8]. In contrast, our DAG based refinement is used to refine imprecisions that arise due to the join operator at merge nodes. In [9], Fischer et. al. used predicated dataflow lattices to improve precision lost by join operation. However, the dataflow lattices considered in [9] are of finite height and hence do not require a widen operator.

Our approach, like those of [12, 22, 16], benefits from cheap image/preimage operations of abstract domains like octagons and polyhedra, as opposed to expensive image/preimage computations in predicate abstraction. In [18], McMillan showed how abstract exploration for predicate abstraction can be performed by way of computing interpolants, thus eliminating the need for the expensive image computation. While this is a powerful technique, it does not benefit from predicates that can be easily discovered as invariants by widen but are more difficult to obtain as interpolants, and that are also crucial for proving a property. Beyer et al [5] introduced path programs to help discover such relevant predicates. If we view this as an advanced interpolation technique, our approach, like other predicate abstraction techniques, can only benefit from the predicates thus computed. Interestingly, our abstraction refinement algorithm can also be used to compute relevant predicates by analyzing path programs.

The remainder of the paper is organized as follows. In Section 2 we present the interpolated widen operation and discuss implicit handling of disjuncts. Section 3 discusses DAG-based refinements. Section 4 presents and analyzes experimental results from our tool DAGGER, and Section 5 concludes the paper.

2   Refinement: Interpolated Widen and Implicit Disjuncts

Let V be a finite set of variables. A state s is a valuation to all variables in V. Let Σ be the (possibly infinite) set of all possible states. A program P_V over a set of variables V is a six-tuple $(L, E, R, l_0, \mathsf{Image}^\flat)$, where (i) L is a finite set of control locations in the program, representing possible valuations to the program counter, (ii) $E \subseteq L \times L$ is a set of control flow edges, (iii) $R \subseteq L$ is a set of error locations, (iv) l_0 is the initial program location, which is not in R, and cannot be the target of any control flow edge, and (vi) $\mathsf{Image}^\flat$ is a function from $2^\Sigma \times L \times L$ to 2^Σ, where $\mathsf{Image}^\flat(\sigma, l, l')$ is the set of states obtained by starting at some state in the set of states σ and executing the statements along the control flow edge (l, l'). The preimage operation $\mathsf{Preimage}^\flat$ is defined as the inverse of the image operation. We overload the $\mathsf{Image}^\flat$ and $\mathsf{Preimage}^\flat$ operations to operate over a sequence of edges in the obvious way.

We assume that the control flow graphs of our programs are connected reducible graphs, and that every location has at most two incoming control flow edges. An edge $e \in E$ is a *backedge* if it closes a cycle during a depth first traversal of the graph $\langle L, E \rangle$, starting at location l_0. A location l is called a *merge* location if it has two incoming edges, neither of which is a backedge. A location l is called a *loophead* if it has two incoming edges, and exactly one is a backedge.

A control location l is said to be reachable if there exists a path $(l_0, l_1, \ldots, l_n, l)$ in the control flow graph and a state $\sigma_0 \in \Sigma$, such that $\mathsf{Image}^\flat(\{\sigma_0\}, (l_0, l_1, \ldots, l_n, l))$ is not $\emptyset$. Our goal is to check if any error location $l_e \in R$ is reachable. A true counterexample is a sequence of control flow locations $(l_0, l_1, \ldots, l_n, l_e)$ such that $l_e \in R$ and there exists $\sigma_0 \in \Sigma$ satisfying $\mathsf{Image}^\flat(\{\sigma_0\}, (l_0, l_1, \ldots, l_n, l_e)) \neq \emptyset$. The counterexample is called spurious if $\mathsf{Image}^\flat(\{\sigma_0\}, l_0, l_1, \ldots, l_n, l_e) = \emptyset$ for every $\sigma_0 \in \Sigma$. The length of a counterexample $(l_0, l_1, \ldots, l_n, l_e)$ is one less than the length of the sequence $(l_0, l_1, \ldots, l_n, l_e)$.

Following [7], we use abstract interpretation of a program P_V over an abstract domain $\langle \Sigma^\sharp, \sqsubseteq, \top, \bot, \sqcup, \sqcap \rangle$, which is a complete lattice. In particular, we consider abstract domains where elements of $\Sigma^\sharp$ are formulas over V in a fragment of first order logic closed under Craig interpolation [14]. Every formula represents a set of states. The abstract image operation $\mathsf{Image}(s, l, l')$ takes an abstract element s and the control flow edge (l, l') and returns the abstract element s' obtained by abstractly executing the statements along the control flow edge (l, l'). The abstract $\mathsf{Preimage}$ operation is analogously defined. In the following discussion, we will assume that the Image and $\mathsf{Preimage}$ operations are exact. The effects of overapproximating Image and $\mathsf{Preimage}$ operations are briefly discussed later.

Widen. The widen [7] operator $\nabla : \Sigma^\sharp \times \Sigma^\sharp \to \Sigma^\sharp$ is a binary operator such that for all $A, B \in \Sigma^\sharp$, we have (i) $A \sqsubseteq A\nabla B$, (ii) $B \sqsubseteq A\nabla B$, and (iii) for any strictly increasing sequence $A_0 \sqsubset A_1 \sqsubset \ldots$, if we define $B_0 = A_0$, $B_1 = B_0\nabla A_1$, $B_2 = B_1\nabla A_2, \ldots$, then there exists $i \geq 0$ such that $B_j = B_i$ for all $j > i$.

The *bounded widen* or *widen up-to* [13] operator with respect to a set T of abstract elements, $\nabla_T : \Sigma^\sharp \times \Sigma^\sharp \to \Sigma^\sharp$, is a widen operator such that for any $C \in T$, if $A \sqsubseteq C$ and $B \sqsubseteq C$ then $A\nabla_T B \sqsubseteq C$.

Interpolant. For any two elements $A, E \in \Sigma^\sharp$ such that $A \sqcap E = \bot$, $I \in \Sigma^\sharp$ is said to be an interpolant [14] of A and E if (i) $A \sqsubseteq I$, (ii) $I \sqcap E = \bot$, and (ii) the formula representing I has only those variables that are common to the formulae representing A and E.

The widen operator $A\nabla B$ is used to guarantee termination when computing an abstract fixpoint. However, the imprecision introduced by widen may lead to false errors. This can happen if, for an abstract error state E, $(A \sqcup B) \sqcap E = \bot$, but $(A\nabla B) \sqcap E \neq \bot$. In this case, we propose to pick an interpolant I of $A \sqcup B$ and E, and use a bounded widen operator $A\nabla_{\{I\}} B$ to compute the abstract

```
/* Global: program P_V, interpolant set T,       2. RefineTREE (n_e)
abstract computation tree */                     1: ψ ← ⊤; curr ← n_e; i ← Depth(n_e)
1. AbstractTREE                                  2: while i > 0
1:  n_0 ← ⟨l_0, ⊤⟩; T ← ∅; i ← 0;                3:    Let ⟨l', s'⟩ = curr and ⟨l, s⟩ = Parent(curr)
2:  loop                                         4:    if Image(s, l, l') ⊓ ψ = ⊥
3:    for all n = ⟨l, s⟩ such that Depth(n) = i   5:      /* curr is a refinement node */
4:      for all edges (l, l') in cfg             6:      s' ← ApplyRefinement(l', ⟨l, s⟩, ψ)
5:        img ← Image(s, l, l')                  7:      DeleteDescendents(curr)
6:        if ¬Covered(l', img)                   8:      return i − 1
7:          if l' is loophead                    9:    ψ ← Preimage(ψ, l, l')
8:            s'' ← Sel(l', n)                    10:   curr ← Parent(curr); i ← i − 1
9:            img ← s''∇_T(s'' ⊔ img)            11: end while
10:           Add ⟨l', img⟩ as child of n        12: "program incorrect"; exit
11:   if ∃n_e = ⟨l_e, s_e⟩ such that l_e ∈ R
12:     i ← RefineTREE(n_e)                      3. ApplyRefinement (l', ⟨l, s⟩, ψ)
13:   else if ¬∃ node at depth i + 1             1: Let n = ⟨l, s⟩; s'' ← Sel(S_{l',n});
14:     "program correct"; exit                  2: img ← Image(s, l, l')
15:   else                                       3: if (s'' ⊔ img) ⊓ ψ = ⊥ then
16:     i ← i + 1                                4:    T ← T ∪ Interpolate(s'' ⊔ img, ψ)
17: end loop                                     5:    return s''∇_T(s'' ⊔ img)
                                                 6: else
                                                 7:    return img
```

Fig. 2. Refinement using Interpolated Widen

fixpoint. Such a bounded widen operator that uses interpolants as bounds is called *interpolated widen*. A primary insight of this paper is that if the parameter T of a bounded widen operator contains an interpolant, then a false error that occurs due to the imprecision of widen can be avoided.

Lemma 1. Let $A, B, E \in \Sigma^\sharp$ be such that $(A \sqcup B) \sqcap E = \bot$. Let $I \in \Sigma^\sharp$ be an interpolant of $(A \sqcup B)$ and E, and let $T \subseteq \Sigma^\sharp$ be any set such that $I \in T$. Then $(A \sqcup B) \sqsubseteq (A\nabla_T B) \sqsubseteq I$ and $(A\nabla_T B) \sqcap E = \bot$.

In the polyhedra abstract domain, bounding widen with constraints from the convex hull has been used in earlier work [12,22]. Although such constraints separate the forward reachable states from the error, they may not be interpolants. Since interpolants often give succinct reasons for eliminating counterexamples, we choose to use them to bound widen.

For several abstract domains like polyhedra and octagons, the $\sqcup$ operation is inexact, in addition to having inexact ∇. Powerset extensions of these domains however have exact $\sqcup$. A primary drawback of powerset domains is the increased complexity of interpolation and other abstract domain operations. We therefore propose ways to avoid these operations on powerset domains, while using base abstract domains with inexact $\sqcup$ operator. The abstraction refinement algorithm using interpolated widen and tree based exploration is shown in Figure 2.

During the abstract fixpoint computation, procedure AbstractTREE stores the intermediate states as a tree (N, A, n_0) where N is the set of nodes, A is the set of edges and n_0 is the root node. Each node in N represents an abstract state during the computation, stored as a pair $\langle l, d \rangle \in L \times \Sigma^\sharp$. The tree thus constructed gives a model to perform counterexample driven refinement whenever an error location is reached during the abstract computation.

Let the function Parent : $N \setminus \{n_0\} \to N$ give for each node $n \in N \setminus \{n_0\}$ its unique parent n' in the tree. Let the function Depth : $N \to \mathbb{N}$ give for each node n the number of edges along the path from n_0 to n. Let $\mathsf{Covered}(l, s)$ be a predicate that returns True iff either $s = \bot$ or there exists a node $n = \langle l, s' \rangle$ in the tree such that $s \sqsubseteq s'$. Let $S_{l,n}$ denote the set of maximal abstract states among the abstract states at the predecessors of node n with location l. Note that there can be more than one node with maximal abstract state among the predecessors of node n with location l because of refinements as explained later. Given a set of abstract states S, the function $\mathsf{Sel}(S)$ deterministically returns one element from S (using heuristics mentioned in [12]).

Since every node in the abstract tree stores a single abstract state, the image computation in each step of forward exploration along a path in the tree gives a single abstract state. Therefore, when we reach loopheads, we need to widen a set S of abstract states with the set $S \cup \{s\}$, where s is the newly computed abstract state. Given this special requirement, we define an operator $\nabla_T^p : \wp(\Sigma^\sharp) \times \Sigma^\sharp \to \wp(\Sigma^\sharp)$ that takes a set $S \subseteq \Sigma^\sharp$ and an element $s \in \Sigma^\sharp$, and returns the set of maximal elements in $S \cup \{\mathsf{Sel}(S) \, \nabla_T \, (\mathsf{Sel}(S) \sqcup s)\}$.

Lemma 2. *Let $S_0 \subseteq \Sigma^\sharp$ be a finite set. Consider the sequence $S_1 = S_0 \, \nabla_T^p \, s_0$, $S_2 = S_1 \, \nabla_T^p \, s_1, \ldots$, where $s_i \in \Sigma^\sharp$ for all $i \geq 0$. There exists $u \geq 0$ such that $S_v = S_u$ for all $v \geq u$.*

The computation of $\mathsf{AbstractTREE}$ starts with an abstract tree having a single node $n_0 = \langle l_0, \top \rangle$. Consider a node $n = \langle l, s \rangle$ and control flow edge (l, l'). If $\mathsf{Covered}(l', \mathsf{Image}(s, l, l'))$ returns False, a new node $n' = \langle l', s' \rangle$ is added as a child of n in the tree; otherwise a new node is not added. If (l, l') is not a backedge then s' is obtained as $\mathsf{Image}(s, l, l')$. Otherwise s' is computed using an interpolated widen operation as $s'' \nabla_T (s'' \sqcup \mathsf{Image}(s, l, l'))$, where $s'' = \mathsf{Sel}(S_{l',n})$. In computing s', we must also ensure that the invariant computation for the current path eventually terminates if no refinements are done in between. Lemma 2 gives this guarantee. If a node $n_e = \langle l_e, s_e \rangle$ with $l_e \in R$ gets added to the tree, then an error location is reached, and $\mathsf{RefineTREE}(n_e)$ is invoked. The abstraction refinement procedure terminates when either a fixpoint is reached or refinement finds a true counterexample.

An important property of procedure $\mathsf{AbstractTREE}$, that stems from its depth-wise exploration of nodes is: *if the loop at line 3 gets executed with $i = k$, the program being analyzed has no true counterexamples of length $\leq k$.* This can be proved by induction on k (refer [11]).

Procedure $\mathsf{RefineTREE}$ takes an error node n_e as input and analyzes the counterexample represented by the path from n_0 to n_e in the abstract computation tree. It either confirms the counterexample as true or finds a node for refinement. It initializes the error state at n_e to $\top$ and then uses the abstract $\mathsf{Preimage}$ operation to propagate this error state backward. At a node $n' = \langle l', s' \rangle$ with parent $n = \langle l, s \rangle$, if ψ denotes the backward propagated error state at n', and if $\psi \sqcap s' \neq \bot$, the procedure proceeds in one of the following ways:

(1) Suppose the exact image of the parent, i.e. $\mathsf{Image}(s, l, l')$, does not intersect ψ. Then l' must be a loophead and s' must have been computed as $s'' \nabla_T (s'' \sqcup \mathsf{Image}(s, l, l'))$, where s'' is $\mathsf{Sel}(S_{l',n})$. Furthermore, abstract state

s'' cannot intersect ψ, as otherwise, a true counterexample shorter than the current one can be found – an impossibility by the above mentioned property of AbstractTREE. If $s'' \sqcup \mathsf{Image}(s, l, l')$ doesn't intersect ψ, neither s'' nor $\mathsf{Image}(s, l, l')$ intersects ψ. We refine ∇_T by computing an interpolant between $s'' \sqcup \mathsf{Image}(s, l, l')$ and ψ, and including it in T, to make ∇_T precise enough. The abstract state s' is refined by using the refined ∇_T operation. Lemma 1 ensures that this refined state does not intersect ψ. If $s'' \sqcup \mathsf{Image}(s, l, l')$ intersects ψ we simply refine the abstract state to $\mathsf{Image}(s, l, l')$. This is a valid refinement as the image does not intersect ψ (checked in line 4 of RefineTREE). Note also that this refinement implicitly converts $s'' \nabla_T (s'' \sqcup img)$ to a disjunction of s'' and img, with the disjuncts stored at distinct nodes (with location l') in the tree. This differs from [12] where a set of base abstract domain elements is stored at each node to represent their disjunction. Note that our way of representing disjunctions may result in a node n with location l' having multiple maximal nodes among its predecessors with location l'. After refining node n', we delete its descendents since the abstract states at these nodes may change because of this refinement.

(2) If the exact image $\mathsf{Image}(s, l, l')$ intersects ψ, the abstract error ψ at node n' is propagated backward by the Preimage operation until either a refinement node is identified or n_0 is reached. Since Image and Preimage are exact, $\mathsf{Image}(s, l, l')$ intersects ψ if and only if s intersects $\mathsf{Preimage}(\psi, l, l')$. Therefore it is not necessary to intersect $\mathsf{Image}(s, l, l')$ with ψ before propagating the error backwards. If n_0 is reached during backward propagation we report a true counterexample.

Note that if the Preimage operation is overapproximating, a counterexample reported by RefineTREE may not be a true counterexample. However, if a program is reported to be correct, it is indeed correct. If the Image operation is overapproximating, then a spurious counterexample may not be eliminated because RefineTREE only refines join and widen operations. Consequently AbstractTREE may loop indefinitely, a problem typical of all counterexample guided abstraction refinement tools. This can be rectified by letting RefineTREE improve the precision of Image as well.

3   DAG Refinement

The tree based abstraction refinement technique discussed in the previous section potentially suffers from explosion of paths during forward exploration. Yet another drawback of tree based exploration is that every invocation of RefineTREE analyzes a single counterexample. We propose to address both these drawbacks by adapting the tree based technique of the previous section to work with a DAG. In such a scheme, the abstract computation joins states computed along different paths to the same merge location. It then represents the merged state at a single node in the DAG, instead of creating separate nodes as in a tree based scheme. Subsequently, if it is discovered that merging led to an imprecision that generated a spurious counterexample, the refinement procedure splits the merged node, so that abstract states computed along different paths are represented separately.

The use of a DAG G to represent the abstract computation implies that when an error location is reached at a node n_e, there are potentially multiple paths from the root n_0 to n_e in G. Let the subgraph of G containing all paths from n_0 to n_e be called the counterexample-DAG G_e. Unlike in a tree based procedure, we must now analyze *all* paths in G_e to determine if n_e is reachable. The refinement procedure either finds a true counterexample in G_e, or if all counterexamples are spurious, it replaces a set of imprecise operations by more precise ones along every path in G_e. Refinement proceeds by first computing a *set of abstract error preimages*, $err(n)$, at each node n in G_e. For a node n, $err(n)$ is computed as the set union of the preimage of every element in $err(n')$, for every successor n' of n in G_e.

Unlike in a tree based procedure, a node $n' = \langle l', s' \rangle$ may not have a unique predecessor in the counterexample DAG G_e. We say that node n' is a *refinement node with respect to predecessor* $n = \langle l, s \rangle$ if $\exists e' \in err(n'), s' \sqcap e' \neq \bot$ and $\forall e \in err(n), s \sqcap e = \bot$. The goal of refinement at such a node n' is to improve the precision of computation of s' from s, so that the new abstract state at n' does not intersect $err(n')$. However, the abstract states already computed at descendents of n' in G may be rendered inexact by this refinement, and may continue to intersect the corresponding abstract error preimages. Hence we delete all descendents of n' in G.

Refinement is done at node $n' = \langle l', s' \rangle$ in one of the following ways: (i) If l' is a merge location and n' has predecessors $n_1 = \langle l_1, s_1 \rangle, \ldots, n_k = \langle l_k, s_k \rangle$, then refinement first deletes deletes n' and all its incoming edges. Then it creates k new nodes $m_1, \ldots, m_k$, where $m_i = \langle l', t_i \rangle$ and $t_i = \mathsf{Image}(s_i, l_i, l')$. (ii) If l' is a loophead, then as done in Algorithm RefineTREE, refinement either introduces disjunctions (implicitly) or does interpolated widen with a refined set of interpolants. An interpolant is computed between the joined result at n' and each of the abstract error states from the set $err(n')$. The result of the interpolated widen is guaranteed not to intersect $err(n')$.

Consider a merge node n' that is a refinement node with respect to predecessor n but not with respect to predecessor m. Suppose no ancestor of n is a refinement node while m has an ancestor p that is a refinement node. In this case if we apply refinement at p before n', then node n' will be deleted and no counterexample corresponding to a path through n and n' would have any of its nodes refined. To prevent this, nodes are refined in reverse topological order. This ensures that at least one node along each path in the counterexample-DAG is refined.

Lemma 3. *Let $n_e = \langle l_e, s_e \rangle$ be a node in a counterexample-DAG G_e corresponding to error location l_e. Every invocation of refinement with G_e either finds a true counterexample or reduces the number of imprecise operations on each spurious counterexample ending at n_e in G_e.*

As discussed above, the abstraction procedure aggressively merges paths at merge locations, and refinement procedure aggressively splits paths at merge locations. One could, however, implement alternative strategies, where we selectively merge paths during abstraction and selectively split them during refinement. For example, whenever refinement splits a merge node n into nodes

$n_1, \ldots n_k$, it may be useful to remember that descendents of n_i should not be merged with those of n_j where $i \neq j$ during forward exploration. This information can then be used during abstraction to selectively merge paths leading to the same merge location. Our implementation uses this simple heuristic to prevent aggressive merging of paths. Note also that as an optimization, we store and propagate back only those abstract error preimages s'_e at node $n' = \langle l', s' \rangle$ that satisfy $s'_e \sqcap s' \neq \bot$. This potentially helps in avoiding an exponential blow up of error preimages during refinement.

Progress Guarantees. It would be desirable to prove that our DAG-based abstraction refinement scheme has the following *progress* property: *Once a counterexample is eliminated it remains eliminated forever.* There are two reasons why the abstraction refinement procedure may not ensure this. Firstly, it does not keep track of refinements performed earlier, and secondly, the interpolated widen operation is in general non monotone, i.e., $A' \sqsubseteq A$ and $B' \sqsubseteq B$ does not necessarily imply $(A' \nabla_T B') \sqsubseteq (A \nabla_T B)$. Progress can be ensured by keeping track of all earlier refinements and by using monotone operations. We propose addressing both these issues by using a *Hint* DAG H, which is a generalization of the list based *hints* used in [12]. Monotonicity of interpolated widen is ensured by intersection with the corresponding widened result in the previous abstraction iteration. The details of using *Hint* DAG can be found in [11]. Lemma 3 along with the use of Hint DAG ensures the following: *a counterexample c having k imprecise operations is eliminated in at most k refinement iterations with counterexample-DAGs containing c.* The *Hint* DAG also ensures that *once a counterexample is eliminated, it remains eliminated in all subsequent iterations of abstraction.*

4   Implementation

We have implemented our algorithm in a tool, DAGGER, for proving assertions in C programs. DAGGER is written in ocaml and uses the CIL [6] infrastructure for parsing our input programs. DAGGER uses the octagon and polyhedra abstract domains as implemented in the APRON library [1]. We use flow insensitive pointer analysis provided by CIL to resolve pointer aliases in a sound manner.

We have implemented several algorithms for abstract computation which include the TREE and DAG based exploration with and without interpolated widen. This is done to compare the enhancements provided by each of these techniques. DAGGER keeps track of a separate interpolant set for each program location as opposed to having a single monolithic set of interpolants for all program locations. We outline the interpolation algorithms for the octagon and polyhedra abstract domains, and then explain an optimization of caching abstract error preimages.

Interpolation for the octagon domain. In the octagon abstract domain every non-$\bot$ abstract element is represented by a set of constraints of the form $l \bowtie e \bowtie u$, where $\bowtie \in \{<, \leq\}$, l and u are real or rational constants and e is an expression that is either a single variable, difference of two variables or sum of two variables. We will assume that the set of constraints is in canonical form, i.e., l and u are tight bounds for the expression e. InterpolateOct computes an interpolant I of two non-$\perp$ canonical octagons A and B such that $A \sqcap B = \perp$. This takes time quadratic in the number of program variables. Note that in Algorithm ApplyRefinement (Figure 2) canonicalization would already have been done at line 3 when checking the emptiness of intersection, before InterpolateOct is invoked at line 4.

Interpolation for the polyhedra domain. In this domain, each non-$\perp$ abstract element is represented by a set of non redundant constraints. For an abstract element A, let $var(A)$ be the set of variables occurring in the constraints of A. Function $Project(A, V)$, computes the projection of polyhedra A on a set of variables V, i.e., it existentially quantifies the variables not in V. Given two non-$\perp$ polyhedra A and B such that $A \sqcap B = \perp$, the interpolant can be computed as below.

InterpolateOct **(A,B)**
1: $I \leftarrow \emptyset$
2: **for all** expressions e **do**
3:     Let $al : l_a \bowtie e$ and $au : e \bowtie u_a$ be constraints in A
4:     Let $bl : l_b \bowtie e$ and $bu : e \bowtie u_b$ be constraints in B
5:     **if** $au \sqsubseteq \{\neg bl\}$ **then**
6:         $I \leftarrow I \cup \{\neg bl\}$
7:     **if** $al \sqsubseteq \{\neg bu\}$ **then**
8:         $I \leftarrow I \cup \{\neg bu\}$

InterpolatePoly1 **(A,B)**
1: $I \leftarrow \emptyset$
3: **for all** constraints c in B **do**
4:     **if** $A \sqsubseteq \{\neg c\}$
5:         $I \leftarrow I \cup \{\neg c\}$

InterpolatePoly2 **(A,B)**
1: $V \leftarrow var(A) \cap var(B)$
2: $I \leftarrow Project(A, V)$

InterpolatePoly1 computes an interpolant from the constraints of B. Any $i \in I$ computed by InterpolatePoly1 is implied by A and does not intersect B. It has variables common to the constraints of A and B. Note that there may not be any constraint c in B whose negation is implied by A. In such a case, we obtain interpolants by algorithm InterpolatePoly2. In our implementation, we first try to get an interpolant by InterpolatePoly1 algorithm. If no interpolant is found, then we use InterpolatePoly2. As part of future work, we wish to incorporate interpolation techniques from [17,20] in our tool DAGGER. The correctness proofs and complexity analysis of InterpolatePoly1 and InterpolatePoly2 algorithms can be found in [11].

In each of the above mentioned abstract domains, a non-$\perp$ abstract element is represented as a set of constraints (conjoined implicitly). For any two abstract elements A and B, a simple interpolated widen operator can be defined as: $A \nabla_T B = B$ if $A = \perp$. Otherwise $A \nabla_T B = \{c \in T \mid \gamma(A) \subseteq \gamma(\{c\}) \wedge \gamma(B) \subseteq \gamma(\{c\})\} \cup \{c \in A \mid \gamma(B) \subseteq \gamma(\{c\})\}$.

Caching error states. Our implementation also uses an additional optimization of caching abstract error preimages at refinement points. This optimization has been empirically found to be useful in early detection of imprecisions that lead to errors in future explorations. Compared to [12] where widen is refined by join, the use of interpolated widen can potentially increase the total number of image and preimage computations in the overall abstraction refinement

Table 1. Experimental results. Column I: time (seconds), Column II: number of refinement iterations. '*' denotes non-termination in 2000 sec, '!' denotes inability of tool to discover new predicates, and '-' denotes tool crash.

Pgm	DAGGER I	II	TREE + ∇ I	II	TREE + ∇_I I	II	DAG + ∇ I	II	DAG + ∇_I I	II	BLAST I	II	SLAM I	II	GR06 I	II	ARMC I	II
Sendmail																		
p1-ok	4.64	9	1940	18408	11.2	16	131.5	412	5.76	9	*	*	*	*	*	*	-	-
p2-ok	0.27	4	35.8	3996	0.77	4	64.23	1332	0.39	4	*	*	*	*	*	*	*	*
p3-ok	0.15	0	18.4	1	18.3	1	0.15	0	0.14	0	2.2	4	*	*	*	*	-	-
p1-bad	3.31	11	2.81	33	8	17	3.53	19	21.7	38	1368	46	*	*	12	33	-	-
p2-bad	0.06	1	0.08	1	0.08	1	0.06	1	0.06	1	1.1	7	9.9	12	0.1	1	0.12	1
p3-bad	4.91	49	1735	2402	252	203	30.85	64	101	53	*	*	*	*	*	*	-	-
STING																		
seesaw	0.04	2	*	*	0.05	2	*	*	0.05	2	!	!	1.0	1	0.82	6	*	*
bkley	0.04	1	0.04	0	0.04	0	0.05	1	0.04	1	!	!	2.90	5	0.10	2	4	16
bk-nat	0.06	2	0.09	2	0.06	1	0.11	4	0.07	2	!	!	!	!	0.43	3	3.25	18
hsort	0.14	3	*	*	0.16	3	*	*	0.14	3	!	!	1.10	1	0.72	3	22.5	40
efm	0.09	1	0.09	1	0.09	1	0.08	1	0.09	1	!	!	1.40	1	0.06	0	16.9	35
lifo	0.31	2	0.57	2	0.55	2	0.38	3	0.32	2	!	!	7.50	9	3.3	6	75.3	88
lifnat	0.49	3	*	*	1.46	5	*	*	0.48	3	!	!	6.60	9	29.55	12	!	!
cars	19.5	8	*	*	17.6	8	*	*	19.5	8	!	!	1.80	3	*	*	107	27
barbr	3.46	8	*	*	4.80	7	*	*	3.44	8	!	!	43.9	22	10.5	6	674	205
swim	0.60	2	2.46	13	0.60	2	1.49	9	0.60	2	!	!	!	!	11.1	6	579	137
swim1	0.72	3	2.57	13	0.79	3	1.54	9	0.72	3	!	!	!	!	11.2	6	767	144
hsort1	0.07	1	*	*	0.08	1	*	*	0.15	1	!	!	1.3	1	*	*	0.15	1
barbr1	0.63	2	*	*	1.15	2	*	*	0.62	2	!	!	16.1	11	*	*	570	109
lifnat1	0.59	6	*	*	8.71	23	*	*	0.74	5	!	!	!	!	*	*	!	!
Miscellaneous																		
fla	0.01	0	0.01	0	0.01	0	0.01	0	0.01	0	1.07	12	*	*	0.01	0	*	*
ex1	0.04	1	*	*	0.06	1	*	*	0.04	1	!	!	!	!	*	*	0.62	3
f2	0.07	1	*	*	0.06	1	*	*	0.07	1	!	!	!	!	0.42	2	*	*
ex2	0.03	0	5.4	0	5.4	0	0.03	0	0.03	0	506	132	*	*	5.4	0	1.7	12
JM06	0.02	0	0.02	0	0.02	0	0.02	0	0.02	0	*	*	*	*	0.02	0	*	*
Programs Strengthened with loop invariants obtained by initial widen pass																		
p1-ok'	4.64	9	1948	18413	8.2	13	121	411	4.76	9	200	24	*	*	*	*	-	-
p2-ok'	0.27	4	35.8	3996	0.77	4	64.23	1332	0.39	4	*	*	*	*	*	*	*	*
JM06'	0.02	0	0.02	0	0.02	0	0.02	0	0.02	0	0.07	2	*	*	0.02	0	0.17	1
barbr'	3.46	8	*	*	4.80	7	*	*	3.44	8	!	!	4.7	14	10.5	6	890	153
barbr1'	0.63	2	*	*	1.15	2	*	*	0.62	2	!	!	1.7	5	*	*	767	104
lifnat1'	0.59	6	*	*	6.71	10	*	*	0.74	5	!	!	!	!	*	*	205	71

loop. Caching abstract error preimages helps in mitigating this effect (see [11] for further discussion of this optimization technique).

Experimental Evaluation. We have evaluated our implementation on the suite of buffer overflow programs (adapted from Sendmail) developed by Zitser et al. [23], the set of STING benchmarks [21], and a miscellaneous set of programs. All programs can be obtained from [11]. Our current implementation is intra procedural and we handle multiple procedures by providing procedure summaries by way of annotations. The experiments are performed on an Intel(R) Xeon 3.00 GHz processor with 4GB RAM. The experimental results are given in Table 1.

Benchmark programs. The Sendmail programs have nested while loops with branching structures within the loops. The assertions in these programs check bounds on array accesses. Programs with 'ok' suffix are correct and those with 'bad' suffix have array bound errors. The programs p1-bad and p3-bad have deep counterexamples whose lengths depend on the size of the array. The STING programs have a single while loop with nondeterministic branching in the loop body. We modified the examples to assert for the invariants computed by STING. For the programs hsort1, barbr1 and lifnat1, we dropped some conjuncts in the invariants computed by STING while writing the assertion. Program ex2 has a sequence of if-then-else statements, leading to an exponential explosion of paths. Program JM06 is the benchmark program in [17] that could not be analyzed by BLAST. The programs with primed names in the last six rows were obtained by annotating the corresponding unprimed programs with location invariants obtained from an initial widen based analysis (using "assume" statements) as suggested in [16] suggests. All Sendmail programs and JM06 were analyzed in DAGGER using the octagon abstract domain. All STING programs and f1a, f2, ex1 and ex2 were analyzed in DAGGER using the polyhedra abstract domain.

Description of columns. In Table 1 we compare DAGGER with other abstraction refinement tools (SLAM, BLAST, ARMC), with our earlier tool GR06 [12], and with combinations of DAGGER's constituent optimizations. We could not compare with IMPACT and with the tools mentioned in [22, 16] due to their unavailability. The column DAGGER gives results for a DAG based exploration, as described in Section 3, with the additional optimization of caching abstract error preimages at refinement points. The column TREE + ∇ is for a TREE based exploration with widen refined by $\sqcup$ instead of by interpolated widen. The column TREE + ∇_I gives results for a TREE based exploration, as discussed in Section 2. Similarly, the column DAG + ∇ gives results for a DAG based exploration with widen refined by $\sqcup$ instead of by interpolated widen. The column DAG + ∇_I gives results for a DAG based exploration, as discussed in Section 3.

Advantages of interpolated widen. To understand the effect of interpolated widen, we compare the columns TREE + ∇ and DAG + ∇, where interpolated widen is not used, with the corresponding columns TREE + ∇_I and DAG + ∇_I, where interpolated widen is used. The programs seesaw, hsort, lifnat, cars, barbr, hsort1, barbr1, lifnat1, ex1 and f2 require interpolated widen to compute inductive invariants strong enough to prove the desired properties. For p1-ok and p2-ok, exploration without interpolated widen performs a large number of refinement iterations proportional to the size of the array being processed, as seen in columns TREE + ∇ and DAG + ∇. Interpolated widen eliminates the dependence on array size, as seen in columns TREE + ∇_I and DAG + ∇_I.

Advantages of DAG exploration. For programs p3-ok and ex2, TREE based exploration explores exponentially many paths. However, DAG based exploration avoids this blow up by merging abstract states along different paths at each merge location. DAG based exploration is also effective in detecting true counterexamples. In p3-bad, the TREE based technique explores several spurious counterexamples before discovering a true error. The DAG based technique reduces this effort significantly. It also does not blow up while analyzing multiple counterexamples by backward propagation of error. Interestingly, in p1-bad, the TREE based exploration got lucky and found a true counterexample quickly. The STING benchmarks do not have significant branching structure. Thus, the DAG + ∇ and TREE + ∇ techniques, and also DAG + ∇$_I$ and TREE + ∇$_I$ explorations perform similarly for these examples.

Advantages of caching. For programs p1-bad and p3-bad, the number of image and preimage computations using TREE + ∇$_I$ and DAG + ∇$_I$ grows quadratically with the length of the counterexample. This contrasts with TREE + ∇ and DAG + ∇, where this number grows linearly with the length of the counterexample, leading to much lesser computation times. This discrepancy arises because in TREE + ∇ and DAG + ∇, widens are refined to joins that are more precise than interpolated widens. Thus, once a widen is refined, it does not need to be refined further. By caching error preimages at refinement points, the above drawback can be significantly addressed in interpolated widen based techniques. This can be seen by comparing the DAGGER column with the DAG + ∇$_I$ column for programs p1-bad and p3-bad.

Comparison with other refinement tools. For the Sendmail examples p1-ok, p2-ok, p3-bad and for JM06, none of SLAM, BLAST, GR06 and ARMC are able to find the right predicates. DAGGER's interpolated widen however finds the right predicates in a few iterations. On most of Sendmail examples, GR06 does not terminate due to an explosion in the number of disjuncts. When location invariants obtained from an initial widen based analysis are added to the original program, the performance of other tools does not always improve. The last six rows of Table 1 illustrate this. For BLAST and SLAM, the performance improves for some programs by way of either terminating within 2000s (where it did not terminate earlier), or faster convergence. However for other programs (p2-ok' for BLAST, and p1-ok', p2-ok', JM06' for SLAM) these tools still do not terminate in 2000s. For ARMC the performance improves on some examples (lifnat', JM06') and degrades on others (barbr', barbr1'). For GR06 and DAGGER the performance does not significantly change after adding invariants since these tools can easily discover these invariants. This illustrates that invariants obtained from an initial widen based analysis may be too weak to help refinement, and that interaction between widen and interpolation as implemented in DAGGER is useful.

The refinement engine of BLAST fails for STING programs as it is equipped to generate only difference and bounds constraints, while the STING programs need more expressive invariants. SLAM is unable to make progress on bk-nat, swim, swim1 and lifnat1, as it cannot discover the correct predicates. ARMC takes several more iterations (and longer execution times) compared to DAGGER to generate the right predicates on most of the STING examples. However for the programs seesaw, lifnat and lifnat1, it is unable to generate the right predicates, and hence does not terminate. GR06 is able to compute the correct inductive invariants for many programs in the STING benchmarks. But the programs cars, hsort1, barbr1, and lifnat1 fail with this technique. DAGGER and the constituents of DAGGER that use interpolated widen (namely TREE + ∇_I and DAG + ∇_I) are able to prove these programs correct in a small number of iterations.

Finally, looking at the miscellaneous benchmarks, we find that SLAM fails on all these examples. BLAST fails on ex1, f2 and JM06. GR06 fails on ex1, and ARMC fails on f1a, f2 and JM06. Again, DAGGER and the constituents of DAGGER that use interpolated widen (namely TREE + ∇_I and DAG + ∇_I) are able to prove these programs correct in a small number of iterations.

Tools like BLAST, SLAM, and ARMC use techniques beyond what we have discussed for widen and interpolants. For example, BLAST uses recursive enumeration of predicates, SLAM uses several heuristics to determine a good set of predicates, and both BLAST and ARMC use several sophisticated algorithms to compute interpolants. In contrast, DAGGER uses very simple widen and interpolation operators, and by combining these appropriately (and dynamically), it outperforms these other tools.

5   Conclusion

We presented three new techniques to automatically refine abstract interpretations to tune the precision of fixpoint computations dynamically and reduce the number of false errors produced by abstract interpretation. We have proved that our refinements guarantee progress in a formal sense. However, since assertion checking is undecidable, our procedure is not guaranteed to terminate. In practice, we find that our procedure terminates and outperforms tools available to us on a variety of benchmarks. Though our implementation DAGGER uses polyhedra and octagons, our techniques can be used with any choice of abstract domain, widen, join and interpolation operators.

Acknowledgments. The first author was supported by Microsoft Corporation and Microsoft Research India under the Microsoft Research India PhD Fellowship Award.

References

1. Apron. Numerical Abstract Domain Library, http://apron.cri.ensmp.fr/library/
2. Bagnara, R., Hill, P., Zaffanella, E.: Widening operators for powerset domains. Technical Report 344, University of Parma, Italy (2004)
3. Bagnara, R., Hill, P.M., Ricci, E., Zaffanella, E.: Precise widening opertors for convex polyhedra. In: Cousot, R. (ed.) SAS 2003. LNCS, vol. 2694, Springer, Heidelberg (2003)
4. Ball, T., Rajamani, S.K.: The SLAM project: debugging system software via static analysis. In: POPL 2002, pp. 1–3 (2002)
5. Beyer, D., Henzinger, T.A., Majumdar, R., Rybalchenko, A.: Path invariants. In: PLDI, pp. 300–309 (2007)
6. CIL. Infrastructure for C Program Analysis and Transformation.
   http://manju.cs.berkeley.edu/cil/

7. Cousot, P., Cousot, R.: Abstract interpretation: a unified lattice model for static analysis of programs by construction or approximation of fixpoints. In: POPL 1977, pp. 238–252 (1977)

8. Esparza, J., Kiefer, S., Schwoon, S.: Abstraction refinement with craig interpolation and symbolic pushdown systems. In: Hermanns, H., Palsberg, J. (eds.) TACAS 2006. LNCS, vol. 3920, pp. 489–503. Springer, Heidelberg (2006)

9. Fischer, J., Jhala, R., Majumdar, R.: Joining dataflow with predicates. In: ESEC/SIGSOFT FSE, pp. 227–236 (2005)

10. Gopan, D., Reps, T.W.: Lookahead widening. In: Ball, T., Jones, R.B. (eds.) CAV 2006. LNCS, vol. 4144, pp. 452–466. Springer, Heidelberg (2006)

11. B. S. Gulavani, S. Chakraborty, A. V. Nori, and S. K. Rajamani. Automatically refining abstract interpretations. Technical Report TR-07-23, CFDVS, IIT Bombay, 2007. http://www.cfdvs.iitb.ac.in/~bhargav/dagger.html

12. Gulavani, B.S., Rajamani, S.K.: Counterexample driven refinement for abstract interpretation. In: Hermanns, H., Palsberg, J. (eds.) TACAS 2006. LNCS, vol. 3920, pp. 474–488. Springer, Heidelberg (2006)

13. Halbwachs, N., Proy, Y.E., Roumanoff, P.: Verification of real-time systems using linear relation analysis. FMSD 11(2), 157–185 (1997)

14. Henzinger, T., Jhala, R., Majumdar, R., McMillan, K.: Abstractions from proofs. In: POPL (2004)

15. Henzinger, T.A., Jhala, R., Majumdar, R., Sutre, G.: Lazy abstraction. In: POPL, pp. 58–70 (2002)

16. Jain, H., Ivancic, F., Gupta, A., Shlyakhter, I., Wang, C.: Using statically computed invariants inside the predicate abstraction and refinement loop. In: Ball, T., Jones, R.B. (eds.) CAV 2006. LNCS, vol. 4144, pp. 137–151. Springer, Heidelberg (2006)

17. Jhala, R., McMillan, K.L.: A practical and complete approach to predicate refinement. In: Hermanns, H., Palsberg, J. (eds.) TACAS 2006. LNCS, vol. 3920, pp. 459–473. Springer, Heidelberg (2006)

18. McMillan, K.L.: Lazy abstraction with interpolants. In: Ball, T., Jones, R.B. (eds.) CAV 2006. LNCS, vol. 4144, pp. 123–136. Springer, Heidelberg (2006)

19. Rybalchenko, A., Podelski, A.: Armc: The logical choice for software model checking with abstraction refinement. In: PADL (2007)

20. Rybalchenko, A., Sofronie-Stokkermans, V.: Constraint solving for interpolation. In: Cook, B., Podelski, A. (eds.) VMCAI 2007. LNCS, vol. 4349, pp. 346–362. Springer, Heidelberg (2007)

21. Sankaranarayanan, S., Sipma, H., Manna, Z.: Constraint based linear-relations analysis. In: Giacobazzi, R. (ed.) SAS 2004. LNCS, vol. 3148, pp. 53–68. Springer, Heidelberg (2004)

22. Wang, C., Yang, Z., Gupta, A., Ivancic, F.: Using counterexamples for improving the precision of reachability computation with polyhedra. In: Damm, W., Hermanns, H. (eds.) CAV 2007. LNCS, vol. 4590, pp. 352–365. Springer, Heidelberg (2007)

23. Zitser, M., Lippmann, R., Leek, T.: Testing static analysis tools using exploitable buffer overflows from open source code. In: FSE, pp. 97–106 (2004)

Sviss:
Symbolic Verification of Symmetric Systems*

Thomas Wahl[1], Nicolas Blanc[1], and E. Allen Emerson[2]

[1] Computer Systems Institute, ETH Zurich, Switzerland
[2] Department of Computer Sciences, The University of Texas at Austin, USA

Abstract. Sviss is a flexible platform for incorporating efficient symmetry reduction into symbolic model checking. The tool comes with an extensive C++ library for system modeling using BDDs and a rich CTL-based model checking engine. Applications range from communication protocols to computer hardware and multi-threaded software. We believe Sviss to be the first symbolic tool to exploit symmetry in concurrent device-driver verification, which is vital in operating system design.

1 Introduction

Symmetry reduction has proved to effectively curb the complexity of model checking finite-state multi-process systems. Provided the transition relation of the system is invariant under permutations of the participating processes, states that are identical up to permutations can be collapsed into an equivalence class, known as an *orbit*. This can reduce the number of states that need to be kept in memory from exponential to polynomial in the number of processes.

In contrast to its immediate success with explicit-state model checkers such as Murφ [7], symmetry reduction of a system given symbolically as a Binary Decision Diagram (BDD) was first thought to be infeasible in practice due to the *orbit problem*: the BDD representing the symmetry equivalence relation is of intractable size [3]. In this paper, we present a symbolic model checker with symmetry reduction that never builds this BDD and thus avoids the orbit problem: Sviss (historically, "*S*ymbolic *V*erification of *I*nvariants of *S*ymmetric *S*ystems") implements, to our knowledge, the first *efficient* symbolic realization of symmetry reduction, by dynamically mapping each encountered state to a unique representative of its orbit [5].

Sviss comes with a rich C++ library for constructing transition relations. The benefit of a library in a widely known programming language over a specialized input language is flexibility: the library has been used to model systems as diverse as asynchronous communication protocols [5], Boolean abstractions of concurrent software (see section 3), synchronous parallel programs [4], and finite-state machine descriptions of computer hardware. The penalty for this flexibility is that by using C++ constructs outside the library, the user can circumvent

---

* Work supported by the Swiss National Science Foundation under grant 200021-109594, by ETH research grant TH-21/05-1, and by NSF grant CCR-020-5483.

C.R. Ramakrishnan and J. Rehof (Eds.): TACAS 2008, LNCS 4963, pp. 459–462, 2008.

restrictions that ensure symmetry, which are therefore not enforced by the tool (a weakness that SVISS shares with other tools exploiting symmetry including MURφ [7]).

SVISS especially supports experimentation. An input file contains no property specifications. Instead, once the transition relation is built, the tool repeatedly requests CTL-like formulas at a prompt and performs global model checking by computing the set of states satisfying the formula. If the set is small, it can be visualized in a compact format. The intended utility of this feature is to increase confidence in the model by inspecting the set of initial, bad or reachable states of a small instance of a parameterized system.

2   Tool Description and Usage

The state space of the design under investigation is described in SVISS through model parameters, constants, and program variables. The variables can be of type Boolean, finite range, enumeration, record and array. The C++ library offers routines to access these variables, further Boolean operators, simple linear arithmetic, and a set of specialized functions for transition relation construction. An example illustrating the use of the library is provided on the tool website: http://www.inf.ethz.ch/~wahlt/Sviss.

Variables are either global or belong to a *symmetry block*. Each block comprises the local variables of processes forming a symmetric factor of the state space (such as a block of readers and a block of writers in the Readers-Writers problem). A block also specifies the number of replicated components and the symmetry group that is to act within it. SVISS offers reduction with respect to full (arbitrary permutations of components) and rotational symmetry (cyclic shifts), specified by the user individually for each block. Global variables that store process indices (such as a token variable in a resource allocation protocol) are allowed and treated specially by the reduction algorithms.

SVISS first compiles a system model to a customized executable. The model may leave some parameters unspecified, such as the number of process components. These parameter, as well as CTL specifications, can conveniently be supplied later at the command line of the executable or at a prompt. This greatly facilitates experimentation with different parameters and specifications.

SVISS computes the set of states corresponding to an input formula, which can be written in a dialect of CTL, augmented by past-time temporal operators, with or without frontier set optimization. The computation can be done (i) ignoring symmetry, (ii) using dynamic symmetry [5], (iii) using the *orbit relation* [3] and (iv) by way of *multiple representatives* [3].[1] If the result is neither empty nor equal to the entire state space, the set of states (or a few elements of it) can be enumerated. For experimental purposes, SVISS further supports the computation of a set's cardinality, of the corresponding set of symmetry-representative states, and of the corresponding set of symmetry-equivalent states (i.e. the set's orbit).

---

[1] On average, efficiency seems to diminish in the order (ii), (i), (iv), (iii).

SVISS possesses a specialized operator INV, which checks invariant conditions after each step during symbolic reachability analysis, either forward (from *init*) or backward (from *error*). Upon failure, the tool prints an error trace in terms of the original program variables.

SVISS uses the CUDD decision diagram package [9] for BDD manipulations.

3   Applications of SVISS

SVISS has been applied successfully to communication and locking protocols and to systems parameterized by the number of processes, in one fell swoop over a finite range of the parameter. Quantitative results from these experiments are available in the cited literature [5,4], which also compares the performance of SVISS's algorithms with alternative approaches to exploiting symmetry.

In this paper we share our experiences of applying SVISS to concurrent Linux device-driver software. A driver is confronted with a set of processes representing users, the operating system environment and external events. We used DDVerify [11] to obtain a (coarse) Boolean abstraction of the driver software with about 10-12 Boolean predicates per driver. All abstract models contain errors (often spurious), at depths ranging from 100 to 200 instructions.

The histograms in figure 1 show time (top left, log-scale) and space (bottom left) demands for safety-checking eight abstract models with a fixed number of

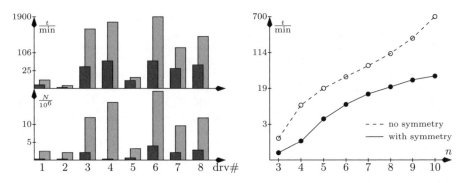

Fig. 1. Comparison of resource demands without and with symmetry across drivers for ten processes (left) and across numbers of components for driver # 3 (right)

ten processes, ignoring (light gray) and exploiting (dark gray) symmetry dynamically [5]. We see tremendous memory savings thanks to symmetry, in all cases.[2] The same holds for the run-time, with a few exceptions (e.g. drivers # 1, 2, 5); the exceptions correspond to shallow errors. The deeper the exploration, the greater the time and space savings of symmetry reduction. A similarly widening gap can be observed for a growing number n of components (graph on the

---

[2] "Memory" = peak number N of allocated BDD nodes. Experiments conducted on a 3 GHz Intel[TM] Pentium[TM] 4 dual-core processor, 2 GB of main memory.

right, only time is shown). After reaching a certain number of allocated BDD nodes, the cost of computing a transition image far exceeds that of symmetry-canonizing the set of successor states. The image computations benefit from a small set of representative states in the case of symmetry.

4   Related Work and Conclusions

Distinguished examples of *explicit-state* model checkers using symmetry include Murφ [7], SMC [8] and Zing [1]. Due to the enumeration, these tools are limited to systems with a manageable number of reachable states. Present-day (partially) BDD-based model checkers that offer symmetry reduction include UPPAAL [6], RULEBASE [2] and RED [10]. To escape the orbit problem, these tools usually fall back on approximate reduction strategies.

Concurrent software verification is still in its infancy. Symmetry reduction can help this effort by (i) increasing the depth up to which programs can be explored in reasonable time, (ii) increasing the number of abstraction-refinement iterations, each of which entails more predicates and thus more resource needs than its predecessor, and (iii) increasing the number of processes to which, say, a device driver can be exposed for verification. A future step is to integrate SViss fully into an abstraction-refinement framework based on Boolean programs.

References

1. Andrews, T., Qadeer, S., Rajamani, S.K., Rehof, J., Xie, Y.: Zing: A model checker for concurrent software. In: Alur, R., Peled, D.A. (eds.) CAV 2004. LNCS, vol. 3114, pp. 484–487. Springer, Heidelberg (2004)
2. Barner, S., Grumberg, O.: Combining symmetry reduction and Under Approximation for symbolic model checking. In: FMSD 2005 (2005)
3. Clarke, E.M., Enders, R., Filkorn, T., Jha, S.: Exploiting symmetry in temporal logic model checking. In: FMSD 1996 (1996)
4. Emerson, E.A., Trefler, R.J., Wahl, T.: Reducing Model Checking of the Few to the One. In: Liu, Z., He, J. (eds.) ICFEM 2006. LNCS, vol. 4260, pp. 94–113. Springer, Heidelberg (2006)
5. Emerson, E.A., Wahl, T.: Dynamic symmetry reduction. In: Halbwachs, N., Zuck, L.D. (eds.) TACAS 2005. LNCS, vol. 3440, pp. 382–396. Springer, Heidelberg (2005)
6. Hendriks, M., Behrmann, G., Larsen, K.G., Niebert, P., Vaandrager, F.W.: Adding symmetry reduction to Uppaal. In: Larsen, K.G., Niebert, P. (eds.) FORMATS 2003. LNCS, vol. 2791, Springer, Heidelberg (2004)
7. Melton, R., Dill, D.L.: Murφ Annotated Reference Manual, rel. 3.1., http://verify.stanford.edu/dill/murphi.html
8. Sistla, A.P., Gyuris, V., Emerson, E.A.: Smc: a symmetry-based model checker for verification of safety and liveness properties. In: ACM ToSEM 2000 (2000)
9. Somenzi, F.: The CU Decision Diagram Package, release 2.3.1, University of Colorado at Boulder, http://vlsi.colorado.edu/~fabio/CUDD/.
10. Wang, F., Schmidt, K., Yu, F., Huang, G.-D., Wang, B.-Y.: Bdd-based safety-analysis of concurrent software with pointer data structures using graph automorphism symmetry reduction. In: IEEE ToSE 2004 (2004)
11. Witkowski, T., Blanc, N., Kroening, D., Weissenbacher, G.: Model checking concurrent linux device drivers. In: ASE 2007 (2007)

RESY: Requirement Synthesis
for Compositional Model Checking*

Bernd Finkbeiner, Hans-Jörg Peter, and Sven Schewe

Universität des Saarlandes
66123 Saarbrücken, Germany
{finkbeiner,peter,schewe}@cs.uni-sb.de

Abstract. The requirement synthesis tool RESY automatically computes environment assumptions for compositional model checking. Given a process M in a multi-process PROMELA program, an abstraction refinement loop computes a coarse equivalence relation on the states of the environment, collapsing two states if the environment of M can either force the occurrence of an error from both states or from neither state. RESY supports three different operation modes: assumption generation, compositional model checking, and front-end to the model checker SPIN. In *assumption generation* mode, RESY minimizes the size of the assumption; small assumptions are useful for program documentation and as certificates for re-verification. In *compositional model checking* mode, RESY terminates as soon as the property is proven or disproven, independently of the size of the assumption. In *front-end* mode, RESY terminates when the size of the assumption falls below a specified threshold, and calls SPIN with the simplified verification problem.

1   Requirement Synthesis

RESY is a tool for the automatic synthesis of requirement automata for safety properties. Requirement automata represent the assumptions an environment makes on the behavior of a component. Typical applications include *program documentation* [1], where the synthesized requirements help the user to understand the interaction of the program components; *program certification* [2], where the synthesized requirements simplify the re-verification of the system (possibly by a different user and a different tool); and *compositional model checking* [3], where the requirement is synthesized and used during the *same* model checking run, in order to avoid the construction of the full product state space.

RESY implements the requirement synthesis algorithm presented in [4]. Given a system $M \| E$, which consists of a process M and its environment E, RESY computes an equivalence relation on the states of M, collapsing two states if E can either force the occurrence of an error from both states or from neither state.

* This work was partly supported by the German Research Foundation (DFG) as part of the Transregional Collaborative Research Center "Automatic Verification and Analysis of Complex Systems" (SFB/TR 14 AVACS).

C.R. Ramakrishnan and J. Rehof (Eds.): TACAS 2008, LNCS 4963, pp. 463–466, 2008.

The requirement automaton is the quotient of M with respect to the equivalence relation.

Key advantages of this approach are that the generated requirement automaton is small (RESY's equivalence is much coarser than language-based equivalences like bisimulation), inexpensive to compute (RESY is often dramatically faster than L*-based requirement learning), and easy to re-verify (implementation and requirement are related by a simple homomorphism).

2   Generating Requirements from Abstractions

Computing the equivalence relation requires two traversals of the state space. In a *forward* traversal, we identify states of the process M that are all either reachable or unreachable, depending on the state in the environment E they are combined with. In a *backward* traversal, we identify states of M that either all have or all do not have a path to the error, depending again on the state in E they are combined with.

To avoid the expansion of the full state graph, RESY considers abstractions of E. The abstractions are computed in an automatic abstraction refinement loop that, starting with the trivial abstraction, incrementally increases the size of the abstraction.

The abstraction $\mathcal{E}$ of the environment is a modal transition system that is defined by an equivalence relation $\simeq$ on E. Replacing E with its abstraction introduces the possibility that two states of M both lead to an error when composed with $\mathcal{E}$, but only one of them leads to an error when composed with E. RESY therefore distinguishes situations that *may* lead to an error (i.e., when the error is reached in the composition with $\mathcal{E}$ but not necessarily in E) from situations that *must* lead to an error (both in composition with $\mathcal{E}$ and in composition with E). Merging two states of M is safe in two cases: (1) if they *both must* lead to an error, and (2) if *neither* of them *may* lead to an error.

The environment abstraction identifies *must* and *may* transitions. In the backward analysis, for example, a transition $([v], a, [v'])$ is a *must* transition if, for all states $w \simeq v$, there is a state $w' \simeq v'$ such that (w, a, w') is a transition of E. Reachability on *must* transitions is a sufficient criterion for reachability in the concrete system; unreachability on *may* transitions is a sufficient criterion for unreachability in the concrete system.

In each abstraction refinement step, RESY uses a heuristic to pick some *may* transition $([v], \sigma, [v'])$ of the forward or backward analysis that is not also a *must* transition, and splits the equivalence class $[v']$ (respectively $[v]$), distinguishing states that either have or do not have the incoming (respectively outgoing) transition in E. By default, RESY picks forward and backward transitions that are closest to the initial state and the error, respectively.

RESY recognizes situations in which further refinements of the environment abstraction will no longer lead to a reduction of the requirement automaton. Depending on RESY's operation mode, the refinement loop may also be interrupted earlier, yielding a sound but not necessarily minimal requirement automaton.

3   Operation Modes of RESY

The input to RESY is a PROMELA program that specifies a distributed system as a parallel composition of modules, and a specification automaton for the safety property. RESY can be executed in the following modes:

- *Assumption generation.* In this mode, RESY minimizes the size of the requirement automaton. This mode is most useful if the automaton is to be used as a certificate.
- *Compositional model checking.* In this mode, RESY terminates as soon as the property is proven or disproven, independently of the size of the requirement automaton generated so far. This mode is most useful if RESY is to be used as a stand-alone model checker.
- *SPIN front-end.* In this mode, RESY also terminates if the size of the requirement automaton falls below a user-defined threshold (for example, 10% of the states of the program M). If the property has not been proven or disproven at this point, RESY replaces M with the requirement automaton and calls SPIN [5] with the modified PROMELA program.

4   Results

Table 1 shows the performance of RESY on a range of benchmarks, including the sliding window protocol (SW), an elevator controller (Elevator), a production cell (Prodcell), and an industrial document flow (workflow). For each benchmark, the table shows the time and memory usage of the assumption generation mode and compares the performance of the compositional model checking mode (CMC) and the SPIN front-end mode using a threshold of 10% (R10%) with the performance of the model checker SPIN alone (SPIN).

The *sliding window* protocol is parameterized by the buffer and window sizes. Property A, B, and C are valid properties (e.g., "the protocol does not invent messages"). Property D ("the receiver never produces any output") does not hold. The *elevator* benchmark is parameterized by the number of floors. (The property states that a door is never open when no elevator is present.) In the *production cell*, two concurrent programs control a plant. The benchmark is parameterized by the number of components of the plant (which may include robot arms, a press, lifts, and grippers). The property requires that there is no arm within the press when it starts working. The *workflow* benchmark models an industrial document flow. It is parameterized by the number of participants.

The results in Table 1 show that compositional model checking with RESY often improves over monolithic model checking with SPIN by more than an order of magnitude. Computing the minimal requirement automaton typically does not add significant cost. The minimal requirement automaton is always much smaller than the original process and often small enough to be presented to the user.

Availability. RESY and the benchmarks used in this paper are available online at http://react.cs.uni-sb.de/resy.

Table 1. Experimental results of RESY on a range of benchmarks. The table shows the performance of the *assumption generation* mode, and compares the performance of the verification modes *compositional model checking* (CMC) and SPIN *front-end* with a threshold of 10% (R10%) to the performance of SPIN. The time (t) and memory usage (m) is given in milliseconds and megabytes, respectively; the sizes of the process M, environment E, and requirement automaton $\mathcal{A}$ are given as the number of states. All benchmarks were measured on an Intel Pentium M processor 2.13 GHz.

	model size		assumption generation			verification CMC		R10%		SPIN	
	M	E	t	m	$\mathcal{A}$	t	m	t	m	t	m
SW 2/1/A	48	26	86	0.4	3	86	0.3	86	0.4	1149	2.7
SW 3/1/A	256	120	2880	2.6	6	2877	2.4	3960	2.7	9017	3.9
SW 3/2/A	256	120	3882	2.7	5	3872	2.5	5366	2.8	9657	4.1
SW 2/1/B	48	26	86	0.4	28	49	0.3	86	0.4	1148	2.7
SW 3/1/B	256	120	3818	2.9	107	1722	1.9	3818	2.9	9050	3.9
SW 3/2/B	256	120	4979	3.0	209	598	1.7	4979	3.0	9613	4.1
SW 2/1/C	48	26	44	0.3	5	53	0.3	44	0.3	1148	2.7
SW 3/1/C	256	120	985	2.2	9	985	2.8	1958	2.7	9069	4.0
SW 3/2/C	256	120	1524	2.2	9	1523	3.0	2978	2.8	9640	4.1
SW 2/1/D	48	26	22	0.4	1	22	0.2	22	0.4	1148	2.7
SW 3/1/D	256	120	84	2.3	1	84	1.4	84	2.3	8890	3.6
SW 3/2/D	256	120	89	2.4	1	89	1.5	89	2.4	9406	3.7
Elevator 2	48	18	68	0.2	11	61	0.1	68	0.2	636	2.6
Elevator 3	192	30	414	1.0	15	407	0.5	414	1.0	860	2.6
Elevator 4	768	42	2633	4.9	22	2615	2.1	5113	4.9	1152	2.6
Prodcell 2	12	12	23	0.1	5	23	0.1	23	0.1	519	2.6
Prodcell 3	24	24	73	0.2	6	65	0.2	73	0.2	681	2.6
Prodcell 4	40	24	111	0.4	6	118	0.3	802	2.6	803	2.6
Prodcell 5	40	40	296	0.6	6	296	0.5	296	0.6	897	2.6
Prodcell 6	40	48	486	0.7	6	486	0.6	486	0.7	973	2.6
Prodcell 7	72	48	902	1.1	6	906	0.8	1831	2.6	1158	2.7
Workflow 2	64	11	35	0.2	4	31	0.1	35	0.2	526	2.6
Workflow 3	512	16	441	2.5	8	50	0.5	441	2.5	619	2.6
Workflow 4	4096	25	20294	62.9	16	409	4.1	20294	62.9	849	2.7

References

1. Giannakopoulou, D., Păsăreanu, C.S., Barringer, H.: Assumption generation for software component verification. In: Proc. ASE, pp. 3–12. IEEE Computer Society, Los Alamitos (2002)
2. Namjoshi, K.S.: Certifying model checkers. In: Berry, G., Comon, H., Finkel, A. (eds.) CAV 2001. LNCS, vol. 2102, pp. 2–13. Springer, Heidelberg (2001)
3. Alur, R., Madhusudan, P., Nam, W.: Symbolic compositional verification by learning assumptions. In: Etessami, K., Rajamani, S.K. (eds.) CAV 2005. LNCS, vol. 3576, pp. 548–562. Springer, Heidelberg (2005)
4. Finkbeiner, B., Schewe, S., Brill, M.: Automatic synthesis of assumptions for compositional model checking. In: Najm, E., Pradat-Peyre, J.-F., Donzeau-Gouge, V.V. (eds.) FORTE 2006. LNCS, vol. 4229, pp. 143–158. Springer, Heidelberg (2006)
5. Holzmann, G.: The Spin Model Checker, Primer and Reference Manual. Addison-Wesley, Reading (2003)

Scoot: A Tool for the Analysis of SystemC Models*

Nicolas Blanc[1], Daniel Kroening[2], and Natasha Sharygina[3]

[1] ETH Zurich, Switzerland
[2] Oxford University, Computing Laboratory, UK
[3] University of Lugano, Switzerland

Abstract. *SystemC* is a system-level modeling language and offers support for concurrency and arbitrary-width bit-vector arithmetic. The existing static analyzers for *SystemC* consider only small fragments of the language. We present SCOOT, a model extractor for *SystemC* based on a C++ frontend. The models generated by SCOOT can serve multiple purposes, ranging from verification and simulation to synthesis. Exemplarily, we report results indicating that our tool can be used to improve the performance of dynamic execution up to a factor of five.

1 Introduction

SystemC is a system-level modeling language implemented as a C++ library. It offers support for concurrency and arbitrary-width bit-vector arithmetic. Along with an event-driven simulation environment, the library provides a notion of timing, which is well-suited for modeling circuits. *SystemC* permits describing a system at several levels of abstraction, starting at a high-level functional description, down to synthesizable gate-level. Due to the complexity of C++, existing static analyzers for *SystemC* consider only small fragments of the language, essentially searching for specific key-words. We present SCOOT, a model extractor for *SystemC*. The tool sypports a wide range of language constructs, as it based on our C++ front-end. The models generated by SCOOT can serve several purposes, ranging from verification and simulation to synthesis. The tool is tightly integrated with verification back-ends for Bounded Model Checking (CBMC) [4] and SAT-based predicate abstraction (SATABS) [2]. Results on applying model checking to models generated by SCOOT have been reported before [5].

As an example of the utility of SCOOT beyond formal verification, we report results indicating that our tool can be used to improve the performance of dynamic execution up to five times.

2 Overview of Scoot

A *SystemC* program consists of a set of *modules*. Modules may declare processes, ports, internal data, channels and instances of other modules. Processes

---

* Supported by ETH research grant TH-21/05-1 and Foundation Tasso, Switzerland.

C.R. Ramakrishnan and J. Rehof (Eds.): TACAS 2008, LNCS 4963, pp. 467–470, 2008.

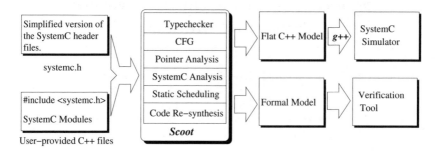

Fig. 1. Overview of SCOOT

implement the functionality of the module, and are sensitive to events. As in Verilog or VHDL, ports are objects through which the module communicates with other modules. Although variables are shared between processes, classic interprocess communication is achieved through predefined channels such as signals and FIFOs.

SCOOT uses a C++ front-end to translate the *SystemC* source files into a control flow graph. The nodes of the graph are annotated with assignments and guards (implemented in the typechecking and CFG-conversion phases in Figure 1). Subsequently, static analysis techniques are used to determine the following information, which is specific to *SystemC*:

- The module hierarchy,
- the sensitivity list of the processes, and
- the port bindings.

The *SystemC* library makes heavy use of virtual functions and dynamic data structures, which are not easily analyzed by static analysis techniques. SCOOT abstracts implementation details of the library by using simplified header files that declare only relevant aspects of the API and omit the actual implementation.

3   Static Scheduling for Dynamic Verification

Technically, *SystemC* modules are plain C++ classes that can be compiled and linked to a runtime scheduler, providing thus a way to simulate the behavior of the system. The model hierarchy is discovered at run-time only and therefore, the compiler is missing opportunities to take advantage of this knowledge. To illustrate the utility of the model generated by SCOOT, we re-synthesize more efficient C++ code from the model.

SystemC has a *co-operative multitasking* semantics, meaning that the execution of processes is serialized by explicit calls to a `wait()` method and that threads are not preempted. The scheduler tracks simulation time and *delta cycles*. The simulation time corresponds to a positive integer value (the clock), while delta cycles are used to stabilize the state of the system. A delta cycle consists of three phases: *evaluate*, *update*, and *notify*.

1. The evaluation phase selects, from the set of runnable processes, a process and triggers or resumes its execution. The process runs immediately up to the point where it returns or invokes the wait function. The evaluation phase iterates until the set of runnable processes is empty. The order in which processes are selected from the set of runnable processes is implementation-defined.
2. In order to simulate synchronous executions, processes can delay change-of-state effects by scheduling update requests. After the evaluation phase terminates, the kernel executes any pending update request. This is called the update phase. Typically, signal-assignments are implemented using the update mechanism. Therefore, signals keep their value for a whole evaluation phase.
3. Finally, during the delta-notification phase, the scheduler determines which processes are sensitive to events that have occurred, and adds all such process instances to the set of runnable processes.

Delta cycles are executed until the set of runnable processes is empty. Subsequently, the simulation time is increased, and processes waiting for the current time-event are notified.

Formally, let S represent the set of states of a *SystemC* model. We write Up to denote the function from 2^S to 2^S that updates a set of states as described by the update phase. Similarly, let $Ev : 2^S \rightarrow 2^S$ denote the evaluation phase. The delta phase performs a fix-point computation defined by $\delta(S) = \delta \circ Up \circ Ev(S)$. Finally, we concisely express the semantics of the scheduler with the function $Sim(t) = \delta \circ Up_{time} \circ Sim(t-1)$ that computes the set of final states at a time t. The function Up_{time} updates the clock.

The standard *SystemC* scheduler contains several sources of inefficiency: first, the scheduler stores data in containers that allocate memory at run-time, and second, it triggers processes using function pointers. SCOOT generates a completely static scheduler by fixing the evaluation order of the processes and resolving dynamic calls. Finally, processes are sequentialized using a similar technique used by KISS [7] that implements context switches with fast goto statements.

Code Re-synthesis. The intermediate representation used by SCOOT was originally designed for model checking, and uses bit-vector arithmetic expressions. After static scheduling, SCOOT translates the intermediate representation back to a flat C++ program that does not rely on the *SystemC* library anymore. The generated model is subsequently passed to g++, which results in a faster simulator.

The following table quantifies the advantages of static scheduling compared to dynamic scheduling on a 3 GHz Intel Pentium 4 processor. We use an AES encryption/decryption core as benchmark. For each module, we report the number of processes, the number of signals, the execution time with dynamic scheduling, the execution time using SCOOT, and the speedup obtained.

Module	# Proc.	# Sig.	Dyn. Sched. [s]	Stat. Sched [s]	Speedup
Byte_Mixcolum	2	7	22.94	4.33	5.3
Word_Mixcolum	7	16	65.82	18.01	3.65
Mixcolum	11	30	75.7	28.6	2.65
Subbytes	15	30	49.73	9.84	5.05
128-bits AES	32	97	319.2	99.73	3.2
192-bits AES	32	99	344.21	105.45	3.26

4   Related Work and Conclusion

Due to the complexity of the C++ language, the development of any tool for
SystemC is a difficult task. Hardware synthesis tools for *SystemC* only consider a
small subset of the C++ syntax [3,1]. In [8], Savoiu et al. propose to use Petri-net
reductions for *SystemC*, and report a speedup of 1.5 for an AES core. In [6], Pérez
et al. present a static-scheduling technique restricted to method processes. Our
sequentialization technique extends the benefits of static scheduling to general
threads by eliminating the overhead caused by context switches.

We provide a tool that extracts formal models from *SystemC* code. The tool
supports a broad subset of the language, as it is built on top of our C++-front-
end. The main applications are formal analysis, e.g., by model checking, and
synthesis. Exemplarily, we show that formal models have value even in dynamic
verification: we show a significant improvement in simulation performance by
using a statically scheduled model.

We are continuing to improve the *SystemC* support of our tool. It currently
handles the most commonly used features of the *SystemC* API. We are also
investigating additional formal techniques to further enhance static scheduling.

References

1. Castillo, J., Huerta, P., Martinez, J.I.: An open-source tool for SystemC to Verilog
   automatic translation. In: SPL, vol. 37, pp. 53–58 (2007)
2. Clarke, E., Kroening, D., Sharygina, N., Yorav, K.: SATABS: SAT-based predicate
   abstraction for ANSI-C. In: Halbwachs, N., Zuck, L.D. (eds.) TACAS 2005. LNCS,
   vol. 3440, pp. 570–574. Springer, Heidelberg (2005)
3. Kostaras, N., Vergos, H.T.: SyCE: An integrated environment for system design in
   SystemC. In: RSP, pp. 258–260. IEEE, Los Alamitos (2005)
4. Kroening, D., Clarke, E., Yorav, K.: Behavioral consistency of C and Verilog programs using bounded model checking. In: DAC, pp. 368–371. ACM, New York (2003)
5. Kroening, D., Sharygina, N.: Formal verification of SystemC by automatic hard-
   ware/software partitioning. In: MEMOCODE, pp. 101–110 (2005)
6. Pérez, D.G., Mouchard, G., Temam, O.: A new optimized implemention of the SystemC engine using acyclic scheduling. In: DATE, pp. 552–557. IEEE, Los Alamitos
   (2004)
7. Qadeer, S., Wu, D.: KISS: keep it simple and sequential. In: PLDI, pp. 14–24. ACM,
   New York (2004)
8. Savoiu, N., Sandeep, S., Rajesh, G.: Improving SystemC simulation through Petri
   net reductions. In: MEMOCODE, pp. 131–140 (2005)

Trusted Source Translation of a Total Function Language

Guodong Li and Konrad Slind

School of Computing, University of Utah
{ligd, slind}@cs.utah.edu

Abstract. We present a trusted source translator that transforms to-tal functions defined in the specification language of the HOL theorem prover to simple intermediate code. This translator eliminates polymorphism by code specification, removes higher-order functions through closure conversion, interprets pattern matching as conditional expressions, etc. The target intermediate language can be further translated by proof to a simple imperative language. Each transformation is proven to be correct automatically. The formalization, implementation and mechanical verification of all transformations are done in HOL-4.

1 Introduction

Giving realistic programming languages such as C and Java correct semantics is difficult. It is more difficult to make such semantics tractable so that we can reason about non-trivial programs in a formal setting. Some widely used functional languages have been given a formal semantics, *e.g.* Scheme has a denotational semantics [19] and ML has a formal operational semantics [14]. However, these semantics do not as yet provide a practical basis for formal reasoning about programs in the languages, although they are extremely valuable as reference documents and for proving meta-theorems (like type preservation).

In order to allow formal reasoning to the maximum extent, we can program applications directly in logic, and then compile the logic to realistic platforms for execution. Specifically, we can specify both the algorithms and the mathematics needed for their verification in higher order logic, and then compile the verified algorithms to low level platforms which are also modeled in the same logic.

The specification language we use is the Total Functional Language (TFL) [20], which is a pure, total functional programming layer on top of higher order logic and implemented in both the HOL-4 [17] and Isabelle [16] systems. TFL enables abstract algorithms to be specified in a mixture of mathematics and programming idioms and then reasoned about using a theorem prover. Roughly speaking, this language comprises ML-style pure terminating functional programs, *i.e.*, those (computable) functions that can be expressed by well-founded recursion in higher order logic. Features like type inference, polymorphism, higher order functions and pattern matching make it a comfortable setting in which to program. This language can express a very wide range of algorithms. The trade-off is that the compilation of logic specifications written in this language is fairly complicated.

C.R. Ramakrishnan and J. Rehof (Eds.): TACAS 2008, LNCS 4963, pp. 471–485, 2008.
© Springer-Verlag Berlin Heidelberg 2008

We have developed a software compiler [11,12], which produces assembly code, and a hardware compiler [21], which synthesizes Verilog netlists, for a small subset of TFL. This subset, named HOL-, is a simple monomorphically-typed functional language handling first order equations where variables range over tuples of booleans and 32-bit words. The software compiler performs normalization, inline expansion, nested function hoisting, register allocation and code generation to convert HOL- programs into assembly. Many transformations are implemented as rewrite rules [12]. The correctness of each transformation is proven on the fly: after a program is translated, a theorem is given as by-product that states the equivalence of the transformed code and this program.

This paper presents an extension of these compilers by strengthening the front end translation to support polymorphism, higher order functions, algebraic datatypes, pattern matching and other advanced features in TFL. As far as we know, it is the first verified translator that compiles logic specifications coded in such advanced functional languages as TFL. We also present an approach to translate HOL- into a simple imperative language. The mechanical correctness proof is performed deductively by synthesizing functions from imperative code and showing that these functions are equivalent to the original HOL- functions. This enables safe source translations from ML-like functional languages to imperative languages.

A TFL program is converted into an equivalent HOL- program via a sequence of transformations, the correctness of each of which is proved automatically in the logic system. Although standard compilation techniques developed for functional programming may be applied here, new challenges are posed due to the fact that (i) the source language is not visible in the logic — it is the logic itself that is taken as the source language; (ii) TFL programs have a set-theoretic semantics rather than an operational or denotational semantics; (iii) all transformations must be formalized and verified in the logic that is compiled. Since TFL and HOL- programs are not defined as datatypes and do not have an evaluation semantics, widely-used techniques that base on structural induction on syntax datatypes and rule-induction over evaluation relations cannot be applied here.

The main contribution of our work is that we construct and verify compilations for logic specifications written in the term language of a widely-used theorem prover. Users can model an application directly in HOL and prove properties about it, then our compilers translate it to low level code with a certificate (proof) showing that this code correctly implements the application. As a consequence, the execution of this code will always guarantee the properties proven on the original application.

2   TFL and HOL-

Both TFL and HOL- are subsets of the higher order logic built in HOL, thus their syntax and the semantics have already been defined. Programs written in them are simply mathematical functions defined in the HOL logic. It is this feature that enables us to use standard mathematics to prove properties of these programs directly in the logic system. This supports much flexibility and allows the meaning of a program to be transparent. In particular, two programs are equivalent when the mathematical functions represented by them are equal.

One immediate advantage of taking TFL as the source language is that many front end tasks are already provided by the HOL-4 system: lexical analysis, parsing, type inference, overloading resolution, function definition, and termination proof (needed to admit recursive functions, since HOL is a logic of total functions). The result of all this activity is a valid HOL function definition, embodied in a possibly recursive equation. From this starting point, a sequence of proof-based transformations pass through intermediate forms, ending in HOL-.

TFL is a polymorphic, higher order, pure and terminating functional language supporting algebraic datatypes and pattern matching. Its syntax is shown in Figure 1, where $[term]_{separator}$ means a sequence of *term*'s separated by the *separator*. HOL- is a simple typed functional language handling first order equations over nested tuples of basic types. Clearly HOL- is a subset of TFL.

τ	$::= T \mid t \mid \tau\, D$		primitive type, type variable and algebraic type
	$\mid \tau \# \tau \mid \tau \to \tau$		tuple type and arrow(function) type
at_c	$::= id \mid id\ \mathbf{of}\ [\tau]_\Rightarrow$		algebraic datatype clause
at	$::= \mathbf{datatype}\ id = [at_c]_\mid$		algebraic datatype
	$\mid [at]_;$		mutually recursive datatype
pt	$::= i \mid v \mid c\ \overrightarrow{pt}$		pattern
e	$::= i : T \mid v : \tau$		constant and variable
	$\mid \overrightarrow{e}$		tuple, i.e.$[e]_,$
	$\mid p\ e$		primitive application
	$\mid c\ e$		constructor application
	$\mid f_{id}$		function identifier
	$\mid e\ e$		composite application
	$\mid \mathbf{if}\ e\ \mathbf{then}\ e\ \mathbf{else}\ e$		conditional
	$\mid \mathbf{case}\ e\ \mathbf{of}\ [(c\ e) \rightsquigarrow e]_\mid$		case splitting
	$\mid \mathbf{let}\ v = e\ \mathbf{in}\ e$		let binding
	$\mid [\lambda\,v].\ e$		anonymous function
f_{decl}	$::= f_{id}\,([pt],) = e$		pattern matching clause
	$\mid [f_{decl}]_\wedge$		function declaration
	$\mid v = e$		top level variable declaration

Fig. 1. The syntax of the total function language TFL

The translator performs transformations that are familiar from existing functional language compilers except that it does so by proof for the term language of HOL. TFL's high-level features such as polymorphism, higher-order functions, pattern matching and composite expressions need to be expressed in terms of HOL-'s much lower-level structures:

- The translator removes polymorphism from TFL programs by making duplications of polymorphic datatype declarations and functions for each distinct combination of instantiating types.
- The translator names intermediate computation results and makes the evaluation order explicit by performing a continuation-passing-style (CPS)

transformation. TFL expressions and functions are simplified to forms suitable for subsequent transformations.
- The translator applies defunctionalization to remove higher-order functions by creating algebraic datatypes to represent function closures and type based dispatch functions to direct the control to top level function definitions.
- The translator converts pattern matching first into nested case expressions, then into explicit conditional expressions.

All intermediate forms of a program are still mathematical functions defined in HOL. The correctness proof of a transformation of a source program p proceeds, in a *translation validation* [18] style, by showing the generated program q computes the same mathematical function as p. Note that the built-in type checker in HOL will type check both p and q to ensure their type safety. Two techniques are used to generate correctness proofs:

1. The transformation is implemented as a rewrite rule based on a theorem that is proven once and for all. In many cases we just need to instantiate this theorem by the input program. Examples include the normalization.
2. A per-run correctness check is performed to show that the transformation ensures semantics preserving on the given program. In general, we convert the source program p into p' using some algorithm, and then compare p and p' w.r.t their semantics. Examples include the monomorphisation and defunctionalization.

3   Trusted Transformation

In this section we describe algorithms of a series of syntax directed transformations; we also show how to prove the correctness of them.

3.1   Monomorphisation

This transformation eliminates polymorphism and produces a simply-typed intermediate form that enables good data representations. The basic idea is to duplicate a datatype declaration at each type used and a function declaration at each type used, resulting in multiple monomorphic clones of this datatype and function. This step paves the way for subsequent conversions such as the type based defunctionalization. Although this seems to lead to code explosion in theory, it is manageable in practice (MLton, a fancy ML compiler, uses similar techniques and reports maximum increase of 30% in code size).

The first step is to build an instantiation map that enumerates for each datatype and function declaration the full set of instantiations for each polymorphic type. A TFL program will be type checked by the HOL system and be annotated with polymorphic type identifiers such as $'a, 'b, \ldots$ when it is defined. In particular, type inference has been done for (mutually) recursive functions. The remaining task is to instantiate the generic types of a function with the actual types of arguments at its call sites.

The notation used in this section is as follows. A substitution rule $R = (t \hookrightarrow \{T\})$ maps an abstract type t to a set of its type instantiations; an instantiation set $S = \{R\}$ is a set of substitution rules; and an instantiation map $M = \{z \hookrightarrow S\}$ maps a datatype or a function z to its instantiation set S. We write $M.y$ for the value at field y in the map M; if $y \notin Dom\ M$ then $M.y$ returns an empty set. The union of two substitution sets $S_1 \cup_s S_2$ is $\{t \hookrightarrow S_1.t \cup S_2.t \mid t \in Dom\ S_1 \cup Dom\ S_2\}$. We write $\bigcup_s \{S\}$ for the combined union of a set of substitution rules. The union of two instantiation maps $M_1 \bigcup_m M_2$ is defined similarly. The composition of two instantiation sets S_1 and S_2, denoted as $S_1\ o_r\ S_2$, is $\{t \hookrightarrow \bigcup \{S_2.t \mid t \in Dom\ S_1\} \mid z \in Dom\ S_1\}$. And, the composition of an instantiation map M and a set S is defined as $M\ o_m\ S = \{z \hookrightarrow M.z\ o_r\ S \mid z \in Dom\ M\}$.

The instantiation information of each occurrence of a polymorphic function and datatype is coerced into an instantiation map during a syntax directed bottom-up traversal. The main conversion rules Γ and Δ shown in Fig. 2 build the instantiation map by investigating types and expressions respectively. The rule for a single variable/function declaration is trivial and omitted here: we just need to walk over the right hand side of its definition. If a top level function f is called in the body of another function top level g, then g must be visited first to generate an instantiation map M_g, and then f is visited to generate M_f; finally these two maps are combined to a new one, *i.e.* $((M_f \circ M_g.f) \cup_m M_g)$. The clauses in mutually recursive functions can be visited in an arbitrary order.

$$
\begin{aligned}
\Gamma[[\tau]] &= \{\}, \quad \text{for } \tau \in \{T, t\} \\
\Gamma[[\tau\ D]] &= \{D \hookrightarrow \mathsf{match\_tp}\ (\mathsf{at\_tp}\ D)\ \tau\} \\
\Gamma[[\tau_1\ op_t\ \tau_2]] &= \Gamma[[\tau_1]] \cup_m \Gamma[[\tau_2]], \quad \text{for } op_t \in \{\#, \rightarrow\} \\
\Delta[[i]] &= \{\} \\
\Delta[[v : \tau]] &= \Gamma[[\tau]] \\
\Delta[[[e],]] &= \bigcup_m \{\Gamma[[e]]\} \\
\Delta[[p\ e]] &= \Delta[[e]] \\
\Delta[[(c : \tau)\ e]] &= \{\mathsf{con2tp}\ c \hookrightarrow \mathsf{match\_tp}\ (\mathsf{con2tp}\ c)\ \tau\} \\
&\quad \cup_m \Gamma[[\tau]] \cup_m \Delta[[e]] \\
\Delta[[(f : \tau)\ e]] &= \{f_{id} \hookrightarrow \mathsf{match\_tp}\ f_{id}\ \tau\} \cup_m \Gamma[[\tau]] \cup_m \Delta[[e]] \\
\Delta[[\text{if } e_1 \text{ then } e_2 \text{ else } e_3]] &= \Delta[[e_1]] \cup_m \Delta[[e_2]] \cup_m \Delta[[e_3]] \\
\Delta[[\text{case } e_1 \text{ of } [((c : \tau)\ e_2) \rightsquigarrow e_3]_!]] &= \Delta[[e_1]] \cup_m \bigcup_m \{\{\mathsf{con2tp}\ c \hookrightarrow \mathsf{match\_tp}\ (\mathsf{con2tp}\ c)\ \tau \\
&\quad \cup_m \Delta[[e_2]] \cup_m \Delta[[e_3]]\}\} \\
\Delta[[\text{let } v = e_1 \text{ in } e_2]] &= (\Delta[[e_1]]\ o_m\ \Delta[[e_2]].v) \cup_m \Delta[[e_2]] \\
\Delta[[[\lambda v.]^* e]] &= \Delta[[e]]
\end{aligned}
$$

Fig. 2. Build instantiation maps for polymorphic components

This algorithm makes use of a couple of auxiliary functions provided by the HOL system. Function $\mathsf{con2tp}\ c$ maps a constructor c to the datatype to which it belongs; $\mathsf{at\_tp}\ D$ returns σ if there is a datatype definition $\mathsf{datatype}\ \sigma = D$ of $\ldots$; when x is either a function name or a constructor, $\mathsf{match\_tp}\ x\ \tau$ matches the original type of x (*i.e.* the type when x is defined) with τ and returns a substitution set.

After the final instantiation map is obtained, we duplicate a polymorphic datatype/function for all combinations of its type instantiations, and replace each call of the polymorphic function with the call to its monomorphic clone with respect to the type. The automatic correctness proof for the transformation is trivial: each duplication of a polymorphic function computes the same function on the arguments of the instantiating types.

Now we give a simple example to illustrate the transformation.

$$\text{datatype } \sigma = C \text{ of } 'a \,\#\, 'b \qquad f\,(x :' a) = x$$
$$g\,(x :' c, y :' d) = \text{let } (h :' d \to ('c \,\#\, 'd)\, \sigma) = \lambda z :' d.$$
$$(C : ('c \,\#\, 'd) \to ('c \,\#\, 'd)\, \sigma)\,((f :' c \to' c)\, x, (f :' d \to' d)\, z) \text{ in } h\,y$$
$$j = (g\,(1 : num, \bot : bool),\, g\,(\bot : bool, \top : bool))$$

The algorithm builds the following instantiation maps:

Investigate j : $M_j = \{g \hookrightarrow \{'c \hookrightarrow \{bool, num\}, 'd \hookrightarrow \{bool\}\}\}$
Investigate g : $M_g = \{f \hookrightarrow \{'a \hookrightarrow \{'c, 'd\}\}, \sigma \hookrightarrow \{'a \hookrightarrow \{'c\}, 'b \hookrightarrow \{'d\}\}\}$
Compose M_g and M_j: $M_{g \circ j} = M_g \circ M_j.g =$
$\{\ f \hookrightarrow \{'a \hookrightarrow \{bool, num\}\},\ \sigma \hookrightarrow \{'a \hookrightarrow \{bool, num\}, 'b \hookrightarrow \{bool\}\}\ \}$
Union M_g and $M_{g \circ j}$: $M_{\{g,j\}} = M_g \cup_m M_j =$
$\{\ f \hookrightarrow \{'a \hookrightarrow \{bool, num\}\},\ g \hookrightarrow \{'c \hookrightarrow \{bool, num\}, 'd \hookrightarrow \{bool\}\},$
$\quad \sigma \hookrightarrow \{'a \hookrightarrow \{bool, num\}, 'b \hookrightarrow \{bool\}\}\ \}$
Investigate f : no changes, $M_{\{f,g,j\}} = M_{\{g,j\}}$

Then for datatype σ, function f and function g, a monomorphic clone is created for each combination of instantiating types. Calls to the original functions are replaced with the appropriate copies of the right type. For example, function j is converted to $j = (g_{num\#bool}\,(1, \bot),\, g_{bool\#bool}\,(\bot, \top))$, where $g_{num\#bool}$ and $g_{bool\#bool}$ are the two clones of g. The correctness of j's conversion is proved based on the theorems showing that g's copies compute the same function as g with respect to the instantiating types: $\Vdash_{thm} g_{num\#bool} = g \land g_{bool\#bool} = g$.

3.2   Normalization

This transformation bridges the gap between the form of expressions and control flow structures in TFL and HOL-. A TFL program is converted to a simpler form such that: (1) the arguments to function and constructor applications are atoms like variables or constants; (2) discriminators in case expressions are also simple expressions; (3) compound expressions nested in an expression are lifted to make new 'let' bindings; (4) curried functions are uncurried to a sequence of simple functions that take a single tupled argument. Primitive expressions such as arithmetic and logical expressions on atoms need not to be converted.

A continuation-passing-style (CPS) transformation is performed to normalize TFL programs. The essence is to sequentialize the computation of TFL expressions by introducing variables for intermediate results, and the control flow is pinned down into a sequence of elementary steps. It extends the one in our software compiler [12] by addressing higher level structures specific to TFL. In the following rules, $C\,e\,k$ denotes the application of the continuation k to an expression e, and its value is equal to $k\,e$. After the conversion, we rewrite with the theorem $C\ e\ k = \mathsf{let}\ x = e\ \mathsf{in}\ k\ x$ to obtain 'let'-based normal forms.

$C\ [[e]]\ k = k\ e,\quad$ when e is a primitive expression
$C\ [[\lambda \overrightarrow{v}.e]] = \lambda \overrightarrow{v}.\ \lambda k.\ C\ [[e]]\ k$
$C\ [[(e_1, e_2)]]\ k = C\ [[e_1]]\ (\lambda x.\ C\ [[e_2]]\ (\lambda y.\ k\ (x, y)))$
$C\ [[op\ e]]\ k = C\ [[e]]\ (\lambda x.\ k\ (op\ x))\quad$ when $op \in \{p, c, f_{id}\}$
$C\ [[(e_1\ e_2)]]\ k = C\ [[e_1]]\ (\lambda x.\ C\ [[e_2]]\ (\lambda y.\ k\ (x\ y)))$
$C\ [[\mathsf{let}\ v = e_1\ \mathsf{in}\ e_2]]\ k = C\ [[e_1]]\ (\lambda x.\ C\ [[e_2]]\ (\lambda y.\ k\ y))$
$C\ [[\mathsf{if}\ e_1\ \mathsf{then}\ e_2\ \mathsf{else}\ e_3]]\ k =$
$\quad C\ [[e_1]]\ (\lambda x.\ k\ (\mathsf{if}\ x\ \mathsf{then}\ C\ [[e_2]]\ (\lambda x.x)\ \mathsf{else}\ C\ [[e_3]]\ (\lambda x.x)))$
$C\ [[\mathsf{case}\ e_1\ \mathsf{of}\ c\ e_{2_1} \rightsquigarrow e_{3_1}\ |\ c\ e_{2_2} \rightsquigarrow e_{3_2}\ |\ \ldots]]\ k =$
$\quad C\ [[e_1]]\ (\lambda x.\ (C\ [[e_{2_1}]]\ (\lambda y_1.\ C\ [[e_{2_2}]]\ (\lambda y_2.\ \ldots,$
$\quad\quad k\ (\mathsf{case}\ x\ \mathsf{of}\ c\ y_1 \rightsquigarrow C\ [[e_{3_1}]]\ (\lambda x.x)\ |\ c\ y_2 \rightsquigarrow C\ [[e_{3_2}]]\ (\lambda x.x)\ |\ \ldots)))))$

The following example illustrates this transformation, where c_1 and c_2 are the two constructors of a datatype.

Original: $f\ (x, y, z) = \mathsf{case}\ x - y - z\ \mathsf{of}\ c_1\ a \Rightarrow f(x - 1, a, y)\ |\ c_2\ b \Rightarrow b + y$
Converted: $f\ (x, y, z) =$
$\quad \mathsf{let}\ v_1 = x - y - z\ \mathsf{in}$
$\quad\quad \mathsf{case}\ v_1\ \mathsf{of}\ c_1\ a \Rightarrow \mathsf{let}\ v_2 = x - 1\ \mathsf{in}\ f(v_2, a, y)\ |\ c_2\ b \Rightarrow b + y$

3.3 Defunctionalization

In this section we convert higher-order functions into equivalent first-order functions and hoist nested functions to the top level through a type based closure conversion. After the conversion, no nested functions exist; and function call is made by dispatching on the closure tag followed by a top-level call.

Function closures are represented as algebraic data types in a way that, for each function definition, a constructor taking the free variables of this function is created. For each arrow type we create a dispatch function, which converts the definition of a function of this arrow type into a closure constructor application. A nested function is hoisted to the top level with its free variables to be passed as extra arguments. After that, the calling to the original function is replaced by a calling to the relevant dispatch function passing a closure containing the values of this function's free variables. The dispatch function examines the closure tag and passes control to the appropriate hoisted function. Thus, higher order operations on functions are replaced by equivalent operations on first order closure values.

As an optimization, we first run a pass to identify all 'targeted' functions which appear in the arguments or outputs of other functions and record them in a side effect variable **Targeted**. Non-targeted functions need not to be closure converted, and calls to them are made as usual. During this pass we also find out the functions to be defined at the top level and record them in **Hoisted**. Finally **Hoisted** contains all top level functions and nested function to be hoisted.

The conversion works on simple typed functions obtained by monomorphisation. We create a closure datatype and a dispatch function for each of the arrow types that targeted functions may have. A function definition is replaced by a binding to an application of the corresponding closure constructor to this function's free variables. Suppose the set of targeted functions of type τ is

$\{f_i\ x_i = e_i \mid i = 1, 2, \ldots\}$, then the following algebraic datatype and dispatch function are created, where tp_of and fv return the type and free variables of a term respectively (and the type builder Γ will be described below):

$$
\begin{aligned}
clos_\tau &= cons^\tau_{f_1}\ \text{of}\ \Gamma[[\text{tp\_of}\ (\text{fv}\ f_1)]] \mid cons^\tau_{f_2}\ \text{of}\ \Gamma[[\text{tp\_of}\ (\text{fv}\ f_2)]] \mid \ldots \\
(dispatch_\tau(cons^\tau_{f_1}, x_1, y_1) &= (f_1 : \Gamma[[\tau]])\ (x_1, y_1))\ \wedge \\
(dispatch_\tau(cons^\tau_{f_2}, x_2, y_2) &= (f_2 : \Gamma[[\tau]])\ (x_2, y_2))\ \wedge \\
&\qquad \cdots
\end{aligned}
$$

As shown in Fig. 3, the main translation algorithm inspects the references and applications of targeted functions and replaces them with the corresponding closures and dispatch functions. Function Γ returns the new types of variables. When walking over expressions, Δ replaces calls to unknown functions (*i.e.* those not presented in <u>Hoisted</u>) with calls to the appropriate dispatch function, and calls to known functions with calls to hoisted functions. In this case the values of free variables are passed as extra arguments. Function references are also replaced with appropriate closures. Finally <u>Redefn</u> contains all converted functions, which will be renamed and redefined in HOL at the top level.

$$
\begin{aligned}
\Gamma[[v : T]] &= T \\
\Gamma[[v : \tau_1 \rightarrow \tau_2]] &= \text{if}\ v \in \underline{\textbf{Targeted}}\ \text{then}\ clos_{\tau_1 \rightarrow \tau_2}\ \text{else}\ \tau_1 \rightarrow \tau_2 \\
\Gamma[[v : \tau\ D]] &= \Gamma[[\tau]]\ D \\
\Gamma[[[v],]] &= [\Gamma[[v]]], \\
\Delta[[v : \tau]] &= \text{if}\ v \in \underline{\textbf{Targeted}}\ \text{then}\ cons^\tau_v\ \text{else}\ v : clos_\tau \\
\Delta[[[e],]] &= [\Delta[[e]]], \\
\Delta[[p\ e]] &= p\ (\Delta[[e]]) \\
\Delta[[c\ e]] &= c\ (\Delta[[e]]) \\
\Delta[[(f : \tau)\ e]] &= \text{if}\ f \in \underline{\textbf{Hoisted}}\ \text{then}\ (\text{new\_name\_of}\ f)\ (\Delta[[e]], \text{fv}\ f) \\
&\qquad \text{else}\ dispatch_\tau\ (f : clos_\tau, \Delta[[e]]) \\
\Delta[[\text{if}\ e_1\ \text{then}\ e_2\ \text{else}\ e_3]] &= \text{if}\ \Delta[[e_1]]\ \text{then}\ \Delta[[e_2]]\ \text{else}\ \Delta[[e_3]] \\
\Delta[[\text{case}\ e_1\ \text{of}\ [c\ e_2 \rightsquigarrow e_3]_i]] &= \text{case}\ \Delta[[e_1]]\ \text{of}\ [(\Delta[[c\ e_2]]) \rightsquigarrow \Delta[[e_3]]]_i \\
\Delta[[\text{let}\ f = \lambda \overrightarrow{v}.\, e_1\ \text{in}\ e_2]] &= (\Phi[[f\,\overrightarrow{v} = e_1]]\ ;\ \Delta[[e_2]]) \\
\Delta[[\text{let}\ v = e_1\ \text{in}\ e_2]] &= \text{let}\ v = \Delta[[e_1]]\ \text{in}\ \Delta[[e_2]] \quad \text{when}\ e_1\ \text{is not a}\ \lambda\ \text{expression} \\
\Phi[[f_{id}\ (\overrightarrow{v} : \tau) = e]] &= \\
&\quad \text{let}\ e' = \Delta[[e]]\ \text{in} \\
&\qquad \underline{\textbf{Redefn}} := \underline{\textbf{Redefn}} + (f_{id} \hookrightarrow \underline{\textbf{Redefn}}.f_{id} \cup \{(f_{id} : \tau \rightarrow \Gamma[[\text{tp\_of}\ e']])\ \overrightarrow{v} = e'\} \\
\Phi[[[f_{decl}]_\wedge]] &= [\Phi[[f_{decl}]]];
\end{aligned}
$$

Fig. 3. Remove higher order functions through closure conversion

Now we show the technique to prove the equivalence of a source function f to its converted form f'. We say that a variable $v' : \tau'$ corresponds $v : \tau$ iff: (1) $v = v'$ if both τ and τ' are closure type or neither of them is. (2) $\forall x \forall x'.\, dispatch_{\tau'}(v', x') = v\ x$ if v' is a closure type and v is an arrow type, and x' corresponds to x; or vice versa. Then f' is equivalent to f iff they correspond to each other. The proof process is simple, as it suffices to simply rewrite with the old and new definitions of the functions.

As an example, the following higher order program

$$f\,(x : num) = x * 2 < x + 10$$
$$g\,(s : num \to bool, x : num) =$$
$$\quad \text{let } h_1 = \lambda y.\,y + x \text{ in if } s\,x \text{ then } h_1 \text{ else let } h_2 = \lambda y.\,h_1\,y * x \text{ in } h_2$$
$$k\,(x : num) = \text{if } x = 0 \text{ then } 1 \text{ else } g\,(f, x)\,(k\,(x - 1))$$

is closure converted to

datatype $clos_{\tau_1} = cons_f^{\tau_1}$
datatype $clos_{\tau_2} = cons_{h_1}^{\tau_2}$ of $num \mid cons_{h_2}^{\tau_2}$ of num
$dispatch_{\tau_1}\,(cons_f^{\tau_1} : clos_{\tau_1}, x : num) = f'\,x\ \wedge\ f'\,x = x * 2 < x + 10$
$dispatch_{\tau_2}\,(cons_{h_1}^{\tau_2}\,y : clos_{\tau_2},\,x : num) = h'_1\,(y, x))\ \wedge$
$dispatch_{\tau_2}\,(cons_{h_2}^{\tau_2}\,y : clos_{\tau_2},\,x : num) = h'_2\,(y, x))\ \wedge$
$h'_1\,(y, x) = y + x\ \wedge\ h'_2\,(y, x) = h'_1(y, x) * x$
$g'\,(s : clos_{\tau_1}, x : num) = \text{if } dispatch_{\tau_1}(s, x) \text{ then } cons_{h_1}^{\tau_2}\,x \text{ else } cons_{h_2}^{\tau_2}\,x$
$k'\,(x : num) = \text{if } x = 0 \text{ then } 1 \text{ else } g\,(cons_f^{\tau_1}, x), (k'\,(x - 1))$
where τ_1 and τ_2 stand for arrow types $num \to bool$ and $num \to num$ respectively

And the following theorems (which are proved automatically) justify the correctness of this conversion:

$$\Vdash_{thm}\ f = f' \qquad \Vdash_{thm}\ k' = k$$
$$\Vdash_{thm}\ (\forall x.\,dispatch_{\tau_1}\,(s', x) = s\,x) \Rightarrow \forall x \forall y.\,dispatch_{\tau_2}\,(g'\,(s', x), y) = (g\,(s, x))\,y$$

3.4   Pattern Matching

This conversion to nested case expressions is based on Augustsson's original work [1], which was adapted by Slind [20] for function description in HOL. A pre-processing pass is first performed to deal with incomplete and overlapping patterns: incomplete patterns are made complete by adding rows for all missing constructors; and overlapping patterns are handled by replacing a value with possible constructors. Note that this approach may make the pattern exponentially larger because no heuristics are used to choose the "best" order in which subterms of any term are to be examined.

The translation rule Δ shown below converts patterns $[pat_i \rightsquigarrow rhs_i]_|$ into a nested case expression. It takes two arguments: a stack of variables that are yet to be matched, and a matrix whose rows correspond to the clauses in the pattern. All rows are of equal length, and the elements in a column should have the same type.

Conversion Δ proceeds from left to right, column by column. At each step the first column is examined. If each element in this column is a variable, then the head variable z in the stack is substituted for the corresponding v_i for the right hand side of each clause. If each element in the column is the application of a constructor for type τ, and τ contains constructor $C_1, \ldots, C_n$, then the rows are partitioned into n groups of size $k_1, \ldots, k_n$ according to the constructors. After partitioning, a row $(C(\bar{p}) :: pats; rhs)$ has its lead constructor discarded, resulting in a row expression $(\bar{p}\,@\,pats; rhs)$. Here :: is the list constructor, and @ appends the second list to the first one. If constructor C_i has type $\tau_1 \to$

$\cdots \rightarrow \tau_j \rightarrow \tau$, then a set ν_i of new variables $v_1, \ldots, v_j$ are pushed onto the stack. Finally the results for all groups are combined into a case expression on the head of the stack.

$$\Delta \left(\frac{z :: stack}{\begin{array}{c} v_1 :: pats_1 \rightsquigarrow rhs_1, \\ \cdots \\ v_n :: pats_n \rightsquigarrow rhs_n \end{array}} \right) = \Delta \left(\frac{stack}{\begin{array}{c} pats_1 \rightsquigarrow rhs_1[z \leftarrow v_1], \\ \cdots \\ pats_n \rightsquigarrow rhs_n[z \leftarrow v_2] \end{array}} \right), \text{ and}$$

$$\Delta \left(\frac{z :: stack}{\begin{array}{c} C_1 \,\overline{p_{11}} :: pats_{11} \rightsquigarrow rhs_{11}, \\ \cdots \\ C_n \,\overline{p_{1k_1}} :: pats_{1k_1} \rightsquigarrow rhs_{1k_1} \\ C_n \,\overline{p_{n1}} :: pats_{n1} \rightsquigarrow rhs_{11}, \\ \cdots \\ C_n \,\overline{p_{1k_n}} :: pats_{nk_n} \rightsquigarrow rhs_{nk_n} \end{array}} \right) = \text{tp\_case } (\lambda \nu_1.M_1) \, \ldots \, (\lambda \nu_n.M_n) \, z$$

$$\text{where } M_i = \Delta \left(\frac{\nu_1 :: stack}{\begin{array}{c} \overline{p_{i1}} \,@\, pats_{k1} \rightsquigarrow rhs_{k1}, \\ \cdots \\ \overline{p_{ik_i}} \,@\, pats_{ik_i} \rightsquigarrow rhs_{ik_i} \end{array}} \right) \text{ for } i = 0, \ldots, n$$

When a datatype tp with n constructors is declared, a case expression theorem $\forall x.\, tp\_case \, f_1 \, \ldots \, f_n \, (C_i \, x) \equiv f_i \, x$ for $i = 1, \ldots, n$ is stored in HOL. For example, the case expression for natural number is $(\text{num\_case } b \, f \, 0 = b) \, \wedge \, (\text{num\_case } b \, f \, (\text{Suc } n) = f \, n)$.

For example, this step translates the Greatest Common Divisor function gcd to a form taking only one argument:

$$gcd \, (0, y) = y \qquad gcd \, (\text{Suc } x, 0) = \text{Suc } x$$
$$gcd \, (\text{Suc } x, \text{Suc } y) = \text{if } y \leq x \text{ then } gcd \, (x - y, \text{Suc } y) \text{ else } gcd \, (\text{Suc } x, y - x)$$
$$\Rightarrow$$
$$gcd \, z = \text{pair\_case } (\lambda v \, v_1.\, \text{num\_case } v_1 (\lambda v_2.\, \text{num\_case } (\text{Suc } v_2)$$
$$(\lambda v_3.\, \text{if } v_3 \leq v_2 \text{ then } gcd \, (v_2 - v_3, \text{Suc } v_3) \text{ else } gcd \, (\text{Suc } v_2, v_3 - v_2)) \, v_1) \, v) \, z$$

In the next step case expressions are interpreted as conditional expressions based on the following theorem

$$\text{tp\_case } (\lambda x.f_1 \, x) \, (\lambda x.f_2 \, x) \, \ldots \, z =$$
$$\text{if is\_}C_1 \, z \text{ then } f_1 \, (\text{destruct}_{C_1} \, z) \text{ else if is\_}C_2 \, z \text{ then } f_2 \, (\text{destruct}_{C_2} \, z) \text{ else} \ldots$$

where operator $\text{is\_}C_i$ tells whether a variable matches the ith constructor C_i, i.e. $\text{is\_}C_i \, (C_j \, x) = \top$ iff $i = j$; and operator destruct_{C_i} is the destructor function for constructor C_i. For example, $\text{destruct}_{\text{Suc}} \, (\text{Suc } x) = x$. These operators will be implemented as datatype access operations in later compilation phases. In addition, an optimization is performed to tuple variables: if an argument x has type $\tau_1 \# \ldots \# \tau_n$, then it is replaced by a tuple of new variables $(x_1, \ldots, x_n)$. Superfluous branches and 'let' bindings are also removed. In this manner the gcd function is converted to

$$gcd\ (z_1, z_2) = \text{if } z_1 = 0 \text{ then } z_2$$
$$\text{else let } v_2 = \text{destruct}_{Suc}\ z_1 \text{ in}$$
$$\text{if } z_2 = 0 \text{ then Suc } v_2 \text{ else let } v_3 = \text{destruct}_{Suc}\ z_2 \text{ in}$$
$$\text{if } v_3 \leq v_2 \text{ then } gcd\ (v_2 - v_3, \text{Suc } v_3) \text{ else } gcd\ (\text{Suc } v_2, v_3 - v_2)$$

4   Producing-by-Proof Imperative Code

Porting pure and terminating ML programs into TFL is easy due to the high similarity in the syntax and semantics of ML and TFL. One of the main issues — the termination proof of the imported ML program — is handled by proving that the generated TFL function is total. Moreover, the imported programs will be type checked by HOL. As the translation from TFL to HOL- eliminates features pertaining to functional languages such as higher order functions and nested expressions, it is natural to consider translating HOL- to realistic imperative languages such as C and Java.

We have developed a method in our software compiler [11] that translates simple normal forms obtained from HOL- programs to a low level imperative language HSL (Heap and Stack Level). HSL supports various structured control statements including blocks, sequential compositions, conditionals, tail recursions, and function calls. However, since HSL is designed to couple tightly with the targeted machine language and accesses registers and heaps directly, it is not a good candidate as the target imperative language.

We extend HSL to a higher level imperative language IL (for *Imperative Language*). The global variables of IL correspond to top level variables in HOL-; and local variables in IL correspond to the administrative redexes (*i.e.* left hand sides) of 'let' expressions in HOL-. IL also inherits the datatypes from HOL-, thus no datatype representation is needed. What's more important is our augmentation of the reasoning mechanism: we maintain a set of separate logic judgments rather than just one judgment (as we did in [11]) and use them to reason about programs. The syntax of IL's control flow structures is shown below.

$$
\begin{aligned}
s ::=\ & v := s & \text{assignment} \\
\mid\ & \textbf{return } v & \text{return} \\
\mid\ & s; s & \text{sequential statement} \\
\mid\ & \textbf{IF } e \textbf{ THEN } s \textbf{ ELSE } s & \text{conditional jump} \\
\mid\ & \textbf{WHILE } e\ s & \text{loop} \\
\mid\ & v :=_f p_{id}\ s & \text{function call} \\
p ::=\ & p_{id}\ (\overrightarrow{v}) = s & \text{programs}
\end{aligned}
$$

We first define an operational semantics (omitted here due to lack of space) for IL and then derive an axiomatic semantics from it. Each axiomatic semantics rule is specified as a Hoare triple $\{precondition\}\ program\ \{postcondition\}$:

$$\frac{\{P\}\ S_1\ \{Q\} \quad \{R\}\ S_2\ \{T\} \quad Q \Rightarrow R}{\{P\}\ (S_1\ ;\ S_2)\ \{T\}} \qquad \frac{\{P\}\ S\ \{P\}}{\{P\}\ (\textbf{WHILE } C\ S)\ \{P \wedge \neg C\}}$$

$$\frac{\{P \wedge C\}\ S_t\ \{Q\} \quad \{P \wedge \neg C\}\ S_f\ \{Q\}}{\{P\}\ (\textbf{IF } C \textbf{ THEN } S_t \textbf{ ELSE } S_f)\ \{Q\}} \qquad \frac{\{P\}\ S_t\ \{Q\} \quad \{P\}\ S_f\ \{R\}}{\{P\}\ (\textbf{IF } C \textbf{ THEN } S_t \textbf{ ELSE } S_f)\ \{\text{if } C \text{ then } Q \text{ else } R\}}$$

In order to connect the semantics of a IL program s with that of a HOL- function f, we introduce the following rule to characterize s's axiomatic semantics as a set of predicates (where $\sigma\langle x \rangle$ returns the value of variable x in state σ; and eval $S\ \sigma$ returns the new state after S's execution):

$$s \vdash \{(\bar{i}_k, f_k\ \bar{i}_k, \bar{o}_k)\} \doteq \forall k \forall \sigma \forall \bar{v}_k.(\sigma\langle \bar{i}_k \rangle = \bar{v}_k) \Rightarrow ((\text{eval } S\ \sigma)\langle \bar{o}_k \rangle = f_k\ \bar{v}_k)$$

The kth predicate $(\bar{i}_k,\ f_k\ \bar{i}_k,\ \bar{o}_k)$ specifies that: if inputs $\bar{i}_k$ have initial values $\bar{v}_k$, then in the state after the execution of s, the values left in outputs $\bar{o}_k$ are equal to applying the function f_i to the initial values $\bar{v}_k$. Such a rule is obtained by instantiating the P and Q in $\{P\}\ s\ \{Q\}$ to $\lambda\sigma.\forall k.\sigma\langle \bar{i}_k \rangle = \bar{v}_k$ and $\lambda\sigma.\forall k.\sigma\langle \bar{o}_k \rangle = f_i\ \bar{v}_k$ respectively. We also write e_k for $f_k\ \bar{i}_k$ if the context is clear. If the judgment embodied by a predicate synthesizes f on inputs $\bar{i}$ and outputs $\bar{o}$, then we claim that s correctly implements f with respect to $\bar{i}$ and $\bar{o}$.

In a preprocessing step, tail recursive HOL- functions are rewritten to equivalent 'while' forms [12], where while $c\ f \doteq \lambda x.\text{if } \neg c\ x \text{ then } x \text{ else while } (f\ x)$. Currently this preprocessing admits only tail recursive programs; mutually recursive functions are not supported yet.

We derive a couple of rules to mechanically synthesize for an IL program the functions it correctly implements. The rules utilize the following definitions. Notation Δ converts a HOL- variables and program fragments to TFL terms. $\bigcup(\bar{i}_k)$ constructs a tuple from the union of $\bar{i}_k$ for all k. As usual, $[\text{let } o_i = f_k\ \bar{i}_k]_{\text{in}}$ stands for a chain of 'let' bindings: let $o_1 = f_1\ i_1$ in let $o_2 = f_2\ i_2$ in $\dots$. Rule refl, assgn and return build basic predicates in accordance to TFL 's semantics. Rule cond, while and application are used to synthesize functions for conditional statements, loops and function calls respectively. The predicate sets are manipulated by the union rule union and the elimination rule elim. As the inputs and outputs of s are tuples of arbitrary arity, we provide a shuffle rule to change the structures of them. This rule is particularly useful when we need to match the inputs and outputs of a synthesized function with those of the original function. The sequential composition rule seq is the most complicated one. For each variable $o1_k$ in s_2's inputs, this rule looks up a predicate $(\bar{i1}_k, e1_k, \bar{o1}_k)$ in Σ_1, and inserts a let binding of $e1_k$ to $\bar{o1}_k$ into the composed expression.

$$\frac{}{\vdash \{(\bar{i}, \bar{i}, \bar{i})\}}\ \text{refl} \qquad \frac{}{out := f\ in \vdash \{(\Delta\ in, \Delta\ (f\ in), \Delta\ out)\}}\ \text{assgn}$$

$$\frac{}{\text{return } out \vdash \{(\Delta\ out, \Delta\ out, \Delta\ out)\}}\ \text{return}$$

$$\frac{s_1 \vdash \Sigma_1 \quad s_2 \vdash \Sigma_2 \quad \{(\bar{i1}_k, e1_k, \bar{o1}_k)\} \subseteq \Sigma_1 \quad (\bar{o1}, e2, \bar{o2}) \in \Sigma_2}{s_1 ; s_2 \vdash \{(\bigcup(\bar{i1}_k), [\text{let } o1_k = e1_k]_{\text{in}}\ e2, \bar{o2})\}}\ \text{seq}$$

$$\frac{s_1 \vdash \Sigma_1 \quad s_2 \vdash \Sigma_2 \quad (\bar{i}, e1, \bar{o}) \in \Sigma_1 \quad (\bar{i}, e2, \bar{o}) \in \Sigma_2}{\text{IF } cnd \text{ THEN } s_1 \text{ ELSE } s_2 \vdash \{(\bar{i}, \text{if } (\Delta\ cnd) \text{ then } e1 \text{ else } e2, \bar{o})\}}\ \text{cond}$$

$$\frac{s \vdash \Sigma \quad (\bar{i}, e, \bar{i}) \in \Sigma}{\text{WHILE } cnd\ s \vdash \{(\bar{i}, \text{while } (\Delta\ cnd)\ e, \bar{i})\}}\ \text{while}$$

$$\frac{s \vdash \Sigma \cup \{(callee.\bar{i}, e, callee.\bar{o})\} \quad (\Delta\ caller.i) = caller.\bar{i} \quad (\Delta\ caller.o) = caller.\bar{o}}{caller.o :=_f s\ caller.i \vdash \{(caller.\bar{i}, e[callee.\bar{i} \leftarrow caller.\bar{i}], caller.\bar{o})\}}\ \text{application}$$

$$\frac{s \vdash \Sigma_1 \quad s \vdash \Sigma_2}{s \vdash \Sigma_1 \cup \Sigma_2} \text{ union} \quad \frac{s \vdash \Sigma \cup \{(\bar{i}, e, \bar{o})\}}{s \vdash \Sigma} \text{ elim} \quad \frac{s \vdash \Sigma \cup \{(\bar{i}, f\,\bar{i}, \bar{o})\} \quad g\,\bar{i}' = f\,\bar{i}}{s \vdash (\bar{i}', g\,\bar{i}', \bar{o})} \text{ shuffle}$$

Basically, a predicate set records the values of live variables during the execution by relating them with other variables' old values. These rules are applied to build relations between specific inputs and outputs during the execution. The application of them is syntax directed, and proceeds in a bottom-up manner. For example, given the following IL program p produced from HOL- function f,

$$p\,(a,b) = c := 2a + b; \text{ IF } c^2 > 1000 \text{ THEN return } c \text{ ELSE } \{c := c * b; \text{ return } c\}$$
$$f\,(a,b) = \text{let } c = 2a + b \text{ in if } c^2 > 1000 \text{ then } c \text{ else let } c = c * b \text{ in } c$$

we first apply rules refl, assgn and return to get $c := c * b \vdash \{((b,c), c * b, c)\}$ and return $c \vdash \{(c,c,c)\}$. Then by applying the seq rule once we have $(c := c * b; \text{ return } c) \vdash \{((b,c), \text{let } c = c * b \text{ in } c, c)\}$. Similarly return $c \vdash \{((b,c), c, c)\}$ is derived. According to the cond rule we have (IF $c^2 > 1000$ THEN return c ELSE $\{c := c * b; \text{ return } c\}) \vdash \{((b,c), \text{if } c^2 > 1000 \text{ then } c \text{ else let } c = c * b \text{ in } c, c)\}$. For brevity we denote it as $S \vdash \{((b,c), e, c)\}$. Now investigating the remaining statement $c := 2a + b$ will generate $c := 2a + b \vdash \{(b,b,b), ((a,b), 2a + b, c)\}$. Then applying the seq once we have $c := 2a + b; S \vdash \{((a,b), \text{let } b = b \text{ in let } c = 2a + b \text{ in } e, c)\}$. Finally, after the superfluous 'let' binding of b is removed through β-reduction, the synthesized function is equal to f. The derivation is syntax-directed and automatic.

This reasoning mechanism can be improved by adopting Myreen and Gordon's idea that uses separation logic [15] to reason about assembly language. We are considering porting their method into our setting to verify the translation from HOL- to IL.

5   Related Work

There has been much work on translating functional languages; one of the most influential has been the paper of Tolmach and Oliva [22] which developed a translation from SML-like functional language to Ada. Our monomorphisation and closure conversion methods are similar, *i.e.*, removing polymorphism by code specialization and higher-order functions through closure conversion. However, we target logic specification languages and perform correctness proofs on the transformations. Our work can be regarded as an extension of theirs by now verifying the correctness of these two conversions.

Hickey and Nogin [7] worked in MetaPRL to construct a compiler from a full higher order, untyped, functional language to Intel x86 code, based entirely on higher-order rewrite rules. A set of unverified rewriting rules are used to convert a higher level program to a lower level program. They use higher-order abstract syntax to represent programs and do not define the semantics of these programs. Thus no formal verification of the rewriting rules is done.

Hannan and Pfenning [6] constructed a verified compiler in LF for the untyped λ-calculus. The target machine is a variant of the CAM runtime and differs greatly from real machines. In their work, programs are associated with operational semantics; and both compiler transformation and verifications are modeled as deductive systems. Chlipala [4] further considered compiling a simply-typed λ-calculus to assembly language. He proved semantics preservation based on denotational semantics assigned to the intermediate languages. Type preservation for each compiler pass was also verified. The source language in these works is the bare lambda calculus and is thus much simpler than TFL, thus their compilers only begin to deal with the high level issues we discuss in this paper.

Compared with Chlipala [4] who gives intermediate languages dependent types, Benton and Benton [2] interprets types as binary relations. They proved a semantic type soundness for a compiler from a simple imperative language with heap-allocated data into an idealized assembly language.

Leroy [3,10] verified a compiler from a subset of C, *i.e.* Clight, to PowerPC assembly code in the Coq system. The semantics of Clight is completely deterministic and specified as big-step operational semantics. Several intermediate languages are introduced and translations between them are verified. The proof of semantics preservation for the translation proceeds by induction over the Clight evaluation derivation and case analysis on the last evaluation rule used; in contrast, our proofs proceed by verifying the rewriting steps.

A purely operational semantics based development is that of Klein and Nipkow [8] which gives a thorough formalization of a Java-like language. A compiler from this language to a subset of Java Virtual Machine is verified using Isabelle/HOL. The Isabelle/HOL theorem prover is also used to verify the compilation from a type-safe subset of C to DLX assembly code [9], where a big step semantics and a small step semantics for this language are defined. In addition, Meyer and Wolff [13] derive in Isabelle/HOL a verified compilation of a lazy language (called MiniHaskell) to a strict language (called MiniML) based on the denotational semantics of these languages. Of course, compiler verification itself is a venerable topic, with far too many publications to survey (see Dave's bibliography [5]).

6   Conclusions and Future Work

We have presented an approach to construct and mechanically verify a translator from TFL to HOL-. The outputs of this translator can be compiled to assembly code and hardware using the verified compilers for HOL- we developed in previous work [11,12,21]. Thus users can write logic specifications in an expressive language TFL and obtain certified low level implementations automatically.

Currently, we are augmenting the compiler to tackle garbage collection, as well as performing a variety of optimizations on intermediate code. We also consider translating by proof a large subset of Java into TFL.

References

1. Augustsson, L.: Compiling pattern matching. In: Conference on Functional Programming Languages and Computer Architecture (1985)
2. Benton, N., Zarfaty, U.: Formalizing and verifying semantic type soundness of a simple compiler. In: 9th ACM SIGPLAN International Symposium on Principles and Practice of Declarative Programming (PPDP 2007) (2007)

3. Blazy, S., Dargaye, Z., Leroy, X.: Formal verification of a C compiler front-end. In: Misra, J., Nipkow, T., Sekerinski, E. (eds.) FM 2006. LNCS, vol. 4085, pp. 460–475. Springer, Heidelberg (2006)
4. Chlipala, A.: A certified type-preserving compiler from lambda calculus to assembly language. In: Conference on Programming Language Design and Implementation (PLDI 2007) (2007)
5. Dave, M.A.: Compiler verification: a bibliography. ACM SIGSOFT Software Engineering Notes 28(6), 2–2 (2003)
6. Hannan, J., Pfenning, F.: Compiler verification in LF. In: Proceedings of the 7th Symposium on Logic in Computer Science (LICS 1992) (1992)
7. Hickey, J., Nogin, A.: Formal compiler construction in a logical framework. Journal of Higher-Order and Symbolic Computation 19(2-3), 197–230 (2006)
8. Klein, G., Nipkow, T.: A machine-checked model for a Java-like language, virtual machine and compiler. ACM Transactions on Programming Languages and Systems (TOPLAS) 28(4), 619–695 (2006)
9. Leinenbach, D., Paul, W., Petrova, E.: Towards the formal verification of a C0 compiler: Code generation and implementation correctnes. In: 4th IEEE International Conference on Software Engineering and Formal Methods (SEFM 2005) (2005)
10. Leroy, X.: Formal certification of a compiler backend, or: programming a compiler with a proof assistant. In: Symposium on the Principles of Programming Languages (POPL 2006), ACM Press, New York (2006)
11. Li, G., Owens, S., Slind, K.: Structure of a proof-producing compiler for a subset of higher order logic. In: De Nicola, R. (ed.) ESOP 2007. LNCS, vol. 4421, pp. 205–219. Springer, Heidelberg (2007)
12. Li, G., Slind, K.: Compilation as rewriting in higher order logic. In: 21th Conference on Automated Deduction (CADE-21) (July 2007)
13. Wolff, B., Meyer, T.: Tactic-based optimized compilation of functional programs. In: Filliâtre, J.-C., Paulin-Mohring, C., Werner, B. (eds.) TYPES 2004. LNCS, vol. 3839, pp. 201–214. Springer, Heidelberg (2006)
14. Milner, R., Tofte, M., Harper, R., MacQueen, D.: The Definition of Standard ML, revised edition. MIT Press, Cambridge (1997)
15. Myreen, M.O., Gordon, M.J.C.: Hoare logic for realistically modelled machine code. In: Grumberg, O., Huth, M. (eds.) TACAS 2007. LNCS, vol. 4424, pp. 568–582. Springer, Heidelberg (2007)
16. Nipkow, T., Paulson, L.C., Wenzel, M.: Isabelle/HOL. LNCS, vol. 2283. Springer, Heidelberg (2002)
17. Norrish, M., Slind, K.: HOL-4 manuals (1998-2006), http://hol.sourceforge.net/
18. Pnueli, A., Siegel, M., Singerman, E.: Translation validation. In: Steffen, B. (ed.) TACAS 1998. LNCS, vol. 1384, Springer, Heidelberg (1998)
19. http://swissnet.ai.mit.edu/~jaffer/r5rs-formal.pdf
20. Slind, K.: Reasoning about terminating functional programs, Ph.D. thesis, Institut für Informatik, Technische Universität München (1999)
21. Slind, K., Owens, S., Iyoda, J., Gordon, M.: Proof producing synthesis of arithmetic and cryptographic hardware. Formal Aspects of Computing 19(3), 343–362 (2007)
22. Tolmach, A., Oliva, D.P.: From ML to Ada: Strongly-typed language interoperability via source translation. Journal of Functional Programming 8(4), 367–412 (1998)

Rocket-Fast Proof Checking for SMT Solvers

Michał Moskal

University of Wrocław, Poland

Abstract. Modern Satisfiability Modulo Theories (SMT) solvers are used in a wide variety of software and hardware verification applications. Proof producing SMT solvers are very desirable as they increase confidence in the solver and ease debugging/profiling, while allowing for scenarios like Proof-Carrying Code (PCC). However, the size of typical proofs generated by SMT solvers poses a problem for the existing systems, up to the point where proof checking consumes orders of magnitude more computer resources than proof generation. In this paper we show how this problem can be addressed using a simple term rewriting formalism, which is used to encode proofs in a natural deduction style. We formally prove soundness of our rules and evaluate an implementation of the term rewriting engine on a set of proofs generated from industrial benchmarks. The modest memory and CPU time requirements of the implementation allow for proof checking even on a small PDA device, paving a way for PCC on such devices.

1 Introduction

Satisfiability Modulo Theories (SMT) [14] solvers check satisfiability of a first order formula, where certain function and constant symbols are interpreted according to a set of background theories. These theories typically include integer or rational arithmetic, bit vectors and arrays. Some SMT solvers support only quantifier free fragments of their logics, other also support quantifiers, most often through instantiation techniques. SMT solvers are often based on search strategies of SAT solvers.

The usage of background theories, instantiation techniques and efficient handling of the Boolean structure of the formula differentiates SMT solvers from first-order theorem provers based on resolution. SMT solvers are efficient for larger mostly ground formulas. This makes them good tools for hardware and software verification.

SMT solvers typically either answer that the input formula is unsatisfiable, or give some description of a model, in which the formula might be satisfiable. In terms of software verification the first answer means that the program is correct, while the second answer means, that an assertion might be violated. The model description is used to identify a specific assertion and/or execution trace.

What is troubling is that we are trusting the SMT solver, when it says the program is correct. One problem is that there might be a bug in the SMT solver, whose implementation can be largely opaque to others than the developer.

C.R. Ramakrishnan and J. Rehof (Eds.): TACAS 2008, LNCS 4963, pp. 486–500, 2008.
© Springer-Verlag Berlin Heidelberg 2008

The other problem is that we might want to provide the evidence of program being correct to someone else, like in Proof-Caring Code [13] scenarios.

It is therefore desirable for an SMT solver to produce the proof of the unsatisfiability of formulas. The problem is that in program verification, the queries are rather huge and so are the proofs. For example formulas in the AUFLIA division of the SMT problem library[1] contain up to 130 000 distinct subterms, with an average of 8 000. The proofs we have generated are on average five times bigger than the formulas. The most complicated proof we have encountered contains around 40 000 basic resolution steps and around 1 000 000 (sub)terms in size. What is worth noting however, is that state of the art SMT solvers are able to check a vast majority of such queries in under a second. As the general expectation is that proof checking should be faster than proof generation, it becomes clear that we need very efficient means of proof checking.

1.1   Contributions

The contributions of this paper are:

- we introduce a simple, yet expressive term rewrite formalism (Sect. 2), and show it is strong enough to encode and check proofs of theory and Boolean tautologies (Sect. 3), and also NNF/CNF conversions with skolemization (Sect. 4),
- we discuss two highly efficient implementations of the proposed rewrite system (Sect. 6). In particular we discuss performance issues (Sect. 6.2) and we describe techniques to help ensure soundness of the rewrite rules (Sect. 6.1).

There are two reasons to use term rewriting as a proof checking vehicle. One is that the term rewriting is a simple formalism, therefore it is relatively easy to reason about the correctness of an implementation of the proof checker. The bulk of soundness reasoning goes at term rewrite rules level, which is much better understood and simpler to reason about than a general purpose (often low level) programming language used to implement a proof checker.

The second reason is memory efficiency, which on modern CPUs is also a key to time efficiency. We encode proof rules as rewrite rules and handle non-local conditions (like uniqueness of Skolem functions) at the meta level, which allows for the rewrite rules to be local. The idea behind the encoding of the proof rules is to take proof terms and rewrite them into the formulas that they prove. This allows for memory held by the proof terms to be immediately reclaimed and reused for the next fragment of the proof tree read from a proof file.

1.2   Proof Search in SMT Solvers

This section gives description of a proof search of an SMT solver based on DPLL and E-matching. It applies to most of the current SMT solvers.

---

[1] Both the library and this particular division are described further in Sect. 6.2.

In order to check unsatisfiability of a formula, an SMT solver will usually first transform it into an equisatisfiable CNF formula, while simultaneously performing skolemization. Subsequent proof search alternates between Boolean reasoning, theory reasoning, and quantifier instantiation. For the Boolean part we use resolution. Also the final empty clause is derived using resolution. Theory reasoning produces conflict clauses, which are tautologies under respective theories, e.g., $\neg(a > 7) \vee a \geq 6$ or $\neg(c = d) \vee \neg(f(c) = 42) \vee \neg(f(d) < 0)$. Quantifier reasoning is based on instantiating universal quantifiers and producing tautologies like $\neg(\forall x.\, f(x) > 0 \rightarrow P(x)) \vee \neg(f(3) > 0) \vee P(3)$. It can be thought of as just another background theory.

To make this search procedure return a proof, we need proofs of: CNF translation, Boolean tautologies and theory tautologies. By taking these three together, we should obtain a proof that the formula is unsatisfiable.

2 Definitions

Let $\mathcal{V}$ be an infinite, enumerable, set of variables. We use x and y (all symbols possibly with indices) as meta-variables ranging over $\mathcal{V}$. Let Σ be an infinite, enumerable set of function symbols, we use meta-variable f ranging over Σ. We define the set of *terms* $\mathcal{T}$, and the set of *patterns* $\mathcal{P} \subseteq \mathcal{T}$ as follows:

$$\mathcal{T} ::= x \mid f(\mathcal{T}_1, \ldots, \mathcal{T}_n) \mid \lambda x.\, \mathcal{T}_1 \mid \mathbf{cons} \cdot (\mathcal{T}_1, \mathcal{T}_2) \mid \mathbf{nil} \cdot () \mid \mathbf{build} \cdot (f, \mathcal{T}_1) \mid$$
$$\mathbf{apply} \cdot (\mathcal{T}_1, \mathcal{T}_2) \mid \mathbf{fold} \cdot (\mathcal{T}_1)$$
$$\mathcal{P} ::= x \mid f(\mathcal{P}_1, \ldots, \mathcal{P}_n)$$

where $n \geq 0$. The notion $s \cdot (\ldots)$ stands for a *special form*, which have particular interpretations in the term rewrite system. We will use $t_1 :: t_2$ as a syntactic sugar for $\mathbf{cons} \cdot (t_1, t_2)$, and $\mathbf{nil}$ for $\mathbf{nil} \cdot ()$.

The set of *free variables* of a term, $FV : \mathcal{T} \rightarrow \mathcal{P}(\mathcal{V})$, is defined as usual:

$$
\begin{aligned}
FV(x) &= \{x\} \\
FV(f(t_1, \ldots, t_n)) &= \textstyle\bigcup_{1 \leq i \leq n} FV(t_i) \\
FV(\lambda x.\, t) &= FV(t) \setminus \{x\} \\
FV(s \cdot (t_1, \ldots, t_n)) &= \textstyle\bigcup_{1 \leq i \leq n} FV(t_i)
\end{aligned}
$$

Note that it is also defined on $\mathcal{P}$, as $\mathcal{P} \subseteq \mathcal{T}$. Let $\mathcal{T}(A, B)$ be a set of terms built from function symbols from the set A and variables from the set $B \subseteq \mathcal{V}$ (i.e. if $t \in \mathcal{T}(A, B)$ then $FV(t) \subseteq B$). A *substitution* is a function $\sigma : \mathcal{V} \rightarrow \mathcal{T}$, which we identify with its homomorphic, capture free extension to $\sigma : \mathcal{T} \rightarrow \mathcal{T}$.

A *rewrite rule* is a pair (p, t), where $p \in \mathcal{P}$, $t \in \mathcal{T}$ and $FV(t) \subseteq FV(p)$. Let $\mathcal{R}$ be set of such rewrite rules, such that for distinct $(p, t), (p', t') \in \mathcal{R}$, p and p' do not unify. We define a *normal form* of a term t, with respect to $\mathcal{R}$ as $\boldsymbol{nf}(t)$, with the rules below. Because the function defined below is recursive it is possible for it not to terminate. If the rules below do not result in a single unique normal form for term t, then we say that $\boldsymbol{nf}(t) = \otimes$. If term has $\otimes$ as subterm, it is itself regarded as equal to $\otimes$. In practice this condition is enforced by limiting running time of the proof checker.

$$\boldsymbol{nf}(x) \;\; = \;\; x$$

$$\boldsymbol{nf}(f(t_1,\ldots,t_n)) \;\; = \;\; \begin{cases} \boldsymbol{nf}(t\sigma) \\ \quad \text{for } (p,t) \in \mathcal{R} \text{ such that} \\ \quad \exists \sigma.\, p\sigma = f(\boldsymbol{nf}(t_1),\ldots,\boldsymbol{nf}(t_n)) \\ f(\boldsymbol{nf}(t_1),\ldots,\boldsymbol{nf}(t_n)) \\ \quad \text{otherwise} \end{cases}$$

$$\boldsymbol{nf}(\lambda x.\, t_1) \;\; = \;\; \lambda x.\, \boldsymbol{nf}(t_1)$$

$$\boldsymbol{nf}(\mathbf{apply} \cdot (\lambda x.\, t_1, t_2)) \;\; = \;\; \boldsymbol{nf}(t_1[x := t_2])$$

$$\boldsymbol{nf}(\mathbf{build} \cdot (f, t_1 :: \cdots :: t_n :: \mathbf{nil}))$$
$$= \;\; \boldsymbol{nf}(f(t_1,\ldots,t_n))$$

$$\boldsymbol{nf}(\mathbf{build} \cdot (f, t_1)) \;\; = \;\; \mathbf{build} \cdot (f, \boldsymbol{nf}(t_1)) \quad \text{if none of the above apply}$$

$$\boldsymbol{nf}(s \cdot (t_1,\ldots,t_n)) \;\; = \;\; s \cdot (\boldsymbol{nf}(t_1),\ldots,\boldsymbol{nf}(t_n)) \quad \text{if none of the above apply}$$

where $t_1[x := t_2]$ denotes a capture free substitution of x with t_2 in t_1[2].

The semantics of the **fold** $\cdot (t)$ is not defined above. Its role is to perform theory-specific constant folding on t. Folding is implemented either inside the proof checker or by an external tool called by the proof checker. In this paper we use integer constant folding (for example $\boldsymbol{nf}(\mathbf{fold} \cdot (\mathtt{add}(20, 22))) = 42$).

The signature used throughout this paper can be divided in four categories:

1. logical connectives: `false, implies, and, or, forall, neg`
2. theory specific symbols: `eq, add, leq, minus` and natural number literals (`0, 1, 2, ...`)
3. technical machinery: `lift_known,` □, `sk`
4. rule names

3   Boolean Deduction

Consider the logical system from Fig. 1. It is complete for Boolean logic with connectives $\rightarrow$ and $\bot$. Three of the derivation rules there ((`mp`), (`absurd`) and (`nnpp`)) fit a common scheme:

$$\frac{\Gamma \vdash \Xi_1(\psi_1,\ldots,\psi_m) \ldots \Gamma \vdash \Xi_n(\psi_1,\ldots,\psi_m)}{\Gamma \vdash \Xi(\psi_1,\ldots,\psi_m)} \; (r)$$

where Ξ_i and Ξ are formulas built from the Boolean connectives and formula meta-variables $\psi_1,\ldots,\psi_m$, while (r) is the name of the rule. We call such rules *standard rules*. Additional Boolean connectives can be handled by adding more standard rules. To encode a standard derivation rule, we use the following rewrite:

$$r(\Box(\Xi_1(x_1,\ldots,x_m)),\ldots,\Box(\Xi_n(x_1,\ldots,x_m)), x_{i_1},\ldots,x_{i_l}) \blacktriangleright$$
$$\Box(\Xi(x_1,\ldots,x_m))$$

---

[2] The actual implementation uses de Bruijn indices, so the "capture free" part comes at no cost.

Proof rule	Rewrite rule
$\dfrac{\Gamma \vdash \psi_1 \to \psi_2 \quad \Gamma \vdash \psi_1}{\Gamma \vdash \psi_2}$ (mp)	$\mathtt{mp}(\square(\mathtt{implies}(x_1, x_2)), \square(x_1)) \blacktriangleright$ $\square(x_2)$
$\dfrac{\Gamma \vdash \bot}{\Gamma \vdash \psi}$ (absurd)	$\mathtt{absurd}(\square(\mathtt{false}), x) \blacktriangleright$ $\square(x)$
$\dfrac{\Gamma \vdash (\psi \to \bot) \to \bot}{\Gamma \vdash \psi}$ (nnpp)	$\mathtt{nnpp}(\square(\mathtt{implies}(\mathtt{implies}(x, \mathtt{false}), \mathtt{false}))) \blacktriangleright$ $\square(x)$
$\dfrac{\Gamma \cup \{\psi_1\} \vdash \psi_2}{\Gamma \vdash \psi_1 \to \psi_2}$ (assume)	$\mathtt{assume}(x_1, x_2) \blacktriangleright$ $\quad \mathtt{lift\_known}(\mathtt{implies}(x_1, \mathbf{apply} \cdot (x_2, \square(x_1))))$ $\mathtt{lift\_known}(\mathtt{implies}(x_1, \square(x_2))) \blacktriangleright$ $\quad \square(\mathtt{implies}(x_1, x_2))$
$\dfrac{\psi \in \Gamma}{\Gamma \vdash \psi}$ (assumption)	

Fig. 1. A complete system for $\to$ and $\bot$

where x_{i_j} are additional technical arguments, to fulfill the condition that the left-hand side of a rule has to contains all the free variables in the right-hand side and r is a function symbol used to encode this particular rule. Therefore we can model (mp), (absurd) and (nnpp) using the rewrite rules listed in Fig. 1.

We are left with the (assume)/(assumption) pair, which is modeled using lambda expressions. There is no explicit rewrite for (assumption) rule. The term x_2 is expected to be of the form $\lambda y. t$, where t is a proof using y in places where (assumption) should be used. This is very similar to the encoding of the IMP-I rule in Edinburgh Logical Framework [10].

We call *restricted* the terms of the form $\square(...)$, $\mathtt{lift\_known}(...)$ or $\mathtt{sk}(...)$ (the last one is used in the next section). We say that $P \in \mathcal{T}$ is a pre-proof (written **preproof**(P)), if it does not contain a restricted subterm, or a subterm which is a $s \cdot (...)$ special form.

Lemma 1. *For any pair* (P, σ), *such that* **preproof**(P), $\forall x \in \mathcal{V}. x\sigma = x \lor \exists \phi. x\sigma = \square(\phi)$ *and* **nf**$(P\sigma) = \square(\psi)$, *there exists a derivation* $\Gamma \vdash \psi$ *where* $\Gamma = \{\phi \mid x \in \mathcal{V}, x\sigma = \square(\phi)\}$.

Proof. The proof is by induction on the size of P. Because $\square(...)$ is not a subterm of P, the head of P must be either:

1. a variable x, in which case $x\sigma$ is $\square(\psi)$ and the (assumption) rule can be used, since $\psi \in \Gamma$,
2. $P = r(P_1, \ldots, P_n, t_1, \ldots, t_m)$, where a rewrite, obtained from a derivation rule (r), is applicable to:

$$r(\mathbf{nf}(P_1\sigma), \ldots, \mathbf{nf}(P_n\sigma), \mathbf{nf}(t_1), \ldots, \mathbf{nf}(t_m))$$

We use the induction hypothesis on (P_i, σ), where $\mathbf{nf}(P_i\sigma) = \square(\psi_i)$ and build the derivation using the (r) rule.

Proof rule	Rewrite rule
$$\dfrac{}{\Gamma \vdash t = t}\ (\texttt{eq\_refl})$$	$\texttt{eq\_refl}(x) \blacktriangleright$ $\quad \Box(\texttt{eq}(x,x))$
$$\dfrac{\Gamma \vdash t_1 = t_2 \quad \Gamma \vdash t_2 = t_3}{\Gamma \vdash t_1 = t_3}\ (\texttt{eq\_trans})$$	$\texttt{eq\_trans}(\Box(\texttt{eq}(x_1,x_2)),\Box(\texttt{eq}(x_2,x_3))) \blacktriangleright$ $\quad \Box(\texttt{eq}(x_1,x_3))$
$$\dfrac{\Gamma \vdash t_1 = t_2}{\Gamma \vdash t_2 = t_1}\ (\texttt{eq\_trans})$$	$\texttt{eq\_symm}(\Box(\texttt{eq}(x_1,x_2))) \blacktriangleright$ $\quad \Box(\texttt{eq}(x_2,x_1))$
$$\dfrac{\Gamma \vdash t_1 = t_2}{\Gamma \vdash \psi(t_1) \to \psi(t_2)}\ (\texttt{eq\_sub})$$	$\texttt{eq\_sub}(\Box(\texttt{eq}(x_1,x_2)),y) \blacktriangleright$ $\quad \Box(\texttt{implies}(\textbf{apply} \cdot (y,x_1), \textbf{apply} \cdot (y,x_2)))$
$$\dfrac{\Gamma \vdash x + x_1 \leq c_1 \quad \Gamma \vdash -x + x_2 \leq c_2}{x_1 + x_2 \leq c_1 + c_2}\ (\texttt{utvpi\_trans})$$	
$\texttt{utvpi\_trans}(\Box(\texttt{leq}(\texttt{add}(x_1,x_2),x_3)),\Box(\texttt{leq}(\texttt{add}(\texttt{minus}(x_1),y_2),y_3))) \blacktriangleright$ $\quad \Box(\texttt{leq}(\texttt{add}(x_2,y_2),\textbf{fold} \cdot (\texttt{add}(x_3,y_3))))$	

Fig. 2. The equality rules, and an example of an UTVPI rule

3. $P = \texttt{assume}(P_1,\psi)$, which rewrites to $\Box(...)$ in two steps, through the $\texttt{lift\_known}(...)$ (which cannot be used explicitly because $\textbf{\textit{preproof}}(P)$). $\textbf{apply} \cdot (P_1,\Box(\psi))$ needs to be reduced to $\Box(...)$ for the $\texttt{lift\_known}(...)$ to be applied, so $\textbf{\textit{nf}}(P_1) = \lambda x.\, P_2$, for some P_2. Because no rule can result in a rewrite to a lambda term (all of the rewrite rules have a term of the form $f(...)$ as their right hand side), then not only $\textbf{\textit{nf}}(P_1)$, but also P_1 itself needs to start with a lambda binder. Therefore $P_1 = \lambda x.\, P_3$, for some P_3. In this case we use the induction hypothesis on $(P_3,\sigma[x := \Box(\psi)])$, and then use the (assume) rule to construct the implication.

There are no other cases, since no other rewrite rule has $\Box(...)$ as the right-hand side. $\qquad\qquad\square$

Applying this lemma with $(P,\emptyset)$ gives the theorem.

Theorem 1. *For any P, such that $\textbf{\textit{preproof}}(P)$ and $\textbf{\textit{nf}}(P\sigma) = \Box(\psi)$ there exists a derivation $\vdash \psi$.*

Theory Conflicts. Proving theory conflicts clearly depends on the particular theory. Fig. 2 lists rules for the theory of equality. The encoding is the same as for the standard rules from Fig. 1. For arithmetic we currently support the UTVPI fragment [11] of integer linear arithmetic. It consists of inequalities of the form $ax + by \leq c$, where $a, b \in \{-1,0,1\}$ and c is an integer. The decision procedure closes set of such inequalities, with respect to a few rules, of the form similar to the one listed in Fig. 2. Again, the encoding is the same as for ordinary deduction rules.

4 Skolemization Calculus

Fig. 3 lists rules for a skolemization calculus. The $\uplus$ is disjoint set union (i.e. $A \cup B$ if $A \cap B = \emptyset$ and undefined otherwise). The intuition behind $S; Q \vdash \psi \rightsquigarrow \phi$

Proof rule	Rewrite rule
$\dfrac{\emptyset; Q \vdash \neg\psi(f(Q)) \rightsquigarrow \phi}{\{f\}; Q \vdash \neg\forall x.\, \psi(x) \rightsquigarrow \phi}$ (skol)	$\mathbf{sk}(y, \mathbf{skol}(f, y_1), \mathbf{neg}(\mathbf{forall}(x))) \blacktriangleright$ $\mathbf{sk}(y, y_1, \mathbf{neg}(\mathbf{apply} \cdot (x, \mathbf{build} \cdot (f, y))))$
$\dfrac{S; Q, x \vdash \psi(x) \rightsquigarrow \phi(x)}{S; Q \vdash \forall x.\, \psi(x) \rightsquigarrow \forall x.\, \phi(x)}$ (skip$_\forall$)	$\mathbf{sk}(y, \mathbf{skip}_\forall(y_1), \mathbf{forall}(x_1)) \blacktriangleright$ $\mathbf{forall}(\lambda x.\, \mathbf{sk}(x :: y, y_1, \mathbf{apply} \cdot (x_1, x)))$
$\dfrac{}{\emptyset; Q \vdash \psi \rightsquigarrow \psi}$ (id)	$\mathbf{sk}(y, \mathbf{id}, x_1) \blacktriangleright x_1$
$\dfrac{S_1; Q \vdash \psi_1 \rightsquigarrow \phi_1 \quad S_2; Q \vdash \psi_2 \rightsquigarrow \phi_2}{S_1 \uplus S_2; Q \vdash \psi_1 \wedge \psi_2 \rightsquigarrow \phi_1 \wedge \phi_2}$ (rec$_\wedge$)	$\mathbf{sk}(y, \mathbf{rec}_\wedge(y_1, y_2), \mathbf{and}(x_1, x_2)) \blacktriangleright$ $\mathbf{and}(\mathbf{sk}(y, y_1, x_1), \mathbf{sk}(y, y_2, x_2))$
$\dfrac{S_1; Q \vdash \psi_1 \rightsquigarrow \phi_1 \quad S_2; Q \vdash \psi_2 \rightsquigarrow \phi_2}{S_1 \uplus S_2; Q \vdash \psi_1 \vee \psi_2 \rightsquigarrow \phi_1 \vee \phi_2}$ (rec$_\vee$)	$\mathbf{sk}(y, \mathbf{rec}_\vee(y_1, y_2), \mathbf{or}(x_1, x_2)) \blacktriangleright$ $\mathbf{or}(\mathbf{sk}(y, y_1, x_1), \mathbf{sk}(y, y_2, x_2))$
$\dfrac{S_1; Q \vdash \neg\psi_1 \rightsquigarrow \phi_1 \quad S_2; Q \vdash \neg\psi_2 \rightsquigarrow \phi_2}{S_1 \uplus S_2; Q \vdash \neg(\psi_1 \vee \psi_2) \rightsquigarrow \phi_1 \wedge \phi_2}$ (rec$_{\neg\vee}$)	$\mathbf{sk}(y, \mathbf{rec}_{\neg}\vee(y_1, y_2), \mathbf{neg}(\mathbf{or}(x_1, x_2))) \blacktriangleright$ $\mathbf{and}(\mathbf{sk}(y, y_1, \mathbf{neg}(x_1)), \mathbf{sk}(y, y_2, \mathbf{neg}(x_2)))$
$\dfrac{S_1; Q \vdash \neg\psi_1 \rightsquigarrow \phi_1 \quad S_2; Q \vdash \neg\psi_2 \rightsquigarrow \phi_2}{S_1 \uplus S_2; Q \vdash \neg(\psi_1 \wedge \psi_2) \rightsquigarrow \phi_1 \vee \phi_2}$ (rec$_{\neg\wedge}$)	$\mathbf{sk}(y, \mathbf{rec}_{\neg}\wedge(y_1, y_2), \mathbf{neg}(\mathbf{and}(x_1, x_2))) \blacktriangleright$ $\mathbf{or}(\mathbf{sk}(y, y_1, \mathbf{neg}(x_1)), \mathbf{sk}(y, y_2, \mathbf{neg}(x_2)))$
$\dfrac{S_1; Q \vdash \psi_1 \rightsquigarrow \phi_1}{S_1; Q \vdash \neg\neg\psi_1 \rightsquigarrow \phi_1}$ (rec$_{\neg\neg}$)	$\mathbf{sk}(y, \mathbf{rec}_{\neg\neg}(y_1), \mathbf{neg}(\mathbf{neg}(x_1))) \blacktriangleright$ $\mathbf{sk}(y, y_1, x_1)$

Fig. 3. The skolemization calculus

is that for each model M of $\forall Q.\, \psi$ there exists an extension of M on the symbols from S that satisfies $\forall Q.\, \phi$. We formalize it using second order logic with the following lemma:

Lemma 2. *Let* $Q = \{x_1, \ldots, x_n\}$ *and* $S = \{f_1 \ldots f_n\}$. *If* $S; Q \vdash \psi \rightsquigarrow \phi$ *where* $\psi \in \mathcal{T}(\Sigma, Q)$, $\phi \in \mathcal{T}(\Sigma \uplus S, Q)$, *then* $\models \exists^2 f_1 \ldots \exists^2 f_n.\, \forall x_1, \ldots, x_n.\, \psi \to \phi$.

The key point of the proof is that for the rules of the common form:

$$\dfrac{S_1; Q \vdash \Xi_1(\psi_1, \ldots, \psi_k) \rightsquigarrow \phi_1 \quad \ldots \quad S_m; Q \vdash \Xi_m(\psi_1, \ldots, \psi_k) \rightsquigarrow \phi_m}{S_1 \uplus \ldots \uplus S_m; Q \vdash \Xi(\psi_1, \ldots, \psi_k) \rightsquigarrow \Xi'(\psi_1, \ldots, \psi_k, \phi_1, \ldots, \phi_m)} \quad (r)$$

where ψ_j and ϕ_j range over first order formulas it is enough to show the following:

$$\forall Q : \mathbf{Type}.\, \forall S_1 \ldots S_n : \mathbf{Type}.$$
$$\forall \psi_1 \ldots \psi_k : Q \to \mathbf{Prop}.$$
$$\forall \phi_1 : S_1 \times Q \to \mathbf{Prop}.\, \ldots \forall \phi_m : S_m \times Q \to \mathbf{Prop}.$$
$$\bigwedge_{i=1 \ldots m} (\exists f_i : S_i.\, \forall x : Q.\, \Xi_i(\psi_1(x), \ldots, \psi_k(x)) \to \phi_i(f_i, x)) \to$$
$$(\exists f_1 : S_1.\, \ldots \exists f_m : S_m.\, \forall x : Q.\, \Xi(\psi_1(x), \ldots, \psi_k(x)) \to$$
$$\Xi'(\psi_m(x), \ldots, \psi_k(x), \phi_1(f_1, x), \ldots, \phi_m(f_m, x)))$$

which is much like the formula from the lemma, except that there is only one Skolem constant f_i per premise and also there is only one free variable in all the formulas, namely x. However these symbols are of arbitrary type, so they can be thought of as representing sequences of symbols.

We prove such formulas for each rule, the reader can find the proof scripts for Coq proof assistant online [1].

Rewrite encoding. The common form of a rule is encoded as:

$$\mathbf{sk}(y, r(y_1, \ldots, y_m), \Xi(x_1, \ldots, x_k)) \blacktriangleright$$
$$\Xi'(x_1, \ldots, x_k, \mathbf{sk}(y, y_1, \Xi_1(x_1, \ldots, x_k)), \ldots, \mathbf{sk}(y, y_m, \Xi_m(x_1, \ldots, x_k)))$$

The first argument of sk(...) is the list of universally quantified variables in scope. The second argument is a rule name, along with proofs of premises. The third argument is the formula to be transformed.

The encoding of non-common rules (as well as the common rules used here) is given in the Fig. 3.

Lemma 3. *If* $\boldsymbol{preproof}(P)$, $\boldsymbol{nf}(\text{sk}(x_1 :: \cdots :: x_n :: \textbf{nil}, P, \psi)) = \psi'$, *and for each occurrence of* $\text{skol}(f)$ *as a subterm of* P, *the function symbol* f *does not occur anywhere else in* P *nor in* ψ, *then there exists* S, *such that* $S; x_1, \ldots, x_n \vdash \leadsto \psi\psi'$.

Proof. By structural induction over P. $\qquad\square$

Theorem 2. *If* $\boldsymbol{preproof}(P)$, $\boldsymbol{nf}(\text{sk}(\textbf{nil}, P, \psi)) = \psi'$, *and for each occurrence of* $\text{skol}(f)$ *as a subterm of* P, *the function symbol* f *does not occur anywhere else in* P *nor in* ψ, *and* ψ' *is unsatisfiable then* ψ *is unsatisfiable.*

Proof. By Lemmas 2 and 3. $\qquad\square$

5   The Checker

The proof checker reads three files: (1) rewrite rules describing the underlying logic; (2) a query in SMT-LIB concrete syntax; and (3) the proof. The concrete syntax for both the rewrite rules and the proof term is similar to the one used in SMT-LIB. The proof term language includes the following commands:

- **let** $x := t_1$: bind the identifier x to the term $\boldsymbol{nf}(t_1)$
- **initial** t_1 t_2: check if $\text{skol}(f)$ is used in t_1 only once with each f, that the f symbols do not occur in t_2, compares t_2 against the query read from the SMT-LIB file and if everything succeeds, binds $\square(\boldsymbol{nf}(\text{sk}(\textbf{nil}, t_1, t_2)))$ to the special identifier **initial**; this command can be used only once in a given proof
- **final** t_1: checks if $\boldsymbol{nf}(t_1) = \square(\texttt{false})$, and if so reports success and exits
- **assert_eq** t_1 t_2: checks if $\boldsymbol{nf}(t_1) = \boldsymbol{nf}(t_2)$ (and aborts if this is not the case)
- **assert_ok** t_1 t_2: checks if $\boldsymbol{nf}(t_1) = \square(\boldsymbol{nf}(t_2))$ (and aborts if this is not the case)
- **print** t_1: prints a string representation of t_1

The last three commands are used to debug the proofs.

The proofs, after initial skolemization, are structured as a sequence of clause derivations, using either resolution, theory conflicts, instantiation or CNF-conversion steps. All these clauses are **let**-bound, until we reach the empty clause. Basically we end up with a proof-tree in natural deduction, deriving the Boolean false constant from the initial formula. The tree is encoded as a DAG, because **let**-bound clauses can be used more than once.

Proof rule	Rewrite rule
$\dfrac{\Gamma \vdash \psi_1 \wedge \psi_2}{\Gamma \vdash \psi_1}$ $(\mathtt{elim}_{\wedge 1})$	$\mathtt{elim}_{\wedge 1}(\Box(\mathtt{and}(x_1, x_2))) \;\blacktriangleright$ $\quad \Box(x_1)$
$\dfrac{\Gamma \vdash \psi_1 \wedge \psi_2}{\Gamma \vdash \psi_2}$ $(\mathtt{elim}_{\wedge 2})$	$\mathtt{elim}_{\wedge 2}(\Box(\mathtt{and}(x_1, x_2))) \;\blacktriangleright$ $\quad \Box(x_2)$
$\dfrac{\Gamma \vdash \psi_1 \vee \psi_2}{\Gamma \vdash \neg \psi_1 \rightarrow \psi_2}$ $(\mathtt{elim}_\vee)$	$\mathtt{elim}_\vee(\Box(\mathtt{or}(x_1, x_2))) \;\blacktriangleright$ $\quad \Box(\mathtt{implies}(\mathtt{neg}(x_1), x_2))$
$\dfrac{\Gamma \vdash \neg\psi \quad \Gamma \vdash \psi}{\Gamma \vdash \bot}$ $(\mathtt{elim}_\neg)$	$\mathtt{elim}_\neg(\Box(\mathtt{neg}(x_1))), \Box((x_1)) \;\blacktriangleright$ $\quad \Box(\mathtt{false})$
$\dfrac{\Gamma \vdash \psi}{\Gamma \vdash \neg\neg\psi}$ $(\mathtt{add}_{\neg\neg})$	$\mathtt{add}_{\neg\neg}(\Box(x_1)) \;\blacktriangleright$ $\quad \Box(\mathtt{neg}(\mathtt{neg}(x_1)))$
$\dfrac{\Gamma \vdash \psi \rightarrow \bot}{\Gamma \vdash \neg\psi}$ $(\mathtt{intro}_\neg)$	$\mathtt{intro}_\neg(\Box(\mathtt{implies}(x_1, \mathtt{false}))) \;\blacktriangleright$ $\quad \Box(\mathtt{neg}(x_1))$
$\dfrac{\Gamma \vdash \neg\psi \rightarrow \bot}{\Gamma \vdash \psi}$ $(\mathtt{elim}_{\neg\rightarrow})$	$\mathtt{elim}_{\neg\rightarrow}(\Box(\mathtt{implies}(\mathtt{neg}(x_1), \mathtt{false}))) \;\blacktriangleright$ $\quad \Box(x_1)$
$\dfrac{\Gamma \vdash \forall x.\, \psi(x)}{\Gamma \vdash \psi(t)}$ $(\mathtt{inst})$	$\mathtt{inst}(y, \Box(\mathtt{forall}(x))) \;\blacktriangleright$ $\quad \Box(\mathbf{apply} \cdot (x, y))$

Fig. 4. Additional rules for the example

All those steps are best described through an example[3]. Fig. 4 lists rules not previously mentioned in this paper, that were used in the proof. The real proof system has more rules. As described in Sect. 6.1, we mechanically check all rules. Our example formula is:

$$P(c) \wedge (c = d) \wedge (\forall x.\, \neg P(x) \vee \neg(\forall y.\, \neg Q(x, y))) \wedge (\forall x.\, \neg Q(d, x))$$

The first step is the initial skolemization:

let $q_1 := \mathtt{forall}(\lambda x.\, \mathtt{or}(\mathtt{neg}(P(x)), \mathtt{neg}(\mathtt{forall}(\lambda y.\, \mathtt{neg}(Q(x, y))))))$
let $q_2 := \mathtt{forall}(\lambda x.\, \mathtt{neg}(Q(d, x)))$
let $f_{in} := \mathtt{and}(P(c), \mathtt{and}(\mathtt{eq}(c, d), \mathtt{and}(q_1, q_2)))$
let $sk := \mathtt{rec}_\wedge(\mathtt{id}, \mathtt{rec}_\wedge(\mathtt{id}, \mathtt{rec}_\wedge(\mathtt{skip}_\forall(\mathtt{rec}_\vee(\mathtt{id}, \mathtt{skol}(f, \mathtt{rec}_{\neg\neg}(\mathtt{id})))), \mathtt{id})))$
initial $sk\ f_{in}$

Here our expectation, as the proof generator, is that $\forall x.\, \neg P(x) \vee \neg(\forall y.\, \neg Q(x, y))$ will be replaced by $\forall x.\, \neg P(x) \vee Q(x, f(x))$, which we express as:

> **let** $q_3 := \mathtt{forall}(\lambda x.\, \mathtt{or}(\mathtt{neg}(P(x)), Q(x, f(x))))$
> **let** $f_{sk} := \mathtt{and}(P(c), \mathtt{and}(\mathtt{eq}(c, d), \mathtt{and}(q_3, q_2)))$
> **assert_ok initial** f_{sk}

The first step of the actual proof is a partial CNF-conversion. Our CNF conversion uses Tseitin scheme, which introduces proxy literals for subformulas. This

---

[3] The proof presented here is not the simplest possible of this very formula. However it follows the steps that our SMT solver does and we expect other SMT solvers to do.

produces equisatisfiable set of clauses, yet the proof maps the proxy literals back to the original subformulas. Then the defining clauses of proxy literals become just basic Boolean facts. We therefore derive clauses of the form $f_{sk} \to \neg\psi \to \bot$, where ψ is one of the conjuncts of f_{sk}, for example:

let $c_1 := \mathsf{assume}(f_{sk}, \lambda f.\, \mathsf{assume}(\mathsf{neg}(\mathsf{eq}(c,d)), \lambda p.\, \mathsf{elim}_\neg(p, \mathsf{elim}_{\wedge 2}(\mathsf{elim}_{\wedge 1}(f)))))$
assert_ok c_1 $\mathsf{implies}(f_{sk}, \mathsf{implies}(\mathsf{neg}(\mathsf{eq}(c,d)), \mathsf{false}))$

and similarly we derive:

$$\textbf{assert\_ok}\ c_0\ \mathsf{implies}(f_{sk}, \mathsf{implies}(\mathsf{neg}(P(c)), \mathsf{false}))$$
$$\textbf{assert\_ok}\ c_2\ \mathsf{implies}(f_{sk}, \mathsf{implies}(\mathsf{neg}(q_3), \mathsf{false}))$$
$$\textbf{assert\_ok}\ c_3\ \mathsf{implies}(f_{sk}, \mathsf{implies}(\mathsf{neg}(q_2), \mathsf{false}))$$

Next we instantiate the quantifiers:

let $c_4 := \mathsf{assume}(q_2, \lambda q.\, \mathsf{assume}(Q(d, f(c)), \lambda i.\, \mathsf{elim}_\neg(\mathsf{inst}(f(c), q), i)))$
assert_ok c_4 $\mathsf{implies}(q_2, \mathsf{implies}(Q(d, f(c)), \mathsf{false}))$
let $i_1 := \mathsf{or}(\mathsf{neg}(P(c)), Q(c, f(c)))$
let $c_5 := \mathsf{assume}(q_3, \lambda q.\, \mathsf{assume}(\mathsf{neg}(i_1), \lambda i.\, \mathsf{elim}_\neg(i, \mathsf{inst}(c, q))))$
assert_ok c_5 $\mathsf{implies}(q_3, \mathsf{implies}(\mathsf{neg}(i_1), \mathsf{false}))$

Then we need to clausify i_1:

let $c_6 := \mathsf{assume}(i_1, \lambda i.\, \mathsf{assume}(P(c), \lambda o_1.\, \mathsf{assume}(\mathsf{neg}(Q(c, f(c))), \lambda o_2.$
$\mathsf{elim}_\neg(o_2, \mathsf{mp}(\mathsf{elim}_\vee(i), \mathsf{add}_{\neg\neg}(o_1))))))$
assert_ok c_6 $\mathsf{implies}(i_1, \mathsf{implies}(P(c), \mathsf{implies}(\mathsf{neg}(Q(c, f(c)), \mathsf{false})))$

Then we do some equality reasoning:

let $c_7 := \mathsf{assume}(\mathsf{neg}(Q(d, f(c))), \lambda l_n.\, \mathsf{assume}(\mathsf{eq}(c,d), \lambda e.\, \mathsf{assume}(Q(c, f(c)), \lambda l_p.$
$\mathsf{elim}_\neg(l_n, \mathsf{mp}(\mathsf{eq\_sub}(e, \lambda x.\, Q(x, f(c))), l_p)))))$
assert_ok c_7 $\mathsf{implies}(\mathsf{neg}(Q(d, f(c))), \mathsf{implies}(\mathsf{eq}(c,d), \mathsf{implies}(Q(c, f(c)), \mathsf{false})))$

What remains is a pure Boolean resolution. The resolution is realized by assuming the negation of the final clause and then using unit resolution of the assumed literals and some previous clauses, to obtain new literals, and as a last step, the **false** constant. We first resolve c_4 with c_7:

let $c_8 := \mathsf{assume}(q_2, \lambda l_1.\, \mathsf{assume}(\mathsf{eq}(c,d), \lambda l_2.\, \mathsf{assume}(Q(c, f(c)), \lambda l_3.$
$\mathsf{mp}(\mathsf{mp}(\mathsf{mp}(c_7, \mathsf{intro}_\neg(\mathsf{mp}(c_4, l_1))), l_2), l_3)$
assert_ok $c_8 \mathsf{implies} q_2, \mathsf{implies}\, \mathsf{eq}(c,d), \mathsf{implies}\, Q(c, f(c)), \mathsf{false}$

and finally we derive (also through resolution) the false constant:

let $kq_2 := \mathsf{elim}_{\neg\to}(\mathsf{mp}(c_3, \mathsf{initial}))$
let $kq_3 := \mathsf{elim}_{\neg\to}(\mathsf{mp}(c_2, \mathsf{initial}))$
let $kp := \mathsf{elim}_{\neg\to}(\mathsf{mp}(c_0, \mathsf{initial}))$
let $ke := \mathsf{elim}_{\neg\to}(\mathsf{mp}(c_1, \mathsf{initial}))$
let $kq := \mathsf{elim}_{\neg\to}(\mathsf{mp}(\mathsf{mp}(c_6, \mathsf{elim}_{\neg\to}(\mathsf{mp}(c_5, kq_3))), kp))$
let $c_9 := \mathsf{mp}(\mathsf{mp}(\mathsf{mp}(c_8, kq_2), ke), kq)$
final c_9

6   Implementation

We have implemented two versions of the proof checker: one full version in OCaml and a simplified one written in C. Proof generation was implemented inside the Fx7 [1] SMT solver, implemented in the Nemerle programming language. The solver came second in the AUFLIA division of 2007 SMT competition, being much slower, but having solved the same number of benchmarks as the winner, Z3 [6].

An important point about the implementation, is that at any given point, we need to store only terms, that can be referenced by **let**-bound name, and thus the memory used by other terms can be reclaimed. As in our encoding the proof terms actually rewrite to formulas that they prove, there is no need to keep the proof terms around. We suspect this to be the main key to memory efficiency of the proof checker. The C implementation exploits this fact, the OCaml one does not.

Both implementations use de Bruijn [5] indices in representation of lambda terms. We also use hash consing, to keep only a single copy of a given term. We cache normal forms of the terms, we remember what terms are closed (which speeds up beta reductions). Also a local memoization is used in function computing beta reduction to exploit the DAG structure of the term. The rewrite rules are only indexed by the head symbol, if two rules share the head symbol, linear search is used.

All the memoization techniques used are crucial (i.e., we have found proofs, where checking would not finish in hours without them).

The OCaml implementation is about 900 lines of code, where about 300 lines is pretty printing for Coq and Maude formats. The C implementation is 1500 lines. Both implementation include parsing of the proof and SMT formats and command line option handling. The implementations are available online along with the Fx7 prover.

6.1   Soundness Checking

The OCaml version of the checker has also a different mode of operation, where it reads the rewrite rules and generates corresponding formulas to be proven in the Coq proof assistant. There are three proof modes for rules:

- for simple facts about Boolean connectives, arithmetic and equality, the checker generates a lemma and a proof, which is just an invocation of appropriate tactic
- for other generic schemas of proof rules from Sect. 3 and 4, the checker produces proof obligations, and the proofs need to be embedded in the rule descriptions
- for non-generic proof rules, the user can embed both the lemma and the proof in the rule description file, just to keep them close

This semiautomatic process helps preventing simple, low-level mistakes in the proof rules. The checker provides commands to define all these kinds of rules and associated proofs.

Directory	Total	UNSAT	% UNSAT	Fake	% Fake	Fail	% Fail
front_end_suite	2320	2207	95.13%	101	4.35%	12	0.52%
boogie	908	866	95.37%	25	2.75%	17	1.87%
simplify	833	729	87.52%	44	5.28%	60	7.20%
piVC	41	17	41.46%	10	24.39%	14	34.15%
misc	20	16	80.00%	0	0.00%	4	20.00%
Burns	14	14	100.00%	0	0.00%	0	0.00%
RicartAgrawala	14	13	92.86%	0	0.00%	1	7.14%
small_suite	10	8	80.00%	0	0.00%	2	20.00%

Fig. 5. Results on the AUFLIA division of SMT-LIB

6.2 Performance Evaluation

When running Fx7 on a query there are five possible outcomes:

- it reports that the query is unsatisfiable, and outputs a proof
- it reports that the query is unsatisfiable, but because the proof generation is only implemented for the UTVPI fragment of linear arithmetic, the proof is correct only if we assume the theory conflicts to be valid (there is typically a few of them in each of such "fake" proofs)
- it reports the query is satisfiable, timeouts or runs out of memory

Tests were performed on AUFLIA benchmarks from the SMT-LIB [14]. This division includes first order formulas, possibly with quantifiers, interpreted under uninterpreted function symbols, integer linear arithmetic and array theories. They are mostly software verification queries. The machine used was a 2.66GHz Pentium 4 PC with 1GB of RAM, running Linux. The time limit was set to ten minutes.

The results are given in Fig. 5. The "Total" column refers to the number of benchmarks marked unsatisfiable in the SMT-LIB; "UNSAT" refers to the number of cases, where the benchmark was found unsatisfiable and a correct proof was generated; "Fake" is the number of benchmarks found unsatisfiable, but with "fake" proofs; finally "Fail" is the number of cases, where Fx7 was unable to prove it within the time limit. It should be the case that UNSAT + Fake + Fail = Total. The percentages are with respect to the Total.

With the **C implementation**, proof checking a single proof never took more than 7 seconds. It took more than 2 seconds in 4 cases and more than 1 second in 19 cases (therefore the average time is well under a second). The maximal amount of memory consumed for a single proof was never over 7MB, with average being 2MB.

We have also tested the C implementation on a Dell x50v **PDA** with a 624MHz XScale ARM CPU and 32MB of RAM, running Windows CE. It was about 6 times slower than the Pentium machine, but was otherwise perfectly capable of running the checker. This fact can be thought of as a first step on a way to PCC-like scenarios on small, mobile devices. Other devices of similar computing power and, what is more important, RAM amount include most smart phones and iPods.

The **OCaml implementation** was on average 3 times slower than the C version, it also tends to consume more memory, mostly because it keeps all the terms forever (which is because of our implementation, not because of OCaml).

We have also experimented with translating the proof objects into the **Maude syntax** [3]. We have implemented lambda terms and beta reduction using the built-in Maude integers to encode de Bruijn indices and used the standard equational specifications for the first order rules. The resulting Maude implementation is very compact (about 60 lines), but the performance is not as good as with the OCaml or C implementation — it is between 10 and 100 times slower than the OCaml one. It also tends to consume a lot more memory. The reason is mainly the non-native handling of lambda expressions. Beta reductions translate to large number of first order rewrites, which are then memoized, and we were unable to instrument Maude to skip memoization of those.

We have performed some experiments using **Coq metalogic** as the proof checker. We did not get as far as implementing our own object logic. The main obstacle we have found was the treatment of binders. Performing skolemization on a typical input results in hundreds of Skolem functions. When using a higher order logic prover, such functions are existentially quantified and the quantifiers need to be pushed through the entire formula to the beginning. Later, during the proof, we need to go through them to manipulate the formula. This puts too much pressure on the algorithms treating of binders in the higher order prover. In our approach Skolem functions are bound implicitly, so there is no need to move them around. This is especially important in SMT queries, where the vast majority of the input formula is ground and quantified subformulas occur only deep inside the input. We can therefore keep most of the formula binder-free. We were not able to perform any realistic tests, as Coq was running out of memory.

Both Maude and Coq are far more general purpose tools than just proof checkers. However relatively good results with Maude suggest that using a simple underlying formalism is beneficial in proof checking scenarios.

7   Related and Future Work

CVC3 [2] and Fx7 were the only solvers participating in the 2007 edition of the SMT competition to produce formal proofs. The proof generation in CVC3 is based on the LF framework. We are not aware of a published work evaluating proof checking techniques on large industrial benchmarks involving quantifiers.

Formalisms for checking SMT proofs have been proposed in the past, most notably using an optimized implementation [15] of Edinburgh Logical Framework [10]. However even with the proposed optimizations, the implementations has an order of magnitude higher memory requirements than our solution. Also the implementation of the checker is much more complicated.

Recently a Signature Compiler tool has been proposed [16]. It generates a custom proof checker in C++ or Java from a LF signature. We have run our proof checker on a 1:1 translation of the artificial EQ benchmarks from the paper. It is running slightly faster than the generated C++ checker. The memory requirements of our implementation are way below the size of the input file on those benchmarks. The checkers remain to be compared on real benchmarks involving richer logics and quantifiers.

In context of the saturation theorem provers it is very natural to output the proof just as a sequence of resolution or superposition steps. What is missing here, is the proof of CNF translation, though proof systems has been proposed [8], [7] to deal with that.

Finally, work on integrating SMT solvers as decision procedures inside higher order logic provers include [12], [9], [4]. The main problem with these approaches is that proof generation is usually at least order of magnitude faster than proof checking inside higher order logic prover. The Ergo [4] paper mentions promising preliminary results with using proof traces instead of full proofs with Coq for theory conflicts. It is possible that using traces could also work for CNF conversion and skolemization. Yet another approach mentioned there is verifying the SMT solver itself.

An important remaining problem is the treatment of theory conflicts. One scenario here is to extend the linear arithmetic decision procedure to produce proofs. It should be possible to encode the proofs with just a minor extensions to the rewrite formalism. Another feasible scenario is to use a different SMT solver as a oracle for checking the harder (or all) theory conflicts. This can be applied also to other theories, like bit vectors or rational arithmetic.

8   Conclusions

We have shown how term rewriting can be used for proof checking. The highlights of our approach are (1) time and space efficiency of the proof checker; (2) simplicity of the formalism, and thus simplicity of the implementation; and (3) semiautomatic checking of proof rules. The main technical insight is that the proof rules can be executed locally. Therefore the memory taken by proofs trees can be reclaimed just after checking them and reused for the subsequent fragments of the proof tree.

The author wishes to thank Joe Kiniry, Mikoláš Janota, and Radu Grigore for their help during the work on the system, and Nikolaj Bjørner as well as anonymous TACAS reviewers for his help in getting the presentation of this paper better.

This work was partially supported by Polish Ministry of Science and Education grant 3 T11C 042 30.

References

1. Fx7 web page, `http://nemerle.org/fx7/`
2. Barrett, C., Berezin, S.: CVC Lite: A new implementation of the Cooperating Validity Checker. In: Alur, R., Peled, D.A. (eds.) CAV 2004. LNCS, vol. 3114, pp. 515–518. Springer, Heidelberg (2004)

3. Clavel, M., Durán, F., Eker, S., Lincoln, P., Martí-Oliet, N., Meseguer, J., Quesada, J.F.: Maude: Specification and programming in rewriting logic. Theoretical Computer Science (2001)

4. Conchon, S., Contejean, E., Kanig, J., Lescuyer, S.: Lightweight Integration of the Ergo Theorem Prover inside a Proof Assistant. In: Second Automated Formal Methods workshop series (AFM 2007), Atlanta, Georgia, USA (November 2007)

5. de Bruijn, N.G.: Lambda-calculus notation with nameless dummies: a tool for automatic formula manipulation with application to the Church-Rosser theorem. Indag. Math. 34(5), 381–392 (1972)

6. de Moura, L., Bjorner, N.: Efficient E-matching for SMT solvers. In: Proceedings of the 21st International Conference on Automated Deduction (CADE-21), Springer, Heidelberg (to appear, 2007)

7. de Nivelle, H.: Implementing the clausal normal form transformation with proof generation. In: fourth workshop on the implementation of logics, Almaty, Kazachstan, University of Liverpool, University of Manchester, pp. 69–83 (2003)

8. de Nivelle, H.: Translation of resolution proofs into short first-order proofs without choice axioms. Information and Computation 199(1), 24–54 (2005)

9. Fontaine, P., Marion, J.-Y., Merz, S., Nieto, L.P., Tiu, A.: Expressiveness + automation + soundness: Towards combining SMT solvers and interactive proof assistants. In: Hermanns, H., Palsberg, J. (eds.) TACAS 2006. LNCS, vol. 3920, pp. 167–181. Springer, Heidelberg (2006)

10. Harper, R., Honsell, F., Plotkin, G.: A framework for defining logics. In: Proceedings 2nd Annual IEEE Symp. on Logic in Computer Science, LICS 1987, Ithaca, NY, USA, June, 22–25, 1987, pp. 194–204. IEEE Computer Society Press, New York (1987)

11. Harvey, W., Stuckey, P.: A unit two variable per inequality integer constraint solver for constraint logic programming (1997)

12. McLaughlin, S., Barrett, C., Ge, Y.: Cooperating theorem provers: A case study combining HOL-Light and CVC Lite. In: Armando, A., Cimatti, A. (eds.) Proceedings of the 3rd Workshop on Pragmatics of Decision Procedures in Automated Reasoning (PDPAR 2005), Edinburgh, Scotland, January 2006. Electronic Notes in Theoretical Computer Science, vol. 144(2), pp. 43–51. Elsevier, Amsterdam (2006)

13. Necula, G.C.: Proof-carrying code. In: Conference Record of POPL 1997: The 24th ACM SIGPLAN-SIGACT Symposium on Principles of Programming Languages, Paris, France, January 1997, pp. 106–119 (1997)

14. SMT-LIB: The Satisfiability Modulo Theories Library. http://www.smt-lib.org/

15. Stump, A., Dill, D.: Faster Proof Checking in the Edinburgh Logical Framework. In: 18th International Conference on Automated Deduction (2002)

16. Zeller, M., Stump, A., Deters, M.: A signature compiler for the Edinburgh Logical Framework. In: Proceedings of International Workshop on Logical Frameworks and Meta-Languages: Theory and Practice (2007)

SDSIrep: A Reputation System Based on SDSI*

Ahmed Bouajjani[1], Javier Esparza[2], Stefan Schwoon[2],
and Dejvuth Suwimonteerabuth[2]

[1] LIAFA, University of Paris 7, Case 7014, 75205 Paris cedex 13, France
[2] Technische Universität München, Boltzmannstr. 3, 85748 Garching, Germany

Abstract. We introduce SDSIrep, a reputation system based on the
SPKI/SDSI authorization system. It is well-known that a system of
SPKI/SDSI certificates corresponds to the formal model of a pushdown
system (PDS). Our system, SDSIrep, allows principals to express trust
and recommendations in the form of so-called certificates with weights.
By interpreting weights as probabilities, we obtain a random-walk model
of the reputation of a principal. Thus, SDSIrep represents an application
of the theory of probabilistic PDSs to the field of computer security. We
present an algorithm to compute the reputation of each principal. An
extension of SDSIrep also provides for so-called intersection certificates,
by which, loosely speaking, a principal gains reputation if recommended
by all members of a given group of principals. On a formal-methods
level, this extension makes SDSIrep correspond to probabilistic alternating PDSs, and we extend the underlying theory of PDSs to handle this
case. As an example we sketch a small academic reputation system that
combines information from different reputation sources, like conferences,
coauthors, and rankings.

1 Introduction

In many Internet applications, notions of trust and reputation play an important
role. In particular, in an open-world scenario where we do not know all the
participants beforehand, we often need to decide whether to trust other persons
without having met them before. Examples include systems like Ebay, where
hitherto unknown participants engage in financial transactions; peer-to-peer file-
sharing networks where people download files from one another and the academic
world, where one often needs to assess a candidate's scientific merit.

If one cannot judge somebody else's trustworthiness oneself, a common solution is to assess their reputation: while *trust* is a "local" notion about the
relation between two parties, *reputation* means somebody's "global" standing
within some community. In the first two of the above scenarios, so-called *reputation systems* can be employed where a participant's reputation is computed
from the experiences that other participants have made in prior transactions.
A survey of reputation systems can be found in [1]. A concrete, well-known

---

* This work was partially supported by SFB 627 Nexus, Project A6.

C.R. Ramakrishnan and J. Rehof (Eds.): TACAS 2008, LNCS 4963, pp. 501–516, 2008.
© Springer-Verlag Berlin Heidelberg 2008

example of a reputation system is the one used by Ebay, where every transaction can be assigned a rating that is stored in a central server, which can then authoritatively compute each participant's reputation. Such a system, which is based on the ratings users give to each other, is also called *user-driven*. In contrast, some domain-specific reputation systems such as the one proposed for rating Wikipedia contributors [2] are called *content-driven*, because they rate users based on how their contributions evolve in the system. Our proposal is not geared towards any specific domain, and we follow the user-driven approach.

People often place trust in individuals and in the recommendations given by well-reputed institutions. (Notice that trust and recommendations are closely related: normally, we would recommend a person if we trust them to be good at something.) For instance, when a well-reputed university hires a new researcher, we can interpret this as a recommendation that the university gives to the researcher. Likewise, when a well-reputed magazine publishes papers by a certain author, it implicitly recommends the contents of those papers, enhancing the reputation of the author. Such recommendations tend to "add up"; the more such sources of reputation we know of, the more we would trust a researcher.

In the following, we propose a framework for expressing trust and reputation in such a scenario. This framework allows to make statements that express trust in individuals as well as in (hierarchical) organizations. For instance, one can state that one recommends the employees of a certain university, or the coauthors of one's own papers. Moreover, such statements can be given weights to denote the degree of the recommendation.

For this, we borrow from and modify the SPKI/SDSI framework [3]; we therefore call our system SDSIrep. SPKI/SDSI was designed to denote naming policies in a distributed environment. Simply put, it allows to define groups of principals, which are described in distributed, hierarchical name spaces, and this idea is well suited for our purposes. We also show, by re-interpreting the notion of delegation in SPKI/SDSI, how an important distinction can be made between our trust of a person and our trust of their ability to judge the reputation of others. Our framework also borrows ideas from EigenTrust [4], a reputation system that has been proposed for peer-to-peer networks. We discuss the similarities and differences in Sections 3 and 6.

Previous work has shown that SPKI/SDSI has a strong connection to the theory of pushdown systems [5,6]. Moreover, SPKI/SDSI (and the associated pushdown theory) has been extended with weights, allowing to solve authorization problems with quantitative components. However, the extensions considered so far were not powerful enough to capture situations where trust "adds up" along multiple paths as in our scenario (see above). For example, the framework in [6] can express the fact that a certain level of trust exists if there is at least one path to support it; however, it cannot express the idea that the level of trust increases if multiple such paths exist. Recently, however, new results on probabilistic pushdown systems [7] open up the opportunity for such an extension.

Our paper makes the following contributions:

- We describe a new framework, called SDSIrep, that can be used to build a reputation system suitable for modelling trust relationships in an open-world scenario. Moreover, SDSIrep allows to distinguish between the trust one has in a person and in their recommendations. We then show how these trust values can be aggregated to measure each participant's reputation.
- We expose the relationship between SDSIrep and probabilistic pushdown systems and extend the probabilistic approach to *alternating* pushdown systems. This solution allows to handle so-called intersection certificates, increasing the expressiveness of the SDSIrep framework at practically no extra computational cost.
- As a small case study, we design a system for measuring academic reputation. We implement the algorithms for computing reputations in this example and report on their performance.

We proceed as follows: In Section 2 we recall basic notions of SPKI/SDSI. We then present SDSIrep, our reputation system, in Section 3, and solve the associated trust and reputation problem. In Section 4 we extend SDSIrep with intersection certificates. We present some experimental results in Section 5 before discussing related work and concluding in Section 6.

2 Background

This section provides some background on SPKI/SDSI and pushdown systems.

2.1 A Brief Introduction to SPKI/SDSI

The SPKI/SDSI standard was proposed in [3] and formalised in first-order logic in [8]. We present a subset of SPKI/SDSI that has been considered in most of the work on this topic. The full SPKI/SDSI standard also provides for so-called threshold certificates, which we treat later in Section 4.

SPKI/SDSI was designed to denote authorization policies in a distributed environment. A central notion of SPKI/SDSI are *principals*. A principal can be a person or an organisation. Each principal defines his/her own namespace, which assigns *rôles* to (other) principals. For instance, principal *Fred* can define the rôle `friend` and associate principal *George* with this rôle. Such associations are made in SPKI/SDSI by issuing so-called *name certificates* (*name certs*, for short). A special feature is that principals may reference the namespace of other principals in their certificates. For instance, *Fred* may state that all of *George*'s friends are also his own friends. In this way, SPKI/SDSI allows to associate a rôle with a group of principals described in a symbolic and distributed manner. SPKI/SDSI then allows to assign permissions to rôles using so-called *authorisation certificates* (or *auth certs*).

The SPKI/SDSI standard also uses a public-key infrastructure that allows for certificates to be signed and verified for authenticity. Public-key infrastructure does not play a major rôle in our approach, but we shall re-use the ideas behind the naming scheme.

More formally, a SPKI/SDSI system can be seen as a tuple (P, A, C), where P is a set of *principals*, A is a set of *rôle identifiers* (or identifiers, for short) and $C = Na \uplus Au$ is a set of certificates. Certificates can be either *name certificates* (contained in Na), or *authorization certificates* (contained in Au).

A *term* is formed by a principal followed by zero or more identifiers, i.e., an element of the set PA^*. A term t is interpreted as denoting a set of principals, written $[\![t]\!]$, which are defined by the set of name certificates (see below).

A name certificate is of the form p a $\rightarrow t$, where p is a principal, a is an identifier, and t is a term. Notice that p a itself is a term. The sets $[\![t]\!]$, for all terms t, are the smallest sets satisfying the following constraints:

- if $t = p$ for some principal p, then $[\![t]\!] = \{p\}$;
- if $t = t'$ a, then for all $p \in [\![t']\!]$ we have $[\![p\ \mathsf{a}]\!] \subseteq [\![t]\!]$;
- if p a $\rightarrow t$ is a name certificate, then $[\![t]\!] \subseteq [\![p\ \mathsf{a}]\!]$.

For instance, if *Fred* and *George* are principals and friend is an identifier, then *Fred* friend $\rightarrow$ *George* expresses that George is a friend of Fred, and *Fred* friend $\rightarrow$ *George* friend means that all of George's friends are also Fred's friends, and *Fred* friend $\rightarrow$ *Fred* friend friend says that the friends of Fred's friends are also his friends.

An authorisation certificate has the form $p\ \square \rightarrow t\ b$, where p is a principal, t is a term, and b is either $\square$ or $\blacksquare$. Such a certificate denotes that p grants some authorisation to all principals in $[\![t]\!]$. If $b = \square$, then the principals in $[\![t]\!]$ are allowed to delegate said authorisation to others; if $b = \blacksquare$, then they are not. (Auth certs in SPKI/SDSI contain more details about the authorisation that they confer; this detail is not important for our approach.)

More formally, authorisation certs define a smallest relation $aut \colon P \times P$ between principals such that $aut(p, p')$ holds iff p grants an authorisation to p':

- if there is an auth cert $p\ \square \rightarrow t\ b$, for $b \in \{\square, \blacksquare\}$, and $p' \in [\![t]\!]$, then $aut(p, p')$;
- if there is an auth cert $p\ \square \rightarrow t\ \square$, $p' \in [\![t]\!]$, and $aut(p', p'')$, then $aut(p, p'')$.

For instance, the certificate *Fred* $\square \rightarrow$ *George* friend $\blacksquare$ means that Fred grants some right to all of George's friends, however, George's friends are not allowed to delegate that right to other principals.

The *authorisation problem* in SPKI/SDSI is to determine, given a system (P, A, C) and two principals p and p', whether p' is granted authorisation by p, i.e., whether $aut(p, p')$.

2.2   SPKI/SDSI and Pushdown Systems

Certificates in SPKI/SDSI can be interpreted as prefix rewrite systems. For instance, if p a $\rightarrow p'$ b c and p' b $\rightarrow p''$ d e are two certificates interpreted as rewrite rules, then their concatenation rewrites p a to p'' d e c. In SPKI/SDSI, a concatenation of two or more certificates is called a *certificate chain*. It is easy to see that the authorisation problem, given principals p and p', reduces to the problem of whether there exists a certificate chain that rewrites $p\ \square$ into either

p' □ or p' ■ (in the first case, p' also has the right to delegate the authorisation further, in the second case he has not).

Moreover, it is well-known that the type of rewrite systems induced by a set of SPKI/SDSI certificates is equivalent to that of a pushdown system (PDS), see, e.g. [5,6,9,10]. For example, a cert like p a $\rightarrow p'$ b c is interpreted as a pushdown transition, where p, p' are states of the finite control and where the stack content a is replaced by bc. Then, the SPKI/SDSI authorisation problem reduces to a pushdown reachability problem, i.e., whether from control location p with the symbol □ on the stack (and nothing else) one can eventually reach control location p' with empty stack.

In the following, we present our system, SDSIrep, which extends SPKI/SDSI with weights on certificates and with so-called intersection certificates. In pushdown-automata theory, these extensions correspond to weighted pushdown systems [6] and alternating pushdown systems [9]. For brevity, we will not elaborate on these correspondences any further, and we simply apply the appropriate pushdown theory to SDSIrep. Notice, however, that the combination of weighted and alternating systems employed in this paper is novel.

3   A SDSI-Based Reputation System

We now explain the model of trust and reputation employed by SDSIrep, which motivates the design of our system, given in Section 3.2. We then proceed to show how to compute trust and reputation values in this system. In Section 4 we introduce an extension that further improves the expressiveness of the system.

3.1   A Numerical Model of Trust

Many reputation systems allow participants to express degrees of trust numerically. A common problem with this is that malicious participants may attempt to "spam" the system and boost each other's reputations with arbitrarily high values. The solution employed here is to normalise trust values. In SDSIrep, each principal has a total trust of 1 at his/her disposal, fractions of which can be allocated freely to other principals.

Like in EigenTrust [4], this approach lends itself to a probabilistic interpretation, similar to the "Random Surfer" model used in Google's PageRank [11]. We interpret a SDSIrep system as a Markov chain whose states are the participants, and where the trust that participant A has in B (expressed as a fraction between 0 and 1) serves as the probability of going from A to B. Then, one way to find reputable participants is to perform a random walk on this Markov chain: after a "long enough" period of time, one is more likely to be at a well-reputed participant than not. In particular, each party's reputation is taken as their value in the stationary vector of the Markov chain. Thus, even though all participants can distribute a total trust value of 1 to others, this does mean that the opinions of all participants have the same influence. Well-reputed participants will be visited more often in a random walk than less-reputed ones, giving more weight to their opinions.

What distinguishes SDSIrep from EigenTrust is the way peer-to-peer ratings are specified: principals can assign their trust to *groups of* principals that are defined indirectly, using name certificates like in SPKI/SDSI. Membership in a group is associated with a numeric value, in a kind of fuzzy logic. Suppose, for instance, that a researcher wants to recommend those researchers whose findings have been published in a certain journal. Then, somebody with 10 papers in that journal could be considered to belong more strongly to that group than somebody with just one paper. SDSIrep allows to make such distinctions.

In the terminology of [1], PageRank, EigenTrust, and SDSIrep are all examples of *flow models*. In a flow model, participants can only increase their reputation at the cost of others. This property is obviously satisfied by SDSIrep, because the sum of the reputation values over all participants is bounded by 1. Thus, the absolute reputation values computed within the SDSIrep framework have no meaning in themselves; they only indicate how well-reputed each participant is in comparison with others.

3.2 SDSIrep Certificates

Our system is based on the design of SPKI/SDSI, i.e. a SDSIrep system is again a triple (P, A, C) with (almost) the same meaning as in Section 2. However, in SDSIrep, we are not concerned with authorisation problems. Rather, we reinterpret authorisation certificates as *recommendations*, which express trust in certain groups of principals.

Another change is the addition of weights to certificates. Adding weights drawn from the set $[0, 1]$ to recommendation certs allows to express the degree of recommendations. Similarly, weights on name certs express the degree of membership to a set. We provide only simple examples in this section; a more elaborate example of a SDSIrep system is presented in Section 5.

Weighted recommendation certs allow to recommend all members of a group by issuing one single cert. This reflects common situations in which a principal recommends a group even though the members of the group change along time, or even though he or she does not know many of its members.

A weighted recommendation cert has the form $p \square \xrightarrow{x} t \blacksquare$, where $x \in [0, 1]$ is its weight. Such a cert states that the principal p recommends the principals of the set $[\![t]\!]$ with weight x. The cert $p \square \xrightarrow{x} t \square$ states that p recommends not the principals of $[\![t]\!]$ themselves, but *their recommendations* with weight x.

As an example, suppose that researcher A wants to give 50% of his "share" of recommendations to the authors of journal J. This could be stated by the cert $A \square \xrightarrow{0.5} J$ aut $\blacksquare$. To explain the semantic difference between $\square$ and $\blacksquare$, imagine a reputation system for film directors with directors and critics as principals. Film critics will not be recommended for their directing skills, only for their recommendations. A similar distinction exists in PGP, which separates the trust that principals have in the authenticity of some person's public key from the trust they have in the ability of that person to correctly judge the authenticity of other people's keys.

Notice that there is no certificate with ■ on the left-hand side. Thus, a chain starting with a recommendation cert of the form $p \, \square \xrightarrow{x} t$ ■ necessarily ends when t has been rewritten to an element of $[\![t]\!]$, whereas a chain starting with $p \, \square \xrightarrow{x} t \, \square$ allows to apply further recommendation certs at that point. This corresponds to the idea that $\square$ expresses a recommendation of somebody's recommendations, whereas ■ expresses a recommendation of that person as such.

To normalise the trust values in the system, and in order to enable a probabilistic interpretation as discussed in Section 3.1, we additionally demand that the weights on each principal's recommendation certs add up to 1.

Weighted name certs have the form $p \, \mathtt{a} \xrightarrow{x} t$, where $x \in [0,1]$. Intuitively, such a cert states a fuzzy membership relation: the elements of $[\![t]\!]$ belong to the set $[\![p \, \mathtt{a}]\!]$ with membership degree x.

As an example, consider a journal J and an identifier $\mathtt{aut}$ such that $[\![J \, \mathtt{aut}]\!]$ are the authors that have published in J. Then, if the journal has published 100 papers and B has authored 10 of them, B might be considered to belong to $[\![J \, \mathtt{aut}]\!]$ with degree 10%, expressed as $J \, \mathtt{aut} \xrightarrow{0.1} B$. In order to uphold the fuzzy-set interpretation we demand that for all pairs $p \, \mathtt{a}$, the sum of the weights on all name certs with $p \, \mathtt{a}$ on the left-hand side is 1.

3.3 Certificate Chains and Markov Chains

Consider the certs $A \, \square \xrightarrow{0.5} J \, \mathtt{aut}$ ■ and $J \, \mathtt{aut} \xrightarrow{0.1} B$. If A gives 50% of his recommendations to the authors of J, and B has authored 10% of the papers in J, then a natural interpretation is that 5% of A's recommendations go to B. Thus, the weight of the certificate chain formed from the two certs is obtained by multiplying their individual weights.

To find out how much trust A puts into B, we are interested in the certificate chains going from $A \, \square$ to B ■. In general, there could be more than one such chain. Thus, one needs to find all these chains in order to determine the degree of recommendation A gives to B. The following example shows that the number of such paths can in fact be infinite:

$$A \, \square \xrightarrow{1} A \, \mathtt{friend} \; \blacksquare \quad (1) \qquad A \, \mathtt{friend} \xrightarrow{x} B \quad\quad\quad (3)$$

$$B \, \square \xrightarrow{1} A \; \blacksquare \quad\quad\quad (2) \qquad B \, \mathtt{friend} \xrightarrow{1} A \quad\quad\quad (4)$$

$$A \, \mathtt{friend} \xrightarrow{1-x} A \, \mathtt{friend \, friend} \, (5)$$

Cert (5) is the crucial one. It states that the friends of A's friends also belong to A's friends, albeit with smaller weight. Notice that whenever this cert can be applied, it can be applied arbitrarily often. So A recommends B through many possible chains: for instance, we can apply the cert (1), then cert (5) $2n$ times, and then certs (3) and (4) alternatingly n times each.

We can now define the two algorithmic problems related to SDSIrep. The *trust problem* in SDSIrep is as follows: Given two principals p and p', compute the sum of the weights of all certificate chains that rewrite $p \, \square$ into p' ■. The *reputation problem* is to compute, for each principal, their value in the stationary vector of the Markov chain in which the transition probabilities are given by the solutions to the pairwise trust problems. We discuss solutions for the trust and reputation problems in Section 3.4.

3.4   Solving the Trust and Reputation Problems

It is easy to see that a system of SDSIrep certificates corresponds to a probabilistic pushdown system (pPDS) [7]. The trust problem in SDSIrep then reduces to a pPDS reachability problem, i.e., given p and p', compute the probability of reaching control location p' with stack content ■ when starting from p and □.

Following [7], the solution to this is given by an equation system (see also [12] for the same result using a different but equivalent model). Given a SDSIrep system (P, A, C), the variables are elements of the set $\{\, [p, \mathsf{a}, q] \mid p, q \in P,\ \mathsf{a} \in A \,\}$, where $[p, \mathsf{a}, q]$ denotes the probability of rewriting the term $p\,\mathsf{a}$ into q. To solve the trust problem, we also add an artificial certificate $p' \,■ \xrightarrow{1} \bar{p}'$, where $\bar{p}'$ is a fresh control location; since $p'\,■$ does not appear on any other left-hand side, the solution of $[p, □, \bar{p}']$ gives us the trust placed by p in p'.

Each variable $[p, \mathsf{a}, q]$ has the following equation:[1]

$$[p, \mathsf{a}, q] = \sum_{p\mathsf{a} \xrightarrow{x} p'\mathsf{bc}} x \cdot \sum_{r \in P} [p', \mathsf{b}, r] \cdot [r, \mathsf{c}, q] + \sum_{p\mathsf{a} \xrightarrow{x} p'\mathsf{b}} x \cdot [p', \mathsf{b}, q] + \sum_{p\mathsf{a} \xrightarrow{x} q} x \quad (6)$$

Intuitively, equation (6) sums up the probabilities for all the possible ways of reaching q from $p\,\mathsf{a}$. We just explain the first half of the expression; the other cases are simpler and analogous: if $p\,\mathsf{a}$ is replaced by $p'\,\mathsf{b}\,\mathsf{c}$ (with probability x), then one first needs to rewrite this term to $r\,\mathsf{c}$ for some $r \in P$, which happens with the probability computed by $[p', \mathsf{b}, r]$, and then $r\,\mathsf{c}$ needs to be rewritten into q, which is expressed by the variable $[r, \mathsf{c}, q]$.

For instance, consider the system consisting of rules (1) to (5) in Section 3.3. Some of the resulting equations are (abbreviating f for friend):

$$[B, \mathsf{f}, A] = 1 \qquad\qquad [B, □, B] = 1 \cdot [A, ■, B]$$
$$[A, \mathsf{f}, B] = x + (1 - x) \cdot ([A, \mathsf{f}, A] \cdot [A, \mathsf{f}, B] + [A, \mathsf{f}, B] \cdot [B, \mathsf{f}, B])$$

This equation system has a least solution, and the elements of this least solution correspond to the aforementioned probabilities. Notice that the equation system is non-linear in general. We discuss the resulting algorithmic problems in more detail in Section 5.3. The following theorem now follows from the definitions and the results of [7,12].

Theorem 1. *The solution to the trust problem for principals p and p' is equal to the value of variable $[p, □, \bar{p}']$ in the least solution of the equation system (6).*

---

[1] We show the equation system for the case where the terms on the right-hand side of each cert consist of at most two identifiers; however, this is not a restriction as any system can be converted into a system observing this rule with linear overhead [5].

In general, the least solution cannot be computed exactly, but can be approximated to an arbitrary degree of precision using standard fix-point computation methods [7]. We give more details on this computation when discussing our experiments in Section 5. Notice that the equation system actually gives the probabilities (and hence the trust values) for all pairs of principals, therefore all values in the Markov chain used for solving the reputation problem can be obtained from just one fixpoint computation.

As discussed in Section 3.1, a measure of the "reputation" of principals in the system can be obtained by computing the stationary vector of the Markov chain whose states are the principals and whose transition probabilities are given by the solutions of the trust problems. Computing the stationary vector amounts to solving a linear equation system, using well-known techniques.

However, for the stationary vector to exist, the Markov chain needs to be irreducible and aperiodic. This is not guaranteed in general: e.g., if there is a clique of participants who trust only each other, the Markov chain contains a "sink", i.e., it is not irreducible. This type of problem is also encountered in other models based on random walks, e.g. EigenTrust or PageRank, and the solutions employed there also apply to SDSIrep. For instance, the irreducibility and aperiodicity constraint can be enforced by allowing the random walk to jump to random states at any move with small probability. Notice that the example in Section 5 does not exhibit this kind of problem; therefore, we did not use this trick in our experiments.

4   Intersection Certificates

The SPKI/SDSI standard provides for so-called *threshold certificates*, which consist of, say, an auth cert of the form $p \square \rightarrow \{t_1 b_1, \ldots, t_n b_n\}$, where $b_1, \ldots, b_n \in \{\square, \blacksquare\}$, and an integer $k \leq n$. The meaning of such a cert is that p grants authorisation to principal p' if there is a certificate chain to p' from at least k out of $t_1 b_1, \ldots, t_n b_n$. Threshold certificates for name certs could be defined analogously. We restrict ourselves to the case where $k = n$ and use the more suggestive name *intersection certificate* instead.[2]

In this section we show how intersection certificates can be added to SDSIrep and define the corresponding trust problem and a probabilistic interpretation for SDSIrep with intersection certificates. We then show that the equation system from Section 3.4 can be modified to accomodate this extension.

Algorithms for authorisation in SPKI/SDSI with intersection were studied in [5] and [9]. In the latter, the problem was reduced to reachability in *alternating pushdown systems* (APDS). It turns out that the authorisation problem with

---

[2] In the case *without* weights, any certificate where $k < n$ can be replaced by a set of certificates, one for each k-sized subset of the right-hand side. In the case *with* weights, this can also be done, but the degree to which a participant belongs to the right-hand side can be interpreted in different ways. This question of interpretation is beyond the scope of the paper.

intersection is EXPTIME-complete in general, but remains polynomial when intersection is restricted to authorisation certs. This distinction translates directly to SDSIrep; therefore, we restrict intersection to recommendation certs.

4.1   Intersection Certs in SDSIrep

Sometimes one wishes to recommend principals belonging to the intersection of two or more groups. For instance, researcher A may wish to recommend those of his co-authors that have published in journal J. In SDSIrep, we model this by a certificate such as $A \; \Box \xrightarrow{x} \{A \text{ coaut } \blacksquare, \; J \text{ aut } \blacksquare\}$. In general, intersection certificates have the form $p \; \Box \xrightarrow{x} \{t_1 \; b_1, \ldots t_n \; b_n\}$, where $b_1, \ldots, b_n \in \{\Box, \blacksquare\}$, and express that p recommends the set $\bigcap_{i=1}^{n} [\![t_i]\!]$ with weight x.

The trust problem for the case without intersection certs consists of computing the values of certificate chains. When intersection certs come into play, we need to think of certificate trees instead, where each node is labelled by a term, and a node labelled by term t has a set of children labelled by T if T is the result of applying a rewrite rule to t. For instance, if in addition to the previous intersection certificate we have $A \text{ coaut } \xrightarrow{y} B$ and $J \text{ aut } \xrightarrow{z} B$, then we have the following certificate tree:

$$A \; \Box \xrightarrow{x} \left\{ \begin{array}{l} A \text{ coaut } \blacksquare \xrightarrow{y} B \; \blacksquare \\ J \text{ aut } \blacksquare \xrightarrow{z} B \; \blacksquare \end{array} \right.$$

In the probabilistic interpretation, the probability for this tree is $x \cdot y \cdot z$. Thus, the *trust problem for SDSIrep with intersection* is as follows: Given principals p and p', compute the sum of the probabilities of all trees whose root is labelled by $p \; \Box$ and all of whose children are labelled by $p' \; \blacksquare$. Notice that the solution for the associated *reputation problem* remains essentially unchanged, as the addition of intersection certs merely changes the way peer-to-peer trust is assigned.

4.2   Solving the Trust Problem with Intersection Certs

We now extend the equation system from Section 3.4 to the case of intersection certificates. (In terms of [9], we extend the solution to probabilistic APDSs.)

Let $\Xi := \{\blacksquare, \Box\}$. Since intersection is restricted to recommendation certs, the following important properties hold: (1) if $p \; \Box$ is the root of a certificate tree, then all nodes are of the form $t \; b$, where $b \in \Xi$ and t does not contain any symbol from Ξ; (2) if a term t of a certificate tree has more than one child, $t = p \; \Box$ for some p. It follows that if a term pw is the root of a tree and w does not contain any occurrence of $\blacksquare$ or $\Box$, then every term of the tree has at most one child, and so the tree has a unique leaf. We exploit this fact in our solution.

Let (P, A, C) be a SDSIrep system with intersection certificates. The variables of the new equation system are of the form $[p, \bot, q]$ or $[p, w, q]$, where $p, q \in P$, $\bot \in \Xi$, $w \in A^*$, and w must be a suffix of the right-hand side of a cert. Notice that, by definition, w contains no occurrence of $\blacksquare$ or $\Box$. The variable $[p, \bot, q]$ represents the probability of, starting at $p\bot$, eventually reaching a tree where all leaves are labelled with q. The variable $[p, w, q]$ represents the probability of, starting at pw, reaching a tree whose unique leaf (here we use the fact above) is labelled with q. We add (as in Section 3.4) an artificial rule $p' \blacksquare \xrightarrow{1} \overline{p}'$, which is the only rule consuming the $\blacksquare$ symbol.

For $p, q \in P$ and $\gamma \in A \cup \Xi$, we have:

$$[p, \gamma, q] = \sum_{p\gamma \xrightarrow{x} p'w} x \cdot [p', w, q] \quad +$$

$$\sum_{p\gamma \xrightarrow{x} \{p_1 w_1 \perp_1, \ldots, p_n, w_n \perp_n\}} x \cdot \sum_{q_1, \ldots, q_n \in P} \prod_{i=1}^{n} [p_i, w_i, q_i] \cdot [q_i, \perp_i, q] \quad (7)$$

(Notice that if $\gamma \in A$ then the second sum is equal to 0 by property (2) above.) Moreover, we set $[p, \varepsilon, q] = 1$ if $p = q$ and 0 otherwise, and $[p, \gamma w, q] = \sum_{q' \in P} [p, \gamma, q'] \cdot [q', w, q]$ for every two $p, q \in P$, $\gamma w \in (A \cup \Xi)^+$. Notice that γw is a suffix of the right-hand side of some cert, and therefore so is w.

The intuition for these equations is the same as in the case without alternation, see Section 3.4. The corresponding equation system also has the same properties and can be solved in the same way.

Theorem 2. *The solution to the trust problem for principals p and p' in a SDSIrep system with intersection certificates is equal to the solution of variable $[p, \square, \overline{p}']$ in the least solution of the equation system (7).*

5 Experiments

For demonstration purposes, we have used SDSIrep to model a simple reputation system for the PC members of TACAS 2008. We have chosen this example because the reader is likely to be familiar with the sources of reputation in academia, in particular in computer science. We do not claim that our experiments say anything really relevant about the actual reputation of the PC members, in particular, because part of the required data (the personal preferences of the PC members, see below) was not available to us.

In this section, we give some details on this system, and report on the performance of our solver for the equation systems given in Sections 3.4 and 4.2.

5.1 A Small System for Academic Reputation

Principals and identifiers. The set of principals contains the 28 members of the TACAS programme committee, 6 of the main conferences on automated verification (CAV, ICALP, LICS, POPL, VMCAI, TACAS), and 3 rankings: the CiteSeer list of 10,000 top authors in computer science (year 2006) [13], denoted `CiteSeer`, the CiteSeer list of conferences and journals with the highest impact factors [14], denoted `Impact`, and the list of h-indices for computer scientists [15], denoted `H-index`. The identifiers are `aut`, `publ`, `coaut`, and `circ`, with the following fuzzy sets as intended meaning:

- $[\![c \text{ aut}]\!]$: researchers that publish in conference c;
- $[\![r \text{ publ}]\!]$: conferences in which researcher r has published;
- $[\![r \text{ coaut}]\!]$: r's co-authors;
- $[\![r \text{ circ}]\!]$: r's "circle", defined as r's coauthors, plus the coauthors of r's coauthors, and so on (the degree of membership to the circle will decrease with the "distance" to r).

Name certs. Some illustrative examples of the certs in our system are shown in Figure 1. For the sake of readability, we present them without having normalised the weights (normalized values are more difficult to read and compare). So, to set up the equation system, one has to take all the certs with the same tuple p a on the left-hand side, say $p \text{ a} \xrightarrow{x_1} t_1, \ldots, p \text{ a} \xrightarrow{x_n} t_n$, and then replace each x_i by $x_i / \sum_{i=1}^n x_i$. In this way, all weights are normalised.

Two certs describe to which degree a PC member is an author of a conference and which share each conference has in the PC member's publication list. In both cases, the weight (before normalisation) is the number of papers the author has published in the conference, obtained from DBLP [16]. For instance, for TACAS and Kim Larsen (KL), we have certs (8) and (9).

Another set of certs describes which PC members are coauthors of each other. The weight is the number of jointly written papers, obtained again from DBLP. For instance, cert (10) denotes that KL has written 22 papers with PP.

Finally, each PC member has a circle of fellow researchers, composed of the member's coauthors, the coauthors of the member's coauthors, and so on. We define KL's circle by means of certs (11) and (12).

$$\text{TACAS aut} \xrightarrow{10} \text{KL} \qquad (8) \qquad \text{H-index} \ \square \xrightarrow{34} \text{KL} \ \blacksquare \qquad (14)$$

$$\text{KL publ} \xrightarrow{10} \text{TACAS} \qquad (9) \qquad \text{CiteSeer} \ \square \xrightarrow{2023} \text{KL} \ \blacksquare \qquad (15)$$

$$\text{KL coaut} \xrightarrow{22} \text{PP} \qquad (10) \qquad \text{KL} \ \square \xrightarrow{4} \text{KL publ aut} \ \blacksquare \ (16)$$

$$\text{KL circ} \xrightarrow{0.8} \text{KL coaut} \qquad (11) \qquad \text{KL} \ \square \xrightarrow{3} \text{KL circ} \ \blacksquare \qquad (17)$$

$$\text{KL circ} \xrightarrow{0.2} \text{KL circ circ} \quad (12) \qquad \text{KL} \ \square \xrightarrow{2} \text{Impact} \ \square \qquad (18)$$

$$\text{Impact} \ \square \xrightarrow{1.24} \text{TACAS aut} \ \blacksquare \quad (13) \quad \text{KL} \ \square \xrightarrow{3} \text{CiteSeer} \ \square \wedge \text{H-index} \ \square \ (19)$$

Fig. 1. Name and recommendation certificates for the example

Recommendation certs. The system contains one recommendation cert for each conference, in which **Impact** recommends the authors of the conference with the weight given by its impact factor. For TACAS we have cert (13).

The next two certs, (14) and (15) express that the h-index and CiteSeer lists recommend a PC member (in this case KL) with a weight proportional to his h-index and to his number of citations in the list, respectively.

Finally, each PC member issues four more certs. The certs for KL are given in (16)–(19). Intuitively, they determine the weight with which KL wishes to recommend his circle, the authors of the conferences he publishes in, and how much trust he puts in the Citeseer and h-index rankings. In a real system, each PC member would allocate the weights for his/her own certs; in our example we have assumed that all PC members give the same weights. In order to illustrate the use of intersection certs we have assumed that KL only recommends researchers on the basis of their ranking values if they appear in *both* CiteSeer's list and in the h-index list (19). Moreover, observe that in certs (18) and (19), KL places trust in the *recommendations* given by the rule targets (signified by □), whereas in the other rules he expresses trust in the principals themselves.

In the following two sections we describe the running times and some interesting aspects of solving the equation systems computing the reputation of each researcher. All experiments were performed on a Pentium 4 3.2 GHz machine with 3 GB memory.

5.2 Experiment 1

We have written a program which takes as input the set of SDSIrep certificates described above, generates the equation system of Section 4.2, and computes its solution. We can then compute the degree to which researchers recommend one another. From the result we build a Markov chain as described in Section 3.3. The stationary distribution of the Markov chain, given at the top of Table 1, can be interpreted as the (relative) reputation of each researcher when compared to the others in the system. The lower part of Table 1 shows how the running

Table 1. Stationary distribution for TACAS PC members (values multiplied by 1000) and statistics for different numbers of researchers

PB	EB	TB	RC	BC	BD	PG	OG	AG	FH	MH	JJ	KJ	JK	BK	MK	KL	NL	KN	PP	SR	CR	JR	AR	SS	SS	BS	LZ
26	18	19	78	45	6	56	60	30	19	45	19	5	23	10	30	88	26	37	33	64	22	45	6	54	15	80	41

scientists	10	20	30	40	50	60	70	76
variables	627	1653	3089	4907	7126	9752	12777	14779
time (s)	0.47	2.07	6.85	12.55	23.90	44.89	78.35	106.55

time scales when the number of researchers is increased. For this experiment we have put together the PCs of TACAS, FOSSACS, and ESOP, with a total of 76 members, adding FOSSACS and ESOP to the list of conferences. We have computed the stationary distribution for subsets of 10, 20, ..., 76 PC members. The first line of the table shows the number of variables in the system (which is also the number of equations), and the second shows the time required to solve it and compute the stationary distribution.

Notice that the equation system used here is non-linear (see Section 4.2). Following [12], we solve it using Newton's iterative method, stopping when an iteration does not change any component of the solution by more than 0.0001.

5.3 Experiment 2

In contrast to other trust systems, in which trust is assigned from one individual to another, our choice of SDSI allows to assign trust measures to sets of principals using multiple levels of indirection. For instance, *A* can transfer trust to

B because B is a coauthor of C, and C publishes in the same conference as A. This added expressiveness comes at a price. Certs like (12) or (16), with more than one identifier on the right-hand side, cause the resulting equation system to become non-linear (see Section 3.4). Likewise, intersection certs also cause non-linear equations (see Section 4.2).

On the other hand, if the system does not contain these two types of certs, the resulting equation system is linear, and instead of Newton's method more efficient techniques can be applied, e.g. the Gauß-Seidel method.

In the following, let us assume that intersection certs are absent. Consider cert (12). The certificate is "recursive" in the sense that it can be applied arbitrarily often in a certificate chain, rewriting KL circ to KL circ^n, for any $n \geq 1$. Thus, the length of terms to which KL circ can be rewritten is unbounded. (In pushdown terms, the "stack" can grow to an unbounded size.) If the set of certs is such that this effect cannot happen, then each term can be rewritten into only *finitely many* different other terms. Therefore, we can apply a process similar to that of "flattening" a PDS into a finite-state machine and derive a *larger*, but *linear*, equivalent equation system. If there are recursive certs, we can still choose an arbitrary bound on the length of terms and ignore the contributions of larger terms. In this case, the "unflattened" and "flattened" systems do not have the same solution, but the solution of the "flattened" system converges to the solution of the "unflattened" one when the bound increases.

This provokes the question of whether the performance of the equation solver can be improved by bounding the maximal term length, "flattening" the non-linear system into a linear one, and solving the linear system. In order to experimentally address this question, we again took the system introduced in Section 5.1, but without cert (19). We fixed the maximal term depth to various numbers, computed the corresponding linear flattened systems, and solved them using the Gauß-Seidel method. (We omit the details, which are standard.)

We found that in this example flattening works very well. Even with stack depth 2 we obtained a solution that differed from the one given by Newton's method by less than 1% and can be computed in 1.23 seconds instead of 5.83. Table 2 shows the results for stack depths up to 8, i.e. the size of the equation system obtained for each stack depth and the time required to solve it. Notice that in this case, the growth of the equation system as the stack depth grows is benign (only linear); in general, the growth could be exponential.

This result might suggest that using Newton's method could always be replaced by flattening in the absence of intersection certs. However, some caution is required. When we tried to repeat the experiment for the case with 76 researchers, our solver was able to solve the unflattened system within two minutes, but ran out of memory even for a flattened stack depth of 2.

Table 2. Size of equation system and running times for flattened systems

	Unflattened	Depth 2	Depth 3	Depth 4	Depth 5	Depth 6	Depth 7	Depth 8
vars	2545	5320	7059	8798	10537	12276	14015	15754
time	5.83	1.23	3.32	6.39	10.34	18.78	32.18	42.97

6   Discussion and Related Work

There is a large and growing body of literature on trust and reputation systems, see e.g. [1,17]. In this paper, we have proposed a new framework, SDSIrep, that is novel (to the best of our knowledge) in the way it expresses transitive trust relations in an open-world scenario. More specifically, trust can be assigned to principals based on their memberships in a group described by specific attributes, e.g. co-authors of a researcher or employees of a certain university. We believe that this mimics an important facet of how reputation is usually perceived.

Most trust and reputation systems collect peer-to-peer trust ratings and aggregate a global reputation from these ratings. EigenTrust [4] is an example of a system that also takes transitive trust into account, and it shares some similarities with SDSIrep. Both EigenTrust and SDSIrep allow individual users to express and quantify their personal trust relationships. In EigenTrust, principals express how much they trust their peers, and trust in a peer automatically translates into trusting the peer's recommendations, and so on. In the terminology of [1], EigenTrust is an example of a *flow model*. SDSIrep falls into the same category, but differs in the means in which trust between principals is defined. In SDSIrep, trust can be assigned to groups of principals (see above), and we allow to distinguish between how much we trust a person and how much we trust their recommendations.

Both SDSIrep and EigenTrust make use of a probabilistic interpretation by which these recommendations are aggregated into a measure of reputation. In both cases, this measure is obtained from a Markov chain whose entries are given by the peer-to-peer recommendations. In EigenTrust, the values of this Markov chain are supplied directly by the users, whereas in SDSIrep they are obtained by evaluating the certificates. Thus, roughly speaking, every SDSIrep system has an equivalent EigenTrust system. However, the translation from SDSIrep to EigenTrust is not completely straightforward, it requires to solve the equation systems from Sections 3.4 and 4.2. In fact, providing these equation systems is one of the contributions of this paper.

EigenTrust was designed for *distributed* computation of global trust values in a peer-to-peer network with minimal overhead. We have not investigated this aspect. For the purposes of this paper, we have assumed that some central authority can collect relevant certificates and carry out the computation. In [10], it was shown how authorization questions in SPKI/SDSI can be solved when the relevant certificates are distributed among multiple sites. Our system is also based on SPKI/SDSI, so it is conceivable that ideas from [10] could be lifted to SDSIrep.

We assume that the certificates used in the computations represent the current preferences of the users, and therefore the results of our algorithms reflect the current situation. It is conceivable that users' preferences change over time, and that they will eventually want to redistribute their trust values to reflect their new preferences. (Analogous effects occur, e.g., in PageRank or EigenTrust.) Such dynamics are beyond the scope of this paper. For our purposes, we simply assume that there exists some mechanism that allows the users to manage their certificates and make their current certificates available to the computation engine.

References

1. Jøsang, A., Ismail, R., Boyd, C.: A survey of trust and reputation systems for online service provision. In: Decision Support Systems (2005)
2. Adler, T., de Alfaro, L.: A content-driven reputation system for the Wikipedia. In: Proc. 16th WWW Conference, ACM, pp. 261–270 (2007)
3. Ellison, C., Frantz, B., Lampson, B., Rivest, R., Thomas, B., Ylönen, T.: RFC 2693: SPKI Certificate Theory. In: The Internet Society (1999)
4. Kamvar, S.D., Schlosser, M.T., Garcia-Molina, H.: The EigenTrust algorithm for reputation management in P2P networks. In: Proc. 12th WWW Conference (2003)
5. Jha, S., Reps, T.: Model checking SPKI/SDSI. JCS 12(3–4), 317–353 (2004)
6. Schwoon, S., Jha, S., Reps, T., Stubblebine, S.: On generalized authorization problems. In: Proc. CSFW, pp. 202–218. IEEE, Los Alamitos (2003)
7. Esparza, J., Kučera, A., Mayr, R.: Model checking probabilistic pushdown automata. In: LICS 2004, IEEE, Los Alamitos (2004)
8. Li, N., Mitchell, J.C.: Understanding SPKI/SDSI using first-order logic. In: Proc. CSFW, pp. 89–103. IEEE, Los Alamitos (2003)
9. Suwimonteerabuth, D., Schwoon, S., Esparza, J.: Efficient algorithms for alternating pushdown systems with an application to the computation of certificate chains. In: Graf, S., Zhang, W. (eds.) ATVA 2006. LNCS, vol. 4218, pp. 141–153. Springer, Heidelberg (2006)
10. Jha, S., Schwoon, S., Wang, H., Reps, T.: Weighted pushdown systems and trust-management systems. In: Hermanns, H., Palsberg, J. (eds.) TACAS 2006. LNCS, vol. 3920, pp. 1–26. Springer, Heidelberg (2006)
11. Page, L., Brin, S., Motwani, R., Winograd, T.: The PageRank citation ranking: Bringing order to the web. Technical report, Stanford Digital Library Technologies Project (1998)
12. Etessami, K., Yannakakis, M.: Recursive Markov chains, stochastic grammars, and monotone systems of nonlinear equations. In: Diekert, V., Durand, B. (eds.) STACS 2005. LNCS, vol. 3404, Springer, Heidelberg (2005)
13. CiteSeer: Top 10,000 cited authors in computer science
    http://citeseer.ist.psu.edu/allcited.html
14. CiteSeer: Estimated impact of publication venues in computer science
    http://citeseer.ist.psu.edu/impact.html
15. Hirsch, J.E.: An index to quantify an individual's scientific research output. Proceedings of the National Academy of Sciences 102, 165–169 (2005)
16. Ley, M.: DBLP bibliography, http://www.informatik.uni-trier.de/~ley/db/
17. Jøsang, A., Marsh, S., Pope, S.: Exploring different types of trust propagation. In: Stølen, K., Winsborough, W.H., Martinelli, F., Massacci, F. (eds.) iTrust 2006. LNCS, vol. 3986, pp. 179–192. Springer, Heidelberg (2006)

Author Index

Printing: Mercedes-Druck, Berlin
Binding: Stein+Lehmann, Berlin

Lecture Notes in Computer Science

Sublibrary 1: Theoretical Computer Science and General Issues

For information about Vols. 1–4630
please contact your bookseller or Springer

Vol. 4769: A. Brandstädt, D. Kratsch, H. Müller (Eds.), Graph-Theoretic Concepts in Computer Science. XIII, 341 pages. 2007.

Vol. 4763: J.-F. Raskin, P.S. Thiagarajan (Eds.), Formal Modeling and Analysis of Timed Systems. X, 369 pages. 2007.

Vol. 4759: J. Labarta, K. Joe, T. Sato (Eds.), High-Performance Computing. XV, 524 pages. 2008.

Vol. 4746: A. Bondavalli, F. Brasileiro, S. Rajsbaum (Eds.), Dependable Computing. XV, 239 pages. 2007.

Vol. 4743: P. Thulasiraman, X. He, T.L. Xu, M.K. Denko, R.K. Thulasiram, L.T. Yang (Eds.), Frontiers of High Performance Computing and Networking ISPA 2007 Workshops. XXIX, 536 pages. 2007.

Vol. 4742: I. Stojmenovic, R.K. Thulasiram, L.T. Yang, W. Jia, M. Guo, R.F. de Mello (Eds.), Parallel and Distributed Processing and Applications. XX, 995 pages. 2007.

Vol. 4739: R. Moreno Díaz, F. Pichler, A. Quesada Arencibia (Eds.), Computer Aided Systems Theory – EUROCAST 2007. XIX, 1233 pages. 2007.

Vol. 4736: S. Winter, M. Duckham, L. Kulik, B. Kuipers (Eds.), Spatial Information Theory. XV, 455 pages. 2007.

Vol. 4732: K. Schneider, J. Brandt (Eds.), Theorem Proving in Higher Order Logics. IX, 401 pages. 2007.

Vol. 4731: A. Pelc (Ed.), Distributed Computing. XVI, 510 pages. 2007.

Vol. 4728: S. Bozapalidis, G. Rahonis (Eds.), Algebraic Informatics. VIII, 291 pages. 2007.

Vol. 4726: N. Ziviani, R. Baeza-Yates (Eds.), String Processing and Information Retrieval. XII, 311 pages. 2007.

Vol. 4719: R. Backhouse, J. Gibbons, R. Hinze, J. Jeuring (Eds.), Datatype-Generic Programming. XI, 369 pages. 2007.

Vol. 4711: C.B. Jones, Z. Liu, J. Woodcock (Eds.), Theoretical Aspects of Computing – ICTAC 2007. XI, 483 pages. 2007.

Vol. 4710: C.W. George, Z. Liu, J. Woodcock (Eds.), Domain Modeling and the Duration Calculus. XI, 237 pages. 2007.

Vol. 4708: L. Kučera, A. Kučera (Eds.), Mathematical Foundations of Computer Science 2007. XVIII, 764 pages. 2007.

Vol. 4707: O. Gervasi, M.L. Gavrilova (Eds.), Computational Science and Its Applications – ICCSA 2007, Part III. XXIV, 1205 pages. 2007.

Vol. 4706: O. Gervasi, M.L. Gavrilova (Eds.), Computational Science and Its Applications – ICCSA 2007, Part II. XXIII, 1129 pages. 2007.

Vol. 4705: O. Gervasi, M.L. Gavrilova (Eds.), Computational Science and Its Applications – ICCSA 2007, Part I. XLIV, 1169 pages. 2007.

Vol. 4703: L. Caires, V.T. Vasconcelos (Eds.), CONCUR 2007 – Concurrency Theory. XIII, 507 pages. 2007.

Vol. 4700: C.B. Jones, Z. Liu, J. Woodcock (Eds.), Formal Methods and Hybrid Real-Time Systems. XVI, 539 pages. 2007.

Vol. 4699: B. Kågström, E. Elmroth, J. Dongarra, J. Waśniewski (Eds.), Applied Parallel Computing. XXIX, 1192 pages. 2007.

Vol. 4698: L. Arge, M. Hoffmann, E. Welzl (Eds.), Algorithms – ESA 2007. XV, 769 pages. 2007.

Vol. 4697: L. Choi, Y. Paek, S. Cho (Eds.), Advances in Computer Systems Architecture. XIII, 400 pages. 2007.

Vol. 4688: K. Li, M. Fei, G.W. Irwin, S. Ma (Eds.), Bio-Inspired Computational Intelligence and Applications. XIX, 805 pages. 2007.

Vol. 4684: L. Kang, Y. Liu, S. Zeng (Eds.), Evolvable Systems: From Biology to Hardware. XIV, 446 pages. 2007.

Vol. 4683: L. Kang, Y. Liu, S. Zeng (Eds.), Advances in Computation and Intelligence. XVII, 663 pages. 2007.

Vol. 4681: D.-S. Huang, L. Heutte, M. Loog (Eds.), Advanced Intelligent Computing Theories and Applications. XXVI, 1379 pages. 2007.

Vol. 4672: K. Li, C. Jesshope, H. Jin, J.-L. Gaudiot (Eds.), Network and Parallel Computing. XVIII, 558 pages. 2007.

Vol. 4671: V.E. Malyshkin (Ed.), Parallel Computing Technologies. XIV, 635 pages. 2007.

Vol. 4669: J.M. de Sá, L.A. Alexandre, W. Duch, D.P. Mandic (Eds.), Artificial Neural Networks – ICANN 2007, Part II. XXXI, 990 pages. 2007.

Vol. 4668: J.M. de Sá, L.A. Alexandre, W. Duch, D.P. Mandic (Eds.), Artificial Neural Networks – ICANN 2007, Part I. XXXI, 978 pages. 2007.

Vol. 4666: M.E. Davies, C.J. James, S.A. Abdallah, M.D. Plumbley (Eds.), Independent Component Analysis and Signal Separation. XIX, 847 pages. 2007.

Vol. 4665: J. Hromkovič, R. Královič, M. Nunkesser, P. Widmayer (Eds.), Stochastic Algorithms: Foundations and Applications. X, 167 pages. 2007.

Vol. 4664: J. Durand-Lose, M. Margenstern (Eds.), Machines, Computations, and Universality. X, 325 pages. 2007.

Vol. 4661: U. Montanari, D. Sannella, R. Bruni (Eds.), Trustworthy Global Computing. X, 339 pages. 2007.

Vol. 4649: V. Diekert, M.V. Volkov, A. Voronkov (Eds.), Computer Science – Theory and Applications. XIII, 420 pages. 2007.

Vol. 4647: R. Martin, M.A. Sabin, J.R. Winkler (Eds.), Mathematics of Surfaces XII. IX, 509 pages. 2007.

Vol. 4646: J. Duparc, T.A. Henzinger (Eds.), Computer Science Logic. XIV, 600 pages. 2007.

Vol. 4644: N. Azémard, L. Svensson (Eds.), Integrated Circuit and System Design. XIV, 583 pages. 2007.

Vol. 4641: A.-M. Kermarrec, L. Bougé, T. Priol (Eds.), Euro-Par 2007 Parallel Processing. XXVII, 974 pages. 2007.

Vol. 4639: E. Csuhaj-Varjú, Z. Ésik (Eds.), Fundamentals of Computation Theory. XIV, 508 pages. 2007.

Vol. 4638: T. Stützle, M. Birattari, H. H. Hoos (Eds.), Engineering Stochastic Local Search Algorithms. X, 223 pages. 2007.